Clinical Assessment and Diagnosis in Social Work Practice

Clinical Assessment and Diagnosis in Social Work Practice

JACQUELINE CORCORAN

JOSEPH WALSH

OXFORD
UNIVERSITY PRESS
2006

OXFORD
UNIVERSITY PRESS

Oxford University Press, Inc., publishes works that further
Oxford University's objective of excellence
in research, scholarship, and education.

Oxford   New York
Auckland   Cape Town   Dar es Salaam   Hong Kong   Karachi
Kuala Lumpur   Madrid   Melbourne   Mexico City   Nairobi
New Delhi   Shanghai   Taipei   Toronto

With offices in
Argentina   Austria   Brazil   Chile   Czech Republic   France   Greece
Guatemala   Hungary   Italy   Japan   Poland   Portugal   Singapore
South Korea   Switzerland   Thailand   Turkey   Ukraine   Vietnam

Copyright © 2006 by Oxford University Press, Inc.

Published by Oxford University Press, Inc.
198 Madison Avenue, New York, New York 10016

www.oup.com

Oxford is a registered trademark of Oxford University Press

Library of Congress Cataloging-in-Publication Data
Corcoran, Jacqueline.
Clinical assessment and diagnosis in social work practice / Jacqueline Corcoran,
Joseph Walsh.
p. cm.
Summary: "Guides social workers in developing competence in the American
Psychiatric Association's Diagnostic and Statistical Manual of Mental Disorders
(DSM-IV-TR) system of diagnosis, and assists them in staying attuned during
client assessment to social work values and principles." Provided by publisher.
ISBN-13 978-0-19-516830-3
1. Mental illness—Classification.   2. Mental illness—Diagnosis.
3. Diagnostic and statistical manual of mental disorders.   4. Psychiatric social work.
5. Social service. I. Walsh, Joseph, 1952–. II. Title.
[DNLM: 1. Diagnostic and statistical manual of mental disorders.   2. Social
work, psychiatric—methods.   3. Mental Disorders—diagnosis.   4. Mental Disorders—classification.   WM 30.5 C793c 2006]

RC455.2.C4C72 2006
616.89'075—dc22   2005027740

9 8 7 6 5 4 3

Printed in the United States of America
on acid-free paper

To my parents, Myra and Patrick Corcoran
—Jacqueline

To Ruth and Gus Simpson, for their kindness and
support over so many years
—Joe

ACKNOWLEDGMENTS

We wish to acknowledge the valuable help of several of our students who offered case studies: Catherine Johnson, Sarah Koch, Susan Parrott, Benjamin Smith, Silvana Starowlansky-Kaufman, Candace Strother, and Amy Wooley. We also thank Jennifer Crowell, Liat Katz, and Amy Waldbillig for their contributions to chapters and Susan Munford for her input on chapter 3. Finally, we extend our appreciation to Patrick Corcoran for his painstaking proofreading efforts and hard work.

CONTENTS

1 Introduction   3

2 Social Work and the DSM: Person-in-Environment Versus
   the Medical Model   11

I **Disorders with Onset in Childhood**

3 Mental Retardation   35
   WITH LIAT KATZ

4 Autism   64

5 Oppositional Defiant Disorder and Conduct Disorder   90

6 Attention-Deficit/Hyperactivity Disorder   129

7 Posttraumatic Stress Disorder   164

8 Anxiety Disorders   191

II **Disorders with Onset in Adolescence**

9 Eating Disorders   231

10 Depression   261

11   Substance Use Disorders   304

12   Sexual Disorders: Pedophilia   349

III   Disorders with Onset in Adulthood

13   Bipolar Disorder   381

14   Schizophrenia and Other Psychotic Disorders   412

15   Personality Disorders   448

IV   Disorders with Onset in the Elderly

16   Cognitive Disorders   479

      Index   507

Clinical Assessment and Diagnosis in Social Work Practice

1 Introduction

Social workers in clinical settings need to demonstrate facility with client diagnosis. The *Diagnostic and Statistical Manual of Mental Disorders* (*DSM*) is the preeminent diagnostic classification system among clinical practitioners in this country. Knowledge of the *DSM* is critical so that social workers can be conversant with other mental health professionals and are eligible to receive reimbursement for services they deliver. The challenge for a social work book on mental, emotional, and behavior disorders is to teach social workers competence and critical thinking in the diagnostic process, while also considering diagnosis in a way that is consistent with social work values and principles. These values include a strengths-based orientation, concern for the worth and dignity of individuals, and an appreciation for the environmental context of individual behavior.

To meet these challenges, this book will integrate several perspectives:

- The *DSM*
- A critique of the *DSM*
- The risk and resilience biopsychosocial framework
- Evidence-based practice
- A life-span approach
- Measurement tools for assessment and evaluation

Here we discuss in general terms how these perspectives affect social work diagnosis and how they are integrated into the book.

The *Diagnostic and Statistical Manual*

The *DSM* catalogs, codes, and describes the various mental disorders recognized by the American Psychiatric Association (APA). The manual was first published in 1952 and has undergone continual revisions during the past 50 years. The latest version is *DSM-IV-TR* (Text Revision), published in 2000 (APA, 2000).

Much of the terminology from the *DSM* has been adopted by mental health professionals from all fields as a common language with which to discuss disorders. Chapter 2 provides much more information on the history of the *DSM*. Other chapters cover many of the mental, behavioral, and emotional disorders found in the *DSM*. The disorders that were selected for inclusion are those that social workers may encounter in their employment or field settings.

Critique of the *DSM*

Despite the widespread use of the *DSM*, critiques have emerged from social work and related professions. These are covered in more detail in chapter 2. They include the *DSM*'s lack of emphasis on environmental influences on human behavior (Kutchins & Kirk, 1997). Social work considers the reciprocal impact of people and their environments in assessing human behavior. From this perspective, problems in social functioning might result from stressful life transitions, relationship difficulties, or environmental unresponsiveness. None of these situations needs to assume the presence or absence of "normal" or "abnormal" personal characteristics. In this volume we offer a critique of the diagnosis for each disorder, usually applying to the *DSM* diagnosis.

Risk and Resilience Biopsychosocial Framework

In response to the critique that the *DSM* tends to view mental disorders as arising from pathology inherent to the individual, *Clinical Assessment and Diagnosis in Social Work Practice* draws on the *risk and resilience biopsychosocial framework*. This framework captures "the complex interplay of multiple psychological, social, and biological processes" (Cicchetti & Toth, 1998, as cited in Shirk, Talmi, & Olds, 2000, pps. 836–837) that result in the occurrence of emotional or mental disorders. The risk and resilience aspect of the framework considers the balance of risk and protective factors that interact to determine an individual's propensity toward *resilience*, or the ability to function adaptively despite stressful life events. Although *resilience* has been defined in different ways, it refers to the "absence of significant developmental delays or serious learning and behavior problems and the mastery of developmental tasks that are appropriate for a given age and culture" in spite of exposure to adversity (e.g., Werner, 2000, p. 116). More simply, it is achieving positive outcomes despite hardship. The strengths perspective underlies the concept of "resilience" in that resilient people not only are able to survive and endure but also can triumph over difficult life circumstances.

Risks, on the other hand, can be understood as "hazards in the individual or the environment that increase the likelihood of a problem occurring" (Bogenschneider, 1996). *Protective factors* that exist in the presence of risk factors are the "personal, social, and institutional resources that foster competence, promote successful development, and thus decrease the likelihood of engaging in problem behavior" (Dekovic, 1999). Protective factors may counterbalance or buffer against risk (Pollard, Hawkins, & Arthur, 1999; Werner, 2000). Risk and protective factors are sometimes the converse of each other, however. For instance, at the individual level, difficult temperament is a risk factor, and easy temperament is a protective factor. Indeed, researchers have found many pairs of risk and protective factors that are negatively correlated with each other (Jessor, Van Den Bos, Vanderryn, Costa, & Turbin, 1997).

The biopsychosocial emphasis expands the focus beyond the individual to a recognition of systemic factors that can create and ameliorate problems. The nature of systems is that the factors within and between them have influence on each other. For instance, the presence of a certain risk or protective factor may increase the likelihood of other risk and protective factors. Wachs (2000) provides the example of how an aversive parenting style with poor monitoring increases children's risk for socializing with deviant peers. If parents are overwhelmed by many environmental stressors, such as unemployment, lack of transportation and medical care, and living in an unsafe neighborhood, their ability to provide consistent warmth and nurturance may be compromised. This phenomenon also operates for protective factors. For example, adolescents whose parents provide emotional support and structure the environment with consistent rules and monitoring tend to group with peers who share similar family backgrounds (Steinberg, 2001). Supportive parenting will, in turn, affect the characteristics of the child in that, through receiving it, he or she learns to regulate emotional processes and develop cognitive and social competence (Wachs, 2000). Systemic influences also play themselves out from the perspective of a child's characteristics. A child who has resilient qualities, such as social skills, effective coping strategies, intelligence, and self-esteem, is more likely to attract high-quality caregiving, and attachment patterns formed in infancy tend to persist into other relationships across the life span.

Although precise mechanisms of action are not specified, data have begun to accumulate about the number of risk factors that are required to overwhelm a system and result in negative outcomes (e.g., Fraser, Richman, & Galinsky, 1999; Kalil & Kunz, 1999). The cumulative results of different studies seem to indicate that four or more risk factors represent a threat to adaptation (Epps & Jackson, 2000; Kalil & Kunz, 1999; Runyan et al., 1998; Rutter, Maugham, Mortimore, & Ouston, 1979). However, risk does not proceed in a linear fashion; neither are all risk factors weighted equally (Greenberg, Speltz, DeKlyen, & Jones, 2001). Further, the amount of risk has a stronger relation to variation in problem behavior than amounts of protection have (Dekovic, 1999).

The chapters in this book delineate the unique risk and protective factors that have been identified from the research for both the onset of particular disorders and an individual's adjustment or recovery. Some of the risk and protective factors discussed in each chapter are not specific to that particular disorder; in other words, certain risk and protective factors play a role in multiple disorders. In a prevention and intervention sense, these common risk factors occurring across multiple domains are good targets for reduction or amelioration, and these protective factors are good targets for enhancement.

Case examples illustrate how the risk and resilience biopsychosocial framework can be used for assessment, goal formulation, and intervention planning. The focus is the micro (individual and family) level of practice.

Evidence-Based Practice and Measurement

In the past decade, social work, like other disciplines, has become focused on *evidence-based practice*. This movement is related to social work's increased emphasis on accountability to clients and third-party payers, such as insurance companies and government agencies, and its desire to further the knowledge base of the profession. In evidence-based practice, the worker evaluates the appropriateness of a certain approach for a particular disorder by considering the results of treatment outcome studies (Cournoyer & Powers, 2001; Roberts & Yeager, 2004). Social workers also assess clients individually to determine that they are responding in the desired way to the intervention.

This book addresses the first component of evidence-based practice by including information from recently conducted longitudinal studies, epidemiological research, and treatment outcome studies with clinical populations. Another important source of evidence is the *meta-analysis*, a statistical technique for aggregating the quantitative results of different studies. Literature reviews that attempt to summarize and synthesize the results of many studies are problematic because some studies report statistical significance and others do not. Studies also vary by sample size, type of design used, and other methodological features, as well as the demographic characteristics of the sample, among other variables. Meta-analysis can address some of these issues by putting the quantitative results of studies into a standardized form called the effect size, which is then weighted by sample size for each study and averaged across studies. The *effect size* indicates the strength of the relationship between variables, for instance, between a particular type of intervention and the outcome of interest. The larger the effect size, the greater the impact of the intervention. The size of an effect is usually demonstrated by the following benchmarks: .2 and lower is small, .5 to .3 is medium, and over .5 is considered large (Cohen, 1988). Many of the studies cited in this book were meta-analyses.

For the second component of evidence-based practice—evaluating the progress of individual clients—information on measurement tools for particular disorders is presented in each chapter. Social workers can use these measures as appropriate to assess the effects of their practice. This book emphasizes client self-report measures and ones that do not involve specialized training on the part of the social worker.

A Life-Span Approach

This book is organized according to a life-span approach, which means that disorders typically appearing in childhood and adolescence are discussed first, followed by those with an onset in adulthood, and then those that begin in older age. Despite the assignment of disorders to different phases of the life span, each chapter shows how the particular disorder is manifested across the life span, with accompanying assessment and intervention considerations.

The section on childhood includes autism, mental retardation, oppositional defiant disorder, attention-deficit/hyperactivity disorder, posttraumatic stress disorder, and anxiety disorders. Most of these disorders begin in childhood. However, conduct disorder may begin either in childhood or in the adolescent years. (It is discussed along with oppositional defiant disorder because the symptoms of these two disorders, as well as the research, overlap considerably.) Posttraumatic stress disorder and anxiety disorders are included in the childhood section; although anxiety disorders can occur at any stage of the life span, we balance our discussion in these two chapters on how the disorder presents in both childhood and adulthood, with assessment and intervention considerations specific to particular developmental stages.

The section on disorders in adolescence refers to disorders with typical onset in adolescence: eating disorders, depression, substance use disorders, and sexual disorders (pedophilia). We recognize that onset is not always in adolescence for these disorders, and there is much discussion in each of these chapters on presentation in adulthood.

Disorders in adulthood comprise bipolar disorder, schizophrenia and other psychotic disorders, and personality disorders (borderline and antisocial personality disorders). Disorders associated with older adulthood include the dementias.

Disorders chosen for inclusion in this book had to meet the following criteria:

- They are disorders that clinical social workers may encounter, irrespective of clinical setting.
- They have sufficient research backing them to warrant discussion. For instance, reactive attachment disorder and intermittent explosive disorders were not included because of the lack of research information on them.
- They do not contribute to discrimination or oppression. For instance, gender identity disorder is a *DSM* diagnosis, but social work is committed to the rights of transgendered, as well as lesbian and gay, populations.

Format of the Book

The second chapter provides a historical overview of the *DSM*, its principles and components, and critiques of the *DSM* and its biological basis. Each of the subsequent chapters on the mental, emotional, and behavior disorders includes the following:

- A summary description of the particular mental disorder, including its prevalence, course, and common comorbid disorders
- Assessment factors, including goal formulation and relevant measurement instruments
- The risk and protective factors for both the onset and course of the particular disorder
- Evidence-based interventions
- A critique of the diagnosis from the social work perspective
- A case study and illustration of the multiaxial diagnostic system, with a suggested treatment plan

Our goal in developing this format was to guide you through the assessment and intervention process with various mental, emotional, and behavior disorders that may occur throughout the life span. You will gain in-depth knowledge about important aspects of these disorders and the social work roles connected with them. Most important, you will learn about diagnosis and disorders in a way that is consistent with social work principles and values.

References

American Psychiatric Association. (2000). *Diagnostic and statistical manual of mental disorders* (4th ed., text rev.). Washington, DC: Author.

Bogenschneider, K. (1996). An ecological risk/protective theory for building prevention programs, policies, and community capacity to support youth. *Family Relations: Journal of Applied Family & Child Studies, 45*, 127–138.

Cohen, J. (1988). *Statistical power analysis for the behavioral sciences* (2nd ed.). Hillsdale, NJ: Erlbaum.

Cournoyer, B., & Powers, G. (2001). Evidence-based social work: The quiet revolution continues. In A. R. Roberts & G. J. Greene (Eds.), *Social workers' desk reference* (pp. 798–807). New York: Oxford University Press.

Dekovic, M. (1999). Risk and protective factors in the development of problem behavior during adolescence. *Journal of Youth & Adolescence, 28*, 667–685.

Epps, S., & Jackson, B. (2000). *Empowered families, successful children*. Washington, DC: American Psychiatric Association.

Fraser, M., Richman, J., & Galinsky, M. (1999). Risk, protection, and resilience: Toward a conceptual framework of social work practice. *Social Work Research, 23*, 131–143.

Greenberg, M., Speltz, M., DeKlyen, M., & Jones, K. (2001). Correlates of clinic referral for early conduct problems: Variable- and person-oriented approaches. *Development & Psychopathology, 13*, 255–276.

Jessor, R., Van Den Bos, J., Vanderryn, J., Costa, F. M., & Turbin, M. S. (1997). Protective factors in adolescent problem behavior: Moderator effects and developmental change. In G. A. Marlatt & G. R. Van Den Bos (Eds.), *Addictive behaviors: Readings on etiology, prevention, and treatment* (pp. 239–264). Washington, DC: American Psychological Association.

Kalil, A., & Kuntz, J. (1999). First births among unmarried adolescent girls: Risk and protective factors. *Social Work Research, 23*, 197–208.

Kutchins, H., & Kirk, S. A. (1997). *Making us crazy. DSM: The psychiatric bible and the creation of mental disorders*. New York: Free Press.

Pollard, J., Hawkins, D., & Arthur, M. (1999). Risk and protection: Are both necessary to understand diverse behavioral outcomes in adolescence? *Social Work Research, 23*, 145–158.

Roberts, A. R., & Yeager, K. (2004). Systematic reviews of evidence-based studies and practice-based research: How to search for, develop, and use them. In A. R. Roberts & G. J. Greene (Eds.), *Evidence-based practice manual: Research and outcome measures in health and human services* (pp. 3–14). New York: Oxford University Press.

Runyan, D. K., Hunter, W. M., Scololar, R. R., Amaya-Jackson, L., English, D., Landsverk, J., et al. (1998). Children who prosper in unfavorable environments: The relationship to social capital. *Pediatrics, 101*(1), 12–19.

Rutter, M., Maugham, N., Mortimore, P., & Ouston, J. (1979). *Fifteen thousand hours*. Cambridge, MA: Harvard University Press.

Shirk, S., Talmi, A., & Olds, D. (2000). A developmental psychopathology perspective on child and adolescent treatment policy. *Development and Psychopathology, 12*, 835–855.

Steinberg, L. (2001). We know some things: Parent-adolescent relationships in retrospect and prospect. *Journal of Research on Adolescence, 11*, 1–19.

Wachs, T. (2000). *Necessary but not sufficient*. Washington, DC: American Psychiatric Association.

Werner, E. (2000). Protective factors and individual resilience. In J. Shonkoff & S. Meisels (Eds.), *Handbook of early childhood intervention* (2nd ed., pp. 115–132). New York: Cambridge University Press.

2   Social Work and the *DSM*

Person-in-Environment Versus the Medical Model

This book is organized around the *DSM* (APA, 2000) classification system because it is a standard resource for clinical diagnosis in this country and has been for more than half a century. The purpose of the *DSM* is to "provide clear descriptions of diagnostic categories in order to enable clinicians and investigators to diagnose, communicate about, study, and treat people with various mental disorders" (APA, 2000, p. xi). However, the *DSM* represents only one of many possible perspectives on human behavior, a medical perspective. There has always been a tension between the social work profession's person-in-environment perspective and the requirement in many settings that social workers use the *DSM* to "diagnose" mental, emotional, or behavioral disorders in clients. The purpose of this chapter is to explore this uneasy relationship of social work to the DSM. As an introduction to the process, the concept of *disorder* is reviewed from four professional perspectives.

▓▓▓▓ The Concept of "Disorder"

Many of the human service professions, all of which have their own unique value and knowledge bases, develop formal standards for evaluating and classifying the behavior of real or potential clients as *normal* or *abnormal*, *healthy* or *unhealthy*, *sane* or *insane*, *rational* or *irrational*. They use different criteria for doing so, however. Since its beginnings, the profession of social work has made efforts to put forth such classification systems (one of which is described later in the chapter), but at the same time it has always been uncomfortable with the act of labeling behavior. Still, for social workers, the current approach is preferable to the way that three other professional perspectives—medical, psychological, and sociological—regard disorder.

The Medical (Psychiatric) Perspective

There is no single definition of *normalcy* in any discipline. The current definition of *mental disorder* utilized by the American Psychiatric Association (2000) is a "significant behavioral or psychological syndrome or pattern that occurs in an individual and that is associated with present distress (e.g., a painful symptom) or disability (i.e., impairment in one or more important areas of functioning) or with significantly increased risk of suffering death, pain, disability, or an important loss of freedom" (p. xxxi). The syndrome or pattern "must not be merely an expectable and culturally sanctioned response to a particular event . . ." (p. xxxi). Whatever its cause, "it must currently be considered a manifestation of behavioral, psychological, or biological dysfunction in the individual" (p. xxxi). Neither deviant behavior nor conflicts between an individual and society are to be considered disorders unless they are symptomatic of problems within the individual.

The medical definition thus focuses on underlying disturbances within the person and is sometimes referred to as the *disease model* of abnormality. This implies that the abnormal person must experience changes within the self (rather than create environmental change) in order to be considered normal again.

Psychological Perspectives

The social science of psychology studies the internal mental functions of people without giving primary consideration to organic processes. Some psychologies of human development postulate stage theories, in which a universal sequence of life stages contributes to normal or abnormal development and behavior (e.g., Bjorklund & Pellegrini, 2002). The time context becomes important, as normality is assessed with a consideration of stages that a person is expected to pass through at certain biological ages. Erikson's (1979) work provides an example of one well-known stage theory. These eight psychosocial stages and their associated challenges are infancy (trust vs. mistrust), early childhood (autonomy vs. shame and doubt), play age (initiative vs. guilt), school age (industry vs. inferiority), adolescence (identity vs. identity diffusion), young adult (intimacy vs. isolation), adulthood (generativity vs. self-absorption), and mature age (integrity vs. disgust and despair). Each new stage of personality development builds on previous stages and assumes the relevance of interpersonal influences on one's progression.

Thus, normal behavior is reflected in one's satisfactory passage through stages. Any unsuccessful transition from one stage to the next can result in the onset of abnormal behavior, as evidenced by a deviant pattern of coping with challenges. An unsuccessful struggle through one stage implies that the person will experience difficulties in mastering subsequent developmental stages.

The Sociological Approach: Deviance

There are a variety of approaches to the study of abnormality, or deviance, in the field of sociology. One example is the theory of *symbolic interactionism* (Hewitt, 1994). From this perspective, people who cannot constrain their behaviors within acceptable social roles (e.g., parent, student, employee, church member) in the eyes of others become labeled as deviant. That is, *deviance* is a negative label that results from one's being considered by a majority of significant others in a community or society—those people with whom the individual has substantive relationships—to be in violation of the prescribed social order (Traub & Little, 1994). Those significant others are unable to grasp the perspective from which the deviant person thinks and acts. Put more simply, the behavior may make sense to the individual, but it does not make sense to observers.

If the individual's behavior is labeled as *deviant*, the significant others conclude that their inability to understand the perspective of the other is due to that person's shortcomings, rather than to their own rigidity. They cannot relate to the individual's behavior and thus reject it for being at odds with social conventions. The deviance label may be mitigated if the individual accepts that he or she should think or behave otherwise and if the person makes efforts to conform to the social order.

The Social Work Perspective: Social Functioning

The profession of social work is characterized by the consideration of *systems* and the reciprocal impact of people and their environments (the psychosocial perspective) on human behavior (Andreae, 1996). Social workers tend not to classify individuals as abnormal or disordered but instead consider the *person-in-environment* (PIE) as an ongoing transactional process that facilitates or blocks one's ability to experience satisfactory social functioning. The quality of a person's social functioning is related to the biological, psychological, and social factors in his or her life. Three types of PIE situations likely to produce problems in social functioning include stressful life transitions, relationship difficulties, and environmental unresponsiveness (Germain & Gitterman, 1996). All of these are transactional and do not emphasize the presence or absence of "normal" personal characteristics.

Social work interventions may focus on the person *or* on the environment. Still, clinical social workers specialize in work with client populations at the "micro" level of the PIE spectrum. The National Association of Social Workers (1994) defines *clinical social work practice* as "the application of social work theory and methods to the treatment and prevention of psychosocial dysfunction, disability, or impairment, including emotional and mental disorders, in individuals, families, and groups. It is based on an application of human development theories within a psychosocial context." The fact that this definition includes references to emotional and mental disorders helps to underscore the tension noted earlier between the philosophy of the profession and the work of its clinical practitioners.

Classifying Mental, Emotional, and Behavioral Disorders

The first edition of the *DSM* (APA, 1952)[1] reflected the influence of two previous works that had been widely used in the United States during the prior 30 years. Each of these volumes was the result of efforts to develop a uniform nomenclature of disease. First, the American Medico-Psychological Association and National Council for Mental Hygiene collaborated to produce a standard reference manual in 1918 (initially titled the *Statistical Manual for the Use of Institutions for the Insane*). It included 22 categories of mental illness and reflected this country's primary focus on psychiatric hospitals and severe forms of mental illness. In addition, the New York Academy of Medicine published the *Standard Classified Nomenclature of Disease* in 1933, which, although focused on medical diseases, made great strides in developing a uniform terminology.

The *Statistical Manual*, responsibility for which was eventually assumed by the American Psychiatric Association, was used until World War II. During the war, observations of relatively mild mental disorders among soldiers uncovered the manual's limitations. Psychiatrists began to treat problems such as personality disturbances, psychosomatic disorders, and stress reactions. The *Statistical Manual* was not helpful for diagnosing these cases, and the Armed Forces and Veterans Administration actually developed their own supplemental nomenclatures. In 1948, with the war over, the APA initiated new action for the standardization of diagnosis. The need for change was felt most strongly by practitioners in clinics and private practice, reflecting the movement of psychiatry out of institutions and into communities. The result was publication of the first edition of the *DSM* in 1952 (Grob, 1991).

Since its beginning, the *DSM* has relied on symptom clusters as the basis for diagnosis. There are other ways that the process could be advanced, however (Clark, Watson, & Reynolds, 1995). For example, clients could be classified on the basis of dimensions of behavioral characteristics. From this perspective, human behavior occurs on a continuum of severity, from normal through problematic. Dimensions may refer to the severity of defined sets of symptoms, individual traits, or underlying vulnerabilities. That is, a client might not be diagnosed as having a certain disorder but rather with exhibiting certain characteristics to a problematic degree. A dimensional system would probably result in fewer categories of disorder and reflect the reality that similar behaviors may serve different functions across individuals. (In acknowledgment of the dimensional approach, we have included in this book measurement instruments that can be used for each disorder.) Neither the dimensional approach, which many researchers advocate, nor any other alternative to the *DSM* approach, is explored in this book, but it is important for you to understand that there is nothing "sacred" in the system developed for the *DSM*.

The Relationship Between Social Work and the *DSM*

All social workers in direct practice need to diagnose clients. That is, they have to make judgments upon which to take professional actions for which they will be held accountable. One of these important judgments is whether a person falls into a *DSM* category. If the person does not, a diagnosis may still need to be made in order to provide services to that person. Many times, then, the use of a diagnosis can facilitate intervention, and at other times it may be problematic from an ethical perspective. It is our view that the *DSM* thus has its benefits *and* limitations with respect to clinical practice. The *DSM* classification system is a product of the psychiatric profession and as such does not fully represent the knowledge base or values of the social work profession. Still, it is extensively used by social workers and many other human service professionals nationwide for the following reasons:

- Worldwide, the medical profession is preeminent in setting standards for mental health practice. Thus, social workers, along with members of other professions, are often expected by agency directors to use the *DSM* in their work.
- Competent use of the *DSM* helps social workers claim expertise similar to that of the other professions (Brubeck, 1999).

- Practitioners from various disciplines can converse in a common language about disorders.
- Social workers are extensively employed in mental health settings, where clinical diagnosis is considered necessary prior to selecting appropriate intervention. In fact, social workers account for *more than half* of the mental health workforce in the United States (Gambrill, 2002; O'Neill, 1999).
- The *DSM* perspective is incorporated into professional training programs offered by members of a variety of human service professions.
- Portions of state social worker licensing exams require knowledge of the *DSM* (Biggerstaff, 1994).

Throughout the remainder of this chapter, we examine the manual with regard to both its utility and its limitations.

The Evolution of *DSM*

As noted previously, the presenting problems of clients are often categorized from the perspective of the *DSM*, and social workers' decisions about diagnoses are important in understanding those problems and selecting intervention strategies. Because the "medical" perspective may sometimes be at odds with social work's person-in-environment perspective, it is important for social workers to understand the development and evolution of the manual. Social workers can see how some diagnostic categories have social as well as medical and psychological origins. They can also get a sense about the relative validity of the various types of diagnoses.

DSM-I

The first edition of the *DSM* (1952) was constructed by a small committee of APA members who prepared drafts of the material and sent them to samples of members of the APA and other related organizations for feedback and suggestions. The final product included 106 diagnoses, each of which had descriptive criteria limited to several sentences or a short paragraph. The manual had a psychodynamic orientation, reflected in the wide use of the term *reaction*, as in "schizophrenic reaction" or "anxiety reaction." It included many new diagnoses specifically intended for use with outpatient populations.

DSM-I's two major categories were (a) disorders caused by or associated with impairment of brain tissue function and (b) disorders of psychogenic origin without clearly defined physical cause or structural change in the brain. The former category included acute and chronic brain disorders

resulting from such conditions as infection, dementia, circulatory disturbance, and intoxication. The latter category included problems resulting
from a more general inability to make successful adjustments to life demands. It included psychotic disorders (such as manic depression, paranoia, schizophrenia), autonomic and visceral disorders, psychoneurotic disorders (anxiety, dissociative, conversion, phobic, obsessive-compulsive, and
depressive reactions), personality disorders, and transient situational personality disorders.

DSM-II

The *DSM* was revised for the first time in 1968, following 3 years of preparation. The APA's decision to do so was justified by its desire to bring
American nomenclature into closer alignment with that of the *International
Classification of Diseases* (*ICD*), the worldwide system for medical and psychiatric diagnosis that was updated and published that same year. Still, the
DSM-II was not so much a major revision as an effort to reflect current
psychiatric practice. The committee wanted to record what it "judges to be
generally agreed upon by well-informed psychiatrists today" (APA, 1968,
p. viii). Its process of construction was similar to that of *DSM-I*. Following
its adoption by APA leadership, it attracted little attention from the general
public. Psychiatry at that time was far less a social force than it was to
become during the next 10 years.

The *DSM-II* included 182 diagnoses in 10 classes of disorder described
in less than 40 pages:

- Mental retardation
- Psychotic organic brain syndromes (such as dementia, infection, and cerebral)
- Nonpsychotic organic brain syndromes (epilepsy, intoxication, circu-latory)
- Psychoses not attributed to physical conditions (schizophrenia, major affective disorders)
- Neuroses
- Personality disorders
- Psychophysiology (somatic) disorders
- Transient situational disturbances
- Behavior disorders of childhood and adolescence
- Conditions without manifest psychiatric disorder

The term *reaction* was eliminated from the manual, but the *neurosis* descrip-
tor was retained for some categories, indicating the ongoing psychodynamic influence.

Through *DSM-II*, there was no serious effort on the part of psychiatry to justify its classifications on the basis of scientific evidence. The manual was vague, inconsistent, and empirically weak with regard to validity and reliability (Kirk & Kutchins, 1992). Nevertheless, it was popular among clinical practitioners and far more useful to them than it was to researchers.

After the publication of *DSM II*, a conflict erupted within psychiatry over whether homosexuality should be classified as a mental illness (Kutchins & Kirk, 1997). Although it was generally considered to be a disorder up to that time, it first appeared as a separate diagnostic category in *DSM II*. The gay rights movement had become quite powerful by the early 1970s, however, and protests were directed against the APA for its perceived stigmatization. The psychiatry profession was divided about the issue, and the conflict reached a resolution only in 1974, when a vote of the APA membership (note how far the APA had to go to live up to any claims of science) resulted in homosexuality being deleted from further editions of the manual. Still, as a kind of compromise measure, it was retained in subsequent printings of *DSM-II* as "sexual orientation disturbance" and in *DSM-III* as "ego dystonic homosexuality." The diagnoses were intended for use only with those who were uncomfortable with their homosexuality and wanted to live as heterosexuals. This episode is a prime example of the "politics" of mental illness.

DSM-III

The publication of the *DSM-III* in 1980 represented a major turning point in the evolution of the classification system and for the field of psychiatry in general. This edition represented a clear effort to portray psychiatry as an empirical scientific enterprise. It also promoted a nontheoretical approach to diagnosis, a five-axis diagnostic system, and behaviorally defined criteria for diagnosing disorders. For the first time, the *DSM* included an official definition of *mental disorder* (presented earlier in this chapter). It included 265 disorders, and for each of them information was presented about diagnostic features, coding information, associated features, age at onset, course, impairment, complications, predisposing factors, prevalence, and sex ratio. It was a much larger manual than its spiral-bound predecessors were. Disorders were classified into 17 categories, usually by shared phenomenological features, although there was some inconsistency in this process. For example, there were two chapters devoted to "not elsewhere classified" groups of disorders, and the infant, child, and adolescent disorders were all classified together.

The development of *DSM-III* was far more intensive, and involved far more participants, than development of the earlier editions. It was put forth as a scientific document, based on research findings. Even so, the APA recognized that supporting these claims was difficult. In addition to literature reviews and field trials, criteria for the inclusion of many disorders were based on whether they were used with relative frequency, whether interested professionals offered positive comments about it, and whether it was useful with outpatient populations. This final criterion indicates the psychiatry profession's desire to continue moving away from its roots in the public mental hospitals.

The multiaxial system of diagnoses (Table 2.1) introduced in *DSM-III* is still in use, although in amended form. Its justifications were a desire to make the process of diagnosis more thorough and individualized and recognition of the medical and psychosocial factors that contribute to the process of diagnosis.

One rationale for differentiating Axis I, which covers clinical or mental disorders and other conditions that may be a focus of clinical attention, from Axis II, which covers personality disorders, mental retardation, and other developmental disorders, was the perceived etiology of the disorders. Transient disorders, those for which a client would be more likely to seek intervention, were placed on axis I, and more "constitutional" conditions on axis II. Other rationales for differentiating Axes I and II were their formal structure (psychological versus organic components) and their temporal stability (those on axis II were presumed to be either long-term or permanent) (APA, 1980). The division was also intended to highlight the personality disorders that had become of great interest to psychiatrists for the first time. Over the years, however, critics have found less conceptual support for the distinction between the axes (Clark et al., 1995).

Axes IV and V, which bring attention to environmental influences on a client's functioning, should be of great interest to social workers. However, in Axis IV no method was presented to systematically identify and record these factors. It was left to the practitioner to briefly describe the

Table 2.1		
The *DSM* Classification of Mental Disorders		
Axis I	Clinical or mental disorders	
	Other conditions that may be a focus of clinical attention	
Axis II	Personality disorders	
	Mental retardation and other developmental disorders	
Axis III	General medical conditions	
Axis IV	Psychosocial and environmental problems	
Axis V	Global assessment of functioning	
Source: Adapted from the American Psychiatric Association (2000).		

stressor and then rate its severity on a scale of 1 to 7 between "none" and "catastrophic." This approach changed over subsequent editions. Further, there was confusion over whether the identified stressors were intended to represent a *cause* or a *consequence* of the Axis I disorder (Brubeck, 1999). To regard the stressors as a consequence of a disorder contradicted social work's interest in person–situation interactions as contributing to the development of problems in living; social workers are more likely to consider stressors as causes of disorders. Axis V, the *global assessment of functioning* (GAF), also broadened the scope of diagnosis, as the practitioner was asked to summarize the level of a client's social, occupational, and leisure functioning on a scale between 1 (superior) and 7 (grossly impaired).

Another innovation of the *DSM-III* that was conceptually appealing to the social work profession was the introduction of *V-codes*, "conditions attributable to a mental disorder that are a focus of attention or treatment" (APA, 1980, p. 331). They include *relational* problems and thus represent the only coding category for problems that are recognized to exist outside the individual. V-codes include interpersonal issues that complicate the treatment of another disorder or arise as a result of it. Listed on Axis I when they will be a major focus of the intervention, they include:

- Problem related to a general mental disorder or general medical condition (a client's main difficulty is related to interaction with a relative or significant other who has a mental disorder or physical disease)
- Parent–child relational problem (symptoms or negative effects on functioning are associated with how a parent and child interact)
- Partner relational problem (symptoms or negative effects on functioning are associated with the way a client and spouse/partner interact)
- Sibling relational problem
- Relational problem not otherwise specified (for example, with a neighbor or coworker)

The V-codes also include problems related to abuse or neglect, such as the physical abuse of a child or adult, the sexual abuse of a child or adult, and the neglect of a child.

DSM-III reflected a major expansion of psychiatric turf in the United States. Unlike other editions of the manual, it was a target of criticism from some social workers and other mental health professionals for its perceived lack of validity and reliability (Kirk & Kutchins, 1992). Its authors defended against these criticisms by presenting it as a work in progress (Kutchins & Kirk, 1997).

DSM-III-R

The APA justified the publication of *DSM-III-R* (APA, 1987), the *R* standing for "revised," because of the lengthy time lag between *DSM-III* and the projected publication date of *DSM-IV* (approximately 5 years away). The editors stated that accumulated research findings indicated a need for revisions in the descriptions and criteria for some disorders and a clarification or updating of information about others. All diagnoses were reviewed for consistency, clarity, and conceptual accuracy by appointed committees. The participants were initially asked to limit their criticisms and input to improving existing descriptions of disorders, but many new disorders were eventually included. No new reliability studies were conducted, however, to substantiate evidence for the existence of these disorders.

The new manual reflected more than minor adjustments. There were 292 mental disorders included in the product. The manual introduced the *hierarchical exclusionary rules*, which were estimated to affect 60% of diagnoses (Clark et al., 1995). That is, a diagnosis was to be excluded from consideration if it was judged to occur during the course of a coexisting disorder that had a higher position in the hierarchy. For example, a person with schizophrenia who developed depression would not be given the latter diagnosis, because many symptoms of depression are implicit in the former diagnosis. Axes I and II now permitted *specifiers* of the severity of a disorder (mild, moderate, and severe). On Axis IV (psychosocial stressors), *DSM-III-R* provided separate scales for children and adolescents and adults. It also offered 11 types of psychosocial stressors to choose from. These were now to be coded on a 1 (none) to 6 (catastrophic) scale and described as predominantly *acute* (less than 6 months) or *enduring*. Axis V was now to be coded along a continuum from 0 to 100, with anchor descriptors at every 10 points. Two scores were now required, reflecting the client's GAF at present and his or her highest level during the past year. These changes did seem to enhance the client's clinical description.

Much controversy emerged, however, about the proposed inclusion of three new diagnoses. All of them were strongly criticized by feminist groups (and others) for alleged gender biases (Figert, 1995; Franklin, 1987; Lerman, 1996). The proposed sexual disorder of paraphilic rapism received strong objections, as it appeared to make the act of rape—or, more specifically, repeated rape—a disorder and thus an act for which perpetrators might conceivably not be held legally accountable. Premenstrual dysphoric disorder described a type of depression experienced by women before menstruation. This diagnosis might stigmatize women as mentally unstable during their menstrual cycles. Masochistic personality disorder, characterized by a recurrent need to experience interpersonal suffering, might label as disordered women who have difficulty separating from abusers. There was clearly a concern among the general public that psychiatry was again about to pathologize behavior that had been previously conceptualized as either normal or criminal. In the end, the editors of *DSM-III-R* did not include any of these three diagnoses in the text, but they did put them into an appendix as conditions that merited further study.

DSM-IV

The *DSM-IV* was published in 1994, and, like the second and third editions, it represented a major effort to update the state of diagnostic knowledge in the United States. Additionally, the editors continued to work toward terminological and coding consistency with the ICD. The massive effort was conducted with a 16-member task force and 13 work groups, each consisting of 50 to 100 people who had expertise in particular topic areas. The editors claimed that the manual benefited from the "substantial increase in research on diagnosis" and that "most diagnoses now have an empirical literature or available data sets that are relevant to decisions" related to manual revisions (APA, 1994, p. xviii). Preparations for the new manual included 150 reviews of the published literature, reanalysis of 50 data sets already collected, and 12 issue-focused field trials to test diagnostic options. New diagnoses were included only if there was research support, although categories already scheduled to be included in the 10th edition of the *ICD* were given priority. An effort was also made to simplify diagnostic criteria to make the manual more user-friendly for practitioners.

The final product included approximately 340 mental disorders classified into 16 types, which continued the APA's practice of adding disorders to each edition of the *DSM*. Most other changes were minor. The term *rule out* was replaced by *provisional* on Axes I and II. Of interest to social workers, Axis IV was revised to include nine factors representing psychosocial and environmental problems, and the severity codes were deleted. A more controversial change was the inclusion of clinical significance criteria in almost half the diagnostic criteria sets, requiring that symptoms not merely be present but cause clinically significant distress or impairment in important areas of the client's functioning (Spitzer & Wakefield, 1999). Although these criteria were not empirically based, they represented an attempt to make diagnostic criteria stricter. This change was favored by some social workers in that a person did not have a disorder if he or she merely exhibited symptoms, but only if those symptoms created distress in an environmental context.

DSM-IV-TR

This "text revision" of the *DSM-IV* that appeared in 2000 was presented, like the 1987 revision, as a compromise between those who felt that the manual is updated too often to facilitate research and those who wanted access to the most up-to-date information about mental disorders (First & Pincus, 2002). The editors reported that with *DSM-V* not due until 2010 (or later), there would be 16 years between editions, too great a gap to accommodate accumulating knowledge about mental disorders. The purposes of the 3-year text revision project were to ensure that the descriptive information about disorders was up to date, correct any errors or ambiguities from *DSM-IV*, and reflect changes in *ICD* coding, required by the U.S. government for reporting health care statistics. The manual included no changes in diagnoses, diagnostic criteria, or organizational structure.

Examples of diagnostic categories where the wording was clarified include pervasive developmental disorder not otherwise specified, the tic disorders, the paraphilias, and polysubstance dependence. Coding changes were made for the cognitive disorders and several others. Instructions for using Axis V, the global assessment of functioning, were clarified. The "current" score was articulated as referring to "the past week," and practitioners were advised to use the lower of two rating scores when there were differences in the quality of a client's functioning among the social, occupational, and leisure domains. *DSM-IV-TR* was not a significant change from its predecessor with respect to clinical usage.

Now that the nature of the *DSM* has been described, we can review how clinical practitioners currently use it. Table 2.2 includes a summary of instructions for the use of the *DSM-IV-TR* (APA, 2000).

Criticisms of the *DSM*

The American Psychiatric Association has always maintained that the *DSM* is not a perfect classification system and that it is a work in continuous process. The editors assert that each edition represents an improvement over the previous one because it incorporates the most complete knowledge available at the time about the nature of mental disorders. Still, the manual has been critiqued as fundamentally flawed by members of the social work and other professions. The most important criticisms for clinical social work practitioners are described here.

The DSM *makes no provisions for recording client strengths.* It is conceivable that a multiaxial classification system might devote one or more axes to strengths. The manner in which the *DSM* has evolved even leads some professionals to believe that disorders are probably more numerous than is acknowledged at present. For example, in his otherwise useful text, *DSM-IV Made Easy* (1995), Morrison writes: "The fact that the manual omits a disorder doesn't mean it doesn't exist. With each new edition of the *DSM*, the number of listed mental disorders has increased. . . . The conclusions

Table 2.2

Procedures for Completing a *DSM* Diagnosis

General Guidelines

a. Sufficiently investigate the presenting symptoms to ensure that they are genuine.
b. List diagnosis first that is most responsible for the current evaluation.
c. When uncertain if a diagnosis is correct, use the "provisional" qualifier.
d. When appropriate, use the following severity criteria. They are required for mood, substance abuse, mental retardation, and conduct disorder, but can be used for any Axis I or II diagnosis.
   1. Mild: minimum criteria
   2. Moderate: intermediate; between mild and severe
   3. Severe: many more symptoms than minimum criteria; some are especially severe; social functioning is especially compromised
   4. In partial remission: the client previously met full criteria; some symptoms remain but there are too few to fulfill criteria currently
   5. In full remission: the client has been symptom-free for a period of time that seems clinically relevant
   6. Prior history: the client appears to have recovered, but the clinician feels it is important to mention it

Hierarchic Principles

a. Disorders due to a general medical condition (such as panic attacks due to hypoglycemia) and substance-induced disorders (psychotic episode during an amphetamine binge) preempt a diagnosis of any other disorder that could produce the same symptoms.
b. When a more pervasive disorder has essential or associated symptoms that are defining symptoms of a less pervasive disorder, the more pervasive disorder is diagnosed if its diagnostic criteria are met. For example, if dysthymia is present when schizophrenia is present, then only schizophrenia should be diagnosed. If oppositional defiant and conduct disorders are both present, use the conduct disorder diagnosis.

Axis II (Personality Disorders, Mental Retardation)

If the personality disorder is the most important reason for the client's seeking evaluation, add the "principal diagnosis" term.

Axis III (General Medical Conditions)

a. These may have a direct bearing on client's Axis I diagnoses (especially true of cognitive disorders).
b. In other cases, physical illness may affect (or be affected by) management of Axis I or II diagnosis.
c. Note the source of the information, such as "according to the client" or "confirmed in chart by a physician."

Axis IV (Psychosocial and Environmental Problems)

a. The duration of the problem is intended to include only the past year.
b. These can be coded on Axis I when they are a focus of evaluation or treatment.
c. A positive stressor may be included if it has caused problems for the client.
d. More than one may be listed. These may include
   1. Primary support group (death of or illness in a relative; divorce or separation; re-marriage of parent; abuse; conflicts with relatives)
   2. Economic (poverty, debt, credit problems, inadequate welfare or child support)
   3. Social environment (loss or death of friend, acculturation problems, racial or sexual discrimination, retirement, living alone)
   4. Access to health care services (inadequate health services, insufficient health insurance, no transportation for health services)
   5. Educational (academic problems, conflicts with classmates or teachers, illiteracy, poor school environment)
   6. Interaction with the legal or criminal systems (arrest, incarceration, suing or being sued, victim of a crime)
   7. Occupational (stressful work conditions, changing jobs, unemployment)
   8. Housing problems (homelessness, poor housing, dangerous neighborhood)
   9. Other psychosocial stressors (conflicts with human service professionals, exposure to war, natural disasters, or catastrophes)

Axis V (Global Assessment of Functioning)

a. These rating are based on the clinician's judgment.
b. The scores reflect the client's overall occupational, psychological, and social functioning (not physical limitations or environmental problems) on a continuum of mental health and illness.
c. Two scores are included: one reflecting the client's current GAF (the past week), and another reflecting the client's highest level during the past year.
d. Scores range from 0 to 100, for example,
90–100: Superior functioning in a wide range of activities
0–10: Persistent danger of severely hurting self or others, persistent inability to maintain minimal personal hygiene, or serious suicidal acts with clear expectation of death.

Source: Adapted from the American Psychiatric Association (2000).

should be obvious: there are probably still more conditions out there, waiting to be discovered" (p. 9). This orientation to human behavior is *hardly* strengths oriented.

It promotes an arbitrarily medical model for thinking about human problems. Disorders are conceptualized as residing *within* clients. Many authors have criticized the tendency of psychiatry to overstate the case for biological causation of some mental disorders (such as attention-deficit/hyperactivity disorder, depression, bipolar disorder, and schizophrenia) and over-emphasize biological rather than psychosocial interventions (Breggin & Cohen, 1999; Healy, 2002; Valenstein, 1998). As discussed earlier, social work considers the reciprocal interactions between the person, including developmental, biological, and psychological aspects, and the environment, including the immediate social environment and wider social influences and forces.

The DSM *views clients in isolation.* It does not address interaction problems and the roles played by systems (sometimes oppressive) in the emergence of problem conditions. Some argue that, rather than being disorders of the person, symptoms may instead be understandable reactions to abnormal stressors (Kutchins & Kirk, 1997). While the V-codes allow practitioners to articulate relational issues, these are not reimbursable by insurance companies and are thus not accorded the same legitimacy as other diagnoses. Axis IV is also helpful in overcoming this bias, but neither does it receive great emphasis from practitioners compared with the issues recorded on Axes I and II.

The DSM *is organized for use in determining a diagnosis prior to intervention.* Social workers, in contrast, regard the assessment process as ongoing throughout intervention, with new hypotheses tested as new information emerges. Although a practitioner can always change a client's *DSM* diagnosis, the manual suggests that a decision about diagnosis should be made early in the clinical process.

The DSM *promotes reductionistic thinking about people.* It tends to minimize the complexity of the human condition, although to be fair this would be true of any similar diagnostic manual. Ongoing use of the *DSM* has an effect on a social worker's heuristics (unconscious decision-making strategies) (Miller, 2002). That is, client behaviors tend to be perceived only in terms of available *DSM* categories. Likewise, the process of diagnosis may be biased by the social worker's awareness of prior diagnoses when previous records exist for a client. The editors of the *DSM* (APA, 1994) do attempt to dispel this notion, stating in an introduction that the manual is "meant to serve as guidelines to be informed by clinical judgment and is not meant to be used in a cookbook fashion" (p. xxiii).

Many mental disorders have tended to become "reified" as concrete entities (such as schizophrenia, major depression, borderline personality disorder, and others), even though the reliability of diagnosis (agreement among practitioners) has been about the same since *DSM-II* (Kutchins & Kirk, 1997). In other words, the manual promotes an illusion among some practitioners that disorders represent specific conditions, when in fact they are conceptual and, in many cases, quite vague.

Despite the efforts of the DSM *editors to more specifically define disorders, there is an acknowledged heterogeneity (within-groups variability) for most of them and an abundance of unclassifiable "boundary cases"* (those that do not quite meet all required symptom criteria). This complicates the process of diagnosis but, more seriously, the process of determining intervention strategies, because people who have the same diagnosis are presumed to benefit from similar interventions. This problem has been dealt with in part by adding new subtypes of disorders, but these tend to demonstrate poor validity and reliability. The introduction of *severity* qualifiers in *DSM-III-R* represented another effort to add descriptive specificity to many disorders. Further, the not otherwise specified (NOS) categories included with many disorders lack fundamental diagnostic specificity due to their absence of clear criteria. This is not a minor issue because the proportion of NOS diagnoses in the mood, dissociative, and personality disorder categories is high (Clark et al., 1995).

The DSM *has become a major moneymaking enterprise for the American Psychiatric Association.* All professional associations, including the National Association of Social Workers, must be concerned with their finances and devise a variety of ways to raise money. Some outsiders, however, remark on the great income-generating potential of each edition of the *DSM* and feel that the APA's frequent updating of the manual has as much to do with revenues as with scientific advances. Publication of the manual is always accompanied by the publication of supplementary books (case study texts and handbooks for differential diagnosis, as examples), and professional development seminars on the use of the manual also draw sizable enrollments (Kirk & Kutchins, 1992; Kutchins & Kirk, 1997).

The expanded classification of disorders in the DSM *also furthers the purposes of pharmaceutical companies.* As more constellations of behaviors are considered mental disorders, they become reimbursable and treatable through medication (Kutchins & Kirk, 1997). The drug companies benefit financially as more reimbursable disorders are discovered. The influence of pharmaceutical companies on the practice of psychiatry is not always recognized. For instance, drug companies sponsor research on medications, block unfavorable results from publication, fund psychiatric conferences and continuing education programs, and are major advertisers for psychiatric journals (Fisher & Greenberg, 1997).

In the context of practitioners seeking diagnostic clarity with the DSM, *the problem of comorbidity, in which a person may qualify for more than one diagnosis on an axis, is significant.* The APA encourages the recording of more than one diagnosis on an axis when the assessment justifies doing so. Still, research indicates that 52 to 91% of clients merit several diagnoses, but practitioners infrequently recorded them (Clark et al., 1995). Social workers (and others) may resist doing so at times in an effort to minimize the perceived stigmatizing aspects of diagnosis.

The *DSM* is likely to continue for many more years as the primary resource for the formal classification of mental, emotional, and behavioral disorders. Although social workers should advocate for *DSM* revisions or other classification systems that are compatible with their value base, they can productively work within the *DSM* framework to help clients with many serious problems in living. Before closing this chapter, we present one example of an alternative classification system that was developed by members of the social work profession.

The Person-in-Environment Classification System

In 1981 the California chapter of the National Association of Social Workers (NASW) initiated an effort to enhance social work's professional identity and value base by developing a new classification system for problems in living. The PIE classification system was developed to describe, classify, and code the social functioning problems of the adult clients of social workers (Karls & Wandrei, 1994). The purposes of PIE were similar to some of the purposes of the *DSM*: clarify the practice domain of social work, provide a basis for gathering data to measure service needs, encourage clearer communication among social workers, and promote common descriptions of client situations to facilitate intervention.

The PIE system was developed and field-tested between 1981 and 1984 (with efforts to establish interrater reliability and content validity), but because of funding problems the project was dropped, and NASW has not endorsed further work on it. Although the PIE is not currently in use, it serves as a reminder that social workers can participate in the development of classification systems that attend more thoroughly than the *DSM* to the biopsychosocial components of human functioning. It remains an example of an alternative method for formulating diagnosis, one that is consistent with the perspective of the social work profession.

The PIE (Table 2.3) is intended to balance client problems and strengths and does not endorse any particular theory of human development. It has *social functioning* problems, *environmental* problems, *mental health* problems, and *physical health* problems. Interestingly, and probably reflecting the time of its development, the system does not include a means of explicitly noting client strengths.

One positive development in social work's pursuit of a holistic perspective on problems in living is NASW's participation in field-testing a manual that will help health care professionals learn the World Health Organization's International Classification of Functioning, Disability, and Health (O'Neill, 2004). This coding framework, first published in 2001 but not yet in widespread use, provides a means for professionals to look beyond health care diagnosis and record clients' levels of functioning and disability. The code is based on a biopsychosocial approach and incorporates person-in-environment, ecological, and strengths models of practice.

Table 2.3

The Person-in-Environment Classification System

Factor I: Social Functioning Problems

A. Social role in which each problem is identified
   1. Family (parent, spouse, child, sibling, significant other)
   2. Other interpersonal (lover, friend, neighbor, other)
   3. Occupational (worker/paid, worker/home, worker/volunteer, student, other)
B. Type of problem in social role

1. Power	4. Dependency	7. Victimization
2. Ambivalence	5. Loss	8. Mixed
3. Responsibility	6. Isolation	9. Other

C. Severity of Problem

1. No problem	4. High severity
2. Low severity	5. Very high severity
3. Moderate severity	6. Catastrophic

D. Duration of Problem

1. More than 5 years	4. 2 to 4 weeks
2. 1 to 5 years	5. 2 weeks or less
3. 6 months to 1 year	

E. Ability of Client to Cope with Problem

1. Outstanding coping skills	4. Somewhat inadequate
2. Above average	5. Inadequate
3. Adequate	6. No coping skills

Factor II: Environmental Problems

A. Social system where each problem is identified

1. Economic/basic needs	4. Health, safety, social services
2. Education/training	5. Voluntary association
3. Judicial/legal	6. Affectional support

B. Specific type of problem within each social system
C. Severity of problem
D. Duration of problem

Factor III: Mental Health Problem

A. Clinical syndromes (Axis I of *DSM*)
B. Personality and developmental disorders (Axis II of *DSM*)

Factor IV: Physical Health Problem

A. Disease diagnosed by a physician (Axis III of *DSM*)
B. Other health problems reported by client and others

Note

1. Unless otherwise indicated, information on the history of the *DSM* has been drawn from Kutchins and Kirk's (1997) excellent review.

Conclusion

Clinical social workers need to understand and be able to use the *DSM* for the diagnosis of their clients in mental health agencies. The manual is well established as the standard document for diagnosis in the United States and is used by practitioners from many professions who work in mental health settings. It enhances the assessment process in many ways but is also at odds with the social work profession's philosophy of person-in-environment transactions as determining the quality of a client's social functioning. By appreciating the *DSM*'s limitations, social workers are more likely to bring to the assessment process other aspects of a client's situation, including strengths and resources. They will also maintain awareness that the *DSM* is not representative of "truth" but offers one system of classification among many possible systems.

Regarding the issue of clinical assessment from the social work perspective, Miller (2002) emphasizes that the process should include attention to a client's vulnerability factors, the environmental context of the presenting problem, family and community data, and biopsychosocial variables. She also reminds social workers that their profession is distinguished by *ongoing* assessment following the initial designation of a *DSM* diagnosis.

In the rest of the book, the risk and resilience biopsychosocial framework is explored as a way to understand all of the *DSM* disorders. Factors related to the individual and the social environment are discussed in terms of their influence on clients' strengths and limitations in managing challenges associated with mental, emotional, and behavioral functioning.

References

American Psychiatric Association. (1952). *Diagnostic and statistical manual of mental disorders*. Washington, DC: Author.

American Psychiatric Association. (1968). *Diagnostic and statistical manual of mental disorders* (2nd ed., text rev.). Washington, DC: Author.

American Psychiatric Association. (1980). *Diagnostic and statistical manual of mental disorders* (3rd ed.). Washington, DC: Author.

American Psychiatric Association. (1987). *Diagnostic and statistical manual of mental disorders* (3rd ed., rev.). Washington, DC: Author.

American Psychiatric Association. (1994). *Diagnostic and statistical manual of mental disorders* (4th ed.). Washington, DC: Author.

American Psychiatric Association. (2000). *Diagnostic and statistical manual of mental disorders* (4th ed., text rev.). Washington, DC: Author.

Andreae, D. (1996). Systems theory and social work treatment. In F. J. Turner (Ed.), *Social work treatment* (4th ed., pp. 601–616). New York: Free Press.

Biggerstaff, M. A. (1994). Licensing, regulation, and certification. In R. L. Edwards (Ed.), *Encyclopedia of Social Work* (pp. 1616–1624). Silver Spring, MD: National Association of Social Workers.

Bjorklund, D. F., & Pellegrini, A. D. (2002). *The origins of human nature: Evolutionary and developmental psychology*. Washington, DC: American Psychological Association.

Breggin, P., & Cohen, D. (1999). *Your drug may be your problem: How and why to stop taking psychiatric drugs.* Reading, MA: Perseus.

Brubeck, M. (1999). Social work and the DSM. In F. J. Turner (Ed.), *Adult psychopathology* (2nd ed., pp. 121–135). New York: Free Press.

Clark, L. A., Watson, D., & Reynolds, S. (1995). Diagnosis and classification of psychopathology: Challenges to the current system and future directions. *Annual Review of Psychology, 46*, 121–154.

Erickson, E. H. (1979). *Identity and the life cycle.* New York: Norton.

Figert, A. E. (1995). The three faces of PMS: The professional, gendered, and scientific structuring of a psychiatric disorder. *Social Problems, 42*(1), 56–73.

First, M. B., & Pincus, H. A. (2002). The *DSM-IV* text revision: Rationale and potential impact on clinical practice. *Psychiatric Services, 53*(3), 288–292.

Fisher, S., & Greenberg, R. (1997). What are we to conclude about psychoactive drugs? Scanning the major findings. In S. Fisher & R. Greenberg (Eds.), *From placebo to panacea: Putting psychiatric drugs to the test* (pp. 359–384). New York: Wiley.

Franklin, D. (1987). The politics of masochism. *Psychology Today, 21*(1), 52–57.

Gambrill, E. (2002). Encouraging transparency. *Journal of Social Work Education, 38*(2), 211–214.

Germain, C. B., & Gitterman, A. (1996). *The life model of social work practice: Advances in theory and practice* (2nd ed.). New York: Columbia University Press.

Grob, G. N. (1991). *From asylum to community: Mental health policy in modern America*. Princeton, NJ: Princeton University Press.

Healy, D. (2002). *The creation of psychopharmacology*. Cambridge, MA: Harvard University Press.

Hewitt, J. P. (1994). *Self and society: A symbolic interactionist social psychology* (6th ed). Boston: Allyn & Bacon.

Karls, J. M., & Wandrei, K. E. (Eds.). (1994). *Person-in-environment system: The PIE classification system for social functioning problems.* Washington, DC: National Association of Social Workers.

Kirk, S. A., & Kutchins, H. (1992). *The selling of DSM: The rhetoric of science in psychiatry.* Hawthorne, NY: Aldine de Gruyter.

Kutchins, H., & Kirk, S. A. (1997). *Making us crazy. DSM: The psychiatric bible and the creation of mental disorders.* New York: Free Press.

Lerman, H. (1996). *Pigeonholing women's misery: A history and critical analysis of the psychodiagnosis of women in the twentieth century.* New York: Basic.

Miller, J. (2002). Social workers as diagnosticians. In K. J. Bentley (Ed.), *Social work practice in mental health: Contemporary roles, tasks, and techniques* (pp. 43–72). Pacific Grove, CA: Brooks/Cole.

Morrison, J. (1995). *DSM-IV made easy: The clinician's guide to diagnosis.* New York: Guilford.

National Association of Social Workers. (1994). *Social work speaks: NASW policy statements* (3rd ed.). Washington, DC: NASW Press.

O'Neill, J. V. (1999). Women gain in clinical fields. *NASW News, 46*(6), 1–2.

O'Neill, J. V. (2004). New diagnosis framework: NASW involved in setting codes for functioning. *NASW News, 49*(1), 9.

Spitzer, R. L., & Wakefield, J. C. (1999). *DSM-IV* diagnostic criteria for clinical significance: Does it help solve the false positives problem? *American Journal of Psychiatry, 156,* 1856–1864.

Traub, S. H., & Little, C. B. (Eds.). (1994). *Theories of deviance* (4th ed.). Itasca, IL: Peacock.

Valenstein, E. (1998). *Blaming the brain: The truth about drugs and mental health.* New York: Free Press.

Disorders with Onset in Childhood

3   Mental Retardation

WITH LIAT KATZ

Mental retardation (MR) is a complex diagnosis that takes into account a person's interaction with his or her environment. The diagnosis of MR used to be based solely on IQ, but the diagnosis has changed over the years; the current definition uses level of adaptive functioning as well as IQ. The two most widely accepted diagnostic criteria for MR are the American Association of Mental Retardation's (AAMR) criteria and the criteria published in the *Diagnostic and Statistical Manual of Mental Disorders, Fourth Edition, Text Revision* (*DSM IV-TR*) (APA, 2000).

AAMR is the major professional organization internationally in the mental retardation field. It was first established in 1876 and has been defining mental retardation since 1921. As an advocacy body, AAMR points out that mental retardation is not something a person *has* or *is*, nor is it a medical or mental disorder. Rather, it is characterized by both limitations in intellectual functioning and adaptive skills that are shaped by the person's environmental supports. The AAMR defines the following five assumptions as essential to the diagnosis of MR (AAMR, 2002):

1. Limitations in present functioning must be considered within the context of community environments typical of the individual's age, peers, and culture.
2. Valid assessment considers cultural and linguistic diversity, as well as differences in communication, sensory, motor, and behavioral factors.
3. Within an individual, limitations often coexist with strengths.
4. An important purpose of describing limitations is to develop a profile of needed supports.

5. With appropriate personalized supports over a sustained period, the life functioning of the person with mental retardation generally will improve (AAMR, 2002).

The diagnostic category of mental retardation in the *DSM-IV-TR* (APA, 2000) essentially follows AAMR guidelines for diagnosis but is more specific. With an onset before the age of 18, the MR diagnosis is listed and subclassified according to its severity under Axis II in the multiaxial scale. The classifications include mild (IQ level is from 50–55 to approximately 70), moderate (35–40 to 50–55), severe (20–25 to 35–40), and profound mental retardation (below 20 or 25), as well as mental retardation, severity unspecified. The etiology, if known (e.g., lead poisoning, Down syndrome), is coded on Axis III. A "borderline intellectual functioning" (V62.89) code may be used on Axis II if an individual's IQ level is around 70 (APA, 2000). Although the *DSM-IV-TR* does speculate as to what deficits and what achievements people at each severity level may gain, without knowledge of the individual's attitude, strengths, and support system, it is impossible to accurately gauge the capabilities of a particular individual.

Like the AAMR, in addition to IQ level, the *DSM-IV-TR* specifies that an individual diagnosed with MR must have concurrent deficits in adaptive functioning in at least two of the following areas: self-care, communication, home living, social/interpersonal skills, use of community resources, self-direction, functional academic skills, work, leisure, health, and safety. Adaptive skills tend to vary most widely in those diagnosed with mild MR (Hodapp & Dykens, 1996).

Differential Diagnosis

Although the term *developmental disability* is often used interchangeably with *mental retardation*, especially in reference to services or entitlement, *developmental disability* is a legal concept rather than a medical diagnostic category (Szymanski & King, 1999 [1]). Developmental disabilities involve a broad spectrum of disorders, including MR, autism, and epilepsy, although MR is the most common. The disorders classified as developmental disabilities can relate to mental and/or physical impairment that manifests before a person is 22 years of age.

In the *DSM-IV-TR*, several other clinical classifications, including learning disorders and pervasive developmental disorders (PDD) (e.g., autistic disorder, Asperger's disorder), share some degree of cognitive or adaptive functioning impairment; however, they are differentiated from mental retardation by certain features. Learning disorders are characterized by subaverage academic functioning in a particular academic area. Although a

PDD is often comorbid with MR, social interaction—related criteria distinguish it from MR. In PDD, impairment in reciprocal social interaction exists, as well as in the development of communication skills. (See chapter 2.) In both learning disorders and the PDDs, the individual need not necessarily show impairment in general intellectual development or in other domains of adaptive functioning.

Comorbid Disorders

Mental retardation has many possible comorbid disorders. These include most of the "disorders usually diagnosed in infancy, childhood, and adolescence" listed in the *DSM-IV-TR* under Axis I (APA, 2000). The disorders that are frequently comorbid include pervasive developmental disorders, attention-deficit/hyperactivity disorder, feeding and eating disorders, tic disorders, and elimination disorders. Learning and communication disorders, however, are not associated with MR (APA, 2000).

With MR, there is often significant frequency of other comorbid disorders not necessarily diagnosed in childhood: mental disorders due to a general medical condition; schizophrenia and other psychotic disorders; mood disorders; anxiety disorders, such as posttraumatic stress disorder and obsessive-compulsive disorder; and eating disorders.

Physiological disorders are also frequently associated with MR. The greater the severity of the retardation, the higher the prevalence of associated disorders. Fifteen to 30% of people diagnosed with severe or profound MR have seizure disorders. Twenty to 30% of people with severe or profound MR also have motor-related disorders, such as cerebral palsy, and 10 to 20% of people with severe or profound MR have sensory impairments, such as hearing and vision loss (McLaren & Bryson, 1987; Szymanski & King, 1999).

Prevalence

The prevalence of mental retardation is estimated at about 1 to 3% of the general population (APA, 2000; Hodapp & Dykens, 1996; Szymanski & King, 1999). The majority have mild MR (about 85–90%), 10% have moderate MR, 3 to 4% of those diagnosed have severe MR, and 1 to 2% have profound MR (APA, 2000). Although MR is diagnosed across lines of racial, ethnic, educational, social, and economic backgrounds, some distinct trends exist. More boys than girls are affected, and mild MR is more prevalent in lower socioeconomic groups and in African Americans than among Caucasians or Hispanics (Hodapp & Dykens, 1996; Watson & Gross, 1997).

Assessment

The assessment process should be undertaken with the goal being the determination of the individual's diagnosis, strengths and abilities, and possible physiological interventions and general support needs. The overall goal for the assessment and subsequent treatment plan is to maximize independence, taking into account the individual and the family's needs and desires.

The assessment process should start with a comprehensive physical examination to determine the physical manifestation and possible etiology of the symptoms. Testing for cognitive development and adaptive functioning should follow. In addition, interdisciplinary teams should evaluate individuals for their other ancillary support needs. These elements of assessment are discussed in more depth here.

Physical Examination

Because children with MR generally reach their developmental milestones (e.g., walking and talking) later than the general population, the pediatrician is often one of the first professionals to suggest further testing. Initially, if a diagnosis of MR is suspected, a comprehensive physical exam and a medical, family, developmental, health, social, and educational history should be taken to discover any possible organic cause of symptoms and to understand the individual's manifestation of symptoms. Some disorders that can cause MR symptoms are treatable, such as phenylketonuria (PKU) and hyperthyroidism. However, in a significant percentage of cases—between a quarter and a third—no brain abnormality or etiology can be found (Arc, 2004).

Depending on initial findings, laboratory tests may include a chromosomal analysis; appropriate brain imaging tests; an electroencephalogram; tests for urinary amino acids, blood organic acids, and lead level; and biochemical tests for inborn errors of metabolism. The necessity for these tests must be balanced with the individual's tolerance of the procedures involved.

Cognitive Assessment

For both diagnostic and educational purposes, testing should be completed to assess the individual's intellectual functioning and learning abilities. Some of the standard tests utilized are the Stanford-Binet Intelligence Scale, the Kaufmann Assessment Battery for children, and the Weschler Intelligence Scales (there are separate tests for children and adults). For infants, the Bayley Scales of Infant Development are used to assess language, personal and social, motor, and problem-solving skills (Bayley, 1993). In the choice of testing instruments as well as in the interpretation of the results, the individual's sociocultural background and native language should be taken into account (APA, 2000).

Adaptive Functioning Assessment

Because MR is now seen as a product of the interaction between the individual and his or her environment, it is critically important to examine the individual's level of support and subsequent adaptive functioning level. The social worker can play a key role in this assessment. The first step in this process is comprehensively interviewing the individual and his or her parents or other caregivers to assess the person's daily living, communication, social, and behavioral skill level. Guidelines for the interview include the following:

- Interviews should be conducted in the natural environment: home, school, or community residence.
- Most often, reassurance, support, and concrete and clear communication will yield needed information.
- The person's understanding of the disability, the reasons for referral, unique strengths and resources, ability to relate, expression of affect, and attention span should be assessed.
- People with MR may deny their disability, as they want to present themselves in the best light possible.
- Open-ended questions should be relied on as much as possible, as people with MR may not provide accurate information to leading questions (they may want to please the interviewer) or to closed-ended questions that require a yes or no response (they may be likely to respond with the choice that has been presented last).

When people evidence poor communication skills, the social worker will have to increasingly rely on caregivers for information, as well as behavioral observation. Measurement instruments can also assess adaptive functioning. See appendix I. It should be noted that all scales lack some accuracy in depicting an individual's actual skill level, because they rely on subjective informant reporting. Scales should, therefore, be supplemented with historical data, clinical interviews, and direct observation (Watson & Gross, 1997). Finally, the level of support the individual is currently receiving and the support required to achieve maximum independence should be assessed.

Assessment of Comorbid Mental, Emotional, and Behavior Problems

Comorbid psychiatric disorders affect adjustment and quality of life. Particularly detrimental are behavioral issues; as inappropriate behavior increases, so does the risk of compromising employment and residential opportunities. In addition, relatively few mental health clinicians receive training specific to the needs of this population. White et al. (1995) note that clinicians treating people with dual diagnoses of MR and a mental illness tend to emphasize the individual's MR diagnosis and underemphasize the mental illness. Thus, the individual may not receive adequate treatment. People with MR and co-occurring mental illnesses are also at risk for longer inpatient stays than people diagnosed with a mental illness alone (Saeed, Ouellette-Kuntz, Stuart, & Burge, 2003). See appendix II for measures assessing mental, emotional, and behavior problems.

Multidisciplinary Teams

To address the comprehensive needs of people with MR, ideally a multidisciplinary team should perform the assessment (Szymanski & King, 1999; Watson & Gross, 1997). Psychologists are needed to perform cognitive assessments. Developmental pediatricians and clinical geneticists complete physical diagnostic evaluations, and psychiatrists and behavioral psychologists assess the psychological and behavioral abilities of the individual. Other members of an interdisciplinary team that would be helpful in diagnosing the individual's comprehensive needs are speech and language therapists, physical therapists, educational specialists, school social workers, occupational specialists (if adults), recreational therapists, social workers in child protective services (mental retardation is represented among both parents and children in the CPS system), and workers from home-based skills-training programs, behavioral support agencies, residential programs, and mental health settings.

Some developmental disorders clinics are available for such comprehensive interdisciplinary assessments. The Association of University Centers on Disabilities is a national resource for consumer-focused facilities that provide training programs to agencies in the developmental disabilities field and technical assistance to individuals, families, and advocates. They also strive to perform the most up-to-date research on MR and other developmental disabilities (Association of University Centers on Disabilities, 2004).

Individualized Plans

Following assessment, individualized support plans are written up with the individual. These plans have a variety of names depending on the support agency: individualized education plans (IEPs) for children in school, individualized support plans (ISPs) or individual treatment plans (ITPs) for adults in residential or vocational support settings, or consumer service plans (CSPs) for case coordination services. These plans are usually required by the regulatory and/or funding agencies that oversee support agencies. The plans typically include the individual's personalized long-term goals and measurable and achievable short-term objectives, and they delineate the support services the individual will receive to accomplish the goals and objectives. The plans typically have a time frame and specifics written in the plan for reassessing the individual's progress and revising the plan accordingly.

Risk and Protective Factors for Onset

In a significant percentage of cases—between a quarter and a third—the cause of the MR symptoms is not known. In about 35% of people diagnosed with MR, a genetic causation is found; in fewer than 10%, a malformation syndrome of unknown origin may be identified. The most common genetic cause of MR is Down syndrome, an abnormality in the development of chromosome 21. In addition to Down syndrome, the other major causes of MR are fetal alcohol syndrome and fragile X. The categories of risk include genetic conditions, problems during pregnancy, problems at birth, problems after birth, and poverty and cultural deprivation. These are reviewed by Arc (2004). See Table 3.1 and also the Web site http://www.nlm.nih.gov/medlineplus/ency/article/001523.htm for links that provide more information on specific conditions and syndromes contributing to MR.

Genetic conditions result from abnormalities of inherited genes, problems when certain genes combine, or other errors in genes caused during pregnancy by such events as infections and exposure to x-rays. At least 500 genetic diseases have been associated with MR. Chromosomal disorders, such as Down syndrome, are in this category and include structural changes in chromosomes or when there are too few or too many chromosomes. Fragile X is a gene abnormality on the X chromosome and is an inherited condition, unlike Down syndrome. The fact that boys are overrepresented in MR diagnoses has to do with particular sex-related disorders of which the most prevalent is fragile X syndrome (Hodapp & Dykens, 1996).

Certain maternal behaviors during pregnancy may increase the risk for MR. These include excessive alcohol intake in the first 12 weeks of pregnancy, which may result in fetal alcohol syndrome. A pregnant mother's prenatal drug use, cigarette smoking, and malnutrition are other risk factors for the onset of MR. A pregnant woman's exposure to contaminants or

Table 3.1	
Risk and Protective Factors for Onset of Mental Retardation	
Risk	Protective Factors
Biological	
Prenatal illnesses and conditions	Regular prenatal care
Maternal behaviors during pregnancy	Prenatal screening and genetic counseling, if needed
Birth defects	
Genetic abnormalities	Routine newborn developmental screenings.
Childhood illnesses and trauma	
Male gender	Childhood immunizations against such diseases as measles and Hib
	Specific treatment of an underlying condition
	Proper diet for pregnant woman and child.
Social	
Lower socioeconomic status	Dissemination of educational information by community organizations on preventable aspects of MR
African-American heritage	
Environmental conditions, such as exposure to lead.	Government programs to provide for the nutritional needs of young children
	Early intervention and education
	Child safety seat laws

Source: If not otherwise cited in text, information in this table is drawn from APA (2000); Rush & Frances (2000); Szymanski & King (1999); Watson & Gross (1997).

illnesses, such as rubella and syphilis, may also pose risk for the developing child. In addition, if a woman has HIV, she may pass it to her child, causing possible neurological damage.

Problems at birth most commonly include prematurity and low birth weight as risk factors. Problems after birth are childhood diseases, such as whooping cough, chickenpox, measles, and Hib disease; a blow to the head or near drowning; and exposure to lead, mercury, or other environmental toxins. Poverty is a risk factor for MR because of its association with malnutrition, disease, inadequate prenatal and medical care, and environmental health hazards. Extreme deprivation of nurturance and of social, linguistic, and other stimulation may also contribute to MR. African American children are more likely to be diagnosed than Caucasian individuals; the reasons for this phenomenon are unresolved, but the overrepresentation of

African Americans among those living in poverty certainly plays a large role (Hodapp & Dykens, 1996).

Several protective factors may offset the identified risks (Arc, 2004): regular prenatal care, childhood immunizations, and routine developmental screenings. Prenatal care involves regular visits to a physician, ultrasounds, and education by the physician about appropriate behavioral changes, such as the benefits of smoking and drinking cessation and dietary needs during pregnancy. Education about the importance of folic acid supplementation in pregnancy can also prevent neural tube defects that can cause MR. Pediatric HIV infection can be reduced by the pregnant mother's treatment with zidovudine (AZT). Removal of lead from the environment and other preventive interventions, such as child safety seats and bicycle helmets, reduce the risk of brain damage (Arc, 2004).

Specific treatment of an underlying condition, if known, can prevent or minimize brain injuries that result in MR. Examples of such preventive measures include changing the diet for a child diagnosed with PKU and inserting a shunt in the case of hydrocephalus.

▨▨▨▨ Risk and Protective Factors for the Course of the Disorder

The course and continued diagnostic eligibility for the mental retardation diagnosis are contingent on continuous reevaluation of the individual's adaptive skills and the level of support required to achieve these skills. Although IQ may remain unchanged, if the level of adaptive functioning increases, the individual's quality of life can improve, perhaps to the point where the individual no longer meets criteria for MR. Adaptive skills can be enhanced by the availability of environmental supports, such as individualized habilitative, educational, medical, residential, and other supportive services. The quality and expectations of the support givers and the amount of empowerment opportunities given to an individual can also be key environmental factors in achieving higher levels of adaptive functioning.

Another factor for the course of MR is the naturally occurring psychosocial supports by community members and family members that can enrich individuals' lives and provide the resources and emotional support needed to enhance adaptive functioning. In particular, family support is critical, and without a repertoire of effective coping strategies, parents are unable to give adequate support to their child with MR. In their study, Taanila, Syrjala, Kokkonen, and Jarvelin (2002) found the following coping strategies used by parents: obtaining information about MR and their child's specific co-occurring issues, having a realistic and accepting attitude about the diagnosis, enlisting cooperation among family members, possessing solid social network support, and openly expressing feelings and affection. Family therapy may be one method used to develop support and coping skills. The Arc (formerly the Association for Retarded Citizens), comprising a national organization as well as local and state chapters, is also available for family members. Originally formed by parents of children with mental retardation 50 years ago, the Arc provides both service delivery and advocacy functions.

Adaptive skill level may be based not only on support received but also on health status and psychological functioning. Biomedical causes of MR may continue to manifest problems for the individual in terms of abilities and, ultimately, life span. However, even biomedical conditions encompass a heterogeneous course that cannot be entirely predicted. People with MR are also at risk for certain health conditions, such as epilepsy, which occurs in 15 to 30% of people with MR (Watson & Gross, 1997). MR is found in 50 to 75% of cases of people with cerebral palsy (Ratey et al. 2000), which can hamper motor stimulation and development. Regular physical exams should be done as a protective measure to rule out any physical problems and to manage those that are present. See Table 3.2.

Table 3.2

Risk and Protective Factors for the Course of the Disorder

Risk	Protective
Biological	
Co-occurring physiological disorders	Medications to combat symptoms from MR or co-occurring disorders
	Regular physical exams
Psychological	
Presence of aggression, self-injury, mood disorders, or other psychiatric conditions	Individual's own strengths and attitude
	Communication skills
Presence of autistic disorder and other pervasive developmental disorders	
Social	
Life stressors	Individual and family has adequate coping strategies
Lack of adequate support system	
Lack of familial support and resources	Educational supports and interventions that concentrate on the principles of empowerment, normalization, and independence
Vulnerability to abuse	
Stigma	
	Skills training in independent living and job skills

Source. Greenbaum & Auerbach (1998); Jancin (2003); Rush & Frances (2000); Szymanski & King (1999); Taanila et al. (2002); Watson & Gross (1997).

Individual life stressors, such as interpersonal loss or rejection, environmental stressors, transitional phases, parenting and social support problems, illness or disability, and stigmatization because of physical or intellectual problems, also act as risk factors (Rush & Frances, 2000). Another risk present for those diagnosed with MR is their vulnerability to sexual or physical abuse or to being taken advantage of financially. People with MR are also vulnerable to more subtle dangers, such as limited opportunities for development, because those around them have lowered expectations for people diagnosed with MR. Life stressors cause us all undue stress and affect our ability to function, and with diminished cognitive abilities and/or communication difficulties, life stressors can have a stronger impact on people diagnosed with MR and trigger behavioral problems.

At the same time, an individual's own strengths and attitude can be a protective factor for the course of MR, because it is through such strengths that an individual has the motivation to learn, develop, and grow his or her own talents, despite any limitations presented by a diagnosis of mental retardation.

Intervention

Forty years ago, most people with MR lived in institutional settings where they were not involved in their own care or treatment planning. The shift from institutional living to community-based programs was prompted in part by supportive legislation and litigation (Cuvo & Davis, 2001). Federal legislation—for example, the Individuals with Disabilities Education Act (IDEA)—entitles children with MR from ages 3 to 21 to free testing and appropriate individualized education and skills training within school systems. Most states have also established early intervention programs (EIPs) for children under age 3. Special education programs within school systems include the provision for an individualized education plan (IEP) that acts as a protective factor when established and implemented properly. Properly written IEPs include objectives that are individualized, measurable, and achievable; address appropriate class placement and support services; and are created by using input from the student, teachers, support staff, and the student's family member(s) and advocates. Despite mandates, the cost of such services can be astronomically expensive, and many parents, school systems, and municipalities cannot afford to provide them (Rush & Frances, 2000).

Most programs that are currently involved in the habilitation and "treatment" of MR are grounded in self-determination, community integration, person-centered planning, strengths-based approaches, and normalization. This last term refers to making conditions normal for the person with MR rather than making the person "normal." The goals of these support organizations (e.g., residential, educational, vocational, recreational) are to empower and educate individuals with MR so that they can live the most meaningful and independent lives in their own communities as possible.

Because effective protocols are based on individualized treatment for the particular manifestations of MR, demonstrated adaptive functioning level, the strengths and skills, the supports needed, and the specific goals the individual wants to achieve, it is difficult to describe global effective treatment strategies. With the additional caveat that intervention strategies will not be effective for each individual, some general approaches have been found effective, in addition to individualized treatment strategies.

1. Enlist the cooperation and support of the individual diagnosed with MR and his or her family so they are invested and part of the treatment approach (Rush & Frances, 2000).
2. Treat the underlying condition, if known, to prevent or minimize brain injury that results in MR.
3. Diagnose and treat the comorbid physical conditions, such as hypothyroidism, congenital cataracts, or heart defects in children with Down syndrome and seizures in people with tuberous sclerosis.
4. Provide education and supportive therapies (such as physical, occupational, and language therapies).
5. Provide needed supports, such as child care specific to children with disabilities, residential support, behavioral training, appropriate support systems in school, day support, vocational support, and respite support (Watson & Gross, 1997).
6. To make sure that all of the individual's needs are coordinated, continuity of care and easy and timely access to services, which can take the form of case management or case coordination, must be assured.
7. Psychosocial stressors need to be minimized, as they can lead to higher levels of impairment and behavioral issues due to frustration.
8. Select an individually tailored residential arrangement in the least restrictive setting possible.
9. Treat the symptoms of mental illnesses and the problem behaviors that often accompany a diagnosis of MR. Internalizing symptoms and social maladjustment tend to be more amenable to intervention than externally destructive behaviors (Didden, Duker, & Korzilius, 1997).

Medications can combat some of the symptoms that may arise from MR or co-occurring disorders. However, in a meta-analysis of interventions for problem behaviors, medication was the least effective treatment (Didden et al., 1997). In addition, it is both unethical and ineffective in the long term to use medication as a simple behavioral compliance tool. Because of abuses encountered with the use of medication in people with mental retardation (Bernet, 1999, as cited in Szymanski & King, 1999), the following guidelines are recommended:

1. A treatment plan should be in place that addresses all relevant aspects of the individual and his or her environment; medication should be one part of an overall plan.
2. The person's functional status should not be diminished as a result of the medication.
3. The person should receive the lowest effective dose possible, and dose reductions should be periodically attempted at least once a year.
4. Side effects and adverse results should be continually assessed.
5. The use of medication should lead to the desired outcome, otherwise, there is no need to continue with that particular medication indefinitely.

For psychosocial intervention for behavior problems and co-occurring psychiatric disorders, first-line treatments are client and family education, applied behavior analysis, and managing the environment (Rush & Frances, 2000). Cognitive-behavioral therapy is also recommended as a first-line treatment for some co-occurring mental disorders, including major depressive disorder, posttraumatic stress disorder, and obsessive-compulsive disorder.

Applied behavior analysis involves delineating sequences of behaviors, such as self-care and communication, into their constituent parts, managing stimulus and reinforcement conditions, and gradually fading prompts and reinforcement for the behavior. Indeed, training parents and teachers in behavioral methods, using accelerating differential reinforcement procedures, and teaching social skills and communication skills to clients can be used across different severity levels both of MR and of symptoms accompanying MR (Rush & Frances, 2000).

Managing the environment refers to alteration of conditions that might trigger behavior problems: activities required (e.g., restructuring a job to make it easier), physical conditions (e.g., noise, temperature, lighting, crowding), and social conditions (e.g., changes in social grouping or enrichment through social stimulation) (Rush & Frances, 2000).

Although most of the writing on psychotherapy is anecdotal, consensus in the field is that individuals with mild MR can benefit from individual, family, and group therapy if necessary language skills are in place and approaches are modified as appropriate. Most of the time, a concrete, skills-oriented approach is taken. For example, teaching how to handle peer pressure is critical so the individual can protect himself or herself against exploitation and behaviors that can be inappropriate or cause harm. One important goal is the development of a positive self-image and an understanding of limitations as a "lack of talent" in certain domains that is counterbalanced by knowledge of unique strengths and talents. Contextual interventions are also key aspects of intervention. For instance, a way to build self-esteem may be by changing a frustrating classroom experience or a job that does not fit with the client's abilities.

Regarding family intervention, the needs of the family vary, depending on when the diagnosis is made and the developmental stage of the child. Parents of young children who have just been diagnosed need education about the child's condition, an opportunity to express feelings of loss and anger, and information and referral about services and early intervention. The Arc can be an important source of information and referral.

Parents of older children need guidance and support in managing their children's behaviors and in generalizing to the home gains made in school interventions. At the same time, a focus on the child's strengths and abilities and on development of a positive self-image must be maintained. Parents may also need assistance and advocacy relevant to receipt of educational supports provided under federal and local laws. Families with adolescents need help in adjusting to the youth's sexuality and increasing independence from the family. Depending on the culture of the family, parents of adults with MR may need help to find appropriate out-of-home community placements and to separate from their children emotionally, with resolution of any accompanying guilt for doing so. Parents who are elderly may require resources and support if their children are still living in the home.

To summarize, for treatment approaches to be effective, they need to be individualized, they need to involve the individual and his or her family in treatment planning, and they need to look for the presence of psychosocial factors that affect the individual's development. These treatment approaches are most effective when they exist within a framework of a normalizing community-based setting. These recommendations will help individuals reach their general goals of maximum independence and their individualized personal goals as well.

Critique

Although the designation of the MR diagnosis is important for professional communication between clinicians as well as for provision of adequate services, it should be noted that the MR diagnosis could be construed as negative. The connotation and the colloquial use of the word *retarded* do not address a person's needs or skills; rather, it is used as an insult and utilized like other terms such as *stupid* to degrade another person.[2] Thus, the power of the MR diagnostic label should be considered, and an individual's adaptive skill level should be frequently reevaluated to see if this label can be removed (Watson & Gross, 1997). Moreover, the term *MR* encompasses different subgroups of dysfunction with varying etiologies and outcomes. Therefore, alternatives to the label "MR" could be used, such as an "intellectual" or "cognitive" disability (Batshaw & Shapiro, 1997).

At present, the American Psychiatric Association, the American Association on Mental Retardation, and the World Health Organization each maintain separate definitions of the disorder. While these distinctions are subtle, they embody differences in philosophical orientation with implications for treatment, insurance coverage, and the self-concept of persons with mental retardation and their families (Hodapp & Dykens, 1996). For example, the APA, in an effort to provide a more empirical basis for the diagnosis and to allow for greater comparability between individuals, has mainly tied the diagnosis to scores on standardized tests. This emphasis places mental retardation more firmly within a medical model. In addition, critics of these tests claim that they do not measure innate intellectual ability, but rather the degree of fit between the individual and the class cultural norms of the white, middle class U.S. educational system. However, the *DSM* criteria also stipulate that concurrent adaptive impairments be present in at least two domains; this can be viewed as an effort to mitigate the focus on IQ by providing a more comprehensive parameter of retardation.

The AAMR, which often functions in an advocacy capacity, has tried to make the diagnosis less stigmatizing and more politically palatable to both persons with mental retardation and the public at large. The efforts of the AAMR have transformed the concept of mental retardation from an inherent trait or defect to a disability, arising from the interaction of the individual and his or her environment (Nanson & Gordon, 1999). As such, it can be ameliorated with appropriate supports, lending greater hope to persons with mental retardation and their families.

Case Illustration

The case used for this chapter involves a 41-year-old African American woman, Ms. Rochelle Hunt, who had been diagnosed as a child with MR. During her school years, she had been in special education services, and a variety of IQ tests taken over time had consistently placed her in the "mild" range of MR (about 65).

Ms. Hunt first entered into case management services through her county's Mental Retardation Services Department 11½ years ago, when she was pregnant. At that time, she came to the county government center for help, as her father had asked her to leave his house, where she had been living, because he disapproved of her having a baby out of wedlock. Since then, Ms. Hunt has received services intermittently, returning of her own accord when she needed additional help.

Throughout the years, Ms. Hunt has been involved in an on-again, off-again relationship with her daughter's father, who has hit her multiple times. Ms. Hunt's daughter was diagnosed with MR and has been receiving case management services from the same case manager as Ms. Hunt. Although Ms. Hunt's daughter (now age 11) had some of the protective factors for the onset of MR (developmental screenings, up-to-date immunizations, and regular physical examinations), she had a genetic risk for MR and many environmental risk factors, such as the absence of good cognitive and psychosocial stimulation, which precipitated her diagnosis of MR.

Most recently, Ms. Hunt sought help because she lost her job (because of not showing up for work on some days) and was being evicted from her apartment.

Ms. Hunt had left food out in her kitchen, which led to an insect problem. The landlord was forced to respond because others tenants were complaining. The landlord also reported a particular incident in which either Ms. Hunt or her boyfriend had defecated over her back porch. In addition, Ms. Hunt's neighbors had complained to the landlord that frequent yelling and what sounded like physical altercations could be heard between Ms. Hunt and her boyfriend.

These two areas of diminished adaptive functioning (home living and work), combined with her IQ and the onset of symptoms before age 18, allowed her to continue to be diagnosed with MR. Because Ms. Hunt had come into services as an adult and there were no records of her developmental milestones, it is not clear what risk and protective factors she had for the onset of MR. However, Ms. Hunt possessed certain risk factors for the course of her MR. She had suffered a number of life stressors, such as eviction from her apartment, losing her job, raising her daughter, and dealing with domestic violence. Ms. Hunt's support system was not always adequate to her needs. On occasion, Ms. Hunt decided that she could do things on her own without any support and would refuse services. Ms. Hunt's father and sisters all had significant physical, cognitive, and mental health issues that prevented them from responding to Ms. Hunt's support needs. Several times throughout the years, Ms. Hunt had sought vocational support services from the county agency. Because of inadequate funds, the agency was unable to serve her, and her name was placed on a waiting list. Another possible risk for Ms. Hunt was that she had not had a physical exam since the last time she'd received services 2½ years ago. She explained that she had not known how to access and use her health benefits.

Protective factors for the course of MR include Ms. Hunt's self-confidence that she could do things relatively independently and the fact that she was able to take care of her daughter. In addition, Ms. Hunt's religious beliefs and the emotional support she felt from her church congregation were protective factors. Ms. Hunt's self-confidence was enhanced by her belief that God was taking care of her, and the church provided her with some friendships and recreational opportunities.

A multidisciplinary team was used to assess Ms. Hunt and develop a treatment plan on an annual basis as long as Ms. Hunt wanted services. The team consisted of a vocational support provider, a case manager, a representative from the local office of the national advocacy group, the Arc, anyone else Ms. Hunt chose to bring, and, most important, Ms. Hunt herself. As an example of the assessment process, the case manager helped Ms. Hunt acquire a primary care doctor and assisted her in sorting out health insurance and transportation issues. The subsequent physical examination indicated that Ms. Hunt had hypertension. She was provided with education about diet and exercise and was given medication to manage her condition.

The team assessed her goals for the future, her strengths, and the support needs that she will require to accomplish those goals. Upon coming back into services, Ms. Hunt came up with the goals of dating a different boyfriend, getting a new affordable place to live, finding and maintaining meaningful employment, and participating in more recreational activities. She stated that her ultimate goal was to own her own home. As for Ms. Hunt's strengths, the team determined that she was able to do most things in her life independently (e.g., shop, take care of her daughter, perform activities of daily living). She was self-confident, had the support of the agency, had a steady income (Social Security and SSI), and had a fulfilling spiritual life.

The following multiaxial diagnosis was made:

Axis I: 309.24 Adjustment Disorder with Anxiety
Ms. Hunt said her "nerves" were bothering her after the eviction notice and being fired, and she was having a hard time sleeping.
Axis II: 317. Mild Mental Retardation
Axis III: Hypertension
Axis IV: Occupational problems (loss of job)
Housing problems (eviction from apartment)
Problems with primary support group (domestic violence by boyfriend)
Axis V: GAF: 60

The team, including Ms. Hunt, concluded that she needed some help to find a job and an apartment, education about the dynamics of domestic violence, financial counseling, and assistance in making a Section 8 housing application. Each representative from the various agencies and departments (e.g., vocational services, the Arc representative, case management services) stated what support that agency could offer and proposed it to Ms. Hunt.

Each department or agency then developed an individualized support plan with Ms. Hunt that addressed the strengths and supports she needed to achieve her goals for that particular part of her life (i.e., vocational, case management, recreational). The case manager coordinated the services to ensure that plans jibed with the others and addressed Ms. Hunt's goals.

Treatment Strategy

The treatment strategy for Ms. Hunt was grounded in self-determination and person-centered planning. Ms. Hunt was involved in every step of the treatment planning process—she was asked about her goals and her desired level of support, and she was involved in the writing of the plan itself. When she brought up the domestic violence situation, the treatment team respected that it was her choice to remain with her boyfriend (i.e., the team did not make value statements or rescue her from the situation) and counseled her on her options. The treatment team had been schooled in the fact that even people with mental retardation deserve the dignity of risk[3] to make choices (even choices others might deem as poor). However, Ms. Hunt was informed that if her daughter was harmed by the situation in her home, someone on the team might be obligated to call child protective services.

The case manager further ensured that each plan had long-term goals and measurable and achievable short-term objectives. The plans also had to include a list of support services that were needed to achieve the goals and objectives. An example of a long-term goal that was written is "Ms. Hunt will gain meaningful and steady employment." An example of an achievable and measurable objective that was written was "Ms. Hunt will pick up three job applications per week from neighborhood stores with 80% success by 3 months from the writing of this plan." Eighty percent effectiveness referred to the fact that after 3 months Ms. Hunt would have had to pick up three applications per week for 80% of the weeks in that quarter to be considered successful in that objective. Another objective was "Ms. Hunt will attend a Section 8 housing informational meeting by 1 month from now." There were many such goals and objectives written. The team agreed to meet again in 3 months to assess Ms. Hunt's progress.

At that time, Ms. Hunt proudly announced that she was able to get Section 8 housing assistance. She attended the Section 8 informational meeting, and her case manager helped her fill out the appropriate forms. With the assistance of her case manager, she called several apartments and was waiting to hear back from them. She also reported that she had been getting some job applications (she had not quite met that particular objective yet because she rarely went three times in a week). Her job coach helped her fill out the applications and prepare for interviews, and Ms. Hunt had two interviews scheduled for the following week in an elementary school cafeteria. She was excited about working in a school. She noted that she was still with her boyfriend but had convinced him to go to counseling sessions with her at the county's mental health clinic. The team congratulated her for the hard work she had done, reassessed her goals and support needs, and set a date to evaluate Ms. Hunt's progress in another 3 months.

Appendix I. Measures of Adaptive Behavior

Adaptive Behavior Scale—Residential and Community, 2nd ed. (ABS-RC:2)
AMR Adaptive Behavior Scale—School, 2nd ed. (ABS-S:2)
Lambert, Nihira, & Leland (1993)

- Assesses the ability of individuals who are mentally retarded, emotionally maladjusted, or developmentally disabled to cope with the natural and social demands of their environment. Two forms for this scale: one for school (ABS-S:2) and the other for residential and community settings (ABS-RC:2).
- Completed by parents, teachers, nurses, and institutional aides, as well as psychologists, social workers, and speech and language professionals.
- Item types are scored "yes/no" or "select which statement best applies."
- Part 1 is designed to evaluate coping skills considered important to personal independence and responsibility in daily living and is grouped into 9 behavior domains (independent functioning, physical development, economic activity, language development, numbers and time, prevocational/vocational activity, self-direction, responsibility and socialization).
- Part 2 measures personality and behavior disorders and is grouped into 7 domains (Social Behavior, Conformity, Trustworthiness, Stereotyped and Hyperactive Behavior, Self-Abusive Behavior, Social Engagement, and Disturbing Interpersonal Behavior).

- ABS-S assesses the same domains, except domestic ability and inappropriate body exposure.

Reliability: Adaptive Behavior Full Scales—School Version

- Internal consistency for all scores exceed .90.
- Split-half reliability for ages 8–9 was .91.
- Test-retest reliability for ages 6–13 was .66 (same interviewer 2–4 weeks apart).
- Interrater reliability for ages 6–18 years was .74 (two interviewers).

Reliability: Problem Behavior Scales—School Version

- Split-half reliability for ages 8–9 was .94.
- Test-retest reliability for ages 6–13 was .83 (same interview 2–4 weeks apart).
- Interrater reliability for ages 6–8 was .57 (two interviewers).

Validity: Adaptive Behavior Full Scales—School Version

- Adaptive behaviors were highly correlated with age 0–18 (.41), indicating construct validity.
- Adaptive behaviors were positively correlated with IQ (.41–.72), indicating criterion validity. Correlations ranged from high for heterogeneous groups of handicapped children to low for nonhandicapped adults.
- Positive correlations with other adaptive behaviors scales (.53–.61), indicating criterion validity.

Inventory for Client and Agency Planning (ICAP)

(Bruininks, Hill, Weatherman, & Woodcock, 1986; http://www.cpinternet .com/~bhill/icap/)

- 16-page booklet that assesses adaptive and maladaptive behavior and gathers additional information to determine the type and amount of special assistance that people with disabilities may need
- Takes 15 minutes to complete
- Administered to a parent, teacher, or a caregiver of the individual
- Targets infants through adults
- 77 adaptive behaviors divided into four categories: motor skills, social and communication skills, personal living skills, and community living skills

- 8 categories of maladaptive behavior in four dimensions (the description of specific problem behaviors, frequency of occurrence, severity, and the usual management response by others)
- Service Score is provided that combines the overall score of the adaptive and maladaptive behaviors (0–100)

Reliability: Adaptive Behaviors

- Split-half reliability for 8–9 year-olds was .84.
- Test-retest reliability for 6–13 year-olds (same interviewer 2–4 weeks apart) was .98.
- Interrater reliability for 6–18 year-olds (2 interviewers) was .95.

Validity: Adaptive Behaviors

- Adaptive behaviors were highly correlated with age 0–18 (.91), indicating construct validity.
- Adaptive behaviors were positively correlated with IQ (.20–.78), indicating criterion validity.
- Positive correlations with other adaptive behaviors scales (.66–.81), indicating criterion validity.

Reliability: Maladaptive Behaviors

- Test-retest reliability at 6–13 years is .86.
- Interrater reliability at 6–18 years (2 interviewers) is .83.

Validity: Maladaptive Behaviors

- Criterion validity correlation with other maladaptive scales is .09–.58.

Appendix II. Measures for Emotional, Behavioral, and Mental Problems

Aberrant Behavior Checklist (ABC)

(Aman & Singh, 1986; Brown, Aman, & Havercamp, 2002)

- Symptom checklist for assessing problem behaviors of children and adults with mental retardation, including moderate to severe MR, in different settings: at home, in residential facilities, and in work training centers.

- ABC–Residential version includes 58 items rated on a 4-point scale divided into 5 subscales: irritability/agitation, lethargy/social withdrawal, stereotypic behavior, hyperactivity/noncompliance, and inappropriate speech.
- ABC–Community version contains the same item content except that home, school, and workplace are listed as the relevant settings.
- Checklist completed by parents, special educators, psychologists, direct caregivers, nurses, and others with knowledge of the person being assessed.

Reliability

- Across studies, internal consistency for subscales ranged from .76 to .94.
- Interrater reliability ranged from .39 to .67 for staff providers; parent–teacher agreement ranged from .39 to .45.
- Test-retest reliability ranged from .55 to .83 for care providers and .50 to .67 for teacher ratings.

Validity

- Established convergent and divergent validity with the Behavior Problems Inventory (Rojahn, Aman, Matson, & Mayville, 2003)

Behavioral and Emotional Rating Scale (BERS)

(Epstein & Sharma, 1998)

- 52-item scale administered on a 4-point Likert scale
- 5 subscales: interpersonal strength, family involvement, intrapersonal strength, school functioning, and affective strength
- Completed by teachers, parents, counselors, or others knowledgeable about the child in approximately 10 minutes
- Focuses on child's strengths

Reliability

- Internal consistency is strong: All alpha coefficients for subscales were above .80, and half were above .90.
- Interrater and test-retest reliability were evaluated in two separate studies in which teachers or teachers' aides rated individuals with emotional and behavioral disturbance; the results showed stability over time and consistency between raters, with all correlations over .80 and half over .90.

- Convergent validity has been examined in two studies: Correlations between the BERS Subscales and total score from the Walker Mc-Connell Scale of Social Competence and School Adjustment–Adolescent Version were generally moderate to high (.50 to .75). Correlations between the BERS and the five competence scales, the broad-band dimensions, and the total problem score of the teacher report of the Child Behavior Checklist were moderate to high (.39–.72).

Behavior Problems Inventory

(Rojahn, Matson, Lott, Esbensen, & Smalls, 2001)

- 49-item rating instrument for individuals with mental retardation and other developmental disabilities: 14 self-injurious behavior items, 24 stereotyped behavior items, and 11 aggressive/destructive behavior items
- Items scored on two scales: a 5-point frequency scale (never, monthly, weekly, daily, hourly) and a 4-point severity scale (no problem, a slight problem, a moderate problem, a severe problem)
- Questions read by interviewer to the staff and takes approximately 2–5 minutes to complete

Reliability

- Interrater agreement on the full scale scores were excellent.
- Test-retest reliability of the frequency BPI-01 full scale and subscales were good to excellent.
- Internal consistency coefficients were .61, .79, .82, and .83 for self-injurious behavior, stereotyped behavior, and aggressive/destructive subscales and full scale, respectively.

Validity

- Established convergent and divergent validity with the Aberrant Behavior Checklist (Rojahn et al., 2003)

Reiss Scales for Children's Dual Diagnosis

(Reiss & Valenti-Hein, 1994)

- Instrument designed as a children's version of the Reiss Screen for Maladaptive Behavior.

- Scale is completed by caretakers, teachers, parents, and others who know the child.
- 60-item instrument that produces scores on a total score, 10 psychometric scales (anger/self-control, anxiety disorder, attention deficit, autism, conduct disorder, depression, poor self-esteem, psychosis, somatoform behavior, and withdrawn/isolated), and 10 rare behavior problems (crying spells, enuresis/encopresis, hallucinations, involuntary motor movements, lies, obese, pica, sets fires, sexual problem, and verbally abusive).

Reliability

- Internal consistency was .92 for the total score and an average of .75 for the psychometric scales.

Validity

- Factor analysis supports the construct validity of the instrument.

Reiss Screen for Maladaptive Behavior

(Reiss, 1988)

- Screens for mental health problems in persons with mental retardation.
- Uses caretakers', teachers', work supervisors', or parents' ratings of behavior and symptoms for an individual with mental retardation age 16 and older.
- Raters indicate the extent to which each of 36 carefully defined symptoms of psychiatric disorder are "no problem," "a problem," or "a major problem."
- Five item scales produce scores for aggressive behavior, autism, psychosis, paranoia, depression (behavioral signs), depression (physical signs), dependent personality disorder, and avoidant disorder; in addition, "special maladaptive behavior" items assess drug/alcohol, sexual problems, stealing, self-injury, overactivity, and suicidal tendencies.
- Screens for psychiatric disorder in three different ways (severity of challenging behavior, diagnosis, and rare but significant symptoms such as suicidal behavior).
- A positive result indicates that the person should be referred for professional help.
- Takes 10 minutes to complete.

Reliability

- Good interrater reliability, modest to good test-retest reliability, and good internal consistency with a random sample of 60 adults with moderate to profound mental retardation who were living in an institutional setting; however, the autism, depression (physical signs), and depression (physical signs–revised) scales showed only marginal or unacceptable degrees of reliability (Sturmey, Burcham, & Perkins, 1995).
- Reliability adequate for internal consistency, ranging from .57 to .84, and for interrater reliability, ranging from .61 to .84 for a series of research samples: a national sample (306), a Chicago sample (205), and three smaller samples (Prout, 1993).
- Internal reliability for 6 of 8 clinical scales and the total score is fairly high, ranging from .73 to .84, with the exceptions of the autism and depression (physical) scales, which were .58 and .54, respectively (Johns & McDaniel, 1998)

Validity

- Modest to good concurrent validity with the Psychopathology Inventory for Mentally Retarded Adults, the Aberrant Behavior Checklist, and patterns of service use (Sturmey & Bertman, 1994)
- Criterion validity established for the scales by showing that the subjects with a dual diagnosis scored highest on the scales that were most relevant to their specific mental health diagnosis in a diverse sample of 306 adolescents and adults with mental retardation (Havercamp & Reiss, 1997)

Psychopathology Inventory for Mentally Retarded Adults (PIMRA)

(Matson, Kazdin, & Senatore, 1984; Senatore, Matson, & Kazdin, 1985. Information on the PIMRA was also obtained from http://www.idspublishing.com/pimra.htm.)

- Assesses *DSM-III* psychiatric conditions in individuals with mild mental retardation age 16 and older.
- Two structured interviews: one conducted with a parent, teacher, caregiver, or work supervisor; the other interview is with the subject.
- PIMRA yields a total score as well as separate scores for adjustment disorder, affective disorder, anxiety disorder, inappropriate adjust-

ment, personality disorder, psychosexual disorder, schizophrenia, and somatoform disorder.
- Takes 20 minutes to complete

Reliability

- Internal consistency for the self-report version total score was .85 and .83 for the informant version.
- Spearman-Brown split-half reliability was .83 for the self-report version and .65 for the informant version.
- Both versions indicate adequate test-retest correlations, with the informant version having a higher degree of stability.

Validity

- Subjects with diagnosed psychopathology based on institutional records had higher PIMRA total scores than subjects with no psychiatric diagnosis, thus providing evidence for criterion validity of the total score.
- Total scores on the PIMRA and the Checklist of Emotional Problems of Mentally Retarded Adults were correlated at .83, thus providing evidence for the concurrent validity of the PIMRA total score.

Notes

1. Unless otherwise noted, this chapter draws substantially from the excellent review by Szymanski & King (1999).

2. Grateful acknowledgment to Susan Munford for her contribution to this section.

3. This term is frequently used in the field of MR and refers to giving people the opportunity to make their own choices and to learn from their mistakes.

References

American Association on Mental Retardation (AAMR). (2002). *Definition of mental retardation*. Retrieved April 15, 2004, from http://www.aamr.org/Policies/faq_mental_retardation.shtml.

American Psychiatric Association. (2000). *Diagnostic and statistical manual of mental disorders* (4th ed., text rev.). Washington, DC: Author.

Arc (2004). Introduction to mental retardation. Retrieved on June 29, 2004, from http://www.thearc.org/faqs/mrqu.html.

Association of University Centers on Disabilities. (2004). About AUCD. Retrieved June 1, 2005, from http://www.aucd.org/aucd_about.htm.

Batshaw, M., & Shapiro, B. (1997). Mental retardation. In M. Batshaw (Ed.), *Children with disabilities* (4th ed., pp. 335–359). Baltimore: Paul H. Brookes.

Bayley, N. (1993). *Bayley scales of infant development* (2nd ed.). San Antonio, TX: Psychological Corporation.

Cuvo, A. J., & Davis, P. K. (2001). Behavioral acquisition by persons with developmental disabilities. In I. Bremmer & J. Gavin (Eds.), *Blackwell handbook of infant development* (pp. 39–60). Malden, MA: Blackwell.

Didden, R., Duker, P., & Korzilius, H. (1997). Meta-analytic study on treatment effectiveness for problem behaviors with individuals who have mental retardation. *American Journal on Mental Retardation, 101*, 387–399.

Greenbaum, C. W., & Auerbach, J. G. (1998). The environment of the child with mental retardation: Risk, vulnerability, and resilience. In J. A. Burack, R. M. Hodapp, & E. Zigler (Eds.), *Handbook of mental retardation and development* (pp. 583–605). New York: Cambridge University Press.

Hodapp, R., & Dykens, E. (1996). Mental retardation. In E. Mash & R. Barkley (Eds.), *Child psychopathology* (pp. 362–389). New York: Guilford.

Jancin, B. (2003). Developmental disorders respond to quetiapine: Moderate to high dose. *Pediatric News, 37*, 16–17.

King, B., State, M., Shah, B., Davanzo, P., & Dykens, E. (1997). Mental retardation: A review of the past 10 years. Part I. *Journal of the American Academy of Child and Adolescent Psychiatry, 36*, 1656–1663.

McLaren, J, & Bryson, S. E. (1987). Review of recent epidemiological studies of mental retardation: Prevalence, associated disorders, and etiology. *American Journal on Mental Retardation, 92*, 243–254.

Nanson, J. L., & Gordon, B. (1999). Psychosocial correlates of mental retardation. In V. Schwean, & D.H. Saklofske (Eds.), *Handbook of psychosocial characteristics of exceptional children. Plenum series on human exceptionality* (pp. 377–400). Dordrecht, Netherlands: Kluwer Academic Publishers.

Ratey, J. R., Dymek, M. P., Fein, D., Joy, S., Green, L. A., & Waterhouse, L. (2000). Neurodevelopmental disorders. In B. S. Fogel, R. B. Schiffer, & S. M. Rao (Eds.), *Synopsis of neuropsychiatry* (pp. 245–271). Philadelphia: Lippincott, Williams & Wilkins.

Rojahn, J., Matson, J. L., Lott, D., Esbensen, A. J., & Smalls, Y. (2001). The Behavior Problems Inventory: An instrument for the assessment of self-injury, stereotyped behavior, and aggression/destruction in individuals with developmental disabilities. *Journal of Autism and Developmental Disorders, 31*(6), 577–588.

Rush, A. J., & Frances, A. (Eds.). (2000). Expert consensus guideline series: Treatment of psychiatric and behavioral problems in mental retardation. *American Journal on Mental Retardation, 105*, 159–228.

Saeed, H., Ouellette-Kuntz, H., Stuart, H., & Burge, P. (2003). Length of stay for psychiatric inpatient services: A comparison of admissions of people with and without developmental disabilities. *Journal of Behavioral Health Services & Research, 30*, 406–418.

Szymanski, L., & King, B. H. (1999). Summary of the practice parameters for the assessment and treatment of children, adolescents, and adults with mental retardation and comorbid mental disorders. *Journal of the American Academy of Child and Adolescent Psychiatry, 38*(Suppl.), 5S–31S.

Taanila, A., Syrjala, L., Kokkonen, J., & Jarvelin, M. R. (2002). Coping of parents with physically and/or intellectually disabled children. *Child: Care, Health, & Development, 28*(1), 73–86.

Watson, G. S., & Gross, A. M. (1997). Mental retardation and developmental disorders. In R. Ammerman & M. Hersen (Eds.), *Handbook of prevention and treatment with children and adolescents: Intervention in the real world context* (pp. 495–520). New York: Wiley.

White, M. J., Nichols, C. N., Cook, R. S., Spengler, P. M., Walker, B. S., & Look, K. K. (1995). Diagnostic overshadowing and mental retardation: A meta-analysis. *American Journal on Mental Retardation, 100*(3), 293–298.

References for Mental Retardation Measures

Aman, M., & Singh, N. (1986). *Aberrant behavior checklist: Manual.* East Aurora, NY: Slosson.

Brown, E., Aman, M., & Havercamp, S. (2002). Factor analysis and norms for parent ratings on the Aberrant Behavior Checklist–Community for young people in special education. *Research in Developmental Disabilities, 23,* 45–60.

Bruininks, R., Hill, B., Weatherman, R., & Woodcock, R. (1986). *Inventory for client and agency planning (ICAP): The examiner's manual.* Itasca, IL: Riverside.

Epstein, M. H., & Sharma, J. (1998). *Behavioral and emotional rating scale: A strength-based approach to assessment.* Austin, TX: PRO-ED.

Havercamp, S. M., & Reiss, S. (1997). The Reiss screen for maladaptive behavior: Confirmatory factor analysis. *Behaviour and Research Therapy, 35*(10), 967–971.

Johns, M., & McDaniel, W. (1998). Areas of convergence and discordance between the MMPI-168 and the Reiss Screen for Maladaptive Behavior in mentally retarded clients. *Journal of Clinical Psychology, 54*(4), 529–535.

Lambert, N., Nihira, K., & Leland, H. (1993). *AMR adaptive behavior scale–residential and community* (2nd ed.) (ABS-RC:2). *Examiner's manual.* Lutz, FL: PAR.

Matson, J. L., Kazdin, A. E., & Senatore, V. (1984). Psychometric properties of the Psychopathology Inventory for Mentally Retarded Adults. *Applied Research in Mental Retardation, 5,* 881–889.

Prout, H. T. (1993). Assessing psychopathology in persons with mental retardation: A review of the Reiss Scales. *Journal of School Psychology, 31,* 535–540.

Reiss, S. (1988). *The Reiss Screen for Maladaptive Behavior test manual.* Worthington, OH: IDS.

Reiss, S., & Valenti-Hein, D. (1994). Development of a psychopathology rating scale for children with mental retardation. *Journal of Consulting and Clinical Psychology, 62,* 28–33.

Rojahn, J., Aman, M., Matson, J., & Mayville, E. (2003). The Aberrant Behavior Checklist and the Behavior Problems Inventory: Convergent and divergent validity. *Research in Developmental Disabilities, 24,* 391–404.

Rojahn, J., Matson, J. L., Lott, D., Esbensen, A. J., & Smalls, Y. (2001). The Behavior Problems Inventory: An instrument for the assessment of self-injury, stereotyped behavior, and aggression/destruction in individuals with developmental disabilities. *Journal of Autism and Developmental Disorders, 31,* 577–588.

Senatore, V., Matson, J., & Kazdin, A. (1985). An inventory to assess psychopathology of mentally retarded adults. *American Journal of Mental Deficiency, 89,* 459–466.

Sturmey, P., & Bertman, L. J. (1994). Validity of the Reiss Screen for Maladaptive Behavior. *American Journal on Mental Retardation 99*(2), 201–206.

Sturmey, P., Burcham, K., & Perkins, T. S. (1995). The Reiss Screen for Maladaptive Behaviour: Its reliability and internal consistencies. *Journal of Intellectual Disability Research,* 39, 191–195.

4   Autism

Autism is a pervasive developmental disorder (PDD) with an early childhood onset. It is characterized by marked abnormal development in social interaction and communication; a stereotypical, repetitive range of ritualized behaviors such as rocking, toe-walking, flapping, clapping, and whirling; and an obsessive desire for sameness. The disorder was first identified in the literature by Leo Kanner in 1943, and since then autism has become one of the most well-studied behavior disorders in childhood (Smith, Magyar, & Arnold-Saritepe, 2002). Its *DSM-IV* criteria include 12 symptoms divided among three categories: social interaction, communication/play/imagination, and limitations of interests and behaviors (Volkmar & Klin, 1999). Still, there is great variability in possible symptoms among people with autism. Relatively few (10–40%) display any particular behavioral marker, regardless of the diagnostic system being used. No common neural or cognitive deficits, behavior patterns, or life courses have been found among people with the disorder, nor is there a typical response to behavioral or drug intervention.

Despite differences in individual presentation, impairments in social relatedness underlie and define the clinical disorder (Peliosa & Lund, 2001; Volkmar & Klin, 1999). These include a lack of awareness of the feelings of others, an impaired capacity to imitate and express emotion, and the absence of capacity for social and symbolic play. Even in infancy, children with autism may lack reciprocal social engagement and are unable to maintain eye contact with another person (Volkmar & Klin, 1999). As the child grows older, these social disabilities persist, as indicated by difficulty in forming friendships, showing empathy, and understanding the rules and expectations that are a part of daily social interaction (Volkmar & Klin, 1999).

Deficits in communication in those with autism include muteness (seen in 50% of clients), echolalia (repetition of words or phrases), abnormal prosody (atypical speech rhythm, stress, intonation, and loudness), and pronoun reversal (for instance, the person refers to "you" as himself or herself and to the other person as "me"). These impairments are most pronounced in the pragmatic or social aspects of language use. People with autism may present irrelevant details, inappropriately persevere on a topic, suddenly shift to new topics, and ignore others' attempts to initiate conversation (Kaplan & Sadock, 2003). Deficits also involve language comprehension; speech is interpreted in overly concrete and literal ways. In fact, people with autism have more difficulty with understanding language than they do with learning the structures necessary to produce language. Thus, half the autistic population does not develop speech; a majority fails to use speech functionally (Peliosa & Lund, 2001). Persons with autism do, however, often possess characteristic "pockets" of ability, such as memorization, visual and spatial skills, and attention to details (Peliosa & Lund, 2001).

Some authors believe that the pervasive developmental disorders (PDD) classified in the *DSM-IV-TR* represent a continuum of autistic-like features and, as a result, call them autistic-spectrum disorders (Smith et al., 2002). This chapter focuses on autism, with some brief discussion of the other pervasive developmental disorders.

Prevalence of Autism

In the past few years, the reported incidence of autism has increased at a remarkably high rate across the world. The cause may be broader boundaries of the definition, more frequent inclusion of high-functioning persons with autism (and Asperger's syndrome), and the increase in diagnosis of very young children (Marcus, Garfinkle, & Wolery, 2001). Rates of autism range from 7–13 to 10–20 cases per 10,000 people, if atypical autism is included (Croen, Grether, & Selvin, 2002; Smith et al., 2002).

Both epidemiological and clinic-based studies indicate that autism spectrum disorders occur more often in males than in females, with ratio estimates ranging from 2:1 to 5:1 (Smith et al., 2002). Females tend to be more severely affected by the disorder because of a greater likelihood of mental retardation. However, females with autism without mental retardation are usually less impaired than males. The only autistic-spectrum disorder that seems to be more prevalent in females than in males is Rett's disorder (Smith et al., 2002).

In earlier reports, families of high socioeconomic status (SES) were overrepresented in cases of autism. This finding was apparently due to selection bias in that high-SES parents were more likely to seek treatment. Now it is generally believed that autism is represented in all social classes and races (Volkmar & Klin, 1999). Race may be a factor in the age of diagnosis, however. In a study of Philadelphia Medicaid mental health claims for 406 children, Caucasian children received a diagnosis of autism at an average age of 6.3 years, and African American children were diagnosed at a mean age of 7.9 years (Mandell, Listerud, Levy, & Pinto-Martin, 2002). Caucasian children thus began receiving services earlier than African American children. These disparities in diagnosis and intervention may result from clinician behaviors and differences in families' help-seeking behaviors, advocacy efforts, and support for services.

Assessment of Autism

A recent trend is early diagnosis of autism so that intervention can begin as soon as possible. Autism does not appear any later than the age of 3 (Volkmar & Klin, 1999) and is usually diagnosed by age 4 (Smith et al., 2002). When delays do occur, the reasons include a dearth of knowledge about the disorder (even among primary health care physicians) and a lack of easily applied screening tools (Volkmar & Klin, 1999). Practice guidelines adopted by the American Academy of Pediatrics call for pediatricians to examine babies and toddlers for signs of autism (Smith et al., 2002).

Social workers should never diagnose autism by themselves, because the process is complex and requires interprofessional collaboration. A comprehensive assessment should include input from the fields of psychiatry, medicine, psychology, social work, speech/language/communication therapy, occupational therapy, and physical therapy (Volkmar, Cook, Pomeroy, Realmuto, & Tanguay, 1999).

Although biochemical tests may soon distinguish at least some of the conditions within the autistic spectrum, identification at present is made through behavioral symptoms. Yet behavior by itself is a poor guide to diagnosis, because no single behavior or even set of behaviors unequivocally denotes autism (Jordan, 2001). Symptom patterns occur in different areas of functioning, which is why assessment involves professionals from different areas of expertise.

It is essential throughout the assessment process to involve parents and, as appropriate, other family members. The goal is to set the stage for a long-term collaborative relationship and help parents become better informed advocates for their child.

Psychiatric and Medical Assessment

Psychiatric and medical assessments focus on gathering historical information regarding the child's social relatedness and development of language, communication, and motor skills. Medical information must be gathered about the mother's pregnancy, labor, and delivery and the child's early neonatal course. Parents should be asked when they first had concerns about their child and the nature of these concerns. Medical history and neurological exams (including an EEG or MRI) should look for evidence of possible seizures, sensory deficits such as hearing or visual impairment, and other medical conditions. The family history should be reviewed for the presence of other developmental disorders.

Another critical aspect of the assessment is the child's physical examination, which involves identifying treatable medical conditions that sometimes produce symptoms suggestive of PDD. Visual and audiological examinations should be performed if there are concerns about possible sensory problems. The family may report frequent ear infections, but in some cases chronic ear infections are recognized late because of the language delay related to PDD. Lead levels should also be checked, if the child has had exposure.

The physical examination should also assess any inherited medical conditions. For example, the presence of dysmorphic features (small body deformities) may suggest the need for genetic screening for inherited metabolic disorders. Other metabolic causes of developmental delays include fragile X syndrome, which is the most common cause of genetically inherited mental retardation (National Fragile X Foundation, 2003). Its symptoms of hyperactivity are similar to those of autism. Tuberous sclerosis is another relevant genetic condition, in which small substances form and calcify on the child's brain surfaces (Tuberous Sclerosis Association, 2003). Its effects range from mild to serious, but it can cause epilepsy, developmental delays, and autistic-like behavior. Although no definitive laboratory tests are available for autism, these other disorders can be identified medically, and thus the diagnosis of autism may be supported or ruled out.

Psychological Assessment

Psychologists are often in the best position to assess the child's intellectual ability and learning styles and to develop plans for modifying behavior. Assessment of the child's cognitive ability helps to establish his or her overall levels of function. (These are required in many states to determine eligibility for some services.)

When possible, separate estimates of verbal and nonverbal IQ should be obtained. Individuals with autism typically perform better on nonverbal and visual-spatial tasks than on verbal tasks. In addition, assessment of the client's adaptive skills is essential to document the possible presence of any associated mental retardation.

Speech and Language Assessment

The speech and language therapist assesses the child's understanding of all aspects of language and communication by reviewing grammatical level, semantic knowledge, pragmatic ability, and language learning style. This information is vital for planning a program for the child to learn communication and for his or her future educational placement.

Social Work Assessment

The social worker's examination includes observation of the child in structured and unstructured settings, such as the home and school. Observations of the child's interaction with parents and siblings provide important information about the child, the levels of stress experienced by the family in response to the child's symptoms, and the effectiveness of parental interventions.

Information on family support and stress is important. Studies have demonstrated that the family stress associated with having a child with autism is greater than that of having a child diagnosed with mental retardation, Down syndrome, or chronic physical illness (Gabriels, Hill, Pierce, Rogers, & Wehner, 2001).

The social worker should also assess the child's developmental level, as well as symptoms in the areas of social interaction, communication/play, restricted and unusual interests, and any unusual behaviors (for example, excessive hand-washing). The social worker should note the presence of specific problem behaviors that may interfere with intervention programs, such as aggression, self-injury, and other behavioral oddities.

The social worker should further examine the child's prior response to any educational programs or behavioral interventions. This information may be ascertained from previous evaluations for educational and other services, information from standard rating scales and symptom checklists, and narrative reports of teachers and care providers.

Other Assessments

Occupational and physical therapy assessments may be indicated for children with suspected autism, particularly if sensitivity to the environment is excessive or dulled or if motor skill development is impaired (Volkmar et al., 1999). Some diagnostic centers can include even wider assessments. A music therapy assessment, for example, can determine the child's ability to participate in and form relationships through structured musical activities. In summary, the goal of an assessment of autism is not merely to determine whether a child has the disorder but also to gain some idea of the child's potential and to offer guidance on forms of education and treatment that are likely to be beneficial (Jordan, 2001).

Other Pervasive Developmental Disorders

Other than autism, which is the defining pervasive developmental disorder, other PDDs in the *DSM-IV-TR* include Asperger's disorder, Rett's disorder, childhood disintegrative disorder, and pervasive developmental disorder not otherwise specified (also known as atypical autism).

Asperger's Disorder

In Asperger's disorder, early development (both cognition and language) is apparently normal, but the child often has unusual interests that are pursued with great intensity (Holter, 2004). The child's approaches to peers and novel adults may be unusual or idiosyncratic, but attachment patterns to family members are well established. Social deficits become more prominent as the child enters preschool and is exposed to peers. The current criteria for Asperger's disorder emphasize impairments in social interaction and nonverbal communication similar to those found in autism but without the unusual behaviors and environmental responsiveness. Referral for assessment is usually later than in cases of suspected autism. Symptoms of depression are associated with Asperger's disorder and may be the cause for initial psychiatric referral.

Of the various pervasive developmental disorders newly included in *DSM-IV*, Asperger's disorder has been the most controversial (Kasari & Rotheram-Fuller (2005). Until quite recently, the diagnosis of Asperger's was used to refer to adults with autism or to higher cognitively functioning individuals with autism.

Although limited data exist on the course of Asperger's disorder, individuals with the condition have generally a better outcome than those with high-functioning autism: They are more likely to have gainful employment, live independently, and establish a family (Volkmar & Klin, 1999). However, the social difficulties of Asperger's disorder are apparently lifelong.

Rett's Disorder

In Rett's Disorder, which occurs exclusively in females, a brief period of normal development precedes decelerated head growth, loss of purposeful hand movements, and development of severe psychomotor retardation (American Psychiatric Association, 2000). The child has a normal head circumference at birth, and prenatal and infant development is apparently normal to at least age 6 months. Subsequently, the child's head and body growth decelerate, and previously acquired skills are lost, replaced by stereotyped hand movements, such as wringing or washing, and a lack of interest in the environment. This disorder usually has its onset in the latter half of the first year of life, and diagnostic criteria require that it occur before age 4. Its potential for confusion with autism is greatest in the preschool years because of the stereotyped movements and limited or deteriorating language, social, and motor skills.

The course of Rett's disorder is predictable, and the prognosis poor. By the time the child reaches school age, autistic-like features are less prominent. The child reaches a temporary developmental plateau characterized by severe mental retardation, seizures, motor problems, breathing difficulties (hyperventilation, breath-holding spells, air swallowing), grinding of teeth, motor problems, and early scoliosis (curvature of the spine) (Volkmar et al., 1999). Apnea (a temporary cessation of breathing) may alternate with hyperventilation. Subsequently, an even more marked period of developmental deterioration occurs. Although motor problems are pronounced, most children remain ambulatory until the final phase of the disorder, when motor problems and scoliosis increasingly limit mobility. With the disorder comes an increased risk of sudden death and a decreased life expectancy. Adults with this disorder require very high levels of support and supervision.

Smith et al. (2002) suggest that because Rett's disorder has a distinct etiology, presentation, course, and response to treatment, it should be classified separately in future editions of the *DSM*, as it already is in the *International Classification of Diseases, 10th Revision* (World Health Organization, 1992).

Childhood Disintegrative Disorder

Childhood disintegration disorder (CDD) is rare and poorly understood (Peliosa & Lund, 2001). In children with the disorder, a period of at least 2 years of normal development occurs, with age-appropriate communication, social relatedness, play, and adaptive behaviors. The onset of CDD typically occurs between 3 and 4 years of age and can be gradual (over a period of some weeks or months) or abrupt (days to weeks). The disorder is marked by a deterioration and clinically significant loss of at least two skills in the areas of receptive or expressive language and social, toileting, play, and motor skills. The child also develops abnormal functioning in at least two of the areas of behavioral disturbance observed in autism (social relatedness, language and communication, or restricted interests and activities). Thus, a child who previously had appeared perfectly normal loses language, self-help, and other skills and comes to exhibit behaviors suggestive of autism.

Three patterns in the clinical course of CDD have been reported. In about 75% of cases, the child's development and behavior deteriorate to a much lower level of functioning and then reach a plateau, after which developmental gains are minimal. Less frequently, the developmental regression is followed by limited recovery; a child who had become totally mute may regain an ability to speak in single words or, occasionally, phrases or sentences. Sometimes the developmental regression is progressive, and death is the eventual outcome. In most cases, life expectancy is normal.

Pervasive Developmental Disorder Not Otherwise Specified

The term pervasive developmental disorder not otherwise specified (PDD-NOS), sometimes termed atypical PDD or atypical autism, encompasses subthreshold cases with, for example, marked impairment of social interaction or communication or stereotyped behavior patterns or interests, but the full features of autism or of another defined PDD in each of these domains are not met. This category is defined on the basis of the clinician's judgment. The natural history of PDD-NOS has been rarely studied. Although deficits in social and other skills have been noted, these problems are less severe than in classical autism. The issue of whether meaningful subtypes might be defined within the broad PDD category remains a topic of debate.

PDD-NOS is more commonly seen than autism, with a prevalence of perhaps one in several hundred school-age children (Volkmar et al., 1999). The limited data suggest that individuals with PDD-NOS have a better prognosis than those with autism, but social, communicative, or adaptive and behavioral problems may be prominent during the school years. In adolescence and adulthood, increased risk for anxiety and mood disorders emerges for these individuals.

Differential Diagnosis and Comorbidity for Autism

In diagnosing autism, other disorders must also be considered. Table 4.1 addresses some disorders that share characteristics with autism that must

Table 4.1	
Differential Diagnosis of Autism	
Differential Diagnosis	Distinctions Between Diagnoses
Mental retardation	Individuals with autism show specific impairments in reciprocal attention, imitation, and symbolic play.
Developmental language disorders	Children with autism show more pervasive verbal communication difficulties, nonverbal communication impairment, and social difficulties.
Schizophrenia	Schizophrenia is rare in childhood; usually a period of normal development precedes the appearance of hallucinations and delusions.
Stereotypic movement disorders	These disorders involve motor mannerisms (stereotypies) and mental retardation. The diagnosis is not made if the individual has a PDD.
Schizoid personality disorder	The individual suffers from isolation but is able to relate to others in some situations
Reactive attachment disorder	The individual has a history of severe neglect; the social deficits typically remit with a more responsive environment.

Source: Volkmar et al. (1999); Volkmar & Klin (1999).

be ruled out before autism is diagnosed. Some of these alternative diagnoses may be comorbid with autism. In addition, individuals with autism have an increased risk for psychiatric problems because of the broadly debilitating features of autism, cognitive impairment, the frequent presence of comorbid medical disorders, and problematic life experiences related to having autism (Lainhart, 1999).

Two professional viewpoints are prominent in diagnosing conditions that are comorbid with autism (Volkmar, 2001). Some clinicians are reluctant to assign additional diagnoses. From this perspective, autism encompasses not only its core clinical features but also many associated problems, including attention difficulties and behavioral rigidity. Other clinicians prefer to assign multiple diagnoses and make each one a specific target for behavioral or drug intervention. As a general guideline, additional diagnoses should not be made if their symptoms are contained within the diagnosis of autism (Lainhart, 1999). For instance, generalized anxiety disorder should not be diagnosed separately, as obsessive thinking and ritualized, compulsive behaviors are part of the diagnostic criteria for PDD.

For several reasons, estimates of the frequency of comorbid disorders and psychiatric symptoms in persons with autism vary widely (Holmes, 1998). First, the majority of studies rely on clinical rather than epidemiological samples. Second, studies include differences in the way samples are selected, the age of participants, the method of inquiry, and the clinical experience of the interviewers. Third, different instruments and diagnostic measures are used to diagnose the other disorders. Fourth, as noted earlier, the features of autism and Asperger's disorder can make the diagnosis of other psychiatric disorders difficult (Lainhart, 1999). Table 4.2 lists common comorbid disorders that have been established.

Risk and Protective Factors for Autism

Risk and protective factors for autism are generally accepted to be factors for not only autism but also the autistic-spectrum disorders. However, few studies have addressed questions about the magnitude of risk or the proportion of autism that is accounted for by specific factors (Nelson, 1991).

Table 4.2	
Common Co-Occurring Disorders with Autism	
Comorbid Disorder	*Prevalence and Features*
Mental Retardation	Severe or profound in 50% of persons with autism, mild to moderate in 30%, and within the normal IQ range in 20%
Seizure disorders	Present by early adulthood in 25 to 30% of persons with autism
Depression	Rates of 4.4 to 57.6% in persons with autism
Anxiety (agoraphobia, separation anxiety, and simple phobias)	Present in 7 to 84% of persons with autism
Overactivity and/or attentional problems	Present in 21 to 72% of persons with autism
Tic Disorders	Present in 7 to 29% of persons with autism

Source: Aman & Langworthy (2000); Bernard et al. (2002); Volkmar et al. (1999); Lainhart (1999); Richdale (1999); Schopler (2001).

Neither have research studies used multivariate analytic techniques to examine the risks associated with one factor while simultaneously adjusting for others (Tager-Flusberg, Joseph, & Folstein, 2001). With these caveats in mind, the generally accepted risk factors for autism appear in Table 4.3.

Onset

Its precise etiology is not known, but research suggests that autism is a genetic, neurobiological disorder (Bailey et al., 1995). There is no association of autism with any psychological or social factors, including parenting styles. Approximately 60 to 70% of people with autism manifest distinct neurological abnormalities and various levels of mental retardation. Although brain abnormalities exist in a majority of diagnosed individuals, 30 to 40% of people with autism have an anatomically intact central nervous system and no indication of mental retardation (Peliosa & Lund, 2001).

Thus, autism has many etiologies, including the following:

- Genetic conditions
- Viral infections (such as congenital rubella, a type of mental retardation that results from infection during pregnancy)
- Metabolic conditions (such as abnormalities of purine synthesis, the amino acid that energizes many physical reactions)
- Congenital anomaly syndromes (such as Williams syndrome, a genetic disability characterized by outgoing behavior and intellectual and developmental impairments)

None of the identified etiologies is invariably associated with autism, however, and knowledge of these causes has not clarified the neuropsychological basis of the disorder (Peliosa & Lund, 2001).

Table 4.3	
Risk and Protective Factors for the Onset of Autistic Disorder	
Risk	*Protective*
Biological	
Genetic loading	
Brain abnormalities	
High levels of serotonin	
Male gender	

Brain Development

Several brain abnormalities have been identified in persons with autism, but which of the anomalies are both specific and universal to the disorder is still unclear. The most consistent findings point to disruptions in the limbic system and the cerebellum and its circuits (Holter, 2004). Structural and functional brain imaging studies have also indicated that autism may be associated with enlarged overall brain size and decreased size and activity in specific areas of the brain. One of these areas may be the midsagittal area of the cerebellum, thought to be involved in the sequencing of motor activities. Another is the lower hippocampus (in the midbrain), which is associated with complex learning processes. A third area is the amygdala (located in the temporal lobe), which is believed to contribute to the recognition of faces and emotional expression. A final area is the brain stem, in a section associated with attention.

Regarding brain development, it is also hypothesized that boys are four to five times likelier to develop autism than girls because its symptoms are an exaggeration of their "natural" way of thinking. That is, in a context of multiple intelligences, boys tend to be more advanced in systematizing activities, whereas girls are more advanced in empathizing functions (Baron-Cohen, 2003).

With regard to deficits in brain functioning, autism has been conceptualized in a variety of ways (Tager-Flusberg et al., 2001). It may be a disorder of central coherence in which the person is unable to holistically process information and develops a bias toward part-oriented processing. It may be a disorder of executive function in which the person is not able to process bits of information or regulate behavior and thus is inclined toward rigid, repetitive behaviors and impoverished social interaction. It may be a deficit in social cognition in that the internal mental states of other people are not understood. Today, however, most research on brain deficits in autism focuses on language and communication, involving the difficulties in using and comprehending words and their meanings.

Neurotransmitters

Children with autism may have an overgrowth of neurons, coupled with an underdeveloped organization of neurons into specialized systems in some areas of the brain. These findings have not been consistently replicated across studies, however, and therefore must be viewed with caution (Smith et al., 2002).

Research has also indicated that children with autism may have high levels of the neurotransmitter serotonin in the midbrain and brain stem

(Anderson, 2002). Genes that promote serotonin may thus facilitate the multiple neuron interactions that are prerequisites for developing autism. Again, any conclusions about these processes are speculative at this time.

Heredity

In twin studies, the concordance rate for autism in identical twins ranges from 36 to 91% (Veenstra-Vanderweele & Cook, 2003). In other family studies, 2 to 4% of siblings also develop autism, which is 50 times more likely than in the general population. An even greater proportion of siblings (up to 90%) are diagnosed with one of the other pervasive developmental disorders (Santangelo & Folstein, 1999).

Parents of individuals with autism perform worse than controls on measures of executive function and subtle measures of their ability to apprehend the mental states of significant others. Studies also suggest that relatives of individuals with autism show elevated rates of psychiatric disorders, specifically major depression and anxiety disorders (Tager-Flusberg et al., 2001). Rates of major depression throughout a lifetime range from 20 to 37% for first-degree relatives; these depressive episodes are not limited to the period after the birth of the child and are not fully accounted for by the stress of caring for a child with autism (Lainhart, 1999).

The research suggests that different genes and the variety of ways they can be manifested contribute to different symptoms of autism (Smith et al., 2002). In addition, there are probably a few genes that must interact with each other to cause the characteristics of autism (Santangelo & Folstein, 1999). Autism involves perhaps 3 to 10 or more genes altogether, with 2 to 4 genes that must interact to produce symptoms. Thus, in genetic studies, one would expect to find evidence for genes at more than one locus. To date, there is some evidence for three loci: chromosomes 7q, 13q, and 15q (Tager-Flusberg et al., 2001). In the search for causes, researchers have come to appreciate the great complexity of the genetic interactions that appear to produce autism (Veenstra-Vanderweele & Cook, 2003).

Prenatal and Perinatal Complications

A small minority of children with autism have experienced identifiable prenatal or perinatal (immediately after birth) events linked to autism (Smith et al, 2002). These complications, however, are more closely associated with mental retardation than with autism. The association between autism and maternal age has varied in studies, with preliminary evidence suggesting that maternal age is not a factor (Croen et al., 2002).

Recovery and Adjustment

Although the etiology of autism appears to be largely genetic and biological in nature at this point, it is not completely understood (Smith et al., 2002). Hopefully, advances in nervous system assessment will eventually permit early (and perhaps even prenatal) intervention, but for now and probably for years to come, social workers can best focus on the adjustment of individuals diagnosed with autism.

Evidence suggests that with early detection and intervention, the prognosis for autism improves significantly. Studies conducted in the 1960s and 1970s revealed that only 1 to 2% of individuals with autism were able to attain personal and job independence (Volkmar et al., 1999). During that time, however, specialized services were sparse and began only when children were school age.

Currently, a third of people with autism ultimately achieve some level of independence and self-sufficiency in adulthood. Adults with autism who are able to live independently and hold jobs typically have high levels of cognitive and communicative skills, although they still demonstrate social deficits (Volkmar et al., 1999). Intervention before the age of 5 now seems critical for a better outcome; even age 6 may be too late to produce significant gains (Erba, 2000; Ozonoff & Cathcart, 1998; Volkmar & Klin, 1999). Today, two thirds of those diagnosed with autism require intensive care as adults. Hopefully, with earlier intervention and the greater current emphasis on life skills and vocational training, outcomes in adulthood will improve as well (Volkmar & Klin, 1999).

Other than the timing of intervention, protective factors for the course of autism and the other developmental disorders are related to the age of onset, the severity of the condition, and comorbid conditions. Later age of onset (after 24 months) predicts better outcome. The child's early acquisition of nonverbal communication and functional play skills has been linked to subsequent gains in language skills. In addition, intelligible speech capacity acts as a protective factor (Volkmar & Klin, 1999). Children with higher IQs (over 60) are more responsive to intervention. IQ stabilizes after 5 years and correlates with later academic and work achievement (Volkmar & Klin, 1999).

Risk factors for the course of autism include the child's aggression and self-injury (head banging, finger or hand biting, head slapping, and hair pulling), which compromise home and community placements (Lainhart, 1999). Aggressive behaviors are rarely intentional; rather, they are due to the following reasons.

- Cognitive and emotional impairments, which lead to impulsivity, low frustration tolerance, poor emotional and behavioral regulation, and difficulties with adaptive and coping skills

- The inability to communicate anger verbally
- Difficulty with negotiating change
- Learned behaviors to avoid tasks or certain situations
- Misreading of others' intent as threatening
- Seizures or other biological factors

Another protective factor identified for the course of the disorder is the quality of parents' interactions with their children, which may affect the development of children's language skills over time. In one 16-year longitudinal study, parents' level of synchronization (parallel participation) during play with their children seemed to have a positive impact on the development of their child's language skills (Siller & Sigman, 2002). Table 4.4 presents the factors that affect the course of autism.

Table 4.4	
Risk and Protective Factors That Affect the Course of Autistic Disorder	
Risk	Protective
Age of Onset	
Earlier age of onset (before 24 months)	Later age of onset (after 24 months)
Psychological	
Aggression and self-injury	Nonaggressive
Unintelligible speech	Intelligible speech
IQ under 60	IQ over 60
	Early nonverbal communication and functional play skills
Social	
Family	
Parents' lack of involvement in intervention	Parental involvement in intervention
Parents do not engage in parallel play with their children	Parents engage in play activities along with their children
Services	
Late detection	Early detection
Lack of services available	Early, intensive, behavioral intervention

No intervention has yet been shown to change the core features of autism to the extent that the individual is able to achieve normative levels of functioning. But after a thorough diagnostic evaluation, some steps may be taken to help the individual function better. The range of interventions should include special education, family support, and behavioral management. Medications may also be used, if necessary, to control behavioral symptoms, although considerable caution should be exercised when doing so, and the child's response should be monitored closely (Volkmar et al., 1999). Intervention programs should be comprehensive and include professionals from a variety of disciplines.

Parental involvement should be encouraged to enhance consistency in approaches at home and at school and to facilitate the child's generalization of skills across settings. Professionals should work with parents to obtain appropriate educational placement and help them become aware of other community resources, such as respite care. Finally, family members can be invited to join various parent and family groups for information and support. Many parents of children with autism feel guilt, sorrow, anger, and stress, and siblings may also be affected (Magda, Schopler, Cueva, & Hallin, 1996). The family, in almost every case, must adjust to the needs of the child's disability.

Federal law 94-142 mandates the provision of an appropriate educational plan for all children in the United States. As part of this educational plan, ancillary services are often required, including speech or language therapy, occupational therapy, and physical therapy. Sustained, continuous programming is more effective than episodic programming; summer programming may also be needed because children with autism often regress in the absence of such services. Professionals should be prepared to consult and collaborate with teachers and other school personnel (Volkmar et al., 1999) and have a working knowledge of state and federal laws and policies related to services (Holter, 2004). The possibility of new federal mandates for the provision of remedial services beginning in infancy and continuing through the child's life may increase the availability of services for families (Volkmar, 2001).

Thirty years of research have shown the beneficial effects of behavioral interventions in home and school settings (Peliosa & Lund, 2001). These interventions significantly improve clients' skill areas, such as receptive and expressive language, social and play activities, and self-help. Many children with autism also acquire functional academic skills, such as basic reading and math skills, and many can learn vocational skills, such as assembling objects and filing documents. Other demonstrated improvements as a result of behavioral interventions include persistent gains in IQ, daily living skills, and the ability to socialize. Behavioral problems that are often responsive to intervention include tantrums, aggression, and sleep problems. The training manuals developed by Lovaas (1987) for home-based behavior modification provide one example of interventions of this type.

Simeonsson, Olley, and Rosenthal (1987) reviewed four comprehensive early intervention programs and concluded that the critical factors of success were behavioral treatment, parental involvement, early and intensive intervention (at least 15 hours per week, low student-to-staff ratio), and a focus on generalizing the child's skills to new settings. Other studies have suggested the importance of educational interventions to foster the acquisition of basic social, cognitive, communicative, and adaptive skills. Educational programs should be highly structured and oriented to the individual needs of the child (Marcus et al., 2001; Newsom, 1996). Inclusion of occupational therapy services and the presence of normally developing peers have also been recommended.

For adolescents, emphasis should be placed on adaptive and vocational skills to prepare the individual for independent living. In his review, Holter (2004) notes that sexual development in adolescence brings with it some additional behavioral problems, which may be addressed by using sexual education and behavioral techniques.

Among adults, the identification of community resources and support in planning for long-term care is critical. In many states, adults with pervasive developmental disorders are not eligible for services that provide supported employment and residential living arrangements unless they also have mental retardation (Volkmar et al., 1999).

Drug and Behavioral Intervention for Specific Symptoms

The symptoms of autism that respond to medications do not represent the core features of autism—that is, basic deficits in social interaction and communication. Rather, drug intervention may help with aggression, self-injury, inattention, and stereotyped movements, and behavioral improvement may help the individual become more amendable to education (Volkmar, 2001).

For the client's anxiety, selective serotonin reuptake inhibitor (SSRI) drugs may help. Behavior programs, desensitization, predictability in everyday life, and steps to minimize failure and other stressful situations may help as well (Lainhart, 1999).

General attention in autistic children may be improved through the use of stimulants and other medications, but controlled studies are limited, and adverse effects may outweigh benefits in some cases. Empirical evidence for significant reductions in hyperactive symptoms is strongest for the antipsychotics (particularly risperidone), psychostimulants, and naltrexone, an opiate antagonist (Aman & Langworthy, 2000; Schopler, 2001). SSRIs may also be helpful (Lainhart, 1999).

For reducing aggression, risperidone may be effective, often without inducing severe adverse reactions. Olanzapine and clozapine have also been recommended (Bernard, Young, Pearson, Geddes, & O'Brien, 2002). In addition, naltrexone has been posited to block opioids that may be released during self-injurious repetitive behaviors.

Behavioral interventions are the first choice for treating language and social functioning deficits. Although seldom used in this country, biopterin appears to elicit small improvements in language and social functioning in some autistic individuals, with few side effects reported. For sleep problems, which are common in children with autism, behavioral measures are applied initially, possibly along with the administration of melatonin, light therapy, or chronotherapy (time structuring) (Richdale, 1999). For intractable cases of sleep impairment, medication may be a necessary component.

Summary of Interventions

Unfortunately, even the most effective interventions for autism work in only 50 to 60% of cases. Efforts to identify clinical subgroups that may respond to specific interventions have been hampered by the small size and heterogeneity of most study samples, prominent placebo responses, and the lack of widely agreed-upon standards for rating scales to assess potential improvements. Finally, almost all studies are relatively short in duration, even though autism is a chronic disorder requiring lifelong intervention (Schopler, 2001).

Critique of the Diagnosis

Autistic disorder first appeared as a formal diagnosis in *DSM-III* (APA, 1980). Interestingly, it was initially formulated as an Axis II disorder but was moved to Axis I in *DSM-IV*. A high rate of false-positive cases (meaning more people are diagnosed than truly warrant the diagnosis) have been identified using the *DSM* criteria, indicating their low validity and reliability (Peliosa & Lund, 2001).

Because of symptom overlap with other developmental disorders and a lack of clear demarcation between diagnostic categories, debate has ensued over whether autistic disorder, Asperger's syndrome (which first appeared in *DSM-IV*), and PDD-NOS are truly separate. Indeed, the validity of other PDDs has been questioned (Peliosa & Lund, 2001). Research efforts have until recently been focused almost exclusively on autism. However, the advent of formal definitions in *DSM-IV* and *ICD-10* of the other PDDs has already begun to stimulate additional research. It is likely that the definitions of these conditions will be further refined.

Case Illustration: Jacob's Autism

Jacob was a 2½-year-old Latino boy who lived with his mother and father in an urban neighborhood. Jacob's father supported the family financially, while his mother stayed at home and served as Jacob's primary caregiver. Suspecting autism, the family's pediatrician had suggested that Jacob undergo a formal assessment at a clinic specializing in services to children and adults with autism.

The initial assessment for the child was administered in the home under the assumption that a child will feel most comfortable in his or her natural environment. During the interview, Jacob's parents reported that he engaged in several inappropriate behaviors, including excessive mouthing of objects, inappropriate toy use (such as trying to throw or bounce stationary objects), and excessive tantrums. His parents handled his tantrums by trying to console him. Jacob's parents also stated that he did not communicate and had difficulty listening and following through on requests. As a result, they tended to complete tasks for him. Jacob also lacked social skills and refused to eat many foods, so his parents gave him only foods he enjoyed, such as pudding and cookies.

While interviewing Jacob's parents, the social worker also observed his behaviors and the parent–child interactions. Jacob lacked both verbal and nonverbal communication skills. He did not make any sounds, point to desired objects, or shake his head in response to questions or requests. Additionally, Jacob did not make eye contact, and he had deficits in imitation and fine motor skills. Last, Jacob did not show any affection toward either parent.

Jacob's usual routine was to stay home with his mother doing whatever he desired, including engaging in self-stimulus behaviors and watching excessive amounts of a particular television show. His inappropriate behaviors were not interrupted, and in fact, he was permitted to hand-flap or spin car wheels for several minutes at a time.

Multiaxial Diagnosis

Axis I.   299.00 Autistic Disorder: The first criterion involves qualitative impairment in social interaction, for which Jacob manifested all the symptoms. The second criterion involves qualitative impairments in communication, for which he also demonstrated all symptoms. He further met criteria for having restricted repetitive and stereotyped patterns of behavior, interests, and activities. The delays occurred prior to age 3, and he did not meet criteria for Rett's disorder or childhood disintegrative disorder.

Axis II. V71.09 No Diagnosis: Testing did not reveal the presence of mental retardation.

Axis III. None: Unlike many other children with autism, Jacob did not have any comorbid medical conditions.

Axis IV. None

GAF. 30: Jacob's severe impairments included many areas of functioning, including communication, social functioning, and feeding.

Risk and Protective Factors

Jacob's male gender was his only observable risk factor for the onset of autism. He may have had a genetic propensity for autism and brain abnormalities, but these could be only indirectly assessed through his behaviors. Jacob did have several important risk factors for the course of autism. He had an early age of onset (prior to 2 years old), a low IQ, and demonstrated aggressive behaviors and unintelligible speech.

While these factors were discouraging, Jacob had some protective social factors. His autism was detected early, and his parents enrolled him into an early, intensive behavioral intervention. His parents were also quite involved in the intervention process and did not support Jacob's isolative behaviors; instead, they engaged in parallel play with him.

Goal Formulation and Treatment Planning

Because of the severity of Jacob's disorder, both his pediatrician and the early interventionist believed it was necessary to begin behavior therapy, occupational and sensory integration therapy, speech therapy, and physical therapy immediately after he was diagnosed. The family and social worker agreed that the most important behaviors to address were those that set Jacob apart developmentally from other children. His parents believed that his lack of communication was hindering him in other developmental areas, most clearly that of socialization.

It was important to validate the parents' feelings, but at the same time, it would be detrimental to give them false hope. Jacob made no sounds, and there was a possibility that he could never expressively converse without some type of communication system.

The social worker helped Jacob's parents understand that it is often difficult to pinpoint the needs of a nonverbal child; therefore, addressing difficulties relating to all five of the developmental domains would be necessary. Agreed-upon initial treatment goals involved the basic areas of feeding and learning readiness skills.

Interventions

Feeding goals included tasting new foods, chewing textured foods (such as breads and fruits), and transitioning from a bottle to a cup. Learning readiness skills included simple one-step commands (e.g., sit down, stand up, come here), appropriate sitting (no tantrums or self-stimulus behaviors), object manipulation, gross motor imitation, and eye contact.

After mastering the goals with the primary therapist, Jacob needed to be able to generalize to other individuals. The social worker would teach Jacob's parents to apply the techniques to the home setting. The parents were linked to the agency's ongoing support group and to the Autism Association of America for ongoing resources as well.

Appendix. Measures for Autism

The three scales included here—Children's Social Behavior Questionnaire, Autism Screening Questionnaire, and Autism Behavior Checklist—were chosen for their psychometric properties (meaning that they have proven reliability and validity). Scales that did not have adequate support and were in need of further development were not included, even though they may be cited commonly in the literature (e.g., Gilliam, 1995).

Children's Social Behavior Questionnaire (CSBQ)

Luteijn, Jackson, Volkmar, & Minderaa (1998); Luteijn, Luteijn, Jackson, Volkmar, & Minderaa, (2000)

Description

- 96-item questionnaire designed to examine behavioral problems in children with mild variants of PDD.
- Evaluates five categories of behaviors:
  1. acting-out
  2. social contact problems
  3. social insight problems
  4. anxious/rigid behaviors
  5. stereotypical behaviors

Reliability

Interrater reliability between parents of the same child was satisfactory. Test-retest reliability (4-week) was also satisfactory. Internal consistency was satisfactorily high.

Validity

The five subscales of the CSBQ yield high correlations with the Autism Behavior Checklist and the Autism Behavior Checklist. However, discriminant analyses have indicated that only about 27% of children diagnosed with pervasive developmental disorder not otherwise specified can be correctly classified on the basis of the CSBQ, with almost 29% misclassified as autistic and 24% misclassified as having attention-deficit/hyperactivity disorder. In addition, correlations between CSBQ scales and *DSM-IV* criteria for pervasive developmental disorder were reportedly weaker than expected.

Autism Screening Questionnaire (ASQ)

Berument, Rutter, Lord, Pickles, & Bailey (1999)

Description

- Commonly used and accepted parental questionnaire for autism.
- 40-item screening measure developed from the Autism Diagnostic Interview Revised (ADI-R) for use by the primary caregiver focuses on three areas of functioning:

  1. reciprocal social interaction
  2. language and communication
  3. repetitive and stereotyped behaviors

Reliability

Based on the ADI-R, this instrument is thought to have good reliability.

Validity

The ASQ has been found to have good discriminative validity, separating pervasive developmental disorders from nonpervasive developmental disorders at all IQ levels; the cutoff of 15 was most effective.

Autism Behavior Checklist (ABC)

Krug, Arick, & Almond (1980a)

Description

- Part of a broader tool, the Autism Screening Instrument for Educational Planning
- Completed by caregivers of persons suspected of having autism
- 57 items grouped into 5 subscales: Sensory, Relating, Body and Object Use, Language, and Social and Self Help
- Identifies either the absence or presence of autistic characteristics in individuals

Reliability

Eaves, Campbell, & Chambers (2000)
ABC reports an average internal consistency with a coefficient alpha of .87. Interrater reliability between teachers and parents is low, but other interrater reliability is high.

Validity

Concurrent and construct validity evidence is mixed; one example of concurrent validity is provided by Yirmiya, Sigman, & Freeman (1994), who found that children identified by their parents as having severe autistic behaviors on the ABC also had medical records that signified serious symptoms. Although it successfully screens for the presence of autism, the ABC might overclassify cases of autism (Volkmar, Klin, & Cohen, 1997).

References

Aman, M., & Langworthy, K. (2000). Pharmacology for hyperactivity in children with autism and other pervasive developmental disorders. *Journal of Autism and Developmental Disorders, 30*(5), 451–459.

American Psychiatric Association. (2000). *Diagnostic and statistical manual of mental disorders* (4th ed., text rev.). Washington, DC: Author.

Anderson, G. (2002). Genetics of childhood disorders: XLV. Autism, part 4: Serotonin in autism. *Journal of the Academy of Child and Adolescent Psychiatry, 41*(12), 1513–1516.

Bailey, A., Le Couteur, A., Gottesman, I., Bolton, P., Simonoff, E., Yuzda, E., et al. (1995). Autism as a strongly genetic disorder: Evidence from a British twin study. *Psychological Medicine 25*, 63–77.

Baron-Cohen, S. (2003). *The essential difference: The truth about the male and female brain.* Boulder, CO: Perseus.

Bernard, L., Young, A. H., Pearson, J., Geddes, J., & O'Brien, G. (2002). Systematic review of the use of atypical antipsychotics in autism. *Journal of Psychopharmacology, 16*(1), 93–101.

Croen, L. A., Grether, J. K., & Selvin, S. (2002). Descriptive epidemiology of autism in a California population: Who is at risk? *Journal of Autism and Developmental Disorders, 32*(3), 217–224.

Erba, H. W. (2000). Early intervention programs for children with autism: Conceptual frameworks for implementation. *American Journal of Orthopsychiatry, 70*(1), 82–92.

Gabriels, R. L., Hill, D., Pierce, R., Rogers, S., & Wehner, B. (2001). Predictors of treatment outcome in young children with autism. *Autism: The International Journal of Research and Practice, 5*(4), 407–429.

Holmes, D. (1998). *Autism through the lifespan*. Bethesda, MD: Woodbine.

Holter, M. (2004). Autistic spectrum disorders: Assessment and intervention. In P. Allen-Meares & M. Fraser (Eds.), *Intervention with children and adolescents: An interdisciplinary perspective* (pp. 205–228). Washington, DC: NASW Press.

Jordan, R. (2001). Multidisciplinary work for children with autism. *Educational and Child Psychology, 18*(2), 5–14.

Kanner, L. (1943). Autistic disturbances of affective content. *Nervous Child, 2*, 217–250.

Kaplan, H. I., & Sadock, B. J. (2003). *Synopsis of psychiatry: Behavioral sciences/clinical psychiatry* (9th ed.). Baltimore: Williams & Wilkins.

Kasari, C., & Rotheram-Fuller, E. (2005). Current trends in psychological research on children with high-functioning autism and Asperger disorder. *Current Opinion in Psychiatry, 18*, 497–501.

Lainhart, J. (1999). Psychiatric problems in individuals with autism, their parents and siblings. *International review of Psychiatry, 11*, 278–298.

Lovaas, O. I. (1987). Behavioral treatment and normal education and intellectual functioning in young autistic children. *Journal of Consulting and Clinical Psychology, 55*(1), 3–9.

Magda, C., Schopler, E., Cueva, J. E., & Hallin, A. (1996). Treatment of autistic disorder. *Journal of the American Academy of Child and Adolescent Psychiatry, 35*(2), 134–143.

Mandell, D. S., Listerud, J., Levy, S. E., & Pinto-Martin, J. A. (2002). Race differences in the age at diagnosis among Medicaid-eligible children with autism. *Journal of the American Academy of Child and Adolescent Psychiatry, 41*(12), 1447–1454.

Marcus, L., Garfinkle, A., & Wolery, M. (2001). *The research basis for autism intervention*. New York: Plenum.

National Fragile X Foundation. (n.d.). *What is fragile X syndrome?* Retrieved November 17, 2003, from http://www.fragilex.org/html/what.htm

Nelson, K. B. (1991). Prenatal and perinatal factors in the etiology of autism. *Pediatrics, 87*(5), 761–767.

Newsom, C. (1996). Autistic disorder. In T. Mash & R. Barkley (Eds.), *Treatment of childhood disorders* (2nd ed., pp. 416–467). New York: Guilford.

Ozonoff, S., & Cathcart, K. (1998). Effectiveness of a home program intervention for young children with autism. *Journal of Autism and Developmental Disorders, 28*(1), 25–31.

Peliosa, L., & Lund, S. (2001). A selective overview of issues on classification, causation, and early intensive behavioral intervention for autism. *Behavior Modification, 25*(5), 678–697.

Richdale, A. (1999). Sleep problems in autism: Prevalence, cause, and intervention. *Developmental Medicine and Child Neurology, 41*(1), 60–66.

Santangelo, S. L., & Folstein, S. E. (1999). Autism: A genetic perspective. In H. Tager-Flusberg (Ed.), *Neurodevelopmental disorders: Developmental cognitive neuroscience* (pp. 431–447). Cambridge, MA: MIT Press.

Schopler, E. (2001). Treatment for autism: From science to pseudo-science or anti-science. In E. Schopler, N. Yirmiya, et al. (Eds.), *The research basis for autism interventions* (pp. 9–24). New York, NY: Kluwer Academic/Plenum Publishers.

Siller, M., & Sigman, M. (2002). The behaviors of parents with children with autism predict the subsequent development of their children's communication. *Journal of Autism & Developmental Disorders, 32*(2), 77–89.

Simeonsson, R. J., Olley, J. G., & Rosenthal, S. L. (1987). Early intervention for children with autism. In M. J. Guralnick & F. C. Bennett (Eds.), *The effectiveness of early intervention for at-risk and handicapped children* (pp. 275–296). Orlando, FL: Academic Press.

Smith, T., Magyar, C., & Arnold-Saritepe, A. (2002). *Autism spectrum disorder*. New York: Wiley.

Tager-Flusberg, H., Joseph, R., & Folstein, S. (2001). Current directions on research on autism. *Mental Retardation and Developmental Disabilities Research, 7*(1), 21–29.

Tuberous Sclerosis Association. (n.d.). *Tuberous sclerosis*. Retrieved November 17, 2003, from http://www.tuberous-sclerosis.org/publications/tsc.shtml.

Veenstra-Vanderweele, J., & Cook, E. H. (2003). Genetics of childhood disorders: XLVI. Autism, part 5: Genetics of autism. *Journal of the Academy of Child and Adolescent Psychiatry, 42*(1), 116–119.

Volkmar, F. (2001). Pharmacological interventions in autism: Theoretical and practical issues. *Journal of Clinical Child and Adolescent Psychology, 30*(1), 80–87.

Volkmar, F., Cook, E., Pomeroy, J., Realmuto, G., & Tanguay, P. (1999). Practice parameters for the assessment and treatment of children, adolescents, and adults with autism and other pervasive developmental disorders. *Journal of the American Academy of Child & Adolescent Psychiatry, 38*, 32–54.

Volkmar, F., & Klin, A. (1999). *Autism and other pervasive developmental disorders*. New York: Guilford.

World Health Organization (1992). *International statistical classification of diseases and related health problems* (10th rev.). Geneva: World Health Organization.

References for Autism Measures

Berument, S., Rutter, M., Lord, C., Pickles, A., & Bailey, A. (1999). Autism screening questionnaire: Diagnostic validity. *British Journal of Psychiatry, 175*, 444–451.

Eaves, R., Campbell, H., & Chambers, D. (2000). Criterion-related and construct validity of the pervasive developmental disorders rating scale and the autism behavior checklist. *Psychology in the Schools, 37*, 311–321.

Gilliam, J. (1995). *Gilliam autism rating scale*. Austin, TX: Pro-Ed.

Krug, D., Arick, J., & Almond, P. (1980a). *Austism Screening Instrument for Educational Planning. Portland*, O: ASIEP Educational.

Luteijn, E., Jackson, A., Volkmar, F., & Minderaa, R. (1998). The development of the children's social behavior questionnaire: Preliminary data. *Journal of Autism and Developmental Disorders, 28,* 559–565.

Luteijn, E., Luteijn, F., Jackson, S., Volkmar, F., & Minderaa, R. (2000). The children's social behavior questionnaire for milder variants of PDD problems: Evaluation of the psychometric characteristics. *Journal of Autism and Developmental Disorders, 30,* 317–330.

Volkmar, F., Klin, A., & Cohen, D. (1997). Diagnosis and classification of autism and related conditions: Consensus and issues. In D. J. Cohen & F. R. Volkmar (Eds.), *Handbook of autism and pervasive developmental disorders* (2nd ed., pp. 5–40). New York: Wiley.

Yirmiya, N., Sigman, M., & Freeman, B. J. (1994). Comparison between diagnostic instruments for identifying high functioning children with autism. *Journal of Autism and Developmental Disorders, 24,* 281–291.

5 Oppositional Defiant Disorder and Conduct Disorder

Although oppositional defiant disorder (ODD) and conduct disorder (CD) are empirically shown to be separate disorders (Loeber, Burke, Lagey, Winters, & Zera, 2000), they are discussed together in this chapter because they overlap considerably. They both feature anger, defiance, rebellion, lying, and school problems (Biederman, et al., 1996; Loeber et al., 2000). The distinction between them is that children with ODD do not seriously violate the basic rights of others. CD, on the other hand, includes aggression toward people or animals, destruction of property, or a pattern of theft or deceit (American Psychiatric Association, 2000).

Another reason for discussing both disorders together is that ODD is often a developmental antecedent to CD. Almost all children with CD have had an earlier ODD diagnosis (Kronenberger & Meyer, 2001), and about a quarter of youth with ODD eventually develop more serious behavioral problems in the form of CD (Hinshaw & Anderson, 1996). CD, in turn, is a risk factor for antisocial personality disorder in adulthood (Kronenberger & Meyer, 2001).

Yet ODD and CD are different diagnoses. Oppositional defiant disorder is characterized by a pattern of negativistic, hostile, and defiant behaviors toward authority figures such as parents and teachers. At least four of the following behaviors must be present (APA, 2000). The child often

- Loses his or her temper
- Argues with adults
- Actively defies or refuses to comply with adults' requests or rules
- Deliberately annoys people

- Blames others for his or her mistakes or misbehavior
- Is touchy or easily annoyed by others
- Is angry and resentful
- Is spiteful or vindictive

These behaviors persist for at least 6 months and occur more frequently than is typically observed in children of a comparable age and developmental level. ODD is usually evident before age 8 and not later than early adolescence.

Conduct disorder also involves an entrenched pattern of behavior, but in this diagnosis the basic rights of others or major age-appropriate societal norms or rules are violated (APA, 2000). This pattern involves four categories of behaviors:

- Aggressive conduct either causing or threatening harm to people or animals
- Nonaggressive conduct leading to property loss or damage
- Deceitfulness or theft
- Serious violations of rules

At least three of these behaviors need to have been present in the past year, with at least one behavior demonstrated in the past 6 months. The *DSM-IV* acknowledges that these behaviors may be a reaction to the immediate social context, such as living in a high-crime area, and thus would not be symptoms of CD. It is often difficult to discriminate, however, between the child's internal dysfunction and reactions to social contexts (Loeber et al., 2000).

Because so many types of offender acts are symptomatic of CD, we must selectively present information from the literature in this chapter (see also Loeber et al., 2000). Keep in mind, however, that to warrant a diagnosis of CD, an individual must be engaged in a pattern of behavior over time that consistently violates the rights of others and societal norms.

The *DSM-IV* includes subtypes of conduct disorder based on age of onset and the number and intensity of symptoms. These include childhood-onset conduct disorder, in which at least one criterion is present before age 10, and adolescent-onset conduct disorder, in which no criterion emerges before the age of 10. Investigators have confirmed these age-of-onset patterns in longitudinal studies of antisocial behavior as well, for both males and females (Moffitt & Caspi, 2001).

Yet symptoms do vary by sex. Males seem to engage in more confrontational behavior than females do (Lahey et al., 2000). Females manifest more indirect or relational aggression, such as the exclusion of others; threats of withdrawal from relationships; efforts to alienate, ostracize, or defame others; and rumor spreading (Ledingham, 1999; Loeber et al., 2000).

Because these behaviors are not listed in the *DSM* as criteria for CD, some have suggested that the diagnostic criteria should be modified for females (Loeber et al., 2000).

Antisocial behaviors in childhood and adolescence are important to study because of the tremendous costs they incur at the societal level in terms of property destruction, law enforcement, remedial education, foster and residential care, and other mental health services (Kazdin, 1997; Prinz & Miller, 1991). Indeed, public services for those with CD cost 10 times more than those for adolescents with no conduct problems. In addition, personal costs are involved: the emotional and physical harm to victims of antisocial behavior and the distress that behavior-disordered youth and their families experience (Kazdin, 1997; Prinz & Miller, 1991).

Prevalence of ODD and CD

ODD, which also includes attention-deficit/hyperactivity disorder and CD, is more common than either CD or antisocial personality disorder, with a prevalence rate of between 2 and 16% in the general population (APA, 2000). Females present with ODD at a rate of 2 to 9%; males have a higher rate (6–16%) (APA, 2000). The disorder is more prevalent in males than in females before puberty, but rates appear equal after puberty (APA, 2000), possibly because females after that time tend to become involved with antisocial males as partners (Burke, Loeber, & Birmaher, 2002; Moffit, Caspi, Rutter, & Silva, 2001).

In population studies, rates of CD range between 1 and 10% (APA, 2000). The female presentation of CD tends to be less noticeable because nonaggressive, covert behaviors are involved (Hinshaw & Anderson, 1996). Longitudinal research indicates that behavior-disruptive girls commit offenses much less often (3.2%) than do boys (42%). Although women typically have lower rates of criminality than men, they are more frequently arrested for nonaggressive, covert crimes, such as shoplifting and fraud (Loeber et al., 2000).

Assessment of ODD and CD

Assessment for ODD and CD requires a multimethod approach for several reasons (Fonagy & Kurtz, 2002). Youths may act differently depending on the setting (the *DSM* criteria for CD require behavior problems in more than one setting).

Moreover, self-reports by children tend to be unreliable. Children downplay their own symptoms, especially hyperactivity, attention problems, and oppositional behavior (Loeber et al., 2000). Symptom reports from parents and teachers are usually preferable, although even these two sources have their biases. Loeber et al. (2000) reported in their literature review that teachers were more accurate than mothers in identifying child symptoms of hyperactivity and inattentiveness, and parents were better informers of their children's oppositional behavior. At the same time, depressed mothers (and mothers of conduct-disordered children are at risk of depression) may attribute more negative behaviors to their children than are reported by mothers with no mental health problems (Najman et al., 2000).

Valid and reliable structured interviews designed to assess ODD and CD are available for use with parents and teachers after the child has reached a certain age (see measurement section in appendix). In addition to collecting information on child behavior, social workers can seek information on relevant biopsychosocial risk and protective factors (highlighted in a later section of this chapter).

Here are some additional guidelines for making *DSM* diagnoses (APA, 2000):

- Because transient oppositional behavior is common in preschool children and adolescents, caution should be exercised in diagnosing ODD during these developmental periods.
- Oppositional behaviors in children and adolescents should be distinguished from the disruptive behavior resulting from inattention and impulsivity that is associated with attention-deficit/hyperactivity disorder (Carlson, Tamm, & Gaub, 1997).
- A diagnosis of ODD or CD should not be made when the symptomatic behavior is *protective* for a child living in an impoverished, high-crime community.
- ODD should be distinguished from a failure to follow directions that is the result of impaired language comprehension due to hearing loss or a learning disability.
- In cases in which both CD and ODD are present, only CD should be diagnosed.
- When ODD or CD is diagnosed, a child and family relational problem (which would appear as a V-code) should not be included because the ODD or CD diagnosis includes conflict.
- A less severe diagnosis should be considered initially—either an adjustment disorder with disturbance of conduct in response to an identifiable stressor or the V-code for "child or adolescent antisocial behavior."
- Conduct disorder should be diagnosed in adults older than 18 only if the criteria for antisocial personality disorder are not met.

Course of ODD and CD

In about a quarter of cases, youths with oppositional disorder end up developing conduct disorder (Hinshaw & Anderson, 1996). In clinical samples, nearly all youths who develop CD before puberty first meet the criteria for ODD, and the symptoms of ODD are usually retained rather than outgrown (Loeber et al., 2000). Longitudinal research indicates that about half of the children diagnosed with CD overcome their symptoms by adolescence (Lahey, Loeber, Burke, & Rathouz, 2002). The course of the disorders might be different, depending on the age of onset. In a longitudinal study conducted in New Zealand, with participants followed until age 26, the childhood-onset group had the most severe personality, mental-health, substance use, financial, and work problems (Moffitt, Caspi, Harrington, & Milne, 2002). They also produced more children and exhibited higher rates of drug-related and violent crime, including violence against women and children. That is not to say that adolescent-onset ODD and CD are benign, however. The adolescent-onset group still showed problems with impulsivity, mental health, finances, substance dependence, and property offenses. The adolescent-onset men were indeed suffering significant impairment and expressed little hope for their future.

As adults, the group of young men in the study who had childhood but not adolescent ODD or CD presented as low-level chronic offenders with accompanying anxiety, depression, and social isolation. They had problems with work and finances, and few were college educated. Only 15% of these 87 individuals had no adjustment problems. Therefore, it appears that even those who had recovered from the disorder were impaired in critical ways.

The onset of puberty is associated with the beginning of distinctly different trajectories for antisocial boys and girls. Aggressive girls are more likely than aggressive boys to enter into a relationship with a deviant partner, and being involved with a deviant partner is highly associated with the likelihood that antisocial behavior will remain stable into adulthood (Ledingham, 1999). In a review of longitudinal studies, girls with adolescent conduct disorder were more than five times likelier than others to have entered a cohabiting relationship by age 21, many of these with deviant men. These relationships tended to cause further problems for the females; by their early 20s, almost half of them had suffered some form of physical violence at the hands of a partner (Maughan & Rutter, 2001).

Although a history of conduct problems predicts earlier sexual involvement for both boys and girls, the consequences of sexual behavior are more serious for girls because they may become pregnant and drop out of school (Ledingham, 1999). Mothers with conduct disorder exhibit poor parenting practices and are especially likely to use force in interacting with their children (Capaldi & Patterson, 1994; McMahon, 1994).

Comorbidity for CD and ODD

Conduct disorder poses an enhanced risk for other mental, emotional, and behavioral disorders (Loeber et al., 2000). ODD often correlates with attention-deficit/hyperactivity disorder (ADHD); according to a review of longitudinal studies, 35 to 60% of children who are clinic-referred for ADHD will meet the diagnostic criteria for ODD by the age of 7 (Abikoff & Klein, 1992). Depression and conduct disorder may also co-occur, especially for girls (Loeber et al., 2000). Therefore, girls with either disorder may be at heightened risk for substance abuse as a way to self-medicate the symptoms (Loeber et al., 2000).

Risk and Protective Factors for ODD and CD

Extensive research has been conducted on risk factors for CD. Not as much work centers on ODD, but both disorders share similar risk factors and may have a common underlying genetic basis (Burke et al., 2002). Carlson, Tamm, and Hogan (1999) conducted a literature review to determine whether CD and ODD should be considered separately with regard to risk and protective factors. In some risk domains, the ODD groups were similar to the CD groups. In others, the ODD groups did not experience as many risk factors as the CD groups, but they were still at greater risk than control groups.

Risk and protective factors, therefore, are discussed here for both disorders. Table 5.1 outlines the factors related to the onset and course of ODD and CD; Table 5.2, which appears in the Interventions section, outlines the risk and protective factors for interventions that involve parent training. In this section we discuss only the major risk and protective factors from Table 5.1.

Onset Factors

The risk and protective factors for developing ODD and CD are intertwined. In addition, early risk factors set the stage for greater vulnerability to succeeding factors (Caspi & Moffitt, 1995). Moffitt (1993) hypothesizes that a neurologically vulnerable and difficult child develops disruptive behavior in the context of interactions with parents. A child may be initially

Table 5.1

Risk and Protective Factors for Oppositional Defiant and Conduct Disorder

Risk Factors	Protective Factors
Biological Factors	
Heritability	
Difficult temperament	Behavioral inhibition (e.g., anxiety and shyness)
Low autonomic nervous system reactivity	
Male gender	Female gender
Maternal smoking during pregnancy	Mother nicotine-free during pregnancy
Psychological Factors	
Hyperactivity[a]	
Early aggression	
Lack of guilt	
Lack of empathy	
Low harm avoidance	
High stress and poor coping (for girls)	
Negative attributional bias (external locus of control)	
Social Factors	
Family Composition	
Large family size (4 or more)[b]	Smaller family size (less than 4)
Single parenthood	Two-parent home
Inconsistent parental figures	Consistent parental figures
	Family stability
	Stable couple relationship
	Social support for parents
Family Functioning	
Family instability	
Parental conflict, including discord, separation, and family violence	
Parental stress[c]	Consistent and effective discipline strategies[d]
Parent–Child Relationship	
Poor parent–child attachment	Early parent–child attachment, particularly for males
Parental rejection of the child	Parental acceptance

Risk Factors	Protective Factors
Lack of supervision	
Lack of involvement in child's activities	
Inconsistent use of discipline	
Failure to use positive change strategies	
Excessive use of corporal punishment	
Physical and sexual abuse	
Parental Psychopathology	
Parental depression, substance abuse, antisocial personality disorder, or other psychiatric disorders[e]	
Criminal offending in parents	
Peers	
Low social cognition	Social skills
Peer rejection	Acceptance by and feelings of closeness to peers
Social withdrawal	
Delinquent peer relationships	Positive peer relationships
Negative attributional bias	
Academic/School	
Low IQ	High IQ
Poor academic performance	Good academic performance
Verbal deficits	Verbal skills
Community	
Low socioeconomic status, particularly in urban areas	Rural areas
	Middle to upper SES
Community violence and crime	Neighborhood cohesion
Church/Religious Involvement	
Religious involvement[f]	

[a]Cote, Tremblay, Nagin, Zoccolillo, & Vitaro (2002)
[b]Werner (2000).
[c]Loeber et al. (1998).
[d]Steinberg (2001).
[e]APA (2000).
[f]Johnson, Jang, Li, & Larson (2000); Johnson, Jang, Larson, & Li (2001)

Source: Burke et al. (2002), Hill (2002), Holmes et al. (2001).

difficult because of irritable temperament and cognitive deficits, which may be biological or hereditary. These factors may lead to impulsivity, reactivity, or deficits in executive functioning and verbal skills (Loeber & Coie, 2001), which in turn evoke negative reactions from parents. These responses then heighten the child's tendency toward difficult behavior. At the same time, parents who abuse substances or who are themselves diagnosed with antisocial personality disorder tend to have children at an earlier age than other parents do and demonstrate less effective parenting practices (Loeber et al., 2000). Family poverty, neighborhood crime, inadequate social support, and limited community resources may also inhibit their parenting effectiveness (Loeber & Coie, 2001). Parents may eventually attempt to avoid the negative interchanges and the strain involved in taking care of a child with conduct problems (Bussing et al., 2003). Rejection and avoidance of the child further erode discipline and supervision (Capaldi & Patterson, 1994; Reid, 1993).

Negative interactions with the home environment eventually extend into the realm of school and peer groups (Conduct Problems Prevention Research Group [CPPRG], 1992; Moffitt, 1993). Difficulties with teachers may contribute to poor school performance. Alienation from the norms of the school system may develop, and by the time such children are about 10 or 11 years of age, they bond together in deviant peer groups (McMahon, 1994). If such individuals live in poverty, they have restricted opportunities and are therefore more likely to seek out deviant means to obtain fulfillment and a sense of identity (Prinz & Miller, 1991).

The following discussion treats some of the more important risk and protective factors in Table 5.1 in more detail. The first seven are individual biological and psychological factors; the last four are social factors. Familial and social factors predict the diagnosis of conduct disorder better than individual characteristics of the child, according to a study of 508 families with adolescent children (Dekovic, 1999).

Genetics

A meta-analysis of 12 twin studies comprising 3,795 twin pairs and 3 adoption studies comprising 338 adoptees found that genetic effects explain half of the variance in antisocial behavior (Mason & Frick, 1994). The effect of heredity was greater in cases of severe antisocial behavior and was effectively zero with less extreme patterns of conduct problems. None of the other moderating factors—age, gender, race, country from which the sample was drawn—influenced the severity of antisocial behavior.

The absence of significant age effects in this study is surprising, given that early-onset conduct disorder has been associated with a more severe and chronic pattern than late-onset CD. However, children with a greater predisposition to CD are more likely to encounter environments that foster antisocial behavior (Loeber et al., 2000). In particular, children who are predisposed to CD are likely to be raised by ineffective (and sometimes abusive) parents with histories of antisocial behavior, psychopathology, and substance abuse problems.

Temperament

In a review covering both cross-sectional and longitudinal studies and clinical and community samples, Sanson and Prior (1999) found that early difficult temperament—defined as negative emotionality, intense and reactive responding, and inflexibility—predicts conduct problems in late childhood. Conversely, an inhibited or approach-withdrawal temperament is protective against behaviors that impinge on others (Burke et al., 2002).

A lack of consensus on what constitutes temperament and the challenge of differentiating between temperament and early signs of conduct problems have hampered research on the role of temperament in ODD and CD (Burke et al., 2002). In addition, studies typically rely on parent reports for both temperament and problem behaviors, and these can be biased by parents' own psychological adjustment (Hill, 2002) and stress levels (Huizink, De Medina, Mulder, Visser & Buitelaar, 2002). Thus, it is not clear whether temperament is a biologically based factor or psychosocial in nature (Sanson & Prior, 1999).

Maternal Smoking

A well-documented association has been found between maternal smoking during pregnancy and conduct problems for children in later childhood (Shirk, Talmi, & Olds, 2000; Wakschlag & Hans, 2002). Mothers who smoked more than half a pack of cigarettes daily during pregnancy are significantly more likely to have a child with CD than mothers who did not smoke during pregnancy (Loeber et al., 2000).

A number of hypotheses have been offered to establish the causal link between maternal smoking and ODD/CD, but the precise mechanisms are not understood (Shirk et al., 2000; Wakschlag & Hans, 2002). Quite possibly, no causal link exists between smoking and these behavioral disorders, and instead a genetic influence may be operating. Mothers with antisocial behaviors may be more likely to smoke, and it may be the genetic influence of antisocial behavior that is increasing the risk of CD in children.

Intelligence

Low IQ is a risk factor for antisocial behavior, over and above the effects of socioeconomic status and race. Wachs (2000) cites evidence that youths with IQ scores one standard deviation lower than normal have three times the risk for developing conduct disorders. However, Hogan (1999) claimed, from a review of 27 studies controlling for ADHD, that the relationship of

CD with IQ failed to reach significance. IQ is also linked to low achievement in school, which is connected to antisocial behavior (Farrington, 1995).

In addition, high intelligence does not necessarily protect against conduct problems. High verbal IQ has been related to boys' "growing out of" CD only when a parent did not have antisocial personality disorder (Lahey et al., 2002).

Language-Based Verbal Skills

Extensive documentation of the relationship between deficits in verbal ability and conduct problems is widely available, but the reasons for the link are not well understood (Hill, 2002). One hypothesis is that children who are unable to reason verbally may use aggression to manage social dilemmas. Poor verbal abilities may also make it harder for children to identify emotions in themselves and others. If children cannot reflect on their emotional states, they may react in physical or aggressive ways rather than by talking about their feelings, seeking comfort, or engaging in problem-solving activities.

Autonomic Nervous System Reactivity

A low resting pulse rate has also been related to antisocial behavior, although the connection is unclear (Hill, 2002). Low autonomic reactivity may indicate a suppressed behavioral inhibition system, which in turn may result in difficulty with controlling impulsive and aggressive activity. Low autonomic reactivity could further result from habituation to punishment because of constant misbehavior, or it could be related to habituation to the stress of living in difficult family situations. In these latter scenarios, low pulse rate may not play a causal role in conduct problems.

Social Cognitive Problem Solving

Cognitive processing refers to the way people perceive and code their experiences (Kazdin, 2001). Youths who are aggressive tend to display the following distortions in the way they perceive and code their social experiences:

- Inability to produce a variety of strategies to manage interpersonal problems
- Difficulty in figuring out ways to achieve a particular desired outcome
- Difficulty with identifying the consequences of a particular action and its effects on others
- Tendency to attribute hostile motivations to the actions of others
- Misunderstanding of how others feel

The combination of perceived threat and limited options for managing social situations makes antisocial youths more likely to respond with aggression rather than other problem-solving strategies.

Parent–Child Attachment

The evidence is mixed on whether the quality of the parent–child bond is related to ODD and CD. Insecure and disorganized attachment styles have been linked to CD in some studies, although other research has reported no such link (Burke et al., 2002; Greenberg, Speltz, & DeKylen, 1993). Other factors, such as temperament, early behavior problems, or family problems, may act in combination with poor attachment to produce conduct disorders.

Abuse

Longitudinal studies have shown that physical abuse within the family is associated with the child's later externalization of problems (Hill, 2002; Stouthamer-Loeber, Loeber, Homish, & Wei, 2001). Even physical discipline (not just abuse) correlates with child aggression for Caucasian children, although not for African American children (Deater-Deckard & Dodge, 1997). Historical factors of slavery, such as the norm of physical punishment, and the current threat of oppression and societal punishment may lead African American families to view physically harsh discipline as an acceptable part of a positive parent–child relationship, sometimes necessary to prevent economic and social failure for a child growing up in an unforgiving society. Harsh physical discipline is not as strongly associated with child aggression outcomes when it occurs in the context of a warm parent–child relationship (Deater-Deckard & Dodge, 1997). However, harsh physical discipline, or physical abuse, is equally deleterious for all children, whether they grow up in African American families or Caucasian families.

Child sexual abuse is also associated with conduct problems, after controlling for other childhood adversities such as socioeconomic status, family stability, parent–child relationships, parental psychiatric disorder, and parental criminality (McGee & Williams, 1999). However, childhood sexual abuse is a general risk factor for many psychiatric disorders, including depression, anxiety, and substance abuse (Hill, 2002).

Possible mechanisms to explain the connection between child maltreatment and conduct problems include insecure parent–child attachments and impaired child self-concept and distortions of self-concept. Abuse may further result in children encoding experiences as threatening and attributing hostile intent to others in social situations. Aggression in children may also be acquired by modeling.

Peer Relationships

Peer relationships can serve as either a risk or protective factor for the onset of CD (Hill, 2002) and recovery from CD (Dekovic, 1999). Children diagnosed with CD often experience rejection by peers for their aggression and lack of social skills (Holmes, Slaughter, & Kashani, 2001). Because of their impulsivity and attention problems, these children disrupt other children's activities, and as a consequence other children become annoyed and rejecting (Miller-Johnson, Coie, Maumary-Gremaud, & Bierman, 2002).

On the other hand, peers may unwittingly reinforce aggression by acquiescing to a child's demands and demonstrations of force. Peers may alternately respond with aggression in kind, confirming the child's negative view of others and contributing to continuing aggression in future encounters (Holmes, Slaughter, & Kashani, 2001; Morrison, Macdonald, & Leblanc, 2000).

Neighborhood and Socioeconomic Factors

Living in poor and disadvantaged communities poses substantial risks for antisocial behavior in children. Such risks include poverty, unemployment, community disorganization, availability of drugs, the presence of adults involved in crime, community violence, and racial prejudice (Hill, 2002; Loeber et al., 2000; McGee & Williams, 1999). Positive family processes, such as parents' positive marital functioning and parenting abilities, can override the effects of social disadvantage (Hill, 2002). However, even in the presence of protective factors, living in public housing poses a substantial risk for antisocial behavior (Wikström & Loeber, 2000).

Parenting abilities are often challenged by the many stressors that attend living in a low socioeconomic environment, including unemployment, underemployment, the lack of safe childcare, the lack of transportation, inadequate housing, and exposure to crime. These stressors may not only negatively affect parenting but also inhibit access to treatment resources. Impaired parenting abilities elicit further behavior problems in youth (Burke et al., 2002).

Recovery and Adjustment

The risk and protective factors for recovering from ODD or CD and subsequent social adjustment are essentially the same as those involved with the onset of these disorders. However, other child factors (comorbid ADHD, severity of symptoms, younger age of onset, low verbal intelligence) and family factors (low socioeconomic status, presence of an antisocial biological parent, and a teenage mother) bode poorly for the course of the disorder (Hinshaw, Lahey, & Hart, 1993; Lahey et al. 2000; Loeber et al., 2000).

Interventions for ODD and CD

A number of treatments for ODD and CD were comprehensively reviewed by Fonagy and Kurtz (2002). An important point needs to be made about these studies, however: Most of them have focused on boys rather than girls. And although research has been conducted on the effectiveness of various interventions for children from different ethnic groups, problems in research design make conclusions elusive.

In one literature review, Brestan and Eyberg (1998) found a much larger proportion of boys than girls represented in studies, at a ratio of 5 to 1. The authors concluded, given the lack of study on differential male and female response to treatment, that little valid information exists to guide treatment decisions for girls. Clearly, there is a need for research into gender-specific treatment outcomes, because CD in girls may result in serious consequences, such as antisocial personality disorder, involvement with an antisocial partner, and teen pregnancy, which in turn increase the risk for behavior problems in offspring (Loeber et al., 2000).

In the area of intervention for members of ethnic and racial groups, a host of conceptual and methodological problems have hampered research. These include a lack of sufficient data on ethnic groups and subgroups, difficulties in accurately classifying ethnicity and acculturation, problems with access to immigrant or out-of-school youth, biased instrumentation, a focus on risk factors to the exclusion of protective factors, the confounding of the effects of ethnic background with social class, and low sample sizes (Hinshaw & Park, 1999). In the 29 treatment outcome studies reviewed by Brestan and Eyberg (1998), fewer than half provided data on the socioeconomic status and race of sample subjects.

A notable exception to the study of the impact of programs on minorities is a meta-analysis of 305 studies conducted by Wilson, Lipsey, and Soydan (2003). These researchers found that programs for juvenile offenders were equally effective for minority youths as they were for Caucasian youths. Unfortunately, these programs, in general, had only a modest impact on delinquency. The salient issue for effectiveness was not type of program but how successfully programs were implemented.

From this discussion on the generalizability of interventions to special populations, we will explore particular interventions available.

Family Interventions

Family factors seem to be a critical variable in the formation of conduct problems. Therefore, treatments often have a family emphasis. One of the most prevalent treatments is parent training, but more clinical therapies may be required, and in extreme cases, foster care is called for.

Parent Training

The most highly investigated family treatment model for conduct problems is parent training. In this model, parents are taught various skills, including

- Specifying goals for behavioral change
- Tracking target behaviors
- Positively reinforcing pro-social conduct through the use of attention, praise, and point systems
- Employing alternative discipline methods, such as withdrawal of attention, time out from reinforcement, imposition of costs on inappropriate behavior, and removal of privileges

This educational material is generally presented through a variety of formats, including lessons, interactive discussion, modeling, role play, and feedback (Miller & Prinz, 1990). Training sessions give parents the opportunity to see how various techniques should be implemented, practice employing these methods, and evaluate the progress of newly learned behaviors in the home (Kazdin, 1993).

Evidence from reviews of parent training has supported its effectiveness (Brestan & Eyberg, 1998). From a review of 50 studies, Fonagy and Kurtz (2002) concluded that when parent training is used, about two thirds of children under the age of 10 improve. A meta-analysis has also been conducted on parent training, using only studies that included both an experimental and a control group (Serketich & Dumas, 1996). Most of the studies centered on samples of preschool children. Of the 36 trials, the average effect sizes were .86 overall, .84 when parents reported the results, .85 with observer reports, .73 with teacher reports, and .44 when measuring parental adjustment. These are impressive findings.

Another advantage of parent training is that several empirically validated training manuals and programs are in existence: *Helping the Noncompliant Child* (ages 3–8) (Forehand & McMahon, 1981), *Living with Children* (ages 3–12) (Patterson & Gullion, 1968), and *The Incredible Years* (ages 2–8) (Webster-Stratton, 2001). The *Incredible Years* program has been found to be the most cost-effective, but it has been more helpful for child behaviors in the home than in the school (Fonagy & Kortz, 2002). The series is based on modeling theory. Behavioral techniques for parents are demonstrated through videotaped vignettes in the context of a discussion group. The treatment dose can be increased by including a child-oriented component (Webster-Stratton & Hammond, 1997). Such self-administered videotape monitoring can be sufficient for primarily middle-class families and less severe child conduct problems (Fonagy & Kurtz, 2002).

However, more severe problems in children and older children may require more than parent training to help manage conduct problems involving parent–child interaction, address child problem-solving deficits, or intervene in other family problems. For school-age children, a child problem-solving component has been offered in addition to parent training. These programs generally focus on the thought processes children use in approaching interpersonal situations, teaching children step-by-step how to solve problems and fostering pro-social behaviors through modeling and reinforcement (Kazdin, 2001). The combined parent training and problem-solving skills training program for children have a greater impact than parent training only or child problem solving only (Kazdin, Siegel, & Bass, 1992).

When children have behavior problems in the classroom, the addition of classroom-based contingency management programs should be considered in addition to family-based treatments. Classroom contingency management methods are effective in controlling the behavior of children with conduct problems in school, but they have not yet been shown to generalize beyond the classroom or to persist beyond the termination of the program. Parent-administered reinforcements may enhance classroom contingency management.

Parent training has primarily been validated for preschool and school-age children; its outcomes are unfortunately less clinically significant with adolescents (Fonagy & Kurtz, 2002). Adolescents referred for treatment tend to be more severely and chronically impaired. One study has shown, however, that parent training treatment can be effective with adolescents in the juvenile justice system (Bank, Marlowe, Reid, Patterson, & Weinrott, 1991).

The demands of learning and implementing parent training procedures in the home may overwhelm some parents, who then attend sessions sporadically, drop out of treatment, or fail to practice the skills they learn (Fonagy & Kurtz, 2002). Table 5.2 delineates more of the risk and protective factors that have an impact on the outcome of parent training. A good outcome is defined as parent participation in treatment, measurable improvements, and maintenance of gains.

Community-based parent training is said to be both less expensive and more effective than clinic-based programs (e.g., Cunningham, Bremner, & Boyle, 1995; Fonagy & Kurtz, 2002; Thompson, Ruma, Schuchman, & Burke, 1996). Social workers should thus consider how to integrate parent training with other home- and community-based services.

Multisystemic Therapy

Multisystemic treatment has been developed specifically for adolescents in the juvenile justice system. Drawing on family systems theory and Bronfenbrenner's (1979) ecological model as the theoretical basis, multisystemic treatment (MST) views the juvenile offender as embedded in a context of multiple and interrelated systems (Henggeler, Schoenwald, Borduin, Rowland, & Cunningham, 1998). The child's own intrapersonal system (i.e.,

Table 5.2	
Risk and Protective Factors for Outcome of Parent Training	
Risk Factors	Protective Factors
Individual	**Individual**
• Older age of the child • Comorbid disorders • Severe conduct problems	• Younger age • Absence of other disorders • Mild to moderate conduct problems
Social	**Social**
Family	Family
• Maternal problems (i.e., chemical addiction, depression) • Maternal attachment insecurity • Many negative life events • High levels of parental negativity toward the child	• Two-parent households • Low family stress • High social support • Absence of antisocial characteristics • Parental perception of the need for treatment
Socioeconomic status	Socioeconomic status
• Low socioeconomic status, particularly when combined with social isolation	• Middle-to-high SES

Source: Fonagy & Kurtz (2002).

cognitive ability, social skills), the parent–child system, the family system, the school system, peers, and the neighborhood system are targeted for intervention.

MST also draws on several other models. It shares with the family preservation model the central aim of retaining the adolescent in the home. The client's ability to generalize new behaviors is key, and thus treatment is usually delivered in the home or a community setting. MST also takes an individualized approach in recognizing participants' strengths and limitations. In contrast to the family preservation model, however, multisystemic therapy is systematically applied through the use of manualized treatment. Although MST includes family systems interventions (structural and strategic), it also focuses on nonsystemic interventions derived from cognitive-behavioral therapy, such as parent training, social skills training, problem-solving training, and behavior therapy.

MST has been extensively studied; approximately 800 families have participated in the intervention (Henggeler, Schoenwald, Rowland, & Cunningham, 2002). Several prominent national organizations—including the National Institute of Mental Health, the National Institute on Drug Abuse, the Center for Substance Abuse Prevention, and the Office of Juvenile Justice and Delinquency Prevention—promote MST as a model community program because of its strong empirical support (Henggeler et al., 2002). However, a more recent, systematic analysis of the data indicates that treatment outcomes are not as strong as previously reported (Littell, Popa, & Forsythe, 2005). Indeed, among the various outcome measures across studies, only in number of arrests did the treatment group show significant reductions from "treatment as usual." Because training and supervision in the MST model is costly, agency personnel need to be aware of these most recent findings.

Functional Family Therapy

Functional family therapy (FFT), which has also been applied with juvenile offenders, integrates systems, cognitive, and behavioral theories (Alexander & Parsons, 1982). From this perspective, juvenile offending and other clinical problems are conceptualized from the standpoint of the functions they serve for the family system and its members. The goal of functional family therapy is to alter maladaptive interaction and communication patterns so that more direct means of fulfilling these functions can develop (Alexander & Parsons, 1982). Functional family therapy combines knowledge about parent–child interactions and social learning, along with knowledge about the individual cognitive styles that influence juvenile offending. The model has also been referred to as behavioral-systems family therapy (Gordon, Arbuthnot, Gustafson, & McGreen, 1988).

Relatively few outcome studies have evaluated FFT. The available studies have focused on difficult-to-treat populations (e.g., adjudicated delinquent adolescents, multiple-offender delinquents) and have demonstrated relatively clear positive effects. In controlled study comparisons, FFT has led to greater change than other treatment techniques (e.g., client-centered family groups, psychodynamic family therapy) and various control conditions (e.g., group discussion and expression of feeling, no-treatment control groups). The benefits of treatment have been reflected in improved family communication and interactions and lower rates of referral to and contact of youth with the courts. Gains have been evident in separate studies up to 2.5 years after treatment (Kazdin, 2001). Further, the Washington State Institute for Public Policy found that FFT produces a net gain of $13,908 when taking into account both taxpayer and crime victim costs avoided (Aos, Barnoski, & Lieb, 1998).

Treatment Foster Care

Treatment foster care (TFC) is an intervention model that offers an alternative to group residential care for serious chronic juvenile offenders. TFC differs from most group care settings in several important ways:

- Community families are recruited, trained, and supported to provide placements.
- Children generally attend public schools.
- No more than two youngsters are placed in a home.
- Most programs include a family therapy component with biological parents or relatives or other aftercare resources.

Studies have found that the majority of placements in TFC programs were completed as planned, that participants improved on behavioral indicators of adjustment, and that 60 to 89% of the children and adolescents were discharged to less restrictive living settings (Chamberlain, 1999). TFC for children with chronic delinquency has been shown to be relatively effective in reducing their recidivism rates. A meta-analysis was conducted of 40 studies involving 12,000 youths (Reddy & Pfeiffer, 1997). Substantial effects were shown for TFC in terms of lengthening time in placement for hard-to-place adolescents and increasing their social skills. The reduction of behavior problems and improvement in psychological adjustment were more moderate. TFC is consistently shown, however, to be less costly than group care.

Individual Interventions

Generally speaking, individual treatment for conduct problems is not as effective by itself as family interventions are, except with mild conduct problems (Brestan & Eyberg, 1998). Individual treatment may more effectively serve as a component of a broader treatment program targeting several risk domains.

Relationship-based and psychodynamic interventions are often applied in clinical work with children and adolescents with ODD and CD. These treatments continue to be intuitively attractive to many social workers, but none has been identified as effective through empirically supported outcome evaluations (Kazdin, 2001). Thus, these interventions will not be reviewed here.

Cognitive-Behavioral Treatments

A meta-analysis has been conducted on cognitive-behavioral treatments, mainly delivered in the group setting, for antisocial youth (Bennett & Gibbons, 2000). Studies were included if they used "anger management, assertiveness training, cognitive restructuring, relaxation, social problem solving or social skills training as interventions" (p. 3) and employed cognitive-behavioral methods, such as rehearsal, modeling, and coaching, to deliver content. Findings were that such interventions were slightly to moderately effective in ameliorating conduct problems. None of the moderating variables, such as age or duration of treatment, had a significant impact on effects.

Of the cognitive-behavioral treatments for children, problem-solving skills training has been the most rigorously studied, and many treatment manuals are available (i.e., Feindler & Ecton, 1986; Finch, Nelson, & Ott, 1993; Shure, 1992). However, youths with additional diagnoses and academic and reading delays, and who live in families with parent psychopathology, stress, and conflict, do not fare as well in programs using problem-solving skills training as youths with less dysfunction (Fonagy & Kurtz, 2002).

For adolescents, social skills training and problem-solving skills training are the two main derivatives of cognitive-behavioral therapy used. Social skills–oriented training programs appear to improve the social functioning of delinquent adolescents. (For a list of resources on social skills training, see Alberg, Petry, & Eller, 1994.) Training in social problem solving appears effective in reducing aggressive behavior, although the long-term maintenance of gains is limited. Perspective-taking programs (focused on helping antisocial youth understand the feelings of others) are widely used, but the evidence basis for them is lacking. Training in moral reasoning seems to succeed in improving such reasoning, but a reduction in conduct disturbance does not necessarily follow (Fonagy & Kurtz, 2002).

Anger control training is a popular intervention approach in clinical settings, given the obvious problems of impulsiveness and aggression among youth diagnosed with ODD and CD. However, improvements as a result of such programs have not yet generalized to clinically significant behavioral problems. Anger, as a target for intervention, is probably not sufficiently central to conduct problems to be an appropriate goal on its own (Fonagy & Kurtz, 2002). Nevertheless, Kavale, Forness, and Walker (1999) have compiled a resource list of anger control programs:

- *Anger Management for Youth* (Eggert, 1994)
- *Helping Kids Handle Anger: Teaching Self-Control* (Huggins, 1992)
- *Stress Inoculation Training* (Maag, Parks, & Rutherford, 1988; Meichenbaum, 1985)
- The Think-Aloud cognitive-behavioral approach (Camp, Blum, Hebert, & Van Doomick, 1977)
- *Adolescent Anger Control* (Feindler & Ecton, 1986)

For adolescents, multidimensional cognitive-behavioral treatments have also been developed. These include *Aggression Replacement Training* (Goldstein & Glick, 1987), which combines social skills training, anger control, and moral reasoning training and has been used with institutionalized adolescents. The intervention has shown to have a high benefit-cost ratio (Aos, Phipps, Barnoski, & Lieb, 2001).

Group treatment is a commonly used intervention modality for CD and ODD. However, it may actually be contraindicated, as group members are exposed to, and may reinforce, antisocial behaviors (Burke et al. 2002; Chamberlain, 1999).

Medication

Low doses of antipsychotic medications are commonly prescribed to youths with aggression problems in inpatient and day treatment settings, but there is a lack of evidence to support this treatment (Pappadopulos et al., 2003). Burke et al. (2002) caution that with adolescents who have CD, prescribed medication may at times be abused. First-line interventions should always involve a psychosocial approach, and this should continue even if medications are prescribed. Medication should primarily be provided to treat comorbid conditions that may have a stronger empirical rationale for such intervention. As indicated earlier, ADHD is a common comorbid condition. Connor, Glatt, Lopez, Jackson, & Melloni (2002) reported in a meta-analysis of 28 studies that stimulants diminish overt aggression at a .84 level effect size and covert aggression at a .69 effect size in children with ADHD. Both of these effect sizes indicate substantial impact. Further, the MTA Cooperative Group Study, discussed in chapter 6, indicated that ADHD and comorbid oppositional and aggressive symptoms were treated more effectively with stimulants than with psychosocial treatment alone (Swanson et al., 2001). However, when psychosocial treatment was added to medication, outcomes improved by 20%.

The newer antipsychotic medications (such as risperidone, olanzapine, quetiapine, and ziprasidone) can then be prescribed for severe and persistent aggression if psychosocial interventions and medication for other conditions are not helpful. Although these antipsychotic drugs should produce fewer side effects than the traditional antipsychotic drugs, possible side effects should be regularly assessed (Pappadopulos et al., 2003).

Children should be treated, if at all possible, with one medication at a time. Doctors can thus evaluate the response to and side effects of the medication, uncomplicated by the presence of other medications. This practice may also assist with compliance by reducing the complexity of the regimen that the client and his or her family have to follow. In general, adherence to treatment needs to be monitored, given the low compliance rates of youths with conduct disorder (Pappadopulos et al., 2003).

Case Illustration: Janine's Conduct Disorder

Janine is a 12-year-old African American female in foster care. Janine is an attractive, well-developed young lady who is outspoken and athletic. She enjoys playing basketball and other sports and listening to music.[1]

Janine entered the foster care system at age 10, when she reported that her biological uncle was sexually abusing her and her brother. Janine is the oldest of five; all the children have the same mother but different biological fathers. Janine states that her uncle drinks a lot and that he was drunk when he sexually abused her. At the time of removal, Janine and her siblings were living with their grandmother, uncle, and biological mother. They resided in a housing project in an area known for high crime, drug trafficking, and gang violence. Janine was responsible for making the call to child protective services (CPS) to report her uncle's abusive behaviors. When family members discovered that she had initiated the call, they refused to speak with her.

Although Janine's biological mother lived in the home, Janine's grandmother was her primary caregiver. Janine's mother was a teenager at Janine's birth, so her grandmother had assumed a lot of the responsibility for Janine's care from the beginning. Janine's grandmother described her as an overactive, hard-to-control child.

During the past 2 years, Janine has lived in five separate foster homes. Each time she has been removed because of outbursts that begin as verbal tirades and then progress to hitting. She has also stolen money from various foster parents. In addition, she has reportedly stolen from her classmates at school (money, clothes). More recently, she was caught stealing from the convenience store across the street. Janine at times has rationalized her stealing, stating that if people didn't want her to take their things, then they shouldn't leave them out where she could get at them.

Janine has lived in her current foster home, which is located in a working-class neighborhood, for 6 months. Her foster mother is African American, unmarried, and employed full-time. Janine appears to have become attached to her foster mother. However, her foster mother says that Janine often argues with her and has, on occasion, become violent. Janine's foster mother is willing to keep her if Janine's aggression and lying can be controlled. According to her foster mother, teachers, and social workers, Janine often lies to avoid doing things ("I've already done it" when asked to do chores or tasks at school) or to get out of trouble (blaming others for starting physical altercations she initiated). Janine's foster mother is worried that because she has to work until dinnertime, she is unable to supervise Janine adequately the frequent times Janine has been suspended from school.

Janine's CPS worker reported that if Janine is asked to leave her current foster home, she will be sent to a residential placement. Janine has begged her caseworker and foster mother not to send her away. Janine's brother, Kyle, attends a therapeutic day treatment center and is in the process of being returned to his biological father's home. Janine has questioned her caseworker about returning to her own biological father. However, her father has now married another woman who has children of her own. He and his wife are reluctant to have Janine come into their home and potentially disrupt their lives and set a bad example for the other children.

Recently, Janine's CPS worker referred her to a therapeutic day treatment center after she was expelled from public school for violent outbursts, fights with peers, and poor academic performance. The poor school performance seems partially attributable to frequent suspensions, but Janine also seems to have difficulty with concentrating and focusing on her work, according to teacher reports relayed to the foster mother. Her foster mother has also noted similar qualities when Janine attempts homework.

Multiaxial Diagnosis

The following diagnosis was given at the intake interview for the day treatment program. Janine, the foster mother, and the CPS caseworker provided information necessary for the diagnosis.

Axis I: 312.89 Conduct Disorder Unspecified Onset, Mild Severity
V61.21 Sexual Abuse
314.01 Attention-Deficit/Hyperactivity Disorder, Predominantly Inattentive Type (see chapter 6 for more information on the ADHD)
Axis II: V71.09 No diagnosis
Axis III: None
Axis IV: Problems with primary support group (sexual abuse, removal from the home, foster care, inadequate discipline); educational problems (academic failure, discord with teachers and classmates); problems related to the social environment (lack of friendships)
Axis V: Global Assessment of Functioning: 51

The first required criterion for CD is that disruptive behaviors must be present for at least a year. Furthermore, the client must exhibit at least three of the behaviors listed for CD in the *DSM*, with at least one occurring within the past 6 months. Janine's conduct problems became apparent 2 years ago and have persisted during that time frame. It is possible, based on Janine's grandmother's description of Janine as an overactive, out-of-control child, that Janine met criteria for conduct disorder in early childhood. However, the grandmother's report might have been tainted in an attempt to discredit Janine for the sexual abuse allegations. Therefore, the age of onset is unknown (unspecified onset). Janine exhibited four of the listed behaviors, and each of these occurred within the past 6 months. The first two behaviors are threatening or bullying others and starting fights. Janine often initiates fights both at home and at school, with her foster mother, with peers, and with teachers. Although the majority of her fights have been verbal, some of them have extended to physical violence. Two other behaviors listed under conduct disorder that Janine displays involve theft without confrontation and frequent lying. The severity specifier "mild" is given because Janine barely meets the conduct problems criteria with only four symptoms, and the impact on other people is "intermediate" (i.e., most of the fighting she displays involves verbal argument).

The second required criterion for a CD diagnosis is that the behaviors must seriously impair academic and social functioning. Janine's academic record is poor (several failing grades), and over the past school year she has often been absent because of frequent fights. In the social realm, Janine has failed to remain in a foster home for any length of time because of these behaviors. Moreover, Janine admits that she does not have friends.

The *DSM* cautions that when conduct behaviors are protective against a dangerous environment, such as in a low-income, high-crime, over-crowded urban area, then the diagnosis of CD should not be given. Since foster care, Janine has been living in safe neighborhoods, but before that time, she lived in a dangerous area. Conduct problems, if they existed prior to the current 2-year period, might have served a protective function in such a neighborhood. However, in the past 2 years, she has had no need to rely on such behaviors to maintain her safety.

When examining other diagnoses that may better encapsulate her symptoms, it must be noted that Janine also meets the criteria for ODD. She often loses her temper, argues with adults, refuses to follow adult rules, blames others for misbehavior, is touchy or easily annoyed by others, and is angry and resentful. Thus, Janine meets six of the behaviors listed under ODD, whereas only four are required to make the diagnosis. However, Janine's behaviors meet the diagnosis for CD, leading one to rule out ODD on the basis of the *DSM*'s guidelines.

In addition to ODD, adjustment disorder is a possibility. The criteria for adjustment disorder with disturbance of conduct require that the client's behaviors surface within 3 months of a stressor and impair social and academic performance. Other criteria for adjustment disorder are that the behaviors cannot be attributed to bereavement and the behaviors can last no longer than 6 months. Janine's case history is notable for sexual abuse and foster care placement. Janine acted out aggressively almost immediately after being placed into foster care, leading one to the conclusion that her behaviors were a reaction to severe life stressors. Furthermore, her reactions have impaired her school performance and relationships. Although her symptoms have persisted for longer than 6 months, one can argue that the stressors involved have been ongoing. Janine faces continual rejection from her family of origin because of their reaction to her allegations of sexual abuse; they make only sporadic attempts to comply with the CPS case plan for reunification. Being forced to live in foster care is another chronic stressor. Hence, a diagnosis of adjustment disorder with disturbance of conduct could be justified, although most clinicians would probably concur with a diagnosis of CD.

Sexual abuse has also been listed under Axis I because Janine is still facing the aftermath of abuse by her uncle. However, this diagnosis has been placed second. It is the aggressive and acting-out behaviors that have received more attention, requiring her to attend a day treatment program.

Because of Janine's sexual and physical abuse history, another diagnosis to possibly explore is posttraumatic stress disorder.

- Criterion A for posttraumatic stress disorder could be justified by Janine's exposure to traumatic events. The second part of Criterion A is that the child's response is expressed in disorganized or agitated behavior. It could be argued that her aggression represents agitated behavior.
- Criterion B involves reexperiencing of the trauma. However, Janine denies thinking about the sexual abuse or having dreams related to it. She also denies flashbacks and does not appear to experience psychological distress or physiological reactivity to any particular cues associated with the abuse.
- Criterion C, involving avoidance and numbing, could be reflected in Janine's avoidance of thoughts, feelings, or conversations associated with the trauma. She says she can't remember important aspects of the sexual abuse, although it is unclear whether her stating so is a posttraumatic symptom or reflects embarrassment, oppositionality, or irritation at having to repeat her story. Janine does display a restricted range of affect, in that anger and aggression seem to be her primary feelings.
- Criterion D, involving arousal symptoms, could also be involved in Janine's case. She has frequent bouts of irritation and anger, she has difficulty concentrating, and her seeing threat in other people's actions could be interpreted as hypervigilance.

Although Janine seems to meet several of the criteria related to PTSD, the reexperiencing component does not seem to be present, and so she does not receive this diagnosis.

The justification of the ADHD diagnosis in Janine's case is taken up in chapter 6. The rationale for the GAF score of 51 (the low end of "moderate" symptoms) is as follows: Janine has no friends, her academic performance is poor, she has been expelled from school, and she has recently stolen from a convenience store; she has also had difficulty maintaining a stable placement because of her behavior.

Janine's risk and protective factor assessment is displayed in Table 5.3. Goal and intervention planning have been placed within the context of this assessment.

Table 5.3		
Janine's Risk and Protective Factors Assessment		
Risk	Protective	Goals
Biological Factors		
Maternal smoking during pregnancy: *Janine's mother smoked during her pregnancy.*		Sexuality education and pregnancy prevention. (Janine is at risk for early sexual involvement and becoming involved with antisocial males.)
Psychological Factors		
Early aggression: Janine's grandmother said that Janine has always been overactive and "hard to control."	*Positive coping mechanisms include listening to music when she she feels "mad," as it has a calming effect, and playing basketball.*	Help Janine examine sexual abuse experience and its aftermath in a graduated fashion, accompanied by the development of coping skills, such as cognitive restructuring and developing appropriate attributions (she was not responsible for abuse, but she is responsible for her actions now). Possibly use a system of rewards, such as time playing basketball or other physical activity in therapy sessions after she has spent time processing the abuse.
High stress and poor coping: *Janine has suffered from a number of highly stressful life events, including sexual abuse, rejection from her biological family, the absence of her biological father, and placement in a number of different foster homes. Her coping methods include externalizing behaviors; she avoids talking about the abuse and doesn't have friends.*	*Janine was able to stop the abuse from happening by initiating a call to Child Protective Services.*	
Negative attributional bias: *Janine blames the physical fights on others' provocation; she sees her stealing as justified in that "if people didn't want me to take their stuff, they shouldn't leave it out."*		

continued

Table 5.3 (*continued*)

Janine's Risk and Protective Factors Assessment

Risk	Protective	Goals
Social Factors		
Family		
Large family size: Janine is one of five children *in her biological family.*	Smaller family size: *Janine is the only child in her foster home.*	Work toward getting an effective discipline strategy in the home, as well as increasing positive interactions and providing empathy for Janine's feelings.
Single parenthood: *Janine's foster mother is a single parent;* while her biological mother is also a single *parent, Janine's grandmother was also available in the home as a parent figure.* Inconsistent parental figures: *Since she has been removed from her home, Janine has been in several foster placements.*	Social support for parents: *Janine's foster mother has informal (family, friends) and formal (CPS) supports.*	Janine will attend a day treatment program so that treatment and structure will be provided on a consistent basis.
Poor parent–child attachment: *The quality of infant-child attachment is unknown, but a risk is that Janine's mother was a teenager when she was born, and her grandmother assumed a lot of the caregiving.*		Have an aggressive plan in place to involve Janine's biological mother and grandmother in belief and support of Janine; if unworkable, then develop a permanency plan for placement.
Parental rejection of the child: *Not only Janine's mother, but her whole biological family has rejected her.*		
Lack of supervision: *Foster mother works until dinnertime, so she is unable to supervise Janine the frequent times she has been suspended from school.*		

Risk	Protective	Goals
Inconsistent use of discipline: *Foster mother has found Janine's aggression and noncompliance difficult to manage.*		
Sexual abuse: *Janine was sexually abused by her mother's brother for 2 years.*		
Peers		
Low social cognition		*As above, attribution retraining, increase perspective taking; develop social problem-solving skills and other social skills.*
Peer rejection		
Social withdrawal: *Janine has few social skills and lacks friends; she sees others as initiating and provoking negative interactions.*		
Academic/School		
Poor academic performance: *Janine is failing several classes.*	*Janine has refrained from grouping with other delinquent peers.*	Involve in extracurricular activities, such as basketball and other sports.
		Work on maintaining foster care placement, so she can remain at current school.
		Refer for testing for IQ and learning disabilities.
Community		
With her biological family, Janine lived in a low-income urban area afflicted with violence and crime.	Janine attends the Baptist Church with her foster mother.	
	In her current foster home, Janine lives in a workingclass neighborhood.	

Critique of the Diagnosis

According to the *DSM-IV*, excessive and continuing displays of aggressive behavior can be considered a mental disorder and formally labeled as conduct disorder (CD). As one reviews Janine's case, it is clear that she meets the criteria for CD. However, a social work practitioner must question the validity of applying a *DSM-IV* diagnosis to Janine.

Although Janine displays many of the behaviors listed under CD, it is imperative to explore other motivations behind her aggressive behaviors. As stated in the case history, Janine has been a victim of sexual abuse and over the past 2 years has been rejected by five different foster homes. In their critique of the *DSM-IV*, Kutchins and Kirk (1997) emphasize the importance of distinguishing between behavior as a dysfunction within a person and behavior as a reaction to life stressors. Although it is possible that Janine's behavior signifies a dysfunction within Janine, it is more probable that Janine is reacting negatively to her circumstances. It is unfair to expect a child to react appropriately after being sexually abused, rejected by parents, and forced to live in numerous unstable environments—all within the context of poverty. As one examines Janine's situation, it seems likely that her behaviors can be attributed to the stressors in her life.

The *DSM* view of disorders is that they evolve from individual dysfunction. Indeed, the *DSM–IV-TR* states, "Consistent with the *DSM-IV* definition of mental disorder, the Conduct Disorder diagnosis should be applied only when the behavior in question is symptomatic of an underlying dysfunction within the individual and not simply a reaction to the immediate social context" (p. 96). However, the literature on ODD/CD identifies coercive family factors and other social environment variables as key to the development of these disorders. The *DSM* definition is therefore not in line with what has been empirically validated as contributing to these disorders.

Appendix. Measures for Conduct Disorder/Oppositional Defiant Disorder

Self-Report Delinquency Scale

Elliott, Huizinga, & Ageton (1985)

Description

- 47-item version for 11- to 19-year-olds derived from offenses in Uniform Crime Reports.
- Also assesses for substance use.
- Report of frequency of each behavior in past year.
- 40-item version used in National Youth Survey includes a General Delinquency scale giving a summary measure of criminal offenses and an Index Offense scale that includes only relatively serious offenses.

Reliability

- Test-retest reliabilities range from .80 to .99.

Validity

- Good discriminant and predictive validity with chronic offenders (Dunford & Elliott, 1984) and serious offenders (Elliott et al., 1985).

Youth Self-Report

Achenbach (1991)

Description

- Assesses 11- to 18-year-olds' self-reports of their own problems and competencies for the last 6 months.
- Items are parallel to Child Behavior Checklist.
- 3-response format (0/ "not true," 1/ "somewhat" or "sometimes true," 2/ "very true" or "often true")
- 17 competence items include:

  1. Activities
  2. Social
  3. Mean of youth's self-report of academic performance

- 103 problem items

  1. Thought problems
  2. Attention problems
  3. Self-destructive/identity problems (oapnly for boys)
     Internalizing
  4. Withdrawn
  5. Somatic complaints
  6. Anxious/depressed
     Externalizing
  7. Delinquent behavior
  8. Aggressive behavior

Reliability

- 1-week test-retest reliabilities: mean .76 for competence scores and mean .72 for problems scores
- 6-month test-retest reliability: mean of .69 for problem scores
- 7-month test-retest reliabilities: mean of .50 for competence scales and .49 for problem scales

Validity

• Discriminates between referred and nonreferred youth

Eyberg Child Behavior Inventory

Eyberg (1992)

Description

• A parent-completed, 36-item, behavior rating scale developed to assess disruptive behaviors in children ages 2–16 years
• 2 scales:

1. Intensity ("never"/1 to "always"/7): how often the behaviors currently occur
2. Problem ("yes"/"no"): identifies the specific behaviors that are currently problems

• Takes 10 minutes to complete

Reliability

• Interparent agreement .86 for Intensity and .79 for Problem scales.
• Internal consistency was .98 for both Intensity and Problem scales for nonreferred pediatric clinic sample and for pediatric clinic adolescents.
• Test-retest reliability was .86 for Intensity and .88 for Problem scales over 3 weeks, .80 for Intensity and .85 for Problem scales over 3 months, and .75 for Intensity and .75 for Problem scales.

Validity

• Valid across ethnic groups (Collett, Ohan, & Myers, 2003).
• Scores were correlated with observational measures of parent–child interactions.

• Problem (.67) and Intensity (.75) scores were correlated with Externalizing scale of the Child Behavior Checklist and with Internalizing scale (Problem = .48; Intensity = .41).
• Problem (.62) and Intensity (.59) scores correlated with Parenting Stress Index child domain scores and with parent domain scores (Problem = .62; Intensity = .59).
• When comparing preschool disruptive children and a comparison group without such problems and adolescents who were disruptive

versus adolescents who were not, mean Intensity and Problem scores differentiated between groups.
- Scale appears to be sensitive to treatment change in young children

Child Behavior Checklist

Achenbach (1991)

Description

- Parent-report checklist assessing child (ages 4–18) functioning with response set ("0" not true/ "2" very or often true) in last 6 months
- Written at fifth-grade reading level and requires 20 minutes to complete
- A briefer version available for 2- to 3-year-olds
- Assesses 2 primary areas:
  1. Social competence (20 items): amount and quality of child's participation in extracurricular activities, school functioning, jobs, chores, friendships, and other activities
  2. Behavior problems (118 behaviors): 8 syndromes under 2 broad groupings:
     Internalizing
     Withdrawn, somatic complaints, anxious/depressed
     Externalizing
     Delinquent behavior, aggressive behavior
     Social problems, thought problems, attention problems, sex problems

Reliability

- 1-week test-retest reliability ranged from .70 to .95.
- 1-year test-retest reliability was a mean correlation of .62 for competence scales and .75 for problem scales.
- 2-year test-retest reliability was a mean correlation of .56 for competence scales and .71 for problem scales.

Validity

- Correlations between Child Behavior Checklist and Connors Parent Questionnaire ranged from .59 to .86 with total problem scores correlating .82.
- Correlations between Child Behavior Checklist and Quay-Peterson Revised Behavior Problem Checklist ranged from .59 to .88 with total problem scores correlating .81.

- Discriminates between clinic and nonclinic children.
- Sensitive to treatment effects

Note

1. This case will also be continued in chapter 6.

References

Abikoff, H., & Klein, R. G. (1992). Attention-deficit hyperactivity and conduct disorder: Comorbidity and implications for treatment. *Journal of Consulting and Clinical Psychology, 60,* 881–892.

Alberg, J., Petry, C., & Eller, A. (1994). *A resource guide for social skills interaction.* Longmont, CO: Sopris West.

Alexander, J., & Parsons, B. V. (1982). *Functional family therapy.* Monterey, CA: Brooks/Cole.

American Psychiatric Association. (2000). *Diagnostic and statistical manual of mental disorders* (4th ed., text rev.). Washington, DC: Author.

Aos, S., Barnoski, R., & Lieb, R. (1998). *Watching the bottom line: Cost-effective interventions for reducing crime in Washington.* Olympia, WA: Washington State Institute for Public Policy.

Aos, S., Phipps, P., Barnoski, R., & Lieb, R. (2001). *The comparative costs and benefits of programs to reduce crime.* Olympia, WA: Washington State Institute for Public Policy.

Bank, L., Marlowe, J. H., Reid, J. B., Patterson, G. R., & Weinrott, M. R. (1991). A comparative evaluation of parent-training interventions for families of chronic delinquents. *Journal of Abnormal Child Psychology, 19,* 15–33.

Bennett, D., & Gibbons, T. (2000). Efficacy of child cognitive-behavioral interventions for antisocial behavior: A meta-analysis. *Child and Family Behavior Therapy, 22,* 1–15.

Biederman, J., Farone, S., Milberger, S., Jetton, J., Chen, L., Mick, R., et al. (1996). Is childhood oppositional defiant disorder a precursor to adolescent conduct disorder? Findings from a four year follow-up study of children with ADHD. *Journal of the American Academy of Child and Adolescent Psychiatry, 35,* 1193–1204.

Brestan, E., & Eyberg, S. (1998). Effective psychological treatments of conduct-disordered children and adolescents: 29 years, 82 studies, and 5,272 kids. *Journal of Clinical Child Psychology, 27,* 180–189.

Bronfenbrenner, U. (1979). *The ecology of human development: Experiments by nature and design.* Cambridge, MA: Harvard University Press.

Burke, J., Loeber, R., & Birmaher, B. (2002). Oppositional defiant disorder and conduct disorder: A review of the past 10 years, part II. *Journal of the American Academy of Child and Adolescent Psychiatry, 41,* 1275–1294.

Bussing, R., Gary, F.A., Mason, D. M., Leon, C. E., Sinha, K., & Garvan, C. W. (2003) Child temperament, ADHD and caregiver strain: Exploring relationships in an epidemiological sample. *Journal of the American Academy of Child & Adolescent Psychiatry, 42*, 184–192.

Camp, B., Blum, G., Hebert, F., & Van Doomick, W. (1977). "Think-aloud": A program for developing self-control in aggressive young boys. *Journal of Abnormal Child Psychology, 5*, 152–159.

Capaldi, D. M., & Patterson, G. R. (1994). Interrelated influences of contextual factors on antisocial behavior in childhood and adolescence for males. In D. C. Fowles, P. Sutker, & S. H. Goodman (Eds.), *Progress in experimental personality and psychopathology research* (pp. 165–198). New York: Springer.

Carlson, C. L., Tamm, L., & Gaub, M. (1997). Gender differences in children with ADHD, ODD, co-occurring ADHD/ODD identified in a school population. *Journal of the American Academy of Child and Adolescent Psychiatry, 36*(12), 1706–1714.

Carlson, C., Tamm, L., & Hogan, A. (1999). The child with oppositional defiant disorder and conduct disorder in the family. In H. Quay & A. Hogan (Eds.), *Handbook of disruptive behavior disorders* (pp. 337–352). New York: Kluwer Academic/Plenum.

Caspi, A., & Moffitt, T. E. (1995). The continuity of maladaptive behavior: From description to understanding in the study of antisocial behavior. In D. Cicchetti, & D. J. Cohen (Eds.), *Developmental psychopathology, Vol. 2: Risk, disorder, and adaptation. Wiley series on personality processes* (pp. 472–511). Oxford, England: John Wiley & Sons.

Chamberlain, P. (1999). Residential care for children and adolescents with oppositional defiant disorder and conduct disorder. In H. Quay & A. Hogan (Eds.), *Handbook of disruptive behavior disorders* (pp. 495–506). New York: Kluwer Academic/Plenum.

Conduct Problems Prevention Group. (1992). A developmental and clinical model for the prevention of conduct disorder: The FAST Track program. *Development and Psychopathology, 4*, 509–527.

Connor, D.F., Glatt, S. J., Lopez, I. D., Jackson, D., & Melloni, R. H. Jr.. (2002) Psychopharmacology and aggression. I: A meta-analysis of stimulant effects on overt/covert aggression-related behaviors in ADHD. *Journal of the American Academy of Child & Adolescent Psychiatry, 41*, 253–261.

Cote, S., Tremblay, R., Nagin, D., Zoccolillo, M., & Vitaro, F. (2002). Childhood behavioral profiles leading to adolescent conduct disorder: Risk trajectories for boys and girls. *Journal of the American Academy of Child and Adolescent Psychiatry, 41*, 1086–1095.

Cunningham, C. E., Bremner, R., & Boyle, M. (1995). Large group community-based parenting programs for families of preschoolers at risk for disruptive behaviour disorders: Utilization, cost effectiveness, and outcome. *Journal of Child Psychology & Psychiatry, 36*, 1141–1159.

Deater-Deckard, K., & Dodge, K. (1997). Spare the rod, spoil the authors: Emerging themes in research on parenting and child development. *Psychological Inquiry, 8*, 230–235.

Dekovic, M. (1999). Risk and protective factors in the development of problem behavior during adolescence. *Journal of Youth & Adolescence, 28,* 667–685.

Eggert, D. (1994). *Anger management for youth: Stemming aggression and violence.* Bloomington, IN: National Educational Service.

Farrington, D. P. (1995). The challenge of teenage antisocial behavior. In M. Rutter (Ed.), *Psychosocial disturbances in young people: Challenges for prevention.* (pp. 83–130). New York, NY: Cambridge University Press.

Feindler, E., & Ecton, R. (1986). *Adolescent anger control: Cognitive-behavioral techniques.* Elmsford, NY: Pergamon.

Finch, A., Nelson, W., & Ott, E. (1993). *Cognitive-behavioral procedures with children and adolescents: A practical guide.* Needham Heights, MA: Allyn & Bacon.

Fonagy, P., & Kurtz, Z. (2002). Disturbance of conduct. In P. Fonagy, M. Target, D. Cottrell, J. Phillips, & Z. Kurtz (Eds.), *What works for whom? A critical review of treatments for children and adolescents.* New York: Guilford.

Forehand, R. L., & McMahon, R. J. (1981). *Helping the noncompliant child: A clinician's guide to parent training.* New York: Guilford.

Goldstein, A., & Glick, B. (1987). *Aggression replacement training.* Champaign, IL: Research Press.

Gordon, D. A., Arbuthnot, J., Gustafson, K. E., & McGreen, P. (1988). Home-based behavioral-systems family therapy with disadvantaged juvenile delinquents. *American Journal of Family Therapy, 16,* 243–255.

Greenberg, M., Speltz, M., & DeKylen, M. (1993). Attachment security in preschoolers with and without externalizing behavior problems. *Development and Psychopathology, 5,* 191–213.

Henggeler, S. W., Schoenwald, S. K., Borduin, C., Rowland, M., & Cunningham, P. B. (1998). Multisystemic treatment of antisocial behavior in children and adolescents. New York: Guilford.

Henggeler, S., Schoenwald, S., Rowland, M., & Cunningham, P. (2002). Serious emotional disturbance in children and adolescence: Multisystemic therapy. NY: Guilford.

Hill, J. (2002). Biological, psychological and social processes in conduct disorders. *Journal of Child Psychology and Psychiatry, 43*(1), 133–164.

Hinshaw, S., & Anderson, C. (1996). Conduct and oppositional defiant disorders. In E. Mash & R. Barkley (Eds.), *Child psychopathology* (pp. 113–149). New York: Guilford.

Hinshaw, S., Lahey, B., & Hart, E. (1993). Issues of taxonomy and comorbidity in the development of conduct disorder. *Development & Psychopathology, 5,* 31–49.

Hinshaw, S., & Park, T. (1999). Research problems and issues: Toward a more definitive science of disruptive behavior disorders. In H. Quay & A. Hogan (Eds.), *Handbook of disruptive behavior disorders* (pp. 593–620). New York: Kluwer Academic/Plenum.

Hogan, A. E. (1999). Cognitive functioning in children with oppositional defiant disorder. In H. C. Quay & A. E. Hogan (Eds.), *Handbook of disruptive behavior disoders* (pp. 317–335). New York: Kluwer Academic.

Holmes, S. E, Slaughter, J. R., & Kashani, J. (2001) Risk factors in childhood that lead to the development of conduct disorder and antisocial personality disorder. *Child Psychiatry & Human Development, 31,* 183–193.

Huggins, P. (1992). *Helping kids handle anger: Teaching self-control.* Longmont, CO: Sopris West.

Huizink, A., De Medina, P., Mulder, E., Visser, G., & Buitelaar, J. (2002). Psychological measures of prenatal stress as predictors of infant temperament. *Journal of the American Academy of Child and Adolescent Psychiatry, 41,* 1078–1086.

Johnson, B. R., Jang, S. J., Larson, D., & Li, S. D. (2001). Does adolescent religious commitment matter? A reexamination of the effects of religiosity on delinquency. *Journal of Research in Crime and Delinquency, 38,* 22–43.

Johnson, B. R., Jang, S. J., Li, S. D., & Larson, D. (2000). The "invisible institution" and black youth crime: The church as an agency of local social control. *Journal of Youth and Adolescence, 29,* 479–498.

Kavale, K., Forness, S., & Walker, H. (1999). Interventions for oppositional defiant disorder and conduct disorder in the schools. In H. Quay & A. Hogan (Eds.), *Handbook of disruptive behavior disorders* (pp. 441–454). New York: Kluwer Academic/Plenum.

Kazdin, A. (2001). Treatment of conduct disorders. In J. Hill & B. Maughan (Eds.), *Conduct disorders in childhood and adolescence* (pp. 408–448). New York: Cambridge University Press.

Kazdin, A. E. (1993). Treatment of conduct disorder: Progress and directions in psychotherapy research. *Development and Psychopathology, 5,* 277–310.

Kazdin, A. E. (1997). Practitioner review: Psychosocial treatments for conduct disorder in children. *Journal of Child Psychology and Psychiatry, 38,* 161–178.

Kazdin, A. E., Siegel, T. C., & Bass, D. (1992). Cognitive problem-solving training and parent management training in the treatment of antisocial behavior in children. *Journal of Consulting and Clinical Psychology, 60,* 733–747.

Kronenberger, W. S., & Meyer, R. G. (2001). *The child clinician's handbook* (2nd ed.). Needham Heights, MA: Allyn & Bacon.

Kutchins, H. & Kirk, S. A. (1997). *Making us crazy. DSM: The psychiatric bible and the creation of mental disorders.* New York: Free Press.

Lahey, B., Miller, T., Schawb-Stone, M., Goodman, S., Waldman, I., Canino, G., et al. (2000). Age and gender differences in oppositional behavior and conduct problems: A cross sectional household study of middle childhood and adolescence. *Journal of Abnormal Psychology, 109,* 488–503.

Lahey, B. B., Loeber, R., Burke, J., & Rathouz, P. J. (2002). Adolescent outcomes of childhood conduct disorder among clinic-referred boys: Predictors of improvement. *Journal of Abnormal Child Psychology, 30*(4), 333–349.

Ledingham, J. (1999). Children and adolescents with oppositional defiant disorder and conduct disorder in the community: Experiences at school and with peers. In H. Quay & A. Hogan (Eds.), *Handbook of disruptive behavior disorders* (pp. 353–370). New York: Kluwer Academic/Plenum.

Littell, J. H., Popa, M., & Forsythe. B. (2005). Multisystemic Therapy for social, emotional, and behavioral problems in youth aged 10–17 (Cochrane Review). In: The Cochrane Library, Issue 3. Chichester, UK: John Wiley & Sons, Ltd.

Loeber, R., Farrington, D., Stouthamer-Loeber, M., & Van Kammen, W. B. (1998). *Antisocial behavior and mental health problems: Explanatory factors in childhood and adolescence.* Mahwah, NJ: L. Erlbaum Associates.

Loeber, R., Burke, J. D., Lagey, B. B., Winters, A., & Zera, M. (2000). Oppositional defiant and conduct disorder: A review of the past 10 years, part I. *Journal of the American Academy of Child and Adolescent Psychiatry, 39*(12), 1468–1484.

Loeber, R., & Coie, J. (2001). Continuities and discontinuities of development, with particular emphasis on emotional and cognitive components of disruptive behaviour. In J. Hill & B. Maughan (Eds.), *Conduct disorders in childhood and adolescence* (pp. 379–407). New York: Cambridge University Press.

Maag, J., Parks, B., & Rutherford, R. (1988). Generalization and behavior covariation of aggression in children receiving stress inoculation therapy. *Child and Family Behavior Therapy, 10*, 29–47.

Mason, D., & Frick, P. (1994). The heritability of antisocial behavior: A meta-analysis of twin and adoption studies. *Journal of Psychopathology and Behavioral Assessment, 16*, 301–323.

Maughan, B., & Rutter, M. (2001). Antisocial children grown up. In J. Hill & B. Maughan (Eds.), *Conduct disorders in childhood and adolescence* (pp. 507–552). New York: Cambridge University Press.

McGee, R., & Williams, S. (1999). Environmental risk factors in oppositional-defiant disorder and conduct disorder. In H. Quay, C. Herbert & A. Hogan (Eds), *Handbook of disruptive behavior disorders* (pp. 419–440). Dordrecht, Netherlands: Kluwer Academic Publishers.

McMahon, R. J. (1994). Diagnosis, assessment, and treatment of externalizing problems in children: The role of longitudinal data. *Journal of Consulting and Clinical Psychology, 62*, 901–917.

Meichenbaum, D. (1985). *Stress inoculation training*. New York: Pergamon.

Miller, G. E., & Prinz, R. J. (1990). Enhancement of social learning family interventions for childhood conduct disorder. Psychological Bulletin, 108, 291–307.

Miller-Johnson, S., Coie, J. D., Maumary-Gremaud, A., & Bierman, K. (2002). Peer rejection and aggression and early starter models of conduct disorder. *Journal of Abnormal Child Psychology, 30*(3), 217–231.

Moffitt, T., & Caspi, A. (2001). Childhood predictors differentiate life-course persistent and adolescence-limited antisocial pathways among males and females. *Development and Psychopathology, 13*, 355–375.

Moffitt, T., Caspi, A., Harrington, H., & Milne, B. (2002). Males on the life-course-persistent and adolescence-limited antisocial pathways: Follow-up at age 26 years. *Development and Psychopathology, 14*, 179–207.

Moffitt, T., Caspi, A., Rutter, M., & Silva, P. (2001). *Sex differences in antisocial behavior: Conduct disorder, delinquency, and violence in the Dunedin longitudinal study.* Cambridge: Cambridge University Press.

Moffitt, T. E. (1993). Adolescence-limited and life-course-persistent antisocial behavior: A developmental taxonomy. *Psychological Review, 100*, 674–701.

Morrison, M., Macdonald, G., & Leblanc, T. (2000) Identifying conduct problems in young children: Developmental pathways and risk factors. *International Social Work 43*(4), 467–480.

Najman, J., Williams, G., Nikles, J., Spence, S., Bor, W., O'Callaghan, M., et al. (2000). Mothers' mental illness and child behavior problems: Cause-effect association or observation bias? *Journal of the American Academy of Child and Adolescent Psychiatry, 39*(5), 592–602.

Pappadopulos, E., MacIntyre, J., Crismon, M., Findling, R., Malone, R., Derivan,

A., et al. (2003). Treatment recommendations for the use of antipsychotics for aggressive youth (TRAAY). Part II. *Journal of the American Academy of Child and Adolescent Psychiatry, 42,* 145–162.

Patterson, G., & Guillon, M. (1968). *Living with children: New methods for parents and teachers.* Champagne, IL: Research Press.

Prinz, R. J., & Miller, G. E. (1991). Issues in understanding and treating childhood conduct problems in disadvantaged populations. *Journal of Clinical Child Psychology, 20,* 379–385.

Reddy, L. A., & Pfeiffer, S. I. (1997). Effectiveness of treatment foster care with children and adolescents: A review of outcome studies. *Journal of the American Academy of Child & Adolescent Psychiatry,36,* 581–588.

Reid, J. B. (1993). Prevention of conduct disorder before and after school entry: Relating interventions to developmental findings. *Development and Psychopathology, 5,* 243–262.

Sanson, A., & Prior, M. (1999). Temperament and behavioral precursors to oppositional defiant disorder and conduct disorder. In H. C. Quay & A. E. Hogan (Eds.), *Handbook of disruptive behavior disorders* (pp. 397–417). New York: Kluwer Academic.

Serketich, W., & Dumas, J. (1996). The effectiveness of behavioral parent training to modify antisocial behavior in children: A meta-analysis. *Behavior Therapy, 27,* 171–186.

Shirk, S., Talmi, A., & Olds, D. (2000). A developmental psychopathology perspective on child and adolescent treatment policy. *Development and Psychopathology, 12,* 835–855.

Shure, M. (1992). *I can problem solve (ICPS): An interpersonal cognitive problem solving program.* Champaign, IL: Research Press.

Steinberg, L. (2001). We know some things: Parent-adolescent relationships in retrospect and prospect. *Journal of Research on Adolescence, 11,* 1–19.

Stouthamer-Loeber, M., Loeber, R., Homish, D., & Wei, E. (2001). Maltreatment of boys and the development of disruptive and delinquent behavior. *Development & Psychopathology, 13,* 941–955.

Swanson, J. M., Kraemer, H. C., Hinshaw, S. P., Arnold, L. E., Conners, C. K., Abikoff, H. B., et al. (2001). Clinical relevance of the primary findings of the MTA: Success rates based on severity of ADHD and ODD symptoms at the end of treatment. *Journal of the American Academy of Child & Adolescent Psychiatry, 40,* 168–179.

Thompson, R. W., Ruma, P. R., Schuchmann, L. F., & Burke, R. V. (1996). A cost-effectiveness evaluation of parent training. *Journal of Child & Family Studies, 5,* 415–429.

Wachs, T. (2000). *Necessary but not sufficient.* Washington, DC: American Psychological Association.

Wakschlag, L. S., & Hans, S. L. (2002). Maternal smoking during pregnancy and conduct problems in high-risk youth: A developmental framework. *Development & Psychopathology, 14*(2), 351–369.

Webster-Stratton, C. (1981; revised 2001). *Incredible years parents and children training series.* Retrieved November 7, 2003, from http://www.incredibleyears.com.

Webster-Stratton, C., & Hammond, M. (1997). Treating children with early-onset conduct problems: A comparison of child and parent training interventions. *Journal of Consulting and Clinical Psychology, 65*, 93–109.

Werner, E. (2000). Protective factors and individual resilience. In J. Shonoff & S. Meisels (Eds.), *Handbook of early childhood intervention* (2nd ed., pp. 115–133). Cambridge: Cambridge University Press.

Wikström, P. O., & Loeber, R. (2000). Do disadvantaged neighborhoods cause well-adjusted children to become adolescent delinquents? *Criminology, 38*, 1109.

Wilson, S., Lipsey, M., & Soydan, H. (2003). Are mainstream programs for juvenile delinquency less effective with minority youth than majority youth? A meta-analysis of outcomes research. *Research on Social Work Practice, 13*, 3–26.

References for ODD/CD Measures

Achenbach, T. M. (1991). *Manual for the Child Behavior Checklist/4-18 and 1991 profile*. Burlington: University of Vermont Department of Psychiatry.

Collett, B., Ohan, J., & Myers, K. (2003). Ten-year review of rating scales. VI: Scales assessing externalizing behaviors. *Journal of the American Academy of Child and Adolescent Psychiatry, 42*, 1143–1171.

Dunford, F., & Elliott, D. (1984). Identifying career offenders using self-reported data. *Journal of Research in Crime and Delinquency, 21*, 57–86.

Elliott, D., Huizinga, D., & Ageton, S. (1985). *Explaining delinquency and drug use.* Beverly Hills, CA: Sage.

Eyberg, S. (1992). Assessing therapy outcome with preschool children: Progress and problems. *Journal of Clinical Child Psychology, 21*, 306–311.

6 Attention-Deficit/Hyperactivity Disorder

Attention-deficit/hyperactivity disorder (ADHD) is characterized by a persistent pattern (6 months or more) of *inattention* and/or *hyperactivity* and *impulsive behavior* that is more frequent and severe than what is typically observed in others at a comparable developmental level (American Psychiatric Association, 2000). ADHD is characterized in children by a lack of self-control and ability to sustain direction. These children are distractible, do not often finish what they start, and are irritable and impatient, often interrupting and pestering others. Adults with the disorder are usually not hyperactive but are impatient, restless, and moody. They have difficulty managing their time and priorities.

The *DSM* delineates three subtypes of ADHD, depending on which symptoms predominate: the *hyperactive/impulsive, inattentive,* and *combined* types. Younger children are more likely to be diagnosed with the hyperactive/impulsive type, and not as much research has been conducted with the primarily inattentive type (Root & Resnick, 2003). To be diagnosed, the child must have demonstrated symptoms before the age of 7, although the age-of-onset criterion has been debated (Cuffe et al., 2001; Loeber, Green, Lahey, Frick, & McBurnett, 2002; Willoughby, Curran, Costello, & Angold, 2000).

ADHD is considered to be one of the disruptive behavior disorders (along with conduct disorder and oppositional defiant disorder), and the *DSM* diagnosis is made on the basis of behavioral symptoms. The disorder has recently been redefined by some researchers, however, as a pattern of cognitive or neuropsychological impairment (Tannock & Brown, 2000). Various theories about its nature have evolved, most of which describe problems in the frontal lobe functioning of the brain. The exact nature of the deficits is unknown, but current proposals include deficits associated with self-regulation, response delay or inhibition, and executive control (Barkley, 1998).

For social workers in clinic and school settings, children with ADHD are a substantial proportion of their caseloads: as much as 30 or 40% of clinic referrals (Barkley, 1998). In addition, 4 to 12% of cases seen in primary care settings involve ADHD (American Academy of Pediatrics, 2000), with ADHD-related outpatient visits to general practitioners increasing from 1.6 to 4.2 million per year during the years 1990 to 1993 (Swanson, McBurnett, Christian, & Wigal, 1995).

Prevalence of ADHD

Reports of the prevalence of ADHD in adolescence and adulthood differ, depending on the measures used, the population being studied, the diagnostic criteria employed, and the type of informant (Barkley, 1998; Cantwell, 1996; Cuffe et al., 2001). A trend toward increasing prevalence has resulted from the change in *DSM* criteria between the third and fourth editions (Cuffe et al., 2001). For the school-age population, prevalence rates for the United States and other countries are estimated at 3 to 9%, although it is difficult to make comparisons across cultures because of the different criteria and methodology employed (Gingerich, Turnock, Litfin, & Rosen, 1998). This translates to about 2 million cases of ADHD for school-age children (Barkley, 2000). The lifetime prevalence rate of ADHD in adults is 8.1% (Kessler, Berglund, Demler, et al., 2005).

Estimates of the ratios of male to female cases of ADHD vary greatly—from 2:1 to 9:1. Boys with ADHD may show noncompliance; therefore, they more often come to the attention of professionals. In clinic samples, more boys tend to be seen, and thus more research has been done on boys with ADHD (Rucklidge & Tannock, 2001). A meta-analysis of 18 studies of gender differences in ADHD revealed that, in the general population, girls with ADHD are less impaired than boys, but they show similar behavior patterns to boys in clinic samples (Gaub & Carlson, 1997).

Some researchers claim that, in the United States, prevalence rates are similar across ethnic groups and socioeconomic strata (Barkley, 1998). Others present evidence that low-income, African American children and other individuals living in low socioeconomic status show an increased incidence (Gingerich et al., 1998). Living in chronically stressful and unstable environments may lead to symptoms of agitation, reactivity, and difficulty in concentrating, among others. Another hypothesis for the possible overrepresentation of ADHD children in low socioeconomic strata is social drift related to problems with education and employment (Barkley, 1990).

The Course of the Disorder

Childhood to Adolescence

According to longitudinal studies, at least two thirds of males in their early to mid-teens continue to meet diagnostic criteria for ADHD, demonstrating academic, cognitive, or behavioral problems (Mannuzza & Klein, 1999). In late adolescence, 40% of youth may still display clinically problematic symptoms. Attentional problems in adolescents with ADHD place them at significant risk of driving accidents, injury, drinking and driving, and other traffic violations (Woodward, Fergusson, & Horwoord, 2000). Antisocial behaviors may become more common at this time to include 25 to 33% of youth with the disorder (Mannuzza & Klein, 1999). Two thirds will have had contact with the juvenile justice system, and drug abuse may be a problem for some. For the 50% who no longer qualify for the diagnosis in late adolescence, minor problems may persist in academics, self-esteem, and peer relationships. In other areas, however, such as substance abuse and antisocial activities, they will not be different from their classmates who did not have ADHD as children (Mannuzza & Klein, 1999).

In Adulthood

Studies on long-term outcome focus mainly on clinical samples followed over time (Cuffe et al., 2001), with declines noted in the rates of persistent ADHD. Continuance rates from childhood to adulthood are estimated at two fifths (Mannuzza, Klein, Bessler, Malloy, & LaPadula, 1998) or one third (Weiss & Hechtman, 1993) of child clinical samples. In older studies, ADHD was not always disentangled from conduct problems, given the high level of concordance between the disorders. This tended to inflate rates of substance abuse and antisocial problems in adults diagnosed with ADHD as youths (Langstroem, 2002). When ADHD is combined with conduct problems, there is a heightened risk for negative consequences in adulthood, including problems with relationships, substance abuse and dependence, and antisocial behavior (Langstroem, 2002).

In their review of longitudinal studies, Mannuzza and Klein (1999) found that, in comparison with those who were never diagnosed with ADHD, adults with childhood ADHD had lower educational achievement, held lower ranking occupations, were at increased risk for antisocial personality disorder, experienced self-esteem impairments, and displayed deficits in social skills. Half were still showing symptoms of ADHD in their mid-20s. On the positive side, most of these adults were employed and showed fewer emotional and behavioral problems than they did in adolescence. A majority (two thirds) of them were not diagnosed with any mental disorder.

Comorbidity of Other Disorders with ADHD

A significant proportion (44%) of children with ADHD are diagnosed with another mental disorder. Approximately one third of them have *two* other disorders, and 10% have *three* other disorders (Langstroem, 2002). The most frequent co-occurring diagnosis is another of the disruptive disorders. Estimates indicate that ODD and CD are present in 40 to 70% of children with ADHD (Newcorn & Halperin, 2000). Substantial comorbidity also exists between ADHD and mood disorders (15–75%) and ADHD and anxiety disorders (25%) (Pliszka, 2000). Learning disabilities are also common comorbid conditions for children with ADHD. The overlap between the disorders is approximately 20% when rigorous diagnostic criteria are employed (Tannock & Brown, 2000).

Diagnosing ADHD

This section considers the salient diagnostic issues regarding ADHD at each developmental stage, beginning with preschool children and ending at adulthood. ADHD generally begins before the age of 4 or 5. Although earlier assessment can inform intervention that might minimize later problems, difficulties abound in diagnosing ADHD in preschool-age children (Shepard, Carter, & Cohen, 2000). For instance, valid and reliable instruments for assessing ADHD are lacking. Caution must also be exercised in diagnosing ADHD in preschool because the child may be reacting to a difficult environment, displaying anxiety symptoms, or experiencing other problems with emotional regulation (Shepard et al., 2000). As a result, most children are not diagnosed until elementary school.

Assessment at the school-age stage has several components, as there is no definitive biological or neurological test that establishes the diagnosis (Root & Resnick, 2003):

- A physical examination, to rule out possible medical causes of symptoms.
- Clinical interviews with key informants including the child, parents,

and teachers. Problems related to trauma, stress, depression, and anxiety should be ruled out.

- The completion of rating scales by parents and teachers. The validity of teacher reports in the diagnosis of ADHD has been demonstrated through long-term follow-up (Mannuzza, Klein, & Moulton, 2002). In other words, teacher reports are extremely important in making the diagnosis.
- A review of school records, including report cards, achievement tests, and attendance.
- A review of health records, including both medical and psychological reports.
- Psychological testing to assess cognitive ability, visual-motor integration, and attention (Shepard et al., 2000).
- Behavioral observations of the child and of parent–child interactions.

The social worker should advise parents about the assessment process. He or she may find that many parents, suspecting ADHD in their children, have brought their children to their primary care provider, who has then diagnosed the child with ADHD and prescribed medication. However, because of time constraints on primary providers and their lack of background, this is not an appropriate procedure to follow.

Although the social worker can take on certain aspects of this assessment—including clinical interviewing of the child and parent, assessing parent–child interactions, interviewing teachers, and administering measures—other aspects, including medical and psychological evaluation, require referrals. Social workers should also be familiar with the child study process in the school districts in which they work. (Information is typically available on state education Web sites.)

Regarding diagnosis in adults, the following components are involved (American Academy of Child and Adolescent Psychiatry, 2002):

- A clinical interview, with discussion of ADHD symptoms present in childhood.
- History taking of drug and alcohol use, because ADHD can be comorbid with substance abuse and dependence.
- Information from collateral sources (parents, significant others), who may be more accurate reporters of symptoms.
- A medical history and physical examination to rule out physical conditions.
- The completion of rating scales such as the Wender Utah Rating Scales (Wender, Reimherr, & Wood, 1981), the Brown Attention-Deficit Disorder Scale for Adults (Brown, 1996), and the Conners Adult ADHD Rating Scale (Conners, 1990).

The social worker must be alert to other diagnoses that might better account for the symptom presentation, such as learning disorders, borderline intellectual functioning, bipolar disorder, depression, or a personality disorder. In addition, practitioners working with children who have ADHD should be alert to the fact that between 25 and 50% of their parents will have ADHD as well (Weiss, Hechtman, & Weiss, 2000).

Risk and Protective Factors

Risk and protective factors for both the onset of ADHD and its course, in terms of persistence and severity, are listed in Tables 6.1 and 6.2, respectively. In the following section, some of the risk and protective factors are further elaborated. Like many disorders discussed in this volume, research on protective factors is more limited than information on risk factors (Whalen & Henker, 1999).

Onset

Biological Factors: Genetics

Having a parent with ADHD places a child at risk for ADHD. As noted, 25 to 50% of parents with an ADHD child also have ADHD (Weiss et al.,

Table 6.1	
Risk and Protective Factors for the Onset of ADHD	
Risk	Protective
Biological	
Genetic predisposition	No genetic predisposition
Maternal smoking, alcohol and drug use during pregnancy	Mother doesn't smoke or use substances during pregnancy
Complications during pregnancy and delivery	Complication-free pregnancy and delivery
Social	
Family	
Lack of an attachment bond, coupled with low maternal social support	High levels of maternal social support and a strong mother–child attachment bond
Low socioeconomic status	High socioeconomic status

Table 6.2	
Risk and Protective Factors for the Course of ADHD	
Risk	Protective
Psychological	
Comorbid oppositional defiant disorder or conduct disorder	No comorbid diagnosis or a comorbid anxiety disorder
Social	
Family	
Parent with ADHD	Parents do not have ADHD
Coercive and inconsistent parenting	Effective child management strategies
Single-parent home	Two-parent home

2000). Reviews of twin studies find varying rates of the extent genetic factors account for the variance in ADHD: 30–80% (Samudra & Cantwell, 1999), 64–91% (Root & Resnick, 2003), and 55–97% (Barkley, 2000). The precise genetic mechanisms are not known, but a dopamine transmitter gene (DAT-1) and a dopamine receptor gene (DRD-4), among others, have been linked to ADHD children and families (Maher, Marazita, Ferrell, & Vanyukov, 2002). However, correlation should not be confused with causality. The higher rates of dopamine seen in children with ADHD may be a consequence rather than a precursor of the disorder (Leo & Cohen, 2003).

Prenatal and Perinatal Risk Factors

Complications during pregnancy and delivery may place individuals at risk for ADHD (Root & Resnick, 2003; Samudra & Cantwell, 1999). Children who are born preterm are at twice the risk for ADHD as children who are full term (Bhutta, Cleves, Casey, Cradock, & Anand, 2002).

Maternal smoking in pregnancy is also associated with a risk of ADHD in children (Linnett, et al., 2003). In addition, maternal drinking during pregnancy, especially in the first trimester and binge drinking, may act as a predisposing factor (Samudra & Cantwell, 1999). However, a recent review of nine studies indicates mixed findings on the effects of maternal drinking on ADHD (Linnett et al., 2003). Research on maternal drug use in pregnancy is limited, although heroin dependence and cocaine use have been associated with ADHD (Samudra & Cantwell, 1999). Still, variables such as poverty and poor prenatal care, rather than drug use per se, may be the more significant factors.

Caregiving Factors

Some researchers posit that attachment patterns between a parent and child contribute to the onset of ADHD. According to one model, in parent–child interactions, stimulation and arousal is often pushed on the infant while the child's own cues and signals regarding environmental interactions are ignored (Sroufe, 1989). Infants with this experience over time may not learn that their behavior can be reorganized following stimulation. In one study, children who were adopted with a history of severe institutional deprivation experienced high rates of inattention and overactivity compared with those who were adopted without such a history (Kreppner, O'Connor, & Rutter, 2001). Part of the deprivation involved a lack of attachment with consistent caregivers. The symptoms of inattention and overactivity were more pronounced when the children were 6 years old than when they were 4. At that point, they had been with their adoptive families for an average of 2½ years, suggesting the persistence of symptoms.

Carlson, Jacobvitz, and Sroufe (1995) conducted an 11-year prospective longitudinal study of 191 children of mothers in low socioeconomic circumstances and found that, for children in elementary school, early caregiving characteristics and socioeconomic variables independently predicted hyperactivity. This relationship remained even after controlling for early distractibility (Samudra & Cantwell, 1999).

Summary of Risk Factors for Onset

Although ADHD is considered to be, in large part, an inherited, neurosychological disorder, genetic factors may not be the only way that children may be at risk for the disorder. Alternative pathways to ADHD may include other biological factors (e.g., exposure to substances), gene–environment interactions, or social factors, such as parent–child attachment patterns, parental isolation, lack of social support, stressful life events, low socioeconomic status, and combinations of these variables (Samudra & Cantwell, 1999; Whalen & Henker, 1999; Wilens, Spencer, & Biederman, 2000). Possibly, distinct subgroups of ADHD may each have unique symptom clusters, neurobiology, response to pharmacological intervention, and prognosis (Shepard et al., 2000).

Adjustment and Recovery

Even though ADHD is considered a neuropsychological disorder, its persistence, severity, treatment responsiveness, and long-term outcomes are influenced by psychosocial variables (Langstroem, 2002; Whalen & Henker, 1999). According to Barkley, Fischer, Edelbrock, and Smallish (1990), little evidence supports a purely psychosocial explanation of ADHD, but environmental factors may well shape the nature and severity of a genetic predisposition toward poor impulse control. In particular, the risk for certain comorbid disorders, such as oppositional defiant disorder and conduct disorder, are largely related to family factors (Barkley, Fischer, Edelbrock, & Smallish, 1990). Any parental psychopathology, marital conflict, and family difficulties that contribute to inconsistent, coercive, or decreased efforts at managing the child's behavior may serve to increase problem behaviors in the child with ADHD (Weiss & Hechtman, 1993).

Having a parent with ADHD has already been discussed as a risk factor for the onset of a child's ADHD; it also presents a risk for the child's response to treatment. Parents with ADHD may have difficulty keeping appointments, attending to information provided in visits, remembering instructions, and following through with a behavior program at home because of their lack of consistency and organization (Weiss et al., 2000). They may also monopolize the practitioner's attention with their own problems. Indeed, Sonuga-Barke, Daley, and Thompson (2002) reported that parent training outcomes for 3-year-old children were compromised when mothers had high levels of ADHD symptoms.

Another factor identified in families involves household composition. Studies find that children with severe ADHD are less likely to have families with two parents (Cuffe et al., 2001), possibly because of the stress involved. A two-parent home may be a protective factor because two parents are more likely to successfully manage the stress related to having a child with ADHD (Cuffe et al., 2001). Pervasive child problems demand considerable parental resources. These demands often result in failure, fatigue, demoralization, isolation, strained marital relationships, and neglect or overindulgence of siblings (Whalen & Henker, 1999). Indeed, Barkley (2000) likens the difficulties parents of children with ADHD face to those experienced by parents of children with autism. For these reasons, the social worker's empathic understanding and support of parents can facilitate constructive family interactions.

Intervention

The treatment needs of children with ADHD and their families require multimodal approaches, including medication, school-based interventions, and psychosocial interventions for both child and parents (Multimodal Treatment Study of Children with Attention-Deficit/Hyperactivity Disorder Cooperative Group [MTA], 1999). Based on a survey of 50 psychologists and 51 physicians with expertise in the area of ADHD (Conners, March, Frances, Wells, & Ross, 2001), guidelines have been developed for deciding between behavioral-psychosocial and medication treatment (Conners et al., 2001). See Table 6.3. If parents prefer, a medication-only approach has em-

Table 6.3

Guidelines for Treatment

Behavioral treatment should be used in the following instances:
- For milder cases of ADHD
- For preschool-age children
- When there are accompanying internalizing disorders, such as anxiety and depression
- When the child's behavior indicates social skill deficits
- When the family prefers psychosocial treatment

Combined medication and behavioral treatment should be used in most cases, particularly in the following situations:
- The ADHD symptoms are severe.
- There are accompanying externalizing disorders, such as oppositional defiant disorder and conduct disorder, mental retardation, or central nervous system problems (e.g., epilepsy, migraine).
- The child exhibits severe school problems.
- The symptoms cause family problems.
- A rapid intervention response is required.
- The person is diagnosed with the "combined" subtype of ADHD.

pirical validation for the treatment of core ADHD symptoms (Klassen, Miller, Parminder, Lee, & Olsen, 1999; MTA, 1999). A combined intervention approach, however, involving both medication and behavioral-psychosocial treatments, enhances treatment compliance and addresses the various co-orbid problems experienced by so many children with ADHD (Root & Resnick, 2003). Specific aspects of both medication and psychosocial treatment are explored next.

Psychosocial Interventions

Psychosocial interventions comprise those targeted toward parents, children, and the school system. Empirically validated interventions typically operate from the theoretical perspective of behavioral and cognitive-behavioral theories.

Family Interventions

A multimodal intervention approach requires that parents are knowledgeable about the aspects of care needed, including information about ADHD, its medications, effective parenting practices, how to reinforce children's coping strategies, and how to manage parental stress. As described previously, parenting practices can play a large role in determining the outcome of ADHD for a child. Because of problems children have with listening and following through with directions, interactions between children and their caregivers may easily turn coercive. Such parent–child exchanges are, in turn, linked to the development of conduct problems (Patterson, 1982, 1986; Patterson, DeBaryshe, & Ramsey, 1989).

The empirical literature on family intervention for ADHD mainly discusses parent training, which was initially developed to address conduct problems (see chapter 5). Children learn pro-social behavior (for example, following directions, completing homework, doing household chores, getting along with siblings) by positive reinforcement through praise, token economies, and rewards. Parents are taught to respond to children's negative behaviors by ignoring or punishing the child so that he or she will have to suffer negative consequences (for example, time out from reinforcement, the loss of points and privileges, or work duty) for engaging in the behavior. Parents are taught these principles through didactic instruction, behavioral rehearsal, modeling, and role plays.

Parent training is a brief treatment model with about 12 sessions in either individual or group formats. The strategies learned must be enacted consistently long after treatment is over so that the child does not revert to previous undesirable behaviors. If parents also have ADHD, then certain modifications in this process may be necessary. Instruction may need to be home based and hands-on, and the behavioral system should be kept simple (Weiss et al, 2000).

Because children with ADHD have problems with schoolwork, other interventions for parents include structuring the home environment (so that the child has a quiet, uncluttered place to work relatively free of distractions, perhaps with a parent sitting nearby), regular teacher verification of satisfactory homework completion, and a home-based reinforcement system featuring regular school–home note exchanges (DuPaul & Power, 2000). In such a system, the teacher evaluates the child once per day (0 = work harder, 1 = OK, 2 = good job!) on selected target behaviors (such as completion of work, attention to instruction, and speaking at appropriate times). Parents review the teacher rating and provide incentives for goal attainment and punishment for failing to make agreed-upon changes (DuPaul & Power, 2000).

Individual Interventions

One of the primary treatment goals is for students with ADHD to gain more control over their behavior and academic performance while relying less on support from teachers, parents, and peers. Three major self-directed strategies that have been used with this population are self-instruction, self-monitoring, and self-reinforcement (DuPaul & Power, 2000). Although these techniques are widely accepted as helpful by practitioners, empirical investigations have yet to consistently support their efficacy with this population. Self-instruction typically involves training youth for the completion of tasks in the following steps: (a) the practitioner modeling a task approach by stating thoughts aloud prior to each action, (b) having the student duplicate this strategy by stating thoughts *aloud* while completing a task, (c) having the student gradually *reduce the volume* of thought statements, and (d) asking the student to engage in reflective thought *covertly* while completing work.

Self-monitoring involves students observing and recording the occurrence of their own behaviors. Self-reinforcement involves teaching children to track and assess their own performance and to provide appropriate feedback to themselves (DuPaul & Power, 2000).

School Interventions

School-based services for children with ADHD rest on a foundation provided by several federal laws. The way each law addresses the educational needs of children with ADHD is briefly described next, referencing the work of DuPaul and Power (2000), Root and Resnick (2003), and Tannock and Brown (2000). Section 504 of the 1973 Rehabilitation Act prohibits schools from discriminating against people with handicaps. The Individuals with Disabilities Education Act (IDEA) of 1990 (the reauthorization of the Education for All Handicapped Children Act, PL 94-142) includes several relevant provisions for persons with ADHD. It qualifies children with ADHD for special education services under the disability category (such as a learning disability or the category of "other health impairment") when symptoms affect alertness, which, in turn, limits school performance. It also provides free and appropriate public education for children with ADHD and a multidisciplinary evaluation process toward the development of an individualized educational plan. The Americans with Disabilities Act (ADA) ensures that reasonable accommodations must be made for individuals who have a substantial limitation of a major life activity, such as learning. Social workers, as well as parents of children with ADHD, can find more information about these laws and their enactment at state departments of education. If it is necessary for parents to seek legal services for better enforcement of the laws, they should be referred to local bar associations, which have listings of attorneys who specialize in these cases (Root & Resnick, 2003).

The types of interventions required by a student with ADHD to perform well in school depend on multiple factors: the settings where the impairment is occurring; the level of functional impairment; the resources available in the home, school, and community; the motivation of the student to change; the presence of comorbid psychiatric conditions; and the child's prior response to educational, behavioral, or pharmacological interventions (DuPaul & Power, 2000). Children and adolescent students with

ADHD are typically placed in general education classrooms, which is appropriate as long as modifications are implemented effectively by the general education teacher. Indeed, research reviews have documented mixed findings for the use of special education with students with ADHD. Acceptability of treatment procedures may be enhanced if the general education teacher is provided with information about ADHD and successful interventions for the disorder. Several books may be helpful in this regard (see Barkley, 1994; DuPaul & Stoner, 2003; Parker, 1992; Pfiffner, 1996).

A meta-analysis of 63 studies of school-based interventions indicated that contingency management programs and academic interventions were more effective than cognitive-behavioral interventions for affecting the classroom behavior of children with ADHD (DuPaul & Eckert, 1997). However, academic performance was more difficult to change through intervention. Barkley (1998) and DuPaul and Power (2000) have suggested the following modifications to instruction:

- Repeating instructions frequently
- Presenting information in color
- Remaining on one topic for only a brief time
- Presenting material quickly
- Providing frequent breaks
- Representing time limits in concrete ways, such as the use of a timer on the child's desk
- Requiring an active motor response from the child, such as pressing a button
- Giving the child frequent opportunities to receive feedback for performance
- Giving a menu of possible assignments, such as completing a worksheet, doing problems on the computer, or practicing problems with a classmate
- (For adolescents and young adults) providing instruction in note-taking, study, and test-taking skills

Management of behavior in the classroom involves providing brief, firm reprimands immediately following an undesired behavior and making sure that verbal praise is given at least three times as often as reprimands. However, praise may not sufficiently galvanize children with ADHD, who may suffer impairments in motivation (Barkley, 1998). As a result, tokens, which can be exchanged for rewards, can be more effective because they represent concrete, external sources of motivation (DuPaul & Power, 2000). Tokens can also be used for "response cost" strategies, in which they are withdrawn from a child's "account" for unacceptable behavior. The social worker may also play the role of mentor or identify a mentor within the school system. This person spends a great deal of one-on-one time with the child through the school day. The purposes of mentoring are to develop a relationship of support and trust with the child, design an organizational system so that the child can track materials and assignments, negotiate behavioral contracts, monitor academic performance (with frequent input from teachers), and help teachers structure classroom interventions (DuPaul & Power, 2000).

Medication

During the last decade in the United States, the rate of stimulant prescriptions has risen steeply. The vast majority of children (90%) seeking help for ADHD-related concerns from primary care providers received prescriptions (National Institutes of Health [NIH], 2000). The increase in production of stimulants and the numbers of prescriptions written could be in response to improved recognition of ADHD by physicians, an increase in the prevalence of ADHD, or an easing of the standards for making the ADHD diagnosis. At the same time, great variability across communities and physicians exists in the use of medication for ADHD. Surveys have indicated that in some communities, children diagnosed with ADHD were not medicated adequately, whereas in others, a majority of children on stimulants failed to earn a diagnosis of ADHD (NIH, 2000).

The primary psychostimulant drugs are methylphenidate, the amphetamines (including dextroamphetamine and methamphetamine, which are more potent substances), and pemoline. They are classified (except for pemoline) as Schedule II drugs by the Drug Enforcement Agency because of their abuse potential. For example, Ritalin is pharmacologically similar to cocaine in its impact on brain biochemistry, though not in its molecular structure (DeGrandpre, 1999). Schedule II is the most restrictive classification for medications, prohibiting both their prescription by phone and the writing of refills. The psychostimulants are currently approved for the treatment of ADHD, narcolepsy, and obesity (Lawrence, Lawrence, & Carson, 1997). At present they account for 95% of ADHD medication therapy in the United States. In this country the majority of children (71%) with ADHD take methylphenidate, because it is effective, has been available the longest (since 1958), and has been tested most thoroughly (NIH, 2000). As well as showing a strong effect on the core symptoms of ADHD (attention, impulsivity, and hyperactivity), the stimulants also seem to be effective in reducing aggression (Connor, Glatt, Lopez, Jackson, & Melloni, 2002). In a review of the randomized controlled trials of the use of stimulants in ADHD, involving 5,899 patients, improvement in core ADHD symptoms occurred in 65 to 75% compared with 5 to 30% of those taking a placebo (McClellan & Werry, 2003). As a result of the accumulated evidence, stimulants are the first-line treatment for both children and adults (McClellan & Werry, 2003; Weiss & Weiss, 2004). The fact that a stimulant improves attention in those who take it is not diagnostic, however, as most people, if given stimulants, show better focus and concentration (DeGrandpre, 1999). Further, stimulant treatment does not appear to alter the adolescent or adult outcome of ADHD, despite well-established therapeutic gains in childhood (Jacobvitz, Sroufe, Stewart, & Leffert, 1990; Mannuzza & Klein, 1999).

The common adverse effects of the stimulants are generally transient and include loss of appetite, weight loss, irritability, insomnia, and abdominal pain (Sadock & Sadock, 2003). Less common adverse effects include depression, increased blood pressure, tachycardia, nightmares, tics, skin rashes, toxic psychosis, and liver toxicity. All of the drugs except pemoline carry a "rebound" effect, meaning that the symptoms of ADHD tend to recur dramatically after the drug is eliminated from the consumer's body. They may stunt physical growth among children and adolescents, but there is a rebound growth to normal height during drug holidays or after the drug is discontinued (Sadock & Sadock, 2003).

Although the stimulants have traditionally been the drugs of first choice in treating ADHD, alternatives are necessary. Many individuals either do not respond to the primary medications or experience intolerable adverse reactions. Evidence for the effectiveness of other medications for treating ADHD is emerging. See Tables 6.4, 6.5, and 6.6 for more information on stimulants and other medications prescribed for ADHD.

Table 6.4				
Medications for ADHD: Preparation, Daily Dosage, Age Approved				
Drug	Trade Name	Preparation	Age for Use	Daily Dose(mg.)
Psychostimulants				
Amphetamine	Adderall	Tablet	3+	20–40
Methylphenidate	Ritalin	Tablet	6+	20–40
	Concerta	Tablet		18–36
Dextroamphetamine	Dexedrine	Tablet, Capsule	3+	5–60
Pemoline	Cylert	Tablet	6+	56–75
Other				
Clonidine[a]	Catapres	Tablet, Patch	Not specified	0.5–3
Atomoxetine	Strattera	Capsule	6+	20–60
[a] Not FDA approved for treatment of ADHD				

Table 6.5

Psychostimulant Medications: Action, Advantages, and Disadvantages

Amphetamine

- Rapid onset with 2–6 hour effect; beneficial for symptoms of inattention, hyperactivity-impulsivity, and aggression.

Advantages

- May need only one daily dose; may be helpful for those who don't respond to other amphetamines.

Disadvantages

- Potential for abuse and diversion to illicit drug market; common transient symptoms include loss of appetite, weight loss, irritability, and insomnia.

Methylphenidate

- Releases stored dopamine, decreases dopamine reuptake, and inhibits monoamine oxidase activity.

Advantages

- Most widely used and most studied; relative to other stimulants, has less of an appetite suppression effect.

Disadvantages

- Because of short half-life, might need to be taken 2–4 times daily; while a time-release form is available, some evidence that it may be less effective (Fitzpatrick, Klorman, Brumaghim, & Borgstedt, 1992); its slower absorption results in delayed onset and also increases sleep.

Dextroamphetamine

- Increases dopamine and norepinephrine transmission and inhibits monoamine oxidase activity.

Advantages

- Least expensive of psychostimulants; fast acting; with a half-life of 6 hours, needs to be taken only twice daily.

Disadvantages

- Potential for abuse and diversion to illicit drug market; higher likelihood of anorexia, insomnia, and cardiovascular effects than Ritalin.

Pemoline

- Structurally different from Ritalin and the amphetamines; seems to act through dopamine mechanisms in ways that are not yet well understood.

Advantages

- Needs to be taken only once daily and is available in a chewable tablet; thus may be easier for children and families to manage; the lesser stimulant effect reduces its abuse potential and produces less anorexia and insomnia; only psychostimulant that produces no rebound effect on discontinuation.

Disadvantages

- May require up to 6 weeks of use before therapeutic effect; more expensive than other stimulants; has not been researched as extensively as Ritalin; there have been reports in England of deaths from overdose due to liver toxicity.

Sources: Barkley (1998); Bentley & Walsh (2001); Efron, Jarman, & Barker (1997); Faraone & Biederman (2002); Rodgers (1996); Weiss & Weiss (2004).

Table 6.6

Other Medications to Treat ADHD: Actions, Advantages, and Disadvantages

Clonidine

• Originally developed to lower blood pressure; decreases arousal by decreasing the activity of alpha-2 receptors in the central nervous system and thereby promoting release of norepinephrine; has been effective with children who have severe problems with mood, activity level, cooperation, and frustration tolerance but less effective at improving attention.

Advantages
• Quickly absorbed with a long half-life; effective with symptoms of hyperactivity; can be dispensed with a 7-day patch.

Disadvantages
• Common adverse effects include dry mouth and eyes, fatigue, irritability, sedation, dizziness, hypotension, and constipation. Reports of child deaths when there were existing heart problems. It is not advised to combine clonidine with stimulants.

Tricyclic Antidepressants (imipramine, desipramine, and amitriptyline)
• Between half to a third of individuals (both children and adults) show clinically significant response; possibly useful if people have not responded to the stimulants or atomoxetine.

Advantages
• For adults with a family history of depression.

Disadvantages
• Cardiac monitoring is needed because cardiac problems (tachycardia or arrhythmia) have been reported, as well sudden deaths in children.

Bupropion (Wellbutrin)
• An atypical antidepressant.

Advantages
• May be helpful for individuals for whom stimulants have not worked or who have comorbid depression, have a personal or family history of tics, or are at risk of stimulant abuse.

Disadvantages
• Adverse side effects include insomnia, agitation, confusion, irritability, and possible hypertension. Use of bupropion is contraindicated in those with seizure or eating disorders.

Atomoxetine
• A selective norepinephrine reuptake inhibitor; it's new, and there are no long-term studies available of its positive and adverse effects.

Sources: Barkley (1998); Bentley & Walsh (2001); Brown & La Rosa (2002); Connor, Fletcher, & Swanson (1999); Popper (1997); Weiss & Weiss (2004).

Concerns Related to Medication Prescription for Children

Although pharmacological intervention is certainly less expensive than psychosocial interventions, there are concerns with the use of medication for children and adolescents. Medication for children under 5 years of age is rarely indicated because the main reason to use medications is to help school-age children perform better in school (Shepard et al., 2000). Therefore, the primary use for stimulants with preschool children is behavior control, which might be aptly managed through structuring the environment with parent training skills. In addition, it has been hypothesized that the prefrontal cortex, the brain area that is the primary site of action of psychostimulants, is not fully mature at this young age. Other organ systems that are active in the breakdown and secretion of psychostimulants are also immature (Shepard et al., 2000).

A concern about the use of stimulants with adolescents is that they will be at increased risk for substance use as they become habituated to using medication to regulate their behavior (Gadow, 1991). However, a meta-analysis examining the association between medication use and substance abuse in adolescence and adulthood found that children who took medication were at lower risk for substance abuse than those who had not (Faraone & Wilens, 2003; Wilens, Faraone, Biederman, & Gunawardene, 2003).

An additional safeguard against abuse is provided through the use of longer-acting medications, such as extended-release methylphenidate (e.g., Concerta). With these drugs, the medication need be given only once daily by the parents and not taken to school, where it could be given away or sold. Furthermore, the active ingredient in this extended-release caplet is in the form of a paste, which cannot be ground up or snorted (NIH, 2000).

A final concern with youths is that medication may remove their sense of responsibility and control over their own behaviors. A study of adolescents with ADHD found that they blamed not taking their medication for their failure to follow parent instructions and credited taking their medication for obeying (Ohan & Johnston, 1999). Adolescents, therefore, might be at risk for attributing responsibility for their behavior to medication compliance.

Medication Efficacy for Adults with ADHD

Studies of stimulant-treated adults have produced divergent rates of drug efficacy, ranging from 23% to 75% (Schatzberg & Nemeroff, 1998). This variability may be the result of low stimulant dosages, the high rate of comorbid disorders, or how the diagnosis of ADHD was reached. Of particular concern is the danger of prescribing psychostimulants for adults who have comorbid substance abuse disorders. The tricyclic antidepressants are considered second-choice medications if stimulants are either not effective or contraindicated (Weiss & Weiss, 2004). Another antidepressant, bupropion

(Wellbutrin), has also been suggested. Anecdotal evidence purports that atomoxetine (Strattera) may be useful as well.

Critique

ADHD is considered an inherited neuropsychological disorder, but substantive supporting evidence is lacking (DeGrandpre, 1999). Social influences, such as attachment patterns, parental stress, and poverty, and other biological contributing factors, such as maternal smoking, may be underrecognized.

We must also not underestimate the tremendous profit reaped by drug companies and their influence on prescribing rates, which in some communities are alarmingly high. For instance, it is not widely known that drug companies fund such groups as Children and Adults with Attention Deficit Disorder, where the use of medication is promulgated (DeGrandpre, 1999).

Another problem is that psychopharmacological intervention is often handled by primary care physicians rather than by psychiatrists. The general practitioner commonly sees the parent and child and may make a diagnosis and provide a prescription largely based on parent complaints. As discussed, teacher reports are critical, as are other testing procedures.

A further problem with the diagnosis of ADHD involves the validity of the criteria for females and for adults. As mentioned, fewer girls tend to be diagnosed with ADHD, even controlling for referral bias, because females as a group have a lower base level of inattentiveness and hyperactivity than their male counterparts. Therefore, they have to deviate much further from girls without symptoms in order to be diagnosed (Arnold, 1996). As a result, discussion has been generated on appropriate diagnostic criteria for females.

Finally, adults are now being diagnosed with ADHD at higher rates, but the diagnostic criteria center on the behaviors of children. There have been some attempts to make the criteria more relevant for adults. For instance, for the symptom "often runs about or climbs excessively in situations in which it is inappropriate," a note states that for adolescents or adults, this may be translated into subjective feelings of restlessness (APA, 2000, p. 92). Still, the criteria for adults must not only be made uniformly relevant but also be validated empirically.

Case Example

This case was begun in chapter 5 (ODD/CD) and is continued here. See chapter 5 for details of the case and the other diagnoses that were given.

We focus here only on the diagnosis of attention-deficit/hyperactivity disorder, inattentive type.

To make this diagnosis, several assessment components had to be addressed. Janine had a physical examination, which indicated no physical ailment that would account for symptoms. Janine's foster mother and her teacher at the public school completed their respective versions of the Conners Rating Scales. The teacher version showed higher rates of attention problems and hyperactivity for Janine than the parental version. As you will recall, teacher reports of ADHD have more credence.

At the day treatment program, Janine went through a series of tests for intelligence and learning disabilities. Her IQ was found to be slightly below average, marked by verbal deficits. No learning disabilities were detected.

The CPS worker accessed school records and found that Janine's grades had been poor throughout her school career. Little is known about Janine's developmental history because of the lack of cooperation by her mother and grandmother. Janine's mother did reveal that all three boys living in her home are on Ritalin, which was prescribed by a general physician. Kyle, Janine's brother who was also removed from the home, has been diagnosed with ADHD, as well. The shared diagnosis among siblings might indicate a possible genetic link; however, these children have all faced similar early caregiving difficulties and low socioeconomic status, which may contribute to the development of ADHD.

When examining the diagnostic criteria for ADHD, one important consideration is whether inattention symptoms, such as "often does not seem to listen when spoken to directly" and "often does not follow through on instructions and fails to finish schoolwork or chores," are attributed to oppositionality or to inattention/impulsivity-hyperactivity. The clinician determined that Janine's behaviors were influenced by both these traits, which was confirmed by the rating scales. Other inattention symptoms Janine displayed include: often has difficulty sustaining attention in tasks; often has difficulty organizing tasks and activities; often avoids, dislikes, or is reluctant to engage in tasks that require sustained mental effort; is often easily distracted by extraneous stimuli; and is often forgetful in daily activities. Note that the inattention criterion requires six symptoms and Janine possibly meets seven.

Janine demonstrates a single hyperactivity symptom: often fidgets with hands or feet or squirms in seat. She has two symptoms of impulsivity: often blurts out answers before questions have been completed; and often interrupts or intrudes on others. For hyperactivity and impulsivity symptoms, the client should meet at least six; therefore, Janine does not appear to be hyperactive-impulsive.

See Tables 6.7 and 6.8 for the risk and protective factors assessment for

Table 6.7

Case Example: Janine's Risk and Protective Factors Assessment for Onset of ADHD

Risk	Protective
Biological	
Genetic predisposition is possible because Janine's brothers have been diagnosed with ADHD.	*Other than smoking, Janine's mother denied the use of alcohol and drugs during pregnancy.*
Janine's mother smoked during pregnancy.	
Social	
Family	
Lack of an attachment bond coupled with low maternal social support. *The attachment bond Janine has with her mother might have been compromised. Janine's mother was a teenager when she had Janine, and grandmother did a lot of the caretaking throughout the years, as Janine's mother moved in and out of the home. At this point, the attachment has been damaged because both Janine's grandmother and her mother have cut off contact from her.*	
Low socioeconomic status: *Janine's biological family lives well below the poverty line.*	

Table 6.8

Case Example: Janine's Risk and Protective Factors Assessment for the Course of ADHD

Risk	Protective
Psychological	
Comorbid conduct disorder	
Social	
Family	
Coercive and inconsistent parenting: The different foster homes in which Janine was placed have had difficulty managing Janine's behaviors to the point where she had to leave these homes.	Effective child management strategies: *Janine's current foster mother is working to get effective discipline methods in place.*
Single-parent home: *Janine's foster mother is a single parent.*	

For further information on testing for learning disorders, see Tannock and Brown (2000). If a social worker suspects that a child with ADHD also has a learning disorder, then he or she might educate parents about possible services or refer the child for testing in the school.

both the onset and course of ADHD for Janine. Germane goals have already been discussed in chapter 5.

▓▓▓▓ Appendix. Measures for Attention-Deficit/Hyperactivity Disorder

Much of this information is drawn from Collett, Ohan, & Myers (2003).

Connors Ratings Scales–Revised (Conners, 1997)

Description

- Revision of popular scale with long history in the evaluation of ADHD to address limited normative data and mixed empirical support and to include *DSM-IV* criteria.
- Parent (80-item and 27-item versions), teacher (59-item and 28-item versions), and adolescent (87-item and 27-item versions) for youth, ages 3–17.
- The full forms of all reporter versions provide comprehensive evaluation, whereas the abbreviated forms aid screening or treatment monitoring.
- Measures Cognitive Problems/Inattention, Hyperactivity, Oppositional, Anxious/Shy, Perfectionism, Social Problems, and Psychosomatic.

Reliability

- Internal consistencies for the various subscales were calculated by age and range from moderate to excellent for parent, teacher, and adolescent forms.
- Test-retest reliabilities of 6 to 8 weeks range from poor to high moderate for parent ratings but stronger for teachers and adolescent reports.

Validity

- Gender and age difference are consistent with established patterns (i.e., males score higher on externalizing scales and lower on internalizing scales; disruptive behaviors are lower for older age groups).
- Discriminant validity is shown by the scale's ability to differentiate youths with and without ADHD.

- Parents' form demonstrates excellent sensitivity and specificity.
- The comorbidity subscales have poorer psychometric properties.

The Swanson, Nolan, and Pelham-IV Questionnaire (SNAP-IV)

Swanson (1992); Swanson et al. (2001)

Description

- Parent and teacher versions for children ages 5–11
- Long history in ADHD evaluation, particularly in research; first developed for use with *DSM-III* and updated with each *DSM* revision
- 90 items (full version, takes 20–30 minutes to complete), 31 items (short version, takes 5–10 minutes)
- Available online

Reliability

- Internal consistency good to excellent.
- No information on test-retest reliability.
- Interrater agreement between parents and teachers is poor, although this is typical.

ADHD Rating Scale-IV (ADHD RS-IV)

DuPaul, Power, Anastopoulos, & Reid (1998)

Description

- Updated and directly derived from *DSM-IV* symptom criteria
- Parent (home form) or teacher (school form) for children ages 5–18
- Scale designed for children but can be modified and administered to adults; wording is changed for adults, and "play activities" will be replaced with "leisure activities"
- 18 items
- 5–10 minutes to complete
- Spanish translation available

Reliability

- Internal consistencies for the subscales and total scale range from very good to excellent for both home and school forms.

- Test-retest reliabilities over 4 weeks are at least good for both forms.
- Low interrater agreement between teachers and parents fairly typical for this type of scale.

Validity

- Age and gender patterns consistent with established trends, indicating more symptoms for males and for younger ages of both genders
- Construct validity shown by the scale's basis in *DSM-IV* criteria
- Convergent validity evidenced by low to very good correlations with similar measures and direct observations of children's behavior
- Subscales discriminate between youths with ADHD and both clinical and nonclinical controls
- Hyperactive/Impulsive subscale differentiates children with combined type from inattentive type, with the parent version more useful in this respect than the school form
- Parent report better for sensitivity; teacher report better for specificity

Vanderbilt ADHD Parent Rating Scale (VADPRS)

Wolraich (2003); Wolraich, Feuer, Hannah, Baumgaertel, & Pinnock (1998)

Description

- Relatively new *DSM-IV*-based scales for ADHD; also assesses ODD, conduct disorder, anxiety and depression, and parent perceptions of youth school and social functioning
- 43-items, parent and teacher versions for children ages 6–12
- Available online
- Takes 10–15 minutes
- Spanish and German translations available

Reliability

- Internal consistency is excellent.
- Interrater reliability between parents and teachers is low, as is typical.
- No information on test-retest reliability is available.

Validity

- Concurrent validity is shown by moderate correlations with the ADHD sections of the Diagnostic Interview Schedule for Children-Version 4-Parent Version
- No other validity information is available

ADHD Symptoms Rating Scale (ADHD-SRS)

Holland, Gimpel, & Marrell (2001)

Description

- A recent scale, developed from a review of the literature of descriptors of inattention, hyperactivity, and impulsivity
- Parent and teacher versions for children ages 5–18 years, possibly even preschoolers
- 56 items, takes 15–20 minutes to complete
- Spanish translation available

Reliability

- Excellent internal consistencies and test-retest reliabilities (2 weeks).
- Interrater agreement between parents and teachers is poor, though this is typical.

Validity

- Excellent convergent validity established with similar measures
- Differentiates children with ADHD from nonclinical children

Attention Deficit Disorder Evaluation Scale–Second Edition (ADDES-2)

McCarney (1995a, 1995b)

Description

- An updated version of an established scale developed from diagnosticians and educators of students with ADHD to measure inattention and hyperactivity/impulsivity; includes symptoms from *DSM-IV*
- Widely used in clinical settings
- Parent (50 items) and teacher (56 items) versions for children ages 4–18
- Takes 10–15 minutes to complete
- Spanish translation available

Reliability

- Excellent internal consistencies
- Excellent 30-day test-retest reliabilities

- Interrater agreement is good between teachers and between parents, unusual for similar scales

Validity

- Convergent validity is evidenced by moderate to excellent correlations with comparable scales.
- Discriminant validity between ADHD and nonclinical samples is good.

ACTeRS-Second Edition

Ullman, Sleator, & Sprague (2000)

Description

- Popular in school settings.
- Clinicians and parents of ADHD children provided input to development of scale; 11 items assessing inattention and hyperactivity are comparable to *DSM-IV* descriptions.
- Teacher (24 items), Parent (25 items, includes descriptors of preschool behaviors associated with ADHD), Adolescent Self-Report (35 items, includes measure of social functioning) versions for children ages 5–13
- Measures attention, hyperactivity, social skills, oppositional behavior, early childhood problems, impulsivity, and social adjustment.
- Takes 5–10 minutes to complete.
- Spanish translation available.

Reliability

- Internal consistency is excellent, good, and moderate for the teacher, parent, and self-report version, respectively.
- Moderate interrater reliability between teachers.

Validity

- Discriminant validity for the parent and self-report version is evidenced by higher ratings for youths who have ADHD than those without.
- Teacher version differentiates children with ADHD from those with learning disabilities.

Brown Attention-Deficit Disorder Scales for Children and Adolescents (BADDS)

Brown (2001)

Description

- Unlike scales that focus on ADHD symptoms, the BADDS is said to measure deficits in executive functioning underlying ADHD.
- Separate versions for youths 3–7 years, 8–12, and 12–18 are worded to indicate developmentally relevant manifestations of ADHD. For ages 3–7, separate parent and teacher forms are available (44 items). For ages 8–12, separate versions for parent, teacher, and youth self-report (50 items). The adolescent version can be administered to the adolescent and/or the parent (40 items).
- Scale measures the following: Organizing, Prioritizing and Activating to Work; Focusing, Sustaining and Shifting Attention to Tasks; Regulating Alertness, Sustaining Effort and Processing Speed; Managing Frustration and Modulating Emotions; Utilizing Working Memory and Accessing Recall; and Monitoring and Self-Regulating Action (for ages 3–7 and 8–12).
- Takes 10–15 minutes to administer.

Reliability

- Internal consistencies are acceptable for clinical samples, excellent for the normative sample.
- Interrater agreement between parents and teachers is low to moderate for ages 3 to 7 and 8 to 12, somewhat better than other scales. For ages 8 to 12, agreement between the children's self-report and parent-or-teacher self-report is also low to moderate.

Validity

- Convergent validity for the BADDS is evidenced by moderate to excellent correlations with the parent and teacher versions of the CBCL, the BASC, and Conners Ratings Scales.
- Divergent validity is shown by lower correlations between BADDS and internalizing measures.
- Discriminant validity established by the differences between children with ADHD and the normative samples.

Home Situations Questionnaire

Barkley & Edelbrock (1987)

Description

- Lists 16 different situations for which parents observe and handle their child's behaviors.
- Parents indicate ("yes"/"no") whether problem behaviors occur in these situations; if so, parents rate severity of the problem (1/ "mild" to 9/ "severe").
- Appropriate for children ages 4–11.
- Yields 2 summary scores.

    1. Number of Problem Situations: "an index of the situational diversity of problem behaviors for a given child"
    2. Mean Severity Score: "an index of the severity of problem behaviors across situations"

- Modified versions have been developed to make the scales appropriate for adolescents (Adams, McCarthy, & Kelly, 1995) and specific to problems related to ADHD symptoms (DuPaul & Barkley, 1992).
- Can measure treatment response.

Reliability

- Internal consistency is strong.
- Test-retest reliabilities (4 weeks) shown to be moderate for the number of problem situations and moderate to good for problem behavior severity.

Validity

- Number of Problem Situations correlated with the following scales of the Child Behavior Profile: Aggressive (.83); Hyperactive (.73); Delinquent (.48); Depressed (.62); and Social Withdrawal (.62).
- Mean Severity Score correlated with the following scales of the Child Behavior Profile: Aggressive (.69); Hyperactive (.66); Delinquent (.60); Depressed (.46); and Social Withdrawal (.61).
- Number of Problem Situations correlated with the following Child Domain scales of the Parenting Stress Index: Adaptability (.78); Distractibility/Hyperactivity (.76); Mood (.73); and Demanding (.70).
- Mean Severity Score correlated with the following Child Domain

scales of the Parenting Stress Index: Adaptability (.63); Distractibility/Hyperactivity (.75); Mood (.61); and Demanding (.59).

- Summary scales correlated with the Adjustment, Depression, Hyperactivity, Social Skills, and Psychosis scales of the Personality Inventory for Children, ranging from .72 to .81.

Discriminates between normal children and children diagnosed with attention deficit disorder with hyperactivity and ADHD children and their normal siblings.

The Wender Utah Rating Scale (WURS)

Ward, Wender, & Reimherr (1993)

Description

- 61-item, self-report measure designed for adults to describe their own childhood behavior.
- Purpose in creating scale was to retrospectively establish the childhood diagnosis of ADHD.

Reliability

- Split-half reliability correlations comparing odd/even items were satisfactory.
- Satisfactory internal consistency and temporal stability.

Validity

- A discriminant function analysis correctly classified 64.5%. Among those who did not have ADHD, only 57.5% were correctly classified, compared with 72.1% among those with ADHD. Therefore, the WURS is sensitive in detecting ADHD, but it misclassifies approximately half of those who do not have ADHD.

References

American Academy of Child and Adolescent Psychiatry. (2002). Practice parameter for the use of stimulant medications in the treatment of children, adolescents, and adults. *Journal of the American Academy of Child and Adolescent Psychiatry*, 41(Suppl.), 26S–49S.

American Academy of Pediatrics. (2000). Clinical practice guideline: Diagnosis and evaluation of the child with attention-deficit/hyperactivity disorder. *Pediatrics*, 105, 1158–1170.

American Psychiatric Association. (2000). *Diagnostic and statistical manual of mental disorders* (4th ed., text Rev.). Washington, DC: Author.

Arnold, L. (1996). Sex differences in ADHD. *Journal of Abnormal Child Psychology, 24,* 555–569.

Barkley, R. A. (1990). *Attention deficit hyperactivity disorder: A handbook for diagnosis and treatment.* New York: Guilford.

Barkley, R. A (1994). *ADHD in the classroom: Strategies for teachers.* New York: Guilford.

Barkley, R. A. (1998). Attention-deficit/hyperactivity disorder. In E. J. Mash & R. A. Barkley (Eds.), *Treatment of childhood disorders* (2nd ed., pp. 55–110). New York: Guilford.

Barkley, R. A. (2000). *Taking charge of ADHD* (rev. ed.). New York: Guilford.

Barkley, R. A., & Edelbrock, C. (1987). Assessing situational variation in children's problem behaviors: The home and school situations questionnaires. *Advances in Behavioral Assessment of Children and Families, 3,* 157–176.

Barkley, R. A., Fischer, M., Edelbrock, C., & Smallish, L. (1990). The adolescent outcome of hyperactive children diagnosed by research criteria: I. An 8-year prospective follow-up study. *Journal of the American Academy of Child and Adolescent Psychiatry, 29,* 546–557.

Bentley, K. J., & Walsh, J. (2006). *The social worker and psychotropic medication* (3rd ed.). Pacific Grove, CA: Brooks/Cole.

Bhutta, A., Cleves, M., Casey, P., Cradock, M., & Anand, K. (2002). Cognitive and behavioral outcomes of school-aged children who were born preterm: A meta-analysis. *Journal of the American Medical Association, 288,* 728–737.

Brown, R., & La Rosa, A. (2002). Recent developments in the pharmacotherapy of attention-deficit/hyperactivity disorder. *Professional Psychology: Research and Practice, 33,* 591–595.

Brown, T. (1996). *Brown Attention Deficit Disorder Scales: Manual.* San Antonio, TX: Psychological Corporation.

Cantwell, D. (1996). Attention deficit disorder: a review of the past 10 years. *Journal of American Academy of Child and Adolescent Psychiatry, 35*(8), 978–987.

Carlson, E. A., Jacobvitz, D., & Sroufe, L. A. (1995). A developmental investigation of inattentiveness and hyperactivity. *Child Development, 66,* 37–54.

Conners, C. K. (1990). *Manual for Conners' rating scales.* North Tonawanda, NY: Multi-Health Systems.

Conners, C. K., March, J. S., Frances, A., Wells, K. C., & Ross, R. (2001). Treatment of attention-deficit/hyperactivity disorder: Expert consensus guidelines. *Journal of Attention Disorders, 4,* S1–S128.

Connor, D., Fletcher, K., & Swanson, J. (1999). A meta-analysis of clonidine for symptoms of attention-deficit hyperactivity disorder. *Journal of the American Academy of Child and Adolescent Psychiatry, 38,* 1551–1559.

Connor, D., Glatt, S., Lopez, I., Jackson, D., & Melloni, R. (2002). Psychopharmacology and aggression: I. A meta-analysis of stimulant effects on overt/covert aggression-related behaviors in ADHD. *Journal of the American Academy of Child and Adolescent Psychiatry, 41,* 253–262.

Cuffe, S. P, McKeown, R. E., Jackson, K. L., Addy, C. L., Abramson, R., & Garrison, C. Z. (2001). Prevalence of attention-deficit/hyperactivity disorder in a community sample of older adolescents. *Journal of the American Academy of Child and Adolescent Psychiatry, 40*(9), 1037–1044.

DeGrandpre, R. (1999). *Ritalin nation: Rapid fire culture and the transformation of human consciousness.* New York: Norton.

DuPaul, G. J., & Eckert, T. (1997). The effects of school-based interventions for attention deficit hyperactivity disorder: A meta-analysis. *School Psychology Review, 26,* 5–27.

DuPaul, G. J., & Power, T. J. (2000). Educational interventions for students with attention-deficit disorders. In T. Brown (Ed.), *Attention-deficit disorders and comorbidities in children, adolescents, and adults* (pp. 607–634). Washington, DC: American Psychiatric Press.

DuPaul, G. J., & Stoner, G. (2003). *ADHD in the schools: Assessment and intervention strategies.* New York: Guilford.

Efron, D., Jaman, F., & Barker, M. (1997). Side effects of methylphenidate and dexamphetamine in children with attention deficit hyperactivity disorder: A double-blind, crossover trial. *Pediatrics, 100,* 662–666.

Faraone, S. V., & Biederman, J., (2002). Efficacy of Adderall® for attention-deficit/hyperactivity disorder: A meta-analysis. *Journal of Attention Disorders, 6*(2), 69–75.

Faraone, S., & Wilens, T. (2003). Does stimulant treatment lead to substance use disorders? *Journal of Clinical Psychology, 64,* 9–13.

Fitzpatrick, P., Klorman, R., Brumaghim, J., & Borgstedt, A. (1992). Effects of sustained-release and standard preparations of methylphenidate on attention deficit disorder. *Journal of the American Academy of Child and Adolescent Psychiatry, 31,* 226–234.

Gadow, K. D. (1991). Clinical issues in child and adolescent psychopharmacology. *Journal of Counseling and Clinical Psychology, 59*(6), 842–852.

Gaub, M., & Carlson, C. L. (1997). Gender differences in ADHD: A meta-analysis and critical review. *Journal of the American Academy of Child and Adolescent Psychiatry, 36*(8), 1036–1946.

Gingerich, K., Turnock, P., Litfin, J., & Rosen, L. (1998). Diversity and attention-deficit hyperactivity disorder. *Journal of Clinical Psychology, 54,* 415–426.

Hill, J. C., & Schoener, E. P. (1996). Age-dependent decline of attention deficit hyperactivity disorder. *American Journal of Psychiatry, 153,* 1143–1146.

Jacobvitz, D., Sroufe, L., Stewart, M., & Leffert, N. (1990). Treatment of attention-deficit and hyperactivity problems in children with sympathomimetic drugs: A comprehensive review. *Journal of the American Academy of Child and Adolescent Psychiatry, 29,* 492–518.

Kessler, R., Berglund, P., Demler, O., Jin, R., & Walters, E. (2005). Lifetime prevalence and age-of-onset distributions of DSM-IV disorders in the National Comorbidity survey replication. *Archives of General Psychiatry, 62,* 593–602.

Klassen, A., Miller, A., Parminder, R., Lee, S. K., & Olsen, L. (1999). Attention-deficit hyperactivity disorder in children and youth: A quantitative systematic review of the efficacy of different management strategies. *The Canadian Journal of Psychiatry, 44,* 1007–1016.

Kreppner, J., O'Connor, T., & Rutter, M. (2001). Can inattention/overactivity be an institutional deprivation syndrome? *Journal of Abnormal Child Psychology, 29,* 513–529.

Langstroem, N. (2002). Child neuropsychiatric disorders: A review of associations with delinquency and substance use. In R. R. Corrado (Ed.), *Multi-problem violent youth: A foundation for comparative research on needs, interventions, and outcomes. Series I: Life and behavioral sciences, volume 324* (pp. 91–104). Amsterdam, Netherlands: IOS Press.

Lawrence, J., Lawrence, D., & Carson, D. (1997). Optimizing ADHD therapy with sustained-release methylphenidate. *American Family Physician, 55,* 1705–1712.

Leo, J., & Cohen, D. (2003). Broken brains and flawed studies? A critical review of ADHD neuroimaging research. *The Journal of Mind and Behavior, 24,* 29–56.

Linnett, K., Dalsgaard, S., Obel, C., Wisborg, K., Henriksen, T., Rodriquez, A., et al. (2003). Maternal lifestyle factors in pregnancy risk of attention deficit hyperactivity disorder and associated behaviors: A review of the current evidence. *American Journal of Psychiatry, 160,* 1028–1040.

Loeber, R., Green, S. M., Lahey, B. B., Frick, P. J., & McBurnett, K. (2002). Findings on disruptive behavior disorders from the first decade of the Developmental Trends Study. *Clinical Child and Family Psychology Review, 3,* 37–60.

Maher, B., Marazita, M., Ferrell, R., & Vanyukov, M. (2002). Dopamine system genes and attention deficit hyperactivity disorder: A meta-analysis. *Psychiatric Genetics, 12,* 207–215.

Mannuzza, S., & Klein, R. (1999). Adolescent and adult outcomes in attention-deficit/hyperactivity disorder. In H. Quay & A. Hogan (Eds.), *Handbook of disruptive behavior disorders* (pp. 279–294). New York: Plenum.

Mannuzza, S., Klein, R., & Moulton, J. (2002). Young adult outcome of children with "situational" hyperactivity: A prospective, controlled, follow-up study. *Journal of Abnormal Child Psychology, 30,* 191–198.

Mannuzza, S., Klein, R. G., Bessler, A., Malloy, P., & LaPadula, M. (1998). Adult psychiatric status of hyperactive boys grown up. *American Journal of Psychiatry, 155*(4), 493–498.

McClellan, J., & Werry, J. S. (2003). Evidence-based treatments in child and adolescent psychiatry: An inventory. *Journal of the American Academy of Child and Adolescent Psychiatry, 42,* 1388–1400.

Multimodal Treatment Study of Children with Attention-Deficit/Hyperactivity Disorder Cooperative Group. (1999). A 14-month randomized clinical trial of treatment strategies for attention-deficit/hyperactivity disorder. *Archives of General Psychiatry, 56,* 1073–1086.

National Institutes of Health. Consensus Development Conference Statement: Diagnosis and treatment of Attention-Deficit/Hyperactivity Disorder (ADHD). (2000). *Journal of the American Academy of Child & Adolescent Psychiatry, 39*(2), 182–193.

Newcorn, J., & Halperin, J. (2000). Attention-deficit disorders with oppositionality and aggression. In T. Brown (Ed.), *Attention-deficit disorders and comorbidities in children, adolescents, and adults* (pp. 171–207). Washington, DC: American Psychiatric Press.

Ohan, J. L., & Johnston, C. (1999). Attributions in adolescents medicated for attention-deficit/hyperactivity disorder. *Journal of Attention Disorders, 31*(1), 49–60.

Parker, H. C. (1992). *The ADHD hyperactivity handbook for schools: Effective strategies for identifying and teaching ADD students in elementary and secondary schools.* Plantation, FL: Specialty Press.

Patterson, G. R. (1982). *Coercive family process.* Eugene, OR: Castalia.

Patterson, G. R. (1986). Performance models for antisocial boys. *American Psychologist, 1,* 432–444.

Patterson, G. R., DeBaryshe, B. D., & Ramsey, E. (1989). A developmental perspective on antisocial behavior. *American Psychologist, 44,* 329–335.

Pfiffner, L. J. (1996). *All about ADHD: The complete practical guide for classroom teachers.* New York: Scholastic.

Pliszka, S. (2000). Patterns of psychiatric comorbidity with attention-deficit/hyperactivity disorder. *Child and Adolescent Psychiatric Clinics of North America, 9,* 525–540.

Popper, C. W. (1997). Antidepressants in the treatment of attention-deficit/hyperactivity disorder. *Journal of Clinical Psychiatry, 58* (Suppl. 14), 14–29.

Rodgers, K. (1996). ADHD medication reformulated: An old drug reenters market. *Drug Topics, 140,* 31–32.

Root, R. W. II, & Resnick, R. J. (2003). An update on the diagnosis and treatment of attention-deficit/hyperactivity disorder in children. *Professional Psychology: Research & Practice, 34,* 34–41.

Rucklidge, J. J., & Tannock, R. (2001). Psychiatric, psychosocial, and cognitive functioning of female adolescents with ADHD. *Journal of the American Academy of Child and Adolescent Psychiatry, 40*(5), 530–540.

Sadock, B. J., & Sadock, V. A. (2003). *Kaplan & Sadock's synopsis of psychiatry* (9th ed.). Philadelphia: Lippincott, Williams & Wilkins.

Samudra, K., & Cantwell, D. (1999). Risk factors for attention-deficit/hyperactivity disorder. In H. Quay & A. Hogan (Eds.), *Handbook of disruptive behavior disorders* (pp. 199–230). New York: Plenum.

Schatzberg, A. F., & Nemeroff, C. B. (1998).*The American Psychiatric Press textbook of psychopharmacology.* Washington, DC: American Psychiatric Press.

Shepard, B. A., Carter, A. S., & Cohen, J. E. (2000). Attention-deficit/hyperactivity disorder and the preschool child. In T. E. Brown (Ed.), *Attention-deficit disorders and comorbidities in children, adolescents, and adults* (pp. 407–436). Washington, DC: American Psychiatric Publishing, Inc.

Sonuga-Barke, E., Daley, D., & Thompson, M. (2002). Does maternal ADHD reduce the effectiveness of parent training for preschool children's ADHD? *Journal of the American Academy of Child and Adolescent Psychiatry, 41,* 696–702.

Sroufe, L. (1989). Pathways to adaptation and maladaption: Psychopathology as developmental deviation. In D. Cicchetti (Ed.), *Rochester symposium on developmental psychopathology* (pp. 13–41). Hillsdale, NJ: Erlbaum.

Swanson, J. M., McBurnett, K., Christian, D. L., & Wigal, T. (1995). Stimulant medications and the treatment of children with ADHD. *Advances in Clinical Child Psychology, 17,* 265–322.

Tannock, R., & Brown, T. E. (2000). Attention-deficit disorders with learning disorders in children and adolescents. In T. E. Brown (Ed.), *Attention-deficit disorders and comorbidities in children, adolescents, and adults* (pp. 231–295). Washington, DC: American Psychiatric Publishing.

Weiss, G., & Hechtman, L. T. (1993). *Hyperactive children grown up: ADHD in children, adolescents, and adults* (2nd ed.). New York: Guilford Press.

Weiss, M., Hechtman, L., & Weiss, G. (2000). ADHD in parents. *Journal of the American Academy of Child and Adolescent Psychiatry, 39*, 1059–1061.

Weiss, M., & Weiss, J. (2004). A guide to the treatment of adults with ADHD. *Journal of Clinical Psychiatry, 65*(Suppl. 3), 27–37.

Wender, P. H., Reimherr, F. W., & Wood, D. R. (1981). Attention deficit disorder (minimal brain dysfunction) in adults: A replication study of diagnosis and drug treatment. *Archives of General Psychiatry, 38*(4), 449–456.

Whalen, C., & Henker, B. (1999). The child with attention-deficit/hyperactivity disorder in family contexts. In H. Quay & A. Hogan (Eds.), *Handbook of disruptive behavior disorders* (pp. 139–155). New York: Kluwer Academic/Plenum.

Wilens, T., Faraone, S., Biederman, J., & Gunawardene, S. (2003). Does stimulant therapy of attention-deficit/hyperactivity disorder beget later substance abuse? A meta-analytic review of the literature. *Pediatrics, 111*, 179–186.

Wilens, T. E., Spencer, T. J., & Biederman, J. (2000). Pharmacotherapy of attention-deficit/hyperactivity disorder. In T. E. Brown (Ed), *Attention-deficit disorders and comorbidities in children, adolescents, and adults* (pp. 509–535). Washington, DC: American Psychiatric Publishing, Inc.

Willoughby, M. T., Curran, P. T., Costello, E. J., & Angold, A. (2000). Implications of early versus late onset of attention-deficit/hyperactivity disorder symptoms. *Journal of the American Academy of Child and Adolescent Psychiatry, 39*(12), 1512–1514.

Woodward, L. J., Fergusson, D. M., & Horwoord, L. J. (2000). Driving outcomes of young people with attentional difficulties in adolescence. *Journal of the American Academy of Child and Adolescent Psychiatry,39*, 627–634.

References for ADHD Measures

Adams, C. D., McCarthy, M., & Kelly, M. L. (1995). Adolescent versions of the Home and School Situations Questionnaires: Initial psychometric properties. *Journal of Clinical Child Psychology, 24*, 377–385.

Barkley, R., & Edelbrock, C. (1987). Assessing situational variation in children's problem behaviors: The home and school situations questionnaires. *Advances in Behavioral Assessment of Children and Families, 3*, 157–176.

Brown, T. E. (2001). *Brown Attention-Deficit Disorder Scales for Children and Adolescents*. San Antonio, TX: Psychological Corporation.

Collett, B. R., Ohan, J. L., & Myers, K. M. (2003). Ten-year review of rating scales. V: Scales assessing attention-deficit/hyperactivity disorder. *Journal of the American Academy of Child and Adolescent Psychiatry, 42*(9), 1015–1023.

Conners, C. (1997). *Conners rating scales–Revised technical manual*. North Tonawanda, NY: Multi-Health Systems.

DuPaul, G. J., & Barkley, R. A. (1992). Situational variability of attention problems: Psychometric properties of the Revised Home and School Situations Questionnaires. *Journal of Clinical Child Psychology, 21*, 178–188.

DuPaul, G. J., Power, T. J., Anastopoulos, A. D., & Reid, R. (1998). *ADHD Rating Scale-IV: Checklist, norms, and clinical interpretation*. Eugene, OR: Assessment-Intervention Resources.

Holland M. I., Gimpel, G. A., & Marrell, K. W. (2001). *ADHD symptoms rating scale manual*. Wilmington, DE: Wide Range.

McCarney, S. B. (1995a). *The attention deficit disorders evaluation scale, home version, technical manual* (2nd ed.). Columbia, MO: Hawthorne Educational Service.

McCarney, S. B. (1995b). *The attention deficit disorders evaluation scale, school version, technical manual* (2nd ed.). Columbia, MO: Hawthorne Educational Service.

Swanson, J. (1992). *School based assessments and interventions for ADD students*. Irvine, CA: KC.

Swanson, J., Schuck, S., Mann M., Carlson, C., Hartman, K., Sergeant, J., et al. (2001). Categorical and dimensional definitions and evaluations of symptoms of ADHD: The SNAP and SWAN ratings scales. Retrieved January 9, 2004, from http://www.adhd.net.

Ullman, R. K., Sleator, E. K., & Sprague, R. I. (2000). *ACTeRS teacher and parent forms manual*. Champaign, IL: Metritech.

Ward, M., Wender, P., & Reimherr, F. (1993). The Wender Utah Rating Scale: An aid in the retrospective diagnosis of childhood attention deficit hyperactivity disorder. *American Journal of Psychiatry, 150*(6), 885–890.

Wolraich, M. I. (2003). *Vanderbilt ADHD teacher rating scale (VADTRS) and the Vanderbilt ADHD parent rating scale (VADPRS)*. Retrieved January 9, 2004, from http://www.nichq.org.

Wolraich, M. I., Feuer, I. D., Hannah, J. N., Baumgaertel, A., & Pinnock, T. Y. (1998). Obtaining systematic teacher reports of disruptive behavior disorders utilizing *DSM-IV*. *Journal of Abnormal Psychology 26*, 141–152.

7   Posttraumatic Stress Disorder

WITH AMY WALDBILLIG AND
JENNIFER CROWELL

Posttraumatic stress disorder is a type of anxiety disorder involving anxiety symptoms following exposure to an extreme traumatic stressor (American Psychiatric Association [APA], 2000). The stressor, by definition, includes threatened death or serious injury or other events that involve threat to one's physical integrity, witnessing such events, or learning of such events happening to another person. The three major symptom categories are

1. *Reexperiencing*: The traumatic events are reexperienced through recurrent and/or intrusive thoughts or images, nightmares, and flashbacks.
2. *Avoidance and numbing*: The person, because of the negative affect and arousal associated with reexperiencing, attempts to control or protect against these symptoms.
3. *Increased arousal*: The person is in a state of arousal as indicated by hypervigilance, insomnia, inability to concentrate, and an elevated startle response.

Specifiers for the disorder involve the time frame of symptoms: *Acute* is when symptoms are present for less than 3 months, and *chronic* is when symptoms persist for at least 3 months. Another possible specifier involves delayed onset, in which at least 6 months have passed between the traumatic event and the symptoms. Intense anxiety symptoms that are experienced immediately after the traumatic event and persist for less than 4 weeks are given a different but related diagnosis: *acute stress disorder* (APA, 2000).

Prevalence

Exposure to traumatic events is quite common, occurring to between 39 and 84% of the U.S. population (Foa, Keane, & Friedman, 2000). The prevalence of people affected by trauma is probably even higher in developing countries because of the lack of sufficient material resources to prevent disasters and mitigate their aftermath (Keane, Weathers, & Foa, 2000). Still, only about 25% of people who are exposed to trauma develop PTSD (Perrin, Smith, & Yule, 2000), representing a lifetime rate in the adult population of 6.8% (Kessler, Berglund, Demler, Jin, & Walters, 2005). PTSD ranks behind only substance abuse disorders, major depression, specific phobia, and social phobia in frequency of occurrence among the *DSM-IV* disorders (Keane et al., 2000). The lifetime prevalence rate for elderly people is 2.5% (Kessler et al, 2005), although little is known about PTSD in the older population (Busuttil, 2004). For children, however, estimates vary widely, depending on the type and intensity of the inciting trauma, the length of time between exposure to the trauma and its professional assessment, the demographic characteristics of study subjects, the sampling techniques used, and the manner in which PTSD is assessed (Saigh, Yasik, Sack, & Koplewicz, 1999).

Diagnosis

Children

The validity of the diagnosis of PTSD for children has been questioned. Criteria for the disorder lack sensitivity to the impact of trauma in young children (Perrin et al., 2000), and they rely heavily on children's ability to convey their experience, which is beyond many young children's capacities (Scheeringa, Zeanah, Drell, & Larrieu, 1995). Cohen (1998) asserts that some of the *DSM* criteria may not be relevant to young children, such as visual flashbacks, dissociation, numbing, and traumatic amnesia, although this again may be due to children's difficulties in conveying their experience. Further, clinician observations and interactions with children may not be extensive enough to garner critical information about symptoms.

Because of these challenges, parent reporting is central to the process of diagnosis. Ironically, parents may not always accurately depict impairment in their children (Scheeringa et al., 1995). Cohen (1998) states that parents typically minimize their children's PTSD symptoms. When parents have also suffered exposure to trauma, their manner of perceiving their children's reactions may become biased. The presence of more symptoms in parents tends to be associated with more symptoms in their children.

This could be due to parental bias in reporting or to a real adverse effect of symptomatic parents on children's adaptation (Scheeringa, Peebles, Cook, & Zeanah, 2001).

Both underdiagnosis and overdiagnosis may be of concern with PTSD in children. In addition to parents' potential minimization, children's symptoms may not be apparent at school and thus may not be detected by teachers and other adults, leading to potential underdiagnosis (Cohen, 1998). Overdiagnosis may result from the erroneous belief held among clinicians that reexperiencing trauma and anxiety symptoms alone following exposure to an extreme stressor are sufficient to diagnose PTSD (Cohen, 1998). Diagnostic criteria also permit a great deal of latitude in determining whether a particular stressor is "extreme" (Perrin et al., 2000). Further, the percentage of children receiving the PTSD diagnosis varies greatly, depending on whether a liberal or strict threshold is used to define "persistent" symptoms (McHugo, Mooney, Racusin, Ford, & Fleischer, 2000). Of course, the problem of differential interpretation of criteria is found with many *DSM* diagnoses.

Measurement instruments have been developed for the assessment of PTSD. (See appendixes I and II for a list of measurement tools for children and adults, respectively.) They can assist in diagnosis and treatment planning, along with the following guidelines:

1. As mentioned, the parent is an important source of information about the child's symptoms.
2. The child must also be interviewed directly about the trauma, its effect, and its meaning to the child (Cohen, 1998).
3. The clinician must be knowledgeable about normal developmental behaviors, especially as this pertains to the hyperarousal cluster symptoms (Scheeringa et al., 1995).
4. The child's reexperiencing the event can be facilitated through its reenactment with drawings, stories, and play.
5. Children may experience fears of the dark, bad dreams, nightmares, waking up in the middle of the night, separation anxiety, and fears not directly associated with the trauma, such as a fear of monsters (Cohen, 1998).

Even if the child does not meet criteria for the diagnosis of PTSD, clinicians should offer intervention for clinically significant symptoms (McHugo et al., 2000).

When diagnosing PTSD in either children or adults, the social worker can consider certain other disorders as well. Table 7.1 indicates some of these diagnoses and the ways in which they differ from PTSD.

Other diagnoses, such as a mood disorder or another anxiety disorder, should be considered if the trauma did not precede the PTSD symptoms (Cohen, 1998). In addition, trauma can result in disorders other than PTSD (Foa et al., 2000). During assessment, individuals should be asked about chronic stressors, such as domestic violence or child maltreatment (Cohen, 1998). If the symptom pattern in response to this stressor meets the criteria for PTSD *and* for another disorder, such as major depressive disorder, attention-deficit/hyperactivity disorder, or mixed substance abuse, these other diagnoses should be given in addition to PTSD.

Attention-deficit/hyperactivity disorder (ADHD) is a possible outcome

Table 7.1	
Differential Diagnoses	
Disorder	Characteristics
Acute stress disorder	Must occur and resolve within 4 weeks of the traumatic event
Adjustment disorder	The stressor can be of any severity (rather than extreme), such as a move to a new house or starting a new school or course of study.
	The event involved may be "traumatic" but the requisite number of symptoms for PTSD are not met.
Obsessive-compulsive disorder (OCD)	Recurrent intrusive thoughts occur but are not related to an experienced traumatic event. In OCD, the intrusive thoughts are generally experienced as inappropriate.
Psychotic disorders	Illusions, hallucinations, and other perceptual disturbances are unrelated to exposure to an extreme stressor.
Bereavement	The nontraumatic (anticipated) death of a loved one, characterized by negative feelings and recollections of the loved one.

Source: Perrin et al. (2000).

of childhood traumatization, but there is little evidence to suggest that this is common. Trauma may exacerbate preexisting symptoms of ADHD (Perrin et al., 2000), and a careful history of the client must be taken to ensure that PTSD is not mistaken for ADHD. For example, chronic hyperarousal can present as hyperactivity and poor impulse control and, along with the symptom of intrusive thoughts, can interfere with attention and concentration (Perrin et al., 2000). In addition, some symptoms of PTSD, such as "acting or feeling as if the traumatic event were recurring," "problems concentrating," and "avoiding stimuli associated with trauma," can be confused with symptoms of inattention (Weinstein, Staffelbach, & Biaggio, 2000, p. 368). Other symptoms of trauma might include an "inability to appropriately inhibit response due to hypervigilance" and "physiological reactivity when exposed to cues symbolizing an aspect of the trauma" that resemble symptoms of hyperactivity (Weinstein et al., 2000).

Finally, it is not unusual for children with chronic PTSD to display temper tantrums, school refusal, parental defiance, hostility, and aggression. Such symptoms may suggest diagnoses of oppositional defiant disorder or conduct disorder because they often reflect high levels of irritability, oversensitivity, and extreme avoidance behaviors. Repeated traumatization may also lead to dissociative symptoms, self-injurious and aggressive behaviors, and substance abuse (Perrin et al., 2000).

Comorbidity

In adults, PTSD is often accompanied by other Axis I psychiatric disorders. In the National Comorbidity Survey, Kessler et al. (1995) reported that a majority of individuals (88% of men and 79% of women) with PTSD had at least one other lifetime diagnosis. Major depression was the most common comorbid diagnosis, occurring in just under half of men and women with PTSD (Schnurr, Friedman, & Bernardy, 2002). The co-occurring disorders most prevalent for men with PTSD were alcohol abuse or dependence (51.9%), major depressive episode (47.9%), conduct disorder (43.3%), and drug abuse and dependence (34.5%). The disorders most frequently found with PTSD among women were major depressive episode (48.5%), social phobia (38.4%), simple phobia (29.0%), and alcohol abuse or dependence (27.9%) (Schlenger, Fairbank, Jordan, & Caddell, 1999). In children, PTSD frequently presents in conjunction with mood disorders, anxiety disorders, ADHD, conduct disorder, and enuresis (Saigh, Yasik, Sack, & Koplewicz, 1999).

Although a history of psychiatric disorder is a risk factor for developing PTSD following a traumatic event, PTSD often leads to other psychiatric disorders as well. In the National Comorbidity Survey, PTSD was a primary causal factor for the majority of affective and substance use disorders and also for the development of conduct disorder among females.

Symptom overlap among diagnostic categories helps to explain the high likelihood of lifetime comorbid disorders seen in PTSD. For example, both PTSD and major depression share sleep disturbance, impaired concentration, and diminished interest in one's surroundings. In addition, the emotional detachment and restricted range of affect in persons with PTSD may be confused with depressed mood and psychomotor retardation as seen in major depression. Symptoms found in both PTSD and generalized anxiety disorder include hyperarousal, irritability, hypervigilance, exaggerated startle response, impaired concentration, and insomnia. In addition, people with PTSD and panic disorder both exhibit hyperarousal and dissociation. Perhaps more important, the psychological and physiological reactivity in people with PTSD sometimes can appear to be a full panic attack (Schnurr et al., 2002).

Although high rates of depression and anxiety in individuals with PTSD may be a function of diagnostic criteria overlap between disorders, the high comorbidity of substance use disorders with PTSD may reflect the person's choice of stress reduction strategies. Substances such as alcohol might reduce the symptoms of hyperarousal, and substances such as cocaine might reduce the depressive symptoms (Acierno, Kilpatrick, & Resnick, 1999).

Along with psychiatric comorbidity, poor physical health may also be a consequence of trauma (Schnurr et al., 2002). Trauma survivors, compared with nontraumatized people, report more medical symptoms, use more medical services, have more medical illnesses confirmed by a physician's examination, and display higher mortality (Foa et al., 2000).

Course of the Disorder

Most cases of PTSD are long term. In the National Comorbidity Survey, for approximately 90% of individuals PTSD persisted longer than 3 months, and for over 70%, the disorder lasted longer than a year (Schnurr et al., 2002). More than a third of people never fully recovered. Intervention seems to help the rate of recovery. The median time to remission (the time at which 50% of persons had recovered) was 36 months among those who received intervention and 64 months among those who did not.

Risk and Protective Factors

A couple of meta-analyses have been conducted to determine the predictors for the onset of PTSD (Brewin, Bernice, & Valentine, 2000; Ozer et al., (2003).

Both found that trauma severity and lack of social support showed larger effects than those related to the characteristics of the person pretrauma, such as female gender; social, educational, and intellectual disadvantage; psychiatric history; and various types of previous adversity, including trauma, childhood abuse, and other problems in childhood. Ozer et al. (2003) also reported that dissociation following trauma exposure showed the highest effect in relation to the development of PTSD.

Brewin et al. (2000) noted that a great deal of variation was shown across studies, with the exception of three personal characteristics: psychiatric history, childhood abuse, and family psychiatric history. In addition, direct comparisons within studies indicated that women were more likely to develop PTSD, no matter the type of trauma involved. Implications from this research are that social workers can help individuals who have undergone traumatic events to build and enhance their social supports. They also need to educate people on the adverse effects of dissociation as a coping method for the development of PTSD and to teach more helpful coping strategies.

See Table 7.2 for a listing of risk and protective factors. Some of these factors are described more fully here.

Biological Processes

Physiological processes appear to be associated with PTSD. It is not known to what extent these processes are risk factors for PTSD or result from the person's experiencing certain types of traumatic events (Schnurr et al., 2002). For example, research on people with PTSD includes abnormal findings in the startle reflex. In addition, they exhibit continuously elevated sympathetic nervous system functions even in the absence of an external threat. The adrenergic system appears to have been recalibrated to deal with a permanent life-threatening crisis. Other physiological abnormalities include changes in the sleep cycle, elevations of thyroid gland function, and disturbance in the opioid system (Schnurr et al., 2002). Whether these physiological problems are common to all people with PTSD or only a portion, whether they represent causes or results of the disorder, and whether they will be subject to biological intervention remain open questions that will require much more research to resolve.

Behavioral Factors

Conditioning is a process of developing patterns of behavior through responses to environmental stimuli or specific behavioral consequences (Kazdin, 2000). An initially neutral stimulus comes to produce a conditioned response after being paired repeatedly with a conditioned stimulus. In Pav-

Table 7.2

Risk and Protective Factors for PTSD

Risk	Protective

Features of the traumatic experience

- Degree of exposure to trauma—intensity, duration, and frequency
- Subjective sense of danger

Stressors after the traumatic experience

- Secondary stressors
- Continued adverse events

Type of traumatic event

- War-related events, criminal victimization, exposure to earthquakes, floods, hurricanes, fires, or serious accidents

Biological

Risk	Protective
• Introversion or behavioral inhibition	• Extroversion
• Female	• Male
• Chronic illness or handicapping condition	• Good health
• Genetic risk	

Psychological

Risk	Protective
• Behavioral or psychiatric disorder	• No behavioral or psychiatric disorder
• Diagnosis of ASD	
• Dissociation after trauma	

Social

Family

Risk	Protective
• Family history of psychiatric illness	• No family psychiatric history
• Adverse life events and prior child trauma exposure	• No prior trauma exposure
• Death of a family member	• Positive support

Immediate Social Environment

- Lack of social support

Broader Social Factors

Risk	Protective
• Poverty	• Middle to upper SES
• Immigration to the U.S. because of armed conflict or political repression	

Source: Aciemo, Kilpatrick, & Resnick (1999); Brewin et al. (2000); Debellis (1997); Keane et al. (2000); McNally (1996); Ozer et al. (2003); Saigh, et al. (1999).

lov's famous research, food (the conditioned stimulus) naturally produced salivation (a nonvoluntary response) in dogs. A bell (the unconditioned stimulus) initially failed to evoke salivation. However, after the bell was paired with the food, over time, the dogs started to salivate when presented with the bell alone. The bell at this point attained the status of a conditioned stimulus because it was capable of producing a response by itself.

Classical conditioning plays a role in the understanding of many behavioral problems that clients experience. Many anxiety-related disorders are classically conditioned. An event of sexual abuse in a certain room of a house may evoke overwhelming anxiety when the survivor walks into or near the room, even though she may have no conscious memory of the trigger event.

Although a client's initial symptoms may be directly caused by the trauma, many of the ongoing symptoms result from avoiding the conditioned response and the resultant distress. In this way, repeated negative reinforcement, in which the avoidance leads to a decrease in symptoms, makes the response resistant to extinction (Foa et al., 2000).

Cognitive Factors

Several cognitive theories have branched out from Horowitz's (1976) influential information processing model as reviewed by Calhoun and Resick (1993). In the information processing theory of trauma, adjustment to a traumatic event involves incorporation of the experience into cognitive schemas, which are the structures people use to perceive, organize, store, and retrieve experiences and to make meaning of events. In this model, exposure to trauma may be unable to be processed. Instead, the trauma remains in active memory, which is outside conscious awareness. The defense mechanisms of denial and numbing are activated to prevent the individual from being overwhelmed. The material stays active and is manifested by flashbacks, nightmares, anxiety, and depression. Cycles of denial and numbing alternate with bouts of intrusive thoughts and intense emotion, as the individual attempts to process and integrate the experience into existing cognitive structures.

▨ Intervention

For Children

Few intervention outcome studies have been carried out with children and adolescents who have PTSD, but from the available research, useful intervention guidelines have been developed (Cohen, 1998; Perrin et al., 2000).

First, intervention should include both the parents and the child. Empirical evidence shows that parental emotional reaction to the child's traumatic experience and parental support of the child are powerful mediators of the child's symptoms. It is also helpful to include parents in the intervention so that they can monitor the child's symptoms and implement appropriate behavioral management techniques with the child, both between intervention sessions and after the therapy ends. The social worker's helping parents to resolve their own emotional distress related to the trauma (to which the parent usually has had either direct or vicarious exposure) can help the parent be more perceptive of and responsive to the child's emotional needs. Many parents benefit from direct education about their child's symptoms and how to manage their distressing effects (Cohen, 1998).

A second guideline is that intervention should involve direct exploration of the trauma. Exploration involves the social worker's encouraging a child, through stress management and desensitization procedures, to describe the traumatic event and its aftermath to diminish arousal and distressing emotions. Stress management techniques, such as progressive muscle relaxation, thought stopping, positive imagery, or deep breathing, should be taught to the child prior to detailed discussions of the trauma. Stress management enables the child to gain a sense of control over his or her thoughts and feelings and allows the child to discuss the traumatic event (through desensitization procedures) with confidence that the process will not lead to uncontrollable symptoms and fear. Stress management techniques are also useful to children when they are outside the therapeutic context and begin to reexperience trauma (Cohen, 1998). (See Deblinger and Heflin [1996] for a cognitive-behavioral treatment manual for childhood PTSD related to sexual abuse.)

A third guideline involves the awareness that not all behavioral and emotional problems in children with PTSD are necessarily related to the trauma. In working with children who have PTSD, it is essential to recognize any preexisting or co-occurring disorders and to provide appropriate interventions for them, along with the trauma-focused intervention (Cohen, 1998).

Despite the effectiveness of cognitive-behavioral therapy in the treatment of children with PTSD (in those who have been sexually abused), a survey of 460 therapists indicated that nondirective play therapy was also a popular treatment approach (Cohen, Mannarino, & Rogal, 2001). However, nondirective play therapy has not stood up well to cognitive-behavioral treatment in studies (e.g., Cohen & Mannarino, 1996).

There is also a dearth of empirical evidence for the use of psychotropic medications for treating PTSD, although physicians prescribe a variety of medications for children with the disorder. As a general practice, medication should be selected on the basis of established practice in treating the comorbid conditions (e.g., antidepressants for children with prominent depressive symptoms, psychostimulants for ADHD) (Cohen, 1998). It is important that social workers be aware of the physical and psychological dangers of prescribing any psychotropic drugs for children and adolescents. Psychosocial interventions must always be utilized in conjunction with medication.

For Adults

According to behavioral theory, as well as the information and emotional processing theories of PTSD, key intervention strategies involve *exposure* and *cognitive restructuring* (Foa et al., 2000). Exposure is widely accepted as the primary appropriate intervention for reducing a client's symptoms of arousal and the frequency of reexperiencing the event. Contingency management strategies should also be implemented, however, to manage a client's avoidance and other behavioral problems.

Exposure typically begins with the development of an *anxiety hierarchy*, in which the client lists aspects of the feared situation that initiate different degrees of anxiety. In some forms of exposure (such as flooding), intervention sessions begin with the practitioner initiating a client's exposure to the item rated highest on the hierarchy. Other forms of exposure begin with items rated by the client as provoking moderate anxiety. All exposure methods, however, share the common feature of the client's confronting threatening stimuli until the anxiety is reduced. By continued exposure to a threatening stimulus, the client develops mastery of the situation, and anxiety diminishes. This leads to a decrease in escape and avoidance behaviors that were previously maintained through negative reinforcement.

There are several variants of exposure: symbolic (e.g., through the use of pictures or props), simulated (e.g., through role playing), in vivo (contact with the real situation or stimulus), and imaginal (Velting, Setzer, & Albano, 2004). In *imaginal* exposure, clients confront their memories of the traumatic event. Some imaginal methods involve clients' providing their own narrative by discussing the trauma with the practitioner in detail, and in the present tense, for prolonged periods of time (e.g., 45–60 minutes). The practitioner prompts the client to recall any omitted details. In other forms of imaginal exposure, the practitioner presents a scene to the client based on information he or she has gathered prior to the exposure exercise and helps the client diminish the stress that comes with its presentation. An initial exposure component to this method has the client write a detailed account of the trauma and read it to the practitioner and also at home. The duration and number of exposure sessions may vary.

According to a review by Rothbaum, Meadows, Resick, and Foy (2000), exposure therapy has been tested in 12 studies, several of which were methodologically rigorous and included a variety of types of trauma survivors (for example, Vietnam veterans and female sexual assault survivors). All of these studies had positive results. The strength of evidence for exposure is thus persuasive, and, in fact, no other intervention modality has evidence as compelling to support its efficacy. Still, some trauma survivors are reluctant to confront trauma reminders and tolerate the high anxiety and temporary increase in symptoms that sometimes occur. Thus, not all clients may be good candidates for exposure therapy. In addition, some evidence suggests that exposure is not effective for perpetrators of harm, especially clients whose primary emotion is guilt. Moreover, individuals whose primary emotional response is anger profit less from exposure therapy than those who suffer mainly from anxiety. Still, exposure therapy should be considered as the first line of intervention (Foa, Davidson, & Frances, 1999; Rothbaum et al., 2000).

Cognitive interventions aim to modify a client's automatic thoughts. Strategies used with clients who have PTSD include training them to challenge their problematic cognitions, particularly self-blame and the frustrating attempts to mentally undo the traumatic event. Certain beliefs may result from the trauma and generalize to other aspects of a person's life. These beliefs include a lack of safety, inability to trust, powerlessness, loss of control, poor self-esteem, and doubts about the potential for intimacy. The process for adjusting these beliefs occurs in steps as clients are taught, with the practitioner's help, to identify their dysfunctional thoughts, challenge those that are evaluated as inaccurate or unhelpful, and then replace them with more logical or beneficial thoughts (Rothbaum et al., 2000).

Another treatment for PTSD involves eye movement desensitization and reprocessing (EMDR), a controversial approach that uses a client's eye movements to process traumatic memories. Shapiro, its creator, has outlined the method in her book (Shapiro, 1995) and created a training program for clinicians in EMDR. In a meta-analysis, 34 studies were examined for the effectiveness of EMDR (Davidson & Parker, 2001). The major finding was that EMDR was not more effective than other exposure techniques. Therefore, it remains viable, as exposure treatment has been validated. Indeed, some consider EMDR a form of exposure treatment because clients are asked to keep a traumatic memory in their minds as the clinician elicits the eye movements. However, there was no evidence from the meta-analysis that the eye movements were necessary. In addition, there were no significant differences between studies in which the clinicians had participated in approved training and those in which they had not (Davidson & Parker, 2001), contrary to the claims of its proponents that approved EMDR training is essential.

Medication

Medication is increasingly recognized as a valuable part of a multidimensional intervention approach for adults with PTSD. When successful, medications reduce the severity of core symptoms. In several controlled trials with adult PTSD clients, drugs that affect the neurotransmitter serotonin (especially the selective serotonin reuptake inhibitor antidepressants) have achieved the most positive effects (Stein, Zungu-Dirwayi, Van der Linden, & Seedat, 2003). As noted earlier, many PTSD symptoms are thought to emerge from excessive activity of the central adrenergic system, leading some physicians to use adrenergic blocking agents as well (Perrin et al., 2000). Unfortunately, there are no studies that have systematically examined the value of combining psychosocial interventions with medication (Foa et al., 2000).

Critique

PTSD is one of the disorders in the *DSM* that is conceptualized in terms of problematic functioning in the person–environment system, as a traumatic event, by definition, has had to have occurred (Bradshaw & Thomlison, 1996). However, PTSD is not a unique outcome of trauma; depression is as common a response, and other anxiety disorders, substance use disorders, and eating disorders may develop (Romano, 2004). In addition, in the majority of cases, PTSD is accompanied by another disorder. Symptom overlap among diagnostic categories helps to explain the high likelihood of lifetime comorbid disorders seen in PTSD. These facts indicate that diagnostic clarity is lacking for PTSD.

For the diagnosis of PTSD in childhood, we have already outlined some of the concerns, but to briefly summarize, the questionable accuracy of information on childhood symptoms necessary to make the diagnosis, and also the way that trauma may be experienced differently in children, makes the validity of the diagnosis in childhood questionable.

Case Study

Jacob is a 4-year old Caucasian male who was removed from his birth parent at age 3 because of physical abuse and neglect. He was one of two children born to his mother, who had sexual relations with many men, and his paternity remains unknown. He was placed in regular family foster care shortly after his third birthday. By age 4, Jacob had moved five times, as each foster family reported they were unable to handle his disruptive and aggressive behavior. As a result, Jacob was referred to treatment foster care to receive a higher level of care. Behaviors upon placement included screaming for hours, severe physical tantrums, running into traffic, and punching his hand through a glass window. In addition, Jacob experienced chronic hypervigilance and was often afraid to leave the house or to turn out the lights at bedtime. Other behaviors included reenacting physical abuse on dolls, toileting problems, nightmares, foul language, and frequent refusal to follow adult directives.

Jacob's *DSM-IV* diagnosis is as follows:

AXIS I: Posttraumatic Stress Disorder
AXIS II: None
AXIS III: None
AXIS IV: Primary support group: neglect, abuse, living in foster care
AXIS V: 40

Jacob meets the criteria for posttraumatic stress disorder 309.81 (APA, 2000). For example, criterion A states that an individual must have been exposed to a traumatic event in which two of the following were present: "(1) the person experienced, witnessed, or was confronted with an event or events that involved actual or threatened death or serious injury, or a threat to the physical integrity of self or others and (2) the person's response involved intense fear, helplessness, or horror. Note: In children this may be expressed instead by disorganized or agitated behavior" (pp. 147–148). Jacob met both criteria. First, he experienced life-threatening physical neglect at the hands of his mother. He was malnourished to the extent that his immune system became compromised. Consequently, Jacob suffered from multiple illnesses such as weight loss, influenza, stomach viruses, ear infections, and skin rashes. On occasion, he was treated for these health problems in the emergency room, which initiated the involvement of child protective services (CPS). The second criterion was met because his mother's boyfriend sexually abused him. Jacob was able to convey the forced nature of this abuse through drawing, play, and some verbal expression. What was clear through this communication was the terror he experienced when the "bad man" came to his bed at night. This fear was also evident in his agitated and disorganized behavior, exemplified by his ambivalence in approaching caregivers, extreme anxiety when leaving the house, and an overwhelming dread of bedtime, which often resulted in explosive episodes. While in the care of his mother, he had no way to protect himself or to bring about a response from her. The amount of anxiety produced for such a young mind can be overwhelming and most likely left Jacob distraught and bewildered.

The *DSM-IV* criterion B states that the individual must consistently reexperience the traumatic event in one or more of several ways. In Jacob's case, he experienced four of the five listed symptoms. The first and most disturbing of these is how he would act as if the traumatic event was re-curring. Seeming to enter a dissociative state, Jacob would begin yelling and acting out sexual abuse on a doll or a toy. Swearing at the doll, he would violently reenact a series of sexually abusive behaviors. It was very difficult for Jacob's foster parents to help him move through these episodes and become grounded in the here and now. The second symptom that he often experienced was the visual recollection of the trauma. These were evidenced by his play, such as drawing the bad man. Third were his re-current nightmares, which caused him great agitation. Thus, Jacob had dif-ficulty getting ready for bed or returning to sleep upon awakening from a nightmare. The fourth symptom was the overwhelming psychological stress due to exposure to internal or external cues that represented the trauma. In Jacob's case, this was demonstrated during visitation with his mother. During his visitation, he would display ambivalent behaviors to-ward his mother, such as approaching her for something but then fighting any response she might give. After visits with his mother, he would engage in self-injurious behaviors such as extreme temper tantrums in which he would throw himself into objects or on the floor and sustain injuries. He would also run into traffic, placing himself in grave danger. The visits were discontinued, as there was a clear pattern of self-injurious behavior follow-ing maternal contact. Later, they discontinued visitation with extended fam-ily, as this, too, triggered a trauma reaction in Jacob.

Criterion C states that an individual must demonstrate avoidance of stimuli associated with the trauma that results in numbing and a general lack of responsiveness in at least three ways. Jacob exhibited such symp-tomatology, the first of which was his ambivalence before and during vis-itation with his mother. The second symptom was his avoidance of direct conversations regarding his mother or the bad man. For example, in ther-apy Jacob had chosen dolls to represent his mother and her boyfriend. Jacob would put these dolls away in the therapist's office and retrieve them only when he felt safe to process this trauma. The third symptom was his avoid-ance of going to bed at night, as this used to be a terrifying experience for Jacob.

Criterion D states that an individual must experience increased arousal as indicated by at least two of several symptoms listed. Here again, Jacob experienced three. The first was trouble falling or remaining asleep. The second was his irritability and angry tantrums. The third was his demon-stration of extreme hyperarousal states, in which he would talk about the bad man and how he feared that his foster parents could not protect him. This was further exemplified by Jacob's preoccupation with protective mea-sures, such as locking the door and questioning the safety of the home.

Risk factors associated with Jacob's diagnosis include the intensity of the traumatic event, age of the victim, relationship with perpetrator, personal factors (e.g., hyperarousal states, self-injurious behavior), social support, social functioning, pre/post exposure to trauma and stress, and parent pathology. As already mentioned, Jacob's traumatic events were in some cases life threatening, as indicated by his malnourishment and his fear of the "bad man." These traumas were thought to have begun by age 1, given the mother's historical account. Onset of neglect and abuse at such an early age can increase the severity of the diagnosis and prognosis. Furthermore, Jacob's relationship with his mother suggests little comfort or protection was secured, placing him at grave risk for attachment difficulties. Although Jacob exhibited some personal factors that increased his risk of subsequent pathology, such as hyperarousal states and self-injurious behavior, he also possessed many strengths, as mentioned later. Once placed in foster care, his social support was precarious at best, given the multiple placement disruptions prior to his placement with a treatment family. Too, this instability probably induced subsequent trauma. Other posttraumatic events may have been visits with his birth mother, as Jacob's symptoms would increase and become more violent following visitation. Also, Jacob's social functioning was greatly impaired, as indicated by his aggressive behavior within his peer group. Last, Jacob's birth mother was diagnosed with alcohol dependence and depression and identified herself as being neglected and abused as a child. These factors increased Jacob's predisposition for developing PTSD and further increases the risk of subsequent pathology. As already mentioned, the mother does not know the identity of his father, and no paternal information is available.

Protective factors influencing Jacob's diagnosis include personal factors, social support, treatment, and the prevention of subsequent traumas. Jacob's personal factors included strengths such as a desire to develop attachment relationships, above average intelligence, motivation to learn, and enthusiasm for play. For example, Jacob was approaching his foster parents for comfort (attachment behavior) and slowly building a relationship with them. Also, Jacob's intelligence enabled him to keep pace with his developmental tasks, despite the distraction of his symptomatology. Therefore, he was able to develop competencies at home and at school. This increased his sense of self worth but also kept him functioning at an age-appropriate developmental level. Another personal strength was his propensity to express himself through art and play. This gave Jacob a cathartic medium in which he could communicate and process his past abuse.

Jacob's social supports and services were extensive. He was placed in a two-parent home with no other children. This level of social support included constant supervision, trained therapeutic foster parenting, and undivided attention. The foster parents provided a highly structured, consistent, and nurturing environment. For example, every night at bedtime a foster parent would read to Jacob. The books chosen had themes of safety and stability. Jacob and his foster parents began to develop a trusting relationship upon which Jacob could depend. He attended play therapy weekly with his foster mother. Through this medium, Jacob was able to reenact the abuse through play. Through play, he was able to reorganize his world, expressing his increasing sense of safety. Behavioral therapy was also used during sessions and in the home environment by the treatment foster parents to modify behavior and create structure and safety—for example, time-outs, safety routines, and alternative behavioral options. Other services provided included monthly consultation with an attachment specialist in which the foster parents were instructed in how to cultivate attachment behavior with Jacob. Various assignments were implemented in the home environment. At the same time, Jacob and his foster parents received regular home visits by the treatment foster care social worker, in which they could problem-solve. Jacob also attended a Head Start program with added supports. Last, visitation with his mother was discontinued on account of its negative effect on Jacob. Eventually, termination of parental rights was pursued.

Goal formulation and treatment planning are coordinated by the clinical case manager (CPS worker) by collecting information from collateral sources and from Jacob's treatment team. The treatment team is as follows: CPS worker, foster parents, therapist, psychiatrist, educator, and treatment foster care (TFC) worker. Conceptualized from a person-in-environment framework, the goals and treatment plan are formulated by an assessment of the risk and protective factors and, whenever possible, empirically validated treatment methods used for this diagnosis.

Long-Term Goal

Jacob will build a trusting relationship with his foster parents.

Objectives

1. Jacob will engage in reciprocal behaviors with foster parents and other safe adults.
2. Jacob will follow adult directives.
3. Jacob will allow self to be comforted by his foster parents.
4. Jacob will grieve the primary parental relationship and begin to bond with his foster parents.
5. Jacob will reduce self-injurious behaviors.

Conclusion

This chapter has reviewed aspects of the PTSD diagnosis for both children and adults. It is important for social workers to be aware of this possible diagnosis in children and adults so appropriate intervention is applied. It is also critical for social workers to be aware of the evidence-based treatments for the disorder so that effective intervention is employed, rather than widely used approaches that have not demonstrated their usefulness.

Appendix I. Measures for Child PTSD

Information on PTSD measures was drawn from Ohan, Myers, & Collett (2002).

Children's PTSD-Reaction Index (CPTS-RI)

(Pynoos, 2002)

Description

- 20-item, widely used measure of PTSD symptoms for children and adolescents, although training is required.
- A clinician-administered scale, can also be a self-report scale with youths older than 8.
- Items based on an adult measure of PTSD, derived from the *DSM-III-R*, except, CPTS-RI deviates from *DSM* nomenclature as it asks about subjective experiences.
- 3 subscales: reexperiencing/numbing, fear/anxiety, and concentration/sleep.
- Takes 20–45 minutes to administer and score.

Reliability

- Internal consistency is moderate to good for the reexperiencing/numbing subscale and adequate for the other scales.
- Interrater reliability appears good.
- Test-retest reliability is excellent for short term.

Validity

- Convergent validity is supported by the excellent agreement of CPTS-RI cutoff scores with PTSD diagnoses; subscales highly correlate with trauma exposure and depression.

Trauma Symptom Checklist for Children

Briere (1996)

Description

- Child version (ages 7–16) of the adult Trauma Symptom Inventory to assess distress and related symptoms after trauma.
- Available in 54-item instrument, as well as in shorter forms, 44-item and 40-item version.
- 6 subscales (Anger, Anxiety, Depression, Dissociation, Posttraumatic Stress, and Sexual Concerns) for children 8–15.
- Unlike the Children's Impact of Traumatic Events–Revised, this scale does not orient respondents to their abuse experience and is appropriate for children who have not disclosed abuse, as well as those who have. The scale thus may be useful with children who have experienced multiple types of abuse.
- 20–39 minutes to administer and score.
- Large normative base of ethnically and economically diverse children who do not have a history of trauma.
- Also available is the Trauma Symptom Checklist for Young Children for children ages 3–8, to be completed by parents (Briere et al., 2001).

Reliability

- Alpha values for normed sample ranged from .58 to .89.

Validity

- All subscale scores correlated significantly with each other as well as with the youth and parent versions of the Child Behavior Checklist and with instruments conceptually related to the subscales, including the Child Depression Inventory, the Child Dissociative Checklist, the Children's Impact of Traumatic Events–Revised, and the Child Sexual Behavior Inventory.
- Scale scores were higher among those who had experienced sexual penetration during the abuse.
- Scale scores discriminated between children who had disclosed abuse and children who were evaluated for abuse but for whom abuse was not confirmed (Elliott & Briere, 1994).
- Scale scores were highest for those children who disclosed abuse (credible and partially credible), lowest for children who were believed to have been abused but either had not disclosed or had re-

canted their allegations, and moderate for children who were judged not to have been abused (Elliott & Briere, 1994).

Child PTSD Symptom Scale (CPSS)

(Foa, 2002)

Description

- 24-item, self-report scale specific to the *DSM-IV* concept of PTSD for youths aged 8 to 15 years
- Reexperiencing, Avoidance, and Arousal subscales, with 7 items measuring youths' functional impairment as a result of PTSD
- Takes 15 minutes to administer and score

Reliability

- Internal consistency was very good for the total scale (.89) and moderate to good for the subscales (.70–.80).
- Test and retest reliabilities for the total scales were good (.84) and moderate to good for the subscales (.63–.85).

Validity

- CPSS's correlation with a well-established self-report measure of PTSD symptoms supports good convergent validity.
- CPSS's low to moderate correlations with measures of depression and anxiety support divergent validity from other internalizing symptoms.

The Children's Impact of Traumatic Events Scale

(Wolfe, Gentile, Michienzi, Sas, & Wolfe, 1991)

Description

- A 78-item instrument that measures PTSD symptoms (intrusive thoughts, avoidance, hyperarousal, and sexual anxiety), eroticism, abuse attributions (self-blame and guilt, empowerment, personal vulnerability, and dangerous world), and social reactions (negative reactions by others and social support) in children who have been sexually abused

Reliability

- Internal consistency was varied among the scales: The Dangerous World and Personal Vulnerability scales were questionable, and the others scales were adequate.

Validity

- Construct validity of the abuse attributions scores was varied: Social support scales were mixed: The Self-Blame and Guilt scale performed very well with negative reactions; however, the Personal Vulnerability and Dangerous World scales performed less adequately but demonstrated convergent validity and symptom prediction.

Appendix II. Measures for Adult PTSD

Information is largely drawn from Saigh and Bremner (1999).

PTSD Symptom Scale-Self Report (PSS-SR)

(Foa, Riggs, Dancu & Rothbaum, 1993)

Description

- A self-report counterpart to the PTSD Symptom Scale-Interview, a semistructured interview schedule

Reliability

- Test-retest reliability for total severity over a 1-month interval was .74, and internal consistency was .91.

Validity

- Concurrent validity was supported by the correlation between the PSS-SR and similar measures.
- The scale showed a sensitivity of .62 and an efficiency of .86 for predicting a PTSD diagnosis.

Purdue PTSD Scale–Revised (PPTSD-R)

(Lauterbach & Vrana, 1996)

Description

- 17-item measure corresponding to the *DSM III-R* PTSD criteria.
- Items are rated on a 5-point scale, indicating the frequency of symptoms over the past month.

Reliability

- Test-retest reliability for total severity over a 2-week interval was .72.
- Internal consistency was .91.

Validity

- Convergent validity was supported by moderate to strong correlations with similar scales.
- Scores were higher in participants reporting more severe traumatic events and for those seeking treatment for trauma-related difficulties.

Posttraumatic Stress Diagnostic Scale (PDS)

(Foa, 1995; Foa et al., 1993)

- 49 items.

  - Only self-report measure to assess all six criteria for PTSD in the *DSM-IV*.

- 4-part self-report measure of PTSD:

  - Part 1. 13-item checklist of potential traumatic events.
  - Part 2. 8 items that determine if an event meets the *DSM-IV* definition of Criterion A.
  - Part 3 assesses the frequency over the past month of the 17 PTSD symptoms.
  - Part 4 assesses the impact of symptoms on various aspects of social and occupational functioning.

Reliability

- Test-retest reliability for symptom severity was .83.
- Interrater reliability was .74.

Validity

- PDS had a sensitivity of .82, a specificity of .77, and an efficiency of .79.

- Convergent validity was demonstrated through strong correlations with similar measures.

Davidson Trauma Scale (DTS)

(Davidson, 1996)

Description

- Self-report measure of PTSD, consisting of 17 items corresponding to the *DSM-IV* PTDS symptoms.
- Manual provides a table for converting total DTS scores into a PTSD diagnosis based on the ratio of PTSD cases to noncases at each cutoff score.

Reliability

- Test-retest reliability for total DTS score over a 1-week interval was .86.
- Alpha coefficients for frequency, severity, and total scores were all greater than .90.

Validity

- Good convergent validity, correlating strongly with other trauma measures
- Sensitive to both differences in clinical severity and to improvement in symptoms as a result of treatment

Mississippi Scale for Combat-Related PTSD (Mississippi Scale)

(Keane, Caddell & Taylor, 1988)

Description

- 35-items selected from an initial item pool of 200 items based on the *DSM-III* PTSD criteria and associated features.
- Most widely used measure of combat-related PTSD.
- A civilian version is also available.

Reliability

- Internal consistency of .94 was reported.
- Test-retest (1 week) reliability of .97 was reported.

Validity

- Cutoff of 107 had a sensitivity of .93, a specificity of .89, and an efficiency of .90 against a consensus clinical diagnosis of PTSD.

Penn Inventory for Posttraumatic Stress Disorder (Penn Inventory)

(Hammarberg, 1992)

Description

- 26-item scale based on *DSM-III* and *DSM-III-R* PTSD criteria

Reliability

- Excellent psychometric properties in three samples, including combat veterans and civilian trauma survivors.
- Internal consistency was .94.
- Test-retest reliability was .96.
- A cutoff of 35 yields a sensitivity of .90, a specificity of 1.00, and an efficiency of .94.

Validity

- The Penn Inventory correlated strongly with similar measures and the IES and moderately with level of combat exposure.

References

Acierno, R., Kilpatrick, D., & Resnick, H. (1999). Posttraumatic stress disorder in adults relative to criminal victimization: Prevalence, risk factors, and comorbidity. In P. Saigh & J. Bremner (Eds.), *Posttraumatic stress disorder: A comprehensive text* (pp. 44–68). Needham Heights, MA: Allyn & Bacon.

American Psychiatric Association. (2000). *Diagnostic and statistical manual of mental disorders* (4th ed., text rev.). Washington, DC: Author.

Bradshaw, C., & Thomlison, B. (1996). Posttraumatic stress disorder conceptualized as a problem in the person-environment system. In F. Turner (Ed.), *Adult psychopathology: A social work perspective* (pp. 638–660). New York: Free Press.

Brewin, C., Andrews, B., & Valentine, J. (2000). Meta-analysis of risk factors for posttraumatic stress disorder in trauma-exposed adults. *Journal of Consulting and Clinical Psychology, 68*, 748–766.

Busuttil, W. (2004). Presentations and management of post traumatic stress disorder and the elderly: A need for investigation. *International Journal of Geriatric Psychiatry, 19*, 429–439.

Calhoun, K., & Resick, P. (1993). Post-traumatic stress disorder. In D. H. Barlow (Ed.), *Clinical handbook of psychological disorders: A step-by-step treatment manual* (pp. 48–98). New York: Guilford.

Cohen, J., Mannarino, A., & Rogal, S. (2001). Treatment practices for childhood posttraumatic stress disorder. *Child Abuse and Neglect, 25,* 123–135.

Cohen, J. A. (1998). Summary of the practice parameters for the assessment and treatment of children and adolescents with posttraumatic stress disorder. *Journal of the American Academy of Child and Adolescent Psychiatry, 37*(9), 997–1001.

Cohen, J. A., & Mannarino, A. P. (1996). A treatment outcome study for sexually abused preschool children: Initial findings. *Journal of the American Academy of Child and Adolescent Psychiatry, 35,* 42–50.

Davidson, P., & Parker, K. (2001). Eye movement desensitization and reprocessing (EMDR): A meta-analysis. *Journal of Consulting and Clinical Psychology, 69,* 305–316.

Debellis, M. D. (1997). Postraumastic stress disorder and acute stress disorder. In R. T Ammerman & M. Hersen (Eds.), *Handbook of prevention and treatment with children and adolescents: Intervention in the real world context* (pp. 455–494). New York: Wiley.

Deblinger, E., & Heflin, A. H. (1996). *Treating sexually abused children and their nonoffending parents: A cognitive-behavioral approach.* Thousand Oaks, CA: Sage.

Foa, E. B., Davidson, J., & Frances, A. (1999). The expert consensus guideline series: Treatment of posttraumatic stress disorder. *The Journal of Clinical Psychiatry, 60*(Suppl. 16), 4–76.

Foa, E. B., Keane, T. M., & Friedman, M. J. (Eds.). (2000). *Effective treatments for PTSD: Practice guidelines from the International Society for Traumatic Stress Studies.* New York: Guilford.

Horowitz, M. (1976). *Stress response syndromes.* New York: Aronson.

Kazdin, A. (2000). *Behavior modification in applied settings* (6th ed.). Pacific Grove, CA: Brooks/Cole Publishing.

Keane, T., Weathers, F., & Foa, E. (2000). Diagnosis and assessment. In E. Foa, T. Keane, & M. Friedman (Eds.), *Effective treatments for PTSD* (pp. 18–36). New York: Guilford.

Kessler, R., Berglund, P., Demler, O., Jin, R., & Walters, E. (2005). Lifetime prevalence and age-of-onset distributions of DSM-IV disorders in the National Comorbidity survey replication. Archives of General Psychiatry, 62, 593–602.

Kessler, R., Sonnega, A., Bromet, E., Hughes, M. & Nelson, C. (1995). Posttraumatic stress disorder in the National Comorbidity Survey. *Archives of General Psychiatry, 52,* 1048–1060.

McHugo, G. J., Mooney, D., Racusin, R., Ford, J. D., & Fleischer, A. (2000). Predicting posttraumatic stress after hospitalization for pediatric injury. *Journal of the American Academy of Child and Adolescent Psychiatry, 39*(5), 576–583.

McNally, R. J. (1996). Assessment of posttraumatic stress disorder in children and adolescents. *Journal of School Psychology, 34,* 147–161.

Ozer, E., Best, S., Lipsey, T., & Weiss, D. (2003). Predictors of posttraumatic stress disorder and symptoms in adults: A meta-analysis. *Psychological Bulletin, 129,* 52–73.

Perrin, S., Smith, P., & Yule, W. (2000). Practitioner review: The assessment and treatment of post-traumatic stress disorder in children and adolescents. *Journal of Child Psychology & Psychiatry & Allied Disciplines, 41*(3), 277–289.

Romano, C. J. (2004). Posttraumatic stress disorder: A continuing controversy in neuropsychiatry. *Neuropsychiatry Reviews, 5,* 9–12.

Rothbaum, B., Meadows, E., Resick, P., & Foy, D. (2000). Cognitive-behavioral therapy. In E. Fao, T. Keane, & M. Friedman (Eds.), *Effective treatments for PTSD* (pp. 320–325). New York: Guilford.

Saigh, P., Yasik, A., Sack, W., & Koplewicz, H. (1999). Child-adolescent posttraumatic stress disorder: Prevalence, risk factors, and comorbidity. In P. Saigh & J. D. Bremner (Eds.), *Posttraumatic stress disorder: A comprehensive text* (pp. 18–43). Needham Heights, MA: Allyn & Bacon.

Scheeringa, M. S., Peebles, C. D., Cook, C. A., & Zeanah, C. H. (2001). Toward establishing procedural, criterion, and discriminant validity for PTSD in early childhood. *Journal of the American Academy of Child and Adolescent Psychiatry, 40*(1), 52–60.

Scheeringa, M. S., Zeanah, C. H., Drell, M. J., & Larrieu, J. A. (1995). Two approaches to the diagnosis of posttraumatic stress disorder in infancy and early childhood. *Journal of the American Academy of Child & Adolescent Psychiatry, 34*(2), 191–200.

Schlenger, W. E., Fairbank, J. A., Jordan, B. K., & Caddell, J. M. (1999). Combat-related posttraumatic stress disorder: Prevalence, risk factors, and comorbidity. In P. A.

Schnurr, P. P., Friedman, M. J., & Bernardy, N. C. (2002). Research on posttraumatic stress disorder: Epidemiology, pathophysiology, and assessment. *JCLP/ In Session: Psychotherapy in Practice, 58,* 877–889.

Shapiro, F. (1995). *Eye movement desensitization and reprocessing: Basic principles, protocols and procedures.* New York: Guilford.

Stein, D. J., Zungu-Dirwayi, N., Van der Linden, G. J. H., & Seedat, S. (2003). Pharmacotherapy for posttraumatic stress disorder (Cochrane Review). In *The Cochrane Library,* Issue 1. Oxford: Update Software.

Velting, O., Setzer, N., & Albano, A. M. (2004). Update on and advances in assessment and cognitive-behavioral treatment of anxiety disorders in children and adolescents. *Professional Psychology: Research and Practice, 35,* 42–54.

Weinstein, D., Staffelbach, D., & Biaggio, M. (2000). Attention-deficit hyperactivity disorder and posttraumatic stress disorder: Differential diagnosis in childhood sexual abuse. *Clinical Psychology Review, 20*(3), 359–378.

References for PTSD Measures

Briere, J. (1996). *Trauma symptom checklist for children (TSCC), professional manual.* Odessa, FL: Psychological Assessment Resources.

Briere, J., Johnson, K., Bissada, A., Damon, L., Crouch, J., Gil, E., et al. (2001). The trauma symptom checklist for young children (TSCYC): Reliability and association with abuse exposure in a multi-site study. *Child Abuse & Neglect, 25,* 1001–1014.

Davidson, J. R. T. (1996). *Davidson trauma scale manual*. Toronto, Canada: Multi-Health Systems.

Elliott, D., & Briere, J. (1994). Forensic sexual abuse evaluations of older children: Disclosures and symptomotalogy. *Behavioural Sciences and the Law, 12*, 261–277.

Foa, E. B. (1995). *Posttraumatic stress diagnostic scale manual*. Minneapolis, MN: National Computer Systems.

Foa, E. B. (2002). *The child PTSD symptom scale (CPSS)*. Philadelphia: Center for the Treatment and Study of Anxiety, University of Pennsylvania, School of Medicine, Department of Psychiatry.

Foa, E. B., Riggs, D. S., Dancu, C. V., & Rothbaum, B. O. (1993). Reliability and validity of a brief instrument for assessing post-traumatic stress disorder. *Journal of Traumatic Stress, 6*, 459–473.

Hammarberg, M. (1992). Penn inventory for posttraumatic stress disorder: Psychometric properties. *Psychological Assessment, 4*, 67–76.

Keane, T. M., Caddell, J. M., & Taylor, K. I. (1988). Mississippi scale for combat-related posttraumatic stress disorder. Three studies in reliability and validity. *Journal of Consulting and Clinical Psychology, 56*, 85–90.

Lauterbach, D., & Vrana, S. (1996). Three studies on the reliability and validity of a self-report measure of posttraumatic stress disorder. *Assessment, 3*, 17–25.

Ohan, J. L., Myers, K., & Collett, B. R. (2002). Ten-year review of rating scales, IV: Scales assessing trauma and its effects. *Journal of the American Academy of Child and Adolescent Psychiatry, 41*, 1401–1423.

Pynoos, R. S. (2002). *The child post traumatic stress-reaction index (CPTS-RI)*. Los Angeles: Trauma Psychiatry Service, UCLA.

Saigh, P., & Bremner, D. (Eds.). (1999). *Posttraumatic stress disorder: A comprehensive text*. Needham Heights, MA: Allyn & Bacon.

Wolfe, V., Gentile, C., Michienzi, T., Sas, L., & Wolfe, D. (1991). The children's impact of traumatic events scale: A measure of post-sexual-abuse PTSD symptoms. *Behavioral Assessment, 13*, 359–383.

8   Anxiety Disorders

Anxiety is an unpleasant but normal, functional affect that provides people with warning signs for perceived threats. It includes physiological and psychological symptoms that prepare the individual to confront or avoid the threat (Marks, 1987). The anticipated danger may be internal or external in origin. The symptoms of anxiety include *tension* (trembling, muscle soreness, restlessness, fatigue), *autonomic nervous system hyperactivity* (shortness of breath, feeling smothered, accelerated heart rate, sweating, clammy hands, dry mouth, lightheadedness, abdominal distress, hot flashes or chills, frequent urination, difficulty swallowing, and the feeling of a lump in the throat), and *hypervigilance* (feeling edgy or keyed up, an exaggerated startle response, difficulty concentrating, trouble falling or staying asleep, and irritability) (American Psychiatric Association [APA], 2000).

Anxiety begins as the body's physiological reaction to a threatening stimulus, but the emotions that follow the appraisal of that stimulus can vary. Anxiety becomes problematic when it creates a sense of powerlessness, suggests an impending danger that is unrealistic, produces an exhausting state of vigilance, produces a level of self-absorption that interferes with problem solving, or creates doubt about the nature of reality (Campbell, 1996). Anxiety disorders are characterized by extreme, intense, almost unbearable fear that disrupts social or occupational functioning. These disorders are the most common mental health problems in the United States (Kessler, Chiu, Demler, & Walters, 2005).

Types of Anxiety Disorders

The *DSM* describes 11 different anxiety disorders, as well as separation anxiety disorder, which is listed under disorders of infancy and childhood. The specific anxiety disorders are defined on the basis of the characteristics of the anxious response or the nature of the feared stimulus (Hagopian & Ollendick, 1997). Children can be diagnosed with any of the anxiety disorders with the same criteria used for adults. Particular considerations for children's diagnoses of anxiety disorders are sparse (Hagopian & Ollendick, 1997) but are noted in the following descriptions drawn from the *DSM-IV-TR* and Steketee, Van Noppen, Cohen, and Clary (1998). PTSD has already been covered in chapter 7, and specific phobias are not a focus of this chapter, given that such problems are generally less severe and not encountered as often by social work practitioners.

Separation anxiety disorder features excessive anxiety about separation from a major attachment figure. Note, however, that anxiety upon separation from a caregiver is normal for babies between the ages of 6 and 18 months (Hagopian & Ollendick, 1997). With the disorder, the anxiety at separation may approach a panic level. School refusal is present in the majority of cases (Bernstein & Shaw, 1997). Prevalence rates in the community range from 2 to 4% and appear to be higher in children living in single-parent households (Cronk, Slutske, Madden, Bucholz, & Heath, 2004). Low socioeconomic status has also been cited as a risk factor, but that may reflect the frequent co-occurrence of this variable with single parenting.

Panic disorders involve unpredictable anxiety attacks. They are coded either with agoraphobia (the panic attacks arise from anxiety about being in places or circumstances where escape might be difficult or embarrassing), without agoraphobia (the attacks are not associated with particular situations but are characterized by fears of losing self-control), or agoraphobia without history of panic disorder (in which panic-like symptoms are experienced in places or situations from which escape might be difficult). The lifetime rate of panic disorder (4.7%) is higher than the rate of agoraphobia without panic disorder (1.4%) (Kessler, Berglund, Demler, Jin, & Walters, 2005). Age of first onset is typically in the 20s, and females are at higher risk for these disorders (Gorman et al., 2002).

Although prevalence in African Americans may be similar to that in Caucasians, racial differences in help seeking (African Americans tend to go to medical rather than mental health settings) and symptom presentation (African Americans report more somatic symptoms) may result in misdiagnosis.

The diagnosis of panic disorder is typically not made before puberty. In older adults, although anxiety symptoms are among the most common psychiatric ailments they experience, epidemiological studies suggest that the prevalence of panic disorder in later life may be lower than that in midlife (Gorman et al., 2002).

A phobia features anxiety that is triggered by a specific object or situation. To qualify as a disorder, the subsequent avoidant behavior must impede the person's functioning or result in considerable distress. Estimates of lifetime prevalence rates for phobias in the community range from 10 to 11.3%. The majority of those diagnosed are female.

Social phobia involves anxiety related to social situations; fear of negative evaluation from others is the overwhelming worry. For specific phobia and social phobia, children's symptoms may involve crying, tantrums, paralysis, or clinging. For the diagnosis of social phobia to be made in children, the child must have age-appropriate relationships with familiar people, and the fear of social situations and unfamiliar people must occur with peers, as well as adults. The criterion specifying that the individual recognizes his or her fear as excessive may be omitted for children (Hagopian & Ollendick, 1997).

Like the other disorders discussed thus far, adult females more often experience social phobia than men, although both genders are equally represented in treatment settings. In adolescence, boys are more commonly diagnosed. Social phobia is more common in people from low socioeconomic strata (SES). Social phobia is one of the most common mental disorders among adults with a community lifetime prevalence rate of 12.1% (Kessler, Berglund, et al., 2005) and a 12-month rate of 6.8% (Kessler, Chiu, et al., 2005).

Generalized anxiety disorder (GAD) is characterized by persistent, excessive worry that lasts for at least 6 months, occurring more days than not. The anxiety and worry are accompanied by at least three of the following symptoms: restlessness, fatigue, difficulty concentrating, irritability, muscle tension, and disturbed sleep. Children need to show only one such symptom.

In the *DSM-III-R*, *overanxious disorder* was characterized by general anxiety that may include excessive worry about future and past events and behavior, concerns about competence, and self-consciousness (Bernstein & Shaw, 1997). The disorder was seen as having vague criteria that overlapped with other disorders, so it was subsumed under the GAD diagnosis in *DSM-IV*.

An 8.6% lifetime prevalence rate has been found for generalized anxiety disorder (Kessler, Berglund, et al., 2005), with two thirds female. The disorder is more common in those from lower SES backgrounds, possibly because of the greater number of stressors affecting those in poverty, as well as greater treatment-seeking behavior, higher education, and higher job levels held by people in higher socioeconomic groups. GAD is more common among those who have been previously married than among those who are either currently or never married. Unemployed people and women who work only in the home experience higher rates as well.

Obsessive-compulsive disorder (OCD) involves both recurring thoughts that cause marked anxiety and compulsive behaviors that temporarily serve to neutralize anxiety. The obsessions and compulsions are severe enough to be time consuming (greater than 1 hour per day) or cause marked distress or significant impairment. As with specific phobia and social phobia in children, the criterion that the child should recognize the fear as excessive or unreasonable is omitted (Hagopian & Ollendick, 1997). Lifetime prevalence rates are approximately 1.9% in the community overall (Kessler, Berglund, et al., 2005) and 1% to 3.6% for adolescents. Childhood rates are low—about 1% (Hagopian & Ollendick, 1997). Obsessive-compulsive disorder is equally common in males and females but has an earlier onset in males (age 6–15, compared with 20–29 in females).

No ethnic differences have been found among U.S. youth (King, Leonard, & March, 1998). With both children and adults, the frequency of OCD in clinical samples is lower than in community samples (1.3–5% of children). This discrepancy, which suggests that many individuals with the disorder do not come to clinical attention, may be due to secretiveness about symptoms or a lack of awareness about the disorder and the availability of treatment (King et al., 1998).

Overall, the anxiety disorders are estimated as afflicting 28.8% of the U.S. population over the life span and 18.1% over any 12-month period (Kessler, Chiu, et al., 2005). For children and adolescents in the community, prevalence estimates have ranged from 2.4 to 8.7% (Hagopian & Ollendick, 1997) and from 12 to 20% (Velting, Setzer, & Albano, 2004). Girls have been found to report more fears than boys in community samples, but few sex differences in the prevalence of anxiety disorders during childhood have been observed in clinical samples. During adolescence and early adulthood, sex differences in prevalence begin to emerge. Other than social phobia, which is more common among boys, girls generally have higher rates of anxiety disorders during adolescence (Hagopian & Ollendick, 1997).

Comorbidity

The anxiety disorders share similar patterns of comorbidity on Axis I for both adults and children: Typically depression and other anxiety disorders are comorbid. For example, for people with panic disorder, the lifetime prevalence of major depression is 50 to 70%. The onset of depression precedes the onset of panic disorder in one third of these cases; in the other two thirds, depression is concurrent with or follows the panic disorder

(Gorman et al., 2002). One third of children with an anxiety disorder have two or more (Bernstein & Shaw, 1997). Comorbid major depression is also common, with rates ranging from 28 to 69%. The anxiety disorders are also associated with attention-deficit/hyperactivity disorder.

Substance use disorders may co-occur with anxiety in adults, with both substance use and anxiety serving as risk factors for each other. For example, in a prospective, 7-year study, the presence of an anxiety disorder quadrupled the risk for the onset of alcohol dependence (Kushner, Sher, & Erickson, 1999). At the same time, alcohol dependence increased the risk for an anxiety disorder by three to five times. Longitudinal studies conducted outside the United States also indicate that anxiety disorders may lead to substance use disorders (Goodwin, Fergusson, & Horwood, 2004; Zimmerman et al., 2003).

Obsessive-compulsive disorder seems to be associated with tic disorders. Followed over time, nearly 60% of children and adolescents seeking treatment for OCD develop tics that range from simple, mild, and transient through Tourette's disorder (King et al., 1998). Of those who are diagnosed with Tourette's disorder, 35 to 50% have OCD. There may, in fact, be two subtypes of OCD depending on the presence of a comorbid tic disorder. Tic-related OCD seems to have a childhood onset and is more common in boys. It may also indicate a poorer response to treatment with selective serotonin reuptake inhibitor (SSRI) medications than youths with non-tic-related OCD. In children and adolescents, about half meet the criteria for one of the disruptive disorders, especially ADHD (King et al., 1998). Usually, the disruptive disorder predates the OCD.

Axis II disorders afflict about 50% of people with panic disorder (Gorman et al., 2002). The most common Axis II disorders involve, not surprisingly, the "anxious" cluster—the avoidant, dependent, and obsessive-compulsive types. Despite the high rates of comorbidity found with anxiety disorders, little information exists on optimal intervention methods for these comorbid conditions and how comorbidity affects prognosis.

Assessment of the Anxiety Disorders

Clinical assessment of anxiety should include the following areas of focus (Bernstein & Shaw, 1997; Gorman et al., 2002):

- History of the onset and development of the anxiety symptoms, including the frequency and nature of a person's symptoms.
- Any coexisting psychiatric disorders.
- General medical history and a review of a person's medications, including a physical examination to search for a possible physical basis

for the anxiety. This is especially critical for older adults without a history of anxiety disorders. If there is a physical basis, the appropriate diagnosis is anxiety disorder due to a general medical condition; for a medication- or substance-induced anxiety, the appropriate diagnosis is substance-induced anxiety disorder.
- History of substance use disorders.
- Response to life transitions and major life events and stressors.
- Social, school, occupational, and family history.
- Times when the anxiety symptoms are not present or are more manageable.

Scales may be useful for assessment and tracking symptoms over time. See appendix.

When the client is a child, separate interviews with parents and children are recommended (Velting et al., 2004). Frequently, children report fewer symptoms than their parents. Reasons for this discrepancy include the child's desire to answer questions in a socially desirable manner and the child's limited comprehension of the interview questions. Also, children tend to be less reliable than parents in reporting details about the onset and duration of anxiety symptoms.

Risk and Protective Factors

Determining risk and protective factors that are specific to any of the anxiety disorders is difficult, as is determining whether the risk factors that follow are specific for anxiety or may apply to a number of other diagnoses (Donovan & Spence, 2000). Finally, the risk factors may be concurrent with the anxiety disorder rather than contributing to its cause. As with the other disorders in the *DSM*, the research on protective factors has lagged behind the search for risks. See Table 8.1 for adult factors and Table 8.2 for child factors.

Genetic and Biological Factors

A general predisposition for anxiety, rather than for specific anxiety disorders, is genetically based (Gorman et al., 2002). Results from twin studies suggest that genetic influences are modest, however, ranging between 30 and 40% for anxiety disorders (Hettema, Neale, & Kendler, 2001).

Risk factors related to an individual's temperament are *anxiety sensitivity*, *temperamental sensitivity*, and *behavioral inhibition* (Donovan & Spence, 2000). Anxiety sensitivity is the tendency to respond fearfully to anxiety

Table 8.1

Risk and Protective Factors for Onset of Anxiety Disorders in Adults

Risk	Protective
Biological	
Estimated heritabilities across the disorders are modest (30–40%)	
Prior smoking	
Psychological	
History of separation anxiety disorder (panic disorder)[a]	
Emotional and escape-avoidance coping strategies[b]	Problem-focused coping strategies
Family	
Stressful and/or traumatic life events[c]	
Loss or disruption of relationships or significant life stressor	
Family history of anxiety disorders[c]	

[a]Hayward, Wilson, Lagle, Killen, & Taylor (2004).
[b]Hino, Takeuchi, & Yamanouchi (2002).
[c]Bandelow et al. (2002).

symptoms. Temperamental sensitivity is characterized by a range of emotional reactions toward negativity, including fear, sadness, self-dissatisfaction, hostility, and worry. This tendency predisposes people to both anxiety and depression, which often occur together. Behavioral inhibition involves timidity, shyness, emotional restraint, and withdrawal when introduced to unfamiliar situations (Kagan et al., 1988, as cited in Donovan & Spence, 2000). Behavioral inhibition has been associated with elevated physiological indexes of arousal and has been shown to have a strong genetic component.

An active smoking habit might increase the risk of panic attacks or disorder (Isensee, Wittchen, Stein, Hofler, & Lieb, 2003). Johnson et al. (2000) found in a longitudinal study that adolescents who smoked heavily (20 cigarettes per day) were at an increased risk not only for panic disorder but also for agoraphobia and generalized anxiety disorder. However, the obsessive-compulsive and social phobia disorders were not affected by

Table 8.2

**Risk and Protective Factors for the Onset
of Anxiety Disorders in Children**

Risks	Protections
Biological	
Behavioral inhibition	
Temperamental sensitivity toward negativity	
Anxiety sensitivity	
Psychological	
Anxious-resistant attachment[a]	Problem-focused rather than emotion-focused or avoidant coping strategies
History of major depression	
Separation anxiety disorder	
Family	
Parental anxiety due to inherited child temperament and parenting characteristics	Social support
Traumatic, negative, and stressful life events	

Source: Unless otherwise noted, the information is drawn from Donovan & Spence (2000).
[a]Warren et al. (1997).

smoking. A hypothesis to account for smoking as a risk factor is that carbon monoxide might activate a false alarm for suffocation, and some people overreact to suffocation signals (Breslau & Klein, 1999).

Family Factors

Learning experiences shape anxious behavior (Hagopian & Ollendick, 1997). Through the processes of classical operant and vicarious conditioning, people may learn that certain stimuli are associated with aversive consequences. Fearful and avoidant behaviors may result in certain consequences that are sometimes reinforcing. For instance, if a person once raised a hand to speak in class and was ridiculed, this experience might become conditioned to all classroom experiences. The person might avoid anxiety by never raising a hand in classrooms.

Anxious attachment patterns are a risk factor for anxiety disorders. Anxious attachment is characterized by an infant's becoming distressed and frantically seeking comfort from the attachment figure through clinging and crying when faced with something that the child fears, such as contact with a stranger (Ainsworth, Blehar, Waters, & Wall, 1978). The subsequent contact with the caregiver, however, does not seem to help the child experience a sense of security or reduce the anxiety. In this attachment pattern, the parent is often withdrawn or uninvolved. In a study that tracked children from infancy to adolescence, youths with an anxious attachment pattern in infancy were more likely to suffer from an anxiety disorder as teenagers than those who were securely attached or showed avoidant attachment (Warren, Huston, Egeland, & Sroufe, 1997).

A number of other interpersonal patterns are seen in families of children with anxiety disorders, such as parental overcontrol, overprotection, and criticism (Donovan & Spence, 2002). In addition to their increased risk from genetically based factors, children of anxious parents may be more likely to observe anxious behavior in their parents and to have fearful behavior reinforced by their parents (Hagopian & Ollendick, 1997).

Risk and Protective Factors for Course

Anxiety disorders are common, but because most cases go untreated, many people experience pervasive and lasting impairments (Fonagy, Target, Cottrell, Phillips, & Kurtz, 2002). The specific disorders have different prognoses, but most moderate to severe cases are not likely to remit spontaneously. Panic disorders, for example, tend to run a chronic course with intermittent episodes of attacks; complete remission is rare (Gorman et al., 2002). The course of generalized anxiety disorder is also said to be chronic though fluctuating, and it is often worse during periods of stress (APA, 2000). In studies of youth with obsessive-compulsive disorder, the disorder is persistent both in clinics and in the community populations (King et al., 1998). When anxiety disorders do remit, other disorders sometimes take their place—most often other anxiety disorders or depressive symptoms (Fonagy et al., 2002).

Little has been identified about factors that predict the course of anxiety disorders. One 5-year longitudinal study of 711 people with panic disorder found that while panic severity was not predictive of recovery, moderate to severe agoraphobia posed a risk (Warshaw, Massion, Shea, Allsworth, & Keller, 1997). The researchers also reported that socioeconomic status was a risk for poor outcome. This may be due to the reduced access to treatment for people with lower incomes. On the other hand, lower socioeconomic status may be a result of a more severe illness in which educational and occupational functioning is hampered.

For children, degree of impairment, developmental level, and degree of parental anxiety or psychopathology may affect the outcome of the intervention (Bernstein & Shaw, 1997). For youth with OCD, predictors of a positive response to cognitive-behavioral intervention include motivation to cooperate with treatment, the presence of overt compulsions (such as hand washing) rather than certain thoughts that have to be performed, the ability to monitor and report symptoms, and lack of comorbid disorders. Predictors of negative or partial response to intervention include complicating comorbid factors, family conflict, developmental factors (such as young age, mental retardation, or a pervasive developmental disorder), and showing obsessions rather than compulsions (King et al., 1998). Children from middle- to upper-class families are more likely to receive treatment (Fonagy et al., 2002).

Intervention for the Anxiety Disorders

The health care system is extensively taxed by people with anxiety disorders, even though only 25% obtain treatment (Danton & Antonuccio, 1997). The majority who do receive treatment are seen in the general health system rather than the mental health system, and this means that medication is more often used than psychosocial treatment. Few individuals seeking help receive the empirically validated exposure treatment described later; instead, they receive supportive or psychodynamic therapy or medication (Danton & Antonuccio, 1997). Children often receive psychodynamic therapy or family therapy (Bernstein & Shaw, 1997). No studies have so far examined the effectiveness of family therapy for childhood anxiety disorders, other than cognitive-behavioral therapy delivered in a family format (Fonagy et al., 2002). When compared with individual child cognitive-behavioral therapy, the family condition produced positive changes in the short term but no differences at follow-up, according to a review by Velting et al. (2004).

Psychodynamic therapies are frequently used for people with panic disorder (Gorman et al., 2002). Psychodynamic therapies encompass a range of techniques and theories, not usually directed specifically for treating anxiety disorders. Common elements include achieving an understanding of origins, meanings, and functions of the anxiety; integrating understanding into a larger framework of personality; and developing more adaptive means to achieve the functions served by the symptoms (Gorman et al., 2002). Despite its popularity for people with anxiety disorders, more research is needed to assess the effectiveness of psychodynamic treatment. One study compared emotion-focused treatment (a brief form of supportive psychotherapy) with cognitive-behavioral therapy, imipramine (a tricyclic antidepressant), and a pill placebo (Shear, Houck, Greeno, & Masters, 2001).

The emotion-focused treatment was less effective than cognitive-behavioral therapy and imipramine and equivalent to the pill placebo.

A meta-analysis of treatments for anxiety disorders found that exposure treatment, SSRIs, and combined exposure and medication were equally effective (Kobak, Greist, Jefferson, Katzelnick, & Henk, 1998). Social workers can inform clients of the empirically validated treatments available and the advantages and disadvantages of psychosocial and medication interventions (Tables 8.3 and 8.4). According to Gorman et al.'s (2002) review, more people with panic disorders are comfortable with psychosocial treatment than with drug intervention.

As some general guidelines for specific populations, for older adults, few clinical trials have documented the effectiveness of standard medications or psychosocial treatments (Gorman et al., 2002). If medication is used, the required dose is generally lower than that for younger people, and any increases should be more gradual than with younger adults.

For children, with the exception of OCD, drug therapy should not be used as the sole intervention but as an adjunct to behavioral or psychosocial interventions (Bernstein & Shaw, 1997). For children with OCD, two treatment modalities—cognitive-behavioral therapy and SSRIs—have been shown empirically to have efficacy for the core symptoms (King et al., 1998). Table 8.5 introduces some of the considerations in deciding whether psychotherapy or medication should be the initial approach for children with OCD.

Cognitive-Behavioral Interventions

The purpose of cognitive-behavioral treatment is to adjust the hyperventilation response, the conditioned reactions to physical cues, the fear and

Table 8.3	
Advantages and Disadvantages for Psychosocial Treatment for Adults	
Advantages	Disadvantages
Lacks adverse side effects of medications	Limited availability of exposure (the empirically validated intervention)
No danger of developing physiological dependency	Facing fear is often difficult
	Requires discipline, time, and effort in terms of participation, self-monitoring, and homework completion[a]

[a]10–30% of clients are unable or unwilling to complete the requirements.

Source: Gorman et. al. (2002).

Table 8.4

**Advantages and Disadvantages of Medication
as Treatment for Anxiety Disorders**

Advantages	Disadvantages
Ready availability	Side effects
Less effort required of client	May experience overstimulation[a]
Rapid onset (especially for benzodiazepines)	

[a]In which case, it may be necessary to begin with small dosages and increase gradually.

Source: Gorman et. al. (2002).

avoidance behaviors, and the cognitive aspects of the client's panic attacks and anxiety (Gorman et al., 2002). Twelve-session protocols have been described with both individual and group treatments and are said to be equally effective (Gorman et al., 2002). The treatment of social phobia in adults, however, is recommended in a group format (Hope & Heimberg, 1993).

Although cognitive-behavioral therapy generally involves a "package" of several techniques, whether all are necessary for a positive outcome is unknown (Gorman et al., 2002). The following components complete the package of cognitive-behavioral techniques:

Psychoeducation provides information to clients and perhaps significant others about anxiety, its self-perpetuating nature, how it can be controlled, and available treatments.

Monitoring anxiety symptoms includes being alert to their frequency, duration, and triggers (internal stimuli such as emotions or external stimuli such as substances and particular contexts).

Cognitive restructuring focuses on correcting the client's misappraisal of bodily sensations as threatening. Specific to panic disorders, cues are generally *interoceptive*; that is, people react with alarm to sensations that take place within the body. For example, becoming overly warm may lead a person to think, "I can't breathe. It's too hot. I'm going to pass out" and so on, working himself or herself into an anxiety state. For children, parents are taught to coach their children in questioning the evidence for their thoughts and arriving at coping solutions, rather than to provide excessive reassurance and answers to their children's anxious thoughts (Velting et al., 2004).

Breathing retraining helps clients by distracting them from anxiety symptoms and providing a sense of control over them.

Table 8.5

Deciding on Treatment for OCD in children

Approach	Advantages	Disadvantages
CBT	Durability, less relapse	Time, effort, expense, or anxiety level
	Avoids side effects of medication	Limited availability of exposure/response-prevention treatment
	Favored initial treatment, especially in milder cases and without significant comorbidity	May not be appropriate when a child lacks the cognitive or emotional maturity
	Although family and social problems are not causative for OCD, improving family functioning and the child's functioning at home and school can be beneficial.	May not be appropriate when family lacks support for treatment.
Medication		Relapse is common when person stops taking meds.
		Unclear how long meds should be continued.
		Side effects.

Progressive muscle relaxation is a skill with which the client learns to reduce tension in anxiety-provoking situations by alternately tightening and relaxing certain muscle groups.

Problem solving is a step-by-step approach for generating a variety of practical solutions to life challenges; it is recommended for children and for those with generalized anxiety disorder (Velting et al., 2004).

Exposure is a process in which the client has to face the feared object until the anxiety dissipates. Exposure can take many forms, such as imaginal (e.g., through guided imagery), symbolic (e.g., through the use of pictures or props), simulated (e.g., through role playing), interoceptive (the client is trained to mimic bodily reactions that arouse panic, such as exercise to speed up the heart rate or spinning in a chair to induce dizziness, and develop tolerance to them), and in vivo (contact with the real situation or stimulus). The in vivo method is preferred and the ultimate goal of any exposure program (Velting et al., 2004).

Exposure is typically conducted in a graduated fashion. The practitioner helps the client construct a hierarchy of feared situations from least to worst. The most typical procedure is to work through the items in that order, conquering smaller fears before going on to tackle bigger ones.

Modeling is also used in exposure treatment. In live modeling, the child directly observes another child interacting with the feared stimulus, whereas participant modeling has the model guide the child to engage in successively increased interaction with the feared stimulus.

For OCD, cognitive-behavioral intervention features exposure and *response prevention*, in which the client refrains from avoiding the stimulus or engaging in the ritualistic behavior (King et al., 1998). For example, if a person has an obsession about germs, he is blocked from avoiding what is "germy" or from washing his hands. To help the individual cope during this period, anxiety management skills, such as relaxation training, breathing-control training, and cognitive training, are taught. In contrast to the extensive adult literature, the empirical evidence supporting the approach for children calls for replication and extension.

A support person is usually enlisted to help the client because the exposure and response prevention processes are so difficult to complete otherwise. Treatment is intensive in nature (4–5 hours per day) with a minimum of three sessions per week (Abramowitz, Bridigi, & Roche, 2001; Riggs & Foa, 1993).

According to the Velting et al. (2004) review, the most widely disseminated cognitive-behavioral therapy protocol for childhood anxiety is Philip Kendall's Coping Cat program (Kendall, Kane, Howard, & Siqueland, 1990). This protocol is appropriate for 7- to 16-year-old youths with generalized anxiety disorder, social phobia, or separation anxiety disorder. Individual and group treatment manuals are available, with adaptations for greater involvement of family members.

In one study of the program, 86 participants were evaluated with a 7.4-year follow-up after 16 weeks of intervention (Kendall, Safford, Flannery-Schroeder, & Webb, 2004). The researchers found that the favorable gains measured at posttest were maintained over long-term follow-up. Youths who were successfully treated also showed reduced substance use compared with those who did not receive the treatment.

Intervention manuals have also been developed for school refusal (Kearney & Albano, 2000a, 2000b), OCD (March & Mulle, 1998), phobias, separation anxiety disorder, generalized anxiety disorder (Silverman & Kurtines, 1996), and social phobia in children (Beidel & Turner, 1998; Silverman & Kurtines, 1996) and adolescents (Albano, 1995; Hayward et al., 2000). In all such programs, parental involvement is indicated in the following circumstances (Velting et al., 2004):

- The youth's functioning is seriously compromised by anxiety or comorbidity.
- The child is young in age or developmental level.
- The parents or other family members engage in behavior that accommodates the anxiety.
- A parent has an anxiety disorder or another psychiatric disorder (if so, concurrent individual therapy for the parent is recommended).
- For OCD, there is extensive family involvement in rituals, or there are problems in the family that interfere with the child's individual treatment (King et al., 1998).

Parent–child interventions may include helping parents to encourage the child to face new situations rather than withdraw, to refrain from excessive criticism and intrusiveness, to respond more directly to the child's needs, and to encourage the child to engage in activities despite anxiety. Infant–parent psychotherapy is recommended in cases of impaired attachment (Bernstein & Shaw, 1997). On the other hand, if a teenager presents for treatment but has generally good functioning and no comorbid disorder, less parental involvement is indicated. This helps the teen to address the developmental task of assuming self-responsibility.

For adults, the inclusion of the spouse or significant other in the treatment of agoraphobia may be necessary. In this couples approach, the support person is included in psychoeducation sessions and is given a role as an "assistant" in the client's exposure exercises (Gorman et al., 2002).

Medications

Though several types of antianxiety medication are currently available, the most frequently prescribed for adults are the benzodiazepines (Leonard, 2003). Speculated to have evolved as fear regulators, natural benzodiazepine chemicals may exist in the brain, activated by the GABA neurotransmitter. The benzodiazepine medications are believed to achieve their therapeutic effect by causing the GABA neurotransmitter to bind more completely with its receptor site. GABA receptors in various regions of the brain regulate the antianxiety as well as the sedative and anticonvulsant effects of the benzodiazepines. As a general rule, the benzodiazepines reduce anxiety in lower doses and are sedating in higher doses.

Benzodiazepines are usually taken orally. Quickly absorbed into the gastrointestinal tract, they act rapidly, in many cases within 30 minutes (Julien, 2001). They do not present a risk for overdose. An important characteristic of the benzodiazepines, however, is that with continuous use they can be physically addictive at some dosages. Long-term use (perhaps no more than 2 weeks) can cause production of the body's natural benzodi-azepine compounds to shut down. If the drug is abruptly withdrawn, no natural production of those substances will occur for some time. Clients must be taken off these medications gradually to prevent the effects of physical withdrawal. For these reasons, the benzodiazepines are generally designed for comparatively short-term use, even though physicians some-times prescribe them for up to several years. Benzodiazepines may be used preferentially in situations where rapid symptom control is critical (e.g., the client is about to quit school, lose a job, or require hospitalization) (Gorman et al., 2002). Long-term benzodiazepine use is especially contraindicated for clients with a history of a substance use disorder because of their higher potential for addiction.

Another widely used antianxiety medication is buspirone (Buspar), a drug that enhances the activity of serotonin receptors (Spiegel, 2003). Al-though its impact on anxiety is not yet well understood, serotonin in the hippocampus and limbic areas is believed to reduce anxiety symptoms. To be effective, buspirone must be taken regularly, unlike the benzodiazepines, and it requires several weeks to take effect. Because buspirone is not po-tentially addictive, clients who have taken benzodiazepines for an extended time are often gradually changed over to this medication. Buspirone does have limitations, however. Some recent studies have shown it to be less effective than the benzodiazepines, and specifically less effective for panic disorder (Spiegel, 2003).

An interesting development over the past 10 years is the increased use of medications initially developed as antidepressants to treat anxiety dis-orders. The two classes of these medications used most often for this pur-pose are the tricyclics (TCAs) and the SSRIs. So named because of their chemical structure, the TCAs were the most commonly prescribed antide-pressants through the 1980s. They are believed to work by blocking the reuptake of norepinephrine, serotonin, and, to a lesser extent, dopamine. However, their impact on other areas of the autonomic and central nervous systems may produce discomforting adverse effects, such as dry mouth, constipation, and blurred vision. Fortunately, tolerance develops to some of the adverse effects.

Since the 1990s, SSRIs have been increasingly used for the treatment of anxiety. In a meta-analysis of 43 studies, there were no differences between SSRIs and TCAs on any of the effect sizes, indicating that both groups of antidepressants are equally effective for reducing symptoms of panic, ag-oraphobic avoidance, depression, and general anxiety (Bakker, van Balkom, & Spinhoven, 2002). Also, the percentage of clients free of panic attacks at posttest did not differ. The number of dropouts, however, was significantly lower in the clients treated with SSRIs (18%) than with the TCAs group

(31%). This suggests that SSRIs and TCAs are equal in efficacy for treating panic disorder, but SSRIs are tolerated better with regard to adverse effects.

The physician's selection of a particular medication is guided by several factors, including the client's past history with medications and, if applicable, the comorbidity pattern (Bernstein & Shaw, 1997). For example, a TCA may be prescribed if comorbid enuresis or ADHD is present, whereas an SSRI may be selected if comorbid obsessive-compulsive disorder is present. The side effects profile also guides the physician's choice of medication.

For obsessive-compulsive disorder, clomipramine (Anafranil) is the most extensively studied SSRI medication, and the evidence shows that clomipramine is more effective than the other SSRIs (Kobak et al., 1998). The FDA has approved clomipramine for children ages 10 and up. Clomipramine affects the transmission of both serotonin *and* norepinephrine, whereas most of the other SSRIs tested are mainly selective for serotonin only. This suggests that more than one neurotransmitter system is involved in the biology of OCD.

Dosages of clomipramine must be carefully monitored because of the risk of toxicity, including seizures and cardiac changes that may produce tachycardia. In fact, the adverse effects for clomipramine make the medication disadvantageous. For severe cases, the additional benefit of the medication might outweigh these disadvantages (Kobak et al., 1998). For obsessive-compulsive disorder, other medications have also been approved, including sertraline (Zoloft) (age 6 and older), paroxetine (Paxil) (age 6 and older), and fluvoxamine (Luvox) (age 10 and older).

Several other classes of medications are used to control anxiety, including the beta-blockers, so named because they compete with norepinephrine at certain receptor sites in the brain and peripheral nervous system, sites that regulate cardiac and muscular functions (Stahl, 2000). These medications effectively treat anticipatory anxiety; that is, they lower anxiety by reducing its symptoms of rapid heartbeat, muscle tension, and dry mouth. Because the client does not experience these physiological indicators, his or her subjective experience of anxiety is diminished. The limited number of controlled trials that have been conducted with beta-blockers in panic disorder have provided mixed results, however (Gorman et al., 2002).

Finally, the antihistamines, such as Benadryl, are occasionally used as antianxiety agents (Stahl, 2000). These drugs block histamine receptors associated with anxiety and agitation. Rapidly absorbed, antihistamines maintain a therapeutic effect for at least 24 hours. These drugs tend to sedate the consumer, however, and work effectively as antianxiety agents for only a few months. Though not addictive, they do not alleviate anxiety as effectively as the benzodiazepine drugs.

If a medication has been used effectively, a trial of discontinuation may be attempted after 12 to 18 months. Many clients partially or fully relapse when medication is discontinued and may benefit from prolonged periods of drug treatment. Although data on the percentage of clients who remain well after medication discontinuation are widely divergent, evidence suggests that it is between 30 and 45% (Gorman et al., 2002). Clients who show no improvement within 6 to 8 weeks with a particular medication should be reevaluated with regard to diagnosis, the need for a different treatment, or the need for a combined drug and psychosocial treatment approach.

Bob Case Study

Bob is a single 37-year-old Caucasian male who has come to a social worker employed at a mental health outpatient clinic. Bob looks nervous and is shaking when he enters the social worker's office. When he begins speaking, he blushes. He shows a lack of personal hygiene—his hair is unwashed and looks as if it has been slept on. He smells of unwashed skin, he is unshaven, and his clothes don't match and appear worn.

Bob begins by saying that he gets nervous in public. As he talks to the social worker, he begins to sweat and sounds breathless. His face is very red, and the social worker reassures him to take his time and that he's doing fine.

Bob reveals that he lives by himself in a small, rundown trailer and that his only income is his disability benefits. He reports that his parents live in the area but he does not speak with them much. He also has two siblings and feels that he is the "black sheep of the family." He explains that his siblings are successful in their careers and are married with their own children. Bob often ridicules himself, making comments such as "I can't do anything right" and "I'm not capable."

Bob talks about attending every Agoraphobics Building Independent Lives (ABIL) support group in the local area for the last 10 years. ABIL is a national network for anxiety disorders and promotes the use of support groups. Bob occasionally writes articles and poetry for the organization's newsletter. Despite the number of groups he attends, Bob worries for days before he plans to go to a meeting. As he drives to a session, his heart beats rapidly, he gets dizzy and nauseous, and he reports that he sometimes feels like "I'm dying." Bob's biggest fear centers around "embarrassment" and his perception of what others will think of him if he displays such physiological reactions in public. The support group is the only socializing Bob does, aside from occasional visits to his siblings' families, and he reports gaining some comfort from attendance.

He relates that when he goes grocery shopping or to the bank to cash his checks, he often runs out of the place because of anxiety and usually feels better when he gets back into his car. He tries to fight these feelings by going to the mall or the movie rental store, but he just can't seem to do it. He denies experiencing any of these anxiety symptoms at home.

Bob says that he has been in and out of therapy since he was a teenager and had frequent thoughts of suicide as an adolescent. Bob does not appear to be suicidal at the present time and has not reported having such feelings since adolescence. His last bout of therapy, which he attended for 6 years, ended 4 years ago. That therapist had suggested his attending the support groups. When he was asked what kind of therapy he had received, Bob couldn't identify the particular approach but described talking a lot about his childhood and receiving support for his feelings. He said he finally stopped because he got from the groups what he was receiving from the therapist. However, he realizes his life is still very limited and wants to conquer his fears. Throughout the years, he has also tried an array of "alternative therapies," including hypnosis, which he states have also been ineffective.

Bob has never taken medication for his anxiety disorder because he sees his problem as strictly environmental. He will not give a concrete answer as to why he attributes his problems to environmental causes; however, he often talks about reading self-help books that explain the disorder in this manner.

Bob is reluctant to talk about his past because "that's all the other therapist would talk about" but refers to it as abusive. When asked, he said that none of his other relatives, to his knowledge, has an anxiety disorder. He said that there is, however, substance abuse in his family.

He said there was not a single event that caused the attacks; its onset seemed insidious. He has now displayed these symptoms for 13 years.

Bob reports himself to be physically healthy and does not smoke, drink, or use narcotics. He enjoys hiking and sometimes camps alone.

Multiaxial Diagnosis

Axis I: 300.23 Social Phobia, Generalized
Axis II: 301.82 Avoidant Personality Disorder (Provisional)
Axis III: V71.09 None
Axis IV: Problems related to the social environment (Bob is isolated and has not formed intimate relationships because of his lack of social interaction);
Occupational problems (Bob has been unemployed for years);
Economic problems (Bob lives on a small supplemental income in a low socioeconomic neighborhood)
GAF: 45

Justification for the Axis I diagnosis of social phobia was based upon his meeting full criteria for the disorder, including

> Criterion A: Bob exhibits persistent fear in social situations, demonstrated by blushing, trembling, lack of eye contact, and reports of nausea, dizziness, and feeling like he will die.
>
> Criterion B: Exposure to the feared social situation provokes anxiety, which sometimes takes the form of a panic attack.
>
> Criterion C: Bob recognizes that the fear is excessive and unreasonable.
>
> Criterion D. Bob forces himself to attend support groups but does so with intense anxiety, and he avoids other social contact.
>
> Criterion E. Bob's anxiety interferes significantly with a normal routine (e.g., visiting the grocery store), occupational functioning (he is unable to work), and his social activities and relationships.
>
> Criterion F has to do with youth presentation and therefore is not applicable to this case.
>
> Criterion G: Bob's anxiety is not due to the effects of a substance, a medical condition, or another mental disorder. To rule out panic disorder, Bob reports that he rarely has the unexpected panic attacks that are frequently associated with a diagnosis of panic disorder without agoraphobia. His chief fear is in the social realm; he is deathly afraid of embarrassing or humiliating himself.

The specifier "generalized" has been included because Bob's fears include most social situations.

The *DSM-IV-TR* also suggests consideration of an additional diagnosis of avoidant personality disorder, an Axis II disorder, for individuals with generalized social phobia. Bob has a pervasive pattern, beginning 13 years before, of social inhibition, feelings of inadequacy, and hypersensitivity. He avoids occupational activities because they involve interacting with people (e.g., interviewing, being supervised, and being evaluated). He is unwilling to get involved with people and almost sure that he will not be liked. He has no intimate relationships and is preoccupied with being criticized or rejected in social situations. Bob views himself as socially inept, personally unappealing, and inferior to others, and he is reluctant to take risks or to engage in new activities because they may prove to be embarrassing. Although only four of seven criteria are necessary for the diagnosis, Bob meets all seven. Because the social worker has only had one meeting with Bob, she is making the Axis II provisional at this time.

Bob suffers from certain psychosocial stressors, most of which are consequences of his disorder, as previously described. The social worker assigned Bob a GAF of 45 because Bob suffers such serious impairment in social functioning (the inability to go anywhere there are people) and occupational functioning (inability to hold a job for 13 years).

Risk and Protective Factors Assessment

For onset, Bob's risk factors at the psychological level include escape-avoidance coping strategies and at the family level, stressful life events—abuse as a child. For recovery, Bob's low socioeconomic status may prove a risk; however, he has started to attend a clinic that takes Medicaid for services. On the positive side, Bob's physical health is good, and he has never smoked. He exercises by hiking and mountain climbing, which has been shown to increase mood and decrease anxiety. He is intelligent (reading books) and creative and often writes poetry for an organization's newsletter. These strengths are helping Bob to cope on a daily basis.

Treatment Plan

Although Bob's attendance at support groups is a source of comfort for him, a concern is that almost his entire social life now revolves around his illness. He has also not been able to maintain the social contacts he makes in the groups, even though he has been coming to them for 10 years.

The social worker provides Bob with some education about social phobia, most of which he said was already familiar. She explains exposure therapy as the empirically validated approach. His anxiety spikes in reaction to the idea of facing various public situations. The social worker, in response, reassures him that they will work slowly and in a graduated fashion. She says that she will also teach him skills, such as breathing retraining, progressive muscle relaxation, visualization, cognitive restructuring, and self-talk, so that he is able to relax and distract himself during exposure episodes. Finally, she says that while in vivo exposure will be the ultimate goal, they can begin initially with imaginal exposure, in which he simply thinks about the feared situations.

The social worker will also address Bob's social skills, starting with the basics of physical presentation, saying "hello," and maintaining eye contact. Frequent modeling and rehearsal will take place as he learns these skills.

Medication may be helpful for Bob because he has suffered such severe impairment for such a long duration. Over time, the social worker would work to elicit Bob's perceptions of the advantages and disadvantages of using medication (see Table 8.3) to allow him to make an informed decision. Although Bob reports his physical health as optimal, the social worker will also refer him for a physical examination, as he has not had one in years. If there is any physical basis to his anxiety, this needs to be assessed.

Appendix. Anxiety Measures

This chapter will depart from the others in its presentation of measures. The reason is that Martin Antony, PhD, from the Anxiety Treatment and Research Centre, St. Joseph's Hospital Department of Psychiatry and Behavioural Neurosciences, McMaster University, has compiled a comprehensive list of measures of anxiety. These are provided for both children and adults and are further subdivided into type of anxiety disorder. With Dr. Antony's permission, they have been included in the reference list. For more detailed information on these instruments, the reader is urged to consult Antony, M. M., Orsillo, S. M., & Roemer, L. (Eds.). (2002). *Practitioner's guide to empirically-based measures of anxiety*. New York: Kluwer Academic/ Plenum.

References

Abramowitz, J. S., Bridigi, B. D., & Roche, K. R. (2001). Cognitive behavioral therapy for obsessive compulsive disorder: A review of the treatment literature. *Research on Social Work Practice, 11*(3), 357–372.

Ainsworth, M. D., Blehar, M. C., Waters, E., & Wall, S. (1978). *Patterns of attachment: A psychological study of the strange situation*. Hillsdale, NJ: Erlbaum.

Albano, A. M. (1995). Treatment of social anxiety in adolescents. *Cognitive and Behavioral Practice, 2*, 271–298.

American Psychiatric Association. (2000). *Diagnostic and statistical manual of mental disorders* (4th ed., text rev.). Washington, DC: Author.

Bakker, A., van Balkom, A., & Spinhoven, P. (2002). SSRIs vs. TCAs in the treatment of panic disorder: A meta-analysis. *Acta Psychiatrica Scandinavica, 106*(3), 163–167.

Bandelow, B., Spaeth, C., Tichauer, A., Broocks, A., Hajak, G., & Ruther, E. (2002). Early traumatic life events, parental attitudes, family history, and birth risk factors in patients with panic disorder. *Comprehensive Psychiatry, 43*, 269–278.

Beidel, D., & Turner, S. (1998). *Shy children, phobic adults: Nature and treatment of social phobia*. Washington, DC: American Psychological Association.

Bernstein, G., & Shaw, K. (1997). Practice parameters for the assessment and treatment of children and adolescents with anxiety disorders. *Journal of the American Academy of Child and Adolescent Psychiatry, 36*(Suppl. 10), 69S–84S.

Breslau, N., & Klein, D. (1999). Smoking and panic attacks: An epidemiologic investigation. *Archives of General Psychiatry, 56*, 1141–1147.

Campbell, R. J. (1996). *Psychiatric dictionary* (7th ed.). New York: Oxford University Press.

Cronk, N., Slutske, W., Madden, P., Bucholz, K., & Heath, A. (2004). Risk for separation anxiety disorder among girls: Paternal absence, socioeconomic disadvantage, and genetic vulnerability. *Journal of Abnormal Psychology, 113*, 237–247.

Danton, W., & Antonuccio, D. (1997). A focused empirical analysis of treatments for panic and anxiety. In S. Fisher & R. Greenberg (Eds.), *From placebo to panacea: Putting psychiatric drugs to the test* (pp. 229–280). New York: Wiley.

Donovan, C., & Spence, S. (2000). Prevention of childhood anxiety disorders. *Clinical Psychology Review, 20*, 509–531.

Fonagy, P., Target, M., Cottrell, D., Phillips, J., & Kurtz, Z. (2002). *What works for whom? A critical review of treatments for children and adolescents*. New York: Guilford.

Goodwin, R., Fergusson, D., & Horwood, L. J. (2004). Association between anxiety disorders and substance use disorders among young persons: Results of a 21-year longitudinal study. *Journal of Psychiatric Research, 38*, 295–304.

Gorman, J., Shear, K., Cowley, D., Cross, C. D., March, J., Roth, W., et al. (2002). Practice guideline for the treatment of patients with panic disorder. In *American Psychiatric Association practice guidelines for the treatment of psychiatric disorders. Compendium 2002* (pp. 635–696). Washington, DC: American Psychiatric Association.

Hagopian, L., & Ollendick, T. (1997). Anxiety disorders. In R. Ammerman & M. Hersen (Eds.), *Handbook of prevention and treatment with children and adolescents: Intervention in the real world context* (pp. 431–454). New York: Wiley.

Hayward, C., Varady, S., Albano, A. M., Thieneman, M., Henderson, L., & Schatzberg, A. F. (2000). Cognitive behavioral group therapy for female socially phobic adolescents: Results of a pilot study. *Journal of the American Academy of Child and Adolescent Psychiatry, 39*, 721–726.

Hayward, C., Wilson, K. A. Lagle, K., Killen, J. D., & Taylor, C. B. (2004). Parent-reported predictors of adolescent panic attacks. *Journal of the American Academy of Child and Adolescent Psychiatry, 43*, 613–620.

Hettema, J. M., Neale, M. C., & Kendler, K. S. (2001). A review and meta-analysis of the genetic epidemiology of anxiety disorders. *American Journal of Psychiatry, 1574*, 1568–1578.

Hino, T., Takeuchi, T., & Yamanouchi, N. (2002). A 1-year follow-up study of coping in patients with panic disorder. *Comprehensive Psychiatry, 43*, 279–284.

Hope, D., & Heimberg, R. (1993). Social phobia and social anxiety. In D. Barlow (Ed.), *Clinical handbook of psychological disorders: A step-by-step treatment manual* (pp. 99–136). New York: Guilford.

Isensee, B., Wittchen, H. U., Stein, M., Hofler, M., & Lieb, R. (2003). Smoking increases the risk of panic: Findings from a prospective community study. *Archives of General Psychiatry, 60*, 692–700.

Johnson, J., Cohen, P., Pine, D., Klein, D., Kasen, S., & Brook, J. (2000). Association between cigarette smoking and anxiety disorders during adolescence and early adulthood. *Journal of the American Medical Association, 284*, 2348–2351.

Julien, R. M. (2001). *A primer of drug action: A concise, nontechnical guide to the actions, uses, and side effects of psychoactive drugs* (9th ed.). New York: W. H. Freeman.

Kearney, C. A., & Albano, A. M. (2000a). *When children refuse school: A cognitive behavioral therapy approach. Parent workbook.* New York: Psychological Corporation.

Kearney, C. A., & Albano, A. M. (2000b). *When children refuse school: A cognitive behavioral therapy approach. Therapist's manual.* New York: Psychological Corporation.

Kendall, P., Kane, M., Howard, B., & Siqueland, L. (1990). *Cognitive-behavioral treatment of anxious children: Treatment manual.* (Available from P. C. Kendall, Department of Psychology, Temple University, Philadelphia, PA 19122.)

Kendall, P., Safford, S., Flannery-Schroeder, E., & Webb, A. (2004). Child anxiety treatment: Outcomes in adolescence and impact on substance use and depression at 7.4 year follow-up. *Journal of Consulting and Clinical Psychology, 72,* 276–287.

Kessler, R., Berglund, P., Demler, O., Jin, R., & Walters, E. (2005). Lifetime prevalence and age-of-onset distributions of DSM-IV disorders in the National Comorbidity survey replication. *Archives of General Psychiatry, 62,* 593–602.

Kessler, R., Chiu, W. T., Demler, O., & Walters, E. (2005). Prevalence, severity, and comorbidity of 12-month DSM-IV disorders in the National Comorbidity survey replication. *Archives of General Psychiatry, 62,* 617–627.

King, R., Leonard, H., & March, J. (1998). Practice parameters for the assessment and treatment of children and adolescents with obsessive-compulsive disorder. *Journal of the American Academy of Child & Adolescent Psychiatry, 37* (Suppl. 10), 27S–45S.

Kobak, K. A., Greist, J. H., Jefferson, J. W., Katzelnick, D. J., & Henk, H. J. (1998). Behavioral versus pharmacological treatments of obsessive compulsive disorder: A meta-analysis. *Psychopharmacology, 136,* 211–214.

Kushner, M., Sher, K., & Erickson, D. (1999). Prospective analysis of the relation between *DSM-III* anxiety disorders and alcohol use disorders. *American Journal of Psychiatry, 156,* 723–732.

Leonard, B. E. (2003). *Fundamentals of psychopharmacology.* New York: Martin Duwitz.

March, J. S., & Mulle, K. (1998). *OCD in children and adolescents: A cognitive behavioral therapy manual.* New York: Guilford.

Marks, I. M. (1987). *Fears, phobias, and rituals: Panic, anxiety, and their disorders.* New York: Oxford University Press.

Riggs, D., & Foa, E. (1993). Obsessive compulsive disorder. In D. Barlow (Ed.), *Clinical handbook of psychological disorders: A step-by-step treatment manual* (pp. 189–239). New York: Guilford.

Shear, M. K., Houck, P., Greeno, C., & Masters, S. (2001). Emotion-focused psychotherapy for patients with panic disorder. *American Journal of Psychiatry, 158,* 1993–1998.

Silverman, W. K., & Kurtines, W. M. (1996). *Anxiety and phobic disorders: A pragmatic approach.* New York: Plenum.

Spiegel, R. (2003). *Psychopharmacology: An introduction.* Hoboken, NJ: Wiley.

Stahl, S. M. (2000). *Essential psychopharmacology: Neuroscientific basis and practical applications* (2nd ed.). New York: Cambridge University Press.

Steketee, G., Van Noppen, B., Cohen, I., & Clary, L. (1998). Anxiety disorders. In J.

Williams & K. Ell (Eds.), *Advances in mental health research: Implications for practice* (pp. 118–156). Washington, DC: NASW.

Velting, O., Setzer, N., & Albano, A. M. (2004). Update on and advances in assessment and cognitive-behavioral treatment of anxiety disorders in children and adolescents. *Professional Psychology: Research and Practice, 35*, 42–54.

Warren, S., Huston, L., Egeland, B., & Sroufe, L. A. (1997). Child and adolescent anxiety disorders and early attachment. *Journal of the American Academy of Child & Adolescent Psychiatry, 36*, 637–644.

Warshaw, M., Massion, A., Shea, T., Allsworth, J., & Keller, M. (1997). Predictors of remission in patients with panic with and without agoraphobia: Prospective 5-year follow-up data. *The Journal of Nervous and Mental Disease, 185*, 517–519.

Zimmermann, P., Wittchen, H.-U., Hofler, M., Pfister, H. Kessler, R. C., & Lieb, R. (2003). Primary anxiety disorders and the development of subsequent alcohol use disorders: A 4-year community study of adolescents and young adults. *Psychological Medicine, 33*, 1211–1222.

Assessment of Anxiety Disorders

Principal citations for each measure are indicated with an asterisk (*).

Assessment of Anxiety Disorders in Children and Adolescents

Self Report Measures
Child Anxiety Sensitivity Index

*Silverman, W. K., Fleisig, W., Rabian, B., & Peterson, R. A. (1991). Childhood anxiety sensitivity index. *Journal of Clinical Child Psychology, 20*, 162–168.

Silverman, W. K., Ginsburg, G. S., & Goedhart, A. W. (1999). Factor structure of the childhood anxiety sensitivity index. *Behaviour Research and Therapy, 37*, 903–917.

Fear Survey Schedule for Children (FSSC-R and FSSC-II)

Burnham, J. J., & Gullone, E. (1997). The Fear Survey Schedule for Children–II: A psychometric investigation with American data. *Behaviour Research and Therapy, 35*, 165–173.

*Gullone, E., & King, N. J. (1992). Psychometric evaluation of a revised fear survey schedule for children and adolescents. *Journal of Child Psychology and Psychiatry, 33*, 987–998.

*Ollendick, T. H. (1983). Reliability and validity of the revised Fear Survey for Children (FSSC-R). *Behaviour Research and Therapy, 21*, 395–399.

Leyton Obsessional Inventory—Child Version

*Berg, C. Z., Whitaker, A., Davies, M, Flament, M., & Rapoport, J. (1988). The survey form of the Leyton Obsessional Inventory—Child Version: Norms from an epidemiological study. *Journal of the American Academy of Child and Adolescent Psychiatry, 27,* 759–763.

Multidimensional Anxiety Scale for Children (MASC)

March, J. S. (1999). Test-retest reliability of the Multidimensional Anxiety Scale for Children (MASC). *Journal of Anxiety Disorders, 13,* 349–358.

*March, J. S., Parker, J. D., Sullivan, K., Stallings, P., & Conners, C. K. (1997). The Multidimensional Anxiety Scale for Children (MASC): Factor structure, reliability, and validity. *Journal of the American Academy of Child and Adolescent Psychiatry, 36* (4), 554–565.

Penn State Worry Questionnaire for Children (PSWQ-C)

*Chorpita, B. F., Tracey, S. A., Brown, T. A., Collica, T. J., & Barlow, D. H. (1997). Assessment of worry in children and adolescents: An adaptation of the Penn State Worry Questionnaire. *Behaviour Research and Therapy, 35,* 569–581.

Revised Children's Manifest Anxiety Scale

*Reynolds, C. R., & Richmond, B. O. (1978). What I think and feel: A revised measure of children's manifest anxiety. *Journal of Abnormal Child Psychology, 6,* 271–280.

Screen for Child Anxiety Related Emotional Disorders (SCARED)

*Muris, P., Merckelbach, H., Mayer, B., van Brakel, A., Thissen, S., Moulaert, V., et al. (1998). The Screen for Child Anxiety Related Emotional Disorders (SCARED) and traditional childhood anxiety measures. *Journal of Behavior Therapy and Experimental Psychiatry, 29,* 327–339.

Social Anxiety Scale for Children–Revised

*La Greca, A. M., & Stone, W. L. (1993). Social Anxiety Scale for Children–Revised: Factor structure and concurrent validity. *Journal of Clinical Child Psychology, 22,* 17–27.

Social Phobia and Anxiety Inventory for Children (SPAI-C)

Beidel, D. C., Turner, S. M., & Fink, C. M. (1996). Assessment of childhood social phobia: Construct, convergent, and discriminative validity of the Social Phobia and Anxiety Inventory for Children (SPAI-C). *Psychological Assessment, 8,* 235–240.

*Beidel, D. C., Turner, S. M., & Morris, T. L. (1995). A new inventory to assess childhood social anxiety and phobia: The Social Phobia and Anxiety Inventory for Children. *Psychological Assessment, 7,* 73–79.

Revised Children's Manifest Anxiety Scale (RCMAS)

Reynolds, C. R., & Richmond, B. O. (1985). *Revised Children's Manifest Anxiety Scale (RCMAS) manual.* Los Angeles: Western Psychological Services.

State-Trait Anxiety Inventory for Children
*Spielberger, C. D. (1973). *Manual for the State-Trait Anxiety Inventory for Children*. Palo Alto, CA: Consulting Psychologists Press.

Assessment of Anxiety Disorders in Adults

Panic Disorder and Agoraphobia: Self-Report Scales
Agoraphobic Cognitions Scale (ACS)
*Hoffart, A., Friis, S., & Martinsen, E. W. (1992). Assessment of fear among agoraphobic patients: The Agoraphobic Cognitions Scale. *Journal of Psychopathology and Behavioral Assessment, 14*, 175–187.

Agoraphobic Self-Statements Questionnaire (ASQ)
*van Hout, W. J. P. J., Emmelkamp, P. M. G., Koopmans, P. C., Bögels, S. M., & Bouman, T. K. (in press). Assessment of self-statements in agoraphobic situations: Construction and psychometric evaluation of the Agoraphobic Self-Statements Questionnaire (ASQ). *Journal of Anxiety Disorders*.

Albany Panic and Phobia Questionnaire
*Rapee, R. M., Craske, M. G., & Barlow, D. H. (1994/1995). Assessment instrument for panic disorder that includes fear of sensation-producing activities: The Albany Panic and Phobia Questionnaire. *Anxiety, 1*, 114–122.

Anxiety Control Questionnaire
*Rapee, R. M., Craske, M. G., Brown, T. A., & Barlow, D. H. (1996). Measurement of perceived control over anxiety-related events. *Behavior Therapy, 27*, 279–293.
Zebb, B. J., & Moore, M. C. (1999). Another look at the psychometric properties of the Anxiety Control Questionnaire. *Behaviour Research and Therapy, 37*, 1091–1103.

Anxiety Sensitivity Index (ASI)
Peterson, R. A., & Heilbronner, R. L. (1987). The Anxiety Sensitivity Index: Construct validity and factor analytic structure. *Journal of Anxiety Disorders, 1*, 117–121.
*Peterson, R. A., & Reiss, S. (1993). *Anxiety Sensitivity Index revised test manual*. Worthington, OH: IDS.
Reiss, S., Peterson, R. A., Gursky, D. M., & McNally, R. J. (1986). Anxiety sensitivity, anxiety frequency and the prediction of fearfulness. *Behaviour Research and Therapy, 24*, 1–8.
Taylor, S., Koch, W. J., & McNally, R. J. (1992). How does anxiety sensitivity vary across the anxiety disorders? *Journal of Anxiety Disorders, 6*, 249–259.
Zinbarg, R. E., Barlow, D. H., & Brown, T. A. (1997). Hierarchical structure and general factor saturation of the Anxiety Sensitivity Index: Evidence and implications. *Psychological Assessment, 9*, 277–284.

Anxiety Sensitivity Index–Expanded Version
*Taylor, S., & Cox, B. J. (1998). An expanded Anxiety Sensitivity Index: Evidence for a hierarchic structure in a clinical sample. *Journal of Anxiety Disorders, 12,* 463–483.

Anxiety Sensitivity Profile
*Taylor, S., & Cox, B. J. (1998). Anxiety sensitivity: Multiple dimensions and hierarchic structure. *Behaviour Research and Therapy, 36,* 37–51.

Body Sensations Interpretation Questionnaire
*Clark, D. M., Salkovskis, P. M., Öst, L.-G., Breitholtz, E., Koehler, K. A., Westling, B. E., et al. (1997). Misinterpretation of body sensations in panic disorder. *Journal of Consulting and Clinical Psychology, 65,* 203–213.

Body Sensations Questionnaire (BSQ) and Agoraphobic Cognitions Questionnaire (ACQ)
Arrindell, W. A. (1993). The fear of fear concept: Evidence in favour of multidimensionality. *Behaviour Research and Therapy, 31,* 139–148.

Arrindell, W. A. (1993). The fear of fear concept: Tability, retest artefact and predictive power. *Behaviour Research and Therapy, 31,* 507–518.

Chambless, D. L., Beck, A. T., Gracely, E. J., & Grisham, J. R. (2000). Relationship of cognitions to fear of somatic symptoms: A test of the cognitive theory of panic. *Depression and Anxiety, 11,* 1–9.

*Chambless, D. L., Caputo, G. C., Bright, P., & Gallagher, R. (1984). Assessment of "fear of fear" in agoraphobics: The Body Sensations Questionnaire and the Agoraphobic Cognitions Questionnaire. *Journal of Consulting and Clinical Psychology, 52,* 1090–1097.

Chambless, D. L., & Gracely, E. J. (1989). Fear of fear and the anxiety disorders. *Cognitive Therapy and Research, 13,* 9–20.

Body Vigilance Scale (BVS)
*Schmidt, N. B., Lerew, D. R., & Trakowski, J. H. (1997). Body vigilance in panic disorder: Evaluating attention to bodily perturbations. *Journal of Consulting and Clinical Psychology, 65,* 214–220.

Mobility Inventory (MI)
Arrindell, W. A., Cox, B. J., van der Ende, J., & Kwee, M. G. T. (1995). Phobic dimensions II: Cross-national confirmation of the multidimensional structure underlying the Mobility Inventory (MI). *Behaviour Research and Therapy, 33,* 711–724.

*Chambless, D. L., Caputo, G. C., Jasin, S. E., Gracely, E. J., & Williams, C. (1985). The Mobility Inventory for agoraphobia. *Behaviour Research and Therapy, 23,* 35–44.

Cox, B. J., Swinson, R. P., Kuch, K., & Reichman, J. T. (1993). Dimensions of agoraphobia assessed by the Mobility Inventory. *Behaviour Research and Therapy, 31,* 427–431.

Kwon, S.-M., Evans, L., & Oei, T. P. S. (1990). Factor structure of the Mobility Inventory for Agoraphobia: A validation study with Australian samples of agoraphobic patients. *Journal of Psychopathology and Behavioral Assessment, 12,* 365–374.

Swinson, R. P., Cox, B. J., Shulman, I. D., Kuch, K., & Woszczyna, C. B. (1992). Medication use and the assessment of agoraphobic avoidance. *Behaviour Research and Therapy, 30,* 563–568.

Panic and Agoraphobia Scale

*Bandelow, B. (1995). Assessing the efficacy of treatments for panic disorder and agoraphobia II: The Panic and Agoraphobia Scale. *International Clinical Psychopharmacology, 10,* 73–81.

Bandelow, B. (1999). *Panic and Agoraphobia Scale (PAS) manual.* Seattle, WA: Hogrefe & Huber.

Bandelow, B., Brunner, E., Broocks, A., Beinroth, D., Hajak, G., Pralle, L., et al. (1998). The use of the Panic and Agoraphobia Scale in a clinical trial. *Psychiatry Research, 77,* 43–49.

*Bandelow, B., Hajak, G., Holzrichter, S., Kunert, H. J., & Rüther, E. (1995). Assessing the efficacy of treatments for panic disorder and agoraphobia I: Methodological problems. *International Clinical Psychopharmacology, 10,* 83–93.

Panic Attack Questionnaire–Revised

*Cox, B. J., Norton, G. R., & Swinson, R. P. (1992). *Panic Attack Questionnaire–Revised.* Toronto, Ontario, Canada: Clarke Institute of Psychiatry.

Norton, G. R., Dorward, J., & Cox, B. J. (1986). Factors associated with panic attacks in nonclinical subjects. *Behavior Therapy, 17,* 239–252.

Norton, G. R., Harrison, B., Hauch, J., & Rhodes, L. (1985). Characteristics of people with infrequent panic attacks. *Journal of Abnormal Psychology, 94,* 216–221.

Whittal, M. L., Suchday, S., & Goetsch, V. L. (1994). The Panic Attack Questionnaire: Factor analysis of symptom profiles and characteristics of undergraduates who panic. *Journal of Anxiety Disorders, 8,* 237–245.

Panic Disorder Severity Scale (PDSS)

*Shear, M. K., Brown, T. A., Barlow, D. H., Money, R., Sholomskas, D. E., Woods, S. W., et al. (1997). Multicenter collaborative panic disorder severity scale. *American Journal of Psychiatry, 154,* 1571–1575

Texas Safety Maneuver Scale (TSMS)

*Kamphuis, J. H., & Telch, M. J. (1998). Assessment of strategies to manage or avoid perceived threats among panic disorder patients: The Texas Safety Maneuver Scale (TSMS). *Clinical Psychology and Psychotherapy, 5,* 177–186.

Social Phobia: Self-Report Scales
Fear of Negative Evaluation Scale (FNE) and Social Avoidance and Distress Scale (SADS)

Oei, T. P. S., Kenna, D., & Evans, L. (1991). The reliability, validity, and utility of the SAD and FNE scales for anxiety disorder patients. *Personality and Individual Differences, 12*, 111–116.

Turner, S. M., McCanna, M., & Beidel, D. C. (1987). Validity of the Social Avoidance and Distress and Fear of Negative Evaluation Scales. *Behaviour Research and Therapy, 25*, 113–115.

*Watson, D., & Friend, R. (1969). Measurement of social-evaluative anxiety. *Journal of Consulting and Clinical Psychology, 33*, 448–457.

Shyness and Sociability Scales

*Cheek, J. M., & Buss, A. H. (1981). Shyness and sociability. *Journal of Personality and Social Psychology, 41*, 330–339.

Social Phobia and Anxiety Inventory (SPAI)

Beidel, D. C., Borden, J. W., Turner, S. M., & Jacob, R. G. (1989). The Social Phobia and Anxiety Inventory: Concurrent validity with a clinic sample. *Behaviour Research and Therapy, 27*, 573–576.

Beidel, D. C., Turner, S. M., & Cooley, M. R. (1993). Assessing reliable and clinically significant change in social phobia: Validity of the Social Phobia and Anxiety Inventory. *Behaviour Research and Therapy, 31*, 331–337.

Beidel, D. C., Turner, S. M., & Fink, C. M. (1996). Assessment of childhood social phobia: Construct, convergent, and discriminative validity of the Social Phobia and Anxiety Inventory for Children (SPAI-C). *Psychological Assessment, 8*, 235–240.

Beidel, D. C., Turner, S. M., & Morris, T. L. (1995). A new inventory to assess childhood social anxiety and phobia: The Social Phobia and Anxiety Inventory for Children. *Psychological Assessment, 7*, 73–79.

Beidel, D. C., Turner, S. M., Stanley, M. A., & Dancu, C. V. (1989). The Social Phobia and Anxiety Inventory: Concurrent and external validity, *Behavior Therapy, 20*, 417–427.

Cox, B. J., Ross, L., Swinson, R. P., & Direnfeld, D. M. (1998). A comparison of social phobia outcome measures in cognitive-behavioral group therapy. *Behavior Modification, 22*, 285–297.

Gillis, M. M., Haaga, D. A. F., & Ford, G. T. (1995). Normative values for the Beck Anxiety Inventory, Fear Questionnaire, Penn State Worry Questionnaire, and Social Phobia and Anxiety Inventory. *Psychological Assessment, 7*, 450–455.

Herbert, J. D., Bellack, A. S., & Hope, D. A. (1991). Concurrent validity of the Social Phobia and Anxiety Inventory. *Journal of Psychopathology and Behavioral Assessment, 13*, 357–368.

Ries, B. J., McNeil, D. W., Boone, M. L., Turk, C. L., Carter, L. E., & Heimberg, R. G. (1998). Assessment of contemporary social phobia verbal report instruments. *Behaviour Research and Therapy, 36*, 983–994.

*Turner, S. M., Beidel, D. C., & Dancu, C. V. (1996). *The Social Phobia and Anxiety Inventory manual.* North Tonawanda, NY: Multi-Health Systems.

Turner, S. M., Beidel, D. C., Dancu, C. V., & Stanley, M. A. (1989). An empirically derived inventory to measure social fears and anxiety: The Social Phobia and Anxiety Inventory. *Psychological Assessment: A Journal of Consulting and Clinical Psychology, 1,* 35–40.

Turner, S. M., Stanley, M. A., Beidel, D. C., & Bond, L. (1989). The Social Phobia and Anxiety Inventory: Construct validity. *Journal of Psychopathology and Behavioral Assessment, 11,* 221–234.

Social Phobia Inventory (SPIN)

*Connor, K. M., Davidson, J. R. T., Churchill, E., Sherwood, A., Foa, E. B., & Weisler, R. H. (2000). Psychometric properties of the Social Phobia Inventory (SPIN): A new self-rating scale. *British Journal of Psychiatry, 176,* 379–386.

Social Phobia Scale (SPS) and Social Interaction Anxiety Scale (SIAS)

Brown, E. J., Turovsky, J., Heimberg, R., Juster, H. R., Brown, T. A., & Barlow, D. H. (1997). Validation of the Social Interaction Anxiety Scale and Social Phobia Scale across the anxiety disorders. *Psychological Assessment, 9,* 21–27.

Cox, B. J., Ross, L., Swinson, R. P., & Direnfeld, D. M. (1998). A comparison of social phobia outcome measures in cognitive-behavioral group therapy. *Behavior Modification, 22,* 285–297.

Habke, A. M., Hewitt, P. L., Norton, G. R., & Asmundson, G. (1997). The Social Phobia and Social Interaction Anxiety Scales: An exploration of the dimensions of social anxiety and sex differences in structure and relations with pathology. *Journal of Psychopathology and Behavioral Assessment, 19,* 21–39.

*Mattick, R. P., & Clarke, J. C. (1998). Development and validation of measures of social phobia scrutiny fear and social interaction anxiety. *Behaviour Research and Therapy, 36,* 455–470.

Osman, A., Gutierrez, P. M., Barrios, F. X., Kopper, B. A., & Chiros, C. E. (1998). The Social Phobia and Social Interaction Anxiety Scales: Evaluation of psychometric properties. *Journal of Psychopathology and Behavioral Assessment, 20,* 249–264.

Ries, B. J., McNeil, D. W., Boone, M. L., Turk, C. L., Carter, L. E., & Heimberg, R. G. (1998). Assessment of contemporary social phobia verbal report instruments. *Behaviour Research and Therapy, 36,* 983–994.

Safren, S. A., Turk, C. L., & Heimberg, R. G. (1998). Factor structure of the Social Interaction Anxiety Scale and Social Phobia Scale. *Behaviour Research and Therapy, 36,* 443–453.

Reviews on Self-Report Assessment of Social Phobia

Cox, B. J., & Swinson, R. P. (1995). Assessment and measurement. In M. B. Stein (Ed.), *Social phobia: Clinical and research perspectives.* Washington, DC: Academic Psychiatric Press.

Heimberg, R. G. (1994). Cognitive assessment strategies and the measurement of outcome of treatment for social phobia. *Behaviour Research and Therapy, 32,* 269–280.

McNeil, D. W., Ries, B. J., & Turk, C. L. (1995). Behavioral assessment: Self-report, physiology, and overt behavior. In R. G. Heimberg, M. R. Liebowitz, D. A. Hope, & F. R. Schneier (Eds.), *Social phobia: Diagnosis, assessment, and treatment.* New York: Guilford.

Generalized Anxiety Disorder: Self-Report Scales
Penn State Worry Questionnaire

Brown, T. A., Antony, M. M., & Barlow, D. H. (1992). Psychometric properties of the Penn State Worry Questionnaire in a clinical anxiety disorders sample. *Behaviour Research and Therapy, 30,* 33–37.

Davey, G. C. L. (1993). A comparison of three worry questionnaires. *Behaviour Research and Therapy, 31,* 51–56.

Gillis, M. M., Haaga, D. A. F., & Ford, G. T. (1995). Normative values for the Beck Anxiety Inventory, Fear Questionnaire, Penn State Worry Questionnaire, and Social Phobia and Anxiety Inventory. *Psychological Assessment, 7,* 450–455.

*Meyer, T. J., Miller, M. L., Metzger, R. L., & Borkovec, T. D. (1990). Development and validation of the Penn State Worry Questionnaire. *Behaviour Research and Therapy, 28,* 487–495.

Molina, S., & Borkovec, T. D. (1994). The Penn State Worry Questionnaire: Psychometric properties and associated characteristics. In G. C. L. Davey & F. Tallis (Eds.), *Worrying: Perspectives on theory, assessment, and treatment.* New York: Wiley.

Stöber, J. (1998). Reliability and validity of two widely-used worry questionnaires: Self-report and self-peer convergence. *Personality and Individual Differences, 24,* 887–890.

Stöber, J., & Bittencourt, J. (1998). Weekly assessment of worry: An adaptation of the Penn State Worry Questionnaire for monitoring changes during treatment. *Behaviour Research and Therapy, 30,* 33–37.

Van Rijsoort, S., Emmelkamp, P. M. G., & Vervaeke, G. (in press). The Penn State Worry Questionnaire and the Worry Domains Questionnaire: Structure, reliability, and validity. *Clinical Psychology and Psychotherapy.*

Worry Domains Questionnaire

Davey, G. C. L. (1993). A comparison of three worry questionnaires. *Behaviour Research and Therapy, 31,* 51–56.

Joormann, J., & Stöber, J. (1997). Measuring facets of worry: A LISREL analysis of the Worry Domains Questionnaire. *Personality and Individual Differences, 23,* 827–837.

Stöber, J. (1998). Reliability and validity of two widely-used worry questionnaires: Self-report and self-peer convergence. *Personality and Individual Differences, 24,* 887–890.

*Tallis, F., Eysenck, M., & Mathews, A. (1992). A questionnaire for the measurement of nonpathological worry. *Personality and Individual Differences, 13,* 161–168.

*Tallis, G., Davey, G. C. L., & Bond, A. (1994). The Worry Domains Questionnaire. In G. C. L. Davey & F. Tallis (Eds.), *Worrying: Perspectives on theory, assessment, and treatment*. New York: Wiley.

Van Rijsoort, S., Emmelkamp, P. M. G., & Vervaeke, G. (in press). The Penn State Worry Questionnaire and the Worry Domains Questionnaire: Structure, reliability, and validity. *Clinical Psychology and Psychotherapy*.

Obsessive Compulsive Disorder: Self-Report Scales
Compulsive Activity Checklist (CAC)

Cottraux, J., Bouvard, M., Defayolle, M., & Messy, P. (1988). Validity and factorial structure study of the Compulsive Activity Checklist. *Behavior Therapy, 19*, 45–53.

*Freund, B., Steketee, G. S., & Foa, E. B. (1987). Compulsive Activity Checklist (CAC): Psychometric analysis with obsessive-compulsive disorder. *Behavioral Assessment, 9*, 67–79.

*Philpott, R. (1975). Recent advances in the behavioral measurement of obsessional illness: Difficulties common to these and other instruments. *Scottish Medical Journal, 20*, 33–40.

*Steketee, G., & Freund, B. (1993). Compulsive Activity Checklist (CAC): Further psychometric analyses and revision. *Behavioural Psychotherapy, 21*, 13–25.

Sternberger, L. G., & Burns, G. L. (1990). Compulsive Activity Checklist and the Maudsley Obsessional-Compulsive Inventory: Psychometric properties of two measures of obsessive-compulsive disorder. *Behavior Therapy, 21*, 117–127.

Leyton Obsessional Inventory

*Cooper, J. (1970). The Leyton Obsessional Inventory. *Psychological Medicine, 1*, 48–64.

Stanley, M. A., Prather, R. C., Beck, J. G., Brown, T. C., Wagner, A. L., & Davis, M. L. (1993). Psychometric analyses of the Leyton Obsessional Inventory in patients with obsessive-compulsive and other anxiety disorders. *Psychological Assessment, 5*, 187–192.

Maudsley Obsessive Compulsive Inventory

*Hodgson, R. J., & Rachman, S. (1977). Obsessive compulsive complaints. *Behaviour Research and Therapy, 15*, 389–395.

Sternberger, L. G., & Burns, G. L. (1990). Compulsive Activity Checklist and the Maudsley Obsessional-Compulsive Inventory: Psychometric properties of two measures of obsessive-compulsive disorder. *Behavior Therapy, 21*, 117–127.

Obsessive-Compulsive Inventory

*Foa, E. B., Kozak, M. J., Salkovskis, P. M., Coles, M. E., & Amir, N. (1998). The validation of a new obsessive compulsive disorder scale: The Obsessive-Compulsive Inventory. *Psychological Assessment, 10*, 206–214.

Simonds, L. M., Thorpe, S. J., & Elliott, S. A. (2000). The Obsessive Compulsive Inventory: Psychometric properties in a non-clinical student sample. *Behavioural and Cognitive Psychotherapy, 28*, 153–159.

Overvalued Ideas Scale (OVIS)

*Neziroglu, F., McKay, D., Yaryura-Tobias, J. A., Stevens, K. P., & Tadaro, J. (1999). The overvalued ideas scale: Development, reliability and validity in obsessive-compulsive disorder. *Behaviour Research and Therapy, 37,* 88–902.

Padua Inventory

Kyrios, M., Bhar, S., & Wade, D. (1996). The assessment of obsessive-compulsive phenomena: Psychometric and normative data on the Padua Inventory from an Australian non-clinical student sample. *Behaviour Research and Therapy, 34,* 85–95.

Mancini, F., Gragnani, A., Orazi, F., & Pietrangeli, M. G. (1999). Obsessions and compulsions: Normative data on the Padua Inventory from an Italian non-clinical adolescent sample. *Behaviour Research and Therapy, 37,* 919–925.

McDonald, A. M., & de Silva, P. (1999). The assessment of obsessionality using the Padua Inventory: Its validity in a British non-clinical sample. *Personality and Individual Differences, 27,* 1027–1046.

*Sanavio, E. (1988). Obsessions and compulsions: The Padua Inventory. *Behaviour Research and Therapy, 26,* 169–177.

Sternberger, L. G., & Burns, G. L. (1990). Obsessions and compulsions: Psychometric properties of the Padua Inventory with an American college population. *Behaviour Research and Therapy, 28,* 341–345.

van Oppen, P. (1992). Obsessions and compulsions: Dimensional structure, reliability, convergent and divergent validity of the Padua Inventory. *Behaviour Research and Therapy, 30,* 631–637.

Padua Inventory Washington State University Revision

*Burns, G. L., Keortge, S. G., Formea, G. M., & Sternberger, L. G. (1996). Revision of the Padua Inventory of Obsessive Compulsive Disorder Symptoms: Distinctions between worry, obsessions and compulsions. *Behaviour Research and Therapy, 34,* 163–173.

Responsibility Attitudes and Interpretations Questionnaires

*Salkovskis, P. M., Wroe, A. L., Gledhill, A., Morrison, N., Forrester, E., Richards, C., et al. (2000). Responsibility attitudes and interpretations are characteristic of obsessive compulsive disorder. *Behaviour Research and Therapy, 38,* 347–372.

Yale-Brown Obsessive Compulsive Scale: Self-Report Version

Steketee, G., Frost, R., & Bogart, K. (1996). The Yale-Brown Obsessive Compulsive Scale: Interview versus self-report. *Behaviour Research and Therapy, 34,* 675–684.

Additional Resources on the Self-Report Assessment of OCD

Richter, M. A., Cox, B. J., & Direnfeld, D. M. (1994). A comparison of three assessment instruments for obsessive compulsive symptoms. *Journal of Behavior Therapy and Experimental Psychiatry, 25,* 143–147.

Sternberger, L. G., & Burns, G. L. (1990). Compulsive Activity Checklist and the Maudsley Obsessional-Compulsive Inventory: Psychometric properties of two measures of obsessive-compulsive disorder. *Behavior Therapy, 21*, 117–127.

Taylor, S. (1995). Assessment of obsessions and compulsions: Reliability, validity, and sensitivity to treatment effects. *Clinical Psychology Review, 15*, 261–296.

Taylor, S. (1998). Assessment of obsessive compulsive disorder. In Swinson, R. P., Antony, M. M., Rachman, S., & Richter, M. A. (Eds.). (1998). *Obsessive compulsive disorder: Theory, research, and treatment.* New York: Guilford.

van Oppen, P., Emmelkamp, P. M. G., Van Balkom, A. J. L. M., & van Dyck, R. (1995). The sensitivity to change of measures for obsessive compulsive disorder. *Journal of Anxiety Disorders, 9*, 241–248.

Other Self-Report Measures
Beck Anxiety Inventory (BAI)

Beck, A. T., Epstein, N., Brown, G., & Steer, R. A. (1988). An inventory for measuring anxiety: Psychometric properties. *Journal of Consulting and Clinical Psychology, 56*, 893–897.

*Beck, A. T., & Steer, R. A. (1990). *Manual for the Beck Anxiety Inventory.* San Antonio, TX: Psychological Corporation.

Beck, A. T., & Steer, R. A. (1991). Relationship between the Beck Anxiety Inventory and the Hamilton Anxiety Rating Scale with anxious outpatients. *Journal of Anxiety Disorders, 5*, 213–223.

Beck, A. T., Steer, R. A., Ball, R., Ciervo, C. A., & Kabat, M. (1997). Use of the Beck Anxiety and Depression Inventories for primary care with medical outpatients. *Assessment, 4*, 211–219.

Cox, B. J., Cohen, E., Direnfeld, D. M., & Swinson, R. P. (1996). Does the Beck Anxiety Inventory measure anything beyond panic attack symptoms? *Behaviour Research and Therapy, 34*, 949–954.

De Beurs, E., Wilson, K. A., Chambless, D. L., Goldstein, A. J., & Feske, U. (1997). Convergent and divergent validity of the Beck Anxiety Inventory for patients with panic disorder and agoraphobia. *Depression and Anxiety, 6*, 140–146.

Fydrich, T., Dowdall, D., & Chambless, D. L. (1992). Reliability and validity of the Beck Anxiety Inventory. *Journal of Anxiety Disorders, 6*, 55–61.

Gillis, M. M., Haaga, D. A. F., & Ford, G. T. (1995). Normative values for the Beck Anxiety Inventory, Fear Questionnaire, Penn State Worry Questionnaire, and Social Phobia and Anxiety Inventory. *Psychological Assessment, 7*, 450–455.

Hewitt, P. L., & Norton, G. R. (1993). The Beck Anxiety Inventory: A psychometric analysis. *Psychological Assessment, 5*, 408–412.

Kabacoff, R. I., Segal, D. L., Hersen, M., & van Hasselt, V. B. (1997). Psychometric properties and diagnostic utility of the Beck Anxiety Inventory and the State-Trait Anxiety Inventory with older adult psychiatric outpatients. *Journal of Anxiety Disorders, 11*, 33–47.

Osman, A., Kopper, B. A., Barrios, F. X., Osman, J. R., & Wade, T. (1997). The Beck Anxiety Inventory: Reexamination of factor structure and psychometric properties. *Journal of Clinical Psychology, 53*, 7–14.

Steer, R. A., Ranieri, W. F., Beck, A. T., & Clark, D. A. (1993). Further evidence for the validity of the Beck Anxiety Inventory with psychiatric outpatients. *Journal of Anxiety Disorders, 7*, 195–205.

Wetherell, J. L., & Areán, P. A. (1997). Psychometric evaluation of the Beck Anxiety Inventory with older medical adults. *Psychological Assessment, 9*, 136–144.

Depression Anxiety Stress Scales (DASS)

Antony, M. M., Bieling, P. J., Cox, B. J., Enns, M. W., & Swinson, R. P. (1998). Psychometric properties of the 42-item and 21-item versions of the Depression Anxiety Stress Scales (DASS) in clinical groups and a community sample. *Psychological Assessment, 10*, 176–181.

Brown, T. A., Chorpita, B. F., Korotitsch, W., & Barlow, D. H. (1997). Psychometric properties of the Depression Anxiety Stress Scales (DASS) in clinical samples. *Behaviour Research and Therapy, 35*, 79–89.

*Lovibond, S. H., & Lovibond, P. F. (1995). *Manual for the Depression Anxiety Stress Scales.* Sydney, Australia. The Psychology Foundation of Australia.

Lovibond, P. F., & Lovibond, S. H. (1995). The structure of negative emotional states: Comparison of the Depression Anxiety Stress Scales (DASS) with the Beck Depression and Anxiety Inventories. *Behaviour Research and Therapy, 33*, 335–343.

Endler Multidimensional Anxiety Scales (EMAS)

*Endler, N. S., Edwards, J. M., & Vitelli, R. (1991). *Endler Multidimensional Anxiety Scales (EMAS) manual.* Los Angeles: Western Psychological Services.

Endler, N. S., Parker, J. D. A., Bagby, R. M., & Cox, B. J. (1991). Multidimensionality of state and trait anxiety: Factor structure of the Endler Multidimensional Anxiety Scales. *Journal of Personality and Social Psychology, 60*, 919–926.

Fear Questionnaire (FQ)

Cox, B. J., Parker, J. D., & Swinson, R. P. (1996). Confirmatory factor analysis of the Fear Questionnaire with social phobia patients. *British Journal of Psychiatry, 168*, 497–499.

Cox, B. J., Swinson, R. P., Parker, J. D., Kuch, K., & Reichman, J. T. (1993). Confirmatory factor analysis of the Fear Questionnaire in panic disorder with agoraphobia. *Psychological Assessment, 5*, 235–237.

Cox, B. J., Swinson, R. P., & Shaw, B. F. (1991). Value of the Fear Questionnaire in differentiating agoraphobia and social phobia. *British Journal of Psychiatry, 159*, 842–845.

Gillis, M. M., Haaga, D. A. F., & Ford, G. T. (1995). Normative values for the Beck Anxiety Inventory, Fear Questionnaire, Penn State Worry Questionnaire, and Social Phobia and Anxiety Inventory. *Psychological Assessment, 7*, 450–455.

*Marks, I. M, & Mathews, A. M. (1979). Brief standard self-rating for phobic patients. *Behaviour Research and Therapy, 17*, 263–267.

Mavissakalian, M. (1986). The Fear Questionnaire: A validity study. *Behaviour Research and Therapy, 24,* 83–85.

Oei, T. P. S., Moylan, A., & Evans, L. (1991). Validity and clinical utility of the fear questionnaire for anxiety-disorder patients. *Psychological Assessment: A Journal of Consulting and Clinical Psychology, 3,* 391–397.

Trull, T. J., & Hillerbrand, E. (1990). Psychometric properties and factor structure of the Fear Questionnaire phobia subscale items in two normative samples. *Journal of Psychopathology and Behavioral Assessment, 12,* 285–297.

Frost Multidimensional Perfectionism Scale

Antony, M. M., Purdon, C., Huta, V., & Swinson, R. P. (1998). Dimensions of perfectionism across the anxiety disorders. *Behaviour Research and Therapy, 36,* 1143–1154.

Flett, G. L., Sawatzky, D. L., & Hewitt, P. L. (1995). Dimensions of perfectionism and goal commitment: A further comparison of two perfectionism measures. *Journal of Psychopathology and Behavioral Assessment, 17,* 111–124.

Frost, R. O., Heimberg, R. G., Holt, C. S., Mattia, J. L., & Neubauer, A. L. (1993). A comparison of two measures of perfectionism. *Personality and Individual Differences, 14,* 119–126.

*Frost, R. O., Marten, P., Lahart, C., & Rosenblate, R. (1990). The dimensions of perfectionism. *Cognitive Therapy and Research, 14,* 449–468.

Frost, R. O., & Marten, P. A. (1990). Perfectionism and evaluative threat. *Cognitive Therapy and Research, 14,* 559–572.

Parker, W. D., & Adkins, K. K. (1995). A psychometric examination of the Multidimensional Perfectionism Scale. *Journal of Psychopathology and Behavioral Assessment, 17,* 323–334.

Purdon, C., Antony, M. M., & Swinson, R. P. (1999). Psychometric properties of the Frost et al. Multidimensional Perfectionism Scale in a clinical anxiety disorders sample. *Journal of Clinical Psychology, 55,* 1271–1286.

Stöber, J. (1998). The Frost Multidimensional Perfectionism Scale revisited: More perfect with four (instead of six) dimensions. *Personality and Individual Differences, 24,* 481–491.

Illness Intrusiveness Rating Scale (IIRS)

Antony, M. M., Roth, D., Swinson, R. P., Huta, V., & Devins, G. M. (1998). Illness intrusiveness in individuals with panic disorder, obsessive compulsive disorder, or social phobia. *Journal of Nervous and Mental Disease, 186,* 311–315.

*Devins, G. M., Binik, Y. M., Hutchinson, T. A., Hollomby, D. J., Barré, P. E., & Guttman, R. D. (1983). The emotional impact of end-stage renal disease: Importance of patients' perceptions of intrusiveness and control. *International Journal of Psychiatry in Medicine, 13,* 327–343.

Multidimensional Anxiety Questionnaire

*Reynolds, W. M. (1999). *Multidimensional Anxiety Questionnaire, professional manual.* Odessa, FL: Psychological Assessment Resources.

State-Trait Anxiety Inventory: Form Y (STAI)

Bieling, P. J., Antony, M. M., & Swinson, R. P. (1998). The State-Trait Anxiety Inventory, trait version: Structure and content re-examined. *Behaviour Research and Therapy, 36*, 777–788.

Kabacoff, R. I., Segal, D. L., Hersen, M., & van Hasselt, V. B. (1997). Psychometric properties and diagnostic utility of the Beck Anxiety Inventory and the State-Trait Anxiety Inventory with older adult psychiatric outpatients. *Journal of Anxiety Disorders, 11*, 33–47.

Marteau, T. M., & Bekker, H. (1992). The development of a six-item short-form of the state scale of the State-Trait Anxiety Inventory (STAI). *British Journal of Clinical Psychology, 31*, 301–306.

Oei, T. P. S., Evans, L., & Crook, G. M. (1990). Utility and validity of the STAI with anxiety disorder patients. *British Journal of Clinical Psychology, 29*, 429–432.

*Spielberger, C. D., Gorsuch, R. L., Lushene, R., Vagg, P. R., & Jacobs, G. A. (1983). *Manual for the State-Trait Anxiety Inventory (Form Y)*. Palo Alto, CA: Mind Garden.

Disorders with Onset in Adolescence

9   Eating Disorders

The eating disorders are characterized by disturbances in a person's eating behaviors and distorted perceptions of body weight and shape (American Psychiatric Association [APA], 2000). Pathological fears of becoming overweight lead people with these disorders to engage in drastic, potentially harmful behaviors that are intended to either cause or maintain weight loss (Garfinkel, 1995). *Anorexia nervosa* (AN) and *bulimia nervosa* (BN) are the two primary eating disorders. A third diagnostic category, eating disorder not otherwise specified, is a residual category at present. It is often used to diagnose people who engage in chronic overeating and seek help for that problem. It may become identified in the future as binge eating disorder, but the APA has yet to fully develop the diagnosis. This chapter focuses on the two primary eating disorders.

Anorexia is distinguished by the refusal to sustain a minimal body weight (85% of what is considered normal for body height and age). This is achieved either by restricting or by binge eating and purging, two types of behavior that represent subtypes of the disorder. *Restricting* anorexics maintain low weight through dieting or excessive exercise. *Binge-eating/purging* types engage in binge eating, purging behaviors, or both. Another criterion for the diagnosis of anorexia is the manifestation of an endocrine problem, manifested primarily by amenorrhea in females, which is the absence of at least three consecutive menstrual cycles (APA, 2000).

In bulimia, pathological fears of becoming overweight lead to purging behaviors such as self-induced vomiting and the misuse of laxatives, diuretics, or other medications. Nonpurging clients rely on fasting or excessive exercise to influence their weight. Binge eating and compensatory behaviors must occur about twice weekly for at least 3 months. Although the diagnostic criteria for bulimia and anorexia are distinct, their symptoms typically present along a continuum. Half of clients diagnosed with anorexia eventually develop symptoms of bulimia, and some people who are initially diagnosed with bulimia develop anorexia (Yager et al., 2002[1]).

Prevalence of the Disorders

A review of surveys conducted both in the United States and England indicates a prevalence rate for bulimia nervosa, purging type, of 1 to 3% of adult females. In the United States, a prevalence rate of 3% of high school females has been found (Compas, Haaga, Keefe, Leitenberg, & Williams, 1998). The prevalence of anorexia among females is approximately 0.5%. The prevalence of males with anorexia is 10% of the rate for females (APA, 2000), although some studies suggest that ratios between males and females may differ (Muise, Stein, & Arbess, 2003). Epidemiological studies indicate that in North America bulimia among males is more prevalent than anorexia among females (Yager et al., 2002). Aside from diagnosable eating disorders, widespread body image dissatisfaction exists among females. A 2004 report on the 1998 Minnesota Student Survey ($N = 81,247$) found that more than half of 9th-grade girls (56%) and 12th-grade girls (57%) revealed disordered eating behaviors (Croll, Neumark-Sztainer, Story, & Ireland, 2002). About 30% of males also had engaged in disordered eating.

Comorbidity

There is a high comorbidity rate between eating disorders and other psychiatric disorders. Longitudinal research conducted in a community setting indicates that concurrent disorders occur for a majority (89.5%) of clients and that the comorbid disorder tends to precede the eating disorder (Lewinsohn, Striegel-Moore, & Seeley, 2000). Depression is particularly common; major depression or dysthymia is reported in half to three quarters of individuals with either anorexia or bulimia (Fonagy, Target, Cottrell, Phillips, & Kurtz, 2002; Lewinsohn et al., 2000). Anxiety disorders, particularly social phobia and obsessive-compulsive disorder, are also commonly experienced by people with eating disorders. Among cases of anorexia, lifetime rates of obsessive-compulsive disorder are estimated at 25%. Substance abuse disorders afflict between 30 and 37% of those with bulimia. Problematic impulsive behaviors that are prevalent among persons diagnosed with bulimia include suicide attempts, sexual risk taking, and shoplifting (Thompson, Wonderlich, Crosby, & Mitchell, 1999).

People with eating disorders are often diagnosed with personality disorders as well. Estimates of comorbid personality disorders among the population range from 42 to 75%. Associations have been reported between bulimia and the cluster B and C personality disorders, particularly the borderline and avoidant disorders, and between anorexia and cluster C disorders, particularly avoidant and obsessive-compulsive personality disorders.

As well as mental health problems, people with eating disorders may also suffer from serious health complications (see Rome & Ammerman, 2003, for a comprehensive review). In bulimia, purging behaviors may lead to enlarged salivary glands and the erosion of dental enamel (Hsu, 1990; Mitchell, 1995). Even more seriously, electrolyte imbalances and chronic dehydration increase the likelihood of both cardiac arrhythmia and renal failure. Specific health risks with anorexia include starvation and malnutrition, which affects many bodily systems (Fairburn, 1995; Hsu, 1990). Endocrine problems may include amenorrhea and metabolic abnormalities. Common cardiovascular disturbances include electrolyte imbalances, irregular heart rate, low body temperature, low blood pressure, and heart failure. The client's behaviors may also produce problems in the hematological system (anemia) and the musculocutaneous system (hair covering the body and sensitivity to cold).

As well as co-occurring mental and health problems, a longitudinal study involving 717 teens from New York State communities found that eating and weight problems during adolescence (not necessarily an eating disorder) elevated the risk for poor health (e.g., infectious diseases, neurological symptoms) and mental health disorders (depression, anxiety, suicide attempts) in young adulthood (Johnson, Cohen, Kasen, & Brook, 2002).

Eating Disorders Assessment

Screening for the possibility of an eating disorder should routinely be done during the medical assessment of teenage girls and in situations where adolescents have already been diagnosed with another disorder (Lewinsohn et al., 2000). The assessment of a suspected eating disorder optimally has the following components (Mizes & Palermo, 1997):

- A standard clinical interview
- Client self-monitoring of eating, bingeing, and purging behavior
- Questionnaire measures of eating disorders, body image, and other psychopathology (see appendix for a list of measures)
- A medical evaluation that includes a routine checkup, assessment of

risk due to weight loss and amenorrhea, laboratory tests of electrolyte imbalances, and, for individuals with bulimia, possible referral to
a dentist for problems related to enamel erosion
- Assessment of comorbid disorders
- A developmental history to attend to issues related to temperament
  and the possibility of psychological, sexual, and physical abuse

Risk and Protective Factors for the Development of Eating Disorders

Clinical assessment also includes an examination of the risk and protective
factors associated with the onset of and recovery from eating disorders.
Following the lead of White (2000), we consider anorexia and bulimia together, as they share overlapping risk factors, symptoms, and causes. Unfortunately, research on the etiology of eating disorders tends to lack specificity, and risks have not been established for different stages of child and
adolescent development (Striegel-Moore & Cachelin, 1999; White, 2000). In
addition, some of the risk factors discovered are not specific to eating disorders to the exclusion of other disorders. Finally, little is known at this
time about the relative contributions of different risk factors to the development of eating disorders (Fairburn, Cooper, Doll, & Welch, 1999). Research has tended to focus on each risk area separately—the biological,
psychological, and social—with a lack of integration between them
(Striegel-Moore & Cachelin, 1999). For a complete delineation of risk and
protective factors, see Table 9.1. Some of these factors are further described
next.

Table 9.1	
Risk and Protective Factors for the Onset of Eating Disorders	
Risk	Protective
Biological	
• Heritability	• No parental psychopathology
• Early pubertal maturation	• Late pubertal maturation (14 and over)
• Adolescent developmental stage	
• Obesity (BN)	• Lean body build
• Dieting	• Emphasis on health and fitness rather than weight[b]
• Female gender	• Male gender
• Homosexuality (males)[a]	

Risk	Protective
Psychological	
• Comorbid psychiatric disorders, such as depression and anxiety	• No comorbid disorders
• Traits such as perfectionism, obsessionality, excessive compliance, low self-esteem, and negative affect/attitudes	• High self-esteem and strong sense of identity
• Body dissatisfaction and distortion	• Positive body image
	• Well-developed social and coping skills
	• Positive temperamental disposition
Social	
Family	
• Interactional problems in the family	• Cohesion and positive communication
• Attachment problems	
• Inadequate parenting	• Effective parenting
• Transmission or amplification of societal emphasis on weight and appearance	• Healthy attitudes about weight and shape
• Sexual abuse history	• No abuse history
Extra-curricular activities:	
• Involvement in sports and dance that emphasize very low body fat	
Social Support	
• Social isolation, social anxiety, impoverished relationships, public self-consciousness, and failure to seek social support	• Social connection, social skills
Socioeconomic Status	
• Middle and upper SES	
Societal Values	
• Emphasis on thinness as female beauty	• Participation in cultures or subcultures that do not emphasize thinness as an important aspect of female beauty
• Economic motives to produce body image dissatisfaction to sell products	

For those factors that have not been discussed in the text, see Striegel-Moore & Cachelin (1999).
[a]Muise, Stein, & Arbess (2003).
[b]Kelly, Wall, Eisenberg, Story, & Newmark: Sztainer (2004).

Biological Factors

Few valid biological predictors have been found for the eating disorders (Fonagy et al., 2002). Biological factors under consideration include heritability, early puberty, obesity, and dieting. Of course, these are not solely biological in terms of their probably psychosocial interplay and consequences. Many of the biological features associated with the eating disorders have been attributed to the *effects* of starvation rather than their causes.

Different causal processes within the family environment may be implicated in the development of eating disorders. Whether they are due to genetic mechanisms, childhood experiences, family concerns about weight, family psychopathology, or family transactional patterns, however, is unknown at this time (Cooper, 1995; Wilson, Heffernan, & Black, 1996).

According to the Fonagy et al. (2002) review, heritability is higher in anorexia than in bulimia. Overall, correlational studies indicate that family members of eating-disordered individuals seem to experience an increased risk for both eating disorders and mood disorders, at a rate three times higher than for normal controls (Cooper, 1995). For individuals with bulimia, relatives have an increased risk of substance abuse and obesity (APA, 2000; Fairburn et al., 1999; Hsu, 1990).

An early onset of puberty (before age 11) has been identified as a risk factor, whereas later-onset menarche (age 14 and over) is a protective factor for eating disorders. Girls who mature earlier may be vulnerable for a number of reasons (Mizes & Palmero, 1997; Striegel-Moore, 1993). Early-maturing girls are typically shorter and heavier and therefore further from the current ideal body for women. They are also a target for teasing and experiences for which they may not be psychologically ready, such as dating and pressures for sexual behavior. It may be that early maturation presents particular risks at critical stages of development. In a large longitudinal study, pubertal status was predictive of disordered eating in 5th- and 6th-grade girls but not over a 5-year period when the girls had reached 7th through 10th grade (Leon, Fulkerson, Perry, Keel, & Klump, 1999). Adolescence, when puberty occurs for all girls, is clearly a developmental stage that puts females at risk for developing eating disorders. Anorexia tends to have an earlier age of onset than bulimia (Lewinsohn et al., 2000).

Obesity may increase the risk for eating disorders because of its negative impact on body image (Striegel-Moore & Cachelin, 1999). Studies have indicated that childhood obesity may present a particular risk factor for bulimia (Striegel-Moore & Cachelin, 1999; Mizes & Palmero, 1997) and for males with eating disorders (Muise et al., 2003). Dieting behaviors are also associated with risk (Mizes & Palermo, 1997). In a longitudinal study conducted in 44 secondary schools in Australia, 14- and 15-year-old girls who followed severe weight loss diets were 18 times more likely to develop an eating disorder 3 years later than those who did not diet. Girls who followed moderate weight loss diets were five times as likely to develop a disorder (Patton, Selzer, Coffey, Carlin, & Wolfe, 1999). Restricting food intake almost inevitably leads to bingeing. The self-disgust and fear of weight gain associated with bingeing in turn leads to weight loss behaviors (strict diets, purging, and excessive exercise). However, dieting alone is not sufficient for symptoms of an eating disorder because this behavior is fairly normative among adolescent and adult women.

Psychological Factors

The high rates of comorbidity for eating disorders with other diagnoses such as depression and anxiety have already been discussed. Psychiatric disorders place an individual at risk for the development of eating disorders (Patton et al., 1999). In addition, the presence of certain personality traits, such as perfectionism, obsessional thinking, excessive compliance, low self-esteem (Fairburn et al., 1999), negative mood, or negative attitudes (Leon et al., 1999), may put an individual at risk. Negative self-evaluation and perfectionism appear to be more common in those with anorexia than in those with bulimia (Fairburn et al., 1999). Body dissatisfaction and, to a lesser extent, body distortion are also predictors of eating disorders (Cash & Deagle, 1997). Protective factors include high self-esteem, positive self-regard, a strong sense of identity, well-developed social and coping skills, and a positive temperament (Striegel-Moore & Cachelin, 1999).

Social Factors

There are four aspects of the social context that influence the development of risk and protective factors for eating disorders: family factors, social factors in the immediate environment, socioeconomic status, and the influence of the broader social environment.

Family Factors

Though no specific patterns have been identified, families in which eating disorders develop tend to be more hostile, conflicted, isolated, lacking in cohesion, and enmeshed and less supportive and nurturing (Mizes & Palermo, 1997, p. 580). Another factor involving families is the transmission of the societal emphasis on weight and appearance (Striegel-Moore & Cachelin, 1999). For instance, when parents are excessively concerned about their own and their children's shape and size, they may tease or pressure the child to lose weight (Kotler, Cohen, Davies, Pine, & Walsh, 2001; Mizes & Palermo, 1997).

A history of sexual abuse is found in 20 to 50% of individuals with eating disorders, and often this abuse occurs in the context of the family (Yager et al., 2002). Sexual abuse is more common in those with bulimia than in those with restricting-type anorexia. However, inadequate or abusive parenting and sexual abuse are not specific risk factors for the development of an eating disorder; instead, they raise the risk for problems in general (Striegel-Moore & Cachelin, 1999). Why they contribute to eating disorders in some women and other forms of pathology in others requires further exploration. Conversely, the mere absence of the abuse factor may be highly protective. Further, general factors, such as good parenting and secure attachment to one caregiver, and specific factors, such as the absence of parental weight problems or concern, are likely to contribute to girls' resilience (Striegel-Moore & Cachelin, 1999).

Societal Influences

The vast majority (90%) of people with eating disorders in both clinic and population samples are female (Anderson, 1995; APA, 2000). A review of the research by Mizes and Palmero (1997) has documented the societal overemphasis on thinness for females, including the gradual lowering of relative ideal body weight since the 1960s and 1970s. Media images of excessively thin women are rampant and directed at primarily female audiences. More diet and shape-related content has been found in female- versus male-oriented magazines. Increased exposure to media images of thinness has been shown to be associated with female endorsement of an extreme ideal body weight, thereby creating body image dissatisfaction that leads to increased symptoms of eating disorders (Mizes & Palermo, 1997). Wolf (1991, as cited in Mizes & Palmero, 1997) has pointed out that female-oriented products for thinness and appearance are big business, creating strong inducements for companies to maximize or create markets for products to correct women's presumed flaws.

The tension between the cultural ideal of female beauty and the physical reality of the female body is magnified by female gender role expectations. That is, female identity is defined in relational terms, and beauty is a core aspect of female identity (Striegel-Moore, 1993). Participation in cultures or subcultures that do not emphasize thinness as an important aspect of female beauty appears to protect against developing body image concerns and to reduce the likelihood of dieting (Striegel-Moore & Cachelin, 1999). In terms of resilience, there is some evidence (especially from African American females) that the incidence of eating problems is lower among groups who have strong racial identities. Conversely, acculturation and assimilation, or a weakening of one's sense of racial or ethnic identity, are associated with an increased risk of developing an eating disorder.

In many other countries, eating disorders have increased, even in cultures where they are rare. Japan is the only non-Western country that has had a substantial and continuing increase in eating disorders with statistics comparable to those in the United States. The prevalence of eating disorders is also rising in other non-English-speaking countries, such as Spain, Argentina, and Fiji. In the United States, eating disorders are said to be about as common in young Hispanic women as in Caucasians, more common among Native Americans, and less common among African Americans and Asians. However, a meta-analysis of 18 studies showed that the rates of eating disorders are only slightly higher in Caucasian than in African American female college students (O'Neill, 2003). One hypothesis to explain the relatively comparable rates is that African American females attending college are more acculturated to a Caucasian standard of beauty. O'Neill (2003) reports that the dearth of eating disorder research on Hispanic, Native American, East Indian, and Eastern European women precludes their inclusion in meta-analytic study. Clinical practitioners need to be sensitive to how weight and shape concerns are experienced by all of their clients but especially those who are minorities, from other cultural backgrounds, or who are assimilating into Western societies.

Interestingly, high socioeconomic status does not serve as a buffer against the development of eating disorders in the same way that it does for many other childhood and adolescent disorders (Striegel-Moore & Cachelin, 1999). Females from middle and upper socioeconomic strata may in fact be at greater risk because they experience more demands in the areas of social compliance and perfectionism.

Risk and Resilience Factors for the Course of Eating Disorders

There is wide variation in the course of eating disorders among studies that follow clients over time in terms of weight gain, maintenance of weight gained, establishment of normal eating patterns, and return of regular menses. According to a review of more than 100 longitudinal studies, approximately 20% of individuals still experience significant impairment at follow-up, with about half recovering (Fonagy et al., 2002). Even among those who have good outcomes (defined by restoration of weight and menses), many have other persistent psychiatric symptoms, including dysthymia, social phobia, obsessive-compulsive symptoms, and substance abuse (Yager et al., 2002). Two thirds still suffer from food and weight preoccupation, and approximately 40% show bulimic symptoms. A small proportion may die prematurely from starvation, heart failure, or suicide (APA, 2000). For bulimia nervosa specifically, a review of 88 studies indicated that half of women had fully recovered 5 to 10 years after presentation (Keel & Mitchell, 1997). Twenty percent continued to meet full criteria for bulimia nervosa, while 30% had relapsed into bulimic symptoms. Four years after presentation, risk of relapse seems to abate. Although treatment helps to speed up the recovery process, it does not appear to affect outcome for follow-up periods of less than 5 years.

A poorer prognosis for anorexia has been associated with initially lower minimum weight, the presence of vomiting, failure to respond to previous treatment, disturbed family relationships before the onset of the disorder, and being married (Yager et al., 2002). Clients with anorexia who purge are at a much greater risk for developing serious medical complications. In general, adolescents have better outcomes than adults, and younger adolescents have better outcomes than older adolescents. Many of these prognostic indicators have not been consistently replicated, however, and may be more valid over the short term than over longer time periods.

For bulimia, having a substance abuse or dependence disorder is a risk factor for negative response to treatment (Wilson et al., 1999). Other negative indicators include impulsivity (Keel & Mitchell, 1997) and high baseline frequencies of binge eating and vomiting (Wilson et al., 1999). Not surprisingly, clients who are higher functioning and have milder symptoms have a better prognosis (Yager et al., 2002). Further, relapse may be associated with preoccupation with and ritualization of eating, a lower motivation for change, and having been abstinent for only a short time (Halmi et al., 2002).

Along with longer duration of the disorder and its severity, client resistance and denial form a critical barrier to effective treatment for both anorexia and bulimia (Fonagy et al., 2002). Therefore, enhancing the client's motivation before beginning treatment has gained attention recently and been found to positively affect the rapidity of response to intervention.

Intervention

In community-based samples, only 25% of people with eating disorders receive treatment (Fairburn, 1995). This is partly due to a lack of detection. Based on a review by Hoek (1995), only 43% of clients with diagnosable anorexia are recognized by general practitioners, with three quarters of them referred for treatment. Even fewer cases of bulimia are identified: 11% of probable cases, with half of these being referred for treatment. One reason for the lack of diagnosis is that physicians tend to accept dieting as normal behavior (Mizes & Palermo, 1997). Another challenge to the delivery of appropriate intervention is that mental health providers have not reached a consensus on appropriate treatment strategies and have not been guided by evidence-based methods.

The goals of intervention with clients who have eating disorders should center, of course, on aspects of their weight and eating behaviors. It is also important, however, to address clients' body image dissatisfaction and distorted attitudes about food, shape, and weight, as these factors are connected to relapse (Mizes & Palmero, 1997). Listed here is the range of appropriate goals for clinical intervention (Yager et al., 2002).

- Restoring healthy weight[2]
- Reduction or elimination of binge-eating and purging behaviors
- Treating physical complications
- Enhancing clients' motivation to participate in treatment and cooperate in the restoration of healthy eating patterns
- Providing education on nutrition and healthy eating patterns, including minimization of food restriction and increasing the variety of foods eaten
- Encouraging healthy but not excessive exercise patterns
- Correcting core maladaptive thoughts, attitudes, and feelings related to the eating disorder
- Treating comorbid disorders
- Addressing themes that may underlie eating disorder behaviors, such as developmental conflicts, identity formation, body image concerns, self-esteem in areas unrelated to weight and shape, sexual and aggressive difficulties, mood regulation, gender role expectations, family dysfunction, coping styles, and problem solving
- Enlisting family support and providing family counseling and therapy where appropriate
- Improving interpersonal and social functioning
- Preventing relapse

Treatment Settings

Weight restoration is the first major goal in the treatment of anorexia, and extensive research indicates that weight gain can occur through inpatient hospitalization (Mizes & Palmero, 1997). Inpatient hospitalization is indicated in the following client circumstances (Foreyt, Poston, Winebarger, & McGavin, 1998):

- Serious physical complications, including malnutrition, dehydration, electrolyte disturbances, cardiac dysrhythmia, arrested growth)
- Extremely low body weight
- Suicide risk
- Lack of response to outpatient treatment
- Lack of available outpatient treatment

- Comorbid disorders that interfere with outpatient treatment (e.g., severe depression, obsessive-compulsive disorder)
- A need to be separated from the current living situation

Inpatient services typically take a multidisciplinary approach, involving psychiatry, psychology, nursing, dietetics, occupational therapy, physical therapy, social services, and general medical services (Foreyt et al., 1998). Behavioral reinforcement systems often link weight gain to a client's privileges, including time out of bed or off the unit and permission to exercise or receive visitors (Yager et al., 2002). According to the results of one meta-analysis, behavior therapy results in consistent weight gain and shorter hospital stays. Further, behavioral programs need not be overly strict, such as those in which caloric intake or daily weight is tied to a schedule of privileges; instead, programs in which time out of bed is associated with continued weight gain are generally effective.

Hospital stays have shortened in recent years because of changes wrought by managed care. Shorter hospital stays pose a problem for the client's achieving optimal weight, as weight should be restored at a rate of only 1 to 3 pounds per week. A client who is released before reaching optimal weight[3] may be unable to maintain the weight, and this might necessitate rehospitalization (Mizes & Palmero, 1997). Still, because insurance companies no longer reimburse providers so extensively, the outpatient care of anorexia will increasingly be the norm.

Weight gain can be achieved on an outpatient basis if the client is highly motivated, the family is supportive and cooperative, purging behaviors are absent (Fonagy et al., 2002), symptom duration is brief, and the client is less than 20% below healthy body weight (Yager et al., 2002). Careful monitoring of the client must be in place, however, with the client's understanding that a more restrictive setting may be necessary if progress is not evident in a few weeks.

Partial hospitalization and day hospital programs are being increasingly used in efforts to decrease the length of inpatient stays. For milder cases, these programs are being used in place of hospitalization. Such programs may not be appropriate for clients with lower initial weights—that is, less than 75% of average weight for height. In deciding whether to enroll a client in a partial hospitalization program, the practitioner needs to consider the client's level of motivation to engage in the program and his or her ability to work in a group setting.

Outcome studies of inpatient treatment of bulimia are lacking, but in the majority of cases (95%) outpatient treatment is sufficient (Fonagy et al., 2002). However, weight gain might also be an appropriate goal for individuals with bulimia. Although these clients may be of normal weight, they may also show psychological and biological correlates of semistarvation, such as depression, irritability, and obsessional thinking, and their weight may be below a biologically determined set point.

Psychosocial Interventions

Motivational Interviewing

People with eating disorders tend to deny their problem and need for intervention. The clinical techniques of motivational interviewing can help the practitioner address this possibility. As discussed in chapter 11, motivational interviewing was originally formulated for the treatment of substance use disorders and has been adapted in clinical reports to the treatment of eating disorders (Killick & Allen, 1997; Tantillo, Bitter, & Adams, 2001; Treasure & Ward, 1997). In the one empirical study to date, motivational interviewing performed as well as cognitive-behavioral therapy for reducing bulimic symptoms (Treasure et al., 1999).

Two major psychosocial interventions have received empirical validation: cognitive-behavioral intervention and interpersonal therapy. Cognitive-behavioral treatment is a package of components that includes self-monitoring, social skills training, assertiveness training, problem solving, and cognitive restructuring. The last of these components involves challenging clients' beliefs and distortions, such as: "To be fat is to be a failure, unattractive, and unhappy." "To be thin is to be successful, attractive, and happy." "To exert self-control is a sign of strength and discipline." Some of these beliefs derive directly from social values, and the client can be helped to identify the extent to which they are dysfunctional and the nonadaptive ways clients have allowed these beliefs to dictate their lives.

Recent reviews have supported the effectiveness of cognitive-behavioral treatment for bulimia in terms of binge eating and purging and attitudes related to eating disorders. A meta-analysis of 26 studies indicated that cognitive-behavioral treatments produced an average effect size of .69 for behavior and an average effect size of .67 for attitudes (Lewandowski, Gebing, Anthony, & O'Brien, 1997). About half of study sample participants achieve remission at follow-up (Hay & Bacaltchuk, 2003). Generally, cognitive behavioral therapy shows a superior effect over medication (Whittal, Agras, & Gould, 1999).

In addition, the package of cognitive-behavioral interventions (with the exception of exposure and response prevention, which have not been found helpful) (Hay & Bacaltchuk, 2003) is more effective than its constituent parts delivered alone (Compas et al., 1998). Both individual and group modalities of cognitive-behavioral intervention have been successfully applied. Further, cognitive-behavioral therapy delivered through a self-help, structured format has shown modest positive results and is thus a promising approach (Hay & Bacaltchuk, 2003). Finally, the intervention procedures have been clearly outlined in treatment manuals, facilitating their generalization (Fonagy et al., 2002). (See Fairburn, Marcus, and Wilson [1993] for an example.) Despite these advantages, many experienced clinicians do not find cognitive-behavioral interventions to be as useful as described by researchers (Yager et al., 2002). This may be due to clinician inexperience or discomfort with the methods or differences between clients seen in the community and those who have participated as research subjects.

Individual interpersonal therapy is another empirically validated approach for bulimia (e.g., Fairburn et al., 1991, 1995). Interpersonal therapy is a brief (12–16 session) psychodynamic intervention model with a focus on repairing and resolving the client's relationships that have played a role in the formation of the eating disorder. The client is also helped to learn healthier ways of interpersonal relating. Cognitive-behavioral therapy and interpersonal therapy compare favorably with each other, although interpersonal therapy may take longer to achieve its outcomes.

The discussion up to this point has been limited to bulimia nervosa. Empirical support for psychosocial treatment of anorexia nervosa is lacking. Long-term psychodynamic therapy is most often used for the outpatient treatment of anorexia, although results have not been examined empirically (Mizes & Palermo, 1997).

Family Intervention

The research on family intervention with eating disorders lacks methodological rigor, so it is difficult to draw conclusions about family work. There is, however, a consensus among practitioners that family involvement should be part of the treatment plan, at least for younger adolescents with anorexia (Crisp et al., 1991; Robin, Siegel, & Moye, 1995; Robin et al., 1999). Family involvement means that parents can participate in either collateral (separate from the client) or conjoint sessions (with the client and/or the whole family). Critical comments from parents need to be brought under control before conjoint family work can take place, however, because these are associated with dropout (e.g., Szmukler & Dare, 1991) and poor outcome (e.g., Butzlaff & Hooley, 1998; Szmukler & Dare, 1991; Van Furth et al., 1996). Critical comments are one aspect of *expressed emotion*, a measure of the family's affective communication.

Medication

Psychotropic medications should not be used as the sole or primary treatment of eating disorders, although they may be helpful in many cases as adjunctive interventions (Bacaltchuk, Hay, & Trefiglio, 2003). An assessment of the need for antidepressant medications is usually most appropriate following the client's weight gain, when the psychological effects of malnutrition are resolving. When medications are used, physicians generally prescribe antidepressant drugs because of the high comorbidity of eating disorders with depression and some anxiety disorders. Bacaltchuk and Hay (2003) conducted a review of the use of antidepressants compared with placebo for clients with bulimia. Although the antidepressants were clinically effective, as compared with placebo, there was a higher dropout rate when people took tricyclic antidepressants. These drugs have a problematic side effect profile for many consumers, including dry mouth, blurred vision, and constipation. Apparently, fluoxetine (Prozac) produced better results because the research participants could more easily tolerate it. A relatively high dose of fluoextine (60 mg) is suggested for the treatment of bulimia (Yager et al., 2002).

Medication has been more successful in treating bulimia than anorexia. The average decline in binge frequency achieved during medication treatment is about 50%, and the highest reported rate of remission in studies is only 35% (Fonagy et al., 2002). Although improved, the average client remains significantly symptomatic after a course of antidepressant drugs. Many clients with bulimia who respond well to antidepressant treatment continue to do well if they remain on the medication, but there is also a substantial rate of relapse for clients who continue the medication. Even clients who improve during long-term medication treatment appear prone to relapse when medication is discontinued.

Prevention of Eating Disorders

Few studies have been done on the prevention of eating disorders. Pratt and Woolfenden's (2003) comprehensive review located only eight studies, with no firm conclusions about the impact of programs for children and adolescents. One challenge for practitioners is where to target prevention efforts. Although some high-risk groups have been identified (dancers, models, athletes, people with a family history of eating disorders), and it is known that people who develop eating disorders pass through a period of dieting, only a small percentage of dieters develop these disorders. Little is known about what triggers certain dieters to develop clinical disorders. Thus it is not known if reducing dieting behavior and weight preoccupation among broad groups of females will prevent eating disorders. Targeting females during high-risk developmental periods has also been suggested. Prevention efforts have addressed middle school, high school, and university women. The high prevalence of weight dissatisfaction and dieting in the later elementary school years suggests the need for prevention efforts in the early elementary school years (Mizes & Palermo, 1997). For example, Wertheim, Koerner, and Paxton's (2001) study on adolescents in grades 7,

8, and 10, tracking the girls over 8 months, indicated that eating patterns were stabilized by the time girls reached grade 8. This suggests that prevention programs need to be implemented before this time. Another challenge with prevention programs is the need to strike a balance between reducing the risk of eating disorders in some women while not potentially causing harm to others (e.g., educating individuals on weight loss and dieting) (Pratt & Woolfenden, 2003).

Summary of the Intervention Section

Eating disorders have been a major focus of research attention for the past 25 years. Still, practice effectiveness research is not extensive. Despite evidence that clients with eating disorders can benefit from cognitive-behavioral and interpersonal therapy, practitioners seem to use many other approaches, based apparently on personal preference. Given the high rates of relapse and recurrence with the eating disorders, it must be concluded that current psychosocial treatments are not adequate, and future efforts need to focus on developing new approaches or integrating and evaluating the existing therapies (Fonagy et al., 2002).

Critique of the Diagnoses

A major critique of the diagnostic criteria for anorexia and bulimia is their narrowness. Thus, many people who have serious eating-related problems escape diagnosis and presumably the possibility of help. Many researchers recommend more relaxed criteria (e.g., Kotler et al., 2001). Several rationales are offered to support such a change (Lewinsohn et al., 2000). First, a considerable proportion of those seeking treatment for eating disorders are subthreshold cases, meaning that they do not meet all of the required criteria for formal diagnosis. As a result, "eating disorder not otherwise specified" is a commonly used diagnosis, given to nearly 50% of clients, particularly adolescents (Yager et al., 2002). In addition, research comparing full-syndrome with partial cases reveals few differences in terms of clinical and psychosocial characteristics, including high levels of comorbid depression, suicide attempts, impaired global functioning, and prior treatment. Further, some women who have subthreshold cases eventually develop a full-blown disorder. For adolescents who are still growing, even subclinical cases might result in impaired health (Lewinsohn et al., 2000).

Another critique of the diagnoses that is central to the social work perspective has been the focus on the internal deficits of those with eating disorders rather than emphasizing external social and cultural attitudes (Foreyt et al., 1998; Pratt & Woolfenden, 2003). One of the challenges to prevention efforts is changing the dieting and weight preoccupations that are so central to many females' self-esteem when it is so culturally pervasive (Mizes & Palmero, 1997).

Case Study

Sandra Benitez, age 16, came in with her mother and sister for a session at an outpatient mental health clinic at her school counselor's referral. The school counselor had called Sandra into her office because Sandra had lost 20 pounds, going from 115 to 95. Sandra didn't see this as a problem; she said that she looked like she had always wanted to look ever since she had gained weight when she had entered puberty at age 11. She said she had lost the weight through skipping breakfast, eating yogurt for lunch, and then eating reduced portions at dinner. She'd also stopped going out with her friends for pizza, fast food, and desserts. She exercised each day: 20 minutes of jogging. She used to participate in track every year, but ever since she'd hit puberty, she no longer could run as fast as she used to. She'd tried long-distance running, but she "wasn't any good at it," so she quit and now just ran for exercise.

When asked what she did if she ever overate, she said that every once in a while (every 2 weeks or so), she lost control and would eat almost a whole batch of raw cookie dough, for instance. During those times she would atone the next day by eating even less and upping her exercise routine. She admitted to taking laxatives one time but said that it was "cheating," and "gross," and her stomach had hurt too much.

Despite her weight loss, she says that she still doesn't like her body: Her stomach sticks out, and there is cellulite on her thighs. If she could get the weight off these areas, then she would feel better about herself. She admits to missing one menstrual cycle. She says the worst thing in the world would be if she were fat, and she would kill herself if she got that way. She denies having a problem: "I am not crazy. Everyone wants to be thin."

In heavily accented English, Mrs. Benitez conveyed that her husband couldn't attend the session because of his work. Mr. Benitez was an architect back in Argentina who, after trying several related jobs in the United States without success, became a real state agent. He spends a lot of time working now, including evenings and weekends. As a result, Mrs. Benitez says that she is the primary disciplinarian, although the girls (Sandra and her 15-year-old sister, Bianca) give her no problems. She says the family is "close."

She agrees that Sandra has a problem with her weight but that there is no need for counseling. Mrs. Benitez says that she is praying for her daughter. (The family practices the Catholic religion.) She says with God's help, the family can handle this by themselves. She says that Sandra is a model child in all other ways.

After a number of probing questions, Mrs. Benitez reluctantly admits that she would make herself throw up when she was a young adult to lose weight, and she had a period of time when she was severely underweight. She is now overweight and admits that she hates her body.

Mrs. Benitez explained that the family came to this country for economic reasons when Sandra was 7 and her younger sister 5. However, Mrs. Benitez does not like living in the United States, doesn't like "Americans," and frequently criticizes the culture. She wishes that they could go back home, but she says the economic situation there has become progressively worse, accompanied by an increase in street violence and crime. She says that the only time she worked outside the home was before she was married. She was trained as a teacher in Argentina but says that she is not able to do this in the United States because her credentials don't transfer over. She adds that she likes being home when the girls come home from school so she can talk over their day with them. She says that neither she nor her husband has friends in this country.

Sandra, in a meeting alone with the therapist, says that her mother is obsessed with eating and her weight. During mealtimes, her mother doesn't like anyone to talk to her, so she can "enjoy" her food. She often looks at herself in the mirror, saying she is ugly and fat. Sandra admits that she thinks about food and planning her meals and exercise "a lot." She says that it's better than thinking about "guys," though, and that's what it takes to look the way she does.

Sandra says that her parents have a "terrible" marriage: They haven't slept in the same room for most of her life, and her father calls her mother "fat" and "crazy." However, Mrs. Benitez says that she has a good marriage: Her husband is a good provider. Sandra says that the idea of having a life like her mother's scares her. She says her mother just watches TV all day and cleans. Sandra and her mother do the cooking for the family. Sandra is obsessed with cookbooks and planning meals for the family. They make traditional Argentinean meals, such as *guisos*, *mondongo*, and empanadas, and homemade pasta.

Sandra says that when she was young, she was her daddy's favorite, but since she became a teenager, he now seems to prefer her younger sister, Bianca. She says that he did not notice her weight loss until Bianca pointed it out to him. He thinks she's being silly about not eating and should simply "eat up."

Although Bianca is younger than Sandra, she looks older, as she is taller and of normal weight. Bianca is dressed in flashy, revealing clothes and wears heavy makeup with styled hair. This is in contrast to Sandra, who is wearing jeans and no makeup. Bianca says, "It'll ruin my life," if Sandra dies from starving herself.

Sandra admits to feelings of depression (sadness, crying, feeling "heavy" and "low," feeling like her life is over and that she can't go on living). She says that although she has fantasized about throwing herself in front of a moving car, she wouldn't do anything because of her religious belief that suicide is a sin. She says that her feelings of depression began when she was 14, after a boy she liked for a long time "used" her and dumped her. She says that her feelings of depression fluctuate, depending on the attention the boys she likes give her. She has felt better, she says, now that she exercises regularly and has lost weight. She says she sometimes has difficulty sleeping—initially falling asleep, which might take 2 hours. This occurs on average once a week.

When asked about her other coping mechanisms, she says she talks to her friends, her mother, writes in her diary (mainly about the boys she likes, her grades, and how disgusting she is for eating this or that), cooks, restricts her eating, and exercises. She also likes to spend time reading fashion magazines. Sandra spends a lot of time studying. If she doesn't get an A, she feels terrible about herself. She says that her teachers like her a lot and praise her performance and her good conduct.

Sandra reports no sexual abuse or physical abuse history. She denies using alcohol or any other drugs. She says she is not sexually active, although she thinks her sister might be. Her sister also gets good grades, As and Bs, and is not a discipline problem, although her sister only has one friend.

Sandra has a small circle of friends with whom she hangs around in school, talks on the phone, and goes places on weekends. She has retained her social life, except for eating out with her friends. Two of her friends were so concerned with Sandra's weight loss that they went to their school counselor, which initiated the clinic visit.

Multiaxial Diagnosis for Sandra

Axis I   307.50 Eating Disorder Not Otherwise Specified
          300.4 Dysthmyic Disorder
Axis II   V71.09 No diagnosis
Axis III None (according to client and parents' report)
Axis IV   None
Global Assessment of Functioning: 65

Rationale for Diagnosis

The eating disorder diagnosis is listed because it is the reason clinical attention was sought. Each of the criteria is listed here with Sandra's symptoms in italics:

Criterion A: Refusal to maintain body weight at or above a minimally normal weight for age and height: *Sandra has lost 20 pounds when her body weight was already normal.*

Criterion B: Intense fear of gaining weight or becoming fat, even though underweight: *Sandra says that it would be "the worst thing" if she were fat and that she would kill herself.*

Criterion C: Disturbance in the way in which one's body weight or shape is experienced (*although underweight, she still complains about her stomach and thighs not being thin enough*), undue influence of body weight or shape on self-evaluation (*Sandra feels better about herself now that she is underweight; she feels bad about herself if she overeats*), denial of the seriousness of the current low body weight (*she does not think she has a problem*).

Criterion D: In postmenarcheal females, amenorrhea. *Sandra does not meet this criterion at this time; she has missed one menstrual cycle rather than three consecutive cycles.*

Type—Restricting: *Although Sandra admitted to using laxatives, she used them only once, and she generally relies on restricting her food intake and exercising.*

Because Sandra only meets partial criteria for AN, a diagnosis of eating disorder not otherwise specified is warranted.

Sandra also meets the following criteria for dysthymic disorder:

Criteria A and C: *For a 2-year period, Sandra has experienced feelings of depression (sadness, crying, feeling "heavy" and "low," feeling like her life is over and that she can't go on living). These feelings have persisted most of the day for more days than not during this time frame; she has not been without these symptoms for more than a couple of days. Although Sandra has had these symptoms for 2 years, for children and adolescents, only a 1-year time period is required.*

Criterion B: *Of five descriptors listed, Sandra has insomnia, low self-esteem, and feelings of hopelessness (she needs only two).*

Sandra has not had a major depressive episode (Criterion D), a manic episode (Criterion E), or a psychotic disorder (Criterion F). She does not use substances; neither does she suffer from a medical condition (Criterion G).

Criterion H: *The symptoms cause clinically significant distress.*
Early Onset: *Onset was at age 14.*

The rationale for a GAF score of 65 is that although Sandra suffers from depressed mood and occasional suicidal ideation, she functions well academically and socially and has meaningful interpersonal relationships (her friends, her mother).

Risk and Resilience Assessment and Treatment Plan

A risk and resilience assessment, as well as accompanying goals to reduce risk factors and increase protective factors, is described in Table 9.2. Although Sandra has been diagnosed with a depressive disorder (dysthymia), as well as the eating disorder, the focus of this assessment is on the eating disorder. Sandra has a number of protective factors, but these are outweighed by risk factors for the onset of the eating disorder. Possible goals have been formulated to address risk by different system levels: biological and psychological at the individual level; family and societal pressures at the environmental level. To gain parental support for these goals, the therapist must take a nonblaming stance and emphasize how the parents can join together and change some of their own behaviors to help Sandra heal from her eating disorder.

Many goals can be enacted at the individual level; however, Sandra seems unmotivated to work on the eating disorder. Although she admits she spends a lot of mental energy on food and restraining her intake, she does not see any other negative consequences at this point. She says that losing weight has helped her feel better about herself. Motivational interviewing techniques, therefore, might be the first line of intervention. She also might be more easily engaged in addressing her depressive feelings, which are painful for her. The occasional suicidal ideation is of concern and should be addressed immediately. Both cognitive-behavioral and interpersonal therapies are used to treat depression, as well as eating disorders.

Overall, given the risk and protective factors contributing to her prognosis, Sandra's potential response to treatment seems favorable. Although she has low weight and there seem to be some problems in family functioning, Sandra does not rely upon vomiting, and she is still an adolescent. Problems have yet to become entrenched.

Table 9.2

Sandra's Risk and Protective Factors Assessment

Risk	Protective	Goals
Biological		
Dieting	No history of obesity	1. Educate Sandra on healthy eating and exercise patterns
Female gender		
Heritablity: *Sandra's mother seems to have some eating-disordered attitudes and behaviors; whether Sandra's problems have been inherited is unknown. The transmission of these attitudes and ways of coping might have been learned.*		2. Weight gain
		3. Refer for physical exam to see if health problems have resulted from her disordered eating.
Early pubertal maturation: *Sandra experienced maturation at age 11.*		
Adolescent developmental stage		
Psychological		
Comorbid psychiatric disorders: *Sandra reports feelings of depression and suicidal thoughts.*	Well-developed social and coping skills: *Some of her coping mechanisms are writing in her diary and talking to her friends and her mother.*	1. Increase coping skills
Perfectionism, obsessionality, excessive compliance, low self-esteem, and negative affect/attitudes: *Sandra studies a lot and exercises daily. Her self-esteem depends, in large part, on her weight, boys' approval of her, and grades. Her teachers and her parents say that she has been a model child up until now.*		2. Correcting core maladaptive thoughts, attitudes, and feelings related to E.D.
		3. Reducing and hopefully alleviating depressive feelings.
Body dissatisfaction and distortion: *Despite being underweight at 5 foot 5 inches and 95 pounds, Sandra still feels overweight and is dissatisfied with her body.*		4. Addressing underlying developmental conflicts; idea formation; self-esteem in areas unrelated to weight and shape; sexual and aggressive difficulties; mood regulation; family dysfunction.

Risk	Protective	Goals
Social		
Family		
Interaction problems in the family: *Sandra says that her parents have a "terrible" marriage and that her father calls her mother "fat" and "crazy." However, Mrs. Benitez says that she has a good marriage—her husband is a good provider.*	Cohesion and positive communication: *Mrs. Benitez reports that the family is close and that she and her daughters have good communication.*	1. Work on strengthening the marital relationship and the ability of partners to work as a team to help Sandra.
	Effective parenting: *Mrs. Benitez says that she has no discipline problems with her daughters; they are compliant.*	2. Increase Mr. Benitez's ability to relate to his daughter as a young woman.
Inadequate parenting: *Mr. Benitez is often working and Mrs. Benitez shoulders the burden of parenting.*	No abuse history	3. Work with Mrs. Benitez on her eating-disordered attitudes and behaviors; as Sandra's mother, she is her model for female functioning
Transmission or amplification of societal emphasis on weight and appearance: *Mrs. Benitez seems obsessive about food and has evidenced disordered eating.*	Social connection: *Sandra has a few close friends with whom she regularly socializes.*	4. Increase Mrs. Benitez's social support and range of interests, as she may be overinvolved in her daughters' lives to the exclusion of her own.
		5. Teach family members communication skills.
Wider social environment		
Middle and upper SES: *The Benitez family was of middle SES in Argentina where Mr. Benitez worked as an architect. He now works many hours to maintain their middle-class status.*		1. Build Sandra's awareness of societal values and the extent to which she has internalized these.
Social emphasis on thinness as female beauty: *Both Argentina and U.S. hold these societal values.*		2. Explore and discuss gender role expectations.
Economic motives to produce body image dissatisfaction to sell products: *Both cultures are saturated with media images of thin women and advertisements related to shape and weight. Sandra avidly reads fashion magazines.*		3. Explore and discuss the family's immigration and acculturation process and its possible impact.

The Eating Attitudes Test

Garner & Garfinkel (1979)

Description

- Most commonly used self-report inventory for assessing eating disorders
- 40-item version with 7 factors: food preoccupation, body image for thinness, vomiting and laxative abuse, dieting, slow eating, clandestine eating, and perceived social pressure to gain weight
  26-item version with 3 factors (Garner, Olmsted, Bohr, & Garfinkel, 1982):

  1. Dieting (an avoidance of high-calorie food and a preoccupation with thinness)
  2. Bulimia and food preoccupation (bulimic thoughts and thoughts about food)
  3. Oral control (self-control of eating and perceived pressure from others to gain weight)

- Yields a total score and may be best used as a screening device or as a rough index of treatment progress (Anderson & Williamson, 2002)
- Versions available for children and the non-English-speaking

Reliability

- Overall alpha coefficient = .94
- Alpha coefficients range from .83 to .92 for both the 26-item and 40-item versions (Garner et al., 1982)

Validity

- Although not significantly related to measures of dieting, weight fluctuation, or neuroticism, indicating discriminant validity, scores discriminated between female patients with anorexia nervosa and normal university students.
- Normal-weight females and obese females scored lower than did anorexic patients.
- 26-item version correlates with 40-item version (r = .98) (Garner et al., 1982).

Eating Disorders Examination-Questionnaire Version

(Fairburn & Beglin, 1994)

Description

- 35-item self-report inventory developed from the Eating Disorders Examination, a semistructured interview
- Takes 15 minutes to complete
- 3 subscales: (a) restraint, (b) shape concern, and (c) weight concerns

Reliability

- Very good internal consistency and test-retest reliability, but items measuring the occurrence and frequency of the key behavioral features of eating disorders have somewhat lower stability

Validity

- Concurrent validity is strong between Eating Disorders Examination and the Questionnaire Version on purging, but not for binge eating, and higher levels of disturbance are found on the questionnaire version.

Eating Disorder Inventory-2

(Garner, 1990)

Description

- Self-report measure of the psychological and behavioral characteristics of anorexia and bulimia nervosa
- Designed for people ages 12 and older
- Takes 20 minutes to complete
- Retains the 64 items (grouped into eight scales: Drive for Thinness, Bulimia, Body Dissatisfaction, Ineffectiveness, Perfectionism, Interpersonal Distrust, Interoceptive Awareness, and Maturity Fears) of the EDI and adds 27 new items in three provisional scales: Asceticism, Impulse Regulation, and Social Insecurity
- Attempts to establish the categorical presence or absence of an eating disorder and does not seek to gauge degrees of severity (Schoemaker, Verbraak, Breteler, & van der Staak, 1997)

Reliability

- Internal consistency reliability coefficients for the scales are between .44 and .93; the revised version has lower coefficients.

- Test-retest (1 week) reliabilities of .79 to .95 for all subscales, except Interoceptive Awareness; test-retest (3 weeks) reliabilities were all above .80, excluding Maturity Fears.

Validity

- Sensitive to clinical change.
- Concurrent validity is established based on comparisons with results from *DSM-III-R* and Munich Diagnostic Checklist assessments for eating disorders (Schoemaker et al., 1997).

  - The factor-structure/solution could not be identified for the 3 new scales that were added (Eberenz & Gleaves, 1994).

- Although the original scale was considered valid by item-level factoring, the newly revised one was not (Eberenz & Gleaves, 1994).

Notes

1. This chapter has drawn extensively from this excellent review unless indicated otherwise.

2. For the return of menses and ovulation in females, normal sexual drive and hormone levels in males, and age-appropriate physical and sexual development in children and adolescents.

3. 90% of normal weight so that menstruation can resume.

References

American Psychiatric Association. (2000). *Diagnostic and statistical manual of mental disorders* (4th ed., text rev.). Washington, DC: Author.

Anderson, A. E. (1995). Eating disorders in males. In K. D. Brownell & C. G. Fairburn (Eds.), *Eating disorders and obesity: A comprehensive handbook* (pp. 177–182). New York: Guilford.

Bacaltchuk, J., & Hay, P. (2003). Antidepressants versus placebo for people with bulimia nervosa (Cochrane Review). In *The Cochrane Library*, Issue 1. Oxford: Update Software.

Bacaltchuk, J., Hay, P., & Trefiglio, R. (2003). Antidepressants versus psychological treatments and their combination for bulimia nervosa (Cochrane Review). In *The Cochrane Library*, Issue 1. Oxford: Update Software.

Butzlaff, R. L., & Hooley, J. M. (1998). Expressed emotion and psychiatric relapse. *Archives of General Psychiatry, 55*(6), 547–552.

Cash, T., & Deagle, E. (1997). The nature and extent of body image disturbances in anorexis nervosa and bulimia nervosa: A meta-analysis. *International Journal of Eating Disorders, 22*, 107–126.

Compas, B., Haaga, D., Keefe, F., Leitenberg, H., & Williams, D. (1998). Sampling of empirically supported psychological treatments from health psychology: Smoking, chronic pain, cancer, and bulimia nervosa. *Journal of Consulting and Clinical Psychology, 66,* 89–112.

Cooper, Z. (1995). The development and maintenance of eating disorders. In K. D. Brownell & C. G. Fairburn (Eds.), *Eating disorders and obesity: A comprehensive handbook* (pp. 199–206). New York: Guilford.

Crisp, A. H., Norton, K., Gowers, S., Halek, C., Bowyer, C., Yeldham, D., et al. (1991). A controlled study of the effect of therapies aimed at adolescent and family psychopathology in anorexia nervosa. *British Journal of Psychiatry, 159,* 325–333.

Croll, J., Neumark-Sztainer, D., Story, M., & Ireland, M. (2002). Prevalence and risk and protective factors related to disordered eating behaviors among adolescents: Relationship to gender and ethnicity. *Journal of Adolescent Health, 31,* 166–175.

Fairburn, C. G. (1995). The prevention of eating disorders. In K. D. Brownell & C. G. Fairburn (Eds.), *Eating disorders and obesity: A comprehensive handbook* (pp. 289–293). New York: Guilford.

Fairburn, C. G., Cooper, Z., Doll, H. A., & Welch, S. L. (1999). Risk factors for anorexia nervosa: Three integrated case-control comparisons. *Archives of General Psychiatry, 56*(5), 468–476.

Fairburn, C. G., Jones, R., Peveler, R. C., Carr, S. J., Solomon, R. A., O'Connor, M. E., et al. (1991). Three psychological treatments for bulimia nervosa: A comparative trial. *Archives of General Psychiatry, 48*(5), 463–469.

Fairburn, C. G., Marcus, M. D., & Wilson, G. T. (1993). Cognitive-behavioral therapy for binge eating and bulimia nervosa: A comprehensive treatment manual. In C. G. Fairburn & G. T. Wilson (Eds.), *Binge eating: Nature, assessment, and treatment* (pp. 361–404). New York: Guilford.

Fairburn, C. G., Norman, P. A., Welch, S. A., O'Connor, M. E., Doll, H. A., & Peveler, R. C., et al. (1995). A prospective study of outcome in bulimia nervosa and the long-term effects of three psychological treatments. *Archives of General Psychiatry, 52*(4), 304–312.

Fonagy, P., Target, M., Cottrell, D., Phillips, J., & Kurtz, Z. (2002). *What works for whom? A critical review of treatments for children and adolescents.* New York: Guilford.

Foreyt, J., Poston, W., Winebarger, A., & McGavin, J. (1998). Anorexia nervosa and bulimia nervosa. In E. Mash & R. Barkley (Eds.), *Treatment of childhood disorders* (2nd ed., pp. 647–691). New York: Guilford.

Garfinkle, P. (1995). Classification and diagnosis of eating disorders. In K. D. Brownell & C. G. Fairburn (Eds.), *Eating disorders and obesity: A comprehensive handbook* (pp. 125–134). New York: Guilford.

Halmi, K., Agras, S., Mitchell, J., Wilson, T. G., Crow, S., Bryson, S., et al. (2002). Relapse predictors of patients with bulimia nervosa who achieved abstinence through cognitive behavioral therapy. *Archives of General Psychiatry, 59,* 1105–1109.

Hay, P. J., & Bacaltchuk, J. (2003). Psychotherapy for bulimia nervosa and binging (Cochrane Review). In *The Cochrane Library,* Issue 1. Oxford: Update Software.

Hoek, H. W. (1995). The distribution of eating disorders. In K. D. Brownell & C. G. Fairburn (Eds.), *Eating disorders and obesity: A comprehensive handbook* (pp. 207–211). New York: Guilford.

Hsu, L. K. G. (1990). *Eating disorders.* New York: Guilford.

Johnson, J., Cohen, P., Kasen, S., & Brook, J. (2002). Eating disorders during adolescence and the risk for physical and mental disorders during early adulthood. *Archives of General Psychiatry, 59*, 545–552.

Keel, P., & Mitchell, J. (1997). Outcome in bulimia nervosa. *American Journal of Psychiatry, 154*, 313–321.

Kelly, A., Wall, M., Eisenberg, M., Story, M., & Neumark-Sztainer, D. (2004). High body satisfaction in adolescent girls: Association with demographic, socio-environmental, personal, and behavioral factors [Abstract]. Clinical and research poster presentations. *Journal of Adolescent Health.*

Killick, S., & Allen, C. (1997). "Shifting the balance": Motivational interviewing to help behaviour change in people with bulimia nervosa. *European Eating Disorders Review, 5*, 33–41.

Kotler, L. A., Cohen, P., Davies, M., Pine, D. S., & Walsh, B. D. (2001). Longitudinal relationships between childhood, adolescent, and adult eating disorders. *Journal of the American Academy of Child and Adolescent Psychiatry, 40*, 1434–1441.

Leon, G. R., Fulkerson, J. A., Perry, C. L., Keel, P. K., & Klump, K. L. (1999). Three to four year prospective evaluation of personality and behavioral risk factors for later disordered eating in adolescent girls and boys. *Journal of Youth and Adolescence, 28*, 181.

Lewandowski, L., Gebing, T., Anthony, J., & O'Brien, W. (1997). Meta-analysis of cognitive-behavioral treatment studies for bulimia. *Clinical Psychology Review, 17*, 703–718.

Lewinsohn, P. M., Streigel-Moore, R. H., & Seeley, J. R. (2000). Epidemiology and natural course of eating disorders in young women from adolescence to young adulthood. *Journal of the American Academy of Child and Adolescent Psychiatry, 39*, 1284–1292.

Mitchell, J. E. (1995). Medical complications of bulimia nervosa. In K. D. Brownell & C. G. Fairburn (Eds.), *Eating disorders and obesity: A comprehensive handbook* (pp. 271–277). New York: Guilford.

Mizes, J. S., & Palermo, T. M. (1997). Eating disorders. In R. T. Ammerman & M. Hersen (Eds.), *Handbook of prevention and treatment with children and adolescents: Intervention in the real world context* (pp. 238–258). New York: Wiley.

Muise, A., Stein, D., & Arbess, G. (2003). Eating disorders in adolescent boys: A review of the adolescent and young adult literature. *Journal of Adolescent Health, 33*, 427–435.

O'Neill, S. (2003). African American women and eating disturbances: A meta-analysis. *Journal of Black Psychology, 29*, 3–16.

Patton, G. C., Selzer, R., Coffey, C., Carlin, J. B., & Wolfe, R. (1999). Onset of adolescent eating disorders: Population based cohort study over 3 years. *British Medical Journal, 318*, 765–768.

Pratt, B. M., & Woolfenden, S. R. (2003). Interventions for preventing eating disorders in children and adolescents (Cochrane Review). In *The Cochrane Library*, Issue 1. Oxford: Update Software.

Robin, A. L., Siegel, P. T., & Moye, A. (1995). Family versus individual therapy for anorexia: Impact on family conflict. *International Journal of Eating Disorders, 17*(4), 313–322.

Robin, A. L., Seigel, P. T., Moye, A. W., Gilroy, M., Barker, D. A., & Sikand, A. (1999). A controlled comparison of family versus individual therapy for adolescents with anorexia nervosa. *Journal of the American Academy of Child and Adolescent Psychiatry, 38*, 1482–1489.

Rome, E., & Ammerman, S. (2003). Medical complications of eating disorders: An update. *Journal of Adolescent Health, 33*, 418–426.

Striegel-Moore, R. H. (1993). Etiology of binge eating: A developmental perspective. *International Journal of Social Psychiatry, 32*, 383–387.

Striegel-Moore, R. H., & Cachelin, F. M. (1999). Body image concerns and disordered eating in adolescent girls: Risk and protective factors. In N. G. Johnson, M. C. Roberts, & J. Worell (Eds.), *Beyond appearance: A new look at adolescent girls* (pp. 85–108). Washington, DC: American Psychological Association.

Szmukler, G., & Dare, C. (1991). The Maudsley Hospital study of family therapy in anorexia nervosa and bulimia nervosa. In B. D. Woodside & L. Shekter-Wolfson (Eds.), *Family approaches in treatment of eating disorders. Clinical practice, No. 15.* (pp. 1–21). Washington, DC: American Psychiatric Association.

Tantillo, M., Bitter, C. N., & Adams, B. (2001). Enhancing readiness for eating disorder treatment: A relational/motivational group model for change. *Eating Disorders, 9*, 203–216.

Thompson, K. M., Wonderlich, S. A., Crosby, R. D., & Mitchell, J. E. (1999). The neglected link between eating disturbances and aggressive behavior in girls. *Journal of the American Academy of Child and Adolescent Psychiatry, 38*, 1277–1284.

Treasure, J., Katzman, M., Schmidt, U., Troop, N., Todd, G., & de Silva, P. (1999). Engagement and outcome in the treatment of bulimia nervosa: First phase of a sequential design comparing motivation enhancement therapy and cognitive behavioural therapy. *Behaviour Research and Therapy, 37*, 405–418.

Treasure, J., & Ward, A. (1997). A practical guide to the use of motivational interviewing in anorexia nervosa. *European Eating Disorders Review, 5*, 102–114.

Van Furth, E. F., van Strien, D. C., Martina, L. M. L., van Son, M. J. M., Hendrickx, J. J. P., & van Engeland, H. (1996). Expressed emotion and the predication of outcome in adolescent eating disorders. *International Journal of Eating Disorders, 20*, 19–31.

Wertheim, E. H., Koerner, J., & Paxton, S. J. (2001). Longitudinal predictors of restrictive eating and bulimic tendencies in three different age groups of adolescent girls. *Journal of Youth & Adolescence, 30*(1), 69–81.

White, J. (2000). The prevention of eating disorders: A review of the research on risk factors with implications for practice. *Journal of Child and Adolescent Psychiatric Nursing, 13*, 76–88.

Whittal, M., Agras, W. S., & Gould, R. (1999). Bulimia nervosa: A meta-analysis of psychosocial and pharmacological treatments. *Behavior Therapy, 30*, 117–135.

Wilson, G., Heffernan, K., & Black, C. (1996). Eating disorders. In E. Mash & R. Barkley (Eds.), *Child psychopathology* (pp. 541–571). New York: Guilford.

Wilson, G., Terence L., Loeb, K. L., Walsh, B. T., Labouvie, E., Petkova, E., et al.

(1999). Psychological versus pharmacological treatments of bulimia nervosa: Predictors and processes of change. *Journal of Consulting and Clinical Psychology, 67*(4), 451–459.

Yager, J., Anderson, A., Devlin, M., Egger, H., Herzog, D., Mitchell, J., et al. (2002). Practice guideline for the treatment of patients with eating disorders In *American Psychiatric Association practice guidelines for the treatment of psychiatric disorders: Compendium 2002* (2nd ed., pp. 697–766). Washington, DC: American Psychiatric Association.

References for Eating Disorder Measures

Anderson, D., & Williamson, D. (2002). Outcome measurement in eating disorders. In W. IsHak, T. Burt, & L. Sederer (Eds.), *Outcome measurement in psychiatry: A critical review* (pp. 289–301). Washington, DC: American Psychiatric Publishing.

Eberenz, K. P., & Gleaves, D. H. (1994). An examination of the internal consistency and factor structure of the Eating Disorder Inventory-2 in a clinical sample. *International Journal of Eating Disorders, 16,* 371–379.

Fairburn, C., & Beglin, S. (1994). Assessment of eating disorders: Interview or self-report questionnaire? *International Journal of Eating Disorders, 16,* 363–370.

Garner, D. M. (1990). *Eating Disorder Inventory-2 professional manual.* Odessa, FL: Psychological Assessment Resources.

Garner, D. M., & Garfinkel, P. E. (1979). *The eating attitude test: An index of the symptoms of anorexia nervosa* (9th ed.). Cambridge: Cambridge University Press.

Garner, D. M., Olmsted, M. P., Bohr, Y., & Garfinkel, P. E. (1982). The eating attitudes test: Psychometric features and clinical correlates. *Psychological Medicine, 12,* 871–878.

Schoemaker, C., Verbraak, M., Breteler, R., & van der Staak, C. (1997). The discriminant validity of the Eating Disorder Inventory-2. *British Journal of Clinical Psychology, 36,* 627–629.

10 Depression

A *major depressive episode* is a period of at least 2 weeks during which a person experiences a depressed mood or loss of interest in nearly all life activities. Symptoms are in the following domains:

- affective, including sadness, anxiety, anger, irritability, emptiness, and emotional numbness
- behavioral, including agitation, crying, flatness of expression, and a slowness of physical movement and speech
- attitudes toward the self, including guilt, shame, low self-esteem, helplessness, pessimism, hopelessness, and thoughts of death and suicide
- cognitive, including decreased ability to think and concentrate
- physiological, including an inability to experience pleasure; changes in appetite, weight, and sleep patterns; a loss of energy; feelings of fatigue; decreased sex drive; and somatic complaints

Dysthymic disorder represents a general personality style featuring symptoms that are similar to, but less intense than, those of major depression. Many people with major depression experience this disorder when in remission from the major episode, but it occurs more often by itself. This diagnosis requires 2 years of a continuously depressed mood. It generally has an early age of onset (childhood through early adulthood) and produces impairments in school, work, and social life.

Diagnosis

Information and guidelines follow on the assessment of depression in adolescence, adulthood, and the elderly. Of note is that no biological tests have been identified for the diagnosis of depressive disorders (Birmaher, Ryan, Williamson, Brent, & Kaufman, 1996a). Assessment tools that might be helpful for screening and measuring treatment progress are provided in appendix I (children and adolescents) and appendix II (adults and the elderly).

Adolescence

The criteria for diagnosing depression in children and adolescents are similar to those used for adults, but there are several differences (Waslick, Kandel, & Kakouros, 2002). First, *irritable mood* is a criterion for youths but not for adults, although adults often experience irritability and anger as part of their depression. The *weight loss* criterion is *not* used with children, because children and adolescents are continuing to develop physically and are subject to weight fluctuations regardless of mental status. The *DSM* specifies, however, that youths can meet the appetite and weight disturbance criteria by not sustaining normal standards of growth and weight. For dysthymia, only 1 year's duration is required for adolescents as compared with the 2-year criterion for adults (American Psychiatric Association [APA], 2000). Depression in adolescents is further marked by separation anxiety, somatic complaints, and behavior problems (Birmaher, Ryan, Williamson, Brent, & Kaufman, 1996b). Additional research comparing adult and youth presentations of depression indicate that children and adolescents rarely experience hypersomnia (excess sleep) and are less likely to show psychotic symptoms than adults (Waslick et al., 2002). In other respects, the diagnostic presentations of youths and adults are similar.

For conducting a diagnostic assessment with children and adolescents, a greater reliance on collateral reports from parents and teachers may be necessary (Waslick et al., 2002). This may not result in more reliable information, however, because adolescents tend to be the more accurate reporters of their internal states (Birmaher et al., 1996a), especially if their parents are also depressed (Mufson & Moreau, 1997). Maternal depression colors a mother's perception of her child as more depressed than he or she may be. Current research practice involves counting a symptom as present if *either* the parent or the child reports its existence (Waslick et al., 2002).

Elderly

The elderly do not typically complain of feeling sad, anxious, or hopeless; they may speak instead of physical ailments (Agency for Health Care Policy and Research [AHCPR], 1993; Bird & Parslow, 2002). Indeed, the elderly tend to show more physical signs, such as weight loss, insomnia, and fatigue, as well as cognitive disturbance, such as memory impairment and difficulty concentrating. However, these symptoms are also common to medical conditions that often affect the elderly, such as diabetes, heart disease, Parkinson's, and Alzheimer's. In addition, such symptoms can also be brought on by medication the elderly person takes for physical disorders. Moreover, knowledge about depression is scant among the elderly; many do not believe it is a health problem that can be treated. They may see depression instead as stigmatizing—a character weakness or a sign of being "crazy" (American Association for Geriatric Psychiatry [AAGP], 2002). Further, the majority of the elderly view depression as a normal event in older age (Laidlaw, Thompson, Gallagher-Thompson, & Dick-Siskin, 2003). Depression in the elderly can hence be difficult to diagnose, and as a result, many cases go undetected. The Geriatric Depression Scale can be helpful in this regard as a screening tool for the elderly, even among those with cognitive disorders. See appendix II.

It is important to identify and treat depression in the elderly not only to reduce human suffering but also because health care costs are twice as high for older people with depression because pf increased health services utilization, longer hospital stays, and poor treatment compliance (AHCPR, 1993). Untreated depression can also lead to disability and worsen other physical illnesses, as well as result in premature morbidity and mortality from medical conditions and suicide (AAGP, 2002; AHCPR, 1993).

Prevalence

Adolescents

Reviews have indicated lifetime prevalence rates for adolescent depression ranging from 15 to 20% (Birmaher et al., 1996b; Lewinsohn & Essau, 2002). A recent nationally representative U.S. survey of 13,568 adolescents found that at least 9% of adolescents reported moderate to severe symptoms of depression (Rushton, Forcier, & Schectman, 2002). Point prevalence rates for major depression in adolescents are estimated at between 4 and 8.3%; for dysthymia, point prevalence rates range from 2 to 5% (Birmaher et al., 1996b; Cottrell, Fonagy, Kurtz, Phillips, & Target, 2002). Rates of depression for females are double the rates of males (Birmaher et al., 1996b; Lewinsohn & Essau, 2002).

Adults

Depression is the most prevalent lifetime disorder, and is experienced by 16.6% of the U.S. population (Kessler, Berglund, Demler, Jin, & Walters, 2005). In the last 12 months, major depressive disorder was reported by 6.7% (Kessler, Chiu, Demler, & Walters, 2005). The point prevalence for major depressive disorder in Western industrialized nations is 2.3 to 3.2% for men and 4.5 to 9.3% for women, with a lifetime risk of 7 to 12% for men and 20 to 25% for women (AHCPR, 1993). For the elderly, *DSM-IV* diagnosable depression rates range from 0.8 to 8% (Kraaij, Arensman, & Spinhoven, 2002). The point prevalence for dysthymia is 3%, and the lifetime prevalence is 6% (APA, 2000).

The prevalence of depression has been rising; between the 1950s and the 1990s, the rate increased five times (Kessler, 2003). Prevalence rates for major depressive disorder in adults are said to be unrelated to ethnicity, education, or income (AHCPR, 1993). However, a large study involving 19,219 users of a behavioral health service delivery system in New Jersey found that Latinos were more likely than other ethnic groups to be diagnosed with major depression (Minsky, Vega, Miskimen, Gara, & Escobar, 2003). It is unknown "whether these rates were the result of true differences or in culturally-determined expression of symptoms, clinicians' cultural biases, or problems in the application of *DSM-IV* criterion to Latinos."

Course

Adolescents

Episodes of major depression for treatment-referred children and adolescents last for a median duration of 7 to 9 months (Birmaher et al., 1996b; Cottrell et al., 2002). Community samples typically show a shorter duration, with an estimated mean of 6 months. Although almost all (90%) episodes remit within a 2-year-period, relapse is common. About half of youths experience another episode within 2 years, and a majority (70%) have relapsed at 5 years (Cottrell et al., 2002). Dysthymia takes longer to remit. The recovery rate is 7% 2 years after onset, and its median duration is 3.9 years (Kovacs, Obrosky, Gatsonis, & Richards, 1997). Youths with dysthymia tend to have an episode of major depressive disorder 2 to 3 years later.

Birmaher et al. (1996b) cites evidence that the rate of suicide in youths has quadrupled since 1950; suicide now accounts for 12% of adolescent mortality rates. Suicide attempts have also increased, with 1-year prevalence rates of 1.7 to 5.9% and lifetime prevalence rates of 3 to 7.1%.

Adolescent depression tends to continue into adulthood (Fergusson &

Woodward, 2002), with additional episodes estimated for approximately 60 to 70% of teens (Rao et al., 1995). Adults with an adolescent history of depression experience more relationship and physical health problems than adults who were not depressed (Giaconia, Reinherz, Paradis, Hauf, & Stashwick, 2001). Adolescent depression also puts people at risk in adulthood for bipolar disorder (Fergusson, Horwood, & Lynskey, 1996), anxiety (Fergusson & Woodward, 2002), and substance abuse. In addition to prevention, social workers working with adolescent clients should be knowledgeable about the identification and treatment of depression because rates of depression in youth are substantial and the consequences potentially severe.

Adults

Untreated major depression typically persists for at least a 4-month period (Karasu, Gelenberg, Merriam, & Wang, 2002). Perhaps 50 to 85% of people will suffer another episode, at which time criteria for recurrent major depressive disorder are met. People with major depressive disorder superimposed on dysthymia are at greater risk for having recurrent episodes of major depressive disorder than those without dysthymia.

The course of recurrent major depressive disorder is variable. Some people have episodes separated by many years of normal functioning, others have clusters of episodes, and still others have increasingly frequent episodes as they grow older (Karasu et al., 2002). In a 25-year follow-up of 49 individuals who had been diagnosed in an inpatient setting, the majority (84%) suffered recurrent episodes (Brodaty, Luscombe, Peisah, Anstey, & Andrews, 2001). Some cases are chronic; a large, longitudinal study of primary care patients from clinics around the world found that depression was continuously sustained for a 12-month period for a significant portion (33.5%) of the sample (Barkow et al., 2003). In 20 to 35% of cases, residual symptoms and social or occupational impairment continue between episodes (Karasu et al., 2002).

Comorbidity

Adolescents

The rate of additional mental, emotional, and behavioral disorders for children and adolescents with major depression is high in both community and clinic samples (Waslick et al., 2002). Estimates suggest that 40 to 70% of adolescents with depression have one other disorder and 20% have two or more additional disorders (Birmaher et al., 1996b; Cottrell et al., 2002).

In other words, only a minority of youths with depression do not have another diagnosis (Waslick et al., 2002).

Dysthymia and anxiety disorders are the most common comorbid conditions (Birmaher et al., 1996b). With children and young adolescents, separation anxiety is the most frequent anxiety disorder, with the anxiety preceding depression in two thirds of cases (Goodman, Schwab-Stone, Lahey, Shaffer, & Jensen, 2000). The next most common diagnosis is one of the disruptive disorders: oppositional defiant disorder, conduct disorder, or attention-deficit/hyperactivity disorder (Cottrell et al., 2002). Other concurrent conditions include substance abuse problems, eating disorders, learning disabilities, and medical problems (Waslick et al., 2002). Known guidelines for how to target intervention for these concurrent disorders are described in the next section on adult depression.

Adults

Individuals with major depressive disorder suffer from occupational difficulties and physical disability, including chronic activity restriction, missed days from work, illness (e.g., heart disease) (Rugulies, 2002), increased health care utilization, and mortality (AHCPR, 1993). For comorbidity with other psychiatric disorders, the lifetime rate may reach up to 43%. When comorbidity is present, the social worker has three options, depending on the concurrent disorder:

1. Treat the depression as primary, and when the individual responds, reassess whether the other condition still needs separate treatment (e.g., generalized anxiety disorder).
2. Treat the other condition as primary (for example, eating disorders and substance abuse).
3. Decide which condition predominates (e.g., major depression and panic disorder) (AHCPR, 1993).

Risk Factors for the Onset of Adolescent Depression

Several risk and protective factors have been identified for depression in adolescents. Certain of these are explored in more depth in the following section. Also see Table 10.1 for a detailing of factors.

Adolescent Developmental Stage Factors

Increased vulnerability for depression may occur in adolescence because it is a time of life when the capacity for personal reflection, abstract reasoning,

Table 10.1

Risk and Protective Factors for the Onset of Adolescent Depression

Risk	Protective
Biological	
• Genetic influence	
• Female gender	• Male gender
Cognitive	
• Formal operations	
Psychological	
• Negative attributional style	• Active problem-solving skills
• Ruminative thinking style	
Social	
Family	
• Weak parent–child attachment	
• Parental criticism and hostility	
• Ineffective parenting	
• Enmeshed family relationships	
• Parental psychopathology, particularly depression	
• Child maltreatment	
• Other stressful life events	
Peer	
• Peer rejection	• Peer support and acceptance
Socioeconomic	
• Low socioeconomic status	

and formal operational thought develop. At this stage, youth can first consider *causality* for the events in their lives, and they may develop a negative attribution style (see the next section). Adolescence is also a time in development when a *future orientation* develops; with this ability, the adolescent may experience hopelessness about the future (Abela, Brozina, & Haigh, 2002).

Negative Cognitive Style

Depression is related to significant cognitive distortions, such as Beck's conceptualization of the "cognitive triad" of depression: thoughts about the self as worthless, the world as unfair, and the future as hopeless (Beck, Rush, Shaw, & Emery, 1979). Another aspect of negative thinking patterns involves what has been identified as the "depressive attributional style" (Abramson, Seligman, & Teasdale, 1978). This style attributes negative events to internal, stable, and global attributions ("I failed the test because I was stupid"). Positive outcomes are ascribed to external, transient, and specific reasons ("I passed the test because it was easy"). "Although the mechanisms by which children and adolescents develop cognitive styles are not yet established, studies have suggested that certain factors, such as modeling significant others, perfectionistic standards, criticism, rejection, and experiences with uncontrollable stressful life events, may play a role" (Birmaher et al., 1996b).

Family Factors

Family factors can present risk for the development, maintenance, and relapse of depression in youths (Diamond, Reis, Diamond, Siqueland, & Isaacs, 2002). Several research reviews found that families with an adolescent who is depressed show the following (Diamond et al., 2002): weak attachment bonds (Sund & Wichstrom, 2002), criticism and hostility, parental psychopathology, ineffective parenting, enmeshed family relationships (Jewell & Stark, 2003), and greater family stress (Asarnow, Jaycox, & Tompson, 2001).

Depression in mothers is a particular risk factor. A review of longitudinal studies indicates that by the time a child with a depressed parent reaches age 20, there is a 40% chance that an episode of major depression will have occurred (Beardslee, Versage, & Gladstone, 1998). Maternal depression also appears to result in an earlier onset for child depression (Lewinsohn & Essau, 2002). Girls may be more at risk because of gender role modeling (Goodman & Gotlib, 1999). A mother's parenting may be negatively affected even with mild symptoms of depression (Duggal, Carlson, Sroufe, & Egeland, 2001), although other studies have found that the chronicity and severity of the parent's illness may be linked to higher rates of depression in children (Beardslee et al., 1998).

Many possible reasons may account for the increased risk associated with maternal depression. First, genetic factors may be involved, although evidence for heredity is stronger in adult rather than adolescent samples (Goodman & Gotlib, 1999). Other biological factors may include the abnormal neuroendocrine functioning that has been found in women who are depressed during pregnancy (Goodman & Gotlib, 1999). As a result, the fetus may be exposed to increased cortisol levels and experience a reduced blood flow, leading to slower growth and less movement.

Psychosocial explanations have also been posited (Duggal et al., 2001;

Goodman & Gotlib, 1999; Peterson et al., 1993). Maternal needs for nurturing and care can interfere with a mother's ability to meet children's emotional and social needs. Mothers may be emotionally uninvolved and unavailable and feel a sense of helplessness in the midst of parenting challenges. Parents may model depressive affect, thinking patterns, and behaviors for their children and then reinforce their children's depressive behaviors. Depressed parents also tend to see their children's behavior in a negative light, using low rates of reward and high rates of punishment or responding indiscriminately to the child's behavior. Finally, women with depression often experience high rates of marital discord, which, in turn, exposes children to high levels of parental conflict (Goodman & Gotlib, 1999). Marital problems are also associated with an increased risk for depression in children (Beardslee et al., 1998).

Research over the past five decades has tended to "blame" mothers for a variety of mental, emotional, and behavioral problems in children, so social workers need to be careful not to accept the findings just described as support for that tradition. Social workers should use this knowledge instead to help identify possible depression in parents and apply appropriate services. Evidence is also accumulating that fathers play an important role in families with depressed mothers, either by exacerbating the risk of psychopathology in the child or by protecting the child from the adverse effects of maternal depression (Goodman & Gotlib, 1999). According to a review by Beardslee et al. (1998), other protective factors when children have depressed parents are their ability to engage in interpersonal relationships and their involvement in school and extracurricular activities.

Experiences of Maltreatment

A number of studies have indicated a significant relationship between adolescent depression and childhood physical abuse and sexual abuse (e.g., Fergusson et al., 1996). In one prospective longitudinal study, a majority (64%) of children who were sexually abused were diagnosed with depressive disorders at age 17 years (Egeland, 1997). Researchers in another study tracked 776 randomly selected children at a mean age of 5 years for 17 years, separating out different forms of maltreatment and adverse family risk factors, such as parental conflict and impaired parent–child interactions, that are associated with abuse (Brown, Cohen, Johnson, & Smailes, 1999). They reported that child maltreatment results in a three to four times higher likelihood of depression or suicidality in adolescents and adults. Of all types of maltreatment, sexual abuse poses the greatest risk for depression and suicide (Brown et al., 1999; Fergusson et al., 1996). Between 16.5 and 19.5% of suicide attempts in young adults may be attributed to child sexual abuse (Brown et al., 1999). Physical abuse is also linked to suicide attempts during adolescence and depression in adults (Brown et al., 1999). As noted in other chapters in this book, child maltreatment poses a risk factor not only for the development of depression but also for many other disorders.

Peer Interactions

On the positive side, successful peer relations may mitigate harsh family circumstances. Friends can provide support and enable youths to intimately share and self-disclose in a safe setting. Such acceptance from peers may prevent teens from resorting to risk-taking behaviors (Dekovic, 1999).

SES and Ethnic Minority Status

Ethnic minorities in the United States may be at risk for adolescent depression, although this could be because so many of such youths are living in poverty. The National Longitudinal Studies of Youth indicated that children who lived in poverty at ages 4 to 5 were at increased risk for depression 4 years later compared with children who were not living in poverty (McLeod & Shanahan, 1996). Another survey, involving 2,046 adolescents ages 12 to 15, found rates of major depression for Caucasian youth at 9.6% (without significant behavioral impairment) and 4.3% (with impairment). Higher rates were reported for African American (13.4% without impairment and 6.1% with impairment) and Mexican American youths (16.9% and 9%) (Doi, Roberts, Takeuchi, & Suzuki, 2001). Confounding demographic factors, such as household composition and parent education, however, accounted for much of the variance in rates.

In a study of 810 African American families, risk factors for childhood depressive symptoms (ages 10–12) included uninvolved parenting, racial discrimination, and criminal victimization (Simons et al., 2002). Community ethnic identification seems to be an important as a protective factor, as it is negatively related to depressive symptoms.

Gender

In epidemiological, community, and clinical youth samples, depression is much more prevalent in females than in males (about twice the rate) (Kovacs, 2001). This gender gap, which emerges by age 14, is found internationally—across Canada, Great Britain, and the United States (Wade, Cairney, & Pevalin, 2002)—and persists across the lifespan (Kessler, 2003). It does not appear related to either reporting bias or help-seeking behaviors (Kessler, 2003). Other factors, however, such as age at onset, recovery from the initial episode, risk of another episode, and presence of comorbid disorders, do not demonstrate differential gender patterns (Kovacs, 2001).

Various biological and psychosocial reasons have been hypothesized for the gender gap in depression. Biological theories involve the hormonal shifts females experience during premenses, pregnancy, postpartum, and menopause (Desai & Jann, 2000). For example, a majority of pregnant women (70%) report depressive symptoms, with 15% meeting full criteria for major depression (Desai & Jann, 2000). A recent meta-analysis found that postpartum depression affects 13% of childbearing women (O'Hara & Swain, 1996). However, the specific mechanisms by which hormones exert their influence have not been delineated (Le, Munoz, Ippen, & Stoddard, 2003). It may be instead that hormonal changes intersect with the psychosocial. For example, role changes involved with reproductive events in societies that devalue women's roles may result in depression.

Psychosocial explanations for the gender gap in depression have to do with the stressful life events that females experience, such as sexual abuse and family violence. Sexual abuse in childhood is known to be associated with depression (Brown et al., 1999; Egeland, 1997), and the rate of sexual abuse is higher in females (Bolen & Scannapieco, 1999).

Other stressors come in the form of financial hardship, neighborhood disadvantage, women's work being less highly regarded and paid than men's work, and role overload, as women often assume primary responsibility for taking care of children and the home, even when they are employed outside the home (Le et al., 2003).

Psychological explanations for depression include evidence that females with depression tend to evidence low self-esteem, pessimism, and a ruminative thinking style (Dekovic, 1999; Nolen-Hoeksema, 2002). *Rumination* can be defined as the proclivity to focus on the symptoms of a distressed mood, mulling over the reasons for its occurrence in an incessant and passive way rather than in an active, problem-solving manner (Nolen-Hoeksema, 2002).

Risk and Protective Factors for Adolescent Recovery and Adjustment

Recovery, however, is inhibited by higher levels of depression (Kaminski & Garber, 2002), poor general health, school suspension, weaker family relationships (Rushton et al., 2002), family conflict, parental psychopathology, stressful life events, low SES, and comorbid anxiety (Birmaher et al., 1996a). For both major depression and dysthymia, early onset has typically (but not always) been a poor prognostic factor for the rate of recovery (Goodman et al., 2000; Kovacs et al., 1997).

Risk and protective factors for treatment engagement and outcome have also been identified. Premature dropout from treatment was related to high levels of hopelessness (Brent, Kolko, Birmaher, Baugher, & Bridge, 1999). Positive outcome was associated with the following factors at intake (Brent et al., 1998; Clarke et al., 1992; Hamilton & Bridge, 1999):

- Milder depression
- Lack of comorbid anxiety
- Lack of attention problems
- Higher frequency and enjoyment of positive activities
- Fewer cognitive distortions
- Less hopelessness at intake
- Lack of maternal depression

Given the role of hopelessness in both dropout and outcome from treatment, the social worker should monitor the adolescent's experience of hopelessness and instill a sense of hope in the adolescent. Beyond individual characteristics of the adolescent, recovery has much to do with familial and other environmental factors that the social worker needs to assess and provide services.

Firearms in the household substantially increase the risk of suicide in youth with depression. However, even when parents are warned about this risk, they may not remove guns from the home (Brent, Baugher, Birmaher, Kolko, & Bridge, 2000). Therefore, it is critical that social workers discuss with parents the risk of possessing firearms in the home and monitor parents' behavior around this issue.

Risk and Protective Factors for Adult Depression

Risk and protective factors that are similar for both adolescent and adult depression include gender and negative cognitive style (see Table 10.2). Note that the risk and protective factors for the elderly are similar to those for other adult populations. A meta-analysis of risk factors for depression in the elderly living in the community indicated female gender, previous depression, bereavement, sleep problems, and medical disability (Cole & Dendukuri, 2003). Biological and medical factors are the risk factors discussed here.

Biological Factors

Major depression tends to run in families, which supports, at least in part, a process of genetic transmission. Based on a meta-analysis of five twin studies, the heritability for major depression is significant, in the range of

Table 10.2

Risk and Protective Factors for Onset of Depression in Adults

Risk	Protective
Biological	
• Genetics: a history of depression in first-degree relative	• No first-degree relative history
• Female	• Male
• Medical problems	• Good health
Psychological	
• Negative cognitive style	• Active coping mechanisms
• Insecure attachment style	
Social	
Family	
• Marital problems,[a] poor intimate relationships	• Supportive, intimate relationships
• Low social support and interaction	• Social support and connection
• Stressful life events,[b] especially those involving loss[c]	

[a]Beach & Jones (2002).
[b]Kraaij, Arensman, & Spinhoven (2002).
[c]De Beurs et al. (2001).

31 to 42% (Sullivan, Neale, & Kendler, 2000). However, this also means that the majority of influences (60–70%) are environmental in nature. No specific genetic marker for major depression has been found. The genetic potential for depression may be transmitted as an affective temperament that makes one susceptible to a mood disorder, depending on other internal and external factors. Late-onset depression (after age 60) appears to be less associated with family transmission than early-onset depression (before age 20) (Birmaher et al., 1996b).

Biological theories of depression have been formulated from the hypothesized actions of antidepressants. Many depressions are thought to be associated with "chemical imbalances" or deficiencies of certain neurotransmitters in the limbic area of the brain. These substances are naturally regulated by breaking down in the spaces between cells or through reuptake into transmitting cells.

However, certain limitations apply to these biological theories (Valenstein, 1998). First, there is no test that can establish biological depression.

It is not possible to actually measure the levels of neurotransmitters in the human brain. Only indirect measures can be relied upon, and when these are used, low levels of neurotransmitters considered to be critical are not reliable indicators of depression.

The early antidepressants were thought to work by increasing norepinephrine in the nervous system. The newer antidepressants inhibit the reuptake of serotonin, and it is suspected that all antidepressants have effects on other neurotransmitters such as gamma aminobutyric acid (GABA), dopamine, and the opioids. However, some medications help with depression, even though they affect other transmitters. For instance, the tricyclics tend to work on acetylcholine. "The point is not that an acetylcholine or a dopamine theory of depression would be better than a norepinephrine- or a serotonin-based theory, but rather that all of the biochemical theories presented to explain depression involve a selective perception of the evidence, ignoring some findings and exaggerating and even distorting others" (Valenstein, 1998).

Another problem with theories based on brain chemistry is that medications need a few weeks to demonstrate their impact on mood. However, they produce maximum elevation of neurotransmitter activity in only a couple of days. Because each neuron both receives and transmits from tens of thousands of other neurons, a medication that focuses on one type of neurotransmitter actually exponentiates its effect throughout other chemical systems. Hence, it is difficult to account for the changes that might be responsible for improved mood. In other words, biological theories have not considered the potential complexity involved in the brain (Valenstein, 1998).

Medical Problems

Medical conditions, such as heart attack, cancer, stroke, and diabetes, increase the risk of depression (Karasu et al., 2002; NIMH, 2002). Further, a meta-analysis of 10 studies indicated a significant relationship between positive HIV status and major depressive disorder (Ciesla & Roberts, 2001). In the elderly, symptoms of depression can be precipitated by illnesses common in later life, including Alzheimer's, Parkinson's, heart disease, cancer, and arthritis (NMHA, 2002). Untreated depression can also be a risk factor for recovery from other illnesses. It can increase the level of impairment, interfere with healing, and impede an individual's motivation and ability to follow through with prescribed treatment (NIMH, 2002).

Risk and Protective Factors for Recurrence and Recovery

The risk of recurrence of depression is related to aspects of the disorder: the number of prior episodes that have been experienced and the presence of residual symptoms (Karasu et al., 2002). The risk of recurrence is also associated with the occurrence of concurrent disorders—both medical and psychiatric. Recovery from depression in those seeking outpatient treatment is associated with less severe depression initially, receiving adequate medication treatment, a lack of personality problems, and being married (Barnett et al., 2002).

For the elderly, certain factors may impede optimal treatment response (AHCPR, 1993): an accumulation of negative life events and prolonged and/or unresolved grief. Problems with becoming dependent on others and the role transitions associated with old age may also pose barriers, as might social isolation.

Intervention

The initial part of intervention for those who are depressed is to assess suicidal risk. Consideration of risk and protective factors determines the appropriate treatment setting to protect client safety. For assessment of suicidal risk and options for care, see Table 10.3. Intervention for adolescents is discussed here first, followed by treatment for adults.

Adolescent Intervention

Adolescent intervention includes psychotherapy and medication. Psychotherapies explored here are cognitive-behavioral therapy, interpersonal therapy, and family therapy. Medication, its combination with psychotherapy, and prevention approaches are also covered in this section.

Psychotherapy

Cognitive-Behavioral Therapy
Intervention research has tended to focus on cognitive-behavioral models. *Behavioral* models focus on the development of coping skills, especially in the domain of social skills and choosing pleasant daily activities, so that youths receive more reinforcement from their environments. *Cognitive* models include assessing and changing the distorted thinking that people with depression exhibit, in which they cast everyday experiences in a negative light. Interventions based on cognitive-behavioral models include the following components:

- The identification and restructuring of depressive thinking
- Social skills training (how to make and maintain friendships)
- Communication and social problem solving (how to share feelings and resolve conflict without alienating others)

Table 10.3		
Assessing Suicidal Risk and Intervention		

Assess Risk
- Presence of suicidal or homicidal ideation, intent, or plans
- Access to means for suicide and the lethality of those means
- Presence of psychotic symptoms
- Presence of severe anxiety
- Presence of substance use
- History and seriousness of previous attempts
- Family history of or recent exposure to suicide
- Determine Treatment Setting

Inpatient	Outpatient	If outpatient
• Psychosis is present.	• If psychosis is absent	• Provide education about
• Suicidal or homicidal	• If substance abuse is not a	symptoms of depression
ideation is present, with	problem	and the effectiveness of
significant substance	• Person indicates control	treatment.
abuse, severe	over suicidal thoughts	• Develop a "no harm"
hopelessness, strong		contract."
impulses to act on the		• Advise abstinence from
ideas, or specific suicide		substances, which may
plans.		increase depressive
• Inadequate social support		symptoms and impulsive
for effective outpatient		behaviors.
treatment.		• See clients weekly to
• Complicating psychiatric		monitor suicidal ideation,
or general medical		hopelessness, and
conditions make		substance abuse.
outpatient medication		• Explain to family members
treatment unsafe.		how to respond to
		suicidal ideas.
		• Remove firearms from
		the house.

Source: Agency for Health Care Policy and Research (1993).

- Developing aptitudes pertaining to self-esteem (establishing performance goals)
- Progressive relaxation training to ease the stress and tension that can undercut enjoyment of activities
- Structuring mood-boosting activities into daily life

Interventions involve modeling by the social worker, behavioral rehearsal in the session, and the assignment of homework to practice skills. Narrative reviews (Diamond et al., 2002) and meta-analyses (Cuijpers, 1998; Reinecke, Ryan, & Dubois, 1998) of cognitive-behavioral treatment have indicated positive outcomes in terms of reduction of depression for up to 2 years follow-up.

Some studies, however, have failed to show that cognitive-behavioral interventions outperform simpler treatments, such as relaxation training (Reynolds & Coats, 1986) and therapeutic support (Fine, Forth, Gilbert, & Haley, 1991). In one study, for example, 107 adolescents were randomly assigned to one of three conditions: systemic family treatment, cognitive-behavioral therapy, and a supportive individual therapy control condition (Brent et al., 1997). Cognitive-behavioral therapy was more effective than the other conditions on some measures at posttest, but these differences were not apparent at the 2-year follow-up (Birmaher, et al., 2000).

Interpersonal Therapy

Interpersonal therapy is a relatively brief intervention (approximately 12 sessions) focusing on how current interpersonal relationships have contributed to depression. This perspective considers interpersonal conflicts to be a major source of depression, and the goal of the social worker is to help the client repair these conflicts (Weissman, Markowitz, & Klerman, 2000). The intervention plan focuses on significant role transitions, grief processes, and interpersonal disputes or deficits. The client and social worker devise tasks toward improvements in these areas. This intervention has been adapted for use with adolescents (Moreau, Mufson, Weissman, & Klerman, 1991).

Pretest-posttest studies have shown recovery rates for clients participating in interpersonal therapy as 80% (Santor & Kusumakar, 2001) to 90% (Mufson et al., 1994), with gains maintained at 1-year follow-up (Mufson & Fairbanks, 1996). Santor and Kusumakar (2001) note in their study that service providers had no prior training in interpersonal therapy before they were trained and supervised for the study, suggesting that practitioners can be taught to effectively implement the model.

Randomized studies have recently been conducted that indicate the superiority of interpersonal therapy to clinical monitoring (which includes regular contact but not therapeutic intervention) (Mufson, Weissman, Moreau, & Garfinkel, 1999) and wait-list controls (Rossello & Bernal, 1999) for reducing adolescent depression. In one study with a Puerto Rican sample, both interpersonal therapy and cognitive-behavioral therapy were equally effective in producing clinically significant remittance of symptoms (Rossello & Bernal, 1999).

Family Intervention

Despite the known links between family factors and depression in youth, few studies have explored family-based interventions. In several studies, a parenting component was added to cognitive-behavioral group intervention for adolescents with depression, but no particular benefits were gained by doing so (Clarke, Rohde, Lewinsohn, Hops, & Seeley, 1999; Lewinsohn, Clarke, Hops, & Andrews, 1990). In the Brent et al. (1997) study described earlier, family treatment was not superior to the other conditions. Diamond et al. (2002) designed an attachment-based family intervention that was an integration of various other therapies and tested it on a sample of 32 adolescents with major depressive disorder. The adolescents, who were predominantly female, African American, and low income, were randomized to either the 12-week treatment or a 6-week, minimal-contact, wait-list control group. Although there were some limitations of the study in terms of small sample size and unequal assessments of the groups, the findings were encouraging. At posttest, 81% of the treatment group no longer met the criteria for major depressive disorder compared with 47% of the comparison group. At a 6-month follow-up, 87% of the treatment group continued to demonstrate their improvement.

Medication

In an analysis of service, utilization data from 1987 to 1997, drawing from two nationally representative surveys of the U.S. general population (Olfson et al., (2002), found that outpatient intervention for adolescent depression is much more common. Patterns of treatment have changed, however, with less focus on psychotherapy. Instead, medication is increasingly used. Social workers should thus be aware of medication use with this population so that families can be educated about its benefits and limitations and other appropriate services can be applied. (Unless otherwise indicated, guidelines for the use of medication with child and adolescent depression in this chapter are drawn from Hughes et al. [1999] through the Texas Children's Medication Algorithm Project.)

For adolescent depression, selective serotonin reuptake inhibitors (SSRIs) have shown greater therapeutic effectiveness and fewer adverse effects than tricyclic antidepressants. Indeed, the tricyclic antidepressants are not recommended for children, given the lack of evidence to support their use (Hazell, O'Connell, Heathcote, & Henry, 2003). Early in treatment, the prescribing physician should see clients often (every 1 to 2 weeks) because close monitoring produces greater treatment adherence. It also provides additional opportunities for education and enables clinicians (including social workers) to assess clients for potential worsening symptoms, the emergence of suicidal thinking, and other complicating factors.

Psychotherapy and Medication Combined

Research has not been undertaken on the combination of psychotherapy and medication, despite its common use in practice. One exception is a study by Hamilton and Bridge (1999), who treated 50 youths diagnosed with major depressive disorder at a health maintenance organization. Subjects received nonspecific psychotherapy and selective SSRI medication. At 6 months, 33% of the participants reported improved mood. These recovery rates were not as great as in the more highly structured clinical trials of psychotherapy reported earlier (generally about 60%). A limitation of this study was that only 34% of the sample received the amount of psychotherapy considered to be minimally effective for depressed adolescents, which is six sessions (Wood, Harrington, & Moore, 1996). This study was based in a clinic setting. It is well known that research conducted in clinics yields less positive effects than studies carried out in university settings (Weisz, Donenberg, Han, & Weiss, 1995). University studies involve specially trained therapists with small caseloads using experimental procedures. University studies also rely on pure diagnostic categories of disorders (for instance, screening out those with substance abuse) and lower risk samples (exclusion of those who are suicidal). Social workers typically find themselves in clinic and hospital settings, struggling with comorbid disorders and high-risk problems.

Prevention for Adolescent Depression

Because one of the most readily identifiable risk factors for depression in youths is depression in parents, a few recent studies have attempted to target children of such parents for secondary prevention services. Beardslee, Wright, Salt, and Drezner (1997) conducted a randomized, control trial of a family-based, psychoeducational intervention for parents with depression and their offspring. They found positive intervention effects on child and parent outcomes from participating in the experimental condition. Children learned more about their parents' disorder, with decreasing self-blame and guilt for their parents' condition. The youths also more constructively appraised stressors and improved on their coping methods compared with those in the control condition. In addition, parents showed increased understanding of their children's experience. Despite these positive findings, no information was provided on youth depression outcomes.

Clark and colleagues (Clarke et al., 2001, 2002) used the cognitive-behavioral "Coping with Depression" course (Clarke, Lewisohn, & Hops, 1990) with offspring of parents who were depressed. The results of the 2001 study were largely successful in that the group intervention lessened depression risk in those who were subsyndromal (did not meet full criteria for depression). However, the 2002 study looked at adolescents who met criteria for either major depression or dysthymia. When these adolescents were randomized to either the cognitive-behavioral group intervention or "usual care" (typically antidepressants) at the health maintenance organization where this study took place, the cognitive-behavioral intervention did not present a unique advantage. Recovery rates averaged about 30%. The results of these studies suggest that social workers should be aware of the possible effects of adult depression on teens and intervene accordingly. They might further need to focus their efforts on teens whose depression does not meet full diagnostic criteria or youths who are dysthymic to prevent the onset of major depression (Birmaher et al., 1996b). In addition, Birmaher et al. (1996b) report on other possible prevention strategies. Because substance abuse tends to occur an average of 4.5 years after major depression, there is a window for the prevention of substance abuse for adolescents who are depressed.

Prevention programs have also been a focus of meta-analysis (Merry, McDowell, Hetrick, Bir, & Muller, 2004). Although small positive effects were associated with the psychologically oriented programs just described, these translated into significant decreases in depressive episodes. More educationally driven programs were not deemed successful. Programs applied universally (primary prevention) seemed less effective than those administered to targeted groups (i.e., children of depressed parents) (secondary prevention).

Summary

A few psychotherapy studies with adolescent depression have focused on minority samples (Diamond et al., 2002; Fine et al., 1991; Rosello & Bernal, 1999), and results have been largely positive. This is encouraging, given the fact that adolescents from minority groups may suffer from depression at increased rates.

Overall, in reviewing 13 studies on psychosocial intervention, Diamond et al. (2002) concluded that while results of interventions are positive at posttest, a quarter to half of clients relapse 6 months to 2 years after the intervention. Taking into account both medication and psychosocial intervention studies, Cottrell et al. (2002) noted that almost half (40–50%) of adolescents may not respond. Therefore, although the range of approaches to treatment of adolescent depression needs to be retained, more effective treatments should also be developed. Social workers can be involved in all aspects, including treatment model development, targeting depression in youth, referral, and applying validated prevention and treatment strategies with children and adolescents.

Adult Treatment

There are several options for treatment of adult depression that present certain advantages and disadvantages. These options, discussed in Table

10.4, include psychotherapy, bibliotherapy, and medication. The social worker should be aware, however, that psychotherapy—either cognitive-behavioral or interpersonal therapy—is considered a first-line intervention because of comparable efficacy with medication, lack of side effects, and cost-effectiveness (Antonuccio, Thomas, & Danton, 1997). If treatment is not successful, medication can be used as a supplement, as Antonuccio et al. (1997) found in their cost-effectiveness study that it is more cost-effective to use medication in combination with cognitive-behavioral therapy than alone. Psychotherapy and medication are explored in some detail next. The use of St. John's wort and exercise is also presented.

Psychotherapy

As with the treatment of adolescent depression, cognitive-behavioral psychotherapy directed at the depressive symptoms and interpersonal psychotherapy targeting the interpersonal problems associated with depression appear to work equally well (AHCPR, 1993; Wampold, Minami, Baskin, & Tierney, 2002). Reviews of the meta-analyses (including more than 80 controlled studies) have shown cognitive-behavioral therapy to be more effective than no-treatment control groups, *as well as medication* (Sanderson & McGinn, 2001), even for chronic depression (DeRubeis, Gelfand, Tang, & Simons, 1999). Cognitive-behavioral therapy has also been used to successfully treat depression in the elderly (Arean & Cook, 2002). Finally, cognitive-behavioral therapy seems more effective for preventing relapse than medication (Greenberg & Fisher, 1997). Not everyone is suited to this form of treatment, however. Factors associated with response to cognitive-behavioral treatment include employment, female gender, no comorbidity, and functional attitudes (Karusu et al., 2002).

A meta-analysis on group treatment for depression showed that group therapy is as helpful as individual treatment (McDermut, Miller, & Brown, 2001). Because group treatment is generally more cost-effective, social workers may consider delivering treatment through groups for this population. The meta-analysis also found that group cognitive-behavioral treatment was more effective than psychodynamic group psychotherapy.

A small body of knowledge has also accumulated on the use of cognitive-behavioral marital therapy for depression (Beach & Jones, 2002). Behavioral marital therapy is a skill-building approach following the principles of social learning, cognitive techniques, and behavioral exchange (Beach, Sandeen, & O'Leary, 1990). Partners are taught specific skills to enhance marital support and intimacy and to reduce marital stress and negative expectancies. Cognitive-behavioral marital therapy might be the treatment of choice when the depressed individual views the depression as related to marital functioning. In studies, conjoint therapy has been found to reduce symptoms of depression and to positively affect the couple re-

Table 10.4

Type of Treatments, Benefits, Costs, Indications, and Contraindactions

Type of Treatment	Benefits	Limitations	Indications and Contraindications
Medication	1. Ease of administration 2. Effective for all severity levels of depression (mild, moderate, and severe) 3. Rapid response is possible (4–6 weeks)	1. Need for monitoring for response 2. Side effects 3. Can be used for suicide attempts. 4. Non-adherence is high 5. Not effective in all cases. 6. Often takes a process of trial and error to find the appropriate medication and dosage.	1. History of prior positive response 2. History of first-degree relatives' positive response 3. For severe depression 4. For melancholic depression 5. If there is adherence to medication regime 6. Client preference 7. Experience of doctor with the medication 8. Medical illnesses or other medications that make anti-depressant use risky 9. Cost considerations
Psychotherapy	1. Lack of physiological side effects 2. Individual learns to cope with or avoid factors that precipitate episodes	1. Not recommended as sole treatment for severe depression 2. Many fail to complete course of treatment 3. Need high quality treatment; availability of well-trained practitioners 4. Sessions time-consuming	1. Because of cost-effectiveness, CBT recommended as a first-line treatment (Antonuccio et al., 1997). 2. For mild, moderate, or chronic depression. 3. When psychosocial stress, difficulty coping, and inter-personal problems are present. 4. Client preference. 5. In cases of pregnancy, lactation, or the desire to become pregnant.

Type of Treatment	Benefits	Limitations	Indications and Contraindications
Combined medication and psychotherapy treatment (Arnow & Constantino, 2003)	Same as above	Same as above	1. For severe depression 2. Recommended if psychotherapy alone has not been successful (Antonuccio et al., 1997) 3. A history of psychosocial problems, with and without depression 4. History of problems with treatment adherence
Bibliotherapy (Cuijpers, 1997; Floyd, 2003; Scogin, Hanson, & Welsh, 2003)	1. For mild to &moderate depression 2. Validated for adults and elders, for a 3-year follow-up period (Smith, Floyd, Jamison, & Scogin, 1997) 3. Client can work at own pace at home 4. Client can receive services if geographical or transportation barriers are an issue 5. Cost-effective for those unable to afford medication or psychotherapy 6. Provides skills for coping after treatment has ended	1. Not appropriate for severe depression 2. Not appropriate for those who are unmotivated or have low reading ability or cognitive impairments or who have not responded to individual therapy	*Feeling Good* (Burns, 1999) and *Control Your Depression* (Lewinsohn, Munoz, Youngren, & Zeiss, 1986) have been empirically validated, but many other self-help books available have not been researched.

Source: Karasu et al. (2002); AHCPR (1993).

lationship. (See Corcoran [2003] for a review.) However, the social worker must be aware that the few studies conducted have been primarily with Caucasian, middle-class, married couples who were seen in outpatient settings.

For the elderly, reminiscence and life review therapies may be effective, according to a meta-analysis on the results of 24 studies (Bohlmeijer, Smit, & Cuijpers, 2003). A strong effect was shown for these interventions. The effect was even larger for those with severe depression. Most of the studies were conducted in noninstitutionalized settings, so the results may not generalize to those in nursing homes and extended care facilities.

Medication

Medication is increasingly prescribed as a first-line treatment for depression by managed care health organizations because of its perceived cost-effectiveness. However, in a study of the cost-effectiveness of fluoxetine (Prozac) versus cognitive-behavioral therapy and their combination, Antonuccio et al. (1997) found that fluoxetine involved a 33% higher cost than cognitive-behavioral therapy over a 2-year period. These higher costs were related to the increased rate of relapse with medication, the side effects experienced, and, most seriously, suicide.

Another perception commonly held is that the newer antidepressants, the SSRIs, are more effective than the tricyclic antidepressants. However, a meta-analysis of 102 randomized controlled trials (10,706 patients) found no overall difference in efficacy between SSRIs and tricyclics (Anderson, 2000). The exception is that the tricyclics appear more effective in inpatient settings. The SSRIs are better tolerated, with significantly lower rates of treatment discontinuation overall. In general, it is difficult to predict how a certain individual will react to a particular medication. The process of finding a medication and an appropriate dosage that improves mood is one of trial and error (Healy, 2002).

One controversial finding involving a comprehensive review of the published studies on medication efficacy indicated that medication may be only 25% more effective than inactive placebos (placebos without side effects) (Antonuccio, Burns, Danton, & O'Donohue, 2000). This means that the placebo effect accounted for the bulk of changes reported.

Concerns have been raised about the use of medication with youngsters. For children, cardiac problems may be associated with the tricyclics, and children who are taking tricyclics should be carefully monitored for possible cardiac effects. In the United Kingdom, SSRIs have been banned for people under age 18 because of concerns about suicidality. In examining depression in teens, the SSRIs have been pronounced more effective than the tricyclics.

In addition, the Treatment for Adolescents with Depression Study

(TADS) Team (2004) has examined a 36-week trial in which teens were randomly assigned to take Prozac, cognitive-behavioral therapy, a combination of Prozac and therapy, or a placebo. The combined condition was most helpful, eliciting gains for 71% of that group. Prozac followed in effectiveness, with improved depression in 61% of that group. The cognitive-behavioral group performed only slightly better than placebo (43% of individuals improved versus 35%).

Alternative Treatments

Herbal

St. John's wort is an herbal preparation sometimes used for depression. A review of meta-analyses and studies indicated that St. John's wort is more effective than placebo and has comparable effectiveness to tricyclic antidepressants, with fewer side effects for mild to moderate depression over the short term (1 to 3 months) (Hammerness et al., 2003). Comparisons with SSRIs have been mixed. Some interactions with other medications have been reported, however. For instance, social workers should be aware that for individuals with HIV/AIDS taking protease inhibitors or nonnucleoside reverse transcriptase inhibitors, St. John's wort may reduce concentrations of these medications. Also, women taking oral contraceptives should be warned that St. John's wort may reduce the contraceptive effect. Finally, individuals taking SSRIs should use caution because of some similar actions of the drugs when used together (Hammerness et al., 2003).

Exercise

A meta-analysis of 30 studies on the benefits of exercise for depression found that exercise was as helpful for reducing symptoms as wait-list control, group or individual psychotherapy, behavioral interventions, or social contact (Craft & Landers, 1998). Although time exercised, exercise intensity, and number of days of exercise per week did not seem to make much difference, the number of weeks of exercise contributed to impact. Nine to 12 weeks of exercise produced the largest effect on depression. The moderately to severely depressed group improved even more than those who were mildly depressed.

Critique

One critique of the diagnosis for depression is the validity of the subtypes of depression called melancholic and atypical depressions presented in the *DSM*. Treatment decisions are also not typically made on the basis of these subtypes, and therefore, their usefulness can be questioned.

As with many of the other disorders, the internal nature of dysfunction assumption integral to the *DSM* approach can also be critiqued. The concept of depression as internal dysfunction can be seen in the widespread acceptability of biological theories of depression and the use of medication as treatment. However, this chapter has highlighted some of the critiques of these theories and treatment methods. In addition, the social worker should be aware that although biological susceptibility may play a significant role in the development of depression (perhaps 30%), the majority of contributing factors are psychosocial in nature. Further, psychosocial treatment, despite current managed care approaches, should be considered the first line of intervention for depression.

Case Study

Joseph, a 54-year-old, Caucasian male immigrant from the Czech Republic, was admitted to a psychiatric hospital following a suicide attempt. Admitting records showed that his landlady had found him very disoriented, almost catatonic, unable to function, and with cuts on his left wrist in the house where he rents a room. He had just recently lost his job. The landlady was concerned and called authorities. Upon assessment at a community mental health facility, it was determined he was a potential threat to himself and was committed.

The day after his admission, Joseph met with the treatment team: a psychiatrist, psychologist, social worker, occupational therapist, nurse, and the social worker. Joseph entered the room walking slowly, with a fatigued and visibly drawn countenance. When questioned as to why he was there, he said he didn't know and started to cry. He was unable to provide much information at that meeting except to say his name and where he lived.

Two days later, Joseph was more talkative in a more in-depth assessment conducted by the social worker. The client has been in the United States for 20 years. He has one sister who lives in the area. He attended college in the Czech Republic, and his parents still live there. He has been employed most of his life and recently worked at a tile company driving a truck. However, he lost that job 3 weeks prior to admission to the hospital. He lives alone in a rented room of a house shared with three other men. He has no insurance.

Joseph said he has never previously been hospitalized, and there is no history of mental illness in the family. He has no faith preference now but was raised Catholic. He denies any history of substance abuse or physical or sexual abuse.

Four years ago, Joseph was separated from his wife and later divorced. He had two previous marriages and has a 31-year-old son living in the

Czech Republic from his first wife. He has two sons, 12 and 15 years old, by the third wife, who lives in the area. However, he said that his divorce decreed that he is not allowed to see these children. He was not able to provide further details on the reasons behind the court decision.

Joseph said his youngest son has attention-deficit/hyperactivity disorder, and this caused marital tension because his wife thought he was too firm with the son. His sister also thought so, and he said she sided with his wife in seeking a divorce. He has to pay $1000 a month in child support, and because he has lost his job, he feels overwhelmed with his situation.

Joseph credits his severe depression to intense grief over his divorce, which he says he did not want. He kept saying that it was all his fault. When pressed, he said one night 3 years ago, he and his wife got into an argument when he'd been drinking. She called the police, and he was subsequently charged with a domestic assault. After he attended anger management classes, the charge was dismissed. His wife obtained a restraining order, but he violated it once. He was consequently jailed for 1 day. He has not seen his children in 3 years.

He said the intense loneliness he feels and his remorse over not seeing his children have caused him to feel sad and depressed. Missing his son's birthday a month before was the breaking point. He was in so much emotional pain that he found it difficult to get out of bed and go to work. As a result of absenteeism, he was fired. He despaired of his life and made a half-hearted attempt to slit his wrists.

Despite his obvious despair, Joseph did say he wanted to figure out a way to end his depression and get on with his life. He said he used to have interests in music and played a flute. In addition, he said he likes to garden and wanted to get back into that as well. He said he feels his greatest strength is his ability to pick himself up and keep going, which is what he's done in the past. He also said he wants to eventually be able to see his sons.

Additional Information Needed

The social worker would have liked more information about the circumstances of Joseph's divorce, the restraining order his former wife obtained, and the alleged decree that he is not allowed to see his children. She had attempted to gain more information from Joseph, but he was not forthcoming with details. In addition, the social worker wanted to know the reasons for his other two failed marriages. Finally, the social worker was curious about the extent of Joseph's drinking. He denied alcohol abuse but said alcohol was involved in his domestic fights with his wife. Given the information the social worker had, the following diagnosis was formulated:

Diagnosis

Axis I: 296.2 Major Depressive Disorder, Single episode Severe.
Axis II: V71.09 No diagnosis
Axis III: None
Axis IV: Problems in primary support group. Divorced.
        Problems in social environment. Lives alone, lack of friends
        and family in area.
        Occupational problems. Unemployed
        Economic problems. Inadequate finances to meet expenses,
        lack of insurance
Axis V: GAF 50

Rationale

According to Joseph's self-report, he met seven of the nine symptoms from Criterion A for a major depressive episode (a minimum of five symptoms are needed to make the diagnosis). He experienced the following symptoms for most of the day, nearly every, day for the previous 3 weeks (a minimum of 2 weeks is required for the diagnosis): (a) depressed mood, (b) markedly diminished interest or pleasure in almost all activities, (c) hypersomnia, (d) fatigue or loss of energy nearly every day, (e) feelings of worthlessness or excessive or inappropriate guilt, (f) diminished ability to think or concentrate, and (g) suicide attempt. Further, Criteria B (there was no evidence of a mixed episode), C (the symptoms caused clinically significant distress and impairment in his occupational area of functioning), D (the symptoms were not due to the physiological effects of a substance or a medical condition), and E (the symptoms are not better accounted for by bereavement) were met. He was diagnosed with major depressive disorder, severe because of the number of symptoms and the presence of a suicide attempt. The social worker gave him a GAF of 50 (serious), again because of the suicide attempt that warranted his hospitalization and also his job loss as a result of the depression.

Risk and Protective Factors Assessment and Treatment Formulation

The social worker completed a risk and protective factors assessment for the onset of Joseph's depression and for his recovery. See Table 10.5 for onset. For his recovery, on the positive side, Joseph had not suffered previous episodes, and he has no co-occurring psychiatric or medical condition. On the negative side, he had severe depression on admittance to the hospital, and he is divorced.

Table 10.5

Case Study of Joseph: Risk and Protective Factors Assessment for Onset of Depression

Risk	Protective
Biological	• No first-degree relative history • Good health
Psychological • Negative cognitive style	• Had coping skills before current episode
Social • Marital problems, divorce • Low social support and interaction • Stressful life events, especially those involving loss (job, family, country of origin) • Low socioeconomic status	• Has job skills, previous employment history

Treatment goals included reduction of depressive symptoms, the development of increased social support and coping skills, some resolution of his feelings about his recent marriage, renewed contact with his children, and employment. Interpersonal therapy was the treatment of choice because Joseph's depression seemed tied to loss of relationships and interpersonal problems.

Summary

Social workers should be knowledgeable about the identification and treatment of depression, given the high rates among both the adolescent and adult populations and the potentially severe consequences of depression. Social workers can play an important role, whether or not they are in actual mental health treatment settings, because assessment of depression and appropriate referrals for treatment that has received empirical support are critical to the management of this disorder.

Appendix I. Measures for Childhood and Adolescent Depression

This review was largely drawn from Myers and Winters (2002).

Children's Depression Inventory

(Kovacs, 1992)

Description

- 27-item, self-report inventory for children from ages 8 to 13
- Measuring severity ("0" to "2") of overt symptoms of depression, such as sadness, sleep and eating disturbances, anhedonia, and suicidal ideation
- Modified from the Beck Depression Inventory for adults
- Translated into several languages

Reliability

- Internal consistency is adequate.
- Test-retest reliability varies and is somewhat lower for boys than for girls.

Validity

- Possesses predictive validity for future functioning.
- Shows variable sensitivity to changes during therapy.
- Clinician's ratings of depression from a psychiatric interview correlated with Children's Depression Inventory ($r = .55$).

  - Discriminated between psychiatric sample and nonclinic group and between child guidance and pediatric samples, though with a high false-negative rate
  - Laxity in the CDI's construct for depression, producing poor construct validity—possibly assesses distress rather than depression

- Children who scored high on depression for Children's Depression Inventory made more internal-stable-global attributions for failure and more external-unstable-specific attributions for success as measured by the Attributional Style Questionnaire ($r = .52$) (Kaslow, Rehm, & Siegel, 1984).
- Children's Depression Inventory was negatively correlated with the Coopersmith Self-Esteem Inventory ($r = -.72$) (Kaslow et al., 1984).
- Teachers reported depressed children as more internalizing than nondepressed children but not more externalizing (Kaslow et al., 1984).

Reynolds Adolescent Depression Scale (RADS)

(Reynolds, 1987)

Description

- Measures *DSM-III* criteria for depression over the past 2 weeks
- Has primarily been developed and used with school samples
- Recommended for screening, rather than outcome

Reliability

- Excellent internal reliability
- Very good stability with samples of diverse youth from multiple nationalities, and both clinical and community samples.

Validity

- Rooted in *DSM-III* diagnostic criteria ensures construct validity
- Correlates highly with other depression measures, as well as with measures of related constructs (e.g., anxiety and self-esteem) and has been used as a validation standard for other measures
- Inversely correlated with youth competence

Center for Epidemiologic Studies-Depression for Children and Adolescents

(Weissman, Orvaschel, & Padian, 1980)

Description

- Comprises items empirically derived from other adult depression scales
- Assesses symptoms over the past 2 weeks
- Widely employed with adolescents

Reliability

- Internal reliability is moderate to good.
- Moderate to good correlations stability for adolescents, though not children.

Validity

- Moderate correlations with conduct disorder
- Fails to differentiate youth with depression from psychiatric controls

Beck Depression Inventory II

(Beck, Steer, Ball & Ranieri, 1996)
The reader will note that the BDI is included in both appendixes I and II because the target audience includes both adolescents and adults.

Description

- Self-report measure with 21 items, each having four answer options
- Targeted audience includes depressed adults, adolescents, elderly individuals, inpatients, outpatients, primary care patients, and patients with medical conditions
- Works well with a wide range of ages and cultures, as well as both males and females

Reliability

- Internal consistency of this measure was .93 for college students and .92 for outpatients.
- Variability in test-retest reliabilities.

Validity

- Construct validity of this scale was shown in its .76 correlation to the depression subscale Symptom Checklist 90-Rev and its .60 correlation with the Minnesota Multiphasic Personality Inventory.

Appendix II. Measures for Adult Depression

Zung Self-Rating Depression Scale

(Zung, 1965)
This review draws largely from Burt and Ishak (2002).

Description

- Self-report measure with 20 items, each having four answer options.
- Targeted audience is depressed adults, adolescents, elderly individuals, inpatients, outpatients, primary care patients, and patients with medical conditions.

Validity
(Biggs, Wylie, & Ziegler, 1978)

- Correlates highly with other depression measures.
- Sensitivity was found to be adequate.

Beck Depression Inventory II

(Beck et al., 1996)

Description

- Self-report measure with 21 items, each having four answer options.
- Targeted audience includes depressed adults, adolescents, elderly individuals, inpatients, outpatients, primary care patients, and patients with medical conditions.
- Works well with a wide range of ages and cultures, as well as both males and females.

Reliability

- Internal consistency of this measure was .93 for college students and .92 for outpatients.
- Variability in test-retest reliabilities.

Validity

- Construct validity of this scale was shown in its .76 correlation to the depression subscale Symptom Checklist 90-Rev and its .60 correlation with the Minnesota Multiphasic Personality Inventory

Center for Epidemiologic Studies Depression Scale

(Radloff, 1977)

Description

- Self-report measure with 20 items, all items scored on a 0–3 scale.
- Purpose is to measure frequency and duration (but not intensity) of depression in individuals.
- Targeted population is the general public.
- No cost to use.
- Takes 5–10 minutes to complete.

Reliability

- Internal consistency was .85 in the general population and .90 in the psychiatric population.

Validity

- Correlation with the Hamilton Rating Scale for Depression ranged from .49 to .85. Correlation with the Zung scale was .69, and the correlation to the Symptom Checklist-90 ranged from .73 to .89.

Geriatric Depression Scale

(Yesavage et al., 1982)

Description

- Screens for depression in the elderly
- Can also be used with the cognitively impaired (Burke, Nitcher, Roccaforte, & Wengel, 1992; Feher, Larrabee, & Crook, 1992)
- Can be self-administered or administered by an interviewer in 5–10 minutes
- Available in a 30-item long form or 15-, 10-, 4-, and 1-item short forms
- Items answered either "yes" or "no"
- Available in different languages (Chinese, German, French)

Reliability

- 15-item version has a high internal consistency (Cronbach's alpha = .80) (D'Ath, Katona, Mullan, Evans, & Katona, 1994).
- Cronbach's alpha was .72 for the 10-item form and .55 for the 4-item form.
- Agreement between short scales and the 15-item scales was 95% (10-item), 91% (4-item), and 79% (1-item), respectively.

Validity

- A single item, "Do you feel that your life is empty?" identified 84% of cases of depression (D'Ath et al., 1994).
- Sensitivity of 10-item version was 87% and specificity was 77% (using a cutoff of 3–4); sensitivity of 4-item version was 89% and specificity was 65% (cutoff of 1); sensitivity of 1-item version was 59% and specificity was 75%.
- Has good concurrent validity with the Melancholia scale of the Hamilton Rating Scale for Depression (r = .77) (Salamero & Marcos, 1992).

References

Abela, J. R. Z., Brozina, K., & Haigh, E. P. (2002). An examination of the response styles theory of depression in third- and seventh-grade children: A short-term longitudinal study. *Journal of Abnormal Child Psychology, 30*(5), 515–527.

Abramson, L. Y., Seligman, M. E., & Teasdale, J. D. (1978). Learned helplessness in humans: Critique and reformulation. *Journal of Abnormal Psychology, 87,* 49–74

Agency for Health Care Policy and Research. (1993). *Depression in primary care: Vol. 1. Detection and Diagnosis Clinical Practice Guideline.* Retrieved April 9, 2004, from http://www.mentalhealth.com/bookah/p44-d1.html.

American Association for Geriatric Psychiatry (AAGP). (2002). Depression in late life: Not a natural part of aging. Retrieved August 16, 2003, from http://www.aagpgpa.org/p_c/depression2.asp.

American Psychiatric Association. (2000). *Diagnostic and statistical manual of mental disorders* (4th ed., text rev.). Washington, DC: Author.

Anderson, I. (2000). Selective serotonin reuptake inhibitors versus tricyclic antidepressants: A meta-analysis of efficacy and tolerability. *Journal of Affective Disorders, 58,* 19–36.

Antonuccio, D., Burns, D., Danton, W., & O'Donohue, W. (2000). Rumble in Reno: The psychosocial perspective on depression. *Psychiatric Times, 17*(8). Retrieved March 1, 2003, from http://www.psychiatrictimes.com/p000824.html.

Antonuccio, D., Thomas, M., & Danton, W. (1997). A cost-effectiveness analysis of cognitive behavior therapy and fluoxetine (Prozac) in the treatment of depression. *Behavior Therapy, 28,* 187–210.

Arean, P., & Cook, B. (2002). Psychotherapy and combined psychotherapy/pharmacotherapy for late life depression. *Biological Psychiatry, 52,* 293–303.

Arnow, B. A., & Constantino, M. J. (2003). Effectiveness of psychotherapy and combination treatment for chronic depression. *Journal of Clinical Psychology, 59*(8), 893–905.

Asarnow, J. R., Jaycox, L. H., & Tompson, M. C. (2001). Depression in youth: Psychosocial interventions. *Journal of Clinical Child Psychology, 30*(1) 33–47.

Barkow, K., Maier, W., Ustun, T. B., Gansicke, M., Wittchen, H. U., & Heun, R. (2003). Risk factors for depression at 12-month follow-up in adult primary health care patients with major depression: an international prospective study. *Journal of Affective Disorders, 76,* 157–69.

Barnett, S. M., Sirey, J., Bruce, M., Hamilton, M., Raue, P., Friedman, S., et al. (2002). Predictors of early recovery from major depression among persons admitted to community-based clinics. *Archives of General Psychiatry, 59,* 729–735.

Beach, S., & Jones, D. (2002). Marital and family therapy for depression in adults. In I. Gotlib & C. Hammen (Eds.), *Handbook of depression* (pp. 422–440). New York: Guilford.

Beach, S., Sandeen, E., & O'Leary, K. (1990). *Depression in marriage: A model for etiology and treatment.* New York: Guilford.

Beardslee, W., Versage, E., & Gladstone, T. (1998). Children of affectively ill parents: A review of the past 10 years. *Journal of the American Academy of Child and Adolescent Psychiatry, 37,* 1134–1141.

Beardslee, W. R., Wright, E. J., Salt, P., & Drezner, K. (1997). Examination of children's responses to two preventive intervention strategies over time. *Journal of the American Academy of Child & Adolescent Psychiatry, 36*(2), 196–204.

Beck, A., Rush, A., Shaw, B., & Emery, G. (1979). *Cognitive therapy of depression.* New York: Guilford.

Bird, M., & Parslow, R. (2002). Potential for community programs to prevent depression in older people. *MJA, 7,* 107–110.

Birmaher, B., Brent, D. A., Kolko, D., Baugher, M., Bridge, J., Holder, D. et al. (2000). Outcome after short-term psychotherapy for adolescents with major depressive disorder. *Archives of General Psychiatry, 57*(1), 29–36.

Birmaher, B., Ryan, N., Williamson, D., Brent, D., Kaufman, J., & Dahl, R. (1996a). Childhood and adolescent depression: A review of the past 10 years, Part I. *Journal of the American Academy of Child & Adolescent Psychiatry, 35,* 1427–1439.

Birmaher, B., Ryan, N., Williamson, D., Brent, D., & Kaufman, J. (1996b). Childhood and adolescent depression: A review of the past 10 years, Part II. *Journal of the American Academy of Child & Adolescent Psychiatry, 35,* 1575–1583.

Bohlmeijer, E., Smit, F., & Cuijpers, P. (2003). Effects of reminiscence and life review on late-life depression: A meta-analysis. *International Journal of Geriatric Psychiatry, 18,* 1088–1094.

Bolen, R., & Scannapieco, M. (1999). Prevalence of child sexual abuse: A corrective meta-analysis. *Social Service Review, 73,* 281–301.

Brent, D. A., Baugher, M., Birmaher, B., Kolko, D. J., & Bridge, J. (2000). Compliance with recommendations to remove firearms in families participating in a clinical trial for adolescent depression. *Journal of the American Academy of Child & Adolescent Psychiatry, 39,* 1220–1226.

Brent, D., Kolko, D., Birmaher, B., Baugher, M., & Bridge, J. (1999). Clinical trial for adolescent depression: Predictors of additional treatment in the acute and follow-up phases of the trial. *Journal of the American Academy of Child & Adolescent Psychiatry, 38,* 263–271.

Brent, D. A., Holder, D., Kolko, D., Birmaher, B., Baugher, M., Roth, C., et al. (1997). A clinical psychotherapy trial for adolescent depression comparing cognitive, family, and supportive therapy. *Archives of General Psychiatry, 54*(9), 877–885.

Brent, D. A., Kolko, D. J., Birhamer, B., Baugher, M., Bridge, J., Roth, C., et al. (1998). Predictors of treatment efficacy in a clinical trial of three psychosocial treatments for adolescent depression. *American Academy of Child and Adolescent Psychiatry, 37,* 906–914.

Brodaty, H., Luscombe, G., Peisah, C., Anstey, K., & Andrews, G. (2001). A 25-year longitudinal, comparison study of the outcome of depression. *Psychological Medicine, 31*(8), 1347–1359.

Brown, J., Cohen, P., Johnson, J. G., & Smailes, E. M. (1999). Childhood abuse and neglect: Specificity of effects on adolescent and young adult depression and suicidality. *Journal of the American Academy of Child and Adolescent Psychiatry, 38* (12), 1490–1496.

Burns, D. (1999). *Feeling good: The new mood therapy, revised edition.* New York: Avon.

Ciesla, J. A., & Roberts, J. E. (2001). Meta-analysis of the relationship between HIV infection and risk for depressive disorders. *American Journal of Psychiatry, 158*(5), 725–730.

Clarke, G., Lewinsohn, P., & Hops, H. (1990). The adolescent coping with depression course. Retrieved March 25, 2004, from http://www.kpchr.org/public/news/newACWD.asp.

Clarke, G., Rohde, P., Lewinsohn, P., Hops, H., & Seeley, J. (1999). Cognitive-behavioral treatment of adolescent depression: Efficacy of acute group treatment and booster sessions. *Journal of the American Academy of Child and Adolescent Psychiatry, 38*, 272–279.

Clarke, G. N., Hops, H., Lewinsohn, P., Andrews, J., Seeley, J., & Williams, J. (1992). Cognitive-behavioral group treatment of adolescent depression: Prediction of outcome. *Behavior Therapy, 23*, 341–354.

Clarke, G. N., Hornbrook, M., Lynch, F., Polen, M., Gale, J., Beardslee, W., et al. (2001). A randomized trial of a group cognitive intervention for preventing depression in adolescent offspring of depressed parents. *Archives of General Psychiatry, 58*(12), 1127–1134.

Clarke, G. N., Hornbrook, M., Lynch, F., Polen, M., Gale, J., O'Connor, E., et al. (2002). Group cognitive-behavioral treatment for depressed adolescent offspring of depressed parents in a health maintenance organization. *Journal of the American Academy of Child and Adolescent Psychiatry, 41*(3), 305–314.

Cole, M., & Dendukuri, N. (2003). Risk factors for depression among elderly community studies: A systematic review and meta-analysis. *American Journal of Psychiatry, 160*, 1147–1156.

Corcoran, J. (2003). *Clinical applications of evidence-based family intervention.* New York: Oxford University Press.

Cottrell, D., Fonagy, P., Kurtz, Z., Phillips, J., & Target, M. (2002). What works for whom? A critical review of treatments for children and adolescents. In P. Fonagy, M. Target, D. Cottrell, J. Phillips, & Z. Kurtz (Eds.), *Depressive disorders* (pp. 89–105). New York: Guilford.

Craft, L., & Landers, D. (1998) The effect of exercise on clinical depression and depression resulting from mental illness: A meta-analysis. *Journal of Sport and Exercise Psychology, 20*, 339–357.

Cuijpers, P. (1997). Bibliotherapy in unipolar depression: A meta-analysis. *Journal of Behavior Therapy and Experimental Psychiatry, 28*, 139–147.

Cuijpers, P. (1998). A psychoeducational approach to the treatment of depression: A meta-analysis of Lewinsohn's "Coping with Depression" course. *Behavior Therapy, 29*, 521–533.

De Beurs, E., Beekman, A., Geerlings, S., Deeg, D., Van Dyck, R., & Van Tilburg, W. (2001). On becoming depressed or anxious in late life: Similar vulnerability factors but different effects of stressful life events. *British Journal of Psychiatry, 179*(5), 426–431.

Dekovic, M. (1999). Risk and protective factors in the development of problem behavior during adolescence. *Journal of Youth and Adolescence, 28*(6), 667–685.

DeRubeis, R., Gelfand, L., Tang, T., & Simons, A. (1999). Medications versus cognitive behavior therapy for severely depressed outpatients: Mega-analysis of four randomized comparisons. *American Journal of Psychiatry, 156*, 1007–1013.

Desai, H., & Jann, M. (2000). Major depression in women: A review of the literature. *Journal of the American Pharmaceutical Association, 40*, 525–537.

Diamond, G. S., Reis, B. F., Diamond, G. M., Siqueland, L., & Isaacs, L. (2002). Attachment-based family therapy for depressed adolescents: A treatment development study. *Journal of the American Academy of Child and Adolescent Psychiatry, 41*(10), 1190–1197.

Doi, Y., Roberts, R., Takeuchi, K., & Suzuki, S. (2001). Multiethnic comparison of adolescent major depression based on the DSM-IV criteria in a U.S.–Japan study. *Journal of the American Academy of Child and Adolescent Psychiatry, 40*(11), 1308–1315.

Duggal, S., Carlson, E. A., Sroufe, L. A., & Egeland, B. (2001). Depressive symptomatology in childhood and adolescence. *Development & Psychopathology, 13*(1), 143–164.

Egeland, B. (1997). Mediators of the effects of child maltreatment on developmental adaptation in adolescence. In D. Cicchetti & S. Toth (Eds.), *Rochester symposium on developmental psychopathology: Vol. 8. The effects of trauma on the developmental process* (pp. 403–434). Rochester, NY: University of Rochester Press.

Fergusson, D., Horwood, L., & Lynskey, M. (1996). Childhood sexual abuse and psychiatric disorder in young adulthood: II. Psychiatric outcomes of childhood sexual abuse. *Journal of the American Academy of Child and Adolescent Psychiatry, 35*, 1365–1374.

Fergusson, D., & Woodward, L. (2002). Mental health, educational, and social role outcomes of adolescents with depression. *Archives of General Psychiatry, 59*, 225–231.

Fine, S., Forth, A., Gilbert, M., & Haley, G. (1991). Group therapy for adolescent depressive disorder: A comparison of social skills and therapeutic support. *Journal of American Academy of Child & Adolescent Psychiatry, 30*, 79–85.

Floyd, M. (2003). Bibliotherapy as an adjunct to psychotherapy for depression in older adults. *Journal of Clinical Psychology, 59*(2), 187–195.

Giaconia, R. M., Reinherz, H. Z., Paradis, A. D., Carmola Hauf, A. M., &Stashwick, C. K. (2001). Major depression and drug disorders in adolescence: General and specific impairments in early adulthood. *Journal of the American Academy of Child and Adolescent Psychiatry, 40*(12), 1426–1434.

Goodman, S., Schwab-Stone, M., Lahey, B., Shaffer, D., & Jensen, P. (2000). Major depression and dysthymia in children and adolescents: Discriminant validity and differential consequences in a community sample. *Journal of the American Academy of Child and Adolescent Psychiatry, 39*, 761–770.

Goodman, S. H., & Gotlib, I. H. (1999). Risk for psychopathology in the children of depressed mothers: A developmental model for understanding mechanisms of transmission. *Psychological Review, 106*, 458–461.

Greenberg, R., & Fisher, S. (1997). Mood-mending medicines: Probing drug, psychotherapy, and placebo solutions. In S. Fisher & R. Greenberg (Eds.), *From placebo to panacea: Putting psychiatric drugs to the test* (pp. 115–172). New York: Wiley.

Hamilton, J. D., & Bridge, J. (1999). Outcome at 6 months for 50 adolescents with major depression treated in a health maintenance organization. *Journal of the American Academy of Child and Adolescent Psychiatry, 38*(11), 1340–1346.

Hammerness, P., Basch, E., Ulbricht, C., Barrette, E. P., Foppa, I., Basch, S., et al. (2003). St. John's wort: A systematic review of adverse effects and drug interactions for the consultation psychiatrist. *Psychosomatics, 44,* 271–282.

Hazell, P., O'Connell, D., Heathcote, D., & Henry, D. (2003). Tricyclic drugs for depression in children and adolescents (Cochrane Review). In *The Cochrane Library,* Issue 1. Oxford: Update Software.

Healy, D. (2002). *The creation of psychopharmacology.* Cambridge, MA: Harvard University Press.

Hughes, C. W., Emslie, J. G., Crismon, M. L., Wagner, D. K., Birmaher, B., Geller, B., et al. (1999). The Texas children's medication algorithm project: Report of the Texas consensus conference panel on medication treatment of childhood major depressive disorder. *Journal of the American Academy of Child and Adolescent Psychiatry, 38*(11), 1442–1454.

Jewell, J. D., & Stark, K. D. (2003). Comparing the family environments of adolescents with conduct disorder or depression. *Journal of Child & Family Studies, 12,* 77–89.

Kaminski, K. M., & Garber, J. (2002). Depressive spectrum disorders in high-risk adolescents: Episode duration and predictors of time to recovery. *Journal of the American Academy of Child & Adolescent Psychiatry, 41*(4), 410–418.

Karasu, T. B., Gelenberg, A., Merriam, A., & Wang, P. (2002). Practice guidelines for the treatment of patients with major depressive disorder. In *American Psychiatric Association practice guidelines for the treatment of psychiatric disorder: Compendium 2002* (2nd ed, pp. 463–545). Washington, DC: American Psychiatric Association.

Kessler, Ronald C. (2003). Epidemiology of women and depression. *Journal of Affective Disorders, 74*(1), 5–13.

Kessler, R., Berglund, P., Demler, O., Jin, R., & Walters, E. (2005). Lifetime prevalence and age-of-onset distributions of DSM-IV disorders in the National Comorbidity survey replication. *Archives of General Psychiatry, 62,* 593–602.

Kessler, R., Chiu, W.T., Demler, O., & Walters, E. (2005). Prevalence, severity, and comorbidity of 12-month DSM-IV disorders in the National Comorbidity survey replication. *Archives of General Psychiatry, 62,* 617–627.

Kovacs, M. (2001). Gender and the course of major depressive disorder through adolescence in clinically referred youngsters. *Journal of the American Academy of Child and Adolescent Psychiatry, 40,* 1079–1085.

Kovacs, M., Obrosky, S., Gatsonis, C., & Richards, C. (1997). First-episode major depressive and dysthymic disorder in childhood: Clinical and sociodemographic factors in recovery. *Journal of the American Academy of Child & Adolescent Psychiatry, 36*(6), 777–784.

Kraaij, V., Arensman, E., & Spinhoven, P. (2002). Negative life events and depression in elderly persons: A meta-analysis. *Journals of Gerontology Series B-Psychological Sciences & Social Sciences, 57B*(1), 87–94.

Laidlaw, K., Thompson, L., Gallagher-Thompson, D., & Dick-Siskin, L. (2003). Cognitive behaviour therapy with older people. Chichester, UK: John Wiley.

Le, H. N., Munoz, R., Ippen, C. G., & Stoddard, J. (2003). Treatment is not enough: We must prevent major depression in women. *Prevention and Treatment.* Re-

trieved on December 31, 2003, from http://80-gateway1.ovid.com.proxy
.library.vcu.edu/ovidweb.cgi.

Lewinsohn, P., Clarke, G., Hops, H., & Andrews, J. (1990). Cognitive-behavioral
treatment for depressed adolescents. *Behavior Therapy, 21*, 385–401.

Lewinsohn, P., & Essau, C. (2002). Depression in adolescents. In I. H. Gotlib & C.
Hammen (Eds.), *Handbook of depression* (pp. 541–559). New York: Guilford.

Lewinsohn, P.M., Munoz, R.F., Youngren, M.A., & Zeiss, A.M. (1986). *Control your
depression* (2nd ed.). Englewood Cliffs, NJ: Prentice-Hall.

McDermut, W., Miller, I., & Brown, R. (2001). The efficacy of group psychotherapy
for depression: A meta-analysis and review of the empirical research. *Clinical
Psychology: Science and Practice, 8*, 98–116.

McLeod, J., & Shanahan, M. (1996). Trajectories of poverty and children's mental
health. *Journal of Health & Social Behavior, 37*, 207–220.

Merry, S., McDowell, H., Hetrick, S., Bir, J., & Muller, N. (2004). Psychological and/
or educational interventions for the prevention of depression in children and
adolescents (Cochrane Review). In *The Cochrane Library*, Issue 1.

Minsky, S., Vega, W., Miskimen, T., Gara, M., & Escobar, J. (2003). Diagnostic patterns in Latino, African American, and European American psychiatric patients. *Archives of General Psychiatry, 60*(6), 637–644.

Moreau, D., Mufson, L., Weissman, M., & Klerman, G. (1991). Interpersonal psychotherapy for adolescent depression: Description of modification and preliminary application. *Journal of the American Academy of Child and Adolescent Psychiatry, 30*, 642–651.

Mufson, L., & Fairbanks, J. (1996). Interpersonal psychotherapy for depressed adolescents: A one-year naturalistic follow-up study. *Journal of the American Academy of Child and Adolescent Psychiatry, 35*, 1145–1155.

Mufson, L., & Moreau, D. (1997). Depressive disorders. In R.T. Ammerman & M.
Hersen (Eds.), *Handbook of prevention and treatment with children and adolescents:
Intervention in the real world context* (pp. 403–430). New York: John Wiley &
Sons, Inc.

Mufson, L., Moreau, D., Weissman, M., Wickramaratne, P., Martin, J., & Samilov,
A. (1994). Modification of interpersonal psychotherapy with depressed adolescents (IPT-A): Phase I and II studies. *Journal of the American Academy of Child
and Adolescent Psychiatry, 33*, 695–705.

Mufson, L., Weissman, M., Moreau, D., & Garfinkel, R. (1999). Efficacy of interpersonal psychotherapy for depressed adolescents. *Archives of General Psychiatry,
56*, 573–579.

National Institute of Mental Health (NIMH). (2002). If you're over 65 and feeling
depressed: Treatment brings new hope. Retrieved on October 16, 2002, from
http://www.nimh.nih.gov/publicat/over65.cfm.

NMHA Factsheet (2002). Depression in later life. Retrieved on October 16, 2002,
from Wysiwyg://154/http://www.nmha.org/infoctr/factsheets/22/cm.

Nolen-Hoeksema, S. (2002). Gender differences in depression. In I. H. Gotlib & C.
Hammen (Eds.), *Handbook of depression* (pp. 492–509). New York: Guilford.

O'Hara, M. W., & Swain, A. M. (1996). Rates and risk of postpartum depression: A
meta-analysis. *International Review of Psychiatry, 8*, 37–54.

Olfson, M., Marcus, S. C., Druss, B., Elinson, L., Tanielian, T., & Pincus, H. A.

(2002). National trends in the outpatient treatment of depression. *Journal of the American Medical Association, 287,* 203–209.

Peterson, A., Compas, B., Brooks-Gunn, J., Stemmler, M., Ey, S., & Grant, K. (1993). Depression in adolescence. *American Psychologist, 48,* 155–168.

Rao, U., Ryan, N. D., Birmaher, B., Dahl, R., Williamson, D., Kaufman, J., et al. (1995). Unipolar depression in adolescents: Clinical outcome in adulthood. *Journal of the American Academy of Child and Adolescent Psychiatry, 34,* 566–578.

Reinecke, M., Ryan, N., & Dubois, D. (1998). Cognitive-behavioral therapy of depression and depressive symptoms during adolescence: A review and meta-analysis. *Journal of the American Academy of Child and Adolescent Psychiatry, 37,* 26–34.

Reynolds, W. M., & Coats, K. I. (1986). A comparison of cognitive-behavioral therapy and relaxation training for the treatment of depression in adolescents. *Journal of Consulting & Clinical Psychology, 54*(5), 653–660.

Rossello, J., & Bernal, G. (1999). The efficacy of cognitive-behavioral and interpersonal treatments for depression in Puerto Rican adolescents. *Journal of Consulting and Clinical Psychology, 67,* 734–745.

Rugulies, R. (2002). Depression as a predictor for coronary heart disease: A review and meta-analysis. *American Journal of Preventive Medicine, 23,* 51–61.

Rushton, J., Forcier, M., & Schectman, R. (2002). Epidemiology of depressive symptoms in the national longitudinal study of adolescent health. *Journal of American Academy of Child and Adolescent Psychiatry, 41,* 199–205.

Sanderson, W. C., & McGinn, L. K. (2001). Cognitive-behavioral therapy of depression. In M. M. Weissman (Ed), *Treatment of depression: Bridging the 21st century* (pp. 249–279). Washington, DC: American Psychiatric Publishing, Inc.

Santor, D., & Kusumakar, V. (2001). Open trial of interpersonal therapy in adolescents with moderate to severe major depression: Effectiveness of novice IPT therapists. *Journal of the American Academy of Child and Adolescent Psychiatry, 40*(2), 236–240.

Scogin, F. R., Hanson, A., & Welsh, D. (2003). Self-administered treatment in stepped-care models of depression treatment. *Journal of Clinical Psychology, 59*(3), 341–349.

Simons, R., Murry, V., McLoyd, V., Kueihsiu, L., Cutrona, C., & Conger, R. (2002). Discrimination, crime, ethnic identity, and parenting as correlates of depressive symptoms among African American children: A multilevel analysis. *Development and Psychopathology, 14,* 371–393.

Smith, N., Floyd, M., Jamison, C., & Scogin, F. (1997). Three-year follow-up of bibliotherapy for depression. *Journal of Consulting and Clinical Psychology, 65,* 324–327.

Sullivan, P. F., Neale, M. C., & Kendler, K. S. (2000). Genetic epidemiology of major depression: Review and meta-analysis. *American Journal of Psychiatry, 157*(10), 1552–1562.

Sund, A. M., & Wichstrom, L. (2002). Insecure attachment as a risk factor for future depressive symptoms in early adolescence. *Journal of the American Academy of Child and Adolescent Psychiatry, 41*(12), 1478–1486.

Treatment for Adolescents with Depression Study Team. (2004). Fluoxetine, cognitive-behavioral therapy, and their combination for adolescents with depression: Treatment for adolescents with depression study (TADS) randomized controlled trial. *Journal of the American Medical Association, 292,* 807–820.

Valenstein, E. (1998). *Blaming the brain: The truth about drugs and mental health.* New York: Free Press.

Wade, T. J., Cairney, J., & Pevalin, D. J. (2002). Emergence of gender differences in depression during adolescence: National panel results from three countries. *Journal of the American Academy of Child and Adolescent Psychiatry, 41,* 190–199.

Wampold, B., Minami, T., Baskin, T., & Tierney, S. (2002). A meta-(re)analysis of the effects of cognitive therapy versus "other therapies" for depression. *Journal of Affective Disorders, 69,* 159–165.

Waslick, B. D., Kandel, B. A., & Kakouros, B. S. (2002). Depression in children and adolescents: An overview. In D. Shaffer & B. D. Waslick (Eds.), *The many faces of depression in children and adolescents* (pp. 1–36). Washington, DC: American Psychiatric Publishing.

Weissman, M. M., Markowitz, J. C., & Klerman, G. L. (2000). *Comprehensive Guide to Interpersonal Psychotherapy.* New York, NY: Basic Books.

Weisz, J., Donenberg, G., Han, S., & Weiss, B. (1995). Bridging the gap between laboratory and clinic in child and adolescent psychotherapy. *Journal of Consulting and Clinical Psychology, 63,* 688–701.

Wood, A., Harrington, R., & Moore, A. (1996). Controlled trial of a brief cognitive-behavioral intervention in adolescent patients with depressive disorders. *Journal of Child Psychology and Psychiatry, 87,* 737–746.

References for Depression Measures

Beck, A., Steer, R., Ball, R., & Ranieri, W. (1996). Comparison of Beck Depression Inventories I-A and II in psychiatric outpatients. *Journal of Personality Assessment, 67,* 588–597.

Biggs, J., Wylie, L., & Ziegler, V. (1978). Validity of the Zung Self-Rating Depression Scale. *British Journal of Psychiatry, 132,* 381–385.

Burke, W., Nitcher, R., Roccaforte, W., & Wengel, S. (1992). A prospective evaluation of the Geriatric Depression Scale in an outpatient geriatric assessment center. *Journal of the American Geriatrics Society, 40,* 1227–1230.

Burt, T., & Ishak, W. (2002). Outcome measurement in mood disorders. In T. Burt, L. Sederer, & W. Ishak (Eds.), *Outcome measurement in psychiatry: Critical review* (pp. 155–190). Washington, DC: American Psychiatric Publishing.

D'Ath, P., Katona, P., Mullan, E., Evans, S., & Katona, C. (1994). Screening, detection and management of depression in elderly primary care attenders. I. The acceptability and performance of the 15 item Geriatric Depression Scale (GDS-15) and the development of short versions, *Family Practice, 11,* 260–266.

Feher, E., Larrabee, G., & Crook, T. (1992). Factors attenuating the validity of the Geriatric Depression Scale in a dementia population. *Journal of the American Geriatrics Society, 40,* 906–909.

Kaslow, N., Rehm, L., & Siegel, A. (1984). Social-cognitive and cognitive correlates of depression in children. *Journal of Abnormal Child Psychology, 12,* 605–620.

Kovacs, M. (1992). *Children's Depression Inventory manual*. North Tonawanda, NY: Multi-Health Systems.

Myers, K., & Winters, N. C. (2002). Ten-year review of rating scales II: Scales for internalizing disorders. *Journal of the American Academy of Child and Adolescent Psychiatry, 41*, 634–660.

Radloff, L. (1977). The CES-D Scale: A self-report depression scale for research in the general population. *Applied Psychological Measurement, 1*, 385–401.

Reynolds, W. (1987). *Reynolds adolescent depression scale (RADS)*. Odessa, FL: Psychological Assessment Resources.

Salamero, M., & Marcos, T. (1992). Factor study of the Geriatric Depression Scale. *Acta Psychiatrica Scandinavica, 86*, 283–286.

Weissman, M., Orvaschel, H., & Padian, N. (1980). Children's symptom and social functioning self-report scales: Comparison of mothers' and children's reports. *Journal of Nervous and Mental Disorders, 168*, 736–740.

Yesavage, J. A., Brink, T. L., Owen, R., Lum, O., Huang, V., Adey, M., et al. (1982–1983). Development and validation of a geriatric depression scale: A preliminary report. *Journal of Psychiatric Research, 17*, 37–49.

Zung, W. W. (1965) A self-rating depression scale. *Archives of General Psychiatry, 12*, 63–70.

11 Substance Use Disorders

The *DSM* provides general criteria for *substance abuse* and *substance dependence*, the two types of *substance-related disorders*, rather than separate criteria for each of the 11 classes of substances: alcohol, amphetamines, caffeine, cannabis, cocaine, hallucinogens, inhalants, nicotine, opioids, phencyclidine, and sedatives/hypnotics/anxiolytics (American Psychiatric Association [APA], 2000). The defining characteristic of *abuse* is the negative consequences of use; *dependence* is compulsive use, despite serious consequences, and is often accompanied by tolerance and withdrawal. The *DSM* also describes *substance-induced disorders*, which include intoxication, withdrawal, dementia, amnesia, psychosis, mood, anxiety, sexual dysfunction, and sleep. Alcohol-related disorders in both adolescence and adulthood are a primary focus of this chapter, although other substances are also discussed.

▓▓▓▓ Prevalence

Substance use and abuse disorders are highly prevalent in American society. In 2002, an estimated 22 million Americans (9.4% of the total population age 12 and older) were classified with substance dependence or abuse ("Mental Health," n.d.). For adults, prevalence rates for alcohol dependence are estimated at 15% of the general population. In the elderly, 1-month prevalence rates for alcohol use disorders range from 0.9% to 2.2% ("Mental Health," n.d.). Many adolescents engage in problematic drinking, but only a subset fulfill the criteria for abuse or dependence. For adolescents, three population-based studies found point prevalence alcohol abuse rates ranging from 1 to 14.6%, and marijuana abuse point prevalence rates ranging from 1.4 to 2.9% (Weinberg, Rahdert, Colliver, & Meyer, 1998).

In 2002, among people age 12 or older, the rate of substance dependence or abuse was highest among American Indians/Alaska Natives, at 14.1% ("Mental Health," n.d.). The next highest rate was among biracial persons (13.0%). The rate was similar among African Americans and Caucasians (9.5% and 9.3%, respectively). Among Hispanics, the rate was 10.4%. Although Hispanic males have somewhat higher rates than their Caucasian and African American counterparts, prevalence is lower among Hispanic females than among females from other ethnic groups (APA, 2000).

Asians had the lowest rate of dependence or abuse (4.2%) (Mirin et al., 2002). The low prevalence rates among Asians appear to be related to the deficiency of an enzyme, aldehyde dehydrogenase, that breaks down alcohol after its ingestion. It is estimated that 50% of Japanese, Chinese, and Korean people have this deficiency. When the estimated 10% of individuals with a complete absence of the enzyme consume alcohol, they experience a flushed face and palpitations that can be so severe they will not subsequently drink at all. The 40% of the population with only a relative deficiency experience less intense flushing but still have a significantly reduced risk of developing an alcohol use disorder.

Males are more likely to experience an alcohol use disorder at a rate of 5:1, but this ratio depends on the age sampled (i.e., young adult samples might have closer gaps between men and women). Men are overrepresented in almost all the substance-related disorders, including amphetamine, cannabis, cocaine, hallucinogen, inhalant, opioid, and phencyclidine-related disorders. Women may be at higher risk for prescription drug abuse of sedatives, hypnotics, and antianxiety drugs.

Course of the Disorders

The typical onset for a substance use disorder begins in late adolescence or early adulthood. Having an adolescent substance use disorder puts the individual at risk for continuation into adulthood (Brook, Brook, Zhang, Cohen, & Whiteman, 2002; Rohde, Lewinsohn, Kahler, Seeley, & Brown, 2001). In some cases, substance abuse begins in mid to late adulthood (Mirin et al., 2002). Despite the age of onset, the relationship between the development of alcohol *abuse* into *dependence* is variable, with a minority of abusers (30%) eventually meeting criteria for dependence.

Comorbidity

Psychiatric

Adolescents have a 60% likelihood of being diagnosed with a psychiatric disorder along with a substance use disorder. The disruptive disorders—conduct disorder, oppositional defiant disorder, and attention-deficit/hyperactivity disorder (ADHD)—are most common, followed by depression (Armstrong & Costello, 2002). Estimates for psychiatric comorbid disorders in adults with substance use disorders range widely—between 20% and 90% (APA, 2000). In community samples, while the chance of having a psychiatric disorder is not significantly elevated for those with alcohol abuse, it is for those with alcohol dependence (Petrakis, Gonzalez, Rosenheck, & Krystal, 2002). According to the National Comorbidity Survey (Kessler et al., 1996), more than a quarter (27.9%) had a depressive disorder, and 36.9% had an anxiety disorder in the previous year. Lifetime rates of comorbid schizophrenia were 24%.

Adults in treatment show higher comorbidity than people in the community, and about a third have at least one other substance use disorder (Mirin et al., 2002). Antisocial personality disorder is particularly common in men who abuse substances. The incidence of suicide among people with substance use disorders is three to four times the rate in the general population, with an overall increased risk of 15%.

Because of high comorbidity rates between substance abuse/dependence and other disorders, individuals with other disorders should be routinely questioned about their substance use patterns. The social worker needs to establish the chronology of symptom patterns and assess whether the other disorder was present before the substance use, what the symptoms were like for the client during periods of abstinence, and how the chemical use affected the other disorder. Some authors recommend a period of 3 to 4 weeks after the person has stopped using before diagnosing the presence of another disorder or prescribing medication for that disorder. This recommendation implies that otherwise comorbidity prevalence rates may be artificially elevated by the practice of assigning diagnoses before some symptoms related to the substance use have abated (Miller & Fine, 1993). On the other hand, social workers should monitor clients in the early stages of abstinence for the emergence of symptoms, such as those of posttraumatic stress disorder (PTSD), which may have been masked by the use of substances (Petrakis et al., 2002).

Medical

Substance dependence in the United States (excluding nicotine) annually accounts for 40% of all hospital admissions and 25% of mortality rates, or 500,000 deaths. African Americans have a higher death rate than Caucasians from these disorders. Because the prevalence of alcohol use is higher than any other substance use disorder, medical problems related to drinking are most common. These include gastrointestinal problems (gastritis, ulcers, and, in about 15% of heavy users, cirrhosis of the liver and pancreatitis) and cardiovascular conditions (hypertension and high levels of cholesterol, which increase the risk of heart disease) (Corrao, Bagnardi, Zambon, & Arico, 1999; Mirin et al., 2002).

Women are susceptible to a more rapid onset of addiction and health problems once they begin drinking (Abbott, 1994; Hesselbrock, 1991; Nelson-Zlupko, Kauffman, & Dore, 1995). This progression may be partly due to physiological factors. Because women have a higher ratio of fat and a lower ratio of water in their bodies, alcohol and drugs enter the system at greater concentrations and thus with more potency (Abbott, 1994). The female body's inability to metabolize alcohol means the alcohol is absorbed directly through the protective barrier of the stomach, leading to an increased risk of liver problems and, thus, a higher rate of medical problems and death (Abbott, 1994). In a sample of 10,010 individuals who entered treatment, it was reported that females had more health problems than the males (Wechsberg, Craddock, & Hubbard, 1998). In order of frequency, health concerns for women are respiratory, gynecological, heart, and digestive problems.

Children born to addicted mothers are also at risk for health problems (Abbott, 1994; Nelson-Zlupko et al., 1995). Short-term risks include fetal alcohol syndrome, low birth weight (which itself puts a child at risk for other disorders), the complications of postnatal withdrawal, and HIV infection. These potential short-term effects may also have long-term consequences for children, such as cognitive and motor development problems.

Other than alcohol, some substances are associated with their own health risks. Problems related to cocaine use include weight loss and malnutrition, myocardial infarction, and stroke. Selling cocaine is associated with traumatic injuries from violent attacks. For heroin (opioid) use, transmission of HIV infection from needle use, tuberculosis, malnutrition, and head trauma are prevalent. The death rate is high among those who do not receive treatment—about 10 per 1,000 annually. Death typically results from injuries sustained while buying or selling drugs. HIV infection is another cause of death.

Risk and Protective Factors

Risk and protective factors for the onset of adolescent substance use are described in Table 11.1. One major study found that although psychosocial risk appears to be a more powerful predictor of onset for adolescent use, the relative importance of protective factors is greater for recovery (Latimer, Newcomb, Winters, & Stinchfield, 2000). Risk and protective factors for the onset and recovery of adult substance use disorders are delineated in Tables 11.2 and 11.3, respectively. Risk factors specific to relapse found across studies involve the following factors (McKay, 1999): negative emotional states; increased craving prior to relapse; cognitive factors, such as reduced commitment to abstinence, lower self-efficacy, and the urge to give up; interpersonal problems; and lack of coping efforts during periods of temptation. Social workers should be alert to these factors in helping clients recognize signs of increased susceptibility and how to manage these risks.

Assessment

During clinical assessment, the social worker should focus on the following factors: (Bukstein et al., 1997; Riggs & Whitmore, 1999):

- Onset, progression, patterns, context, and frequency of use of all substances
- Tolerance or withdrawal symptoms
- Major life events
- Other disorders, including the relationship between the onset and progression of the symptoms and substance use
- "Triggers" and context of use
- Perceived advantages and disadvantages of use
- Motivations and goals for treatment
- Number of times the individual has quit and the strategies that were used
- Financial and legal status
- Education and employment status
- Condition of health (a physical examination may be warranted)
- Social support networks
- Coping skills

Also see appendixes I and II for descriptions of self-report measurement tools that can be used with adolescents and adults, respectively.

Adolescents should receive a confidential individual interview and also a parent interview (Riggs & Whitmore, 1999). The social worker, in addition to asking questions about the child, should address the extent of parental

Table 11.1

Risk and Protective Factors for Adolescent Substance Use

System Level	Risk	Protective
Biological	Male	
	Genetics	
Psychological	Impulsivity and ADHD symptoms	
	Early onset of experimentation	
	Aggression and undercontrolled behavior in childhood	
	Sensation-seeking behavior	Goal direction
	Low feelings of guilt	
	Conduct problems and delinquency	
Peers	Social impairment	
	Affiliation with deviant peers	
	Peer substance abuse	Having abstinent friends
School	Low achievement and academic failure	
	Truancy	
	Suspension	
	Low motivation, negative attitude toward school	Positive connection to school
Family	Parental substance abuse	
	Permissive parental values about teen alcohol and drug use	Parental warnings about alcohol use
	Sibling substance abuse	A warm and supportive family environment
	Harsh, inconsistent, and ineffective discipline strategies	Low level of family conflict
	Lack of monitoring and supervision	Parental control and supervision
	Child abuse and other trauma	
	Poor relationships with parents and siblings, low bonding	Being close to parents
	Unemployment, poor education of mother	
	Teens running away from home	
Community	Availability	Clear community prohibitions, such as higher taxes on liquor
Race	Caucasian (alcohol)	
	Hispanic (drug use)	

Sources: Farrell & White (1998); French, Finkbiner, & Duhamel (2002); Hawkins, Catalano, & Miller (1992); Jessor, Van Den Bos, Vanderryn, Costa, & Turbin (1995); Kaplow, Curran, & Dodge (2002); Kilpatrick et al. (2000); Latimer et al. (2000); Loeber, Farrington, Stouthamer-Loeber, & Van Kammen (1998); Martin et al. (2002); National Institute on Drug Abuse (1997).

Table 11.2

Risk and Protective Factors for Onset of Substance Use Disorders

Risks	Protective Factors
Biology	
Genetics (male)[a]	Female
	No family history
	Asian origin
Psychological	
Depression (female)	No prior mental disorder
Antisocial personality disorder (male)	
Social	
Family	
Sexual abuse (particularly for females)	No history of sexual abuse
Peer	
Substance-using peers	Friends who do not support substance use
Neighborhood	
Availability of drugs	Lack of availability

[a]The influence of genetics is low overall, but stronger for males (Walters, 2002).

substance use, parents' attitudes toward their child's use, the amount of monitoring and supervision the youth receives, and the level of attachment and cohesion in the family (Bukstein et al., 1997).

For the elderly, ageist attitudes of health care providers may present obstacles to assessment (Vinton & Wambach, 2005). Providers may not bring up substance abuse; they also may not believe elders can benefit from intervention or that their quality of life would improve as a result. The reliability of elder self-report may also be suspect. Denial, sense of stigma, social desirability effects, and memory loss can affect the accurate recollection or admission of alcohol problems among the elderly. It is sometimes difficult to tell whether physical and cognitive problems found in the elderly are due to the process of aging or the effects of consumption. Screening for alcohol abuse among the elderly includes (a) the quantity and frequency of alcohol consumption, (b) alcohol-related social and legal problems (e.g., housing problems, falls or accidents, poor nutrition, inadequate self- and home care, lack of exercise, and social isolation), (c) alcohol-related health problems, (d) symptoms of drunkenness and

Table 11.3

Risk and Protective Factors for Course of Substance Use Disorders

Risks	Protective Factors
Features of use	
The year after treatment is high risk for relapse	Two years of abstinence
High levels of pretreatment use[a]	
Substance use during treatment	
Biological	
Female	
Life Events	
Physical and/or sexual victimization[b]	
Psychological	
Concurrent disorders, especially personality disorders (borderline and antisocial)	Lack of concurrent disorders
	Motivation
Social	
Family	
Lack of family support	Family support for sobriety
Social Support	
Substance-using peers	Non-substance-using peers
	AA attendance (or at least contact with one member from AA)[c]
	Ability to develop new relationships
Culture	
Ethnic minority	Intervention that integrates culturally relevant beliefs and healing practices
SES	
Low SES	

[a]Karageorge & Wisdom (2001).
[b]Orwin, Maranda, & Brady (2001).
[c]Bond, Kaskutas, & Weisner (2003).

dependence, and (e) self-recognition of alcohol-related problems (Vinton & Wambach, 2005).

Intervention Goals

For people with substance abuse problems, intervention goals include reducing or eliminating substance use, preventing relapse, and improving psychological and social functioning. The last goal involves mending disrupted relationships, reducing impulsivity, building social and vocational skills, and maintaining employment.

For adolescents, intervention should include family involvement and prioritize the improvement of communication among family members (Bukstein et al., 1997). Parents should be helped to consistently provide proper guidance and set limits for the child. Any addiction patterns in the parents must be recognized and, if possible, treated. Intervention should also help adolescents and their families develop an alcohol- and drug-free lifestyle, including recreational activities with non-substance-using peers. Indeed, a treatment plan that includes a comprehensive array of services, including life skills, recreational sessions, and vocational and educational skills training, has been associated with improved outcomes for adolescents (Orwin & Ellis, 2001).

Reducing and Ameliorating Substance Use

For adolescents, abstinence is recommended (Bukstein et al., 1997), but as the person matures into adulthood, controlled alcohol use may be a possibility (Weinberg et al., 1998). However, for adults, controversy surrounds the goal of controlled drinking versus abstinence. For some users, controlled drinking might be an intermediate goal with a long-term goal of abstinence. Controlled use might be unrealistic for others, however, as any further use may pose too high a risk. Those who attain total abstinence show the best prognosis over time because any use may entail disinhibition, increased cravings for other drugs, poor judgment, and an increased risk of relapse.

The following guidelines cited by Mirin et al. (2002) help determine who might be appropriate candidates for controlled drinking. Candidates should be

- In the early stages of alcohol abuse
- Realistically confident that they can control their drinking
- Able to demonstrate improved occupational and psychological functioning as a result of reduced use

Behavioral self-control training has been developed to help people control their drinking. It includes spacing out drinks, prolonging the duration of drinks, and switching to lower-proof drinks. Identifying high-risk situations and self-monitoring are other key components. Walters (2000) conducted a meta-analysis of 17 studies on behavioral self-control training and found that they showed comparative effectiveness with abstinence-based programs. As a result, Walters (2000) maintains that individuals in treatment should be offered a choice of goals.

Relapse Prevention

Reduction in the frequency and severity of relapse is a critical goal of treatment. Specific strategies for practitioners include (see also Larimer, Palmer, & Marlatt, 1999):

- Discussing the client's ambivalence about sobriety
- Identifying the emotional and environmental triggers of craving
- Developing coping strategies to deal with internal or external stressors
- Exploring the chain of decisions leading to the resumption of substance use
- Learning from brief relapse episodes (slips) about triggers leading to relapse and developing effective techniques for early intervention

Relapse prevention has been analyzed in 70 studies representing 9,504 individuals (Irvin, Bowers, Dunn, & Wang, 1999). The overall treatment effect of relapse prevention for alcohol use disorders, substance use disorders, and smoking was $r = .14$, which is low. Relapse prevention was more effective in treating alcohol use ($r = .27$) than some other substance use disorders. The effect on psychosocial adjustment was also larger ($r = .48$). Thus it appears that relapse prevention works better for alcohol than for other substance use, but only in a low to moderate range. Relapse prevention actually seems to produce more of an effect on psychosocial adjustment than on reduced use.

Intervention

Intervention can be very effective for substance abusers, although some people (perhaps 20%) can achieve long-term abstinence without it (APA, 2000). The majority of people who receive treatment for substance dependence either attain abstinence or have only brief episodes of use (as many as 70% in high-functioning samples) (Mirin et al., 2002). Similarly high success rates have been found for those treated for cocaine dependence

(Simpson, Joe, & Broome, 2002). Even in difficult-to-treat populations, such as people who are homeless, a majority (60%) achieve abstinence at 3-month follow-up, and at 1 year, 45% success rates are reported (Mirin et al., 2002). Only a small proportion of people (15–20%) show a chronic, relapsing course over a long period of time (10 to 20 years), requiring numerous interventions.

Regardless of the treatment site or the modalities employed, the frequency, intensity, and duration of treatment participation are positively correlated with improved outcome (Mirin et al., 2002; Prendergast, Podus, & Change, 2000). Length of treatment also seems important for adolescents (Hser et al., 2001; Latimer et al., 2000).

Commonly available treatment settings include hospitals, residential treatment facilities, partial hospital care, and outpatient programs (see Table 11.4). In the United States, inpatient treatment was the modality of choice until recently, when the typical length of stay at inpatient facilities decreased substantially; now the vast majority of those with substance use problems are treated on an outpatient basis (Fuller & Hiller-Sturmhofel, 1999).

Client characteristics that influence decisions about the treatment setting include the potential harm of withdrawal and the extent of environmental support for sobriety. Symptoms of alcohol withdrawal typically begin within 4 to 12 hours after cessation or reduction of alcohol use. They peak in intensity during the second day of abstinence and generally resolve within 4 or 5 days. Serious complications may include seizures, hallucinations, and delirium, although these are now rare. In the past, mortality rates for alcohol withdrawal delirium were as high as 20% but currently are closer to 1% because of improved diagnosis and medical intervention. Still, withdrawal can be life-threatening for elderly people who have significant physical dependence ("Mental Health," n.d.).

Generalized support, reassurance, and frequent monitoring are sufficient interventions for approximately two thirds of those with mild to moderate withdrawal symptoms. Individuals in more severe withdrawal and those who develop hallucinations may require medication. The benzodiazepines have been found effective in reducing withdrawal severity, delirium, and seizures (Mayo-Smith et al., 1997).

The social environment plays a role in attitudes about use and in what circumstances, choice of substances, and also motivation and ability to comply with interventions. Peer and family support are critical factors for recovery. Conversely, significant others who enable use and drug availability bode poorly for outcome. Such risks need to be addressed in treatment with either a high degree of community support or temporary removal from these circumstances through residential treatment.

Table 11.4

Treatment Settings

Setting	Indications
Hospitalization	Severe withdrawal or a documented history of heavy alcohol use and high tolerance
	People who repeatedly fail to cooperate with or benefit from outpatient detoxification
	A drug overdose that cannot be safely treated in an outpatient or emergency room setting
	Severe or medically complicated syndromes
	Comorbid general medical conditions that make ambulatory detoxification unsafe
	A history of not engaging in or benefiting from treatment in a less intensive setting
	Psychiatric comorbidity that markedly impairs the ability to participate in or benefit from treatment, or the comorbid disorder by itself requires hospital care (e.g., depression with suicidal thoughts or acute psychosis)
	Lack of response to less intensive treatment, or when substance use poses an ongoing threat to physical or mental health
Residential (at least 3 months)	People who do not meet criteria for hospitalization but whose lives have come to focus predominantly on substance use and who lack sufficient living skills and social supports to maintain abstinence in an outpatient setting
	Severe withdrawal or a history of heavy alcohol use and high tolerance, placing the person at risk for withdrawal
	People who repeatedly fail to cooperate with or benefit from outpatient detoxification
	Some programs are specifically designed for adolescents, pregnant or postpartum women, and women with young children
Partial hospital care	People who require intensive care but have reasonable probability of refraining from substance use outside a restricted setting
	People leaving hospitals or residential settings who remain at high risk for relapse (insufficient motivation, severe psychiatric comorbidity, or a history of immediate relapse)
	People returning to high-risk environments who have limited psychosocial supports for remaining drug free
	People doing poorly in an intensive outpatient treatment.

continued

Table 11.4 (*continued*)	
Treatment Settings	
Setting	Indications
Therapeutic community (need 12 months)	For opioid users
Outpatient treatment	People whose clinical condition or environmental circumstances do not require a more intensive level of care
	People who are cocaine dependent (but this is applied intensively; more than once a week)

Source: Mirin et al. (2002).

Psychosocial Treatments

One means of conceptualizing intervention for people with substance use disorders is the *transtheoretical stages of change model*. Six stages of change are formulated in this model, based on the individual's readiness to change. Intervention techniques from different theoretical orientations are used to match the relevant stage of change, with a primary focus on building clients' motivation to take action toward their goals. This intervention model is delineated in Table 11.5.

Originators of the stages of change model claim that it is empirically derived and has garnered much research support (e.g., Prochaska, DiClemente, & Norcross, 1994; Velicer, Hughes, Fava, Prochaska, & DiClemente, 1995). According to a recent comprehensive review, however, there is as yet no firm evidence that people progress systematically through each stage of change (Littell & Girvin, 2002). At the same time, a meta-analysis of 47 studies did reveal that cognitive-affective processes were more indicative of the stages of contemplation or preparation (an effect size of .70) and that behavioral processes were more common in the action stage (an effect size of .80) (Rosen, 2000). This generally supports the hypothesized movement of change from a cognitive to a behavioral process as clients become readier to take action toward change.

The treatment models discussed in this chapter—motivational interviewing, AA-based approaches, family therapy, and cognitive-behavioral therapy—are organized according to the stages of change model in Table 11.5. In this way, the social worker can decide when a particular treatment approach can be introduced at an optimal time.

Table 11.5

The Stages of Change and Strategies at Each Stage

Stage of Change	Characteristics	Change Strategies
Precontemplation	Unwilling to do anything about the problem	Link the client with social liberation forces
	Sees the problem behavior as possessing more advantages than disadvantages	Motivational interviewing
		Unilateral treatment
	Usually coerced or pressured to seek help by others	
Contemplation	Client begins to consider there is a problem and the feasibility and costs of changing the behavior	Provide education on the disorder and the recovery process
	Wants to understand the behavior and frequently feels distress over it	Bolster the advantages of changing and problem-solve about how to lessen the disadvantages
	Thinks about making change in the next 6 months	Identify social support systems
		Couples therapy
		Cognitive-behavioral: self-monitoring; functional analysis; consider alternative reinforcers for the problem behavior.
Preparation (Determination)	Person is poised to change in the next month	Couples therapy
		Cognitive-behavioral: Set goals; develop a change plan; develop coping skills
Action	Client has started to modify the problem behavior or the environment in an effort to promote change in the past 6 months	Couples therapy
		Cognitive-behavioral: Appraise high-risk situations and coping strategies to overcome these; apply alternative reinforcers to problem behaviors
		Assess social support systems so others are a resource for change rather than a hindrance

continued

Table 11.5 (continued)

The Stages of Change and Strategies at Each Stage

Stage of Change	Characteristics	Change Strategies
Maintenance	Sustained change has occurred for at least 6 months	Help the individual find alternative sources of satisfaction and continue to support lifestyle changes
		Cognitive-behavioral: Assist the client in practicing and applying coping strategies; remain vigilant for cognitive distortions that might be associated with the problem and ways to counteract them; maintain environmental control
Relapse	The problem behavior has resumed; another cycle has begun, and the client reenters either the precontemplation or the contemplation stage	Cognitive-behavioral: Develop a greater awareness of high-risk situations and coping strategies needed to address these challenges

Source: Adapted from Connors et al. (2001).

Motivational Interviewing

Developed over the last 20 years (Dunn, Deroo, & Rivara, 2001), motivational interviewing is "a client-centered, directive method for enhancing intrinsic motivation to change by exploring and resolving ambivalence" (Miller & Rollnick, 2002, p. 25). Originally for the treatment of substance abuse, it has been used both as a stand-alone treatment and as a way to engage people in other interventions (Walitzer, Dermen, & Conners, 1999). In terms of the stages of change model, motivational interviewing is helpful for those in either the precontemplation (denying the need for change) or contemplation (considering change) stages.

Several guiding principles for the practitioner underlie the techniques of motivational interviewing.

- Listening and expressing empathy
- Developing discrepancies between problem behavior and the client's goals and values

- "Rolling" with resistance, which means avoiding power struggles and instead making statements that help clients argue for change
- Supporting self-efficacy, or the client's sense of confidence that he or she can change
- Developing a change plan

Extensive research has been done on motivational interviewing. Dunn, Deroo, and Rivara (2001) quantitatively reviewed 29 studies focused on substance abuse and found moderate to large effects for the reduction of abuse and dependence, with effects maintained over time. Although studies have largely been conducted on adults, adolescent substance use also showed significantly positive results from motivational interviewing (Burke, Arkowitz, & Dunn, 2002). Overall, motivational interviewing was superior to no-treatment control groups and less viable treatments. It has also been shown to be equivalent to alternatives that were two to three times longer in duration. For example, in the Project MATCH Research Group study (1997, 1998), 952 individuals with alcohol problems from outpatient clinics and 774 from aftercare treatment were provided with either 12-step facilitation (12 sessions), cognitive-behavioral coping skills therapy (12 sessions), or motivational enhancement therapy (4 sessions). Motivational enhancement fared as well as the other two interventions at posttest (Project MATCH Research Group, 1997) and at 3 years later (Project MATCH Research Group, 1998). In the outpatient sample, motivational interviewing was the most effective intervention for clients with high levels of anger (Project MATCH Research Group, 1998).

Cognitive-Behavioral Interventions

Cognitive-behavioral interventions focus on (a) altering the cognitive processes that lead to maladaptive substance use, (b) intervening in the behavioral chain of events that lead to substance use, (c) helping clients deal successfully with drug craving, and (d) promoting and reinforcing the development of social skills and behaviors compatible with remaining drug free. Behavioral interventions reward or punish clients for desirable (such as demonstrating treatment compliance) or undesirable (associated with relapse) behaviors (Carroll, 1999; Higgins & Petry, 1999). Rewards may include vouchers awarded for producing drug-free urine samples that can be exchanged for mutually agreed-on items (e.g., movie tickets) and "community reinforcements," in which family members or peers reinforce behaviors that demonstrate or facilitate abstinence (e.g., participation in positive activities) (Miller, Meyers, & Hiller-Sturmhofel, 1999).

For adolescents, cognitive-behavioral approaches such as rehearsal and social control contracting (Azrin, Donahue, Besalel, Kogan, & Acierno, 1994), problem solving, coping skills training, and relapse prevention techniques show promise, at least for the first few months after the intervention ends (Weinberg et al., 1998). Because so many different interventions for adults fall under the rubric of cognitive-behavioral therapy, space precludes discussion of the research. See Longabaugh and Morgenstern (1999); McCrady (2000); Miller, Meyers, and Hiller-Sturmhofel (1999); and Monti and Rohsenow (1999) for more information. Other cognitive-behavioral treatments are described next as they take place as part of family intervention.

Family Interventions

When possible, family participation is helpful for intervening with a person who has a substance abuse problem. A substantial burden is imposed on families when a member has a substance use disorder. Families also have a tremendous potential impact on perpetuating or ameliorating these problems. Families can clearly affect the abuser's motivation and ability to comply with intervention (Mirin et al., 2002).

Two meta-analyses have been conducted on the use of family therapy, one on alcohol-related disorders (Edwards & Steinglass, 1995) and the other on drug-related disorders (Stanton & Shadish, 1997). Two important conclusions have emerged from these studies. First, regardless of the treatment phase (engagement, treatment, or aftercare), a higher rate of improvement was found when families were involved in treatment compared with when they were not (Edwards & Steinglass, 1995). Second, family intervention (*except* those involving family psychoeducation or support groups) was superior to alternative conditions (individual, treatment as usual, group treatment, or placebo control) in terms of the client's time in treatment and reduced drug use (Stanton & Shadish, 1997).

Another family intervention that has been a focus of research is *unilateral therapy* (Thomas, Santa, Bronson, & Oyserman, 1987), sometimes called *reinforcement training* (Sisson & Azrin, 1986) or the *pressures to change* model (Barber & Gilbertson, 1996). More recently, *community reinforcement* has also been used as a family training approach (Meyers, Miller, Hill, & Tonigan, 1999; Miller, Meyers, & Tonigan, 1999). In this intervention, family members are trained on how to exert influence on the "drinker" so that the person may develop motivation to change. This approach emphasizes that the family member is not responsible for the alcoholic person's behavior. Rather, the family member removes conditions in the environment supportive of drinking, reinforces appropriate behavior of the addict (Sisson & Azrin, 1986; Thomas et al., 1987), gives feedback about inappropriate behavior while drinking (Sisson & Azrin, 1986), and provides consequences if behavior exceeds agreed-upon limits (Barber & Gilbertson, 1996). The length of this intervention ranges from brief models in which family members are seen for 5 (Barber & Gilbertson, 1996) to 7 weeks (Sisson & Azrin, 1986) to models in which family members attend sessions for up to 6 months (Thomas et al., 1987). In the few studies that have been conducted, these models have resulted in the person with substance use entering treatment at a significantly higher rate and with reduced drinking than in the comparison conditions.

The other main approach to family treatment of chemical addiction involves the addict and family member being seen together. The main objective of couples therapy is to alter patterns of interaction that maintain chemical abuse and build a relationship that more effectively supports sobriety (O'Farrell, 1993). These interventions are cognitive-behavioral in nature, entailing building communication skills, planning family activities, initiating caring behaviors, and expressing feelings. Techniques used to learn these skills include homework, role playing, and covert rehearsal. Intervention is generally brief, with 10 (O'Farrell, Choquette, Cutter, Brown, & McCourt, 1993), 12 (Fals-Stewart, Birchler, & O'Farrell 1996), or up to 15 weekly sessions (McCrady et al., 1986). Intervention is delivered in the context of either individual (McCrady et al., 1986) or group couples sessions (O'Farrell et al., 1993) and mostly for alcohol (Epstein & McCrady, 1998) but also for drug use (Fals-Stewart & O'Farrell, 2003; Fals-Stewart et al., 1996). In general, studies indicate that the couple condition produced at least as positive an effect on reduced substance use as individual therapy, and more of an impact on marital functioning, which may be a factor in sustaining abstinence. Cost savings may also be produced by decreased incarcerations and hospitalizations related to alcohol use (O'Farrell & Fals-Stewart, 1999).

Family therapy approaches have received the most attention for adolescent substance abuse disorders (Weinberg et al., 1998). Family systems theory provides the main thrust of intervention with adolescents (Joanning, Thomas, Quinn, & Mullen, 1992; Lewis, Piercy, Sprenkle, & Trepper, 1990; Santisteban et al., 2003; Santisteban, Szapocznik, Kurtines, Murray, & LaPierre, 1996; Szapocznik et al., 1988; Waldron, Slessnick, Brody, Turner, & Peterson, 2001). We will define some of the dominant concepts of systems theory. The concept of *circular causality* means that, rather than blaming the adolescent with the substance problem, each family member is seen as acting and reacting in repeated interaction patterns that have created and maintain the problem (Aponte, 2002; Minuchin, 1974). *Homeostasis* is the way the family system has self-regulated so that the problem behavior retains the "status quo" (Minuchin & Nichols, 1993). Symptoms such as substance use and family resistance to change may represent ways the family maintains homeostasis. Symptoms may also play other *functions* for the system. Substance abuse may, for instance, serve to draw family members together or create more autonomy between them (Alexander & Parsons, 1982). Family *structure* is the organization of interaction patterns that ideally results in a unified parental hierarchy and clear boundaries between sub-systems and the outside world (Minuchin, 1974).

Because of the multidimensional nature of substance use problems in adolescence, most family therapy approaches to treatment are models that integrate several theoretical frameworks. For instance, *brief strategic family therapy* (Szapocznik & Williams, 2000) has both structural and strategic techniques. *Functional family therapy* possesses elements of structural and strategic family systems approaches, as well as behavioral family therapy, with a particular emphasis on the functions of symptoms (Alexander & Parsons, 1982). Both *multidimensional family therapy* (Liddle, 1999) and *multisystemic therapy* (Henggeler, Schoenwald, Borduin, Rowland, & Cunningham, 1998) are presented as "ecologically integrative approaches" (Mirin et al., 2002), because they go beyond family therapy to modify multiple domains of functioning affecting the youth's behavior, including other key supports and systems in the youth's life. (See chapter 5 for more information on multisystemic therapy.)

Multidimensional family therapy, when compared with adolescent group therapy and a multifamily education approach, demonstrated reductions in drug use. At 12-month follow-up, the family therapy group showed improvements that were statistically significant against the education condition but not against the group therapy condition (Liddle et al., 2001). Multisystemic therapy has been employed with juvenile offenders and resulted in higher engagement rates for those who have substance abuse problems (Henggeler, Pickrel, Brondino, & Couch, 1996) and lower self-reported drug use (Henggeler et al., 1991; Henggeler, Melton, Brondino, Scherer, & Hanley, 1997; Henggeler, Pickrel, & Brondino, 1999) than in the comparison or control conditions. Questions have recently been raised, however, about the positive findings of multisystemic therapy in terms of the comparability of the treatment and comparison conditions (Littell, Popa, & Forsythe, 2005).

Alcoholics Anonymous Approaches

Alcoholics Anonymous (AA) self-help groups and treatment-based approaches (the Minnesota model) have tended to predominate in the substance abuse treatment field (Fuller & Hiller-Sturmhofel, 1999; Kelly, Myers, & Brown, 2002; Sheehan & Owen, 1999). We consider these approaches separately here. First, AA self-help groups offer a number of potential advantages[1] (Mirin et al., 2002):

- Referral is appropriate at all stages of the treatment process, even for those who may still actively abuse substances.
- Individuals who attend AA or Narcotics Anonymous regularly receive group support, including reminders of the disastrous consequences of substance use and the benefits of abstinence and sobriety.
- Participants receive straightforward advice and encouragement about avoiding relapse.
- The process of working through the 12 steps with a sponsor provides a structured opportunity for the person to assess the role of past life experiences and personal identity in the development and maintenance of the substance use disorder. A sponsor who is compatible with the individual can provide important guidance and support during the recovery process, particularly during periods of emotional distress and increased craving.
- Opportunities for substance-free social events and interactions are available.
- Members can attend meetings on a self-determined or prescribed schedule—every day if necessary. Periods associated with high risk for relapse, such as weekends, holidays, and evenings, are particularly appropriate for attendance.
- Self-help groups based on the 12-step model are also available for family members and friends (such as Al-Anon, Alateen, and Nar-Anon). Such groups provide support and education about the illness and help to reduce maladaptive enabling behavior in family and friends.

The research on AA self-help groups is scant and methodologically limited. In a meta-analysis, Tonigan, Toscova, and Miller (1996) examined the relationship between AA attendance and drinking in the literature. Although attendance was linked to reduced drinking, the relationship was small. In their meta-analysis, Kownacki and Shadish (1999) indicated that those who voluntarily attended AA did better than those who chose not to utilize AA. Other interventions may also be effective with such persons, however. Kownacki and Shadish (1999) also found that individuals coerced into attending 12-step groups did not reduce their drinking. Regarding AA as part of an inpatient treatment model, few randomized studies have been conducted, and these provide mild support for its helpfulness (Kownacki & Shadish, 1999). Some studies have isolated components of the AA philosophy and procedures and examined their effect on alcohol reduction. Support has been found for the use of the 12 steps, specifically the "honest inventory" (Steps 4 and 5) and the use of recovered alcoholics as counselors.

Other studies show support for AA as a treatment model. For adolescents, abstinence rates for small-scale evaluations of 12-step-based interventions are reported in the range of 50 to 60% (Winters, Stinchfield, Opland, Weller, & Latimer, 2000). In the Project MATCH study described earlier, the 12-step facilitation intervention (a formal treatment approach that guides the individual through the first five steps of AA and encourages AA participation) was as effective as cognitive-behavioral treatment and motivational interviewing. Indeed, individuals in aftercare treatment who were initially severely dependent and individuals in outpatient treatment whose social networks supported drinking had better results with the AA-based treatment than with the cognitive-behavioral and motivational interviewing conditions at 3-year follow-up (Longabaugh, Wirtz, Zweben, & Stout, 1998; Project MATCH Research Group, 1997). In another study, 133 adults were randomly assigned to either a cognitive-behavioral or an AA relapse prevention approach. The latter intervention produced the most favorable substance use outcomes, particularly for those with high initial psychological distress (Brown, Seraganian, Tremblay, & Annis, 2002).

Diversity Issues

Gay men and lesbian women are at increased risk for substance abuse for a number of possible reasons (Beatty et al., 1999). Gay bars, where alcohol is a main feature, are still one of the few legitimate places in most cities for meeting and socializing. A second risk factor for substance abuse among gays and lesbians is that they are not able to fully partake in societal institutions that tend to attenuate substance use among heterosexuals, such as marriage and family life. Third, many gay and lesbian people do not have the full array of support from family, friends, and acquaintances. Loss of peers and acquaintances in the gay network is another burden to which the gay community is susceptible, which might lead to alcohol and drug use for coping with grief.

Fourth, "sexual minority status may entail personal confrontation with prejudicial attitudes, discriminatory behaviors, unfairness and unequal power, hatred, and verbal, emotional, or physical abuse" (Beatty et al., 1999, pp. 545–546). The stress from discrimination may lead some people to cope through the use of alcohol or drugs. Along with the other risks substances pose, for gay males substance use might lower inhibitions and decrease safe sexual practices, which, in turn, might lead to the possibility of HIV infection.

Specialized programming for gays and lesbians is available, though very few programs exist and empirical support for their effectiveness is lacking (Beatty et al., 1999). Social workers should be aware that there are AA groups for gay men and lesbians (LAMBA) in most larger communities.

Ethnic minorities are at risk for lack of engagement in services (Mirin et al., 2002). Although it is recommended that intervention should integrate culturally relevant beliefs and healing practices, taking into account the level of the client's acculturation and the particular group's values (Castro, Proescholdbell, Abeita, & Rodriquez, 1999), guidelines tend to be general in nature and not subject to empirical testing. Future research should ensure that treatment outcome is assessed in terms of ethnicity to examine whether tested interventions have a differential impact on people from different ethnic groups.

It is also possible that gender might crosscut cultural lines in specialized needs for services. For example, Corcoran and Corcoran (2001) found that gender rather than race (African American and Caucasian) was the determining factor in patterns of substance use initiation. Women tend to be underrepresented in treatment. Financial barriers, such as lack of money and health insurance, childcare, and transportation, prevent many women from seeking treatment. Other explanations for women's underutilization of services include their greater perceptions of the social stigma associated with drug and alcohol abuse. Once they are in treatment, women are found to have a higher prevalence than men of primary comorbid depressive and anxiety disorders that require specific intervention. They may also initiate substance abuse more than do men because of problems with coping (Corcoran & Corcoran, 2001). Many women with substance use disorders have a history of physical or sexual abuse (both as children and adults), which may influence their treatment participation and outcomes. For instance, in a report of 4,405 clients in treatment, 42% of the women had been sexually abused (Orwin, Maranda, & Brady, 2001).

Another pattern of women is that they often develop substance use problems in the context of relationships (Ashley, Marsden, & Brady, 2003). Many women have become involved with drugs or alcohol through a partner. Female clients also tend to have more family responsibilities and need more help with family-related problems.

A review of 38 studies on the effect of women-specific substance abuse treatment programming found a consistently positive effect on alcohol and drug use reduction, employment, mental health outcomes, and decreased criminality, among other measures (Ashley et al., 2003). The following components were related to the effectiveness of such programs: childcare provision; prenatal care; women-only admissions; supplemental services that addressed female topics, such as sexuality, parenting, and relationships; mental health programming; and comprehensive services, such as vocational and employment services. These components may not only reduce barriers to treatment entry and retention but also improve outcomes because they address the salient needs of women who abuse substances. In a meta-analysis on 33 studies of women's treatment, more specific results were found (Orwin, Francisco, & Bernichon, 2001). Pregnancy and personal adjustment were the outcomes most affected by women's programming, rather than substance use itself.

Co-Occuring Psychiatric and Substance Use Disorders

As discussed, people with substance use disorders have high rates of co-morbid disorders. Medications are often prescribed for these co-occurring psychiatric disorders (Petrakis et al., 2002; Weinberg et al., 1998). Other guidelines have been presented for the psychosocial treatment of people with co-occurring psychiatric and substance use disorders (Petrakis et al., 2002).

For those with severe mental illness, the immediate goal might be stabilization of the psychiatric illness, followed by motivational interviewing. (See Martino, Carroll, Kostas, Perkins, and Rounsaville [2002] for adapting motivational techniques with this population.) Confrontation, a commonly used technique in many substance abuse treatment settings, may not be effective for those who are potentially psychotic or suicidal (Petrakis et al., 2002), and a supportive approach might be indicated instead. As always, the social worker must attend not only to the psychotherapeutic needs of the individual but also to concrete needs, such as homelessness and physical health. Ongoing case management might be necessary so that the needs of the client will continue to be met and to steer the client through "various mental health, addiction, medical, housing, and entitlement services" (Rosenthal & Westreich, 1999). For those with depression and anxiety, cognitive-behavioral therapy might be indicated because the techniques can address both the psychiatric and substance use concerns (Petrakis et al., 2002). Nevertheless, treatment of comorbid disorders will not spontaneously resolve the substance use disorder. Over time, it often takes on a life of its own (Mirin et al., 2002).

A meta-analysis on interventions for co-occurring disorders found that the overall effect size for programs was low (.22) (Dumaine, 2003). Intensive case management had the highest effect size (.35), and inpatient treatment had the lowest (.13). The low effect size for inpatient treatment might have been the lack of differentiation between integrated (substance abuse and mental disorders) versus nonintegrated (offering only one type of service) treatment.

Pharmacological Interventions

Two types of medications are currently used in substance abuse treatment: aversive medications, designed to deter client drinking, and anticraving medications, which purport to reduce the desire to drink (Fuller & Hiller-Sturmhofel, 1999). The primary aversive drug, disulfiram (Antabuse), inhibits the activity of aldehyde dehydrogenase, the enzyme that metabolizes acetaldehyde, the first metabolic breakdown product of alcohol. In the presence of disulfram, alcohol use results in an accumulation of toxic levels of acetaldehyde, which is accompanied by a variety of unpleasant and potentially dangerous (but rarely lethal) symptoms (Mirin et al., 2002). Abstinence is related to compliance with the medication (Fuller & Hiller-Sturmhofel, 1999).

Medications to prevent relapse are called antidipsotropics. Naltrexone, a drug that is being increasingly used in the United States, is one of these. Naltrexone is an opioid receptor antagonist, a substance that blocks opioid receptors in the brain, so that the individual fails to experience positive effects from substance use. Meta-analyses of studies on naltrexone show that the effects of the medication are small on alcohol relapse (Kranzler & Van Kirk, 2001; Streeton & Whelan, 2001).

Summary of Treatment

Social workers are probably familiar with Alcoholics Anonymous (12-step), as this has been the long-standing approach to treatment for addiction. However, social workers should also be familiar with other available treatments that have shown some evidence basis for their use.

Although 12-step-informed treatment has stood up well to alternative treatments in large-scale evaluations, 12-step self-help groups have not performed as well, despite their widespread use. It could be that 12-step group attendance, while helpful in overcoming social networks that support drinking, should not be substituted as treatment without therapist facilitation. Kownacki and Shadish (1999) warn particularly that court-mandated 12-step group attendance might not be effective and another treatment should perhaps be substituted for coerced populations.

For the partners of people with addictions, Al-Anon has been a traditional approach. However, unilateral therapy may be effective for those who want to reduce drinking in their partners. Couples treatment might be indicated when there is severe marital conflict, as well as substance abuse, and both partners are motivated to participate in this modality. However, the research in this area has mainly focused on marital partners, rather than partners in any other kind of relationship.

Family therapy approaches have been found successful for substance-related disorders and should probably be the treatment of choice for adolescents. The social worker should consider learning the principles and techniques of motivational interviewing because they often work with people—both adolescents and adults—who are mandated to treatment settings. The other benefit of motivational interviewing is that it can be implemented in a brief fashion and can be potentially effective with clients with high levels of anger. Although we have focused here on therapeutic and self-help approaches, social workers should also be aware that case management services provided as part of intervention can improve outcomes for those with substance use disorders and are an essential aspect of services (Gerstein & Zhang, 2001).

Critique

Critiques of the substance-related disorders include their applicability to older adults and adolescents. For the elderly, *DSM-IV* criteria include increased tolerance to the effects of the substance, which results in increased consumption over time. Yet, changes related to physiology and reactions to prescription drugs may alter their drug tolerance as well ("Mental Health," n.d.). Decreased tolerance to alcohol among older individuals may lead to decreased consumption of alcohol with no apparent reduction in intoxication. Diagnostic criteria that relate to the impact of drug use on the typical tasks of young and middle adulthood, such as school or work performance or child rearing, may be largely irrelevant to older adults, who often live alone and are retired. For these reasons, abuse and dependence among older adults may be underestimated.

For adolescents, the symptoms required for psychological dependence, such as impairment of control, craving, and preoccupation with use, have not been examined (Bukstein & Kaminer, 1994). In addition, *DSM* substance abuse criteria largely rest on the negative consequences of use. This criterion may be problematic when applied to adolescents. Rather than substance use leading to negative consequences, often preexisting factors, such as family problems, or concurrent factors, such as another disorder, are responsible for the symptom pattern.

Despite the popularity of a primary disease model of addiction, problematic substance use in adolescents may be better conceptualized as a symptom of a more inclusive pattern of deviant behavior (Jessor & Jessor, 1977). Bukstein and Kaminer (1994) suggest that either the substance use disorders should have criteria specific to adolescents or that substance use patterns should be covered in the criteria for conduct disorder in adolescents.

Case Study

Andrew W. is a 40-year-old Caucasian homosexual male. He was diagnosed HIV-positive 12 years previously as a result of a blood transfusion and is legally blind because of retinal detachments 4 years before that. His CD4 counts are such that he does not have an AIDS diagnosis. He receives services at a comprehensive HIV health clinic, where he sees a psychiatrist, a medical doctor, a nurse, and a social worker, who has been his case manager for 5 years.

Andrew's current medications include protease inhibitors and anti-retrovirals for the HIV, Ritalin for the attention-deficit/hyperactivity disorder with which he was diagnosed as a child, the antidepressant Zoloft for dysthmia (diagnosed by the health center's psychiatrist 3 years previously), and Ambien, a sedative for sleep.

Andrew is unemployed, receiving full disability benefits from the Social Security Administration. He resides in a studio apartment in a working-class neighborhood. Andrew's immediate family consists of his mother and a younger brother. His father is presumably still alive but abandoned the family when Andrew was 9 years old, and no communication exists between them. Andrew's mother, whom Andrew refers to as "an active alcoholic," remarried five more times and is currently single. Andrew and his mother, who lives in another state, speak weekly by telephone, but no visit has occurred in the past 2 years. Andrew's brother is incarcerated on drug charges.

Andrew's local support system is made up of the other residents in his apartment building and two friends who live locally and visit regularly. He's currently not involved in any church or social organizations. He has terminated his church attendance and no longer performs voluntary public speaking on HIV prevention for the health clinic, saying, "What's the point in doing any of these things?" He has begun to spend more and more time alone.

The most significant relationship in Andrew's adult life was his 10-year romantic partnership with Shane, who died of complications of AIDS 5 years before. Andrew has lost numerous friends to AIDS, as well as his partner. His goal is to meet someone; he has placed ads in newspapers and on the Web and has frequented clubs known for sex parties.

After canceling several appointments in a row, he met with the social worker and confessed to thoughts of death. As for other depressive symptoms, he said he found it difficult to sleep at night but then slept very late into the day. Andrew has discontinued taking his HIV medications, no longer wishing to "prolong the inevitable"—that he will die. He said he sees no point to his existence. Other than not taking his medications, Andrew does not admit to having a plan to commit suicide.

Andrew admitted to frequent abuse of his Ritalin and Ambien (three times each per week) and occasional use of illegal street drugs, such as Ecstasy and cocaine (once a week), in combination with increased alcohol consumption (almost every day, an average of a six-pack of beer per day).

Andrew had denied substance use in past visits, when his social worker and the psychiatrist questioned why he'd been getting his prescriptions refilled before they were due. The only reason he had agreed to see the social worker that day was because his visit with the psychiatrist required making contact with his case manager.

Andrew said he had not told the social worker about his substance use because he knows that services depend on his being "clean." (A routine part of the informed consent at the clinic is that the individual will partake in a recovery program if drug and alcohol abuse is present.) Andrew reported that his escalating use in the past year is due to feelings of depression. If he "didn't feel so depressed, then I wouldn't be doing this. Sometimes the pain is unbearable."

The following multiaxial diagnosis was given after this visit:

Axis I   304.80 Polysubstance Dependence
         296.23 Major Depressive Disorder, Single Episode, Severe
             Without Psychotic Features
         296.23 Dysthymic Disorder
         V15.81 Noncompliance with Treatment (HIV)
         314.01 Attention-Deficit/Hyperactivity Disorder,
             Combined Type
Axis II V71.09 No Diagnosis
Axis III Human Immunodeficiency Virus (HIV)
         Retinal detachment
Axis IV Housing Problems—disagreements with neighbors, dissatis-
             faction with housing arrangement
         Problems Related to the Social Environment—social isolation;
             limited support system
Axis V   GAF = 30

The polysubstance dependence diagnosis was made because Andrew has repeatedly used five groups of substances (alcohol, sedatives, cocaine, amphetamines, and hallucinogens) during the last 12-month period. "Further, during this period, the dependence criteria were met for substances as a group but not for any specific substance" (APA, 2000, p. 93). Andrew understands the dangers of mixing his medicines with alcohol or other drugs and taking more medicine than prescribed. He also chose to ignore the risk of losing his psychiatric care if he continued to misuse his medicines. He has also been arguing with his two close friends about his substance use.

Andrew had been diagnosed previously with dysthymia, but his depression seems to have worsened in that he has now discontinued his HIV medicines and no longer cares if he dies. He admits to feelings of worthlessness, he has problems with sleep, and he has markedly diminished interest in activities, such as going to church and partaking in speaking engagements. He said that his depression is so painful and ever-present that he uses substances to cope with it. Therefore, he now meets five of nine symptoms for a major depressive episode. He said that although he has always been a bit depressed throughout his life (dysmthia), he has never felt this kind of excruciating emotional pain; in that case, single episode is coded rather than a recurrent pattern of major depressive episodes. Given the fact that he is threatening his life by not taking his HIV medications, the severe nature of the depression seems important to note.

With this kind of pattern, it is difficult to ascertain whether his alcohol and drug abuse have contributed to the depression. A period of withdrawal from these substances will be necessary to gain a more accurate understanding of his depression. The polysubstance dependence diagnosis was placed first because it has to be treated in order to successfully treat his depression. Noncompliance with treatment is offered as a V-code, and the diagnosis of ADHD was made as a child. The psychiatrist will need to reassess this diagnosis and its applicability for Andrew at this stage of his life; Andrew's depression and substance abuse have also clouded the diagnostic picture.

A risk and resilience assessment on Andrew's substance abuse has been provided in Table 11.6. On balance, it can be seen that Andrew's patterns of risks outweigh any protective factors. Therefore, an intervention plan urgently needs to reduce risk and bolster protection.

The treatment plan involved first a "no harm" contract, which Andrew agreed to sign. He reluctantly agreed to attend the clinic's substance abuse group and also AA groups for gay men and lesbian women in the community. These groups would have the additional potential benefit of bolstering his support system in favor of non-substance-abusing peers.

Although the sedatives and Ritalin were no longer to be prescribed, the prescription of Andrew's psychotropic medications, namely, Zoloft, would be dependent on his abstinence or harm reduction from alcohol. Antidepressants are typically not subject to abuse but do not work if they are mixed with alcohol or other drugs. A consideration is for the psychiatrist to change the antidepressant medication to Effexor, once Andrew has had a couple of weeks of sobriety. Effexor has the advantage of potentially treating both depression and ADHD symptoms in adults.

Motivational interviewing would be used for a dual purpose: both to induce treatment compliance with HIV medications and to shift Andrew's motivation for change of his substance use patterns. His motivation is initially low to stop abusing substances. When he has gained sufficient motivation, cognitive-behavioral treatment is the treatment of choice because it can address the substance use and the depression, as well as the insomnia Andrew complains about. In addition, many of the triggers for substance use are related to his depression. His feelings of grief and loss and how to

Table 11.6

Andrew's Risk and Protective Factors Assessment

Risks	Protective Factors
Biology	
Genetics: Andrew might have a genetic predisposition toward substance use; his mother's and relatives are heavy alcohol users. Andrew has a brother who is currently incarcerated for drug charges. Andrew does not have much information about his father.	
Andrew is male, and males tend to have higher rates of alcohol disorders, as well as most other substance use disorders.	
Psychological	
Depression: Andrew suffers from depression and was diagnosed with ADHD as a child.	Andrew has shown personal resilience in surviving a difficult childhood and living through his partner's death and many of his friends'.
Social	
Family	
Although Andrew wasn't sexually abused as a child, he was physically abused by two different stepfathers. His mother modeled alcohol abuse and subjected Andrew and his brother to unstable relationships.	
Peer	
People he knows from his apartment complex and neighborhood are involved with drugs and alcohol, and alcohol and drugs are readily available.	Andrew's two close friends are not substance using.
Andrew has suffered a number of losses from his friends and partner dying of AIDS.	
Gay bars, where alcohol is available, is a "major social institution in the gay community"[a]	
Neighborhood	
Availability of drugs	
Services	Andrew has access to a comprehensive array of services at the HIV health clinic.

[a]Beatty et al. (1999), p. 545.

manage these painful feelings will be an important aspect of his coping plan.

Conclusion

Even if they are not employed in substance abuse treatment settings, social workers will find themselves working with clients who have substance-related problems. The high comorbidity between substance-related disorders and other disorders means that there is a large amount of overlap between other mental/emotional disorders and substance use. The social worker should know how to assess for the presence of substance use disorders, as well as have knowledge of the full range of treatment approaches available.

Appendix I. Measures for Adolescent Substance Use Disorders

Information on adolescent measures was drawn from Allen and Columbus (1995), Jensen (2004), Rahdert (1991), and Winters and Stinchfield (1995). The National Institute on Drug Abuse (http://www.drugabuse.gov) also has other assessment protocols for adolescents available.

Personal Experience Screening Questionnaire

Winters (1992)

Description

- 18-item self-report with 4-point response option (never/once or twice/sometimes/often) screens for adolescent alcohol and drug problems.
- The test is scored for problem severity, drug use history, and psychological problems. The total score for problem severity gets either a green or a red flag. The red flag score suggests the need for further assessment.

Reliability

- High internal consistency (.90–.91)

Validity

- Differentiates between drug clinic (highest scores), juvenile offender (next highest scores), and normal school groups.

- A discriminant function analysis correctly classified 87% of the school clinic group.
- 87% correct classification of those who need a comprehensive drug abuse assessment.

Personal Experience Inventory

Winters & Henly (1989); Winters, Latimer, Stinchfield, & Henly (1999); Winters, Stinchfield, & Henly (1993)

Description

- Self-report inventory for age 12–18, written at a sixth-grade level.
- 33 scales in 2 major sections: (a) chemical use problem severity, including negative and positive consequences of use, and (b) personal and environmental risk factors.
- A parent version has also been created.
- 45 minutes required.
- Widely used in clinical settings for assessment of adolescent chemical dependency and psychosocial risk.

Reliability

- All scales demonstrated reliability (internal consistency and test-retest).

Validity

- All scales demonstrated construct validity (clinical diagnoses, treatment referral decisions, group status and other measures of problem severity and risk).

Adolescent Alcohol Involvement Scale

Mayer & Filstead (1979)

Description

- 14-item, self-report.
- Takes 15 minutes to complete.
- Assesses type/frequency of drinking, reasons for onset of drinking, the context of drinking, short- and long-term consequences of drinking, the adolescent's perception about drinking, and other people's perceptions.
- Score reveals severity of problems.

Reliability

- Internal consistency ranges from .55 to .76.

Validity

- Scores correlate to diagnosis and ratings from other measures.

Adolescent Drug Involvement Scale

Moberg & Hahn (1991)

Description

- Modification of the Adolescent Alcohol Involvement Scale
- 12-item scale measuring level of drug involvement (defined in terms of consequences, motivations, and sense of control) in adolescents (but has not been tested on minority or inner-city youth).

Reliability

- Internal consistency is alpha coefficient of .85.

Validity

- High correlations with self-reported levels of drug use (.72), teens' perceptions of drug use severity (.79), and clinical assessments (.75).

Appendix II. Measures for Adult Substance Use Disorders

Information for this appendix was drawn from Allen and Columbus (1995).

Michigan Alcoholism Screening Test

Selzer (1971)

Description

- A 24-item index of severity of alcohol misuse, response format 0–1.
- Screens for alcoholism with a variety of populations.
- Useful in assessing extent of lifetime alcohol-related consequences.
- Briefer versions have been developed: the 10-item Brief MAST (Pokorny, Miller, & Kaplan, 1972); the 13-item Short MAST (Selzer, Vinokur, & Van Rooijen, 1975); a geriatric version, MAST-G (Blow, Brower, Schulenberg, et al., 1992); a version for general medical pop-

ulations, Self-Administered Alcoholism Screening Test (Swensen & Morse, 1975); and a version that determines between lifetime and current problems with alcohol, Veterans Alcoholism Screening Test (Magruder-Habib, Harris, & Fraker, 1982).

Reliability

- Coefficient alpha was .93 (Skinner, 1979)

Validity

- Factor analysis yielded five factors, along with a strong unidimensional component (Skinner, 1979):
  1. Recognition of alcohol problem by self and others
  2. Legal, work, and social problems
  3. Help seeking
  4. Marital-family difficulties
  5. Liver pathology

- Correlations with following Personality Research Form constructs: Impulsivity (.24), Affiliation (-.24), Hypochondriasis (.25), Depression (.29), Anxiety (.24), Thinking Disorder (.20), Social Introversion (.24), Self-Depreciation (.32), and Deviation (.26) (Skinner, 1979).
- Scores correlated with lifetime daily average consumption (.58) (Skinner, 1979).

Drug Abuse Screening Test

Skinner (1982)

Description

- 28 items ("yes"/"no") tapping various consequences of drug use
- Parallels items on Michigan Alcoholism Screening Test

Reliability

- Internal consistency = .92

Validity

- Factor analysis indicates a single dimension.
- High scores correlated with stable accommodation, work record, and family contact.

- High scores correlated with more frequent use of cannabis, barbiturates, and opiates other than heroin.
- High scores correlated with Impulse Expression and Social Deviation of Basic Personality Inventory.

Drinking Problems Index (DPI)

Finney, Moos, & Brennan (1991)

Description

- 17-item self-report scale to assess alcohol problems (excessive consumption, dependence symptoms, and escapist drinking) and their consequences (the frequency that different types of problems associated with drinking have occurred in the past year)
- In adults age 55 and older
- Takes 3–5 minutes
- No cost (available through Penney L. Brennan, PhD, Center for Health Care Evaluation, VA Medical Center (1 16A4), 3801 Miranda Avenue, Palo Alto, CA 94304)
- Items measured on a 5-point scale ranging from Never to Often

Reliability

- Internal consistency of .94

Inventory of Drug Use Consequences

Tonigan & Miller (2002)

Description

- 50-item self-administered measure of consequences of alcohol and drug use.
- Parallel to the Drinker Inventory of Consequences.
- Focus on consequences related to (a) Impulse Control, (b) Social Responsibility, and (c) Physical, (d) Interpersonal, and (e) Intrapersonal domains (same for Drinker Inventory of Consequences).
- InDUC is available in versions that capture lifetime problems related to drug use and a Likert-scaled frequency estimate of recent problems (last 90 days).
- Useful for assessment, as well as change over time.

Reliability

- Four of five scales good to excellent stability; intrapersonal consequences reliability poor

Validity

- A confirmatory factor analysis showed that the four scales (Impulse Control, Social Responsibility, Physical, and Interpersonal) conveyed were the larger construct of adverse consequences.
- Sensitive to treatment change.

University of Rhode Island Change Assessment Scale (URICA)

McConnaughy et al. (1983, 1989)

Description

- 32-item scale assesses attitudes toward changing behaviors based on the stages of change model.
- Four 8-item subscales correspond to the four stages of change: precontemplation, contemplation, action, and maintenance.
- Rated on a 5-point Likert scale of 1 (not at all) to 5 (extremely) in response to how important this statement is to them.
- Target group is outpatient and inpatient substance use disorders treatment and adult populations.
- Self-administered test that takes 5–10 minutes to complete.

Reliability
Dozois, Westra, Collins, Fung, & Garry (2004)

- For different samples (outpatient alcohol treatment, self-identified anxious undergraduates, and individuals presenting for the treatment of panic disorder) internal consistency coefficients were found to be good for the subscales: Precontemplation ranged from .69 to 77, Contemplation ranged from .75 to .80, Action ranged from .82 to .90, and Maintenance ranged from .81 to .90.

Validity
Dozois et al. (2004)

- Precontemplation, Contemplation, and Maintenance subscales were associated in expected directions with a number of indexes of symp-

tomatology, self-esteem, hopelessness, perceived costs and benefits of worrying, and actual help-seeking behavior, therefore demonstrating adequate convergent and divergent validity.
- Factor analysis support has been mixed The factor structure provided a moderate fit to four subscales in the subclinical sample and was a poor fit to these scales in the clinical sample.
- Moderate predictive validity in relation to treatment retention and outcome.

Note

1. Although AA might have certain advantages, not everyone will respond to the approach. The social worker should be aware that other self-help groups for addictions exist. Examples include S.M.A.R.T. Recovery (based on Albert Ellis's cognitive-behavioral approach, http://www.smartrecovery.org/) and Women for Sobriety (a self-help group developed specifically for women, http://www .womenforsobriety.org/). A comprehensive review of self-help programs is offered by Nowinski (1999).

References

Abbott, A. A. (1994). A feminist approach to substance abuse treatment and service delivery. *Social Work in Health Care, 19*, 67–84.

Alexander, J., & Parsons, B. V. (1982). *Functional family therapy.* Monterey, CA: Brooks/Cole.

American Psychiatric Association. (2000). *Diagnostic and statistical manual of mental disorders* (4th ed., text rev.). Washington, DC: Author.

Aponte, H. (2002). Structural family therapy. In A. Roberts & G. Greene (Eds.), *Social workers' desk reference* (pp. 263–267). New York: Oxford University Press.

Armstrong, T., & Costello, J. (2002). Community studies on adolescent substance use, abuse, or dependence and psychiatric comorbidity. *Journal of Consulting & Clinical Psychology, 70*, 1224–1239.

Ashley, O., Marsden, M. E., & Brady, T. (2003). Effectiveness of substance abuse treatment programming for women: A review. *American Journal of Drug and Alcohol Abuse, 29*, 19–54.

Azrin, N. H., Donohue, B., Besalel, V. A., Kogan, E. S., & Acierno, R. (1994). Youth drug abuse treatment: A controlled outcome study. *Journal of Child & Adolescent Substance Abuse, 3*, 1–16.

Barber, J. G., & Gilbertson, R. (1996). An experimental study of brief unilateral intervention for the partners of heavy drinkers. *Research on Social Work Practice, 6*, 325–336.

Beatty, R., Geckle, M., Huggins, J., Kapner, C., Lewis, K., & Sandstrom, D. (1999).

Gay men, lesbians, and bisexuals. In B. McCrady & E. Epstein (Eds.), *Addictions: A comprehensive guidebook* (pp. 542–551). New York: Oxford University Press.

Bond, J., Kaskutas, L. A., & Weisner, C. (2003). The persistent influence of social networks and Alcoholics Anonymous on abstinence. *Quarterly Journal of Studies on Alcohol, 64,* 579–588.

Brook, D., Brook, J., Zhang, C., Cohen, P., & Whiteman, M. (2002). Drug use and the risk of major depressive disorder, alcohol dependence, and substance use disorders. *Archives of General Psychiatry, 59,* 1039–1044.

Brown, T., Seraganian, P., Tremblay, J., & Annis, H. (2002). Process and outcome changes with relapse prevention versus 12-step aftercare programs for substance abusers. *Addiction, 97,* 677–689.

Bukstein, O., Dunne, J., Ayres, W., Arnold, V., Benedek, E., Bensenn, R., et al. (1997). Practice parameters for the assessment and treatment of children and adolescents with substance use disorders. *Journal of the American Academy of Child and Adolescent Psychiatry, 36,* 140–157.

Bukstein, O., & Kaminer, Y. (1994). The nosology of adolescent substance abuse. *American Journal on Addictions, 3,* 1–13.

Burke, B., Arkowitz, H., & Dunn, C. (2002). The efficacy of motivational interviewing and its adaptations: What we know so far. In W. R. Miller & S. Rollnick (Eds.), *Motivational interviewing* (2nd ed., pp. 217–250). New York: Guilford.

Carroll, K. (1999). Behavioral and cognitive behavioral treatments. In B. McCrady & E. Epstein (Eds.), *Addictions: A comprehensive guidebook* (pp. 250–267). New York: Oxford University Press.

Castro, F., Proescholdbell, R. J., Abeita, L., & Rodriquez, D. (1999). Ethnic and cultural minority groups. In B. McCrady & E. Epstein (Eds.), *Addictions: A comprehensive guidebook* (pp. 499–526). New York: Oxford University Press.

Connors, G., Donovan, D., & DiClemente, C. (2001). *Substance abuse treatment and the stages of change: Selecting and planning interventions.* New York: Guilford Press.

Corcoran, M., & Corcoran, J. (2001). Retrospective reasons for the initiation of substance abuse: Gender and ethnic effects. *Journal of Multicultural Social Work, 10,* 69–83.

Corrao, G., Bagnardi, V., Zambon, A., & Arico, S. (1999). Exploring the dose-response relationship between alcohol consumption and the risk of several alcohol-related conditions: A meta-analysis. *Addiction, 94,* 1551–1573.

Dumaine, M. (2003). Meta-analysis of interventions with co-occurring disorders of severe mental illness and substance abuse: Implications for social work practice. *Research on Social Work Practice, 13,* 142–165.

Dunn, C., Deroo, L., & Rivara, F. (2001). The use of brief interventions adapted from motivational interviewing across behavioral domains: A systematic review. *Addiction, 96,* 1725–1742.

Edwards, M. E., & Steinglass, P. (1995). Family therapy treatment outcomes for alcoholism. *Journal of Marital and Family Therapy, 21,* 475–509.

Epstein, E., & McCrady, B. (1998). Behavioral couples treatment of alcohol and drug use disorders: Current status and innovations. *Clinical Psychology Review, 18,* 689–711.

Fals-Stewart, W., Birchler, G. R., & O'Farrell, T. J. (1996). Behavioral couples therapy for male substance-abusing patients: Effects on relationship adjustment and drug-using Behavior. *Journal of Consulting and Clinical Psychology, 64*, 959–972.

Fals-Stewart, W., & O'Farrell, T. (2003). Behavioral family counseling and nalrexone for male opioid-dependent patients. *Journal of Consulting and Clinical Psychology, 71*, 432–442.

Farrell, A., & White, K. (1998). Peer influences and drug use among urban adolescents: Family structure and parent-adolescent relationship as protective factors. *Journal of Consulting & Clinical Psychology, 66*, 248–258.

French, K., Finkbiner, R., & Duhamel, L. (2002). *Patterns of substance use among minority youth and adults in the United States: An overview and synthesis of national survey findings.* Fairfax, VA: Caliber Associates.

Fuller, R., & Hiller-Sturmhofel, S. (1999). Alocholism treatment in the United States: An overview. *Alcohol Research and Health, 23*, 69–77.

Gerstein, D., & Zhang, Z. (2001). *Treatment outcomes for different types of substance abuse.* Fairfax, VA: Caliber Associates.

Hawkins, J. D., Catalano, R., & Miller, J. (1992). Risk and protective factors for alcohol and other drug problems in adolescence and early adulthood: Implications for substance abuse prevention. *Psychological Bulletin, 112*, 64–105.

Henggeler, S. W., Borduin, C. M., Melton, G. B., Mann, B. J., Smith, L. A., Hall, J. A., et al. (1991). Effects of multisystemic therapy on drug use and abuse in serious juvenile offenders: A progress report from two outcome studies. *Family Dynamics of Addiction Quarterly, 1*, 40–51.

Henggeler, S. W., Pickrel, S. G., Brondino, M. J., & Crouch, J. L. (1996). Eliminating (almost) treatment dropout of substance abusing or dependent delinquents through home-based multisystemic therapy. *American Journal Psychiatry, 153*, 427–428.

Henggeler, S., Pickrel, S., & Brondino, M. (1999). Multisystemic treatment of substance abusing and dependent delinquents: Outcomes, treatment fidelity, and transportability. *Mental Health Services Research, 1*, 171–184.

Henggeler, S. W., Melton, G. B., Brondino, M. J., Scherer, D. G., & Hanley, J. H. (1997). Multisystemic therapy with violent and chronic juvenile offenders and their families: The role of treatment fidelity in successful dissemination. *Journal of Consulting and Clinical Psychology, 65*, 821–833.

Henggeler, S. W., Schoenwald, S. K., Borduin, C., Rowland, M., & Cunningham, P. B. (1998). *Multisystemic treatment of antisocial behavior in children and adolescents.* New York: Guilford.

Hesselbrock, M. N. (1991). Gender comparison of antisocial personality disorder and depression in alcoholism. *Journal of Substance Abuse, 3*, 205–219.

Higgins, S., & Petry, N. (1999). Contingency management: Incentives for sobriety. *Alcohol Research and Health, 23*, 122–127.

Hser, Y.-I.., Grella, C. E., Hubbard, R. L., Hsieh, S. C., Fletcher, B. W., Brown, B. S., et al. (2001). An evaluation of drug treatment for adolescents in four U.S. cities. *Archives of General Psychiatry, 58*(7), 689–695.

Irvin, J., Bowers, C., Dunn, M., & Wang, M. (1999). Efficacy of relapse prevention: A meta-analytic review. *Journal of Counseling and Clinical Psychology, 67*, 563–570.

Jessor, R., & Jessor, S. L. (1977). *Problem behavior and psychosocial development: A longitudinal study of youth*. New York: Academic Press.

Jessor, R., Van Den Bos, J., Vanderryn, J., Costa, F., & Turbin, M. (1995). Protective factors in adolescent problem behavior: Moderator effects and developmental change. *Developmental Psychology, 31*, 923–933.

Joanning, H., Thomas, F., Quinn, W., & Mullen, R. (1992). Treating adolescent drug abuse: A comparison of family systems therapy, group therapy, and family drug education. *Journal of Marital and Family Therapy, 18*, 345–356.

Kaplow, J., Curran, P., & Dodge, K. (2002). Conduct problems prevention research group. Child, parent, and peer predictors of early-onset substance use: A multisite longitudinal study. *Journal of Abnormal Child Psychology, 30*, 199–216.

Karageorge, K., & Wisdom, G. (2001). *Physically and sexually abused women in substance abuse treatment: Treatment services and outcomes*. Fairfax, VA: Caliber Associates.

Kelly, J., Myers, M., & Brown, S. (2002). Do adolescents affiliate with 12-step groups? A multivariate process model of effects. *Journal of Studies on Alcohol, 63*, 293–305.

Kessler, R., Nelson, C., McGonagle, K., Edlund, M., Frank, R., & Leaf, P. (1996). The epidemiology of co-occurring addictive and mental disorders: Implications for prevention and service utilization. *American Journal of Orthopsychiatry, 66*, 17–31.

Kilpatrick, D. G., Acierno, R., Saunders, B., Resnick, H., Best, C. L., & Schnurr, P. P. (2000). Risk factors for adolescent substance abuse and dependence: Data from a national sample. *Journal of Consulting & Clinical Psychology, 68*, 19–30.

Kownacki, R., & Shadish, W. (1999). Does Alcoholics Anonymous work? The results from a meta-analysis of controlled experiments. *Substance Use and Misuse, 34*, 1897–1916.

Kranzler, H., & Van Kirk, J. (2001). Efficacy of nalrexone and acamprosate for alcoholism treatment: A meta-analysis. *Alcoholism, 25*, 1335–1341.

Larimer, M., Palmer, R., & Marlatt, A. (1999). Relapse prevention: An overview of Marlatt's cognitive-behavioral model. *Alcohol Research and Health, 23*, 151–160.

Latimer, W., Newcomb, M., Winters, K., & Stinchfield, R. (2000). Adolescent substance abuse treatment outcome: The role of substance abuse problem severity, psychosocial, and treatment factors. *Journal of Consulting & Clinical Psychology, 68*, 684–696.

Lewis, R. A., Piercy, F. P., Sprenkle, D. H., & Trepper, T. S. (1990). Family-based inerventions for helping drug-abusing adolescents. *Journal of Adolescent Research, 5*, 82–95.

Liddle, H. (1999). Theory development in a family-based therapy for adolescent drug abuse. *Journal of Clinical Child Psychology, 28*, 521–532.

Liddle, H., Dakof, G., Parker, K., Diamond, G., Barrett, K., & Tejeda, M. (2001). Multidimensional family therapy for adolescent drug abuse: Results of a randomized clinical trial. *American Journal of Drug and Alcohol Abuse, 27*, 651–698.

Littell, J., & Girvin, H. (2002). Stages of change: A critique. *Behavior Modification, 26*, 223–273.

Littell, J. H., Popa, M., & Forsythe. B. (2005). Multisystemic therapy for social, emotional, and behavioral problems in youth aged 10–17 (Cochrane Review). In: *The Cochrane Library*, Issue 3, 2005. Chichester, UK: John Wiley and Sons.

Loeber, R., Farrington, D., Stouthamer-Loeber, M., & Van Kammen, W. B. (1998). *Antisocial behavior and mental health problems: Explanatory factors in childhood and adolescence*. Mahwah, NJ: Erlbaum.

Longabaugh, R., & Morgenstern, J. (1999). Cognitive-behavioral coping-skills therapy for alcohol dependence: Current status and future directions. *Alcohol Research and Health, 23*, 78–85.

Longabaugh, R., Wirtz, P., Zweben, A., & Stout, R. (1998). Network support for drinking: Alcoholics Anonymous and long term matching effects. *Addiction, 93*, 1313–1333.

Martin, C., Kelly, T., Rayens, M. K., Brogli, B. R., Brenzel, A., Smith, W. J., et al. (2002). Sensation seeking, puberty and nicotine, alcohol and marijuana use in adolescence. *Journal of the American Academy of Child & Adolescent Psychiatry, 41*, 1495–1502.

Martino, S., Carroll, K., Kostas, D., Perkins, J., & Rounsaville, B. (2002). Dual diagnosis motivational interviewing: A modification of motivational interviewing for substance-abusing patients with psychotic disorders. *Journal of Substance Abuse Treatment, 23*, 297–308.

Mayo-Smith, M., Cushman, P., Hill, A., Jara, G., Kasser, C., Kraus, M., et al. (1997). Pharmacological management of alcohol withdrawal: A meta-analysis and evidence-based practice guideline. *Journal of the American Medical Association, 278*, 144–151.

McCrady, B. (2000). Alcohol use disorders and the Division 12 task force of the American Psychological Association. *Psychology of Addictive Behaviors, 14*, 267–276.

McCrady, B. S., Noel, N. E., Abrams, D. B., Stout, R. L., Nelson, H. F., & Hay, W. M (1986). Comparative effectiveness of three types of spouse involvement in outpatient behavioral alcoholism treatment. *Journal of Studies on Alcohol, 47*, 459–467.

McKay, J. (1999). Studies of factors in relapse to alcohol, drug and nicotine use: A critical review of methodologies and findings. *Journal of Studies on Alcohol, 60*, 566–576.

Mental health: A report of the surgeon general. Retrieved on July 15, 2005, from http://www.surgeongeneral.gov/library/mentalhealth/home.html.

Meyers, R., Miller, W., Hill, D., & Tonigan, J. (1999). Community reinforcement and family training (CRAFT): Engaging unmotivated drug users in treatment. *Journal of Substance Abuse, 10*, 118.

Miller, N. S., & Fine, J. (1993). Current epidemiology of comorbidity of psychiatric and addictive disorders. *Psychiatric Clinics of North America, 16*, 1–10.

Miller, W., Meyers, R., & Hiller-Sturmhofel, S. (1999). The community-reinforcement approach. *Alcohol Research and Health, 23*, 116–121.

Miller, W., Meyers, R., & Tonigan, J. (1999). Engaging the unmotivated in treatment for alcohol problems: A comparison of three strategies for intervention through family members. *Journal of Consulting and Clinical Psychology, 67*, 688–697.

Miller, W., & Rollnick, S. (2002). *Motivational interviewing: Preparing people to change addictive behavior* (2nd ed.). New York: Guilford.

Minuchin, S. (1974). *Families and family therapy*. Cambridge, MA: Harvard University Press.

Minuchin, S., & Nichols, M. P. (1993). *Family healing: Tales of hope and renewal from family therapy*. New York: Free Press.

Mirin, S., Batki, S., Bukstein, O., Isbell, P., Kleber, H., Schottenfeld, R., et al. (2002). Practice guideline for the treatment of patients with substance use disorders: Alcohol, cocaine, opioids. *American Psychiatric Association practice guidelines for the treatment of psychiatric disorders: Compendium 2002* (pp. 249–348). Washington, DC: American Psychiatric Association.

Monti, P., & Rohsenow, D. (1999). Coping-skills training and cue-exposure therapy in the treatment of alcoholism. *Alcohol Research and Health, 23*, 107–115.

National Institute on Drug Abuse. (1997). *Preventing drug use among children and adolescents* [Booklet]. Washington, DC: Author.

Nelson-Zlupko, L., Kauffman, E., & Dore, M. M. (1995). Gender differences in drug addiction and treatment: Implications for social work intervention with substance-abusing women. *Social Work, 40*, 45–54.

Nowinski, J. (1999). Self-help groups for addictions. In B. McCrady & E. Epstein (Eds.), *Addictions: A comprehensive guidebook* (pp. 328–346). New York: Oxford University Press.

O'Farrell, T. J. (1993). *Treating alcohol problems: Marital and family interventions*. New York: Guilford.

O'Farrell, T. J., Choquette, K. A., Cutter, H. S., Brown, E. D., & McCourt, W. F. (1993). Behavioral marital therapy with and without additional couples relapse prevention sessions for alcoholics and their wives. *Journal of Studies on Alcohol, 54*, 652–666.

O'Farrell, T. J., & Fals-Stewart, W. (1999). Treatment models and methods: Family models. In B. McCrady & E. Epstein (Eds.), *Addictions: A comprehensive guidebook* (pp. 287–305). New York: Oxford University Press.

Orwin, R., & Ellis, B. (2001). *The effectiveness of treatment components in reducing drug use in adolescents and young adults: A Re-analysis of the Job Corps Drug Treatment Enrichment Project*. Fairfax, VA: Caliber Associates.

Orwin, R., Francisco, L., & Bernichon, T. (2001). *Effectiveness of women's substance abuse treatment programs: A meta-analysis*. Fairfax, VA: Caliber Associates.

Orwin, R., Maranda, M., & Brady, T. (2001). *Impact of prior physical and sexual victimization on substance abuse treatment outcomes*. Fairfax, VA: Caliber Associates.

Petrakis, I., Gonzalez, G., Rosenheck, R., & Krystal, J. (2002). Comorbidity of alcoholism and psychiatric disorders: An overview. *Alcohol Research and Health, 26*, 81–90.

Prendergast, M., Podus, D., & Change, E. (2000). Program factors and treatment outcomes in drug dependence treatment: An examination using meta-analysis. *Substance Use and Misuse, 35*, 1931–1965.

Prochaska, J., DiClemente, C., & Norcross, J. (1994). *Changing for good*. New York: Avon.

Project MATCH Research Group. (1997). Matching alcoholism treatments to client heterogeneity: Project MATCH posttreatment drinking outcomes. *Journal of Studies on Alcohol, 58*, 7–29.

Project MATCH Research Group. (1998). Matching alcoholism treatments to client heterogeneity: Project MATCH three-year drinking outcomes. *Alcoholism: Clinical & Experimental Research, 22,* 1300–1311.

Riggs, P., & Whitmore, E. (1999). Substance use disorders and disruptive behavior disorders. In R. Hendren (Ed.), *Disruptive behavior disorders in children and adolescents, Vol. 18, No. 2. Review of psychiatry series* (pp. 133–173). Washington, DC: American Psychiatric Association.

Rohde, P., Lewinsohn, P., Kahler, C., Seeley, J., & Brown, R. (2001). Natural course of alcohol use disorders from adolescence to young adulthood. *Journal of the American Academy of Child and Adolescent Psychiatry, 40,* 83–90.

Rosen, C. (2000). Is the sequencing of change processes by stage consistent across health problems: A meta-analysis. *Health Psychology, 19,* 593–604.

Rosenthal, R., & Westreich, L. (1999). Treatment of persons with dual diagnoses of substance use disorder and other psychological problems. In B. McCrady & E. Epstein (Eds.), *Addictions: A comprehensive guidebook* (pp. 439–476). New York: Oxford University Press.

Santisteban, D., Coatsworth, J., Perez-Vidal, A., Kurtines, W., Schwartz, S., La-Pierre, A., et al. (2003). Efficacy of brief strategic family therapy in modifying Hispanic adolescent behavior problems and substance use. *Journal of Family Psychology, 17,* 121–133.

Santisteban, D., Szapocznik, J., Kurtines, W., Murray, E., & LaPierre, A. (1996). Efficacy of intervention for engaging youth and families into treatment and some variables that may contribute to differential effectiveness. *Journal of Family Psychology, 10,* 35–44.

Sheehan, T., & Owen, P. (1999). The disease model. In B. McCrady & E. Epstein (Eds.), *Addictions: A comprehensive guidebook* (pp. 268–286). New York: Oxford University Press.

Simpson, D., Joe, G., & Broome, K. (2002). A national 5-year follow-up of treatment outcomes for cocaine dependence. *Archives of General Psychiatry, 59,* 538–544.

Sisson, R. W., & Azrin, N. H. (1986). Family-member involvement to initiate and promote treatment of problem drinkers. *Journal of Behavioral Therapy and Experiential Psychiatry, 17,* 15–21.

Stanton, M. D., & Shadish, W. R. (1997). Outcome, attrition, and family-couples treatment for drug abuse: A meta-analysis and review of the controlled, comparative studies. *Psychological Bulletin, 122,* 170–191.

Streeton, C., & Whelan, G. (2001). Naltrexone, a relapse prevention maintenance treatment of alcohol dependence: A meta-analysis of randomized controlled trials. *Alcohol and Alcoholism, 36,* 544–552.

Szapocznik, J., Perez-Vidal, A., Brickman, A. L., Foote, F. H., Santisteban, D., & Hervis, O. (1988). Engaging adolescent drug abusers and their families in treatment: A strategic structural systems approach. *Journal of Consulting and Clinical Psychology, 56,* 552–557.

Szapocznik, J., & Williams, R. A. (2000). Brief strategic family therapy: Twenty-five years of interplay among theory, research and practice in adolescent behavior problems and drug abuse. *Clinical Child and Family Psychology Review, 3,* 117–135.

Thomas, E. J., Santa, C., Bronson, D., & Oyserman, D. (1987). Unilateral family therapy with the spouses of alcoholics. *Journal of Social Service Research, 10,* 145–162.

Tonigan, J., Toscova, R., & Miller, W. (1996). Meta-analysis of the literature on Alcoholics Anonymous: Sample and study characteristics moderate findings. *Journal of Studies on Alcohol, 57,* 65–72.

Velicer, W., Hughes, S., Fava, J., Prochaska, J., & DiClemente, C. (1995). An empirical typology of subjects within stage of change. *Addictive Behaviors, 20,* 299–320.

Vinton, L., & Wambach, K. (2005). Alcohol and drug use among elderly people. In C. A. McNeese & D. DiNitto (Eds.), *Chemical dependency: A systems approach* (pp. 484–502). Boston: Pearson.

Waldron, H., Slessnick, N., Brody, J., Turner, C., & Peterson, T. (2001). Treatment outcomes for adolescent substance abuse at 4- and 7-month assessments. *Journal of Consulting and Clinical Psychology, 69,* 802–813.

Walitzer, K., Dermen, K., & Conners, G. (1999). Strategies for preparing clients for treatment: A review. *Behavior Modification, 23,* 129–151.

Walters, G. (2000). The heritability of alcohol abuse and dependence: A meta-analysis of behavior genetic research. *American Journal of Drug and Alcohol Abuse, 28,* 557–584.

Wechsberg, W., Craddock, G. S., & Hubbard, R. (1998). How are women who enter substance abuse treatment different than men? A gender comparison from the Drug Abuse Treatment Outcome Study (DATOS). *Drugs & Society, 13,* 97–115.

Weinberg, N., Rahdert, E., Colliver, J., & Meyer, G. (1998). Adolescent substance abuse: A review of the past 10 years. *Journal of the American Academy of Child and Adolescent Psychiatry, 37,* 252–262.

Winters, K., Stinchfield, R., Opland, E., Weller, C., & Latimer, W. (2000). The effectiveness of the Minnesota Model approach in the treatment of adolescent drug abusers. *Addiction, 95,* 601–612.

References for Adolescent Substance Use Disorders Measures

Allen, J., & Columbus, M. (1995). *Assessing alcohol problems: A guide for clinicians and researchers.* Bethesda, MD: NIAA.

Jenson, J. (2004). Risk and protective factors for alcohol and other drug use in childhood and adolescence. In M. Fraser (Ed.), *Risk and resilience in childhood: An ecological perspective* (2nd ed.), Washington, DC: NASW Press.

Mayer, J., & Filstead, W. (1979). The adolescent alcohol involvement scale: An instrument for measuring adolescent use and misuse of alcohol. *Journal of Alcohol Studies, 4,* 291–300.

Moberg, D. P., & Hahn, L. (1991). The adolescent drug involvement scale. *Journal of Adolescent Chemical Dependency, 2,* 75–88.

Rahdert, E. (1991). *The adolescent assessment/referral system manual.* Rockville, MD: U.S. Department of Health and Human Services.

Winters, K., & Henly, G. (1989). *Personal Experience Inventory (PEI) test and manual.* Los Angeles: Western Psychological Services.

Winters, K., Latimer, W., Stinchfield, R., & Henly, G. (1999). Assessing adolescent drug use with the Personal Experience Inventory. In M.E. Maruish (Ed.), *The use of psychological testing for treatment planning and outcomes assessment* (2nd ed., pp. 599–630). Mahwah, NJ: Lawrence Erlbaum.

Winters, K., & Stinchfield, R. (1995). Current issues and future needs in the assessment of adolescent drug abuse. In E. Radhert & D. Czechowicz (Eds.), *Adolescent drug abuse: Clinical assessment and therapeutic intervention*. (NIDA monograph 156, pp. 146–170). Rockville, MD: National Institute on Drug Abuse.

Winters, K., Stinchfield, R., & Henly, G. (1993). Further validation of new scales measuring adolescent alcohol and other drug abuse. *Journal of Studies on Alcohol, 54,* 534–541.

Winters, K. C. (1992). Development of an adolescent alcohol and other drug abuse screening scale: Personal experience screening questionnaire. *Addictive Behaviors, 17,* 479–490.

References for Adult Substance Use Disorders Measures

Allen, J., & Columbus, M. (1995). *Assessing alcohol problems: A guide for clinicians and researchers.* Bethesda, MD: NIAA.

Blow, F.C., Brower, K.J., Schulenberg, J.E., Demo-Dananberg, L. M., Young, J. P., and Beresford, T. P. (1992). The Michigan Alcoholism Screening Test–Geriatric Version (MAST-G): A new elderly-specific screening instrument. *Alcoholism: Clinical and Experimental Research, 16,* 372.

Dozois, D., Westra, H., Collins, K., Fung, T., & Garry, J. (2004). Stages of change in anxiety: Psychometric properties of the University of Rhode Island Change Assessment (URICA) scale. *Behaviour Research and Therapy, 42,* 711–729.

Finney, J., Moos, R., & Brennan, P. (1991). The drinking problems index: A measure to assess alcohol-related problems among older adults. *Journal of Substance Abuse, 3,* 395–404.

Magruder-Habib, K., Harris, K., & Fraker, G. (1982). Validation of the Veterans Alcoholism Screening Test. *Journal of Studies on Alcohol, 43,* 910–926.

McConnaughy, E., DiClemente, C., Prochaska, J., & Velicer, W. (1989). Stages of change in psychotherapy: A follow-up report. *Psychotherapy: Theory, Research, Practice, Training, 26,* 494–503.

McConnaughy, E. A., Prochaska, J. O., & Velicer, W. F. (1983). Stages of change in psychotherapy: Measurement and sample profiles. *Psychotherapy: Theory, Research and Practice, 20,* 368–375.

Pokorny, A. D., Miller, B. A., & Kaplan, H. B. (1972). The brief MAST: A shortened version of the Michigan Alcoholism Screening Test. *American Journal of Psychiatry, 129,* 342–345.

Selzer, M. (1971). The Michigan Alcoholism Screening Test: The quest for a new diagnostic instrument. *American Journal of Psychiatry, 127,* 1653–1658.

Selzer, M., Vinokur, A., & Van Rooijen, L. (1975). A self-administered short Michigan alcoholism screening test (SMAST). *Journal of Studies on Alcohol, 36,* 117–126.

Skinner, H. (1979). A multivariate evaluation of the MAST. *Journal of Studies on Alcohol, 40,* 831–843.

Skinner, H. (1982). The drug abuse screening test. *Addictive Behavior, 7,* 363–371.

Swenson, W., & Morse, R. (1975). The use of a self-administered alcoholism screening test (SAAST) in a medical center. *Mayo Clinic Proceedings, 50,* 204–208.

Tonigan, J. S., Miller, W. R. (2002. The Inventory of Drug Use Consequences (InDUC): Test-retest stability and sensitivity to detect change. Psychology *of Addictive Behaviors, 16,* 165–168.

12 Sexual Disorders: Pedophilia

People engage in a wide variety of sexual practices for purposes of procreation, the expression of love, to satisfy their sex drives, and for pleasure. Attempts to categorize sexual behavior as *normal* or *deviant* are often controversial because the process may be characterized by moral biases. The sexual disorders in *DSM-IV* are included as such because the symptomatic behaviors cause considerable distress to the person or to other people who may be victimized by the behavior. In its chapter on sexual and gender identity disorders, the *DSM-IV-TR* includes material on *sexual function* disorders, *gender identity* disorders, and the *paraphilias*. This chapter focuses on pedophilia, a disorder from the third category. Pedophilia is characterized by repeated intense sexual desires, fantasies, or behaviors concerning sexual activity with a sexually immature child (American Psychiatric Association [APA], 2000). It is the most common paraphilia that involves physical contact (Fagan, Wise, Schmidt, & Berlin, 2002). It is almost universally condemned as inappropriate and criminal sexual behavior. Prior to describing pedophilia, we briefly review the paraphilias here.

The Paraphilias

This set of disorders is characterized by recurrent and intense sexual urges, fantasies, or behaviors that involve unusual objects, activities, or situations (APA, 2000). Of all the sexual disorders, it is the clients with paraphilias who most often come to the attention of social workers. The list of specific paraphilias includes:

- Exhibitionism: exposure of one's genitals to others
- Fetishism: use of nonliving objects in sexual activity
- Frotteurism: touching or rubbing one's genitals against a nonconsenting person
- Masochism: voluntarily receiving humiliation or suffering during a sexual act
- Pedophilia: described in the next section
- Sadism: inflicting humiliation or suffering on others (who may be consenting) during a sexual act
- Transvestic fetishism: cross-dressing
- Voyeurism: observing sexual activity by others (who are usually not consenting)

The paraphilias tend to be long term, and in fact the diagnostic criteria mandate that the symptoms are present for at least 6 months. People with any paraphilia tend to engage in several different paraphilias during a lifetime (Sadock & Sadock, 2005). Interestingly, these disorders are almost never diagnosed in females. The only exception is sexual masochism, and even that is estimated to occur at a 20:1 ratio of men to women (APA, 2000).

Persons with paraphilias are careful to conceal their urges or acts (Kendall & Hammen, 1998). The associated fantasies tend to be always present, but the person may or may not act on them, depending on the strength of the urge and the person's efforts to resist it. Symptomatic behaviors may increase in response to psychosocial stressors when accompanied by increased opportunities to engage in the behavior. The deviant behaviors usually disrupt these individuals' potential for long-term bonding with sexual partners. Many people with paraphilias report that their behaviors do not cause them distress; their condition is problematic only because it leads to social limitations due to the reactions of others. Some persons with the disorders, however, do report shame, guilt, and depression regarding the symptoms.

The paraphilias are probably much more prevalent than the frequency of clinical diagnosis suggests, given the large worldwide market in paraphilic pornography and related paraphenalia (O'Grady, 2001). The most common diagnoses in clinics specializing in the treatment of these disorders are pedophilia, voyeurism, and exhibitionism. Sadism and masochism are far less frequently reported. Approximately half of individuals with paraphilias seen in clinics are married. Symptoms may begin in childhood and early adolescence but become more elaborate during late adolescence and early adulthood (Laws & O'Donohue, 1997). Their onset peaks between the ages of 15 and 25 (50% of people with the disorders experience the onset by age 18), and its development is rare after age 50.

Not all unusual sexual behavior is evidence of a paraphilia. These behaviors may also result from a loss of judgment that is symptomatic of other disorders, such as mental retardation, dementia, personality changes due to a medical condition, substance intoxication, a manic episode, and schizophrenia (Laws & O'Donohue, 1997). These other behaviors can be differentiated from a paraphilia in that they are not the person's preferred behavior, they tend to occur in isolation, and the symptoms occur in the context of the other disorder.

There are many possible causes, reflecting a variety of theoretical perspectives, of the paraphilias (Sadock & Sadock, 2005):

- Outlets for sexual and aggressive drives that have been stunted during psychosocial development
- A need to identify with the opposite-sex parent
- A means to calm anxiety related to beliefs about psychological sexual inadequacy by displacing urges onto inappropriate objects
- Modeling the behavior of others (including primary caregivers)
- Lacking punishment for, or reinforcement of, paraphiliac interests at an early age
- A need to dominate and control victims to compensate for feelings of powerlessness (in pedophilia and sadism)
- A sexualization of early experiences of abuse

The prognosis for recovery from a paraphilia is associated with the person's age of onset, frequency of acts, any accompanying substance abuse behavior, attitude about the acts, motivation for change, and the ability to experience conventional sex (Shaw, 1999).

Pedophilia

The term *pedophilia* ironically derives from a Greek word meaning "love of children" (Fagan et al., 2002). As described earlier, pedophilia is characterized by a person's repeated and intense sexual desires, fantasies, or behaviors concerning activity with a sexually immature child. To merit the diagnosis, the person must either act on these desires or be so distressed by them that he experiences significant impairments in work, social, or personal functioning (O'Grady, 2001). People diagnosed with pedophilia must meet the following *DSM-IV-TR* criteria (APA, 2000):

- Over a period of at least 6 months, the person must experience recurrent, intense, sexually arousing fantasies, sexual urges, or behaviors involving sexual activity with a prepubescent child or children (generally age 13 or younger).
- The person has acted on these sexual urges, or the sexual urges or fantasies cause marked distress or interpersonal difficulty.

• The person is at least 16 years old and at least 5 years older than the target child or children.

The diagnosis should include a specifier indicating whether the client is attracted only to children (exclusive type) or is sometimes attracted to adults (nonexclusive type). The practitioner should also note when the pedophilia is limited to incest.

From a review of the literature, Murray (2000) developed a general psychological profile of pedophiles and other child molesters. Personality tests consistently reveal that pedophiles are emotionally immature, have a fear of being unable to function adequately in adult sexual relationships, and are socially introverted. They lack social skills and tend to avoid contact with other adults. They demonstrate inappropriate forms of sexual arousal, usually showing an enduring sexual interest in children. Pedophilia is associated with a lack of sexual and emotional gratification, leading the person to choose children as an outlet for these feelings. Sexual offenders often report taking solace in sexual thoughts and behaviors when confronted with stressful life events (Cortoni, Heil, & Marshall, 1996). The association of alcohol use with pedophilia supports the idea that some people with urges to abuse children can contain those urges until coming under the influence of an intoxicant (Lightfoot & Barbaree, 1993; Travin & Protter, 1993). Pedophiles often justify their inappropriate sexual behaviors by rationalizing that the behaviors are "educational" for the child or that the victim had initiated or readily consented to, and received pleasure from, the acts.

Differential Diagnosis

As noted earlier, not all sex offenders are pedophiles. Such behaviors may also occur in antisocial youth, whose offending behavior represents one aspect of their exploitative behaviors, and in people with neurological disorders that interfere with their ability to regulate aggressive and sexual drives (Shaw, 1999). These other disorders can be distinguished from pedophilia (or another paraphilia) by the fact that the behavior occurs exclusively during the course of the disorder and does not represent the person's preferred sexual pattern.

Varieties of Pedophilia

There are different types of pedophiles. Some only look, and others want to touch or undress the child, but most pedophilic acts involve oral sex or the touching of either the child's or the perpetrator's genitals (Fagan et al.,

2002). In most cases, pedophiles are familiar to the child that they attack; they may be a relative, friend, or neighbor (Nordland, 2001). Less than 3% of all reported sexual abuse cases are perpetrated by strangers who kidnap and then sexually assault the child (Rosenberg, 2002).

People with pedophilia generally express an attraction to children of a certain age range (Murray, 2000). Some prefer males, some prefer females, and some do not have a clear preference. Pedophiles attracted to females usually prefer 8- to 10-year-olds, and those attracted to males usually prefer slightly older children. Pedophilia among females is reported more often, although it may not occur more often. Some pedophiles threaten the target children, and others go to extremes to gain access to desired children and develop elaborate strategies for gaining their trust and compliance. The seduction process may be quite lengthy, and the perpetrator may be attentive to the child's needs in order to gain his or her affection and loyalty. The pedophile usually does not experience distress following his actions.

Several theories and models of the *cycle* of the pedophile's acting out and relapse behaviors have been put forth. All of them attempt to provide a comprehensive description of the cognitive, behavioral, and motivational factors associated with the offense. One such model, offered by Ward and Hudson (1998), assumes that some offenses are associated with a failure of impulse control, whereas others result from the pedophile's careful planning and seeking out of positive emotional experiences. Their model consists of the following phases:

- A stressful life event activates the person's needs, and a desire for deviant sexual activity emerges.
- The person establishes an offense-related goal, accompanied by an inclination to approach or avoid that goal.
- A strategy is selected to achieve the goal, based on one of the following four patterns:

    Avoidant-passive: A desire to avoid offending but a failure to prevent this from happening.

    Avoidant-active: A desire to avoid offending, with clear attempts to control those thoughts and behaviors, although these strategies are ultimately not effective.

    Approach-automatic: The person follows automatic, ingrained cognitive patterns that are designed to impulsively lead to an offense.

    Approach-explicit: The person engages in conscious planning and wellcrafted strategies that result in a sexual offense.

- The high-risk situation is entered.
- The person lapses into behaviors that will lead to the offense.

- The sexual offense occurs, characterized by a focus on the self, the victim, or the relationship.
- The person conducts a postoffense evaluation of the offense, such as guilt about the failure to abstain or a desire for more offending.
- The person develops an attitude toward future offending, resolving at the moment to offend or not to offend.

It is estimated that 15 to 25% of pedophiles convicted for an offense will reoffend within a few years of their release from prison (Morrison, 1995). The recidivism rate for pedophiles involving a preference for males is roughly twice that for those who prefer females.

Assessing Pedophilia

The American Academy of Child and Adolescent Psychiatry have developed practice parameters for clinicians who work with sexually abusive children and adolescents, based on its reviews of the literature (Shaw, 1999). These assessment guidelines are also applicable to adults. The academy asserts that practitioners needs to understand the many biological and psychosocial factors that determine a child's sexual development, gender role, sexual orientation, patterns of sexual arousal, sexual cognitions, sexual socialization, and how sexual and aggressive patterns of behavior may become interrelated for some people. In assessment, practitioners need to gather information about the client's:

- Sexual history, including thought patterns and behaviors regarding sexual activity and its relationship to any aggressive acts
- Developmental and social history
- Legal history
- Medical and psychiatric history
- School and academic history, including intellectual capacities and any learning disabilities that are common to sexual offenders
- Mental status examination, including personality style, coping style, substance use, and inclinations toward self-harm

Formal measures of deviant sexual behavior may be used in this process (see appendix I for a sample of these). Risk assessments of sexual offenders should consider separately, however, the offender's risk for sexual and nonsexual recidivism, because most recidivists engage in nonsexual crimes following program discharge (Hanson & Bussiere, 1998).

In addition to these assessment topics, a *phallometric* assessment is often conducted with sexual offenders. This is a process whereby the person's penile tumescence, or volume change, is measured in response to erotic stimuli. Formally known as a *penile plethysmograph*, this is the most commonly used means of determining male preferences for sex partners of different ages (McGovern, 1991). Following the client's consent, in a comfortable office setting, a strain gauge is placed around his penis to measure its changing circumference in response to various sexual stimuli. The client is then presented with stimuli such as slides, movies, audiotapes of sexual activity, and videotapes of behavioral interactions between men and children. With each presentation, the client is asked to rate his level of arousal on a scale of 0 to 100 while his physiological arousal is measured. Following the assessment, comparisons are made between the client's arousal responses to normal and aberrant materials. Results are immediately shared with the client, because this may be the first time he is made aware of these differential arousal patterns.

Most verbally based assessments of pedophiles may have limited validity because of the individual's tendency to deny deviant thoughts, feelings, and behaviors.

Disorders That Are Comorbid with Pedophilia

People with pedophilia often display additional problem behaviors and *DSM* diagnoses. Adolescent sex offenders experience greater overall psychopathology than nonoffenders, including conduct disorder and the borderline and narcissistic personality disorders (Becker, Kaplan, & Tenke, 1992). Their lives are also characterized by delinquency offenses, unstable family situations, poor social skills, and more school problems than nonoffending adolescents. In one study of 45 adult pedophiles from several intervention programs, 93% met criteria for another disorder as indicated by the Structured Clinical Interview for *DSM-IV* (Raymond, Coleman, Ohlerking, Christenson, & Miner, 1999). These included a 67% lifetime prevalence for a mood disorder, 64% for anxiety disorders, 60% for substance use disorders, 53% for another paraphilia, and 24% for a sexual dysfunction diagnosis. The authors added that 22.5% and 20% of the volunteers met the criteria for antisocial and narcissistic personality disorders, respectively. Finally, as many as 50% of pedophiles have learning disabilities that negatively affect their ability to comprehend social conventions (Cohen et al., 2002).

Risk and Protective Factors

The various biological, psychological, and social risk and protective factors for pedophilia are described next and shown in Tables 12.1 and 12.2.

Table 12.1

Risk and Protective Factors for the Onset of Pedophilia

Risk Factors	Protective Factors
Biological	
Being male	Being female
Elevated plasma epinephrine and norepinephrine levels	
Increased sympathetic nervous system activity	Normal neurotransmitter activity in nervous systems
Low levels of serotonin	
Non-right-handedness (may signify developmental abnormalities)	Right-handedness
Psychological	
Later birth order	Earlier birth order
Sexual abuse as a child	Absence of abuse as a child, including sexual abuse
Disorganized family	
Poor attachment style	Secure attachment to parents
Childhood behavioral problems	
Mother has undergone psychiatric treatment	Presence of nonblaming and emotionally supportive caregivers
Harsh or inconsistent parenting	No history of psychiatric or substance abuse disorder
Lack of empathy	
Lack of problem-solving ability	Good cognitive capabilities
Problems with self-regulation (impulse control)	Good social skills
	Self-regulation capability
Comorbid substance abuse disorder	Capacity for empathy
Living alone or with a parent as an adult	
Difficulties forming adult relationships, including intimate relationships with adult partners	The ability to form and maintain adult relationships, including those with intimacy
Social	
Unemployment or having a low-paying job	Secure employment
Social isolation	Social integration
Exposure to deviant sexual subcultures	

Table 12.2

Risk and Protective Factors for the Course of Pedophilia

Risk	Protection
Earlier age of onset	Later age of onset
Greater frequency of acts	Lesser frequency of acts
Threats in the commission of the crime	Absence of threats in the commission of the crime
Deviant sexual interests	
Choosing strangers as victims (rather than boys known to the perpetrator)	Ability to experience conventional sex
	Choosing boys that the perpetrator knows
Existence of preceding offenses	No prior offenses
Lack of motivation for change	Motivation for change
Blaming of victim	Refusal to blame the victim
History of abuse	No history of abuse
Presence of substance abuse	No substance abuse
Failure to complete treatment	Ability to complete intervention

Risk Factors

Biological

Little research has been done on possible biological risk factors for pedophilia. Many of the studies that have been done had small sample sizes, and their results must thus be considered tentative. There is a consensus among researchers that biological causes may contribute to its etiology, but the relevant factors remain unclear. As noted earlier, almost all pedophiles are men, which suggests hormonal risk factors but could also reflect socialization differences between the sexes. One group of researchers studied a possible association between sexual offending, antisocial personality, and testosterone levels. They studied 10 imprisoned rapists, 10 imprisoned child molesters, and a control group of 31 other males (Aromaki, Lindman, & Eriksson, 2002). The researchers found no significant differences among members of the three groups in levels of testosterone. In the sexual offenders, however, an antisocial personality index was positively correlated with mean saliva testosterone. Intensity of sexual activity in general as determined from self-reports was also significantly related to testosterone in both rapists and child molesters but not in the control males.

Levels of the neurotransmitter serotonin have been associated with impulsive and aggressive behaviors in a variety of *DSM* disorders. In the context of sexual disorders, a study of 8 pedophiles and 11 controls tested the hypothesis that certain deficits in serotonin transmission exist in persons with pedophilia (Maes et al., 2001). The results, which included measures of participants' plasma cortisol, plasma prolactin, and body temperature, supported the hypothesis. The researchers acknowledge the limitation of their small sample size and recommend that future studies on this topic should focus on serotonin's postsynaptic receptor upregulation and lowered presynaptic activity.

Other studies have examined less specific neurodevelopmental abnormalities in those with pedophilia. Researchers at the Quinsy Institute for Sex and Reproduction found (with a sample size of 600) that pedophiles had elevated levels of non-right-handedness (NRH), although the effect size was small (Bogaert, 2001). Most cerebral researchers argue that elevated NRH in clinical groups can result from developmental or central nervous system (CNS) disorders. This finding suggests that pedophiles' behavior is more directly related to CNS developmental abnormalities than to the NRH factor. Further, no relationship was found in this study between the pedophile's educational background and NRH, an association that is sometimes found in general criminal populations. In further consideration of the role of neurodevelopmental characteristics in determining sexual preferences, some researchers propose that early childhood sexual abuse, especially that which occurs prior to age 6, may cause some relevant CNS abnormalities (Blanchard et al., 2002; Cohen et al., 2002). These researchers also suggest that pedophiles may be influenced by genetic factors originating in mothers who have psychiatric problems.

To summarize, the only compelling biological factors that have been identified in the etiology of pedophilia are related to male hormones and the neurotransmitter serotonin. Additional research may eventually identify other factors that are significant in this regard.

Psychological

The strongest risk factors for pedophilia are psychological. Adverse family backgrounds can contribute to a person's later development of inappropriate sexual conduct. Pedophiles generally come from families with marital breakups, parental mental illness, harsh or inconsistent parenting, substance abuse, criminality, and high rates of physical abuse and neglect (Kendall & Hammen, 1998; Lee, Jackson, Pattison, & Ward, 2002; Shaw, 1999). Various types of emotional and physical abuse are also developmental risk factors for the disorder (Shaw, 1999). Further, the presence of childhood behavior problems, particularly those related to high levels of anxiety, is a risk factor. Most of the studies that examine these factors must be interpreted with caution, however, because of the general lack of reliability of client and family self-reports and the failure of some researchers to investigate a range of adverse childhood conditions. Most of these risk factors, when taken in isolation, are not specific to the development of sexual disorders.

Early caregiving is acknowledged as a foundation on which children build their later relationships (Murray, 2000). The child who does not receive affection and a sense of interpersonal security from primary caregivers is at risk for a variety of problems in later relationships outside the family. More specifically, research suggests that insecure attachment is a developmental risk factor for pedophilia (Sawle & Kear-Colwell, 2001). According to attachment theory, infants develop the cognitive schemas (internal perspectives about the environment) of their caregivers and others in the immediate environment, relying on them to predict caregiver behavior and to regulate their own behavior. In this way, the "healthy" infant achieves a feeling of security and ultimately internalizes positive attachment experiences (Bowlby, 1979). Children who experience high levels of separation or rejection when distressed become characteristically less empathetic toward others. The cyclic relationship between parenting styles and attachment appears to contribute to the risk of pedophilia (Sroufe, 1996).

With attachment theory as a background, Sawle and Kear-Colwell (2001) compared 25 pedophiles, 22 nonoffending victims of sexual abuse, and 23 controls with regard to their attachment styles. With multiple measures, they found that both the controls and the victims were more securely attached than the pedophiles, who were insecurely attached. Specifically, the pedophiles had elevated scores on measures of "relationships as secondary" and "lack of confidence." People with these characteristics generally experience a lack of empathy toward others, are emotionally defensive, and are insensitive to interpersonal cues. This makes relationships difficult for them to establish and maintain, producing a risk for pedophilia. These researchers also concluded that the style of intervention with pedophiles should include support and rapport establishment, as well as confrontation, so that the offender's attachment style may be positively influenced during rehabilitation.

A history of sexual abuse is more prevalent in sexual abusers than in the general population and in nonsexual abusers. Reports of sexual victimization in the history of adolescent sex offenders vary from 19 to 82% (Freund & Kuban, 1994). Young victims of abuse may internalize the aggressive and erotic facets of their experiences into patterns of deviant sexual gratification through social learning, imitation, and modeling (Lee et. al., 2002). Adolescents who have been sexually victimized, for example, manifest more deviant erectile responses to sexual stimuli than adolescents who have not been so abused (Becker, Hunter, Stein, & Kaplan, 1989). One study of 64 sex offenders and 33 nonsex, nondrug, and nonviolent property offenders yielded interesting data on this point (Lee et. al., 2002). The researchers hypothesized that childhood sexual abuse, physical abuse, emotional abuse, behavior problems, and family dysfunction are general developmental risk factors for a variety of paraphilias. They also hypothesized that childhood sexual abuse would be a specific risk factor for pedophilia. Both hypotheses were supported. They concluded that male children and adolescents who have been sexually abused are at a greater risk in later years of becoming sexual abusers themselves.

It is important to add that most children who have experienced sexual abuse do not become pedophiles. They are most likely to develop a variety of other psychiatric disorders, such as mood disorders, anxiety disorders, conduct disorders, and suicidal behaviors (Fergusson, Horwood, & Lynskey, 1996). These victim outcomes underscore the seriousness of pedophile behavior.

Combining the risk factors of poor attachment and sexual abuse, it has been hypothesized that people are at risk to sexually abuse children when they cannot get their emotional needs met, regulate their emotional well being, respond empathetically to others, and seek assistance to manage their abusive inclinations (Pithers, Kashima, Cummings, Beal, & Buell, 1988). Early deviant sexual experiences may serve as a template for later deviant sexual behaviors, and inconsistent caregiving may serve to undermine the security of attachments. An adult who has not developed a secure attachment system may construe early abusive sexual experiences as enticing because they represent a form of intimacy, regardless of their deviant nature.

Several other psychological risk factors for pedophilia have been investigated, though with less empirical support. One set of researchers found that the number of older brothers (but not sisters) in a family could lead to sexual deviance, specifically a preference for children or for coercive sex (Bogaert, Bezeau, Kuban, & Blanchard, 1997; Lalumiere, Harris, Quinsey, & Rice, 1998). The proposed reason for this is that later-born male children tend to lack same-sex siblings close in age who might provide appropriate social modeling. It has also been reported that men with arousal patterns to children tend to be of lower intelligence and socioeconomic status (Laws & O'Donohue, 1997). It is hypothesized that both of these characteristics are negatively correlated with mainstream or socially acceptable attitudes and behaviors about sex.

Social

Cultural and social attitudes and practices may have some influence on the potential pedophile's development, although there is little evidence to support this assertion. Although no mainstream organizations support pedophilia, marginal organizations promote sexual behavior between children and adults as positive. One of these is the North America Man/Boy Love

Association (NAMBLA, 2003). Exposure to these groups may provide the learning and modeling needed to support pedophilic behaviors. It has already been noted that pedophiles tend to be socially isolated, so cultures and social environments that reinforce personal isolation may be considered risk factors. Differences among cultures with regard to the age of consent for sexuality and the perceived appropriateness of adult–child physical contact may help to explain why pedophilia is more prevalent among Caucasians and African Americans (Murray, 2000), although this tentative finding may be an artifact of the populations who are studied or the people who most often come to the attention of law enforcement agencies (Murray, 2000). In conclusion, the psychological risk factors for pedophilia described here are considered to be the most relevant to its development and persistence.

Protective Factors

The factors that protect a person from developing pedophilia are largely the opposite of those that put the person at risk for the disorder. Regarding biological factors, being female, the absence of nervous system developmental abnormalities, and normal distributions of serotonin and testosterone are all protective (Aromaki et al., 2002; Blanchard et al., 2002). The most important protective factors are psychological, related to a positive early family environment where the child is able to develop secure attachments to primary caregivers and experience only moderate levels of stress and interpersonal conflict (Finkelhor, 1990; Moncher, 1996; Pithers et al., 1988; Rind, Tromovitch, & Bauserman, 1998). These secure attachments set the stage for the child's development of social competence, flexible strategies for managing emotions and impulses, and empathic responsiveness to others. The absence of sexual molestation as a child is another important protective factor (Laws & O'Donohue (1997). In adulthood, secure employment and social integration are protective (Sawle & Kear-Colwell, 2001).

Intervention with Pedophilia

Deviant sexual arousal and offending, while a very serious presenting problem, is only one aspect of the pedophile's total being. For long-term success, intervention should address a range of dimensions of the client's life, including maladaptive thought processes, low self-esteem, depression, socialization difficulties, and the need for skills in the areas of problem solving, communication, anger management, impulse control, and intimacy (Rosenberg, 2002). The major factors related to the offender's positive response to intervention include a willingness to accept responsibility for his offenses as evidenced by admission of the offense, acceptance of the behavior as a problem, motivation to stop offending, and a willingness to participate in treatment (Rasmussen, 1999). Appendix II lists references for specific intervention manuals and protocols that can be used with members of this client population.

Practitioner and program factors related to the successful engagement of pedophiles have been identified. One pair of researchers rejects confrontational intervention models, arguing that because of the difficulties that pedophiles have with relationships, a more empathic and supportive approach is needed (Kear-Colwell & Boer, 2000). These authors note that pedophiles generally come into treatment unwilling to disclose their problems, because their abusive backgrounds and attachment problems prevent them from forming therapeutic alliances with practitioners. One meta-analysis found a general positive relationship between outcome and therapeutic alliance across a variety of problem issues (Horvath & Symonds, 1991). Pedophiles tend to be socially isolated loners; a significant number of them have negative views about interacting with other adults. They describe their need for contact with children as emotionally and socially important, as well as sexually important. Any adult relationship that demands a degree of intimacy, including those found in intervention programs, can be highly anxiety provoking. Some research from the English prison system supports the idea that empathic practitioner style (along with treatment group cohesiveness) is associated with positive outcomes for pedophiles (Garlick, Marshall, & Thornton, 1996). Thus it appears that the development of trust, a consistent relationship, and a therapeutic alliance may help these clients move toward the idea that change is possible.

Medication

Significant advances in psychotropic medications have been made during the past 20 years to assist in lowering libido and decreasing the incidence of deviant sexual thoughts and actions (Rosenberg, 2002). For example, the selective serotonin reuptake inhibiting antidepressant drugs (SSRIs) all have the common effect of decreasing libido. Although this is an undesired effect for many consumers, it can decrease libido in the pedophile to the extent that he may be better able to resist a sexual fantasy.

A class of medications known as antiandrogen agents is sometimes used to treat pedophilia and the other paraphilias (Gijs & Gooren, 1996). Androgens are male hormones (including testosterone) that are naturally produced in the body and are necessary for normal male sexual development. Androgen drugs are sometimes used to replace the hormones when the body is unable to produce enough on its own. With pedophiles, antiandrogen drugs are prescribed to reduce these hormones and thus reduce the client's sex drive, even while the symptomatic thoughts continue. These drugs have had only modest success, however, in part because of their adverse effects (nausea, diarrhea, breast enlargement, anemia, and erection problems). Further, it is difficult to monitor the client's adherence to such a regimen.

Research is ongoing to develop more effective antiandrogen (sometimes referred to as "chemical castration") drugs that can be used as part of a comprehensive intervention program with pedophiles. A relatively new class of antiandrogen medications, known as gonadotropin-releasing hormone agonists, is being tested (Krueger & Kaplan, 2001). One recent study of 12 people using one such drug, depot leuprolide acetate, for lengths of time spanning 6 months to 5 years, found it to be useful. There was a significant suppression of deviant sexual interests and behavior as measured by client self-report, plus fewer side effects than other acetates. The drug was fairly well tolerated, but 3 of the 12 research participants developed bone degeneration problems. It thus appears that drug therapy will continue to be a limited option in the treatment of the paraphilias in the foreseeable future.

Psychosocial Interventions

Intervention goals with these young people must be comprehensively focused on all of the following:

- Confronting the abuser's denial
- Decreasing deviant sexual arousal
- Facilitating the development of nondeviant sexual interests
- Promoting victim empathy
- Enhancing social and interpersonal skills
- Assisting with values clarification
- Clarifying cognitive distortions

For youth and adult sex offenders, group intervention is always preferred to individual treatment because the abuser is less able to minimize, deny, and rationalize the problem behaviors. Family intervention is essential in cases of incest. Educational intervention modules can provide offenders and families with information about normal sexuality, sexual deviancy, cognitive distortions, appropriate interpersonal behavior, strategies for coping with sexual impulses, victim awareness and empathy, anger management, assertiveness training, social skills training, stress reduction, and relaxation management. Specific behavioral interventions may include the following:

- Covert sensitization: The practitioner guides the client through a process of learning to associate *unpleasant* thoughts and feelings with sexually stimulating deviant imagery, thus extinguishing previously pleasant associations. For example, a client may be shown porno-graphic images of young children and helped to associate these im-ages with such negative thoughts as imprisonment and family rejec-tion. The practitioner must repeatedly walk the client through this process before it becomes ingrained in the client's mind. While artifi-cial, covert sensitization helps the client anticipate and manage the anxiety that he will experience when in actual stimulating situations.

- Assisted covert sensitization: This is similar to the previous process except that the client is provided with external aversive stimuli, such as noxious odors, to associate with the deviant imagery.
- Imaginal sensitization: Teaching relaxation techniques such as deep breathing to interrupt sexually stimulating imagery. If the client can learn to relax, he may be able to interrupt the rise in anxiety associ-ated with deviant imagery.
- Satiation techniques: Prescribing frequent masturbation to the client as a means of lowering his sex drive. Men experience a reduction in sexual tension following ejaculation.
- Sexual arousal reconditioning: Pairing the client's feelings of sexual arousal with appropriate nondeviant sexual stimulation—in other words, finding appropriate outlets for it. This may involve sexual contact with an adult partner or masturbation.
- Relapse prevention through the client's clear awareness of each phase of the sexual assault cycle and its implications.

A final component of intervention is an extended aftercare period, with the practitioner's close monitoring of behavior and the promotion of natural social supports. Recently, the courts have been mandating longer proba-tionary periods and parole sanctions to sexual offenders in general (Fagan et al., 2002).

An analysis of sex offender programs in North America (the number of programs reviewed was not cited) reports that cognitive-behavioral in-tervention strategies such as those listed here are used most commonly (Marshall, 1999). Effective treatment targets both offense-specific and offense-related behaviors. Offense-specific issues are those that are directly related to the disorder, and offense-related issues are broader in scope. They focus on the perpetrator as an abuse survivor, anger and stress manage-ment, new social and living skills, problem solving, sex education, the treat-ment of any comorbid disorders, parenting skills, and substance abuse treatment. Relapse prevention is always a part of these programs.

The author provides a model of how these interventions may be pro-vided, again in group formats. They include the following targets:

- Denial or minimization: Each offender is required to give full disclo-sure of his offenses, including his thoughts and feelings at the time.

The other members of the group challenge the person's tendency to minimize the seriousness of the offense.

- Distorted perceptions: Group members challenge a person's self-serving perceptions of his behavior and distorted beliefs about the feelings of the victim at the time of the offense.
- Victim empathy: This is a lengthy process, facilitated by role plays, of the client's becoming able to recognize the nature of emotions in others and to adopt the other person's perspective during an offense. During these role plays, the client replicates the victim's emotions and takes action to reduce the victim's distress.
- Pro-offending attitudes include negative views of women and children and procrime beliefs. These are challenged as they arise at any time in group discussion.
- Attachment style: Each offender describes his most recent relationship and, if possible, at least one previous relationship, so that his attachment (or relationship) style can be inferred. The group discusses the disadvantages of those ways of relating to significant others. The benefits of appropriate intimacy and appropriate sexual relations are reviewed. The nature of jealousy and how it can be exaggerated is also reviewed. The client is helped to develop social skills to promote a greater potential for intimacy.
- Deviant fantasies (related to the offense): Offenders are required to identify and list their sexual and aggressive fantasies and then monitor their frequency and strength. They must indicate whether and how they attempt to resist the fantasies. Group discussion follows around the meaning of the person's fantasies and the role they play in the offending behavior.
- Relapse prevention: This includes an identification of the client's typical offense cycle, a specification of the factors that increase risk, a delineation of coping skills that may reduce risk, and the establishment of a series of plans to avoid risk. Each offender is required to list and share two warning signs: one that only he can observe (such as fantasies) and another that his parole supervisor or family and friends can observe. The client and designated others actively monitor the potential for relapse by using these warning signs.

Postintervention Recidivism

Recidivism is a major concern with pedophiles, of course, because of the particularly dangerous nature of their actions. A meta-analysis of 61 follow-up studies (with an average of 4–5 years) identified the factors most strongly related to recidivism among sexual offenders (Hanson & Bussiere, 1998). On average, the sexual offense recidivism rate was 13.4% (with

23,393 cases studied). Some subgroups of the sample, however, reoffended at higher rates. Recidivism rates were 18.9% for rapists ($N = 1,839$), 12.7% for child molesters ($N = 9,603$), and 12.2% for nonsexual violent offenders ($N = 7,155$). The authors emphasize that these rates should be considered underestimates, in that many postintervention offenses probably remain undetected.

The strongest predictors of sexual recidivism were factors related to sexual deviance. Other factors associated with general criminal behavior, such as age, prior violent offenses, and juvenile delinquency, were predictive as well but to a much lesser extent. The risk for sexual offense recidivism was increased for those whose deviance was characterized by prior sexual offenses, the victimization of strangers or other people outside the family, the onset of sexual offending at an early age, the selection of male victims, or engagement in diverse sexual crimes. Neither the degree of sexual contact, the force used, nor injuries to the victims were significant predictors of sexual offense recidivism. The sex offenders who failed to complete treatment were at a higher risk for reoffending than those who completed treatment. Sex offenders were more likely to experience general criminal recidivism (crimes not related to sexual offenses) if they ended treatment prematurely, denied their sexual offense, or showed low motivation for treatment. The predictors of recidivism due to both general crimes and nonsexual violent crimes were similar to the predictors of recidivism found among nonsexual offenders.

In their self-regulation model of the relapse process, Ward and Hudson (1998) identify how interventions may be individualized, depending on the offender's relapse pattern. Although not empirically validated, this model is widely used to guide decisions about intervention:

- Avoidance-passive pattern: These clients benefit from increased skills in relationships, problem solving, and mood management. Addressing and changing basic beliefs about personal efficacy may decrease their passivity.
- Avoidance-active pattern: For these clients, the focus should be on increased skill acquisition, changing their general coping styles, and increasing knowledge about the likely outcomes of some stress avoidance strategies.
- Approach-automatic pattern: Through cognitive restructuring, these clients need to develop an increased flexibility in problem solving to reduce their dependence on automatic scripts and strengthen their cognitive control.
- Approach-explicit: These clients must be helped to fundamentally change their personal goals (for offending) and their core beliefs about themselves and the outside world.

There is no disputing that many pedophiles are difficult to treat. Relapse is an ongoing concern, and because of reliability problems in the reporting of offenses, valid data are not available to evaluate long-term (5-year) intervention outcomes. Further, pedophiles are forever distrusted by the society at large. Still, as indicated in the previous discussion, there is not *one* type of pedophile, and intervention successes, as indicated by an absence of future offending, are more common than popularly thought.

Because pedophiles maintain a low social status in most societies, there is not an extensive network of programs for treating them. Interestingly, one group of researchers in Australia performed an extensive cost-benefit analysis of intervention programs (Shanahan & Donato, 2001). They determined that, considering intangible costs (such as the physical health and reduced pain and suffering of victims), an increase in empirically validated programs is likely to save money for a society over the long term (Shanahan & Donato, 2001).

Formal Intervention Guidelines, U.S. Department of Justice

The National Crime Victims Research and Treatment Center and the Center for Sexual Assault and Traumatic Stress have compiled guidelines for the treatment of child physical and sexual abuse (Saunders, Berliner, & Hanson, 2003). These organizations included intervention programs for consideration if they met the following criteria: Significant research data or overwhelming clinical opinion indicates that a disorder is associated with, or results from, sexual or physical abuse; a treatment protocol exists that targets the disorder or problem associated with the abuse; writings describing the treatment protocol are available to practitioners; and the protocols may be used by clinicians working in common treatment settings. The interventions were evaluated and classified as (a) well supported and efficacious, (b) supported and probably efficacious, (c) supported and acceptable, (d) promising and acceptable, (e) innovative, and (f) subject to serious concerns.

We summarize here the organizations' findings with regard to adolescent and adult sex offender intervention. (We have included citations for treatment manual and intervention protocols in appendix II.) Adolescent sex offender treatment is most often carried out in specialized programs and usually includes a variety of cognitive-behavioral techniques that are designed to change clients' offense-supportive beliefs and attributions, improve their handling of negative emotions, teach behavioral risk management, and promote prosocial behaviors. There is no clear scientific evidence that favors a particular approach or demonstrates conclusively that an intervention is effective. Still, short- to moderate-term sexual recidivism rates are not high (less than 10%) after any type of treatment. One point for emphasis is that adolescents tend not to present the same degree of sexual deviancy and psychopathic behavior as adults. Most outcome studies note that nonsexual recidivism is higher than sexual recidivism, which underscores the importance of broad behavioral goals in these interventions.

Adolescent sex offender treatment programs generally include 30 to 75 outpatient sessions. Treatment components usually target awareness of the consequences of abusive behavior, increasing victim empathy, identifying personal risk factors, promoting healthy sexual attitudes and beliefs, social skills training, sex education, anger management, and relapse prevention. The personal history of the offender's sexual victimization must always be addressed, and behavioral techniques or medications should be used to modify deviant sexual arousal. Intervention components for parents should include providing support for behavior change, encouraging supervision and monitoring, teaching recognition of risk signs, and promoting guidance and support to the adolescent.

For adults, the desire to be sexual with a child is rooted in deviant sexual arousal or inadequacy in meeting psychosocial and sexual needs through consensual adult relationships. Adult child molester programs usually include cognitive-behavioral components. These are intended to help offenders develop the motivation and skills to stop sexual offending by replacing harmful thinking and behaviors with healthy thoughts and the skills to make choices that will reduce risk. Sexual molestation is a treatable but not a curable behavior problem, and most offenders require external motivators to successfully complete the treatment process. Effective interventions focus on modifying the factors that support the desire, capacity, and opportunity to offend. Cognitive-behavioral approaches are considered to be the most effective intervention methods, with medication, education, skills building, and self-help methods used as adjunctive interventions. A review of 79 treatment studies (Alexander, 1999) found that treatment of child molesters brought known recidivism rates down to 8.1%, compared with 18.3% for other treatment approaches and 25.8% for untreated offenders.

Interventions that address the specific elements of the offender's beliefs and feelings that lead to sexual offending, and include an individualized relapse prevention component, are considered most likely to decrease new sexual offenses. Core therapeutic tasks include environmental changes to reduce opportunity, personal accountability, management of deviant arousal patterns, the correction of dysfunctional beliefs, identification of the offense cycle, the development of strategies to interrupt the offense cycle and replace past responses with healthy behavior, and the development of victim empathy and motivation to refrain from harming others. Adjunctive tasks may include social and sexual education and skills building, education and support for those who monitor the offender, intervention into any comorbid problem areas, trauma resolution, relationship therapy, and re-unification therapy. Treatment tends to be 1 to 2 years in length, with weekly sessions.

Saunders et. al (2003) stress that, of the 24 types of intervention they reviewed, only one met the highest standard of being "well-supported and efficacious" (trauma focused cognitive-behavioral therapy), and only one other program met the criterion for the second highest standard, "supported and probably efficacious" (adult child molester therapy). More than half were classified as "supported and acceptable." This indicates that despite their best efforts, clinical practitioners are still a long way from being able to fully rehabilitate pedophiles and other child molesters. The interventions with empirical support tend to share characteristics of being goal directed and structured, with an emphasis on skill building to manage emotional distress and behavioral disturbances. A repetitive practice of skills is evident in the more effective programs. For adolescents, key skills to acquire include emotional identification, processing, and regulation; anxiety management; identifying and changing maladaptive cognitions; and problem solving. Parents or caregivers must also be included in the treatment process to support the client's new practices.

Case Illustration

Kurt was a retired 72-year-old Caucasian male, referred to the community mental health center from the county's court services for sex offender treatment. His offense occurred 25 years ago but was revealed only when his stepson, Jim, disclosed detailed information about it during a therapy session. Kurt had served 6 months in jail for his offense.

Kurt grew up in a small rural community in Virginia. Both parents raised him until his father died of a heart attack when he was 8 years old. Without a father in the home, Kurt found himself thrust into the "man of the house" role, taking responsibility for much of its maintenance and functioning. He reported that times were hard because his father's Veterans Administration pension was modest and the nation was at war. Religion played a large role in Kurt's life; his mother saw to it that he regularly attended church. Kurt was involved in high school academics and activities, and he excelled in college, becoming active in various clubs there as well. After graduating from college in 1954, he entered the Army and served in the Korean conflict, which he said changed his life. Kurt stated that war firmed his relationship with God, and he became more involved in church activities. In 1977, Kurt married his wife, who had three children from a previous marriage (Tom, 17; Bob, 15; and Jim, 13). Kurt and Jim became especially close. Kurt stated that he took Jim under his wing and tried to get his stepson, who was socially withdrawn, to become more "masculine" and involved in his community.

During the assessment, Kurt stated: "Following our marriage, we moved into a new home which needed a lot of work. Jim was good with mechanical things and was eager to help out with the handiwork. We worked well together and soon started exercising together as well. I wanted him to lift weights to build up his body. I took pictures to show his progress, and unfortunately some of these were nude photographs. I also did what I guess were inappropriate things with him, but nothing I did was forced. My nerves were bad then. My mother had just died and I had her estate to settle, and I had a nerve-racking job at the Pentagon. My guard was down and I did what I should not have done with Jim." Kurt stated that he was deeply sorry about what he did and that his behavior was anomalous, although it continued periodically while Jim was between the ages of 13 and 15. Kurt remained vague in his descriptions of sexual encounters with his stepson. Since his stepson's disclosure to the therapist one year previously, most of Kurt's family had denounced him. His wife remained the only stable part of his life. Kurt was forbidden to see his grandchildren, who he stated had been the focus of his life.

In later sessions Kurt was able to corroborate court statements, which indicated that he had began photographing his stepson's nude body under the guise of concern for his sexual maturity. Kurt recalled questioning his stepson about masturbation and wet dreams and said he became concerned when his stepson said that he had experienced neither. Without his new wife's knowledge, he took his stepson to the urologist to discern whether there was any physical reason his stepson did not masturbate. He remembered the urologist stating that the boy was normal but perhaps delayed in his sexual maturity. Kurt's sexual acting out increased then over next 6 months and included fondling him to ejaculation, having his stepson watch him masturbate until he ejaculated, and having Jim fondle him. These activities occurred at least weekly and, according to Kurt, without the stepson's protests.

Psychological testing revealed that Kurt scored in the "insignificant" range on the Millon Clinical Multiaxial Inventory, which assesses for personality disorders and major psychiatric disorders (see appendix I, chapter 15). A penile plethysmograph (PPG) reading mapped Kurt's scores in the "below significant" range for deviant sexual arousal.

Diagnosis

Axis I   Pedophilia, Sexual Attraction to Males, Limited to Incest, Nonexclusive Type
Axis II   Deferred
Axis III Arthritis, infective unspecific
Axis IV   Problems with Primary Support Group
          Problems with Legal System
Axis V   GAF= 69

Justification for Diagnosis

Axis I

The client's symptoms were concurrent with the diagnosis of pedophilia in all of the prescribed criteria. Kurt fulfilled criterion (a) because for a period of over 6 months he had recurrent, intense sexually arousing fantasies, sexual urges, and sexual behaviors with a prepubescent child who was 13 years old. Kurt acted on these sexual urges over a period of more than one year and thus met criterion (b). The *DSM-IV-TR* further mandates that the individual be at least 16 years old and 5 years older than the child. At the time of Kurt's first sexual encounter with his stepson, Kurt was 45 and his stepson was reported to be 13, effectively fulfilling criterion (c). Last, the specifiers are warranted, as Kurt targeted his 13-year-old stepson and is married.

Axis II

The presented symptomatology does not constitute a personality disorder, and Kurt's level of functioning clearly refutes the possibility of mental retardation.

Axis III

Kurt reported suffering from arthritis, for which he has received surgeries on his hands, elbows, and shoulder. No further medical conditions were reported. Because of the client's age, however, a medical examination may be necessary to assess for further medical disorders or general medical conditions.

Axis IV

Problems with the primary support system were identified, as Kurt's family members with the exception of his wife have severed all ties to him. He is no longer able to see his grandchildren, with whom he reportedly had good relationships. These circumstances seem to be causing Kurt the greatest stress at this point. He has reported feeling that someone has taken all the meaning out of his life. Kurt has also served 6 weeks in jail and is currently on probation for his sexual offense, justifying the citation of problems with legal system.

Axis V

A GAF score of 69 was assigned because the client is experiencing some difficulty with his family relationships but is generally functioning well. A lower score would have been justified if his marital relationship was in jeopardy.

Additional Information Needed

A genogram of the family's history may be considered in order to gain greater insight into family patterns that may have influenced Kurt's development and current behavior. Because of the penile plethysmograph's (PPG) low validity and reliability, additional sources may be consulted to gain more information on the client system.

Risk and Protective Factors

Kurt exhibits numerous risk and protective factors for his pedophilia. In the biological sphere, Kurt may be at a decreased risk for reoffending because of his age. The client's offensive behaviors date back some 25 years, and the client, who is now 72, may have seen a decline in his sexual stamina with a decline in his testosterone level.

Psychologically, Kurt may be protected by the insignificant scores on psychological tests that assessed for personality and other major psychiatric disorders. Further, penile plethysmograph readings were insignificant and represent a protective factor, which lowers the client's risk of recidivism. The client's cognitive distortions related to his sexual behavior may place him at greater risk for reoffending, as he may not see fault in his sexual acting out and reengage in similar behaviors.

Social protective factors include the client's strong ties to the church community. Although Kurt's disengagement from his family represents a risk factor, his wife's supportive stance exemplifies a protective factor for Kurt. Last, Kurt is not employed in a setting that may expose him to children.

Treatment Plan

The treatment plan may consist of an educational component to inform the client about his disorder, as such knowledge about its patterns may allow the client to control urges and cope with sexual triggers. Desensitization to potential triggers may be included to gradually increase his tolerance of external stimulants. The implementation of cognitive restructuring procedures in the form of cognitive-behavioral therapy may be useful to combat the client's cognitive distortions related to his offensive behavior, and relaxation techniques may also aid in the process. Treatment may also focus on building empathy for the victim, and anger management components may be included to further control for antecedents of sexually offensive behavior.

Critique of the Diagnosis

Disorders with clear or probable biological components, such as schizophrenia, autism, bipolar disorder, the dementias, and major depression, tend to have credibility among the general public as valid mental disorders. Few biological markers have been identified or even speculated as causal for pedophilia. Even so, many people considered it to be a mental disorder on the basis of the grossly deviant sexual thoughts and behaviors that are central to the condition. Pedophile behavior is so harmful to the child victims, so contrary to the values of American society, and so disruptive to the life of the person who has the disorder that the public at large treats it at least in part as a mental disorder. It is also perceived to be a criminal condition, however, and those who are convicted of related behaviors are usually sentenced to prisons rather than treatment facilities. In fact, there seems to be a public fear that conceptualizing pedophilia too strongly as a mental disorder may provide perpetrators with a basis to claim innocence of their associated crimes. Because pedophilia is a chronic condition, citizens are reluctant to allow convicted sexual offenders a "free rein" in the social mainstream after they have served their sentences or completed their intervention programs (Shanahan & Donato, 2001). It may be concluded, then, that pedophilia is accepted by professionals and the public alike as a mental disorder; although unlike almost all other *DSM* diagnoses (and along with some of the other paraphilias), it holds equal status as a criminal condition.

Appendix I. Instruments Used to Assess Pedophilia and Other Sexual Offenders

The Multiphasic Sex Inventory (MSI)

Kalichman, Henderson, Shealy, & Dwyer (1992). Original authors are Nichols & Molinder (1984).

Description

- A 300-item true/false self-report inventory designed to assist in the comprehensive assessment of sex offenders
- Reflects a conceptual framework of sex offender motivational and behavioral characteristics; includes scales for deviant acts, cognitive processes, behavioral aspects of offenses, and deceptive styles

- Includes three sexual deviance scales, five atypical sexual outlet scales, a sexual dysfunction scale (comprised of four subscales), six validity scales, and a scale measuring sex knowledge

Reliability

- Internal consistencies ranged from .53 to .90; scales with heterogeneous content demonstrated lower comparative reliability.

Validity

- Response patterns reflected what was predicted by the researchers based on theoretical and clinical descriptions of sex offenders.
- A negative correlation was found between victim ages and Child Molestation scores.
- Substantial positive correlations were found between distress-related MSI subscales and MMPI distress scales, MSI and MMPI validity scales, and MSI scales and measures of personality type.

The Static-99 Sex Offender Risk Assessment

Hanson & Thornton (2000); Austin, Peyton, & Johnson (2003)

Description

- A 10-item sex offender recidivism risk assessment instrument that is completed through an offender's file review
- Items assess prior sex offenses (charges and convictions), prior sentencing dates, convictions for noncontact sex offenses, index of nonsexual violence, prior nonsexual violence, unrelated victims, stranger victims, male victims, offender age, and offender marital status.
- Offenders are scored with a yes/no response or a structured scale ranging in value from 0 to 3.
- Scores between 0 and 1 are considered "low" risk, 2 to 3 are "medium-low" risk, 4 to 5 are "medium-high" risk, and 6 to 10 are "high" risk.

Reliability

220 offenders were independently rated by two researchers with 81.4–98.6% agreement across items, 40.9% agreement on total score, and 73.2% agreement on risk level.

Validity

Predictive validity was assessed by comparing risk levels of 78 respondents with actual recidivism over a 12-month period; distinct differences in rates were observed among the risk categories.

Appendix II. Treatment Manuals and Protocols

For Adolescents

Henggeler, S. W., Swenson, C. C., Kaufman, K., & Schoenwald, S. K. (1997). *MST supplementary treatment manual for juvenile sex offenders and their families*. Provided to the Institute for Families in Society, University of South Carolina, by the Family Services Research Center, Department of Psychiatry and Behavioral Sciences, Medical University of South Carolina.

Kahn, T. J. (1996). *Pathways: A guided workbook for youth beginning treatment*. Orwell, VT: Safer Society Press.

Kahn, T. J. (1996). *Pathways guide for parents of youth beginning treatment*. Orwell. VT: Safer Society Press.

Marsh, L. F., Connell, P., & Olsen, E. (1988). *Breaking the cycle: Adolescent sexual treatment manual*. Available from St. Mary's Home for Boys, 16535 SW Tualatin Valley Highway, Beaverton, OR 97006.

O'Brien, M. J. (1994). *PHASE treatment manual*. Available from Alpha PHASE, Inc., 1600 University Ave., West, Suite 305, St. Paul, MN. 55104-3825.

Steen, C. (1993). *The relapse prevention workbook for youth in treatment*. Orwell, VT: Safer Society Press.

Way, I. F., & Balthazor, T. J. (1990). *A manual for structured group treatment with adolescent sexual offenders*. Notre Dame, IN: Jalice.

For Adults

Association for the Treatment of Sexual Abusers. (2001). *Practice standards and guidelines for members of the Association for the Treatment of Sexual Offenders*. Beaverton, OR: Author.

Abel, G. G., Becker, J. V., Cunningham-Rather, J., Rouleau, J. L., Kaplan, M., & Reich, J. (n.d.). *The treatment of child molesters*. Atlanta: Author.

Bays, L., & Freeman-Longo, R. (1989). *Why did I do it again? Understanding my cycle of problem behaviors*. Holyoke, MA: NEARI Press.

Bays, L., & Freeman-Longo, R. (1990). *How can I stop? Breaking my deviant cycle*. Holyoke, MA: NEARI Press.

Barbaree, H. E., & Seto, M. C. (1997). Pedophilia: Assessment and treatment. In D. R. Laws & W. O'Donohue (Eds.), *Sexual deviance: Theory, assessment, and treatment* (pp. 175–193). New York: Guilford.

Freeman-Longo, R., & Bays, L. (1988). *Who am I and why am I in treatment?* Holyoake, MA: NEARI Press.

Salter, A. C. (1988). *Treating child sex offenders and victims*. Thousand Oaks, CA: Sage.

References

Alexander, M. A. (1999). Sexual offender treatment efficacy revisited. *Sexual Abuse: A Journal of Research and Treatment, 11*(2), 101–116.

American Psychiatric Association. (2000). *Diagnostic and statistical manual of mental disorders* (4th ed., rev.). Washington, DC: Author.

Aromaki, A. S., Lindman, R. E., & Eriksson, C. J. P. (2002). Testosterone, sexuality and antisocial personality in rapists and child molesters: A pilot study. *Psychiatry Research, 110*(3), 239–247.

Becker, J. V., Hunter, J. A., Stein, R. M., & Kaplan, M. S. (1989). Factors associated with erection in adolescent sex offenders. *Journal of Psychopathology and Behavioral Assessment, 11*, 353–362.

Becker, J. V., Kaplan, M. S., & Tenke, C. E. (1992). The relationship of abuse history, denial, and erectile response profiles of adolescent sexual perpetrators. *Behavior Therapy, 23*, 87–97.

Blanchard, R., Christensen, B., Strong, S., Cantor, J., Kuban, M., Klassen, P., et al. (2002). Retrospective self-reports of childhood accidents causing unconsciousness in phallometrically diagnosed pedophiles. *Archives of Sexual Behavior, 31*(6), 511–516.

Bogaert, A., Bezeau, S., Kuban, M., & Blanchard, R. (1997). Pedophilia, sexual orientation, and birth order. *Journal of Abnormal Psychology, 106*(2), 331–335.

Bogaert, A. F. (2001). Handedness, criminality, and sexual offending. *Neuropsychologia, 39*(5), 465–469.

Bowlby, J. (1979). *The making and breaking of affectional bonds.* London: Tavistock.

Cohen, L. J., Mikiforov, K., Gans, G., Poznansky, O., McGeoch, P., Weaver, C., et al. (2002). Heterosexual male perpetrators of childhood sexual abuse: A preliminary neurospychiatric model. *Psychiatric Quarterly, 73*(4), 313–336.

Cortoni, F., Heil, P., & Marshall, W. L. (1996). *Sex as a coping mechanism and its relationship to loneliness and intimacy deficits in sexual offending.* Paper presented at the 15th annual conference of the Association for the Treatment of Sexual Abusers, Chicago.

Fagan, P., Wise, T., Schmidt, C., & Berlin, F. (2002). Pedophilia. *The Journal of the American Medical Association, 288*(19), 2458–2466.

Fergusson, D. M., Horwood, L. J., & Lynskey, M. T. (1996). Childhood sexual abuse and psychiatric disorders in young adulthood: II. Psychiatric outcomes of childhood sexual abuse. *Journal of the Academy of Child and Adolescent Psychiatry, 35*(10), 1365–1374.

Finkelhor, D. (1990). Early and long-term effects of child sexual abuse: An update. *Professional Psychology: Research & Practice, 21*(5), 325–330.

Freund, K., & Kuban, M. (1994). The basis of the abused abuser theory of pedophilia: A further elaboration on an earlier study. *Archives of Sexual Behavior, 23*(5), 553–563.

Garlick, Y., Marshall, W. L., Thornton, D. (1996) Intimacy deficits and attribution of blame among sexual offenders. *Legal & Criminological Psychology, 1*, 251–258.

Gijs, L., & Gooren, L. (1996). Hormonal and psychopharmacological interventions in the treatment of paraphilias: An update. *Journal of Sex Research, 33*, 273–290.

Hanson, R. K., & Bussiere, M. T. (1998). Predicting relapse: A meta-analysis of sexual offender recidivism studies. *Journal of Consulting and Clinical Psychology, 66*(2), 348–362.

Horvath, A. O., & Symonds, B. D. (1991). Relationship between working alliance and outcome in psychotherapy: A meta-analysis. *Journal of Counseling Psychology, 38*, 139–149.

Kear-Colwell, J., & Boer, D. P. (2000). The treatment of pedophiles: Clinical experience and the implications of recent research. *International Journal of Offender Therapy and Comparative Criminology, 44*(5), 593–605.

Kendall, P. C., & Hammen, C. (1998). *Abnormal psychology: Understanding human problems* (2nd ed.). Boston: Houghton Mifflin.

Krueger, R. B., & Kaplan, M. S. (2001). Depot-leuprolide acetate for treatment of paraphilias: A report of twelve cases. *Archives of Sexual Behavior, 30*(4), 409–422.

Lalumiere, M. L., Harris, G. T, Quinsey, V. L., & Rice, M. E. (1998). Sexual deviance and number of older brothers among sexual offenders. *Sexual Abuse: Journal of Research & Treatment 10*(1), 5–15.

Laws, D. R., & O'Donohue, W. (1997). *Sexual deviance: Theory, assessment, and treatment.* New York: Guilford.

Lee, J. K. P., Jackson, H. J., Pattison, P., & Ward, T. (2002). Developmental risk factors for sexual offending. *Child Abuse & Neglect, 26*(1), 73–92.

Lightfoot, L. O., & Barbaree, H. E. (1993). The relationship between substance use and abuse and sexual offending in adolescents. In H. E. Barbaree, W. L. Marshall, & S. M. Hudson (Eds.), *The juvenile sex offender* (pp. 203–224). New York: Guilford.

Maes, M., van West, D., De Vos, N., Westenberg, H., Van Hunsel, F., Hendriks, D., et al. (2001). Lower baseline plasma cortisol and prolactin together with increased body temperature and higher mCPP-induced cortisol responses in men with pedophilia. *Neuropsychopharmacology, 24*(1), 37–46.

Marshall, W. L. (1999). Current status of North American assessment and treatment programs for sexual offenders. *Journal of Interpersonal Violence, 14*(3), 221–239.

McGovern, K. B. (1991). The assessment of sexual offenders. In B. M. Maletzky, *Treating the sexual offender* (pp. 35–66). Newbury Park, CA: Sage.

McGovern, K. B., & Peters, J. (1988). Guidelines for assessing sexual behaviors. In L. Walker, *Handbook of sexual abuse of children* (pp. 216–246). New York: Springer.

Moncher, F. J. (1996). The relationship of maternal adult attachment style and risk of physical child abuse. *Journal of Interpersonal Violence, 11*(3), 335–350.

Morrison, J. R. (1995). DSM-IV *made easy: The clinician's guide to diagnosis.* New York: Guilford.

Murray, J. B. (2000). Psychological profile of pedophiles and child molesters. *The Journal of Psychology, 134*(2), 311–324.

Nordland, R. (2001). What is a pedophile? Not all of them are child abusers, and they often believe that their victims don't really suffer. Retrieved September 18, 2003, from http://www.newsweek.com

North American Man/Boy Love Association. (2003). Retrieved November 25, 2003, from http://www.nambla1.de/.

O'Grady, R. (2001). Eradicating pedophilia: Toward the humanization of society. *Journal of International Affairs, 55*(1), 123–140.

Pithers, W. D., Kashima, K., Cummings, G. F., Beal, L. S., & Buell, M. (1988). Relapse prevention of sexual aggression. In R. Prentky & V. Quinsey (Eds.), *Human sexual aggression: Current perspectives* (pp. 244–260). New York: New York Academy of Sciences.

Rasmussen, L. A. (1999). Factors related to recidivism among juvenile sexual offenders. *Sexual Abuse, 11*, 69–85.

Raymond, N., Coleman, E., Christenson, G., & Miner, M. (1999). Psychiatric co-morbidity in pedophilic sex offenders. *American Journal of Psychiatry, 156*(5), 786–793.

Rind, B. Tromovitch, P., & Bauserman, R. (1998). A meta-analytic examination of assumed properties of child sexual abuse using college samples. *Psychological Bulletin, 124*(1), 22–53.

Rosenberg, M. (2002). Treatment considerations for pedophilia: Recent headlines aside, this disorder has long confronted the behavioral healthcare community with difficult challenges. *Behavioral Health Management, 22*(4), 38–42.

Sadock, B. J., & Sadock, V. A. (2005). *Kaplan & Sadock's comprehensive textbook of psychiatry.* Philadelphia: Lippincott Williams & Wilkins.

Saunders, B. E., Berliner, L., & Hanson, R. F. (Eds.). (2003). *Child physical and sexual abuse: Guidelines for treatment (Final report: January 15, 2003).* Charleston, SC: National Crime Victims Research and Treatment Center.

Sawle, G. A., & Kear-Colwell, J. (2001). Adult attachment style and pedophilia: A developmental perspective. *International Journal of Offender Therapy and Comparative Criminology, 45*(1), 32–50.

Shanahan, M., & Donato, D. (2001). Counting the cost: Estimating the economic benefit of pedophile treatment programs. *Child Abuse and Neglect, 25*(4), 541–555.

Shaw, J. A. (1999). Practice parameters for the assessment and treatment of children and adolescents who are sexually abusive of others. *Journal of the American Academy of Child and Adolescent Psychiatry, 38*(12), 55S–76S.

Sroufe, L. A. (1996). *Emotional development: The organization of emotional life in the early years.* New York: Cambridge University Press.

Travin, S., & Protter, B. (1993). *Sexual perversion: Integrative treatment approaches for the clinician.* New York: Plenum.

Ward, T., & Hudson, S. M. (1998). A model of relapse prevention in sexual offenders. *Journal of Interpersonal Violence, 1,* 700.

References for Instruments Used to Assess Pedophilla and Other Sexual Offenders

Austin, J., Peyton, J., & Johnson, K. D. (2003). *Reliability and validity study of Static-99/RRASOR sex offender risk assessment instruments.* Final report submitted to the Pennsylvania Board of Probation and Parole. Institute on Crime, Justice, and Corrections, George Washington University, Washington, DC.

Hanson, R. K., & Thornton, D. (2000). Improving risk assessments for sex offenders: A comparison of three actuarial studies. *Law and Human Behavior, 24*(1), 119–136.

Kalichman, S. C., Henderson, M. C., Shealy, L. S., & Dwyer, M. (1992). Psychometric properties of the multiphasic sex inventory in assessing sex offenders. *Criminal Justice and Behavior, 19*(4), 384–396.

Nichols, H. R., & Molinder, I. (1984). *Molinder multiphasic sex inventory.* (Available from Nichols & Molinder, 437 Bowes Drive, Tacoma, WA 98466)

PART III

Disorders with Onset in Adulthood

13   Bipolar Disorder

Bipolar disorder is a disorder of mood in which, over time, a person experiences one or more *manic episodes* that are usually accompanied by one or more *major depressive episodes* (American Psychiatric Association (APA), 2000). During the past three decades, bipolar disorder has been considered primarily a disorder of brain functioning. It is recurrent, chronic, and the sixth leading cause of disability for people age 15 to 44 (Woods, 2000). Medication is always a major, and sometimes the only, intervention for this disorder because of its effectiveness with so many clients. Still, the medicalization of bipolar disorder has tended to obscure the fact that it has an uncertain etiology. Research has continued to support hypotheses that there are psychological and social, as well as biological, components to the onset and course of the disorder.

The Nature of Bipolar Disorder

Bipolar disorder features both manic and depressive episodes (APA, 2000). A *manic episode* is a distinct period in which a person's predominant mood is elevated, expansive, or irritable to the degree that there is serious impairment in occupational and social functioning. Manic episodes may be characterized by any of the following symptoms (at least three are present): unrealistically inflated self-esteem, a decreased need for sleep, pressured speech, racing thoughts, distractibility, an increase in unrealistic goal-directed activity, and involvement in activities with a potential for painful consequences. Manic episodes are rapid in onset and may persist for a few days up to several months.

A *major depressive episode* is a period of at least 2 weeks during which a person experiences a depressed mood or loss of interest in nearly all common life activities. Symptoms may include (five or more must be present) depressed mood, diminished interest or pleasure in most activities, significant and unintentional weight loss *or* gain, insomnia *or* hypersomnia, feelings of physical agitation *or* retardation, loss of energy, feelings of worthlessness or excessive guilt, a diminished ability to think or concentrate, and persistent thoughts of death or suicide.

Another feature of bipolar disorder, one that often disrupts the continuity of intervention, is the *hypomanic* episode (APA, 2000). This refers to the person's gradual escalation over a period of several days to several weeks from a stable mood to a manic state. It is a mild form of mania that may be pleasurable for the client. He or she experiences higher self-esteem, a decreased need for sleep, a higher energy level, an increase in overall productivity, and more intensive involvement in pleasurable activities. Its related behaviors are often socially acceptable, and consequently the hypomanic person may receive positive reinforcement from friends and employers. At these times, however, the client's decreased insight may lead him or her to believe that the bipolar disorder has permanently remitted and there is no need to continue with medication or other interventions. The potential for a full manic episode thus becomes greater. In fact, poor insight, or the lack of awareness of having a mental illness, is a prominent characteristic in the active phases of bipolar disorder (Ghaemi, Stoll, & Pope, 1995).

Subtypes of Bipolar Disorder

There are two types of bipolar disorder (APA, 2000). *Bipolar I* disorder is characterized by one or more manic episodes, usually accompanied by a major depressive episode. *Bipolar II* disorder is characterized by one or more major depressive episodes accompanied by at least one hypomanic episode. In other words, bipolar I disorder features a mix of mood episodes, and in bipolar II disorder, depressive episodes predominate. These subtypes were first introduced in *DSM-IV*. Prior to that time, although it was recognized that people could have varying courses of mood episodes, the disorder was considered to represent a single phenomenology.

There are six subtypes of bipolar disorder, intended to reflect the severity of the most recent mood episode and its aftermath: *mild* (meeting minimum symptom criteria), *moderate, severe* (the client requires almost continuous supervision) *without psychotic features, severe with psychotic features, in partial remission,* and *in full remission.* There are also four specifiers that may be used to more clearly describe the nature of the most recent mood episode: *catatonic* (featuring a pronounced psychomotor disturbance), *melancholic* (referring to the client's presentation during a major depressive episode), *atypical*, and *postpartum* (occurring within 4 weeks of delivery of a child). Bipolar disorder may also be present *with* or *without full interepisode recovery*, *with seasonal pattern*, and *with rapid cycling* (defined as four mood episodes in a 12-month period). The most recent major depressive episode may be *chronic* (meeting full criteria for 2 years or more).

The Frequency of Manic and Depressive Episodes

Bipolar I disorder is highly recurrent, with 90% of those who have a manic episode developing future episodes (Evans, 2000). The number of episodes tends to average four in 10 years (APA, 2000). There are gender differences in the presentation of bipolar I disorder (Hilty, Brady, & Hales, 1999). Its overall prevalence is the same among men and women, but the first mood episode in males is more likely to be manic. In men, the number of manic episodes equals or exceeds the number of depressive episodes, whereas in women depressive episodes predominate. Rapid cycling bipolar disorder is more common in women. Women have an increased risk of developing subsequent episodes of bipolar I disorder in the postpartum period, and some women have their first episode at that time.

The overall prevalence of bipolar disorder is estimated at 1 to 2% (APA, 2000). Bipolar I disorder ranges from 0.04% to 1.6% in community studies, and Bipolar II disorder has a prevalence of 0.05% (Evans, 2000). Between 5 and 15% of people with bipolar II disorder develop a manic episode within 5 years, changing their diagnosis to bipolar I disorder (APA, 2000). The typical age of onset of a manic episode is the mid-20s, but bipolar disorder may begin at any time from childhood through midlife (Brown, 1994). Twenty to 30% of adults with bipolar disorder report that they experienced their first episode before age 20. In one study of a select sample, 59% of respondents reported experiencing their first *symptoms* of bipolar disorder during childhood or adolescence (Lish, Dime-Meenan, Whybrow, Price, & Hirschfeld, 1994).

Approximately 30 to 35% of people experience their first episode of bipolar disorder between the ages of 20 and 30, and 25% report the first episode between ages 40 and 50. The duration between episodes (the *interepisode* period) tends to be longer after the initial episode, decreasing as the illness progresses. Early onset implies a more severe course (Goldberg & Keck, 1999). A first manic episode after the age of 40 is unusual and may be due to a medical condition or to substance abuse.

Half of people with bipolar disorder move through alternating manic and depressed cycles (Brown, 1994). A majority (70–90%) return to a stable mood and functioning capacity between episodes, although more than half experience interpersonal and occupational problems related to the previous episode. Approximately 10% experience "rapid cycling" (APA, 2000), which implies a poorer outcome. Additionally, 40% have a "mixed" type of the disorder, in which a prolonged depressive episode features bursts of mania, perhaps as brief as a few hours in duration.

Bipolar Disorder in Youth

Bipolar disorder can occur in childhood and adolescence, but it almost always appears differently than in adulthood. The childhood disorder presents as a nonepisodic, chronic, rapid-cycling mixed state, featuring agitation, excitability, aggression, and irritability rather than "classic" mania (Carlson, 2002). The child engages in reckless behavior, but this must be distinguished from either "normal" behavior or that which may also be associated with other disorders. Adolescent bipolar disorder often features mood-incongruent psychotic symptoms and thus may be misdiagnosed as schizophrenia or schizoaffective disorder (McClellan & Werry, 1997). Approximately 10 to 15% of adolescents with recurrent major depressive episodes go on to develop bipolar disorder (APA, 2000). The validity of childhood bipolar disorder, however, and its diagnostic criteria are hotly debated (Roberts, Parker, Woogh, Cripps, & Froese, 2000).

Differential Diagnosis

There is a frequent co-occurrence in bipolar disorder of symptoms of other behavioral and developmental disorders, including attention-deficit/hyperactivity disorder (ADHD) and conduct disorder (CD). Some researchers believe that childhood bipolar disorder may represent a type of ADHD. Others believe that it is a distinct disorder but one that should be defined by new *DSM* criteria. Roberts et al. (2000) investigated whether bipolar disorder might be a variant of ADHD with a longitudinal data analysis of 156 children diagnosed with ADHD, conduct disorder, and dysthymia. They found that very few of the people who were later diagnosed with bipolar disorder in adulthood ($N = 20$) had prior diagnoses of ADHD. More of the adults with bipolar disorder had childhood diagnoses of conduct disorder or dysthymia. The researchers concluded that ADHD and bipolar disorder have a separate etiology. In another study of 26 bipolar youth over the age of 12, Kovacs and Pollock (1995) found a 69% lifetime comorbidity and a 54% episodic comorbidity with conduct disorder. The children without the CD comorbidity had a higher rate of primary affective illness, a higher number of bipolar episodes, and a better overall clinical course.

Bipolar disorder must be differentiated from *schizoaffective disorder* (discussed in chapter 14) and other psychotic disorders. This is sometimes difficult, because at both mood extremes the person may experience time-limited hallucinations and delusions. One major difference of bipolar disorder from the psychotic disorders is that the symptoms persist in the absence of hypomanic or depressed mood episodes (Sands & Harrow, 2000). Bipolar disorder is also distinct from two other mood disorders, the *major depressive* and *cyclothymic* disorders. The first of these occurs in the absence of a hypomanic or manic episode. The latter, also considered to be a distinct mood disorder, is characterized by a period of at least 2 years in which the person experiences numerous episodes of hypomanic (but not manic) and depressive symptoms that do not meet the criteria for a major depressive episode. Prevalence rates for cyclothymic disorder are estimated at 0.4% to 1%, and there is a 15 to 50% chance that the person will develop a bipolar disorder (APA, 2000). Because of its relatively benign symptomatology, people with cyclothymic disorder do not often present for intervention. When they do, they are often diagnosed with other disorders.

Clinical practitioners need to participate in a multidisciplinary assessment process and be extremely cautious in their diagnostic formulations for bipolar disorder, especially with children, because of the diagnostic controversy with that population.

Risk and Protective Factors

Genetic Factors

Family history studies, including twin and adoption research, indicate an aggregation of bipolar disorder in families. First-degree biological relatives of people with bipolar I disorder have elevated rates for that disorder (4–24%) as well as for the bipolar II (1–5%) and major depressive disorders (4–24%) (Sadock & Sadock, 2005). People who have a first-degree relative with a mood disorder are likelier to have an earlier age of onset than those without a familial pattern. Twin studies are even more compelling. A study of 30 identical and 37 fraternal twins in which one member of the pair had bipolar disorder showed a concordance rate of 85% (McGuffin et al., 2003). Several decades ago, researchers speculated that the potential for bipolar disorder emanated from a single gene, but this theory has lost support, and studies are now focusing on polygenic models of transmission (Barondes, 1997; Goldberg & Keck, 1999). While genetic research remains promising, the "core" of bipolar disorder remains elusive. The likelihood of genetic factors are complicated by indications that bipolar disorder with late-life onset (after 40 years) has no apparent association with family history (Daly, 1997).

Biological Factors

The limbic system and its associated regions in the brain are thought to serve as the primary site of dysfunction in all of the mood disorders. Four areas under review in the biological study of bipolar disorder include the role of neurotransmitters, the endocrine system, physical biorhythms, and physical complications (Sands & Harrow, 2000; Young & Joffe, 1997). The amount and activity of norepinephrine, serotonin, gamma-aminobutyric acid (GABA), and perhaps other central nervous system nerve tract messengers are clearly abnormal in persons with bipolar disorder. Still, it is unknown what causes these imbalances to occur. One theory proposes that bipolar disorder results from a "kindling" process in limbic system neuron tracts (Schatzberg & Nemeroff, 2001). That is, people with the disorder may experience a chronic, low-grade repetitive firing of electrical impulses in certain cell tracts that occasionally "erupt" into a manic state. Other theories focus on the actions of the thyroid and other endocrine glands to account for nervous system changes that contribute to manic and depressive episodes. Biorhythms, or the body's natural sleep and wake cycles, are erratic in some bipolar clients and may account for, or result from, chemical imbalances that trigger manic episodes. Finally, damage to the limbic system, basal ganglia, and hypothalamus, which are centers of emotional activity in the brain, may contribute to episodes of the disorder. Most researchers agree that these biological processes are significant in the onset and course of bipolar disorder, but there are no brain-imaging techniques (like those available in schizophrenia research) that might provide details about them. Finally, a few studies have associated obstetrical complications with early-onset and severe bipolar disorder (Kinney, Yurgelum-Todd, Tohen, & Tramer, 1998). Risk and protective factors are listed in Table 13.1.

Psychosocial Factors

Stressful life events play an activating role in early episodes of bipolar disorder, with subsequent episodes arising more in the absence of clear external precipitants (Johnson & Roberts, 1995). People with bipolar disorder who have a history of extreme early-life adversity (such as physical or sexual abuse in childhood or adolescence) show an earlier age of onset, faster and more frequent cycling, increased suicidality, and more comorbid conditions, including alcohol and substance abuse (Post, Leverich, King, &

Table 13.1

Risk and Protective Factors for Bipolar Disorder

Risk Factors	Protective Factors
Onset	
Genetic/Biological	
First-degree relative with bipolar disorder	Absence of mood disorders among first-degree relatives
Hypothyroidism	
Neurotransmitter imbalances	
Irregular social or circadian rhythms	
Obstetrical complications	
Psychological	
Postpartum depression	Effective communication and problem-solving skills
Poor sleep hygiene	
Ongoing conflict with family members	Positive family relationships
Traumatic experience during childhood	
Irregular daily living routines	Sense of self-direction, internal rewards
Hypersensitivity	
Self-criticism; low self-esteem	Positive self-esteem
Need for approval from others	
Exaggerated use of denial	
Substance abuse disorders	Absence of substance abuse
Course	
Lack of professional intervention	Ongoing positive alliance with family, mental health professionals
Antidepressant drugs (for bipolar type I)	
Irregular use of medications	Medication adherence
Irregular social rhythms	Knowledge about the disorder
Ongoing conflict with family members	Identification and use of social and community resources
Hypersensitivity	
Self-criticism, low self-esteem	Regular social rhythms and sleep cycle
Need for approval from others	Participation in support groups
Exaggerated use of denial	Willingness to assume responsibility for the disorder
Substance abuse	
Marital conflicts	
Work-related difficulties	

Weiss, 2001). People at risk for bipolar disorder may also have, in addition to stressful life events, an external locus of control orientation and be highly dependent on others for approval and acceptance (Reilly-Harrington, Alloy, Fresco, & Whitehouse, 1999). Dependence on one or a few people for gratification and affirmation can trigger an intense loss when separation from those people occurs. People at risk also tend to use denial or minimization when dealing with conflicts (Ouimette, Klein, & Pepper, 1996). Data also suggest that more severe courses of bipolar disorder are related to early stress experiences.

Clients who experience high levels of life stress in general *after* the onset of bipolar disorder are four times more likely to have a relapse than clients with low levels of life stress (Ellicott, Hammen, Gitlin, Brown, & Jamison, 1990). Events that can cause these episodes include disruptions in daily routines or sleep-wake cycles, such as air travel and changes in work schedules (Malkoff-Schwartz et al., 1998). Stressful life events in social and family support systems appear to affect the course of bipolar disorder, in combination with genetic, biological, and cognitive vulnerabilities (Miklowitz & Alloy, 1999). One study found that relapse risk was related to both the lingering presence of symptoms of mania and also to harsh comments from relatives (Rosenfarb et al., 2001). Clients from families that are high in expressed emotion (critical comments) were likely to suffer a relapse during a 9-month follow-up period. Higher social support is associated with more rapid recovery from bipolar disorder (Johnson, Winett, Meyer, Greenhouse, & Miller, 1999).

There appears to be a mild association between bipolar disorder and the upper socioeconomic classes (Goodnick, 1998). One study suggests two characteristics of people at risk for bipolar disorder that may be common in upper social classes: high achievement ambition and resentment of the perceived obligation to achieve (Peven, 1996).

Risk and Protective Factors for the Course of the Disorder

It should not be surprising that people with bipolar disorder tend to experience serious social and occupational problems: social withdrawal due to low self-esteem, the loss or absence of intimate relationships, increased dependence on others, family conflicts, job loss, and disruptions in social routines (Kahn, 1990). The person's mood swings and erratic behavior may be a source of ongoing turmoil in family, peer, and professional relationships (Johnson et al., 1999). Manic individuals test the limits of their relationships until others are exhausted, frustrated, and drained of empathy. Given the mean age of onset in young adulthood and the higher risk of recurrence as the client ages, most spouses, family, friends, and peers do not experience the client in a manic state until their relationship has already developed. Significant others become confused by perceived changes in the client's personality.

Married people with bipolar disorder are at a high risk for divorce (Clarkin, Carpenter, Hull, Wilner, & Glick, 1998). They become dependent on the spouse for support in times of crisis, but spouses tend to see the mania at least in part as a willful act. The "well" spouse's self-esteem can diminish while being blamed for the family's problems, acting as a buffer between the client and the community, and making many concessions to the client in an effort to maintain family stability. If the marriage continues, other problems may include the "well" spouse's guilt feelings, growing need to control the relationship, and at times even a learned dependence on the client's pathology for the relationship to persist. Further, the client may drain the family's financial resources with spending sprees, debt accumulation, and treatment costs.

These same interpersonal patterns contribute to the bipolar client's occupational problems. One study indicated a stable working capacity in only 45% of clients, and 28% experienced a steady decline in job status and performance (Hirschfeld, Lewis, & Vornik, 2003). Missed work, poor work quality, and conflicts with coworkers all contribute to the downward trend for clients who cannot maintain mood stability. Even though bipolar clients experience lengthy periods of normal mood functioning, occupational functioning can be irreparably damaged by behaviors during mood swings. If the disorder becomes manifest at a young age, the client may not have achieved adequate education and skills to establish a productive work career.

The client and family's denial or lack of insight into the disorder poses another problem (Ouimette et al., 1996). When manic, the client may be reluctant to accept the need for medication and other interventions (Swartz & Frank, 2001). Episodes of mania and depression tend to be brief in comparison with the duration of normal mood activity, and the client may decide after a period of stability that there is no longer a need for precautionary interventions. This is a major concern because it is recommended that most bipolar clients take medication during the active phases of the disorder *and* during periods of stability (Sachs, Printz, Kahn, Carpenter, & Docherty, 2000). This problem is accentuated by the diminished ability of the client to distinguish normal from abnormal mood states. Further, once a manic episode begins, the client's denial becomes more pronounced.

The bipolar client may experience additional emotional problems related to fears of the recurrence of mania and dealing with the loss of relationships and his or her former sense of self. The stigma associated with having bipolar disorder may create problems with self-confidence and esteem (Pardoen, Bauwens, Tracy, Martin, & Mendlewicz, 1993). In fact, the lifetime risk of suicide for those with bipolar disorder is 19%, the highest of any mental disorder (Sands & Harrow, 2000). Suicide attempts may be motivated by several factors, of course, including the wish to die, not to be a burden to others, to punish others, or a nonverbal communication of distress (Miklowitz, 1996).

An adolescent who develops bipolar disorder may experience an arrest in psychological development, acquiring self-efficacy and dependency problems that endure into adulthood (Floersch, 2003). It is also well established that people in both manic and depressive cycles often abuse drugs and alcohol in an effort to "treat" the symptoms. There is a 60% lifetime risk of substance abuse among clients with bipolar disorder (Goodnick, 1998).

Evidence-Based Intervention Strategies

Medications

The medications discussed here are used to treat both types of bipolar disorder. Much of the following discussion is based on the APA's expert consensus guidelines for the drug treatment of bipolar disorder (Sachs et al., 2000). The primary medications used to stabilize a client with bipolar disorder are lithium and valproate, although several other medications have also proven effective. Most physicians recommend that clients take medications even when their mood stabilizes, to reduce the risk of recurrence of another mood episode. When a client is in a manic state, physicians want a quick positive response to a mood stabilizer. If there is no such response within a week, another medication will probably be used. A third drug may be used if a partial response seems to plateau after 2 weeks.

Lithium Carbonate

Lithium, a drug that is available as a tablet, capsule, and injection, is the best studied of the mood-stabilizing drugs. It is relatively inexpensive because it occurs naturally. Pooled response rates from double-blind studies of lithium indicate significant improvement in 70% of clients (Tondo et al., 1998). Lithium reduces manic symptoms by half in 50% of clients after 3 weeks of treatment, and within 2 weeks 20% of clients are completely free of symptoms. It is more effective in treating classic mania than the mixed mania or rapid cycling bipolar disorder. When the full spectrum of bipolar disorders is considered, adequate response rates may be only 50% (Bowden, 1996). With a relatively short half-life, lithium must be taken more than once a day (unless used in time-release form). Lithium takes 2 or more weeks to establish a therapeutic effect. After a client's manic episode recedes, lithium (or any mood-stabilizing medication) is usually still taken to guard against recurrence of an active episode.

Lithium use does not preclude the possibility of a recurrence of mania. It has been shown more effective than placebo in preventing manic relapse (79 to 37%) in clients monitored for up to 1 year (Keck & McElroy, 1996). Longer term studies, however, indicate that a substantial number of clients do not adequately respond to lithium maintenance treatment. A 5-year study of clients who had been symptom-free for 2 years indicated an 83% probability against relapse after 1 year, 52% after 3 years, and 37% after 5 years (Peselow, Fieve, Difiglia, & Sanfilipo, 1994). Other studies determined a 36% recurrence of mania after 5 years (Maj, Pirozzi, & Kemali, 1990) and a 73% rate of relapse into mania or depression among clients followed for an average of 4.3 years (O'Connell, Mayo, Flatow, Cuthbertson, & O'Brien, 1991). Nemeroff (2000) reports a 40% recurrence of mania within 2 years after recovery from an episode and that 55% of lithium users develop resistance to the drug after 3 years. Combination treatments of lithium and other medications (antidepressant, antipsychotic, and anticonvulsant drugs) may improve the long-range outcome, but it is clear that bipolar disorder cannot be fully stabilized with lithium or any other drug.

Like other drugs, lithium is only effective as long as a steady blood level of the drug is maintained. Because the amount of the drug in the client's blood is equal to that in the nervous system, lithium levels are easily monitored. People who take lithium must get their blood drawn regularly. The difference between therapeutic and toxic levels is not great, so monitoring blood levels is particularly important. Routine monitoring of lithium levels may be performed monthly for the first 4 to 6 months. For the remainder of the first year, these measures can be obtained every 2 to 4 months and every 6 months thereafter. At low levels, the medication has no effect, and high levels indicate possible toxicity, which can be physically dangerous.

The high likelihood that clients with bipolar disorder will eventually experience a relapse reflects the nature of the disorder and the limitations of current medication regimens. Clients should be informed that one of the most common reasons for relapse is the discontinuation of an effective medication regimen against medical advice. When a physician recommends discontinuing lithium, it is lowered gradually because of a possible rebound effect (rapid recurrence) of mania or depression with the rapid discontinuation of lithium. After the remission of acute symptoms and a 6- to 12-week continuation stage, lithium treatment of acute mania may be gradually tapered. Physicians differ in their opinions about how long after recovery from a manic phase lithium should be prescribed, but it is generally done for at least 1 year beyond the point of stabilization following a first or second episode. After a client experiences a third mood cycle, the physician may recommend permanent medication use for preventive purposes.

Most of the common side effects of lithium are transient and benign. They need to be carefully monitored, however, particularly with the introduction of the medication or with dosage changes, because serious symptoms may develop. Thirst and weight gain are often experienced, with fatigue, hand tremor, muscle weakness, and confusion being less common. The potentially serious side effects include severe diarrhea, dizziness, nausea, fatigue, slurred speech, and spastic muscle movements. When lithium toxicity is suspected, the social worker should advise the client to discontinue the medication and contact a physician immediately.

Lithium should not be prescribed for women during pregnancy, as it is associated with fetal heart problems (Bowden, 2000). It is excreted in breast milk and thus should not be used by women while breastfeeding. Lithium seems to have an antiaggression effect on children and adolescents (Carlson, 2002). It is not advised for children under age 8, as its effects on them have not been adequately studied. For older children and adolescents, whose systems tend to clear medications quickly, a higher dose may be required to achieve a therapeutic effect. Adolescents appear to tolerate long-term lithium treatment well, but there are concerns about its accumulation in bone tissue and effect on thyroid and kidney function. Their decreased kidney clearance rates put older adults at a higher risk for toxic blood levels (Schatzberg & Nemeroff, 2001). They may be prescribed a smaller dose because they metabolize drugs more slowly.

The Anticonvulsant Medications

Two other medications, formally classified as anticonvulsants, are also effective drugs for the treatment of bipolar disorder (Tohen & Grundy, 1999). They appear to increase the prevalence of the GABA neurotransmitter, which has antimanic properties, in the nervous system. They increase levels of GABA by blocking the effects of GABA antagonists. Valproate is the most thoroughly tested of these drugs, and its effectiveness has resulted in its FDA approval as an antimanic drug. It has become a first-line choice for this purpose, along with lithium. Carbamazepine is a leading alternative to lithium and valproate. A third anticonvulsant drug, lamotrigine, is used less often to treat mania, but it is the only medication that has been shown to be effective for bipolar depression in a large randomized trial. Like lithium, all of these drugs need to be taken more than once daily to maintain a therapeutic level. Their prescription does not require frequent blood tests, however, because they do not share lithium's characteristic of being evenly distributed throughout the circulatory and nervous systems.

These medications offer several advantages over lithium. When effective, they begin to stabilize the consumer's mood in as few as 2 to 5 days (compared to lithium's 14 days). The drugs reduce the frequency of cycles with the same effectiveness as lithium, and there is some evidence that they are more effective maintenance drugs (Nemeroff, 2000). In studies conducted during the 1980s, clients were consistently found to increase remission periods by 60% with the anticonvulsant drugs (Coxhead, Silverstone, & Cookson, 1992). Further, the medications do not seem to potentiate a rebound mood episode with sudden discontinuation.

Valproate is comparable in effectiveness to lithium in treating acute mania, with 60 to 70% of consumers responding to its antimanic actions (Nemeroff, 2000). Results from several studies suggest that valproate decreases the likelihood of relapse or recurrence during maintenance therapy (Tohen & Grundy, 1999). Maintenance doses are similar to its acute-phase doses, given its relatively narrow range of therapeutic effect. Valproate appears to be a better drug than carbamazepine in treating rapid-cycling clients.

There is evidence that carbamazepine has a greater antidepressant effect than lithium, and it is occasionally used as an adjunct with traditional antidepressant drugs (Nemeroff, 2000). Carbamazepine has been found slightly less effective than lithium in treating acute mania. Results across studies demonstrate that 60 to 70% of clients show significant recovery from a manic state with the medication, with an average response rate of 32% for depression and 52% for mania (Sachs et al., 2000). The effectiveness of carbamazepine seems to be greater in non-rapid-cycling clients. A review of studies of the effectiveness of carbamazepine in the maintenance treatment of clients with rapid-cycling bipolar disorder indicates response rates of 57% for depression and 59% for mania (Calabrese et al., 2001). Carbamazepine also has demonstrated efficacy in people with poor response to lithium (Tohen & Grundy, 1999).

There is a trend in psychiatry of prescribing the anticonvulsant drugs more frequently as an initial treatment strategy. Fenn et al. (1996) conducted a 5-year study at a veterans' medical center and found that, although the use of valproate was negligible in 1989, the medication accounted for 25% of standard antimanic treatment for bipolar disorder in 1994, while the rate of lithium therapy declined from 84% to 43% of clients. Lithium and valproate may be used in combination for an additive antimanic effect, as neither interferes with the metabolism of the other. Lithium should not, however, be used with carbamazepine.

The common and generally transient side effects of carbamazepine include dizziness, sedation, short-term anorexia, constipation, diarrhea, and gastric distress resulting in nausea (Leonard, 2003). Acute confusion, double vision, and impaired muscle coordination are less common. Extremely rare but serious adverse effects include anemia and agranulocytosis (lowered white blood cell count). Its side effects tend to be more discomforting than the other drugs, and less than 50% of clients who use the medication are still taking it 1 year later (Nemeroff, 2000). With valproate, common and short-term adverse effects include nausea, sedation, weight gain, tremor, and hair loss. Less common effects include anxiety, depression, hand tremor, headache, and impaired muscle coordination.

The same considerations about lithium for pregnant women, children, and older adults apply to the anticonvulsant medications. However, carbamazepine is used more cautiously with children, as it can precipitate aggression. It has also been associated with developmental and cranial defects in newborns and thus may represent a higher risk for pregnant women than valproate.

Newer anticonvulsant drugs are available, including gabapentin and topiramate, although they are still considered to be experimental (Calabrese, Sachs, Ascher, Monaghan, & Rudd, 1999; Goldberg, 2000). Their use is reserved for those who do not responded to other medications.

Antidepressants

Antidepressant medications are not generally used for the treatment of bipolar I disorder. They have been shown to induce mania in as many as a third of all clients, and a fourth of consumers experience the activation of a rapid-cycling course (Goldberg, Harrow, & Grossman, 1995). These medications are generally used only after nonresponse to mood stabilizers (Goldberg, 2000). In bipolar II disorder, however, antidepressants are used along with an antimania drug for mood stabilization. The selective serotonin reuptake inhibitors can be effective, but venlafaxine and bupropion have demonstrated particularly positive outcomes for these clients. After a first episode of bipolar depression, antidepressant therapy should be tapered in 2 to 6 months, a much shorter continuation period than is advised for nonbipolar depression.

Antipsychotic Medications

We noted earlier that a variety of antipsychotic medications are used with mood-stabilizing medications to control mania until the primary medications take effect. Approximately a third of people with the disorder use these during the maintenance phase of treatment. Among the newer antipsychotic medications, clozapine, risperidone, and quetiapine have been tested as treatment adjuncts for bipolar disorder. Olanzapine became the first atypical antipsychotic drug to be approved by the FDA for the treatment of acute mania, following its positive research results (Berk, Ichim, & Brook, 1999). It is hypothesized that, due to their dopamine and serotonin antagonist activity, these drugs may affect mania and depression as well as psychosis. One study indicated that risperidone was successful in decreasing agitation, psychosis, sleep disturbances, and rapid cycling among clients with bipolar disorder (Stahl, 1996). The mild side-effect profile of the drug makes it a potentially attractive alternative to other antipsychotic medications. Clozapine has been found effective with clients who have schizoaffective disorder, and the overlap of symptoms suggests a possible role in bipolar disorder (Bowden, 1996).

Medications Under Investigation

Drugs from several other classes appear to have potential as antimanic agents, by themselves or as adjuncts to the primary drugs (Tohen & Grundy, 1999). These include benzodiazepines and calcium channel blockers. Research on the effectiveness of these agents is limited, however.

Use of Medications with Children

Lithium, carbamazepine, and valproate are all used in the treatment of children with bipolar disorder. Some pharmacology textbooks indicate that they are generally safe medications. Still, as is true of many psychotropic medications, few studies have been done to establish long-term safety. For example, valproate is suspected of producing liver toxicity in some children (Ghaemi, 2003). The prospects of chronic weight problems and long-term effects on kidney function for all of these medications need to be considered.

Psychosocial Interventions

There is no evidence to suggest that psychotherapy without medication can eliminate the risk for bipolar disorder in persons with other predisposing factors. However, psychosocial interventions have an important role in educating the client about the illness and its repercussions so that it can be controlled (Rothbaum & Austin, 2000). The chronic nature of bipolar disorder is difficult for an individual to come to terms with, and psychosocial interventions can help clients deal with the effects of past episodes on their lives, comprehend the significance of the disorder to their self-image, and make plans to minimize future problems (Jamison, 1991).

Family and Family Group Intervention

Because bipolar disorder is confusing to the client and those close to him or her in the best of circumstances, the social worker should always include didactic education as part of an intervention program (Bauer & McBride, 1996). The goals of psychoeducation are to reduce the high rates of medication nonadherence among clients, enhance social and occupational functioning, recruit family and spouse support as appropriate, and identify psychosocial stresses that may trigger mood episodes (Miklowitz & Goldstein, 1997). The more that a client and those in his or her environment understand about the disorder, the more able they will be to manage it. In earlier sections of this chapter, the etiology and life problems associated with bipolar disorder were described, and this information is appropriate for sharing with clients during the stabilization phase of the disorder.

There is much evidence that expressed emotion (EE), defined as excessive amounts of face-to-face contact and hostile and critical comments between clients and their relatives, is associated with poorer outcomes (Simoneau, Miklowitz, & Saleem, 1998). A variety of family intervention models have been effective in influencing the course of bipolar disorder. One inpatient family intervention program consisted of six 1-hour sessions focused on understanding and accepting the illness, identifying possible precipitating stresses, understanding family interactions that promote stress, planning for stress management, and accepting the need for ongoing intervention after discharge (Clarkin et al., 1990). To study its effectiveness, 21 clients were randomly assigned to experimental and control conditions. Six and 18 months after discharge, clients in the model program demonstrated better outcomes, but the treatment effect was limited to females. The researchers speculated that women may be more socialized to work with their families, whereas men might be prone to move toward independence too quickly.

Family-focused treatment (FFT) is an intervention that attempts to improve family functioning through training members in communication and problem-solving skills and providing education about the illness (Miklowitz & Goldstein, 1997). Three major components to the therapy are family education (about the nature, symptoms, prognosis, and etiology of bipolar disorder), communication training (active listening, delivering positive and negative verbal feedback, and requesting changes in the behavior of others), and problem solving (identifying and defining problems, generating and evaluating solutions, and implementing solutions).

Each component is provided for 2 to 9 sessions depending on the assessed needs of the family. In the authors' research, families received an average of 20 sessions, provided by two cotherapists who had undergone a 2-year training procedure. They received weekly individual and group supervision to ensure adherence to FFT protocols. Intervention sessions occurred weekly for the first 3 months, biweekly for the second 3 months, and monthly for the final 3 sessions. Modeling and behavioral rehearsal in the form of role plays and homework assignments helped clients and family members generalize their new skills to their home settings.

Miklowitz et al. (2000) randomly assigned 101 clients to a 1-year program of FFT or to medication and crisis management. Results indicated that clients receiving FFT achieved longer periods without relapse than clients in the comparison groups. The greatest effects were found for depressive symptoms. Further, after 9 months of FFT, clients and family members were found to be using more positive communication skills, and this appeared to predict later symptom amelioration. Clients from the FFT program were found to have more positive nonverbal interaction patters during a 1-year posttreatment problem-solving assessment than families who received the control intervention (Simoneau, Miklowitz, Richards, Saleem, & George, 1999).

Other researchers have shown that multifamily groups lead to a decrease in expressed emotion among families (Honig, Hofman, Rozendaal, & Dingemans, 1997). In one study, psychoeducation for spouses was found to be more effective than psychoeducation for clients alone with regard to the client's social adjustment and global functioning (Clarkin et al., 1998).

Other Group Interventions

Family members need not participate for groups to have positive outcomes for persons with bipolar disorder. Colom et al. (2003) conducted a randomized trial of the efficacy of group psychoeducation in the prevention of episode recurrences for 120 bipolar clients whose disorders were in remission (the controls attended nonstructured group meetings). Through 21 sessions, group topics focused on medication adherence, coping with environmental stress triggers, and issues related to social and occupational functioning. With 2 years of follow-up, the researchers found that the experimental program significantly reduced the number of client relapses and the number of relapses per client and increased the time span between recurrences of depressive, manic, or mixed episodes. Clients in the experimental group also had fewer and shorter hospitalizations. The authors concluded that the differences between the two groups were due to the experimental group's emphasis on overall treatment adherence, early recognition of symptoms of relapse, and modifications of clients' daily routines (Colom, 2002).

Individual Intervention

Nonmedical interventions cannot alter the chemical processes that contribute to bipolar disorder, but they can help the client organize his or her life to minimize the risk of recurrences and to deal with the interpersonal problems that often result from a manic or depressive episode. One manual-based therapy that focuses on repairing these kinds of conflicts is interpersonal therapy. This therapy is based on the assumption that interpersonal conflicts are a major source of depression for clients, including those with bipolar disorder (Frank et al., 1994). It also assumes that circadian (sleep/wake cycle) and social rhythms influence the course of affective disorders (Frank & Novick, 2002). The therapy focuses on strategies for addressing a client's unresolved grief, interpersonal disputes, interpersonal deficits, and role transitions (Swartz & Markowitz, 1995). During assessment, the practitioner pays particular attention to the client's current relationships with an "interpersonal inventory." The client and practitioner devise tasks toward improvements in these areas. Interpersonal therapy also incorporates behavioral interventions with the assumption that certain life events may trigger manic or depressive episodes by disrupting one's schedule of daily living activities (regular times for sleep, meals, exercise, and work). The client's relationship with the practitioner is used as a model for making changes in other relationships. Studies of interpersonal therapy show that it can bring about increased stability in daily rhythms that are believed to protect against the recurrence of bipolar disorder (Rothbaum & Austin, 2000). The therapy emphasizes the importance of sustaining positive interpersonal relationships with others as a means of maintaining this stability.

In addition to family interventions and interpersonal therapy, cognitive-behavioral interventions can be effective with clients who have bipolar disorder. These interventions challenge a client's cognitions that may activate episodes of mania or depression, and they can also target cognitions related to medication compliance. The effectiveness of these approaches with bipolar disorder has not been tested with controlled trials, but the available literature supports the effectiveness of the technique (Scott, 1996; Swartz & Frank, 2001). Cognitive-behavioral therapy, compared with standard medical treatment, helped to reduce symptoms and increase functional outcome in four studies (Meyer & Hautzinger, 2002). One study with a small sample supported cognitive-behavioral therapy as a means of reducing the residual symptoms of bipolar disorder and enhancing lithium compliance (Fava, Bartolucci, Rafanelli, & Mangelli, 2001).

Case Illustration

Donna was a single, 23-year-old college student in her final undergraduate semester. She was referred to the community mental health center following a 1-month hospitalization for an initial manic episode. She had been psychotic with paranoid delusions during this episode, which was also characterized by sleeplessness, hyperactivity, racing thoughts, hypersexuality, and alcohol abuse. Donna, who had never lived away from her parents, was well stabilized on lithium and thiothixene at the time of her agency intake. She was still quite anxious, frightened by what had happened, and reluctant to resume her normal activities for fear of precipitating another manic episode. She also reported having two periods of depression during the past year. She lost all of her energy, stayed home in her room, took naps, felt tired, and often cried about her inability to force herself to be more active. Donna had not been suicidal. Her parents worried during her depressive phases that Donna was upset about her lack of a clear career path and having few friends.

Donna was the second oldest of six children in a family that experienced much internal tension. Her father was a laborer in a concrete manufacturing company. Still bitter about an early-career bankruptcy, he was a long-term alcohol abuser (an indicator of a possible affective disorder) and was physically abusive of his wife. Most of the children were attractive, socially sophisticated, and outwardly successful, but there was a shared family denial of the father's problem behaviors. Donna stated that she had "no direction" in life. She was by all accounts the child most dependent on her parents and for that reason the scapegoat for the family problems. Her father often said, "If only Donna would grow up, we could all accomplish so much more." Donna became anxious whenever they were out of town and in fact had experienced her manic episode while they were on a vacation.

With only two semesters remaining in her college curriculum, Donna had begun failing or dropping essential courses, apparently postponing graduation and the onset of adulthood. These milestones, viewed by many young adults as exciting accomplishments, symbolized for Donna a troubling end to her adolescence. She had always felt fearful of independent living and liked to rely on her parents for financial and emotional support. She felt personally inadequate and wished to continue living with her parents. Her sleep patterns became fitful; she was often awake and wandered about the house at night. The fact that Donna's bipolar symptoms emerged along with her family's rising expectations of her self-sufficiency seemed significant.

Donna felt bad about herself as she recovered from the manic episode, but she was a willing participant in the agency's services. Her parents seemed supportive of her getting rehabilitation help, even though they had difficulty comprehending what had happened to their daughter.

In summary, Donna's personal and family circumstances included various risk factors for bipolar disorder as well as risk and protective factors for its course. Regarding risks, Donna's father was a long-time alcohol abuser, which may have masked an affective disorder. There were long-standing interpersonal conflicts among all family members, creating an unsettled domestic situation. Most of the children felt alienated from their father, and they seemed to be in competition for their mother's favor, which created an atmosphere of distrust. Donna was extremely dependent on her parents for meeting her basic needs and was afraid of moving away from home. She had little available extended family, as her father had passively allowed those relationships to dissolve over the years. Most people outside the family perceived Donna as friendly, but she had few close relationships with peers and never any boyfriends, so her social skills were not well developed. Finally, she admitted to an irregular sleep-wake cycle when stressed, characterized by bouts of insomnia (3–5 hours of sleep per night) for several weeks at a time.

In speculating about the course of the disorder, Donna had access to several important protective factors. She was a voluntary participant in treatment and willing to take prescribed medications. Her social worker had informational access to a variety of support resources in the community that she could utilize. Donna's parents were interested in her welfare. Some risks were also present, however, including ongoing family conflict, her parents' ambivalence about participating in a psychoeducational group, and Donna's persistently dependent attitudes toward her caregivers.

Diagnosis

Axis I: Bipolar I disorder, most recent episode mixed, severe with psychotic features, in partial remission

Donna has recently experienced both depressive and manic episodes. She had two major depressive episodes in the past year that lasted approximately 3 weeks each. At those times, she had felt extremely sad, became withdrawn, and avoided all activities outside the family. She took regular naps and complained of chronic fatigue. She felt worthless and had occasional crying spells. With her more recent manic episode, the abnormal, elevated mood lasted for 2 full weeks, including the hospitalization. She reported, and hospital records confirmed, that she experienced grandiose self-esteem, got very little sleep, was continuously talkative, had racing thoughts, and was sexually promiscuous. She had delusional ideas about her future as a businesswoman and had been fearful of encountering the Devil, who she thought was pursuing her in human form. Donna's mania had remitted within 1 week of her hospitalization and the introduction of medications.

Axis II: Dependent Personality Features

The social worker was struck by Donna's high level of dependence on others, especially her parents, and believed that these issues would be significant in her counseling. These characteristics included Donna's difficulty in making decisions, need for her parents to assume responsibility for her life, an inability to disagree with others, and difficulty in initiating and sustaining any personal projects because of her lack of confidence. He did not want to diagnose a personality disorder, but by highlighting the presence of features of this disorder, he could make them a part of the focus of the intervention.

Axis III

None. There were no physical causes or contributors to her Axis I or II disorders.

Axis IV: Problems with primary support group and problems related to the social environment

Donna was having difficulty with life transition issues, most prominently her move into adulthood (she was adult by age and with her college degree would be recognized as an adult by her society). She was also aware that her parents, in spite of their support, might begin to have different occupational expectations of her following her college graduation.

Axis V

Current GAF = 60 (moderate symptoms of her disorder, moderate difficulty in social and school functioning); highest GAF during the past year = 70 (no symptoms of bipolar disorder, only slight problems with school and social functioning).

Intervention Plan

Goal: Donna will avoid severe mood swings through the regular use of appropriate medications.

- Objective: Monthly visits with the agency psychiatrist for the prescription and monitoring of lithium and thiothixene
- Objective: Weekly visits with agency clinical social worker for review of mental status and to monitor effectiveness of medications, including any adverse effects

Goal: Donna will reduce the nature of her life stresses that might contribute to bipolar mood episodes.

- Objective: Weekly visits with the agency social worker to explore the nature of predictable life stresses and develop skills for coping with them

Goal: Donna will establish personal goals and begin working toward them.

- Objective: Weekly meetings with the social worker in which the client will (a) be permitted to think about and set her own goals regarding schooling, work, social life, family participation, and work and (b) develop beginning plans for achieving these goals

Goal: Donna and her family will share a supportive family environment.

- Objective: Parents will attend the agency education and support group for relatives of persons with bipolar disorder.
- Objective: Monthly meetings between the social worker, client, and parents to help set mutually agreeable expectations for the client's participation in family and social activities.

Goal: Donna will promote her ongoing mood stability through a structuring of her activities of daily living.

- Objective: Daily completion of the Social Rhythm Metric (see appendix), which will be reviewed in weekly session with the social worker.

Critique of the Diagnosis

The onset of bipolar disorder appears to result from a complex set of biological, psychological, and, to a lesser extent, social factors. Prior to the publication of *DSM-III*, when it was known as manic depression or manic depressive illness, this disorder was conceptualized by many clinical theorists and practitioners as a primarily psychological strategy for dealing with internal and environmental stress. Today, however, research overwhelmingly suggests that biological factors are predominant, and other factors may account more for the timing and course of the disorder than for its onset. Although much remains to be learned about the causes of bipolar disorder, its onset appears to require certain biological processes that occur independently of external factors. For this reason, it has legitimacy within the social work value system as a mental disorder. Its combinations of manic and depressive episodes and cycles (although they may require observation of the client over time to validate) are also unique among disorders in the *DSM*.

Still, there are several controversial aspects to the diagnosis of bipolar disorder. First, the society at large seems to maintain a sense of uncertainty and ambivalence about the role of psychological and social factors in the disorder, as family members and others struggle with how to respond to the disruptive behaviors of clients, particularly when they are in a manic state. Second, the disorder has been diagnosed more often in children and adolescents in the past 20 years. There is much disagreement about the symptom profile in this age group, raising issues of its validity. Another issue, also related to diagnostic validity, is the relationship of bipolar I and bipolar II disorder and of bipolar II disorder and major depression. These distinctions were only established with the publication of *DSM-IV* in 1994, and the differences between these sets of disorders remains somewhat unclear.

Summary

Bipolar disorder is a disorder of mood in which, over time, a person experiences one or more manic episodes that are usually accompanied by one or more major depressive episodes. The disorder is associated with chemical imbalances in the nervous system. Social workers are active in the assessment, intervention, and mental status monitoring of persons with bipolar disorder, because it is a long-term mental illness that can result in a variety of problems in social functioning. Social workers need to be aware of the actions of the mood-stabilizing medications, both positive and negative, because they frequently spend more time providing interventions for clients than the prescribing physicians do. Practitioners also need to be aware of the serious impact of bipolar disorder on a client's sense of self so that they can provide psychosocial interventions to help clients organize and maintain productive lives with minimal symptom recurrence.

Appendix: Instruments Used to Assess Bipolar Disorder

Altman Self-Rating Mania Scale

Altman, Hedeker, Peterson, & Davis (1997)

Description

- A five-item, self-administered multiple-choice scale to measure manic symptoms.
- Each item is rated on a continuum of 0–4.
- Includes subscales for mania, psychosis, irritability.

Reliability

Test-retest reliability of .86 to .89 (with 1- to 7-day intervals for inpatient clients)

Validity

Cronbach's alpha = .79 for the mania subscale, .65 for the psychosis and irritability subscales; correlations of .72 and .77 with the Mania Rating Scale and the Clinician-Administered Altman Scale for Mania.

Clinician-Administered Rating Scale: Mania

Altman, Hedeker, Janicak, & Peterson (1995)

Description

- A 15-item scale for practitioner use in diagnosing and monitoring mania in adults. Each item rates a different symptom of mania.
- The scale includes two factors: mania and psychosis. The first 10 items measure mania, and the final 5 items measure symptoms of psychosis.
- Each item includes a Likert-type rating format from 0–5 and includes 2–4 prompt questions for the interviewer.

Reliability

Interrater reliability = .81 for individual scores, .93 for total scores, .78 for the mania subscale, and .95 for the psychosis subscale (14 clients, 5 raters).

Validity

Concurrent validity with the Mania Rating Scale = .94.

General Behavior Inventory (Adapted)

Youngstrom, Findling, Danielson, & Calabrese (2001)

Description

- A 73-item scale to be administered by parents to measure hypomanic, depressive, and mixed symptoms in children and adolescents.
- Each item rates behavior on a scale of 0–3, with higher scores indicating more severe symptoms.

Reliability

Cronbach's alpha = .97 for the depression subscale, .96 for the hypomania subscale.

Validity

Discriminant function analysis indicated accuracy of placement of respondents into diagnostic groups.

The Internal State Scale

Bauer, Crits-Cristoph, & Ball (1991)

Description

- 17 statements describing characteristics of a person's possible mood states during the past 24 hours.

- Takes 10–15 minutes to administer.
- Includes a "visual analog" response format; the respondent places a mark along a nonanchored continuum from "not at all or rarely" to "very much so or much of the time"; each analog is scored from 0 to 100.
- Includes the four subscales of activation (0–500), perceived conflict (0–500), well-being (0–300), and depression (0–200).
- Cutoff score for depression: less than 125 on the well-being subscale; for hypomania/mania -125 or higher on the well-being subscale and 200 or more on the activation subscale; for remission: 125 or higher on the well-being subscale and less than 200 on the activation subscale.

Reliability

Internal consistency was .84 for the activation subscale, .81 for the perceived conflict subscale, and .92 for the depression subscale.

Validity

- Only the activation subscale correlated with the YMRS (0.6); the depression subscale correlated with the HRDS (.84).
- A discriminant function analysis showed that the subscales assigned 88% of subjects to the correct diagnostic groups.

Social Rhythm Metric (SRM)

Monk, Flaherty, Frank, Hoskinson, & Kupfer (1990)

Description

- A 17-item instrument designed to measure activities that are important to structuring one's day. It is intended for use during the depressive phase of the affective disorder.
- 15 items represent typical daily events, and 2 other items are open-ended.
- The theoretical basis for the instrument is that regularity of social rhythms is important to stable mood.
- The scale should be completed and scored daily by the client for 1 week and then averaged for an overall score.

Reliability

Test-retest reliability for a 1-week period was .44; low but statistically significant.

Validity

Limited to a comparison of scores for four subjects who had recently experienced interruptions in their routines. Their means between the disruptive events and when they returned to their normal routines was 1.95 and
3.06.

Young Mania Rating Scale

Young, Biggs, Ziegler, & Meyer (1978)

Description

- An 11-item scale that measures symptoms of mania. The scale measures manic state rather than manic traits and is not intended to be
  diagnostic.
- Each item is scored along a continuum from 0 (absent) to 4 (extreme). Four items are given twice the weight as the other seven
  items to compensate for poor cooperation from severely ill respondents. Scores may range from 0 to 60.
- Should be administered in the context of a 15–30 minute clinical interview based on the client's report of his or her condition during the
  previous 48 hours and the practitioner's behavioral observations,
  with an emphasis on the latter.

Reliability

Interrater reliability = .93 for total scores, .66–.92 for individual items

Validity

Positive correlations were found with the Beigel-Murphy Scale (.71) and
the Petterson Rating Scale (.89).

References

American Psychiatric Association. (2000). *Diagnostic and statistical manual of mental
    disorders* (4th ed., rev.). Washington, DC: Author.
Barondes, S. H. (1997). *Mood genes: Hunting for origins of mania and depression.* New
    York: W. H. Freeman.
Bauer, M., & McBride, L. (1996). *Structured group psychotherapy for bipolar disorder:
    The life goals program.* New York: Springer.
Berk, M., Ichim, L., Brook, S. (1999) Olanzapine compared to lithium in mania: A
    double-blind randomized controlled trial. *International Clinical Psychopharma-
    cology, 14*(6), 339–343.

Bowden, C. L. (1996). Role of newer medications for bipolar disorder. *Journal of Clinical Psychopharmacology, 16*(2, Suppl. 1), 48–55.

Bowden, C. L. (2000). Efficacy of lithium in mania and maintenance therapy of bipolar depression. *Journal of Clinical Psychiatry, 61*(Suppl. 9), 35–40.

Brown, A. (1994). The treatment of bipolar disorder. *National Alliance for Research on Schizophrenia and Depression Newsletter*, pp. 13–18.

Calabrese, J. R., Sachs, G. S., Ascher, J., Monaghan, E., & Rudd, G. S. (1999). A double-blind, placebo-controlled study of lamotrigine monotherapy in outpatients with bipolar I depression. *Journal of Clinical Psychiatry, 60*, 79–88.

Calabrese, J. R., Selton, M. D., Bowden, C. L., Rapport, D. J., Suppes, T., & Shirley, E. (2001). Bipolar rapid cycling: Focus on depression as its hallmark. *Journal of Clinical Psychiatry, 62*(Suppl. 14), 34–41.

Carlson, G. A. (2002). Bipolar disorder in children and adolescents: A critical review. In D. Shaffer & B. D. Waslick (Eds.), *The many faces of depression in children and adolescents* (pp. 105–123). Washington, DC: American Psychiatric Association.

Clarkin, J. F., Carpenter, D., Hull, J., Wilner, P., & Glick, I. (1998). Effects of psychoeducational intervention for married persons with bipolar disorder and their spouses. *Psychiatric Services, 49*, 531–533.

Clarkin, J. F., Glick, I. D., Haas, G. L., Spencer, J. H., Lewis, A. B., Peyser, F., et al. (1990). A randomized clinical trial of inpatient family intervention: V. Results for affective disorders. *Journal of Affective Disorders, 18*, 17–28.

Colom, F. (2002). The mechanism of action of psychotherapy. *Bipolar Disorders, 4*(Suppl. 1), 102.

Colom, F., Vieta, E., Martinez-Aran, A., Reinares, M., Goikolea, J. M., Beabarre, A., et al. (2003). A randomized trial on the efficacy of group psychoeducation in the prophylaxis of recurrences in bipolar patients whose disease is in remission. *Archives of General Psychiatry, 60*(4), 402–407.

Coxhead, N., Silverstone, T., & Cookson, J. (1992). Carbamazepine versus lithium in the prophylaxis of bipolar affective disorder. *Acta Psychiatry Scandinavia, 85*(2), 114–118.

Daly, I. (1997). Mania. *The Lancet, 349*(9059), 1157–1161.

Ellicott, A., Hammen, C., Gitlin, M., Brown, G., & Jamison, K. (1990). Life events and the course of bipolar disorder. *American Journal of Psychiatry, 147*, 1194–1198.

Evans, D. L. (2000). Bipolar disorder: Diagnostic challenges and treatment considerations. *Journal of Clinical Psychiatry, 61*(Suppl. 13), 26–31.

Fava, G. A., Bartolucci, G., Rafanelli, C., & Mangelli, L. (2001). Cognitive-behavioral management of patients with bipolar disorder who relapsed while on lithium prophylaxis. *Journal of Clinical Psychiatry, 62*, 556–559.

Fenn, H. H., Robinson, D., Luby, V., Dangel, C., Buxton, E., Beattie, M., et al. (1996). Trends in pharmacotherapy of schizoaffective and bipolar affective disorders: A 5-year naturalistic study. *American Journal of Psychiatry, 153*(5), 711–713.

Floersch, J. (2003). The subjective experience of youth psychotropic treatment. *Social Work in Mental Health, 1*(4), 51–69.

Frank, E., Kupfer, D. J., Ehlers, C. L., Monk, T. H., Cornes, C., Carter, S., et al. (1994). Interpersonal and social rhythm therapy for bipolar disorder: Integrating interpersonal and behavioral approaches. *Behavior Therapy, 17*, 143–149.

Frank, E., & Novick, D. (2002). Progress in the psychotherapy of mood disorders: Studies from the Western Psychiatric Institute and Clinic. *Epidemiologia e Psichiatria Sociale, 10*(4), 245–252.

Ghaemi, S. N. (2003). *Mood disorders: A practical guide.* Philadelphia: Lippincott Williams & Wilkins.

Ghaemi, S. N., Stoll, A. L., & Pope, H. G. (1995). Lack of insight in bipolar disorder: The acute manic episode. *Journal of Nervous and Mental Disease, 183*(7), 464–467.

Goldberg, J., & Keck, P. (1999). Summary of findings on the course and outcome of bipolar disorders. In J. Goldberg & M. Harrow (Eds.), *Bipolar disorders: Clinical course and outcome* (pp. 106–127). Washington, DC: American Psychiatric Association.

Goldberg, J. F. (2000). Treatment guidelines: Current and future management of bipolar disorder. *Journal of Clinical Psychiatry, 61*(Suppl. 13), 12–18.

Goldberg, J. F., Harrow, M., & Grossman, L. S. (1995). Course and outcome in bipolar affective disorder: A longitudinal follow-up study. *American Journal of Psychiatry, 152*, 379–384.

Goodnick, P. J. (Ed.). (1998). *Mania: Clinical and research perspectives.* Washington, DC: American Psychiatric Press.

Hilty, D., Brady, K., & Hales, R. (1999). A review of bipolar disorder among adults. *Psychiatric Services, 50*, 201–213.

Hirschfeld, R. M. A., Lewis, L., & Vornik, L. A. (2003). Perceptions and impact of bipolar disorder: How far have we come? Results of the National Depressive and Manic Depressive Association's 2000 survey of individuals with bipolar disorder. *Journal of Clinical Psychiatry, 64*(2), 161–174.

Honig, A., Hofman, A., Rozendaal, N., & Dingemans, P. (1997). Psycho-education in bipolar disorder: Effect on expressed emotion. *Psychiatry Research, 72*, 17–22.

Jamison, K. R. (1991). Manic-depressive illness: The overlooked need for psychotherapy. In B. D. Beitman & G. L. Klerman (Eds.), *Integrating pharmacotherapy and psychotherapy* (pp. 409–420). Arlington, VA: American Psychiatric Publishing.

Johnson, S. L., & Roberts, J. E. (1995). Life events and bipolar disorder: Implications from biological theories. *Psychological Bulletin, 117*, 434–449.

Johnson, S. L., Winett, C. A., Meyer, B., Greenhouse, W. J., & Miller, I. (1999). Social support and the course of bipolar disorder. *Journal of Abnormal Psychology, 108*, 558–566.

Kahn, D. (1990). The psychotherapy of mania. *Psychiatric Clinics of North America, 13*(2), 229–239.

Keck, P. E., & McElroy, S. L. (1996). Outcome in the pharmacologic treatment of bipolar disorder. *Journal of Clinical Psychopharmacology, 16*(2, Suppl. 1), 15S–22S.

Kinney, D., Yurgelum-Todd, D., Tohen, M., & Tramer, S. (1998). Pre- and perinatal complications and risk for bipolar disorder: A retrospective study. *Journal of Affective Disorders, 50*, 117–124.

Kovacs, M., & Pollock, M. (1995). Bipolar disorder and comorbid conduct disorder in childhood and adolescence. *American Academy of Child and Adolescent Psychiatry, 34*(6), 715–723.

Leonard, B. E. (2003). *Fundamentals of psychopharmacology*. New York: Martin Duwitz.

Lish, J. D., Dime-Meenan, S., Whybrow, P. C., Price, R. A., & Hirschfeld, R. (1994). The National Depressive and Manic-Depressive Association (DMDA) survey of bipolar members. *Journal of Affective Disorders, 31*(4), 281–294.

Maj, M., Pirozzi, R., & Kemali, D. (1990). Long-term outcome of lithium prophylaxis in bipolar patients. *Archives of General Psychiatry, 47*(7), 665–671.

Malkoff-Schwartz, S., Frank., E., Andersen, B., Sherrill, J. T., Siegel, L., Patterson, D., et al. (1998). Stressful life events and social rhythm disruption in the onset of manic and depressive bipolar episodes: A preliminary investigation. *Archives of General Psychiatry, 55*, 702–707.

McClellan, J., & Werry, J. (1997). Practice parameters for the assessment and treatment of children and adolescents with bipolar disorder. *Journal of the American Academy of Child and Adolescent Psychiatry, 36*(1), 138–157.

McGuffin, P., Rijsdijk, F., Andrew, M., Sham, P., Katz, R., & Cardino, A. (2003). The heritability of bipolar affective disorder and the genetic relationship to unipolar depression. *Archives of General Psychiatry, 60*, 497–502.

Meyer, T. D., & Hautzinger, M. (2002). Cognitive behavioral therapy in addition to pharmacotherapy for manic depressive disorders: Empirical results. *Nervenartz, 73*(7), 620–628.

Miklowitz, D. J. (1996). Psychotherapy in combination with drug treatment for bipolar disorder. *Journal of Clinical Psychopharmacology, 16*(2, Suppl. 1), 57–65.

Miklowitz, D. J., & Alloy, L. B. (1999). Psychosocial factors in the course and treatment of bipolar disorder: Introduction to the special section. *Journal of Abnormal Psychology, 108*(4), 555–557.

Miklowitz, D. J., & Goldstein, M. (1997). *Bipolar disorder: A family-focused treatment approach*. New York: Guilford.

Miklowitz, D. J., Simoneau, T. L., George, E. A., Richards, J., Kalbag, A., Sachs-Ericsson, N., et al. (2000). Family-focused treatment of bipolar disorder: One-year effects of a psychoeducational program in conjunction with pharmacotherapy. *Biological Psychiatry, 48*, 582–592.

Nemeroff, C. B. (2000). An ever-increasing pharmacopoeia for the management of patients with bipolar disorder. *Journal of Clinical Psychiatry, 61*(Suppl. 13), 19–25.

O'Connell, R. A., Mayo, J. A., Flatow, L., Cuthbertson, B, & O'Brien, B. E. (1991). Outcome of bipolar disorder on long-term treatment with lithium. *British Journal of Psychiatry, 159*(2), 123–129.

Ouimette, P., Klein, D., & Pepper, C. (1996). Personality traits in the first-degree relatives of outpatients with depressive disorders. *Journal of Affective Disorders, 39*, 43–53.

Pardoen, D., Bauwens, F., Tracy, A., Martin, F., & Mendlewicz, J. (1993). Self-esteem in recovered bipolar and unipolar out-patients. *British Journal of Psychiatry, 163*, 755–762.

Peselow, E. D., Fieve, R. R., Difiglia, C., & Sanfilipo, M. P. (1994). Lithium prophylaxis of bipolar illness: The value of combination treatment. *British Journal of Psychiatry, 164*(2), 208–214.

Peven, D. E. (1996). Individual psychology and bipolar mood disorder. In L. Sperry & J. Carlson (Eds.), *Psychopathology & psychotherapy: From DSM-IV diagnosis to treatment* (2nd ed., pp. 77–114). Washington, DC: Accelerated Development.

Post, R. M., Leverich, G. B., King, Q., & Weiss, S. R. (2001). Developmental vulnerabilities to the onset and course of bipolar disorder. *Development and Psychopathology, 13*(1), 581–598.

Reilly-Harrington, N. A., Alloy, L. B., Fresco, D. M., & Whitehouse, W. G. (1999). Cognitive styles and life events interact to predict bipolar and unipolar symptomatology. *Journal of Abnormal Psychology, 108,* 567–578.

Roberts, N., Parker, K., Woogh, C., Cripps, L., & Froese, A. (2000). Bipolar disorder in ADHD children grown up. *American Academy of Child and Adolescent Psychiatry, 39*(6), 678–679.

Rosenfarb, I. S., Miklowitz, D. J., Goldstein, M. J., Harmon, L., Nuechterlein, K. H., & Rea, M. M. (2001). Family transactions and relapse in bipolar disorder. *Family Process, 40*(1), 5–14.

Rothbaum, B. O., & Austin, M. C. (2000). Integration of pharmacotherapy and psychotherapy for bipolar disorder. *Journal of Clinical Psychiatry, 61*(Suppl. 9), 68–75.

Sachs, G. S., Printz, D. J., Kahn, D. A., Carpenter, D., & Docherty, J. P. (2000). *Medication treatment of bipolar disorder.* New York: McGraw-Hill.

Sadock, B. J., & Sadock, V. A. (2005). *Kaplan & Sadock's comprehensive textbook of psychiatry.* Philadelphia: Lippincott Williams & Wilkins.

Sands, J. R., & Harrow, M. (2000). Bipolar disorder: Psychopathology, biology, and diagnosis. In M. Hersen & A. S. Bellack (Eds.), *Psychopathology in adulthood* (2nd ed., pp. 326–347). Needham Heights, MA: Allyn & Bacon.

Schatzberg, A. F., & Nemeroff, C. B. (Eds.). (2001). *Essentials of clinical psychopharmacology.* Washington, DC: American Psychiatric Press.

Scott, J. (1996). The role of cognitive behavior therapy in bipolar disorders. *Behavioral and Cognitive Psychotherapy, 24,* 195–208.

Simoneau, T. L., Miklowitz, D. J., Richards, J. A., Saleem, R., & George, L. (1999). Bipolar disorder and family communication: The effects of a psychoeducational treatment program. *Journal of Abnormal Psychology, 108,* 588–597.

Simoneau, T. L., Miklowitz, D. J., & Saleem, R. (1998). Expressed emotion and interactional patterns in the families of bipolar patients. *Journal of Abnormal Psychology, 107*(3), 497–507.

Stahl, S. M. (1996). *Essential psychopharmacology: Neuroscientific basis and practical applications.* New York: Cambridge University Press.

Swartz, H. A., & Frank, E. (2001). Psychotherapy for bipolar depression: A phase specific treatment strategy. *Bipolar Disorders, 3*(1), 11–22.

Swartz, H. A., & Markowitz, J. C. (1995). Interpersonal psychotherapy. In I. D. Glick (Ed.), *Treating depression* (pp. 95–121). San Francisco, CA: Jossey-Bass.

Tohen, M., & Grundy, S. (1999). Pharmacologic approaches for treatment-resistant mania. *Psychiatric Annals, 28,* 629–632.

Tondo, L., Baldessarini, R. J., Hennen, J., Floris, G., Silvetti, F., & Tohen, M. (1998).

Lithium treatment and risk of suicidal behavior in bipolar disorder patients. *Journal of Clinical Psychiatry,59*, 405–414.

Woods, S. W. (2000). The economic burden of bipolar disease. *Journal of Clinical Psychiatry, 61*(Suppl. 13), 38–41.

Young, L. T., & Joffe, R. T. (Eds.). (1997). *Bipolar disorder: Biological models and their clinical application*. New York: Dekker.

References for Assessment Instruments for Bipolar Disorder

Altman, E. G., Hedeker, D. R., Janicak, P. G., & Peterson, J. L. (1995). The Clinician-Administered Rating Scale for Mania (CARS-M): Development, reliability, and validity. *Biological Psychiatry, 36*(2), 124–134.

Altman, E. G., Hedeker, D. R., Peterson, J. L., & Davis, J. M. (1997). The Altman self-rating mania scale. *Biological Psychiatry, 42*(10), 948–955.

Bauer, M. S., Crits-Cristoph, P., & Ball, W. A. (1991). Independent assessment of manic and depressive symptoms by self-rating: Scale characteristics and implications for the study of mania. *Archives of General Psychiatry, 48*, 807–812.

Monk, T. H., Flaherty, J. F., Frank, E., Hoskinson, K., & Kupfer, D. J. (1990). The social rhythm metric. An instrument to quantify the daily rhythm of life. *Journal of Nervous and Mental Disorders, 178*, 120–126.

Young, R. C., Biggs, J. T., Ziegler, V. E., & Meyer, D. A. (1978). A rating scale for mania: Reliability, validity, and sensitivity. *British Journal of Psychiatry, 133*, 429-435.

Youngstrom, E. A., Findling, R. L., Danielson, C. K., & Calabrese, J. R. (2001). Discriminative validity of hypomanic and depressive symptoms on the General Behavior Inventory. *Psychological Assessment, 13*(2), 267–276.

14 Schizophrenia and Other Psychotic Disorders

Schizophrenia is a mental disorder characterized by a person's abnormal patterns of thought and perception, as inferred from his or her language and behavior. The fact that it is primarily a disorder of *thought* distinguishes it from severe disorders of *mood* such as bipolar disorder. Schizophrenia includes two types of symptoms (American Psychiatric Association [APA], 2000). *Positive* symptoms represent exaggerations of normal behavior. These include hallucinations, delusions, disorganized thought processes, and tendencies toward agitation. The *negative* symptoms represent the diminution of what would be considered normal behavior. These include flat or blunted affect (the absence of expression), social withdrawal, noncommunication, anhedonia (blandness) or passivity, and ambivalence in decision making.

The person with schizophrenia experiences pronounced sensory changes (Benioff, 1995). *Visual* changes include heightened sensitivity to light and color, illusionary changes in faces and objects, and distortions in size. *Auditory* changes include hallucinations, heightened sensitivity to noise, an inability to screen out background noise, the muting of sounds, and distortions of the sounds of voices. *Physical* changes include heightened sensitivity to touch, an inability to interpret internal sensations, and tactile and olfactory hallucinations (described later). *Cognitive* changes include loose associations, the inability to filter out irrelevant information, distractibility, overstimulation of thoughts (flooding), feelings of enhanced mental efficiency, increased *or* decreased speed of thinking, fragmentation (the inability to create a whole from the parts), delusions, and idiosyncratic explanatory systems. Significant memory impairment is common and not associated with the severity of other symptoms (Aleman, Hijman, de Haan, & Kahn, 1998).

Diagnosis

According to the *DSM* (APA, 2000), schizophrenia is characterized by at least 6 months of continuous symptoms. The person must display two or more of the *active* or positive symptoms for at least 1 month. The remainder of the 6 months may feature positive or negative symptoms, and there must also be a decline in the person's social functioning skills. Signs of the disturbance may be limited to negative symptoms during the premorbid (prior to the active phase) or residual (after stabilization from an active phase) periods.

Hallucinations are sense perceptions of external objects when those objects are not present. They may be *auditory, visual, gustatory* (the perception of taste), *tactile* (feeling an object), *somatic* (an unreal experience within the body), or *olfactory* (a false sense of smell). *Delusions* are false beliefs that a person maintains even though they are overwhelmingly contradicted by social reality. They include *persecutory* (people or forces are attempting to bring one harm), *erotomanic* (another person is in love with the individual), *somatic* (pertaining to body functioning), and *grandiose* (an exaggerated sense of power, knowledge, or identity) beliefs, *thought broadcasting* (one's thoughts are overheard by others), *thought insertion* or *withdrawal* (others are putting thoughts into, or taking thoughts out of, one's head), delusions of *being controlled* (thoughts, feelings, or actions are imposed by an external force), and delusions of *reference* (neutral events have special significance for the person).

There are five subtypes of schizophrenia (APA, 2000), which may represent different disease processes, although this is not yet known:

- *Paranoid* schizophrenia features a preoccupation with delusions or auditory hallucinations but a preservation of cognitive functioning and range of mood.
- *Disorganized* schizophrenia is characterized by disorganized speech, behavior, and flat or inappropriate (exaggerated) affect.
- *Catatonic* schizophrenia features disturbances of immobility or excessive mobility, mutism (not speaking), odd gestures, echolalia (repeating the words of others), or echopraxia (repeating the movements of others).
- *Undifferentiated* schizophrenia describes people who exhibit a range of symptoms but do not meet the criteria for any of the previous three subtypes.

- *Residual* schizophrenia describes people who display only negative symptoms after an active episode. This may be transient or persist for many years.

The *DSM* also provides six course specifiers for further detailing the client's unique experience with the disorder: continuous, episodic with (or with no) interepisode residual symptoms, single episode in partial (or full) remission, and unspecified. The reader is referred to the *DSM* for the details of these specifiers.

Schizophrenia must be differentiated from *schizophreniform disorder*, which is similar except for the criterion of duration. That is, if a client has the symptoms of schizophrenia, and the active and residual phases have persisted for more than 1 month but less than 6 months, he or she should receive the latter diagnosis. It may turn out that the client does indeed have schizophrenia, but this cannot be concluded in the absence of the duration criterion. A person with schizophreniform disorder should be given one of two specifiers. The first, *with good prognostic features*, is appropriate if the onset of psychotic symptoms is within 4 weeks of the first noticeable change in the person's behavior and he or she had good prior behavior, is confused at the height of the disorder, and maintains a normal range of mood. Otherwise, the *without good prognostic features* specifier is used, and the client is more likely to have schizophrenia.

Schizophrenia must be also be differentiated from a similar disorder known as *schizoaffective disorder.* A person with that disorder experiences a continuous period of mental illness featuring symptoms that meet criterion A for schizophrenia that are *concurrent* at some time with either a manic, major depressive, or mixed mood episode (see chapter 13 for a description of these). Further, the person's delusions or hallucinations must persist for at least 2 weeks in the absence of prominent mood symptoms, and the symptoms of the mood episodes must be present for a substantial portion of the total duration of the illness. In its presentation, schizoaffective disorder is in some ways "halfway" between schizophrenia and bipolar disorder (although many theorists place it closer to the thought disorder). In fact, it was considered a subtype of schizophrenia through the first two editions of the *DSM*. Another way to conceptualize schizoaffective disorder is that it resembles a bipolar disorder that never quite stabilizes.

Many individuals who develop schizophrenia display what are called *premorbid* or "early warning" signs: a slow, gradual development of symptoms, social withdrawal, a loss of interest in life activities, deterioration in self-care, and a variety of "odd" behaviors. These behaviors are often difficult for families and other loved ones to understand. The signs can exist for many years, but when present they do *not* guarantee the eventual onset of schizophrenia. The person may develop instead a *schizoid* or *schizotypal* personality disorder (see chapter 15) or perhaps no diagnosis.

There is some disagreement about the nature of schizophrenia: whether the symptoms represent a single disorder or several disorders. Some theorists write about the *schizophrenia spectrum* disorders, hypothesized to include a range of disorders that may represent different "degrees" of schizophrenia: schizoaffective disorder and the schizotypal, paranoid, and schizoid personality disorders (Sadock & Sadock, 2005). A person with the genetic potential for schizophrenia may develop one of these related disorders if environmental conditions are protective. Further, some theorists have called for a reformulation of the diagnosis of schizophrenia along a continuum of characteristics that derive in different ways from a "core" deficit called *schizotaxia*, which is still an unspecified biological condition (Tsuang, Stone, & Faraone, 2000). The current *DSM* formulation, however, while not valid beyond dispute, represents an increase in worldwide reliability over the past 50 years, as it corresponds more closely to the World Health Organization's International Classification of Diseases description.

The Prevalence of Schizophrenia

Schizophrenia has an approximate 1% worldwide prevalence (Murray & Jones, 2003). Despite data collection and diagnostic differences, there is remarkable consistency in prevalence among most nations of the world (Murray & Jones, 2003). In some areas, the prevalence is very low (the southwest Pacific region) or very high (western Ireland and Croatia). Data from the National Institute of Mental Health—sponsored Epidemiological Catchment Area research project noted the lifetime prevalence of schizophrenia to be 1.3% of the U.S. population (APA, 2000). The incidence (new cases each year) was estimated at 0.025 to 0.05% of the population.

The prevalence of schizophrenia is twice as high in lower than in higher socioeconomic status (SES) classes (Mulvany, O'Callaghan, Takei, Byrne, & Fearon, 2001). The "downward drift" hypothesis holds that many who develop schizophrenia lose their occupational and social skills and fall into lower SES classes and that others with premorbid personality traits never develop adequate skills to establish themselves in stable social roles. Prevalence differences may also be related to the increased stressors on people in lower SES groups.

Schizophrenia tends to be diagnosed among African Americans more frequently than among Caucasians. Research suggests, however, that this diagnostic difference results from practitioners attributing and weighing particular observations differently for clients of different ethnicities (Trierweiler et al., 2000). That is, clinicians tend to interpret the suspicious attitudes of African Americans as symptomatic of schizophrenia, representing delusions or negative symptoms, rather than learned attitudes for managing uncomfortable situations.

Course of the Disorder

The age of onset of schizophrenia is between 15 and 40 years. Men tend to have their first episodes between the ages of 18 and 26, and women between the ages of 26 and 40 (Seeman, 2003). There is an equal prevalence for males and females, however, and an equal geographical distribution throughout the United States and the world. Women tend to have higher levels of premorbid (prepsychotic) functioning and more positive symptoms than men do. Women also have a better prognosis with regard to their response to intervention and social functioning potential. People with an early age of onset tend to have a poorer premorbid adjustment, more prominent negative symptoms, and more evidence of cognitive impairment (Byrne, Agerbo, & Mortensen, 2002).

Approximately 10% of people with schizophrenia experience its initial onset during late childhood and adolescence (Biederman, Petty, & Faraone, 2004). The disorder is rare before age 11 or 12. In children, delusions and hallucinations are less prominent, and visual hallucinations and disorganized speech may be more common. In diagnosing children, the practitioner must be particularly careful to rule out the possibility of an organic disorder, major affective disorder, pervasive developmental disorder, obsessive-compulsive disorder, and substance use disorder. The duration of schizophrenia is the same regardless of age of onset, although there is a correlation between age of onset and chances for a positive outcome (McClellan, McCurry, Snell, & DuBose, 1999).

Two thirds of people with schizophrenia never marry, and only 34% live in their own home or in a relative's home (Black, Yates, & Andreasen, 1988). Suicide is the number one cause of premature death, as 20 to 40% of people with schizophrenia attempt suicide at some point in their lives, and 10% succeed (Fenton, McGlashan, Victor, & Blyler, 1997). The average life span of people with schizophrenia is approximately 10 years less than the national average in the United States, although this is due to lifestyle factors such as diet, physical health, and risks related to poverty rather than to the neurological features of the disorder (Gottesman, 1991).

Complete remission in schizophrenia is relatively uncommon (Gottesman, 1991), and its course is variable. A person with the disorder may experience a chronic course, with symptoms being more or less florid but never really disappearing, or one in which periods of psychosis are interspersed with periods of remission. As with many physical and mental disorders, an accurate prediction of any individual's course is impossible. Although the causes of schizophrenia are uncertain, there are clues for differentiating better and worse prognoses.

Persons with schizophrenia have a high rate of comorbidity with substance-related disorders (APA, 2000). There is also comorbidity with anxiety disorders (especially obsessive-compulsive and panic disorders) and the schizotypal, schizoid, and paranoid personality disorders.

Risk and Protective Factors for Schizophrenia

The specific causes of schizophrenia are not known. Most research at present is focused in the genetic and biological areas, but psychological factors cannot be ruled out, particularly with regard to the course of the disorder. The *stress/diathesis theory* holds that schizophrenia results from a mix of constitutional factors (perhaps 70% from heritability and biology) and environmental and stress factors (approximately 30%) (Cardno & Murray, 2003). Those external factors, however, are not specific to schizophrenia. They may include insults to the brain, threatening physical environments, emotionally intrusive or demanding experiences, emotional deprivation, and disruptions to cognitive processes. A summary of risk and protective factors for schizophrenia is included in Table 14.1.

Biological Factors

Biological theories of schizophrenia implicate the brain's limbic system, frontal cortex, and basal ganglia as primary sites of malfunction (Conklin & Iacono, 2003). Whether symptoms result from abnormal development or deterioration of function is not clear.

The genetic transmission of schizophrenia is supported by the higher than average risk factors among family members of persons with the disorder (Cardno & Murray, 2003). A *monozygotic* (identical) twin of a person with schizophrenia has a 47% chance of developing the disorder. A *dyzygotic* (nonidentical) twin has only a 12% likelihood, which is the same probability as a child with one parent with schizophrenia. A nontwin sibling has an 8% chance of developing the disorder. Other risk factors include a maternal history of schizophrenia and affective disorder (Byrne et al., 2002).

The age of onset for a child tends to be earlier when the mother has schizophrenia. Further, negative symptoms are frequently seen among nonpsychotic first-degree relatives of people with schizophrenia. In genetically predisposed people, the change from vulnerability to developing psy-

Table 14.1

Risk and Protective Factors for the Onset and Course of Schizophrenia

Risk Factors	Protective Factors
Onset	
Biological	
Genetic vulnerability (family member with a schizophrenia spectrum disorder)	No family history of schizophrenia spectrum disorders
Dopamine hyperactivity	Normal dopamine activity
"Small" limbic system in the forebrain	Normal-size central nervous system components
Abnormal brain development during prenatal months	Normal prenatal development
Enlarged ventricles, decreased brain size	
Premature birth or maternal bleeding	
Age 18–25 for men, 26–40 for women	
Environmental	
Winter or early spring birth	Summer, fall, late spring season of birth
Maternal virus during first trimester	Healthy maternal pregnancy
Traumatic brain injury	Absence of major stressors or traumatic events
Premature birth or excess maternal bleeding	
Traumatic events in childhood	
Low socioeconomic status	
Family dysfunction, poor parenting	
Course	
Poor premorbid adjustment	Later age of onset
Gradual onset (no precipitating events)	Brief duration of active phase
Poor insight about the disorder	Insight
Prominent negative symptoms	Good interepisode functioning (minimal residual symptoms)
Delay of intervention	Absence of brain structure abnormalities
Live in large urban area	Family history of mood disorder
Repeated relapses	Early intervention
Medication absence or noncompliance	Active support system
Absence of a support system	Family participation in interventions
Noncompliance with, or absence of, psychosocial interventions	Participation in a range of psychosocial interventions
	Interest in independent living, assistance with activities of daily living

chosis may be marked by the reduced size and impaired function of the temporal lobe (Johnstone, Cosway, & Lawrie, 2002). Traumatic brain injury, often cited as a contributing cause of the disorder, increases the chances of schizophrenia in families, but only when there is already a genetic loading (Malaspina et al., 2001).

There is growing evidence for deficiencies in neurological development as causal in schizophrenia. Neuropsychological deficits in attention, verbal memory, and the executive functions of planning, organizing, problem solving, and abstracting are prominent in its etiology (Marenco & Weinberger, 2000). Weinberger introduced the neurodevelopment hypothesis of schizophrenia in 1987, using new imaging techniques to observe structural brain changes at the onset of the disorder. He believed that a *lesion* (injury), perhaps involving several brain regions, was activated by an unspecified external factor to trigger its onset. Brain imaging techniques have since revealed enlarged ventricles in many people with schizophrenia that may be a contributing cause through the consequent reduction in brain tissue (Lewis & Higgins, 1996).

Other neurodevelopmental phenomena have been hypothesized to account for its onset (Meinecke, 2001): cellular and molecular mechanisms of central nervous system development, the quality of neural connections, the manner in which sensory-driven and internal neural activities influence the formation of circuits that underlie complex brain functions, and the maturation of the prefrontal cortex dopamine system. A "two-hit" hypothesis holds that genetic or environmental factors may disrupt early central nervous system development, and these factors are affected again during neurological changes later in life to produce a "second hit" (Maynard, Siklich, Lieberman, & La Mantia, 2001). The dopamine hypothesis, established in the 1960s, asserted that schizophrenia results from an excess of that neurotransmitter in the nervous system (Wilson & Claussen, 1993). More recently, causal roles for other neurotransmitters, including serotonin and norepinephrine, have been proposed.

Both brain trauma from birth complications and prenatal viral exposure have also been postulated as causal factors. A meta-analysis of studies that investigated links between obstetrical complications and family history of schizophrenia, age at onset, and gender ($N = 854$ subjects) revealed a significant association between age of onset and obstetrical complications (Verdoux et al., 1997). People with an onset before age 22 were 2.7 times likelier to have had a history of obstetrical complications than those with a later age of onset and 10 times more likely to have had a cesarean birth. There was no association found between obstetric complications and family history of schizophrenia or gender.

There are higher than expected frequencies of prenatal exposure to viruses in individuals who later develop schizophrenia (Kirkpatrick, Herrera Catanedo, & Vazquez-Barquero, 2002). People with schizophrenia tend to be born in winter or early spring, which implies that their mothers were pregnant during a time of year when certain viruses are more prevalent. Postmortem studies show brain abnormalities indicative of developmental problems in the second or third trimester of pregnancy, such as altered cell migration in the hippocampus and prefrontal cortex. This trend seems to hold across time (the past 200 years) and space (pastoral villages to industrial societies). There is some evidence that people with schizophrenia who were born in summer months have more negative than positive symptoms (Kirkpatrick et al., 2002).

Biological factors that protect a person from developing schizophrenia include the absence of a family history of the disorder, normal prenatal development, brief duration of the first episode of positive symptoms, and a normally developed central nervous system. Protective environmental factors include being born during the summer, fall, or late spring months and an absence of physically traumatic events during childhood and adolescence.

Psychological Factors

Various psychological factors have been postulated as significant in the development of schizophrenia. Although they have largely been discredited because of a lack of evidence, they are presented here because they remain a strong part of the legacy of the disorder. Freud (1966) placed neurosis and psychosis on a continuum as resulting from similar psychological mechanisms. He wavered, however, between a defense and deficit theory of schizophrenia. The defense theory conceptualized psychotic symptoms as a means of adapting to internal conflict. Deficit theory implied a nonspecific organic defect resulting in one's inability to sustain attachments to others and instead becoming preoccupied with internal experience.

Developmental theorists assert that mental disorders result from the inability to progress successfully through critical life stages. For example, problems with normal separation from the primary caregiver during the first few years of life may result in schizophrenia if developmental arrests result in an inability to distinguish the self from others (Mahler, Pine, & Bergman, 1975). The failure to make the transition from adolescence to young adulthood, with its challenges of forming of peer relationships, patterning sexual behavior, revising personal values, and developing independent living skills, has also been suggested as producing a regression that may result in schizophrenia (Dawson, Blum, & Bartolucci, 1983). Family theorists have used such terms as "emotional divorce" (Bowen, 1960), "communication deviance" (Singer, Wynne, & Toohey, 1978), the "double-bind" (Bateson, Jackson, Haley, & Weakland, 1963), and family "schisms" and "skews" (Lidz, 1975) to describe problematic parent–child interactions that cause a child to withdraw into psychosis. These have been discounted as causal influences, although family relationships do influence the course of the disorder.

When a person has schizophrenia, a chronic state of emotional burden develops that is shared by all family members (Hatfield & Lefley, 1993). Common reactions include stress, anxiety, resentment of the impaired member, grief, and depression. Spouses tend to blame each other for family turmoil, and children tend to blame parents. There is little time available for family leisure activities, and one adult, usually the mother, becomes the primary caretaker of the impaired member. Siblings have some reactions unique from the parents, including emotional constriction in personality development, isolation from peers, and jealousy about the attention given to the impaired member (National Alliance for the Mentally Ill, 1989).

For these reasons, the concept of family (or caregiver) expressed emotion (EE) has been prominent in the schizophrenia literature for the past 30 years. It has been operationalized to include ratings of family member hostility toward the ill relative, emotional overinvolvement with the relative, and the warmth with which the relative refers to the client; it also includes frequency counts of critical and positive comments about the client (Vaughn & Leff, 1976). Low-EE family environments are associated with fewer symptom relapses and rehospitalizations than high-EE environments are. As a research measure, EE provides one means for determining the kinds of family environments that put people with schizophrenia at risk for symptom relapses or protect them. We should add that many family advocacy groups have objected to the EE measure as blaming them for their family member's illness (Mohr, Lafuze, & Mohr, 2000).

Regarding protective factors, persons with schizophrenia tend to function best with a moderate amount of face-to-face interaction with significant others (Chambless, Bryan, Aiken, Steketee, & Hooley, 1999). Likewise, they manage moderate amounts of social stimulation well. They respond favorably to attitudes of acceptance, reasonable expectations, opportunities to develop social and vocational skills, and a relatively small number but broad range of social supports (family members, friends, neighbors, work peers, school peers, informal community relations, and perhaps church members). Factors that influence the family's coping well or poorly include the severity of the disorder (people actually seem to cope better when the disorder is more severe), the preservation of time for other activities, the ability to be proactive in seeking assistance, and the availability of outside support (Lenoir, Dingemans, Schene, Hart, & Linszen, 2002).

Factors that are protective, or suggest a less severe course of schizophrenia, include a later age of onset, a brief duration of the active phase, and some degree of insight into the disorder (Booth, 1995). Other protective factors include minimal residual symptoms when the disorder is in remission and the ability to experience a range of emotions. Related to intervention, a milder course is more likely when the person receives early intervention, participates in a range of psychosocial interventions, and maintains a desire to work toward independent or minimally supported living. Family participation in the client's intervention is another important protective factor.

Interventions in Schizophrenia

Social workers provide services to people with schizophrenia in hospitals, other psychiatric units, community mental health centers, private clinics, residential centers, group homes, rehabilitation centers, psychosocial clubhouses, and drop-in centers. There is a consensus that the treatment of schizophrenia should always be multimodal and include interventions targeted at specific symptoms as well as at the social and educational needs of the client and family. For children as well as adults, intervention should consist of a thorough psychological and physical assessment, the practitioner's recognition of the phase of the illness (prodromal, acute, recovery, residual, or chronic), a differential diagnosis, medications, and psychosocial interventions (McClellan & Werry, 2000).

Medications

Medication is the primary intervention modality for people with schizophrenia. They are believed to have a relatively high concentration of the neurotransmitter dopamine (five types have been identified) in nerve cell pathways extending into the cortex and limbic system. Dopamine levels are not considered to be causal for the disorder, and other neurotransmitters are also involved in symptom production. The first generation of antipsychotic drugs, most popular between the 1950s and 1980s, act primarily by binding to dopamine receptors and blocking its transmission (Leonard, 2003). The antipsychotic medications differ in their side effect profiles and milligram amounts required in equivalent doses. Most of the first-generation medications target only one of the five types of dopamine (D2) and are more effective at reducing the positive than the negative symptoms of schizophrenia.

The first-generation antipsychotic medications act on all dopamine sites in the brain, but only those in the forebrain produce the symptoms of schizophrenia. The other pathways extend from the midbrain to the basal ganglia, which govern motor activity. A reduction in dopamine in these areas causes adverse effects of *akathisia* (restlessness and agitation), *dystonia* (muscle spasms), *parkinsonism* (muscle stiffness and tremor), and *tardive dyskinesia* (involuntary smooth muscle movements of the face and limbs). *Anticholinergic* medications are often prescribed to combat these effects, even though they have their own adverse effects of blurred vision, dry mouth, and constipation.

The second-generation antipsychotic medications, available in the United States since the late 1980s, act differently than those developed earlier (Julien, 2001). Clozapine, the first of these, is a relatively weak D2 antagonist with a high affinity for D4 receptors, as well as interactions with D1, D3, serotonin, and other receptors (Meltzer, 1991). Clozapine's sites of action are the limbic forebrain and the frontal cortex; thus, it does not carry the risk of adverse effects for the muscular system. In blocking receptors for serotonin, it suggests that this neurotransmitter has a role in the production of symptoms. This medication has been limited in use because it carries the possibility of a rare but serious adverse effect of white blood cell depletion (agranulocytosis).

Other new drugs soon followed. Risperidone, introduced in 1994, also has fewer adverse effects than the first-generation drugs (Stahl, 2000). It has a high affinity for both D2 and serotonin receptors, and it supports the hypothesis that the serotonin antagonists diminish many of the adverse effects noted previously. In a double-blind study involving 397 clients, risperidone was found to be superior to the first-generation drug haloperidol in preventing a relapse of positive symptoms (Csernansky, Mahmoud, & Brenner, 2002). It remains the most frequently prescribed antipsychotic drug.

Olanzapine is an antagonist of all dopamine receptors, some serotonin receptors, and several other receptors. Sertindole is even more specifically targeted, interacting predominantly with D2 receptors, but it does not attach to receptors that produce sedative and anticholinergic effects such as dry mouth, blurred vision, and constipation (Tamminga, 1996). The actions of the newer drugs (such as ziprasidone and quetiapine) cast doubt that any single effect is responsible for their clinical activity (Schatzberg & Nemeroff, 2001). Further, their somewhat better alleviation of negative symptoms suggests that serotonin antagonist activity is significant in this regard.

Both the first- and second-generation medications continue to be used to treat persons with schizophrenia (Essock, 2002). In 1999, 34% of the antipsychotic medication prescriptions paid by Medicaid were first-generation drugs. Of the newer medications prescribed, risperidone was used most frequently (27%), followed by olanzapine (23%), clozapine (11%), and quetiapine (5%). Prescribing practices depend on the physician's preferences and the client's family history and financial status (the older medications are less expensive).

There is approximately a 66% chance that a person with schizophrenia will respond positively to treatment with an antipsychotic medication (Schatzberg & Nemeroff, 2001). Protocols suggest that clients who receive a medication trial for 1 week at therapeutic doses for an acute episode and do not demonstrate any improvement are unlikely to respond with more time, and a new medication should be introduced (Marder et al., 2002). If a person demonstrates a partial remission of active symptoms, the trial should be extended to 12 weeks before a medication change is made. It must be emphasized that adverse effects occur with all antipsychotic medications, and these effects are the primary reason why clients stop using the drugs.

Bentley and Walsh (2006) have outlined six roles for social workers with regard to clients using psychotropic medications. In the role of *physician's assistant*, the social worker supports the recommendations of the client's physician regarding medication use. The *consultant/collaborator* performs preliminary screenings to determine clients' possible needs for medication, makes referrals to physicians, and regularly consults with the physician and client. The *advocate* supports the client's expressed wishes regarding medication and presents them to others in the service milieu. The social worker may also *monitor* the positive and negative effects of medication. The *educator* provides clients and significant others with information about issues relevant to medication use, including actions, benefits, and risks. Finally, the *researcher* uses case reports and other research designs to study how medications affect the lives of clients and families and how they interact with other interventions.

Although almost all physicians recommend antipsychotic medication for people with schizophrenia, there is debate about their effectiveness, their long-term effects, and the relative risks and benefits of their use with regard to the consumer's physical and emotional well-being. The major critic of medication practices in the field of social work is David Cohen (2002), who argues persuasively in his review of the literature that many psychotropic medication studies are methodologically flawed. He concludes that claims of effectiveness are exaggerated and that the development of significant adverse effects is underreported. He urges clinical practitioners to assume a critical attitude toward these drugs in helping clients understand their risks and benefits.

Despite advances in the pharmacological treatment of schizophrenia, the importance of other interventions must not be de-emphasized. Studies that focus on interactions between medications and individual, group, and family behavioral and educational interventions suggest significantly enhanced outcomes for clients on measures of rehospitalization and symptom relapse (Schooler & Keith, 1993).

Psychodynamic Interventions

Psychoanalytic treatment of people with schizophrenia has a long history but is presented as case reports with limited empirical support. Since the 1960s, there have been few controlled studies of individual psychotherapy of any type. In a review of these studies, Gomes-Schwartz (1984) finds that for the most part individual psychodynamic treatment is not effective, with outcome criteria including symptom reduction, reduced hospitalizations, and improved community adjustment. One example of successful analytic therapy with regard to these same measures involved 36 clients with schizophrenia who were treated over a period of 20 months with Rosen's "direct" analysis, which interpreted psychotic communications as expressions of the client's infantile impulses (Karon & VandenBos, 1972). Even so, it was asserted that practitioner characteristics not directly related to analytic technique, such as years of practice experience, being sensitive and tolerant, and having a strong desire to work with people who have schizophrenia, played an important role in those outcomes. In another review of psychotherapy studies, Mueser and Berenbaum (1990) conclude that supportive, reality-oriented approaches appear to be superior to dynamic, insight-oriented therapies on three of four outcome criteria (rehospitalization, vocational adjustment, and social adjustment), but the two general modalities demonstrate no differences related to symptoms.

Cognitive and Behavioral Interventions

Cognitive and behavioral (CB) interventions are increasingly being used to treat people with schizophrenia. These interventions focus on modifying symptoms and their effects by adjusting their meaning to the individual. CB strategies are based on the premise that current beliefs and attitudes largely mediate a person's affect and behavior. With these interventions, practitioners do not generally attempt to "talk people out of" their delusions and hallucinations. Rather, clients are helped to modify dysfunctional assumptions about the self, the world, and the future; improve coping responses to stressful events and life challenges; relabel some psychotic experiences as symptoms rather than external reality; and improve social skills. Such interventions involve client–practitioner conversations about the nature of thoughts and feelings and the formulation of corrective experiences for the client.

Piling, Bebbington, Kuipers, Garety, Geddes et al. (2002b) conducted a meta-analysis of all randomized clinical studies done on cognitive-behavioral interventions for schizophrenia. They were able to locate eight usable studies that included 538 clients. The researchers concluded that CB interventions did improve clients' mental status and decreased rates of treatment dropout and that their positive effects persisted through the follow-up period. Despite these positive outcomes, Hogarty and Flesher (1992) emphasize that people with schizophrenia have difficulty developing a coherent and integrated cognitive schema (way of conceptualizing and organizing the world). They assert that the practitioner must try to understand the clients' cognitive styles before attempting corrective actions.

One type of CB intervention, known as cognitive adaptation training, is also used with people who have schizophrenia, recognizing that they frequently experience deficits in adaptive functioning and role performance as a result of cognitive impairments. Based on neuropsychological, behavioral, and occupational therapy principles, cognitive adaptation training uses an individualized approach to help the client create a daily life routine that is amenable to his or her skill and stress management levels. In a study that compared a standard psychosocial treatment (inpatient supportive group therapy, medication education, occupational therapy, and socialization) with cognitive adaptation training, clients in the experimental group demonstrated greater improvement in adaptation (Velligan, Mahurin, True, Lefton, & Flores, 1996).

Recently, an intervention model known as personal therapy has received much attention because of an outcome study that utilized a randomized control group design (Hogarty, 2002). Personal therapy uses a three-phase approach, focusing on clinical and environmental stabilization, symptom management, and new social and vocational initiatives. The progression of clients through these phases is determined by their rate of progress rather than a prearranged protocol. Both the experimental and control groups in this study received psychological support (empathy, attentiveness, and encouragement), material support (financial support, stable housing, case management), and medication management. In the first phase of personal therapy, a treatment team decides on a medication regimen, joins with the client and family, and educates clients about their illness. In the second phase, practitioners help clients examine the patterns of their illness, precipitants of relapse, and coping strategies for symptom management. In the final stage, practitioners help clients apply coping strategies to new social and vocational initiatives. Both the experimental and control groups showed improvement after 1 year, but the control group's progress leveled off after 1 year whereas the treatment group made additional gains during the next 2 years.

Social skills training (SST) is a type of CB intervention that addresses deficits in interpersonal relating that are frequently found among people with schizophrenia. It provides training on skills needed for successful everyday living. Its research base includes large numbers of both noncontrolled and controlled studies that frequently use single-subject and multiple baseline designs (Pratt & Mueser, 2002). A meta-analysis of research on this topic was conducted by Pilling et al. (2002a), who limited their search to randomized control-group trials with comparisons with other active interventions. This unfortunately resulted in only four studies involving 170 clients. The findings demonstrated no clear evidence of any benefits of SST on relapse rate, global adjustment, social functioning, quality of life, or adherence with other interventions.

With this in mind, several other meta-analyses are presented here that relied on less strict methodologies. In an analysis of 27 studies, Benton and Schroeder (1990) concluded that SST led to major improvements in social behavior when the outcomes were behaviorally defined. Scott and Dixon (1995), in their review of the SST literature, note that some simple behaviors (e.g., improving interpersonal eye contact) can be generalized to novel situations, but it is unclear whether more complex behaviors are transferred. Dobson (1996) concluded from another review, however, that generalization does occur. In a 2-year controlled study, Hogarty et al. (1991) found that significant improvements in client symptom profiles were evident 1 year after SST activities were initiated but that gains were no longer evident after 2 years. In summary, positive outcomes for SST appear to be possible but may be time limited.

Group Interventions

Group interventions include insight-oriented, supportive, and behavioral modalities. They are often used in conjunction with other interventions, such as medication and CB strategies. There are few controlled studies of group therapy. In his review of the descriptive literature on both inpatient and outpatient groups, Kanas (2000) concluded that groups focused on increased social interaction were more effective than insight-oriented groups for people with schizophrenia.

Group interventions are widely used in inpatient settings, but there is little evidence for their effectiveness in stabilizing people who are recently admitted and highly symptomatic. One quasi-experimental study, however, found that participation in a short-term support and education group had a positive effect on the treatment compliance of people with first-episode schizophrenia (Miller & Mason, 2001). Regarding outpatient groups, a meta-analysis of 18 control-group studies produced only modest evidence that group therapy results in reduced symptom severity and increased social and vocational skills (Huxley, Rendall, & Sederer, 2000). One example of a successful intervention is the integrated psychological therapy program, in which people with schizophrenia randomly assigned to a 24-session supportive therapy group (vs. coping-oriented therapy) demonstrated gains in global assessment of functioning over 18 months (Andres, Brenner, Hodel, Pfammatter, & Roder, 2001). Another experimental study of outpatient cognitive-behavioral therapy that included 1 year of biweekly problem-solving groups resulted in members' improved medication compliance, illness concept, and family atmosphere (Klingberg, Wiedemann, & Buckremer, 2001).

Family Interventions

Because the majority of people with schizophrenia reside with or near their families, social workers need to understand what is effective in working with those people to facilitate the adjustment of all family members. The concept of expressed emotion (EE) is significant to this work. Introduced earlier in this chapter, EE can be defined as the negative behaviors of close relatives toward a family member with schizophrenia, including emotional overinvolvement and expressions of criticism and hostility. The concept is not used to blame family members for the course of a relative's illness but to affirm that families need support in coping with this chronic, frustrating disorder. In a meta-analysis by Butzlaff and Hooley (1998) of 27 studies, EE was consistently shown to correlate with symptom relapse. Those authors also found that the relationship was strongest for clients with a more chronic disorder. Family interventions in schizophrenia usually focus in part on producing a more positive atmosphere for all members, which in turn contributes to the ill relative's adjustment.

Pilling et al. (2002b) conducted a meta-analysis of all randomized clinical studies done on family intervention in schizophrenia. For inclusion in this analysis, studies needed to be at least 6 weeks long and include a specific intervention goal. The researchers located 18 usable studies that included 1467 clients. They found that all single-family and family group interventions were more effective at 12 months than the comparison interventions, which usually included some form of "standard care." Single-family interventions reduced readmission rates in the first year. After 2 years, all 18 family interventions lowered the relapse and readmission rates of the relative with schizophrenia and increased medication compliance. There were no effects of family intervention on either client suicide or subjective family burden, however.

During the past 20 years, psychosocial interventions for families of people with schizophrenia have expanded, and some of their effective components can be discerned (Bogart & Solomon, 1999). Effective interventions include crisis-oriented weekly sessions; behavioral family therapy including problem-solving and communication skills training in the family's home; education, discussion, communication, and problem-solving training; and psychoeducational multifamily groups. However, there are no differences in family member functioning based on which type of intervention the family receives. It cannot be concluded, then, that any specific type of family intervention is superior to another.

Key elements in effective interventions include the practitioner's taking a positive approach, establishing a collaborative working relationship, providing structure, focusing on the here-and-now, using family systems concepts, using cognitive restructuring or behavioral approaches, and improving family communication (Lam, 1991). The client's participation in at least some aspect of the intervention is considered to be important. Characteristics of family intervention that appear to produce less positive or poor outcomes include a short-term focus (10 weeks or less), combining families with relatives who have a variety of mental disorders, providing the intervention in a hospital setting, not including the ill relative in meetings, and failing to focus on education and support (Vaughan et al., 1992). In some models of family intervention, services are provided in the home in an effort to secure the participation of all members. There is no evidence, however, that in-home services are more effective than those in clinical settings (Randolph et al., 1994).

Case Management and Community Interventions

Case management is a term used to describe a variety of community-based intervention modalities that attempt to help clients receive a full range of support and rehabilitation services in a timely, appropriate fashion (Rubin, 1992). Although practice activities may differ somewhat depending on the setting, they usually include assessment of client needs, strengths, and limitations; planning for appropriate service acquisition; linkage with service providers from various systems; advocacy on behalf of clients with other providers; monitoring of overall service quality; and evaluation (Kanter, 1995).

Case management interventions are usually carried out in the context of large community-based programs. The most famous of these, assertive community treatment (ACT), was developed by Stein and Test (1980) in Wisconsin and has since been replicated in many other sites around the world. By 1996, there were 397 such programs in the United States (Mueser, Bond, Drake, & Resnick, 1998). The core characteristics of the ACT model of service delivery are assertive engagement, in vivo delivery of services, a multidisciplinary team approach, staff continuity over time, low staff-to-client ratios, and frequent client contacts. Services are provided in the client's home, at shopping malls, at places of work, or wherever the client feels comfortable, and services focus on everyday needs. Frequency of contact is variable depending on assessed client need. Staff-to-client ratios are approximately 1:10. Other kinds of intensive case management programs share some, but not all, characteristics of the ACT model.

According to Mueser et al. (1998), 27 random assignment and 23 uncontrolled studies have been completed on the ACT intervention model. These authors admit that there is much variability in the programs with regard to staffing, types of clients, and resources, and thus comparisons are difficult to make. They conclude, however, that assertive community treatment is consistently more effective than alternative interventions for clients with schizophrenia and other chronic mental disorders in reducing hospitalization rates, symptom severity, and service costs and in enhancing client satisfaction and vocational functioning. Others who survey the literature on this topic have agreed (Burns & Santos, 1995; Olfson, 1990; Scott & Dixon, 1995; Solomon, 1992). It is also agreed, however, that client gains persist only as long as comprehensive services are continued. This raises the question as to whether clients are acquiring skills and resources that promote permanent improvement or are showing short-term gains reflective of intensive support. One critic of the ACT approach states that the research is biased by authors who support the program philosophy and that evaluators may be confusing workers' efforts for clients' efforts (Gomory, 1999). That is, some positive outcomes may be due to administrators refusing hospitalization to clients as an option, and practitioners may be coercing clients to behave in ways that are consistent with program values. In summary, then, ACT programs and other forms of intensive community intervention for people with schizophrenia do produce positive outcomes, but some of these may reflect shifts in resource availability (fewer hospital beds, more short-term crisis residences) and the more pervasive presence of case managers in clients' lives.

Vocational Rehabilitation

Vocational rehabilitation is defined as work-related activity that provides clients with pay and the experience of participating in productive social activity. The goals of vocational programs may be full-time competitive employment, any paid or volunteer job, the development of job-related skills, and job satisfaction. Twamley, Jeste, and Lehman (2003) conducted a meta-analysis of randomized controlled trials of vocational rehabilitation. They located 11 such studies, 9 of which focused on either client placement and support (with training, placement, and occasional contact) or supported employment (more intensive participation of the case manager in the client's job functions) strategies. They concluded that people with schizophrenia benefit from vocational training in terms of their working at any time during the intervention. Programs have a positive influence on work-related activities, such as paid employment, job starts, duration of employment, and earnings. Unfortunately, a diagnosis of schizophrenia is negatively related to the attainment and maintenance of employment when compared with other diagnoses. This finding is consistent with research that correlates successful past employment with a more favorable response to vocational rehabilitation interventions (Lehman, 1995).

Primary Prevention

Primary prevention refers to professional activities that result in the prevention of illness in at-risk individuals. This is not prevalent in any area of mental health, but several efforts have been initiated in this regard with schizophrenia. One recent study in a county in England included attempts to intervene prior to the onset of illness (Falloon, Kydd, Coverdale, & Laidlaw, 1996). Teams of designated mental health practitioners worked closely with family practitioners to educate them about the premorbid symptoms of schizophrenia (such as marked peculiar behavior, speech that is difficult to follow, and preoccupation with odd ideas). When young people were found to have some of these symptoms, they were provided with formal psychoeducation, usually in their own home. Intervention was ongoing and included home-based stress management, problem-solving strategies, and medication, if indicated. Results of this 4-year pilot study demonstrated that the occurrence of the florid psychotic episodes of schizophrenia was noticeably reduced. The authors caution, however, that there is a distinction between avoiding a psychotic episode of schizophrenia and preventing the disorder.

Another example of intervention in the prodromal phase of psychosis, with the goal of preventing or minimizing psychosocial disruption, is a study currently in progress in Australia (Yung et al., 1996). In 1994, a clinic was established to care for and monitor young people between the ages of 16 and 30 who were thought to be at high risk for psychosis. To address issues of stigma, the service was named Personal Assistance and Crisis Evaluation (PACE) and housed in an adolescent health center. Psychosocial treatment was provided with the goal of reducing stress, enhancing coping and problem solving, and emphasizing individualized case management and support. Preliminary results show that it is possible to identify and follow individuals who may be experiencing an early phase of schizophrenia.

Data regarding the risks and benefits of early detection and intervention remain sparse, and the evidence is not sufficient to justify pre-onset treatment as a standard practice (McGlashan, Miller, & Woods, 2001). There are also ethical issues involved in primary prevention efforts, including clinical priorities, screening ethics, stigma, confidentiality, and informed consent (Rosen, 2000).

Schizophrenia is a chronic mental disorder that does not readily respond to interventions that are based on a desire to return clients to a previous level of social and vocational functioning. The various interventions described here can certainly help clients to experience fewer symptoms and enjoy a higher quality of life, but they remain limited in the scope of their impact. It appears that almost all clients with schizophrenia require long-term intervention to maximize their potential.

▨▨▨▨▨ Case Illustration: Rachel

Rachel was a Caucasian 29-year-old single unemployed female, living alone, who was referred to the community mental health center following a short-term hospitalization that was prompted by an exacerbation of psychotic symptoms. Rachel had experienced mental illness for 3 years by this time. Her symptoms included auditory hallucinations, many of which tormented her. She heard the voices of family members (none of whom lived nearby) degrading her as a worthless person doomed to a life of failure. She also heard the voices of angels each night, sometimes being awakened by them as they whispered kindly that she would survive her suffering. Rachel often cried and sometimes screamed for relief when she heard these voices.

Rachel also experienced grandiose and persecutory delusions. She was Jewish and believed herself to be a direct descendant of the biblical Rachel, which accounted for special status in the eyes of God. She believed that God had appointed her to be the spiritual caretaker of her parents, especially her father, to whom she felt particularly attached. In fact, Rachel's stated purpose in life was to sit quietly and concentrate on their well-being for several hours per day. She believed that this would ensure their safety and happiness. Rachel also believed in reincarnation and that she had been repeatedly tortured in previous lives. Most recently, she had been put to death in a gas chamber by Nazis during World War II. She often talked about having vivid flashbacks to these events. Interestingly, while Rachel had some negative symptoms of schizophrenia, these were not prominent. She had a full range of emotional expression.

Rachel had not been able to work or maintain social relationships since the onset of her disorder. Her symptoms were continuous, and she had no insight into them. The symptoms were not *all* present in her thinking *all* the time, but during the course of each day she experienced some of them. During most of her conversations with other people, even those she did not know well, Rachel shared her preoccupations, believing that they would be readily affirmed. Her anxiety required that she spend much of her time alone, away from the sensory stimulation presented by sounds, colors, and people that tended to overwhelm her. Finally, with her lack of insight, Rachel demonstrated poor judgment in her limited social interactions. She liked men, for example, and would openly seduce them while sharing her bizarre thoughts. This led to their rejection of her, although they sometimes exploited her sexually.

Regarding her history, Rachel had been an energetic, personable child, the second of four children born to a physician and his wife. She was a high academic achiever but also unusually moody, given to temper tantrums and frequent interpersonal conflicts. Despite her wishes to the contrary, Rachel had not maintained any long-term relationships with males as an adolescent or young adult, and she often fought with her best girlfriends. Her friends considered her to be demanding and rigid. During adolescence, she developed and was treated for anorexia for several years. Rachel later could not recall any causes for that disorder, saying only that she was a "sad and mixed-up kid." Throughout her life, she had been on fair terms with her family. She idolized her father but did not get along as well with her mother; they argued often, which was her pattern with most people. She had comfortable, but not close, relationships with her siblings. One sister (who was the only family member living nearby—about 75 miles away) described her as an intelligent, temperamental young woman who could be charming but was often "flaky" and had trouble getting along with most people.

Rachel's psychotic symptoms developed when she was about 25, living away from home at a university where she was trying to complete a bachelor's degree in English. She was working long hours on her thesis when she began hearing voices, at first only at night. These terrified her, but she told no one about them. They became worse, occupying her mind to the point that she could no longer concentrate on her schoolwork. Eventually Rachel became so frightened of what was happening that she went to her friends and family and begged them for help. At that point, she experienced the first of her three hospitalizations, and she never returned to school or to independent living. At the time of her community mental health center referral, she was living on limited funds derived from dwindling family savings and a Social Security account. A younger brother was helping her manage her money.

Rachel's Diagnosis

Axis I: Schizophrenia, Paranoid Type, Continuous

Rachel experiences continuous auditory hallucinations. She also has delusional beliefs about being a descendant of key biblical figures. These symptoms have been present every day for the past 3 years. She meets the criteria for paranoid type because she has a preoccupation with delusions, some of which are tormenting, while her cognitive functioning and range of mood are relatively intact. Rachel's quality of social functioning has deteriorated significantly from the onset of her active symptoms. She comes from a prominent family but at present is living in a small apartment with little ready cash.

Rachel's anorexia is not included on Axis I because it was an adolescent disorder from which she recovered.

Axis II: None

Some people who develop schizophrenia have a premorbid history that suggests a paranoid, schizoid, or schizotypal personality disorder, but this is not true of Rachel.

Axis III: Agranulocytosis by History

Rachel had taken the drug clozapine at one time but needed to be switched to another medication because she experienced a depleted white blood cell count.

Avis IV

Problems related to the social environment (the client is living alone but experiences regular interpersonal stress when she tries to interact with others).

Axis V

Current GAF = 30; Highest GAF past year = 40

Her two global assessments of functioning on Axis V reflect Rachel's serious and continuous problems with social, occupational, and leisure functioning but also indicate that she is capable of functioning at a higher level than she is at present. The score of 25 indicates that her behavior is considerably influenced by delusions and hallucinations, she experiences serious impairment in her judgment, and she has difficulties functioning in most areas of her life. At times during the past year, the severity of her symptoms was less pronounced, and her level of functioning somewhat higher as a result.

The Intervention Plan

The following intervention plan was constructed collaboratively by Rachel and her social worker. This accounts for both the client-centered nature of the goals and objectives and the absence of professional terminology. This was an initial plan that would be updated every 3 months, and thus not all of the goals are considered to be long term in nature.

Goal 1: Rachel will develop a comfortable working relationship with the agency social worker.

Objective: Biweekly home visits by the social worker to discuss issues pertinent to Rachel's activities of daily living, including solving problems of concern to the client

Goal 2: To minimize the distress Rachel experiences when hearing the voices of God and her family.

Objectives

1. Monthly meetings with the agency physician for the prescription and monitoring of appropriate medications (Rachel was prescribed the second-generation drug risperidone)
2. Biweekly monitoring of the effects of the medication as reported by the client and observed by the social worker, including positive effects and any adverse physical effects
3. Biweekly consultation of the social worker with the physician to keep the physician updated about the medication's effects

Goal 3: For Rachel's parents and siblings to interact with her in ways that are helpful to her recovery and will preserve positive family relationships.

Objectives

1. Beginning immediately, the social worker will maintain phone contact with parents and other siblings as requested and approved by Rachel to provide them with information about mental illness and its treatment.
2. To inform all family members within 2 weeks of the county chapters of the National Alliance for the Mentally Ill and the Mental Health Association.
3. To invite Rachel's sister living nearby to attend the agency's regularly scheduled family education and support group, now or at any time while Rachel is a client.

Goal 4: To increase Rachel's level of comfort with social activity.

Objective

1. Biweekly meetings with the social worker to discuss and monitor Rachel's social goals and options for meeting people. The social worker will help Rachel select appropriate informal social activities.
2. Referral to formal services such as the agency clubhouse and drop-in center as requested by the client.

Goal 5: To expand the range of Rachel's social network supports.

Objective

1. Within 2 weeks, the social worker will educate Rachel about the county's Center for Vocational Alternatives and refer her there for vocational assessment if desired.
2. Rachel will be educated about the county's Schizophrenics Anonymous self-help group within 1 month and be referred for participation if desired.
3. The social worker will provide Rachel with information about volunteer opportunities in the county as requested.

Critique of the Diagnosis

Schizophrenia remains an enigma. Although it is among the most disabling of all mental disorders, researchers and clinical practitioners are not able to describe exactly what it is, how it is caused, or how it can be effectively prevented or treated. There is a consensus, however, that its primary causes are biological or hereditary (although there remains some debate about the extent of those influences) and that family and social environments are more significant to its course than to its onset. There is also a greater worldwide agreement on its basic symptom profile. Schizophrenia thus appears to be recognized as a "valid" mental disorder, although a clearer differentiation from similar conditions such as schizoaffective disorder and schizotypal personality disorder will further clarify its nature. As more information about its neurobiology is developed, professionals may become able to articulate its core features.

Appendix. Assessment Instruments for Schizophrenia

The Brief Psychiatric Rating Scale (BPRS)

Overall & Gorman (1962); Andersen et al. (1989)

Description

- Measures symptom changes in persons with schizophrenia.
- Not a diagnostic tool but provides a clinical profile at a single point in time.
- Several versions exist; the best known includes 18 items, each rated on a 7-point scale.
- Includes 12 items specific to schizophrenia and 6 for depression.
- Constructed for measuring symptoms of schizophrenia, but along with the depression items may also be considered a schizoaffective scale.

- Scores may be obtained for the four domains of thinking disturbance, withdrawal/retardation, hostility/suspicion, and anxiety/depression.
- Includes recommended cutoff scores for evaluating the severity of symptoms.
- The practitioner assesses most client symptoms at the time of the interview, but six items may be scored on the basis of conditions during the prior 3 days.
- Requires 30 minutes to administer; does not include a standard interview protocol.

Reliability and Validity

- Spearman intraclass coefficients of seven raters was .74 to .83.
- Concurrent validity with one other rating scale (475 respondents) was .93.

The Psychiatric Symptoms Assessment Scale

Bigelow & Berthot (1989)

Description

- A revised version of the BPRS, this 23-item scale uses concrete, behavioral anchor points as guides for practitioner ratings.
- Includes the 18 BPRS items (5 are renamed) with 4 items added to expand the range of ratings for depression, mania, and schizophrenia. Also includes a global "loss of functioning" item.
- All items include guidelines and examples and are rated on a 7-point scale.
- The practitioner is instructed to rate the quality of a given behavior rather than its duration.
- The order of items is intended to reflect the sequence in which information is usually gathered during a clinical interview.

Reliability

- Intraclass correlation coefficients for individual PSAS items were between .328 (this was the only item below .628) and .867.
- Total reliability score for the PSAS was .927.

Validity
Predictive validity was tested by assessing 60 clients with schizophrenia while on medication and then after medications were discontinued. Scores of all but four items changed significantly in the predicted direction.

The Positive and Negative Syndrome Scale for Schizophrenia

Kay, Fiszbein, & Opler (1987)

Description

- Practitioner-administered 30-item scale measures positive and negative symptoms of schizophrenia and general psychopathology.
- Includes 18 items adapted from the BPRS and 12 additional items.
- Each item includes a definition and anchoring criteria for the 7-point ratings.
- Ratings are based on information specific to a time period, usually the previous week. The practitioner derives information primarily from the clinical interview but may utilize input from other professionals and family members.
- The 30–40 minute semiformal interview consists of four prescribed phases: rapport development; probes of pathology; questions about mood, anxiety, orientation, and reasoning; and probes for areas where the client seems ambivalent.

Reliability

Cronbach's alphas = .73 for the positive symptom subscale, .83 for the negative symptom subscale, and .79 for the general psychopathology subscale.

Validity

- Construct validity was supported by the inverse correlation of the positive and negative subscale scores.
- Criterion validity was supported by the relationship of the scale to a variety of external client variables, including history of pathology, family history, cognitive functioning, affective functioning, and subscale scores from the Brief Psychiatric Rating Scale.

The Present State Examination

Wing, Cooper, & Sartorius (1974); Manchanda & Hirsch (1986); Tress, Bellenis, Brownlow, Livingston, & Leff (1987)

Description

- 140 scaled items determine the mental status of clients with schizophrenia and other psychoses.
- Can be used to monitor changes over time.

- Provides scores on 38 syndromes that can be summarized into subscales, two of which are specific to psychotic behavior (delusions/hallucinations and behavior/speech).
- Ratings are based on both client reports and practitioner observation.
- Symptoms observed during the previous month are rated. Most are rated on the basis of frequency and severity.
- Takes 1 hour to complete; suggestions for some interview questions and probes are provided.
- Statistical output provides symptom profiles, subscale scores, a total score, and symptom classification into diagnostic categories.
- Limitations include not addressing organic symptoms, a bias toward reported versus observed behavior, a lack of utility in assessing non-communicative clients, and an insensitivity to mild symptoms.
- Has been amended to function with greater sensitivity as a change rating scale, with symptom ratings expanded to a 7-point range.

Reliability
Interrater reliability = .73 for two-participant repeat interviews ($N = 123$), .67 for test-retest interviews, and .96 for tape-recorded interviews

Validity
Concurrent validity with another general health questionnaire on three occasions was .78, .81, and .77.

The Scale for the Assessment of Negative Symptoms (SANS)
The Scale for the Assessment of Positive Symptoms (SAPS)

Andreasen (1982); Andreasen & Olsen (1982)

Description

- The SANS is a 25-item instrument rated along a 6-point scale with five subscales for affect, poverty of speech, apathy, anhedonia, and impairment of attention.
- The SAPS is a 35-item instrument with four subscales that measure hallucinations, delusions, bizarreness, and positive thought disorder, and one global measure of affect.
- Subscales for both instruments include a global rating index.
- Symptom ratings are to be considered within a time frame of 1 month.
- The SANS and SAPS are designed to be used by a practitioner in conjunction with client interviews, clinical observations, family member observations, reports from professionals, and client self-report.

Reliability

- Internal consistency for total scores was .90 for the SANS and .86 for the SAPS.
- Intraclass correlations produced reliability scores averaging .83 to .92 for the global summary and total scores for both instruments.
- Internal consistency for the global summary scores was .47 for the SANS and .58 for the SAPS.
- Test-retest reliability over a 2-year period ranged between .40 and .50.

Validity

- Factor analysis indicated that the two instruments measure fairly independent dimensions of symptomatology.
- Criterion validity was supported by the fact that outpatients had less severe positive and negative symptomatology than inpatients did, and people without schizophrenia had fewer symptoms than either group.

The UCSD Performance-Based Skills Assessment

Patterson, Goldman, McKibbin, Hughs, & Jeste (2001).

Description

- A performance-based measure that is appropriate for use with middle-aged and elderly people with schizophrenia living in the community.
- Measures five domains of functioning: household chores, communication, finance, transportation, and planning recreational activities.
- Each domain is addressed in terms of one or more tasks assigned to the participant for completion in the presence of the interviewer; the researcher rates successful completion of each task on a Likert scale that ranges between 0–4 and 0–9.
- Requires 30 minutes to complete.

Reliability
Interrater reliability assessed at .91.

Validity
Concurrent validity was partially established through a high correlation of results ($r = .86$) with one other similar measure.

The Quality of Life Interview

Lehman (1988)

Description

- A 45-minute instrument for use with people who have serious mental illnesses, including schizophrenia.
- Provides quality of life measures at a single point in time or measures of change in any of nine domains: living situation, family relations, social relations, leisure, work, finances, legal and safety concerns, and physical and mental health.
- Includes directions and scoring instructions and is highly structured to minimize interviewer effects.
- Scoring is either scaled or dichotomous.
- Organized by first asking the client for demographic information and a rating of general life satisfaction and then proceeding through the life domains, asking first about objective life conditions and then about satisfaction with those conditions. Concludes with another question about life satisfaction and some open-ended probes.
- Interviewing skills are important in setting limits on a respondent's tendency to digress and judging whether a respondent is too disturbed to tolerate the interview or provide valid responses.

Reliability

- Levels of internal consistency ranged from .44 to .90 for subscales.
- Test-retest correlations ranged from .29 to .98.

Validity

- Content validity was established by the selection of scale items from a variety of existing measures.
- Satisfactory construct validity was argued by (a) comparing intercorrelations of objective and subjective quality of life (QOL) measures within each domain, (b) correlating general life satisfaction scores with objective and subjective QOL scores within each domain, and (c) correlating general life satisfaction scores with measure of psychopathology.
- Favorable predictive validity was established by comparing overall predictive capacity of the model with respondents in the general population.

References

Aleman, M. A., Hijman, R., de Haan, E. H. F., & Kahn, R. S. (1998). Memory impairment in schizophrenia: A meta-analysis. *American Journal of Psychiatry, 156*, 1358–1366.

American Psychiatric Association. (2000). *Diagnostic and Statistical Manual of Mental Disorders* (4th ed., text rev.). Washington, DC: Author.

Andres, K., Brenner, H. D., Hodel, B., Pfammatter, M., & Roder, V. (2001). Further advancement of the integrated psychological therapy program for schizophrenic patients: Intervention methods and results. In H. D. Brenner & W. Boeker (Eds.), *The treatment of schizophrenia: Status and emerging trends* (pp. 121–136). Kirkland, WA: Hogrefe & Huber.

Bateson, G., Jackson, D. D., Haley, J., & Weakland, J. H. (1963). A note on the double-bind-1962. *Family Process, 2*, 154–161.

Benioff, L. (1995). What is it like to have schizophrenia? In S. Vinogradov (Ed.), *Treating schizophrenia* (pp. 81–107). San Francisco: Jossey-Bass.

Bentley, K. J., & Walsh, J. (2006). *The social worker and psychotropic medication* (3rd ed.). Pacific Grove, CA: Brooks/Cole.

Benton, M. K., & Schroeder, H. E. (1990). Social skills training with schizophrenics: A meta-analytic evaluation. *Journal of Consulting and Clinical Psychology, 58*, 741–747.

Biederman, J., Petty, C., Faraone, S. V. (2004). Phenomenology of childhood psychosis: Findings from a large sample of psychiatrically reffered youth *Journal of Nervous & Mental Disease, 192*(9), 607–614.

Black, D. W., Yates, W. R., & Andreasen, N. C. (1988). Schizophrenia, schizophreniform disorder, and delusional (paranoid) disorders. In J. A. Talbott, R. E. Hales, & S. C. Yudofsky (Eds.), *The American Psychiatric Press textbook of psychiatry* (pp. 357–402). Washington, DC: American Psychiatric Press.

Bogart, T., & Solomon, P. (1999). Collaborative procedures to share treatment information among mental health care providers, consumers, and families. *Psychiatric Services, 50*(10), 1321–1325.

Booth, G. K. (1995). What is the prognosis in schizophrenia? In S. Vinogradov (Ed.), *Treating schizophrenia* (pp. 125–156). San Francisco: Jossey-Bass.

Bowen, M. (1960). A family concept of schizophrenia. In D. D. Jackson (Ed.), *The etiology of schizophrenia* (pp. 346–372). New York: Basic Books.

Burns, B. J., & Santos, A. B. (1995). Assertive community treatment: An update of randomized trials. *Psychiatric Services, 46*, 669–675.

Butzlaff, R. L., & Hooley, J. M. (1998). Expressed emotion and psychiatric relapse. *Archives of General Psychiatry, 55*, 547–552.

Byrne, M., Agerbo, E., & Mortensen, P. B. (2002). Family history of psychiatric disorders and age at first contact in schizophrenia: An epidemiological study. *The British Journal of Psychiatry, 181*(43), 19–25.

Cardno, A., & Murray, R. M. (2003). The "classic" genetic epidemiology of schizophrenia. In R. M. Murray & P. B. Jones (Eds.), *The epidemiology of schizophrenia* (pp. 195–219). New York: Cambridge University Press.

Chambless, D. L., Bryan, A. D., Aiken, L. S., Steketee, G., & Hooley, J. M. (1999).

The structure of expressed emotion: A three-construct representation. *Psychological Assessment, 11*(1), 67–76.

Cohen, D. (2002). Research on the drug treatment of schizophrenia: A critical reappraisal and implications for social work education. *Journal of Social Work Education, 38*(2), 217–239.

Conklin, H. M., & Iacono, W. G. (2003). At issue: Assessment of schizophrenia: Getting closer to the cause. *Schizophrenia Bulletin, 29*(3), 409–412.

Csernansky, J. G., Mahmoud, R., & Brenner, R. (2002). A comparison of risperidone and haloperidol for the prevention of relapse in patients with schizophrenia. *The New England Journal of Medicine, 346* (16–22).

Dawson, D. F. L., Blum, H. M., & Bartolucci, G. (1983). *Schizophrenia in focus.* New York: Human Sciences Press.

Dobson, D. (1996). Long-term support and social skills training for patients with schizophrenia. *Psychiatric Services, 47*(11), 1195–1199.

Falloon, I. R. H., Kydd, R. R., Coverdale, J. H., & Laidlaw, T. M. (1996). Early detection and intervention for initial episodes of schizophrenia. *Schizophrenia Bulletin, 22*(2), 271–282.

Fenton, W. S., McGlashan, T. H., Victor, B. J., & Blyler, C. R. (1997). Symptoms, subtypes, and suicidality of patients with schizophrenia spectrum disorders. *American Journal of Psychiatry, 154*(2), 199–204.

Freud, S. (1966). *Introductory lectures on psychoanalysis.* New York: W. W. Norton.

Gomes-Schwartz, B. (1984). Individual psychotherapy of schizophrenia. In A. S. Bellack (Ed.), *Schizophrenia: Treatment, management, and rehabilitation* (pp. 307–335). New York: Grune & Stratton.

Gomory, T. (1999). Programs of assertive community treatment: A critical review. *Ethical Human Sciences and Services, 1*(2), 147–163.

Gottesman, I. I. (1991). *Schizophrenia genesis: The origins of madness.* New York: Freeman.

Hatfield, A. B., & Lefley, H. P. (1993). Surviving mental illness: Coping and adaptation. New York: Guilford.

Hogarty, G. E. (2002). *Personal therapy for schizophrenia and related disorders.* New York: Guilford.

Hogarty, G. E., Anderson, C. M., Reiss, D. J., Kornblith, S. J., Greenwald, D. P., Ulrich, R. F., et al. (1991). Family psychoeducation, social skills training, and maintenance chemotherapy in the aftercare treatment of schizophrenia: II. Two-year effects of a controlled study on relapse and adjustment. *Archives of General Psychiatry, 48*(4), 340–347.

Hogarty, G. E., & Flesher, S. (1992). Cognitive remediation in schizophrenia: Proceed with caution. *Schizophrenia Bulletin, 18*(1), 51–57.

Huxley, N. A., Rendall, M., & Sederer, L. (2000). Psychosocial treatment in schizophrenia: A review of the past 20 years. *Journal of Nervous & Mental Disease, 188*(4), 187–201.

Johnstone, E. C., Cosway, R., & Lawrie, S. M. (2002). Distinguishing characteristics of subjects with good and poor early outcome in the Edinburgh high-risk study. *The British Journal of Psychiatry, 181*(43), s26–s29.

Julien, R. M. (2001). *A primer of drug action: A concise, nontechnical guide to the ac-*

tions, uses, and side effects of psychoactive drugs (9th ed.). New York: W. H. Freeman.

Kanas, N. (2000). Group therapy and schizophrenia: An integrative model. In B. Martindale & A. Bateman (Eds.), *Psychosis: Psychological approaches and their effectiveness* (pp. 120–133). London: Gaskell/Royal College of Pharmacists.

Kanter, J. (1995). Case management with long term patients: A comprehensive approach. In Soreff, S. (Ed.), *Handbook for the treatment of the seriously mentally ill* (pp. 169–189). Seattle: Hogrefe and Humber.

Karon, B., & VandenBos, G. R. (1972). The consequences of psychotherapy with schizophrenic patients. *Psychotherapy; Theory, Research and Practice, 9,* 111–119.

Kirkpatrick, B., Herrera Catanedo, S., & Vazquez-Barquero, J. (2002). Summer birth and deficit schizophrenia: Cantabria, Spain. *Journal of Nervous and Mental Disease, 190*(8), 526–532.

Klingberg, S., Wiedemann, G., & Buckremer, G. (2001). Cognitive-behavior therapy for schizophrenic patients: Design and preliminary results of a randomized effectiveness trial. *Zeitschrift fur Klinische Psychologie und Psychotherapie, 30*(4), 259–267.

Lam, D. H. (1991). Psychosocial family intervention in schizophrenia: A review of empirical studies. *Psychological Medicine, 21,* 423–441.

Lehman, A. F. (1995). Vocational rehabilitation in schizophrenia. *Schizophrenia Bulletin, 21*(4), 645–656.

Lenoir, M. E., Dingemans, P., Schene, A. H., Hart, A. A., & Linszen, D. H. (2002). The course of parental expressed emotion and psychotic episodes after family intervention in recent-onset schizophrenia: A longitudinal study. *Social Psychiatry & Psychiatric Epidemiology, 39*(2), 69–75.

Leonard, B. E. (2003). *Fundamentals of psychopharmacology.* New York: Martin Duwitz.

Lewis, S., & Higgins, N. (1996). *Brain imaging in psychiatry.* Cambridge, MA: Blackwell.

Lidz, T. (1975). *The origin and treatment of schizophrenic disorders.* London: Hogarth.

Mahler, M. S., Pine, F., & Bergman, A. (1975). *The psychological birth of the human infant.* New York: Basic Books.

Malaspina, D., Goetz, R. R., Friedman, J. H., Kaufmann, C. A., Faraone, S. V., Tsuang, M., et al. (2001). Traumatic brain injury and schizophrenia in members of schizophrenia and bipolar disorder pedigrees. *The American Journal of Psychiatry, 158*(3), 440–446.

Marder, S. R., Essock, S. M., Miller, A. L., Buchanan, R. W., Davis, J. M., Kane, J. M., et al. (2002). The Mount Sinai conference on the pharmacotherapy of schizophrenia. *Schizophrenia Bulletin, 28*(1), 5–16.

Marenco, S., Weinberger, D. R. (2000). The neurodevelopmental hypothesis of schizophrenia: Following a trial of evidence from cradle to grave. *Development & Psychopathology, 12*(3), 501–527.

Maynard, T. M., Siklich, L., Lieberman, J. A., & La Mantia, A. S. (2001). Neural development, cell-cell signaling, and the "two-hit" hypothesis of schizophrenia. *Schizophrenia Bulletin, 27*(3), 457–476.

McClellan, J., McCurry, C., Snell, J., & DuBose, A. (1999). Early-onset psychotic disorders: Course and outcome over a 2-year period. *Journal of the American Academy of Child and Adolescent Psychiatry, 38*(11), 1380.

McClellan, J., & Werry, J. (2000). Summary of the practice parameters for the assessment and treatment of children and adolescents with schizophrenia. *Journal of the American Academy of Child and Adolescent Psychiatry, 39*(12), 1580–1582.

McGlashan, T. H., Miller, T. J., & Woods, S. W. (2001). Pre-onset detection and intervention research in schizophrenia psychoses: Current estimates of benefit and risk. *Schizophrenia Bulletin, 27*(4), 563–570.

Meinecke, D. L. (2001). Editor's introduction: The developmental etiology of schizophrenia hypothesis: What is the evidence? *Schizophrenia Bulletin, 27*(3), 335–336.

Meltzer, H. Y. (1991). The mechanism of action of novel antipsychotic drugs. *Schizophrenia Bulletin, 17*(2), 71–95.

Miller, R., & Mason, S. E. (2001). Using group therapy to enhance treatment compliance in first episode schizophrenia. *Social Work with Groups, 24*(1), 37–51.

Mohr, W. K., Lafuze, J. E., & Mohr, B. D. (2000). Opening caregiver minds: National Alliance for the Mentally Ill's (NAMI) Provider Education Program. *Archives of Psychiatric Nursing, 14*(5), 235–243.

Mueser, K. T., & Berenbaum, H. (1990). Psychodynamic treatment of schizophrenia. Is there a future? *Psychological Medicine, 20*, 253–262.

Mueser, K. T., Bond, G. R., Drake, R. E., & Resnick, S. G. (1998). Models of community care for severe mental illness: A review of research on case management. *Schizophrenia Bulletin, 24*, 37–74.

Mulvany, F., O'Callaghan, E., Takei, N., Byrne, M., & Fearon, P. (2001). Effects of social class at birth on risk and presentation of schizophrenia: Case-control study. *British Medical Journal, 323*(7326), 1398–1401.

Murray, R. M., & Jones, P. B. (Eds.). (2003). *The epidemiology of schizophrenia.* New York: Cambridge University Press.

National Alliance for the Mentally Ill. (1989). *Siblings and adult children's network: Background information and articles booklet.* Arlington, VA: Author.

Olfson, M. (1990). *The efficacy of assertive community treatment for the severely mentally ill.* Unpublished manuscript.

Pilling, S., Bebbington, P., Kuipers, E., Garety, P., Geddes, J., Martindale, B., et al. (2002a). Psychological treatments in schizophrenia: II. Meta-analysis of randomized controlled trials of social skills training and cognitive remediation. *Psychological Medicine, 32*(5), 783–791.

Pilling, S., Bebbington, P., Kuipers, E., Garety, P., Geddes, J., Orbach, G., et al. (2002b). Psychological treatments in schizophrenia: I. Meta-analysis of family intervention and cognitive behavior therapy. *Psychological Medicine, 32*(5), 763–782.

Pratt, S., & Mueser, K. T. (2002). Social skills training for schizophrenia. In S. G. Hofman & M. C. Thompson (Eds.), *Treating chronic and severe mental disorders: A handbook of empirically supported interventions* (pp. 18–52). New York: Guilford.

Randolph, E. A., Eth, S., Glynn, S. M., Paz, G. G., Leong, G. B., Shaner, A. L., et al. (1994). Behavioral family management in schizophrenia: Outcome of a clinic-based intervention. *British Journal of Psychiatry, 164*, 501–506.

Rosen, A. (2000). Ethics of early prevention in schizophrenia. *Australian & New Zealand Journal of Psychiatry, 34*(Suppl.), S208–S212.

Rubin, A. (1992). Case management. In S. M. Rose (Ed.), *Case management and social work practice* (pp. 5–24). New York: Longman.

Sadock, B. J., & Sadock, V. A. (2005). *Kaplan & Sadock's Comprehensive Textbook of Psychiatry.* Philadelphia: Lippincott Williams & Wilkins.

Schatzberg, A. F., & Nemeroff, C. B. (Eds.). (2001). *Essentials of clinical psychopharmacology.* Washington, DC: American Psychiatric Press.

Schooler, N. R., & Keith, S. J. (1993). The clinical research base for the treatment of schizophrenia. *Psychopharmacology Bulletin, 29*(4), 431–446.

Scott, J. E., & Dixon, L. B. (1995). Assertive case management for schizophrenia. *Schizophrenia Bulletin, 21,* 657–668.

Seeman, M. V. (2003). Gender differences in schizophrenia across the life span. In C. I. Cohen (Ed.), *Schizophrenia into later life: Treatment, research, and policy* (pp. 141–154). Washington, DC: American Psychiatric Publishing.

Singer, M. T., Wynne, L. C., & Toohey, M. L. (1978). Communication disorders and the families of schizophrenics. In L. C. Wynne, R. L. Cromwell, & S. Matthysse (Eds.), *The nature of schizophrenia* (pp. 512–516). New York: Wiley.

Solomon, P. (1992). The efficacy of case management services for severely mentally disabled clients. *Community Mental Health Journal, 28,* 163–180.

Stahl, S. M. (2000). *Essential psychopharmacology: Neuroscientific basis and practical applications (2nd ed.).* New York: Cambridge University Press.

Stein, L. I., & Test, M. A. (1980). Alternative mental hospital treatment: I. Conceptual model, treatment program, and clinical evaluation. *Archives of General Psychiatry, 37,* 392–397.

Tamminga, C. T. (1996, Winter). The new generation of antipsychotic drugs. *National Alliance for Research on Schizophrenia and Depression Newsletter.*

Trierweiler, S. J., Neighbors, H. W., Munday, C., Thompson, E. E., Binion, V. J., & Gomez, J. P. (2000). Clinician attributions associated with the diagnosis of schizophrenia in African-American and non-African American patients. *Journal of Consulting and Clinical Psychology, 68*(1), 171–175.

Tsuang, M. T., Stone, W. S., & Faraone, S. (2000). Toward reformulating the diagnosis of schizophrenia. *American Journal of Psychiatry, 157*(7), 1041–1050.

Twamley, E. W., Jeste, D. V., & Lehman, A. F. (2003). Vocational rehabilitation in schizophrenia and other psychotic disorders: A literature review and meta-analysis of randomized controlled trials. *Journal of Nervous & Mental Disease, 19*(8), 515–523.

Vaughan, K., Doyle, M., McConaghy, N., Blaszczynski, A., Fox, A., & Tarrier, N. (1992). The Sydney intervention trial: A controlled trial of relatives' counseling to reduce schizophrenic relapse. *Social Psychiatry and Psychiatric Epidemiology, 27*(1), 16–21.

Vaughn, C., & Leff, J. (1976). The measurement of expressed emotion in the families of psychiatric patients. *British Journal of Clinical Psychology, 15,* 157–165.

Velligan, D. I., Mahurin, R. K., True, J. E., Lefton, R. S., & Flores, C. V. (1996). Preliminary evaluation of cognitive adaptation training to compensate for cognitive deficits in schizophrenia. *Psychiatric Services, 47*(4), 415–417.

Verdoux, H., Geddes, J. R., Takei, N., Lawrie, S. M., Bovet, P., Eagles, J. M., et al. (1997). Obstetric complications and age at onset in schizophrenia: An international collaborative meta-analysis of individual patient data. *American Journal of Psychiatry, 154*(9), 1220–1227.

Wilson, W. H., & Claussen, A. M. (1993). New antipsychotic medications: Hope for the future. *Innovations & Research, 2,* 3–11.

Yung, A. R., McGorry, P. D., McFarlane, C. A., Jackson, H. J., Patton, G. C., & Rakkar, A. (1996). Monitoring and care of young people at incipient risk of psychosis. *Schizophrenia Bulletin, 22*(2), 283–303.

▉▉▉▉ References for Assessment Instruments for Schizophrenia

Andersen, J., Larsen, J. K., Schultz, V., Nielsen, B. M., Korner, A., Behnke, K., et al. (1989). The brief psychiatric rating scale: Dimension of schizophrenia—reliability and construct validity. *Psychopathology, 22,* 168–176.

Andreasen, N. C. (1982). Negative symptoms of schizophrenia: Definition and reliability. *Archives of General Psychiatry, 39,* 784–788.

Andreasen, N. C., & Olsen, S. (1982). Negative vs. positive schizophrenia: Definition and validation. *Archives of General Psychiatry, 39,* 789–794.

Bigelow, L. B., & Berthot, B. D. (1989). The psychiatric symptom assessment scale (PSAS). *Psychopharmacology Bulletin, 25*(2), 168–179.

Kay, S. R., Fiszbein, A., & Opler, L. A. (1987). The positive and negative syndrome scale for schizophrenia. *Schizophrenia Bulletin, 13*(2), 261–275.

Lehman, A. F. (1988). A quality of life interview for the chronically mentally ill. *Evaluation and Program Planning, 11,* 51–62.

Manchanda, R., & Hirsch, S. R. (1986). Rating scales for clinical studies on schizophrenia. In P. B. Bradley & S. R. Hirsch (Eds.), *The psychopharmacology and treatment of schizophrenia* (pp. 234–260). New York: Oxford University Press.

Overall, J. E., & Gorman, D. R. (1962). The brief psychiatric rating scale. *Psychological Reports, 10,* 799–812.

Patterson, T. L., Goldman, S., McKibbin, C. L., Hughs, T., & Jeste, D. V. (2001). UCSD performance-based skills assessment: Development of a new measure of everyday functioning for severely mentally ill adults. *Schizophrenia Bulletin, 27*(2), 235–245.

Tress, K. H., Bellenis, C., Brownlow, J. M., Livingston, G., & Leff, J. P. (1987). The Present State Examination Change rating scale. *British Journal of Psychiatry, 150,* 201–207.

Wing, J. K., Cooper, J. E., & Sartorius, N. (1974). *The measurement and classification of psychiatric symptoms.* Cambridge: Cambridge University Press.

15　Personality Disorders

The *DSM-IV* category of personality disorders represents an attempt by human service practitioners to identify and help those clients whose chronic problems in social functioning are related to ingrained and persistent patterns of thinking, behaving, and feeling. Although few professionals question the existence of clients with such persistent problems, the idea of a personality as *disordered* is controversial in the social work profession. Some believe that it represents negative labeling and disregards the profession's transactional, person-in-environment perspective on human functioning. In this chapter, we consider the concept of personality disorder and its rationale for inclusion in the *DSM-IV*. We also discuss the nature of one personality disorder that is often encountered by clinical social workers: the borderline type.

Can a Personality Be Disordered?

Personality is an extremely difficult concept to define, even though few people dispute that we all have one. One noted theorist defines *personality* as a stable set of tendencies and characteristics that determine commonalities and differences in people, the psychological behaviors (thoughts, beliefs, actions) that have continuity over time and that may not be easily understood as the sole result of the social and biological pressures of the moment (Maddi, 1996). This definition illustrates the complexity of the concept. Theorists and researchers have developed many models of personality over the years that include different core features, developmental processes, and peripheral characteristics.

There is still no consensus, however, on what a personality is. A problem with the concept of a personality *disorder*, then, is that the primary concept on which it is based is vague (Mattaini, 1994). The ambiguity of the concept is partly related to the fact that it emerged out of psychodynamic theory, which often relies on mental constructs that are difficult to operationalize. Further, social workers should be concerned about using these diagnoses because they appear to describe the *total person*, rather than a particular aspect of the person, and they are generally used in pejorative terms. Even Davis and Millon (1994), arguing in favor of the concept, admit that the notion of a personality disorder as an "entity within a person" is not accurate. They feel more comfortable focusing on personality *patterns*— repetitive behaviors and feelings that are problematic.

Clearly, the term *personality disorder* is misleading and could be replaced with some other term to identify those habits of behavior that create recurrent problems in social functioning for some people. Indeed, many Axis I disorders are persistent as well! As we proceed through this chapter, it should be kept in mind that social and environmental factors always have a significant influence on the thoughts, feelings, and behaviors of clients who exhibit rigid responses to life stress.

Characteristics of Personality Disorders

Several theorists have summarized what they believe are common characteristics of all the personality disorders. According to the American Psychiatric Association (APA) (2000), they are categorized by enduring cognitions and behaviors that:

- Are deviant from cultural standards
- Are pervasive and rigid
- Have an onset in adolescence or early adulthood
- Are stable over time
- Lead to unhappiness and impairment
- Include maladaptive behavior in at least two of the following areas: *affect* (range and intensity of emotions), *cognition* (how the self and others are perceived), *impulse control*, and *interpersonal functioning*

Theorists have attempted to summarize the core features of personality disorders. Millon (1996) asserts three behavioral characteristics that distinguish pathological from normal personalities. First is *tenuous stability*; the person is fragile and lacks resilience under stress. Second is *adaptive inflexibility*, as the person has few strategies for coping with stress. Third are *vicious cycles*, in that the person's maladaptive behavior patterns seem to not only leave current problems unsolved but also generate new problems. Sadock and Sadock (2005) write that people with personality disorders tend to be *irresponsible* (unable to acknowledge their part in things going wrong), *lacking in empathy* (being too driven by their own needs), and *deficient in problem-solving skills*; have an *external locus of control* (seeing control and power as existing outside of themselves); and *generate distress in others* (rather than in themselves). Morrison (1995) writes that their problems in social functioning are often more pervasive than those found in other disorders, their problems are rooted in interpersonal relationships, they tend to "get under the skin" of other people, and they are likely to deny clinical problems and the need for intervention.

The 10 *DSM-IV* personality disorders are listed here, with their primary identifying characteristics:

- Paranoid: distrust and suspiciousness
- Schizoid: detachment from social relationships
- Schizotypal: acute discomfort in close relationships, cognitive or perceptual distortions, and eccentric behavior
- Antisocial: distrust of others and violations of their rights
- Borderline: instability in interpersonal relationships, self-image, affect, and impulse control
- Histrionic: excessive emotionality and attention seeking
- Narcissistic: grandiosity, a need for admiration, and a lack of empathy
- Avoidant: social inhibition, feelings of inadequacy, and hypersensitivity to negative evaluation
- Dependent: submissive and clinging behavior related to an excessive need to be taken care of
- Obsessive-compulsive: preoccupation with orderliness, perfectionism, and control

While subscribing to the concept of discrete personality disorders, the *DSM* does attempt to group them into categories, as described in the next section.

Three Clusters of Personality Disorders

The *DSM* classifies the 10 personality disorders into three clusters, based on shared core characteristics (Woods, 1999). Cluster A includes the *paranoid, schizoid,* and *schizotypal* disorders. People with these disorders are considered by others to be odd and eccentric. These disorders are believed to have a strong genetic base and are more common in the biological relatives of people with schizophrenia. Still, the great majority of people with these disorders never develop an Axis I disorder. The cluster B disorders (*anti-social, borderline, histrionic*, and *narcissistic*) are characterized by dramatic, emotional, and erratic presentations. These disorders may have a partial genetic base in that they have associations with other *DSM* Axis I disorders (such as antisocial personality with substance abuse, borderline personality with mood disorders, and histrionic personality with somatic disorders). The cluster C disorders (*avoidant, dependent*, and *obsessive-compulsive*) feature anxious or fearful presentations. They are associated with the anxiety disorders.

Diagnostic Considerations

All personality disorder diagnoses are recorded on Axis II. If the social worker plans to focus intervention on the personality disorder, the term *principal diagnosis* should be included in parentheses. The cluster A disorders may be specified as *premorbid* if they were present before the symptoms of the Axis I diagnosis (if an Axis I diagnosis will be the primary focus of intervention). This provision reflects the thinking that the cluster A disorders are largely genetic and may be precursors to certain psychotic disorders.

The practitioner must be cautious about diagnosing a personality disorder, partly because he or she will be making judgments about personality functioning in the context of the client's ethnic, cultural, and social background. Some cultures, for example, value interpersonal dependency more than others do. In a related manner, it is known that African Americans are often unjustly diagnosed with paranoid personality disorder (Whaley, 2001).

A personality disorder should rarely be applied to children and adolescents. Personality patterns are evolving during those years, and they are not considered to reach a state of constancy until late adolescence or young adulthood. Borderline personality disorder lacks validity in young people because many of its symptoms have been shown to occur in the course of normal adolescence (Chabrol et al., 2004). To diagnose a personality disorder in a client under age 18, the qualifying symptoms must have been present for a full year.

Other diagnostic challenges are low interrater reliability with personality disorders and their requirement of a longitudinal versus time-limited assessment approach. In fact, the *DSM* acknowledges that its means of classifying personality disorders is debatable. As noted earlier, *DSM-IV* uses a *categorical* approach, in which the disorders are considered to be distinct entities (Millon & Davis, 1999). Other attempts have been made to identify the most fundamental *dimensions* that underlie the entire domain of normal and abnormal personality functioning and to assess clients on a continuum of normalcy and pathology. One model, for example, has five dimensions: neuroticism, introversion versus extroversion, closedness versus openness to experience, antagonism versus agreeableness, and conscientiousness (Costa & Widiger, 2002). In a dimensional system, clients would be assessed as to their position on each of these. The APA asserts that its three clusters (odd-eccentric, dramatic-emotional, and anxious-fearful) may be considered dimensions that appear on continua with Axis I disorders.

With this introduction, we now move into a discussion of borderline personality disorder. People with this disorder are frequently encountered in clinical settings and have historically been difficult for practitioners to effectively treat. Many of the principles of assessment and intervention described here are also relevant to clients with other personality disorders.

Borderline Personality Disorder

Borderline personality disorder (BPD) is characterized by a pattern of instability in interpersonal relationships and self-image and a capacity for frequent and intense negative emotions. Although there is disagreement about the core features of the disorder, most observers agree on the two characteristics of *highly variable mood* and *impulsive behavior*; this was borne out in a large research study by Trull (2001). As described later, the disorder probably results from an interaction of genetic temperament and learned behavior.

Persons with BPD are usually dramatic, energetic, and lively, and they may be personable, charming, and fun at times. They self-disclose to people they like very early in those relationships. When upset, however, their presentation changes abruptly, and they become extremely angry, negative, depressed, and self-destructive in various ways. This is due to their characteristic defense (or coping) mechanism of *splitting*, meaning that they cannot maintain an idea of another person as having both positive and negative qualities. People are judged as being either all good or all bad. For the person with borderline personality disorder, a significant other may be seen as all good and treated as such, but when she or he behaves in a way that is perceived as disappointing, that person becomes all bad and may be completely rejected, temporarily or permanently. In fact, one study found that people with BPD have a strong tendency to view others negatively compared with people with other personality disorders (Arntz & Veen, 2001).

Borderline personality disorder is a significant mental health problem that is present in cultures around the world (APA, 2000). It is the most common personality disorder in clinical settings. BPD is diagnosed in 10%

of clients seen in outpatient mental health clinics, 15 to 20% of psychiatric inpatients, and 3 to 60% of clinical populations who have a personality disorder. It occurs in an estimated 2% of the general population. Because of their interpersonally chaotic lifestyles, these individuals may be found among multiproblem clients in a variety of social service settings. Borderline personality disorder is diagnosed predominantly in women, with an estimated gender ratio of 3:1.

It is paradoxical that although people with BPD have difficulty maintaining relationships, they are extremely social and cannot tolerate being alone. Their perceptions and behaviors involve frantic efforts to avoid abandonment, the possibility of which creates overwhelming anxiety. They experience frequent emotional turmoil and are often in crisis on account of their intense feelings of anger, emptiness, and hopelessness that occur when they are stressed. The person with BPD experiences severe depression when feeling abandoned or mistreated by others, even though these perceptions may be distortions of others' motives.

Other common features of BPD include anxiety, transient psychotic symptoms, suicidal or self-mutilating behaviors, and substance abuse. Up to 55% of inpatients with BPD have histories of suicide attempts, although the actual suicide rate is 5 to 10%, similar to that for people with schizophrenia and major affective disorder (APA, 2000). Up to 80% have committed acts of self-mutilation (such as cutting the forearms or face). Studies have shown that nonsuicidal acts of self-mutilation are intended to express anger, punish oneself, generate normal feelings when experiencing numbness or depersonalization, or distract oneself from painful feelings, whereas suicide attempts are intended to permanently relieve negative emotions (e.g., Brown, Comtois, & Linehan, 2002).

The diagnostic term *borderline* is misleading. When it was first developed for *DSM-III* in the late 1970s, BPD was believed to characterize clients who were on the "border" between psychotic and neurotic disorders. This vague distinction is no longer conceptually useful, but the term has persisted. Suggestions for alternative nomenclature have included *cycloid* and *emotionally unstable* personality disorder (Millon, 1996). The *borderline* term is also misleading in that it tends to be attributed to nonpsychotic clients who are especially difficult for clinical practitioners to engage in a steady, crisis-free intervention, and thus it may be overused.

Risk and Protective Factors

Borderline personality disorder most likely results from a combination of biological and environmental factors (see Table 15.1). It is approximately five times more common among first-degree biological relatives of those

Table 15.1

Risks and Protective Factors: Borderline Personality Disorder

Factors	Risks	Protective Factors
Neurological, biological, and genetic Currently there is more focus on these factors, and more empirical studies are needed.	Tetrogenic prenatal environment[a] Approximately 75% of individuals diagnosed BPD are female Immediate relatives with affective disorders and/or mental illness (an 11.5% risk) A difficult or sensitive temperament	Healthy prenatal environment Being male may not reduce risk, but fewer males are diagnosed with BPD; studies are conflicting No affective disorders or mental illness in immediate or extended family Easy, relaxed temperament, inborn resilience
Family/Caretaker	Chaotic, dysfunctional family with parental substance abuse, legal issues (antisocial disorder or parent in jail or prison), parental psychopathology, and financial problems	Stable family life, with little or no substance abuse, low socioeconomic level, legal issues or psychopathology
Environment	Radical environmental conditions affecting neural development in infancy, seen in extreme neglect, impoverishment, and war-torn areas, Skodol et al. (2002) reports risk at 44–65%. Invalidating environment at home, school, or church[b]	Physically and emotionally safe environment in infancy Validating social and environmental experiences
Psychological and social stressors	Trauma / Sexual Abuse, especially before age 10 and in cases of incest / Physical and /or Verbal abuse during childhood	Little or no trauma or abuse Early comprehensive treatment of psychosocial stressors thought to reduce severity or onset of PDs High intelligence may improve prognosis

[a]Anything adversely affecting normal cellular development in embryo or fetus

[b]Defined as "when communication of private experiences are met with erratic, inappropriate, and extreme responses and personal expressions of thought, emotions, and feelings are punished or trivialized" (Linehan, 1993, p. 49).

with the disorder than in the general population (APA, 2000). There is also a greater familial risk with BPD for substance abuse disorders, antisocial personality disorder, and mood disorders. Still, these risks may be related to environmental conditions as well as personal constitution. One theorist writes that BPD is what happens when the child with a difficult temperament meets an invalidating environment (Linehan, 1993). The person seems to have a predisposition to affective instability and a childhood history of neglect, abuse, loss, or lack of validation.

Biological Factors

The biological causes of BPD are speculative (Johnson, 1999). Certain of the "cardinal" symptoms, including impulsivity, irritability, hypersensitivity to stimulation, emotional lability, reactivity, and intensity, are often associated with a biological foundation. In particular, researchers have studied the link between BPD and two neurotransmitters: serotonin (which is diminished) and norepinephrine (which is overactive) (Gurvits, Koenigsberg, & Siever, 2000). Serotonin has been linked to impulsive external aggression and self-directed aggression. A relationship between the personality and affective disorders has long been argued. People with BPD are said to have a cyclothymic temperament—mood swings that resemble bipolar disorder (the interpersonal conflicts are a differentiating factor). Biological contributors to this process may include elevations of the person's catecholamines (neurotransmitters that mediate mood states and aggression) and dysfunctions in the locus coeruleus (used for information processing and memory), the amygdala in the limbic system (that manages fear and anxiety), and the hippocampus (a center of emotional experience) (Skodol et al., 2002).

Psychological Factors

Despite limited evidence to support their validity, psychoanalytic theorists have produced a rich literature regarding people with borderline personality disorder (St. Clair, 1999). These clients are said to have failed to successfully negotiate the delicate task of separating from primary caregivers while maintaining an internalized sense of being cared for. During their infancy, they either were, or believed themselves to be, abandoned. According to Kernberg (1975), these individuals are fixated at a separation-individuation phase of development and cannot clearly distinguish between the self and other people. They feel that when a parent or other close attachment figure is not physically present or immediately available, he or she is gone forever. The person often experiences intense separation anxiety as a result and thus tends to be dependent and "clingy."

Most empirical research shows a marked relationship between childhood trauma and borderline symptoms (Zanarni & Frankenberg, 1997). Such trauma includes loss, sexual and physical violence, neglect, abuse, witnessing domestic violence, and parental substance abuse or criminality. Ongoing sexual abuse in childhood is the best predictor of the severity of borderline syndromes. One study of 290 people with BPD found a positive association between the severity of childhood sexual abuse and the severity of symptoms and functional impairment (Zanarini et al., 2002). Dissociative symptoms were positively associated with inconsistent treatment by a caregiver, sexual abuse by a caregiver, witnessing sexual violence as a child, and an adult rape history (Zanarini, Ruser, Frankenberg, Hennen, & Gunderson, 2000).

Childhood trauma as a risk factor for BPD also appears to be related to the person's biological sensitivity to environmental stimuli. This is proposed to act through the neurotransmitters described previously during the physical development of people who experience childhood trauma. In studies of predictor variables for the BPD diagnosis, *interpersonal sensitivity* emerged as most significant (Blais, Hilsenroth, & Fowler, 1999). The combination of these two factors may produce a clinical picture of a person who uses impulsive and self-destructive behavior to manage the stress related to her or his hypersensitive reactions to certain stimuli.

In considering general interpersonal factors in the family, Bandelow, B., Krause, J., & Wedekind, D. (2005) list four features in the development of the borderline personality. First is family chaos, which contributes to a sense of drama and unpredictability in the family. Second is traumatic abandonment. The third factor is the family's belief that a member's independence is a negative characteristic, resulting in punishment of children who take initiatives in that direction. Fourth, the client is positively reinforced (cared for) only when he or she is in crisis.

Social Factors

Another risk factor for borderline personality disorder is the structure of Western society, in which the upbringing of most children is limited to one or two primary caregivers, without additional consistent parent figures available to "fill in" when these caregivers prove to be inadequate. This is in contrast to some cultural groups (such as Latinos and African Americans) in which extended family may routinely provide major parenting roles. Western society's reliance on the nuclear family fails to provide opportunities for children to have "second chances" to develop healthy attachments when these might be developmentally beneficial.

Course of the Disorder

Long-term follow-up studies of treated clients with borderline personality disorder indicate that its course is variable. A client's early adulthood is often characterized by chronic instability, with episodes of serious affective and impulse control problems and high levels of use of health and mental health resources. One study of 351 young adults found that BPD predicted negative outcomes in the areas of academic achievement and social maladjustment over the subsequent 2 years, regardless of the presence of any other pathology (Bagge et al., 2004). Later in life, a majority of individuals attain greater stability in social and occupational functioning, in part because their acting-out symptoms decrease (Himelick & Walsh, 2002).

Longitudinal studies indicate that about a third of clients with BPD appear to recover 10 years after the initial diagnosis, solidifying their identity during the intervening years and replacing their self-damaging acts, inordinate anger, and stormy relationships with more mature and modulated behavior patterns (Paris, 2003). After 10 years of intervention, 50% of clients no longer meet the full criteria for the disorder. Longitudinal studies of hospitalized clients with BPD indicate that even though they may gradually attain functional roles 10 to 15 years after admission to psychiatric facilities, only about half of the women and a quarter of the men attain enduring success in intimacy (as indicated by marriage or long-term sexual partnership). Half to three quarters of clients by that time achieve stable, full-time employment. A limitation of these studies is that they concentrated on clients with BPD from middle-class or upper-middle-class families. Clients with the disorder from backgrounds of poverty may have substantially lower success rates in the spheres of intimacy and work.

The social cost for clients with borderline personality disorder and their families is substantial. Recent data indicate that clients with borderline personality disorder show greater lifetime utilization of most major categories of medication and of most types of psychotherapy than clients with schizotypal, avoidant, or obsessive-compulsive personality disorder or major depressive disorder (Zanarini, Frankenburg, Hennen, & Silk, 2004).

Comorbid Disorders

Many disorders are often comorbid with borderline personality disorder, partly because its diagnostic criteria include strong indicators for other disorders. The most commonly seen Axis I disorders include the mood disorders, substance-related disorders, eating disorders (notably bulimia), PTSD and other anxiety disorders, dissociative identity disorder, and attention-deficit/hyperactivity disorder (ADHD). There is overlap among the symptoms of the personality disorders as well, and BPD most often co-occurs with the antisocial and avoidant types (as well as the passive-aggressive and depressive types, which are at present limited to the *DSM-IV* appendix for further study) (Grilo, Sanislow, & McGlashan, 2002). It is sometimes difficult to decide when Axis I symptoms are distinctive enough to diagnose a separate disorder; for that reason, the practitioner should be patient in the assessment phase before making such a determination. When the practitioner combines an Axis I disorder and BPD, intervention should focus on both disorders. The presence of BPD is a risk factor for recovery from an Axis I disorder.

The features that are particularly characteristic of borderline personality disorder are emptiness, self-condemnation, abandonment fears, hopelessness, self-destructiveness, and repeated suicidal gestures. The depressive features may meet criteria for major depressive disorder or dysthymic disorder. A 2-year follow-up study of 58 clients with BPD showed that the exacerbation of an Axis I condition, especially major depressive disorder and substance use, heightens the risk of a client's suicide attempt (Yen et al., 2003). The risk of suicide appears to be highest when clients are in their 20s.

The presence of substance use has major implications for treatment, because clients with BPD who abuse substances generally have a poor outcome and are at a higher risk for suicide and also death or injury from accidents (van den Bosch, Verheul, & van den Brink, 2001). To the extent that clients may use various substances to mask depression, anxiety, and other related symptoms, their willingness to take prescription medications (antidepressants or nonhabituating antianxiety drugs) may alleviate the underlying symptoms and thus reduce their temptation to use alcohol or drugs.

Intervention

Clients with borderline personality disorder are challenging for practitioners to engage in a sustained process of intervention. It is estimated that 40 to 60% of these clients drop out of intervention prematurely (Marziali, 2002). The empirical data to support particular types of intervention are limited. What follows is a review of commonly accepted practices regarding psychosocial and pharmacological intervention (Oldham et al., 2002).

Most clients with borderline personality disorder require ongoing intervention to achieve and maintain improvements in their tolerance of interpersonal relationships and overall functioning. Standard components of intervention include establishing and maintaining a therapeutic framework and alliance, responding to crises and monitoring the client's safety, providing education about the disorder, supplying consistent supportive or insight-oriented therapy, and coordinating intervention provided by other providers (such as physicians and rehabilitation counselors). Some practitioners create a hierarchy of intervention goals (such as first focusing on suicidal behavior).

When possible, group interventions are preferable for persons with BPD (Marziali, 2002), because they:

- Dilute the intensity of client projections onto the practitioner
- Provide opportunities for a variety of client identifications with other members, rather than a single intensive one (with a practitioner)
- Provide more opportunities for learning and experimenting with new patterns of behavior
- Provide more feedback about self-destructive tendencies
- Provide a mutually supportive environment with opportunities for members to provide and receive empathic feedback

The Intervention Contract

Because of clients' labile moods, changing motivation, and self-harm tendencies, the practitioner at the outset of intervention should establish a clear and explicit agreement, or contract, about how the relationship will proceed (Yeomans, Gutfreund, Selzer, & Clarkin, 1993). The practitioner and client can then refer to this agreement during the intervention if the client challenges it. This contract should address (a) when, where, and with what frequency sessions will be held; (b) a plan for crisis management; (c) clarification of the practitioner's after-hours availability; and (d) expectations about such miscellaneous issues as scheduling, attendance, and payment. Because of the potential for impulsive behavior, practitioners must be comfortable with setting limits on self-destructive behaviors. Similarly, practitioners may need to convey to clients the limits of their own capacities. That is, practitioners need to lay out what they see as the necessary conditions to make intervention viable with the understanding that it may not be able to continue if the client cannot adhere to minimal conditions.

Intervention Goals

While validating clients' suffering, practitioners must also help them take appropriate responsibility for their actions. Many clients with BPD who have experienced trauma in the past blame themselves for those experiences. Effective intervention helps clients realize that they were not responsible for the neglect and abuse, but they are responsible for controlling and preventing self-destructive patterns in the present and future (Ryle,

2004). Intervention can become derailed by too much focus on the past trauma instead of attention to current functioning and interpersonal problems. Interpretations of here-and-now behavior as it links to events in the past are useful for helping clients learn about their tendencies toward repetition of maladaptive behavior patterns. Practitioners must have a clear expectation of change as they help clients understand the origins of their suffering.

As previously noted, splitting is a major defense mechanism of clients with borderline personality disorder. The self and others are often regarded as "all good: or "all bad." This phenomenon is closely related to what Beck and Freeman (1990) call "dichotomous" or "all or none thinking." Intervention must be geared toward helping the client begin to experience the shades of gray between these extremes and integrate the positive and negative aspects of the self and others.

Some clients with BPD may need to be seen in protective environments, usually for short periods. Indications for partial or brief inpatient hospitalization include (Oldham et al., 2002):

- Dangerous, impulsive behavior that cannot be managed in an outpatient setting
- Nonadherence with outpatient intervention and a deteriorating clinical picture
- Complex comorbidity that requires intensive clinical assessment of response to intervention
- Symptoms of sufficient severity to interfere with functioning, work, or family life that are unresponsive to outpatient intervention
- Transient psychotic episodes associated with loss of impulse control or impaired judgment

A Review of Interventions

There is a rich intervention literature about clients with borderline personality disorder, most of it (prior to the 1990s) written by psychodynamic thinkers and practitioners. Much of this literature is based on case studies and small samples; empirical research is far less prominent. We review a variety of intervention approaches here.

Psychodynamic Intervention

Psychodynamic intervention involves careful attention to the therapist–client relationship with thoughtfully timed interpretations of transference and resistance. It draws from three major theoretical perspectives: ego psychology, object relations, and self psychology. Psychodynamic intervention is usually conceptualized as operating on an exploratory-supportive continuum of interventions (Berzoff, 1996). On the supportive end of the continuum, goals involve strengthening defenses, shoring up self-esteem, validating feelings, internalizing the therapeutic relationship, and creating a greater capacity to cope with disturbing feelings. At the exploratory end of the continuum, the goals are to make unconscious patterns more consciously available, increase affect tolerance, build a capacity to delay impulsive action, provide insight into relationship problems, and develop reflective functioning toward a greater appreciation of internal motivation in the self and others (Goldstein, 1995). From the standpoint of object relations theory, one major goal is to integrate the split-off aspects of self and object representations so that that client's perspective is more balanced (e.g., seeing others as simultaneously having positive and negative qualities) (Kernberg, 1975). From a self psychology perspective, a major goal is to strengthen the self so that the client experiences a greater sense of internal cohesion (Kohut, 1977).

Medications

Many clients with borderline personality disorder receive medications to manage some of its symptoms, including depression, suicidal ideation, angry outbursts, and impulsive behavior. Prescribing effective medications is difficult, however, because of special challenges presented by this disorder, including its symptom heterogeneity, diagnostic unreliability, the existence of comorbid disorders, the client's labile moods, and the potential for self-destructiveness. A recent review of the empirical literature since 1980 on this topic, in fact, indicates little evidence of positive symptom outcomes for clients (Bornstein, 1997). Looking at double blind, placebo-controlled studies of antidepressant, antianxiety, antipsychotic, anticonvulsant, and lithium medications, the author found either modest or no symptom relief for several medications from each class. He concluded that future drug studies need to be better designed in order to produce more valid findings.

Despite this, drugs are frequently used with clients in an effort to assist with symptom control. Target symptoms typically fall within the three behavioral dimensions of affective instability, impulsive behavior, and cognitive-perceptual difficulties. Specific pharmacological treatment strategies can be targeted to each of these (Bornstein, 1997). Clients who display affective instability exhibit mood lability, sensitivity to rejection, intense anger, depressive "mood crashes," and temper outbursts. These symptoms may at times respond to a selective serotonin reuptake inhibitor (SSRI). For clients displaying problems with impulsive behavior featuring aggression, self-mutilation, or self-damaging behavior (such as promiscuous sex, substance abuse, and reckless spending), SSRIs are also the initial treatment of choice. For clients displaying problems in the cognitive dimension who exhibit suspiciousness, paranoid ideation, illusions, derealization, depersonalization, or transient hallucinations, low-dose antipsychotics are often prescribed. These medications may improve not only their psychotic-like symptoms but also depressed mood, impulsivity, and anger. Unfortunately, because of the absence of consistent research findings, a practitioner cannot be confident that any of these medications will help a particular client.

Empirically Validated Interventions

Fifteen clinical studies of clients with personality disorders that included pretreatment and posttreatment effects were conducted between 1974 and 1998 (Perry, Banon, & Ianni, 1999). All of the studies, which were based on psychodynamic, interpersonal, cognitive-behavioral, and supportive therapies, reported positive outcomes. Four studies focused specifically on borderline personality disorder, and while all of these had limitations, their pooled results indicate a 25% recovery rate per year for clients receiving intervention. With a "natural course" recovery rate from BPD of 3.7% per year, the authors tentatively concluded that clients receiving intervention recover at a rate seven times that of those who do not receive intervention.

Two intervention models for the treatment of clients with BPD have used random, controlled trials to test their efficacy, with positive outcomes. One is Linehan's (1993) dialectical behavior therapy, and the other is interpersonal group psychotherapy (Marziali & Munroe-Blum, 1994).

Dialectical Behavior Therapy

Based on cognitive-behavioral and learning theories, dialectical behavior therapy (DBT) is an intensive, 1-year outpatient intervention that combines weekly individual sessions with weekly skills-training groups that run for 2.5 hours. The term *dialectical* refers to the premises that borderline personality disorder is a product of biological and environmental influences and that intervention needs to address both aspects of the disorder. The purposes of DBT groups are to teach adaptive coping skills in the areas of emotional regulation, distress tolerance, interpersonal effectiveness, and identity confusion and to correct maladaptive cognitions. The individual interventions, provided by the same practitioner, address maladaptive behaviors while strengthening and generalizing coping skills. Some client–practitioner phone contact is permitted between sessions for support and crisis intervention. DBT is a structured intervention comprised of the following five stages:

- Pretreatment: Orientation to the philosophy, structure, and format of the intervention
- Stage 1: Focuses on the client's present behavior and current environmental factors, targeting any life-threatening behavior and increasing the client's basic coping capacities

- Stage 2: Focuses on posttraumatic stress syndrome, including the uncovering and reexperiencing of the client's prior traumatic or emotionally important events
- Stage 3: Focuses on increasing the client's respect for self and capacity to achieve individual goals by synthesizing what has been learned in the group
- Stage 4: Addresses the sense of incompleteness that plagues some clients even after the resolution of problems in living

During the individual component of the intervention, the practitioner's strategies are divided into the following steps:

- Dialectical: to synthesize the biological and environmental aspects of BPD, including the client's struggle to balance self-acceptance with movement toward change
- Validation: to help clients learn how and when to trust themselves and make sense of experiences that appear "irrational" to them
- Problem solving: to resolve problems through such procedures as skills training, contingency management, cognitive modification, and exposure
- Communication skills training: focusing on both sending and receiving skills
- Case management: to help the client manage the physical and social environment to enhance well-being

An important component in DBT is the consultation team. While the practitioner applies DBT strategies to clients, the supervisor applies them to the practitioner, to help that person maintain objectivity during the often-intensive intervention processes.

DBT has empirical support based on a randomized experimental design (Linehan, 1993). Forty-seven women meeting the criteria for BPD were randomly assigned to either 12 months of DBT or to a standard psychodynamic intervention. Results indicated that the DBT clients were less likely to attempt suicide or drop out of intervention than the other clients. They also spent less time in psychiatric hospitals, were better adjusted interpersonally, were less angry, and maintained significantly higher GAF scores.

Interpersonal Group Psychotherapy

Interpersonal group psychotherapy (IGP), designed specifically for people with borderline personality disorder, provides a therapeutic environment in which participants can reflect on and resolve problematic interpersonal interactions (Marziali & Munroe-Blum, 1994). Within this model, the client with BPD is perceived as possessing a self system that incorporates conflicting attitudes. The resulting states of instability are targeted for resolution in the context of relationships. Clients have the opportunity to test modified expectations of the self and others through member–therapist and member–member interactions.

The recommended duration of IGP is 45 sessions that are 90 minutes long, including 40 weekly sessions followed by 5 biweekly sessions. The group process is divided into four phases:

- The search for appropriate interpersonal boundaries
- The establishment of self-control
- The experience of mourning life's losses and disappointments
- Generalizing new learning and experiences

This intervention focuses on observing and processing the meaning of within-group enactments of behavior among clients and cotherapists. Practitioners must be process oriented, affable, and neutral in order to maintain a therapeutic environment during all phases of the group. They avoid attempting to provide definitive explanations of client behavior. Despite the structure of the group, specific topics that are processed are unpredictable.

A test of the effectiveness of IGP was done in a group that compared 30 sessions of group intervention over 35 weeks to open-ended, long-term psychoanalytic therapy. Clients in the experimental group manifested gains on several measures of social functioning based on both client and practitioner reports.

In summary, the studies of DBT and IGP found that participants in both the experimental and control groups made gains that were evident at posttreatment and at also at 1-year follow-up. Cost-benefit analyses, however, favored the group approaches. Incidentally, since its origins, DBT has been expanded for use with other client populations, including substance abusers, suicidal adolescents, people with eating disorders, inmates in correctional settings, depressed older adults, and adults with ADHD (Robins & Chapman, 2004). IGP is also used with a variety of clinical problems that are rooted in negative relationships.

Case Illustration

Shannon was a 19-year-old single working female, referred to the mental health clinic from a psychiatric hospital following a 2-week stay in the crisis unit. She had experienced more than a dozen hospitalizations in the past 18 months, since her high school graduation. All of her hospitalizations were due to depression and suicidal ideation. There was no history of any intervention prior to her high school graduation, however, and no sustained outpatient intervention since then. The client was still taking antidepressant medications as prescribed by the hospital psychiatrist but reported no perceived benefits from them.

The practitioner learned that Shannon was the fourth and youngest girl born to a Roman Catholic couple. The family was middle-class but upwardly mobile. Her parents had a rural background but had moved to a suburban area when Shannon was 5 years old. Shannon did not recall many details of her past but described a childhood of neglect, stating that her parents left all cooking, cleaning, laundering, and other household routines to the children. She remembered her father coming into her room at night, sitting by her bedside and quietly stroking her hair, and that made her extremely uncomfortable. Shannon later stated that she did not get along with any of her siblings and was frequently made the scapegoat for most family conflicts. As a teenager, she took long walks through her neighborhood each night to escape her parents' arguing and her siblings' teasing. She spoke fondly only of a neighborhood policeman whom she often saw on her walks and several aunts and uncles who lived a few miles away.

On the day after her graduation, Shannon moved into the home of an older male friend, his two adolescent children, and two other female acquaintances. She had become acquainted with them while working as an emergency medical technician at the local volunteer fire department. Shannon had developed an early interest in nursing and by age 18 was handling herself skillfully on rescue squad runs. Her work life represented a major strength. Shannon was at best cordial with her own family, however. Her parents refused to attend a joint session at the mental health center. Her mother said to the practitioner on the phone, "Don't let that loser try to blame us for anything."

Shannon's personality style was characterized by superficial pleasantness but a refusal (or inability) to discuss personal information. She had few acquaintances and spent all of her free time with her housemates. Young men showed interest in her at times, but Shannon was anxious about this and avoided getting involved with them. When pressed for detail about these and other personal matters, Shannon became anxious, quiet, and withdrawn. She appeared to dissociate at times, as evidenced by her staring blankly and becoming unresponsive for several minutes. She denied feeling angry about anything, but the practitioner believed that she was keeping it out of her awareness. He believed that keeping her anger inside contributed to her depression. She was passive-aggressive toward the practitioner at times through her tendencies to miss appointments or come late. Shannon engaged in one serious form of self-mutilation: She would sometimes slam her right fist against a wall repeatedly (always when alone), often breaking bones and tearing tendons.

The practitioner saw Shannon as an imminent suicide threat because she was so isolated and depressed, with little evident hope for her betterment. When she did talk, she quietly shared her sense of herself as an evil, worthless, and stupid person. What was most striking was her lack of connection to others, even though she experienced alarming anxiety when alone. These episodes often occurred during her chronically sleepless nights, when she would lie in bed for hours and experience escalating terror about losing control of herself.

After four visits, Shannon prepared a letter for the practitioner and asked that he wait until she left to read it. In the letter she detailed her history of sexual abuse by her father that spanned the ages of 5 through 17. She recalled few details of the incidents and had not discussed them with anyone else. Shannon added that the incest was her own fault, proof that she was a disgusting human being. There was to be no salvation for her, and it meant that she could never become close to anyone.

When they met a few days later, Shannon wept throughout the hour. The practitioner acknowledged reading the letter and expressed his shocked reaction to her revelations. He asked why she had written the letter. Shannon said she never trusted anyone and assumed that anyone who knew her secret would reject her. She admitted to feeling confused by the practitioner's persistent interest in her. She wondered what he had wanted from her and suspected that the motives were sexual. It was only after their first several weeks of work that she considered that he might be interested in her welfare.

Diagnostic Formulation

The practitioner diagnosed Shannon on Axis I with major depression. She met most of the criteria with the following symptoms: feelings of sadness, anxiety, anger, irritability, and emotional numbness; a flatness of expression; feelings of guilt, shame, low self-esteem, helplessness, pessimism, and hopelessness; thoughts of death and suicide; impairment in her ability to think and concentrate; inability to experience pleasure; and poor sleep patterns. The depression was severe. The agency physician supported this diagnosis because he was treating the client with antidepressant medicine.

Shannon was diagnosed with borderline personality disorder on Axis II, and the practitioner considered this to be the principal diagnosis. She met criteria including frantic efforts to avoid abandonment, a pattern of unstable interpersonal relationships, a persistent unstable self-image and sense of self, impulsive behavior (engaging in reckless physical activity), recurrent suicidal and self-mutilating behavior, mood instability, chronic feelings of emptiness, and intense anger that was generally suppressed.

There was no diagnosis on Axis III, given the client's good physical health.

Shannon was noted on Axis IV as having problems with her primary support group and the social environment. She experienced severe and long-term discord with her parents and some siblings, had no close friends, and tended to view others as evil. Further, while she had a job, a place to stay, and some friends, none of these were secure resources. She functioned well as an emergency medical technician but otherwise had a poor work record.

Shannon's current GAF was set at 50. She did not have problems in occupational functioning, but her suicidal ideation was chronic, as were her interpersonal problems.

Summary of Differential Diagnosis

Axis I: Major Depression, recurrent, severe, without psychotic features, without full interepisode recovery

Axis II: Borderline Personality Disorder (principal diagnosis)

Axis III: None

Axis IV: Primary support group (parents, siblings, peers) and social environment (work and social life)

Axis V: Current GAF = 50; highest GAF past year = 50

Critique of the Diagnosis

Borderline personality disorder is a highly problematic diagnostic category. The reasons for this were articulated early in the chapter but are summarized here. First, like the other personality disorders, it is based on a concept (personality) that is itself elusive and difficult to capture. Second, it is a product of the APA's desire to categorize particular personality patterns as discrete personality types, rather than adopting an alternative strategy of articulating relevant dimensions (qualities) of personality that might be more helpful to practitioners in identifying problematic client behavior and intervention targets. Third, BPD has shown to be an invalid and unreliable diagnosis in research studies (Lester, 1998). Clients with the diagnosis may have quite different symptom clusters and as a result present very differently to practitioners. Problems with validity and reliability have rendered progress slow for determining what kinds of intervention might be helpful for clients. Fourth, because one's *personality* is synonymous with the *person*, the borderline personality disorder diagnosis (like the others) seems to present practitioners with an ethical dilemma in reinforcing a strong deficits perspective.

In spite of these concerns, all clients with symptoms of borderline personality disorder have very real, ongoing problems, and practitioners should remain committed to working with them so that they can achieve their goals of improved relationships and social integration.

Appendix. Assessment Instruments for *DSM-IV* Personality Disorders

Dimensional Assessment of Personality Pathology Basic Questionnaire

Livesley, Jackson, & Schroeder (1989)

Description

- 290 item questionnaire
- Measures 18 personality dimensions derived from an analysis of prototypical features of personality disorders
- Items measured on a 5-point Likert scale
- Used in cross-sectional research such as twin studies of the genetics of personality traits

Reliability

- Internal consistency for the clinical sample was high (.84–.94).
- Test-retest reliability ranged from .81 to .93.

Validity

- Correlation with similar scales on the Schedule for Nonadaptive Personality was .53 (range, .01–.78)

Millon Clinical Multiaxial Inventory

Millon, Davis, & Millon (1997)

Description

- Used to assess all *DSM* personality types (from the text and appendix)
- 175 items in true-false format, administered by the client or a clinician
- Divided into 13 personality disorder scales and 9 symptom scales accessing anxiety, depression, thought disorder, and so on
- Requires 20–25 minutes for completion

Reliability

Reliability for the dimension of total personality disorder features was .77 after 1 year and .70 after 3 years.

Validity

Comparison with other instruments yielded low correlation (criterion validity).

NEO Personality Inventory–Revised

Costa & McRae (1992)

Description

- 240-item questionnaire that yields scores on each domain of the five-factor model of personality (neuroticism, extraversion, openness, agreeableness, and conscientiousness) and 30 facets of each domain.
- Each facet is assessed by eight nonoverlapping items with a 5-point scale.
- Two forms are available: one for self-report and the other for peer, spouse, or expert report.
- Requires 35–40 minutes to complete.
- A short form is available (60 items) that assesses only the five domains; this requires 10–15 minutes to complete.
- Results are interpreted by comparing domain and facet scores with an appropriate normative group.

Reliability

- Alpha coefficients for both long forms ranged from .86 to .95 for domain scores and .56 to .78 for facet scores.
- Test-retest reliability was .51 to .91 for the five domains and .51 to .92 for the facets.
- Internal consistency for the short form ranged from .68 to .86; test-retest reliability was .75 to .83.

Validity

- Scale scores correlated well (.60–.69) with a variety of other five-factor measures.
- The various domains and facets of the NEO have correlated moderately well with similar subscales from other instruments.

Personality Assessment Inventory

Morey (1991)

Description

- 344 item questionnaire
- Items scored on a 4-point Likert-type scale (false to very true)
- Used as a general diagnostic aid and measure of psychopathology
- Includes 22 scales, 11 assessing major symptoms, 2 assessing interpersonal phenomena, 5 assessing data useful for treatment consideration, and 4 assessing test validity
- Takes 40–50 minutes to complete

Reliability

- Median internal consistency of the full scales and subscales is good (.82 and .66).
- Short-term stability ranged from .73 to .85 for full scales, .77 to .88 for subscales, and .60 to .90 for the personality scales.

Validity

- Good discriminant validity between borderline features and antisocial features scales in clinical samples.
- Convergent validity has been demonstrated in comparisons with several other personality measures.

Personality Diagnostic Questionnaire for *DSM-IV*

Hyler (1994)

Description

- Assesses the 10 personality disorders in the body of the *DSM-IV* and 2 types in the appendix
- 100 true-false items
- Available in many languages

Reliability

- Good internal consistency (.64) for the Italian version.
- Stability correlation for the number of borderline personality was r = .54; scores were lower after 2 years.

Validity

- Criterion validity is reported as low (but not specifically stated).

Personality Disorder Interview-IV
Schedule for Nonadaptive and Adaptive Personality

Clark (1993)

Description

- A self-report test comprised of 375 true/false items designed to assess trait dimensions in the domain of personality disorders
- Assesses 12 clinical traits and 3 temperament scales, derived from clinically identified personality disorder criteria
- Used in cross-sectional research

Reliability

- Internal consistency = .81, with a range of .71 to .92.
- Test-retest reliability = .79.
- Interscale correlations are low.

Validity

- Convergent validity is good (.53).

The Structured Interview for *DSM-IV* Personality (SIDP-IV)

Pfohl, Blum, & Zimmerman (1997)

Description

- Diagnoses the presence of any of 10 personality disorders.
- To be administered by a clinician, it includes 101 sets of questions divided into 10 topical sections.
- Each *DSM* criterion is scored on a 4-point scale; a criterion is considered to be present if it has been true 50% of the time over the past 5 years; for symptoms to be scored, they must have been present for 5 years.
- Takes 90 minutes to administer.

Reliability

- Interrater reliability for a diagnosis of any personality disorder is k = .58.

Validity

- Compared to best-estimate diagnoses made by a panel of clinicians, level of agreement was 75%, positive predictive validity was .88, and negative predictive ability was .32 (indicating a high proportion of false-negative results).

Wisconsin Personality Inventory

Klein et al. (1993)

Description

- 214-item self-report questionnaire.
- Subjects are asked to rate themselves over the past 5 years on a 10-point scale (never or not at all true to always or extremely true).
- 11 scales represent personality disorder types that are based on themes in the *DSM-III-R* but formulated according to Benjamin's theory of the structural analysis of social behavior.

Reliability and Validity

- Cronbach's alphas for the 11 personality disorders range from .81 to .95.
- High 2-week retest reliability with median .88.
- Stability are scores lower at the 3-4 months (.75).

References

American Psychiatric Association. (2000). *Diagnostic and statistical manual of mental disorders* (4th ed., rev.). Washington, DC: Author.

Arntz, A., & Veen, G. (2001). Evaluations of others by borderline patients. *Journal of Nervous and Mental Disease, 189*(8), 513–521.

Bagge, C., Nickell, A., Stepp, S., Durrett, C., Jackson, K., & Trull, T. J. (2004). Borderline personality disorder features predict negative outcomes 2 years later. *Journal of Abnormal Psychology, 113*(2), 279–288.

Bandelow, B., Krause, J., & Wedekind, D. (2005). Early traumatic life events, parental attitudes, family history, and birth risk factors in patients with borderline personality disorder and healthy controls. *Psychiatry Research, 134*(2), 169–179.

Beck, A. T., & Freeman, A. (1990). *Cognitive therapy of personality disorders*. New York: Guilford.

Berzoff, J. (Ed.) (1996). *Inside out and outside in: Psychodynamic clinical theory and practice in contemporary multicultural contexts*. Northvale, NJ: Jason Aronson.

Blais, M. A., Hilsenroth, M. J., & Fowler, J. C. (1999). Diagnostic efficiency and hierarchical functioning of the *DSM-IV* borderline personality disorder criteria. *Journal of Nervous and Mental Diseases, 187*(3), 167–173.

Bornstein, R. F. (1997). Pharmacological treatments for borderline personality disorder: A critical review of the empirical literature. In S. Fisher & R. P. Greenwood (Eds.), *From placebo to panacea: Putting psychiatric drugs to the test* (pp. 281–304). New York: Wiley.

Brown, M. Z., Comtois, K. A., & Linehan, M. M. (2002). Reasons for suicide attempts and nonsuicidal self-injury in women with borderline personality disorder. *Journal of Abnormal Psychology, 111*(1), 198–202.

Chabrol, H., Montovany, A., Duconge, E., Kallmeyer, A., Mullet, E., & Leichsenring, M. (2004). Factor structure of the borderline personality inventory in adolescents. *European Journal of Psychological Assessment, 20*(1), 9–65.

Costa, P. T., & Widiger, T. A. (2002). *Personality disorders and the five-factor model of personality* (2nd ed.). Washington, DC: American Psychological Association.

Davis, R. D., & Millon, T. (1994). Can personalities be disordered? Yes. In S. A. Kirk & S. D. Einbinder (Eds.), *Controversial issues in mental health* (pp. 40–47). Boston: Allyn & Bacon.

Goldstein, E. G. (1995). *Ego psychology and social work practice (2nd ed.).* New York: Free Press.

Grilo, C. M., Sanislow, C. A., & McGlashan, T. H. (2002). Co-occurrence of *DSM-IV* personality disorders with borderline personality disorder. *Journal of Nervous and Mental Disease, 190*(8), 552–553.

Gurvits, I. G., Koenigsberg, H. W., & Siever, L. J. (2000). Neurotransmitter dysfunction in patients with borderline personality disorder. *Psychiatric Clinics of North America, 23*(1), 27–40.

Himelick, A. J., & Walsh, J. (2002). Nursing home residents with borderline personality traits: Clinical social work interventions. *Journal of Gerontological Social Work, 37*(1), 49–63.

Johnson, H. C. (1999). Borderline personality disorder. In F. J. Turner (Ed.), *Adult psychopathology: A social work perspective* (pp. 430–456). New York: Free Press.

Kernberg, O. (1975). *Borderline conditions and pathological narcissism.* New York: Jason Aronson.

Kohut, H. (1977). *The restoration of the self.* New York: International Universities Press.

Linehan, M. M. (1993). *Cognitive behavioral treatment of borderline clients.* New York: Guilford.

Maddi, S. R. (1996). *Personality theories: A comparative analysis* (6th ed.). Pacific Grove, CA: Brooks/Cole.

Marziali, E. (2002). Borderline personality disorders. In A. R. Roberts & G. J. Greene (Eds.), *Social workers' desk reference* (pp. 360–364). New York: Oxford University Press.

Marziali, E., & Munroe-Blum, H. (1994). *Interpersonal group psychotherapy for borderline personality disorder.* New York: Basic.

Mattaini, M. (1994). Can personalities be disordered? No. In S. A. Kirk & S. D. Einbinder (Eds.), *Controversial issues in mental health* (pp. 48–54). Boston: Allyn & Bacon.

Millon, T. (1996). *Personality disorders: DSM-IV and beyond.* New York: Wiley.

Millon, T., & Davis, R. (1999). *Personality disorders in everyday life.* New York: Wiley.

Morrison, J. (1995). *DSM-IV made easy: The clinician's guide to diagnosis*. New York: Guilford.

Oldham, J. M., Gabbard, G. O., Goin, M. K., Gunderson, J., Soloff, P., Spiegel, D., et al. (2002). Practice guidelines for the treatment of patients with borderline personality disorder. In American Psychiatric Association, *Practice guidelines for the treatment of psychiatric disorders: Compendium 2002*. Washington, DC: Author.

Paris, J. (2003). *Personality disorders over time: Precursors, course, and outcome*. Washington, DC: American Psychiatric Publishing.

Perry, J. C., Banon, E., & Ianni, F. (1999). Effectiveness of psychotherapy for personality disorders. *American Journal of Psychiatry, 156*, 1312–1321.

Robins, C. J., & Chapman, A. L. (2004). Dialectical behavior therapy: Current status, recent developments, and future directions. *Journal of Personality Disorders, 18*(1), 73–89.

Ryle, A. (2004). The contribution of cognitive analytic therapy to the treatment of borderline personality disorder. *Journal of Personality Disorders, 18*(1), 3–35.

Sadock, B. J., & Sadock, V. A. (2005). *Kaplan & Sadock's Comprehensive Textbook of Psychiatry*. Philadelphia: Lippincott Williams & Wilkins.

Skodol, A. E., Siever, L. J., Livesley, W. J., Gunderson, J. G., Pfohl, B, & Widiger, T. A. (2002). The borderline diagnosis II: Biology, genetics, and clinical course. *Biological Psychiatry, 51*(12), 951–963.

St. Clair, M. (1999). *Object relations and self-psychology: An introduction* (3rd ed.). Pacific Grove, CA: Brooks/Cole.

Trull, T. J. (2001). Structural relations between borderline personality disorder features and putative etiological correlates. *Journal of Abnormal Psychology, 110*(3), 471–481.

van den Bosch, L. M., Verheul, R., & van den Brink, W. (2001). Substance abuse in borderline personality disorder: Clinical and etiological correlates. *Journal of Personality Disorders, 15*(5), 416–424.

Whaley, A. L. (2001). Cultural mistrust: An important psychological construct for diagnosis and treatment of African Americans. *Professional Psychology: Theory and Practice, 32*(6), 555–562.

Woods, M. E. (1999). Personality disorders. In F. J. Turner (Ed.), *Adult psychopathology: A social work perspective* (pp. 374–429). New York: Free Press.

Yen, S., Shea, T., Pagano, M., Sanislow, C. A., Grilo, C. M., McGlashan, T. H., et al. (2003). Axis I and axis II disorders as predictors of prospective suicide attempts: Findings from the Collaborative Longitudinal Personality Disorders Study. *Journal of Abnormal Psychology, 112*(3), 375–381.

Yeomans, F. E., Gutfreund, J., Selzer, M. A., & Clarkin, J. F. (1993). Factors related to drop-outs by borderline patients: Treatment contract and therapeutic alliance. *Journal of Psychotherapy Practice and Research, 3*(1), 16–24.

Zanarini, M. C., & Frankenburg, F. R. (1997). Pathways to the development of borderline personality disorder. *Journal of Personality Disorders, 11*(1), 93–104.

Zanarini, M. C., Frankenburg, F. R., Hennen, J., & Silk, K. R. (2004). Mental health service utilization by borderline personality disorder patients and Axis II comparison subjects followed prospectively for six years. *Journal of Clinical Psychiatry, 65*(1), 28–36.

Zanarini, M. C., Ruser, T. F., Frankenberg, F. R., Hennen, J., & Gunderson, J. G. (2000). Risk factors associated with the dissociative experiences of borderline patients. *Journal of Nervous and Mental Disease, 188*(1), 26–30.

Zanarini, M. C., Yong, L., Frankenberg, F. R., Hennen, J., Reich, D. B., Marino, M. F., et al. (2002). Severity of reported childhood sexual abuse and its relationship to severity of borderline psychopathology and psychosocial impairment among borderline inpatients. *Journal of Nervous and Mental Disease, 190*(6), 381–387.

References for Assessment Instruments for *DSM-IV* Personality Disorders

Clark, L. (1993). *Manual for the schedule for nonadaptive and adaptive personality.* Minneapolis: University of Minnesota Press.

Costa, P. T., & McRae, R. R. (1992). *NEO-PI-R professional manual.* Odessa, FL: Psychological Assessment Resources.

Hyler, S. (1994). *Personality diagnostic questionnaire.* New York: New York State Psychiatric Institute.

Klein, M. H., Benjamin, L. S., Rosenfeld, R. R., Treece, C., Hustee, J., & Griest, J. H. (1993). The Wisconsin Personality Disorders Inventory: Development, reliability, and validity. *Journal of Personality Discord, 7,* 285–303.

Livesley, W., Jackson, D., & Schroeder, M. (1989). A study of the factorial structure of personality pathology. *Journal of Personality Discord, 3,* 292–306.

Millon, T., Davis, R., & Millon, C. (1997). Millon Clinical Multiaxial Inventory: I and II. *Journal of Counseling and Development, 70,* 421–426.

Morey, L. (1991). *Personality assessment inventory: Professional manual.* Odessa, FL: Psychological Assessment Resources.

Pfohl, B., Blum, M., & Zimmerman, M. (1997). *Structured interview for DSM personality (SIDP-IV).* Washington, DC: American Psychiatric Press.

PART IV

Disorders with Onset in the Elderly

16   Cognitive Disorders

Cognition can be defined as conscious thinking processes—mental activities of which people are aware. Cognitive processes include a person's taking in relevant information from the environment, synthesizing that information, and formulating a plan of action based on that synthesis (Beck & Weishaar, 1995). Cognitive *disorders* are characterized by deficits in a person's thought processes or memory that are due to brain dysfunction and represent a significant decline from the previous level of functioning. This chapter focuses on two highly debilitating cognitive disorders classified as *dementias* that are experienced mostly by older adults: Alzheimer's disease and vascular dementia. Both are *degenerative* disorders, meaning they involve a progressive decline in the number of functioning neurons in the person's central nervous system. These disorders are *not* a normal part of the aging process.

There are many other types of dementias that, unlike these two, stem from identifiable medical conditions. These include dementias from long-term substance abuse and HIV disease, head trauma, Parkinson's disease (affecting movement), Huntington's disease (affecting cognition, emotion, and movement), Pick's disease (affecting personality, language, social skills, emotions, and behavior), and Creutzfeldt-Jacob disease (a "slow virus" that produces the symptoms of dementia). Other types of cognitive disorders include *delirium* (a time-limited cognitive disturbance) and the *amnestic disorders* (with memory impairment as the only symptom). We do not focus on the latter two disorders in this chapter.

Symptoms of Dementia

Memory impairment is *always* required to make a diagnosis of dementia. Other prominent symptoms may include (American Psychiatric Association [APA], 2000):

- Aphasia: loss of the ability to use words appropriately
- Apraxia: loss of the ability to use common objects correctly
- Agnosia: loss of the ability to understand sound and visual input
- Loss of executive functioning: an inability to plan, organize, follow sequences, and think abstractly

A diagnosis of dementia can be coded as *uncomplicated* (without delusions, delirium, or depression), *with delusions*, *with depression*, or *with delirium*. Approximately 40 to 50% of people with dementia experience symptoms of anxiety and depression (10–20% have a major depressive disorder), 30 to 40% have delusions (often persecutory), and 20 to 30% experience hallucinations (primarily with Alzheimer's disease) (Altman, 2001).

Fifty to 60% of people with dementia have Alzheimer's disease, the most common form of dementia worldwide (Suh & Shah, 2001). Old age is often falsely stereotyped as a stage of life that includes high rates of dementia. In fact, only 5% of people between the ages of 65 and 80 have severe dementia, with another 15% having a mild form of the disorder (Ruitenberg, Ott, van Swieten, Hofman, & Breteler, 2001). Twenty percent of people over 80 have severe dementia. Its highest prevalence occurs above the age of 85. Dementia is rare among children and adolescents, but it can occur at any age as the result of certain medical conditions (APA, 2000). A diagnosis of dementia does not imply an unremitting downward course. There are a variety of reversible dementias, such as those due to pernicious anemia, brain tumors, hypothyroidism, infections, and nutritional deficiencies.

Behavioral problems are the leading reason family members seek medical intervention on behalf of a person with dementia (Finkel, 2001). The following is a list of behaviors that may be evidenced by persons with dementia. Not all people exhibit all of these behaviors, and they may occur with varying degrees of severity:

- Perceptual disturbances including delusions (false beliefs), hallucinations (false sense perceptions), and the misidentification of people
- Mood disturbances (depression and apathy)
- Wandering and other dangerous or careless behavior
- Agitation or rage (including restlessness, hostile behavior, or screaming)
- Sleep disturbances (insomnia or disruptions in sleep rhythm)

- Distressing repetitive behavior
- Inappropriate sexual behavior (fondling, touching, masturbation, verbal remarks)
- Incontinence
- Refusal to eat

Social work interventions are often targeted at reducing or controlling these behaviors, as discussed later in this chapter.

Alzheimer's Disease

Alzheimer's disease, the most common form of dementia, is characterized by the development of cognitive deficits resulting from a diffuse atrophy (wasting away) of tissue in several areas of the brain (Cummings & Cole, 2002). It is named after a 19th-century German physician, Alois Alzheimer, who first formally described the disease in a published case study. Alzheimer's disease (AD) has a gradual onset and progresses with a slow, steady decline in the person's cognitive functioning. The duration of its course is unpredictable and may range from 3 to 20 years, although 5 to 10 years is more common. Its causes are not yet known, and there is no cure, although emerging medical treatments may slow its course. Prevalence estimates range from 1.4 to 1.6% for people age 65 to 69 years, rising to 16 to 25% for those over 85 years old (APA, 2000). Approximately 5 million Americans were diagnosed with AD in 2001, and the number may rise to 15 million (34 million worldwide) by 2050 if effective forms of prevention and treatment are not found. The average age of diagnosis is 80 years, and the symptom of memory loss affects nearly 50% of people over the age of 85 with various levels of severity.

A physician is required to diagnose this disorder. Formally termed *dementia of the Alzheimer's type*, the disorder requires that the client demonstrate a gradual and progressive worsening of short-term memory and at least one of the other brain function impairments listed earlier (APA, 2000). The deficits must account for significant impairment in social and occupational functioning. Identifiable medical conditions that may cause the symptoms need to be ruled out. AD may be recorded as *with early onset* (before age 65) or *with late onset*. A minority of AD patients develop the disorder in their 40s and 50s, and an earlier onset implies a more rapid course. This form of AD often runs in families and is most likely to have a purely genetic cause (Morrison, 1995). The following symptoms of AD are listed in the order in which they develop:

- Loss of recent memory
- Loss of judgment

- Problems with abstract thinking
- Loss of higher order functions (planning)
- Personality changes (exaggerations of normal traits)

Some people with AD experience a phenomenon called *sundowning*—an increase in level of confusion during the late afternoon and evening hours.

Effects on the Family

Only a third of people with dementia in the United States live in nursing homes (Mace & Rabins, 1999), which means that families are the primary caregivers for these individuals. Although the symptoms of Alzheimer's disease are distressing for the affected person, the situation may be equally or more stressful for the caregivers, particularly as the disease progresses. The primary caregiver, usually a member of the client's family, is often required to take the lead in organizing interventions. This often creates an uncomfortable power shift in the relationship. The caregiver is challenged to monitor the client's changing levels of dependence and independence as the disease progresses. He or she must care for the loved one, preserve the client's dignity, and balance his or her own limits on time, energy, and patience. The stress to family member caretakers may be heightened by their fears of loss, guilt over not being an adequate caregiver, ambivalence about the caregiver role, competitiveness with each other, and fears about their own mortality.

The Biology of Alzheimer's Disease

Alzheimer's disease is unfortunately a "rule-out" diagnosis. Rather than being positively identified by medical examination and tests, it is ruled "in" if other possible conditions cannot account for the symptoms (Altman, 2001). This is also true, of course, of many *DSM* diagnoses that are based on observable behavior only. Autopsies of people with AD show that brain cells in the cortex and hippocampus, areas that are responsible for learning, reasoning, and memory, have become clogged with two abnormal structures. *Neurofibrillary tangles* are twisted masses of protein fibers inside cells or neurons, and *plaques* are deposits of a sticky protein called amyloid that is surrounded by debris from deteriorating neurons (Cowley, 2002). Alterations in the composition of blood vessels are also apparent.

A healthy brain contains about 140 billion neurons, all of which generate electrical signals through neurotransmitter activity to help people think, remember, feel, and move. In people with AD, these neurons slowly die. As they die, lower levels of essential neurotransmitters are produced, creating signaling problems among cells. There is, for example, a reduction in the neurotransmitters acetylcholine and norepinephrine and an undesired increase in glutamate.

Although there is no agreement about the primary causes of AD, many agree that its symptoms begin with a protein called amyloid beta (Cummings & Cole, 2002). All people produce the protein, which is harmless in small amounts. It is part of a larger molecule known as the amyloid-precursor protein (APP), a normal protein that extends from a neuron's outer membrane. While performing its normal functions, APP gets "chopped up" by enzymes, leaving residue to dissolve in the brain's watery recesses (the glial cells). Occasionally, and for unknown reasons, a pair of enzymes (beta and gamma secretase) cleaves APP in the wrong places, leaving behind an insoluble amyloid fragment. Some people produce these "junk" neurons faster than others do, but after 70 or 80 years, all brains carry at least a modest amyloid burden.

Some amyloid molecules lose their natural spiral shape and flatten out. They become prone to bind to one another, forming fibrils, like woven carpet fibers, to create larger masses. Amyloid fibrils also bind with proteins like secretase, which makes them less soluble and still harder for the body to clear. Fibrils bind with each other to grow into plaques (thin, hard substances). When these substances reach a certain threshold, the brain can no longer function efficiently.

Risk and Protective Factors

Risk factors for Alzheimer's disease (Table 16.1) include being female, having a first-degree relative with the disorder (a characteristic of 40% of persons with AD), and having a history of head injury or Down syndrome (APA, 2000). Other risk factors include small strokes or cardiovascular disease, being African American, exposure to environmental toxins, poor diet, lack of exercise, and having a depressive disorder before onset. Risk factors are *heavily* weighted toward biology, but there are also some psychological and social risk factors.

Biological Risk Factors

The role of genetics and biology is universally accepted as critical in the etiology and course of AD, although specific information about these processes is lacking. AD may be transmitted genetically, and mutations in any of four genes (located on chromosomes 1, 14, 19, and 21) are associated with its development. Researchers speculate that the protein made by the apolipoprotein-4 (APOE-4) gene promotes the accumulation of amyloid in the brain or interferes with its removal (Stevenson, 1994). The APOE-2 and

Table 16.1

Risk and Protective Factors for the Onset of Alzheimer's Disease

Risk	Protective
Genetic/Biological	
Advanced age (65 and over)	
Family history	No family history of AD
Genetic (chromosome 1, 14 19, 21)	Genetics (APOE e2 allele)
Down syndrome	No Down syndrome
History of head trauma	No history of head trauma
Female gender	Male gender
Small strokes or Cerebrovascular disease	No history of stroke or cardiovascular disease
African American or Hispanic	European American
Lack of exercise	Long-term exercise
Diet (fatty foods, low blood levels of folic acid and vitamin B_{12}, elevated plasma and homocysteine level	Low-fat diet, high in folic acid and vitamin B_{12}, high fish diet
Environmental toxins (water pollutants, aluminum)	No ingestion of toxic metals and chemicals
Smoking cigarettes	No history of smoking
	Moderate wine consumption
	Use of nonsteroidal anti-inflammatory drugs
	Hormonal treatment
	Antihypertensive agents
Psychological	
Depression	Stable mood
Stress	Lower levels of stress
	Early detection and intervention
Social	
Low educational status	Higher educational status
Low occupational status	Higher occupational status

3 proteins appear to protect against AD by strengthening structures vital to nerve cell functioning. Findings for APOE genes have been more consistent for Caucasians than for others. This indicates that APOE may not be the culprit itself but rather may be located near the "culprit" factor or that members of other groups possess other genes that blunt the effect of the genetic risk factors.

A meta-analysis of research on gene properties provides important information about the process of AD transmission (Farrer et al., 1997). This review of 5,930 AD clients and 8,607 healthy volunteers revealed that the APOE-4 gene appears to increase the risk of AD for people in many ethnic groups. The APOE gene located on chromosome 21 causes an increase in abnormal AB peptides. The APOE-2 gene appears to provide a protective effect on the disorder. Presenillin genes (PS1 and PS2) are located on chromosomes 1 and 14, and a mutation in either of them is associated with an increased formation of AB peptides and early-onset AD. A study of five large Colombian families ($N = 3,000$) who had early-onset AD supported the role of a mutation in the PS1 gene located on chromosome 21 (Lopera et al., 1997).

People with Down syndrome, which is related to an extra copy of chromosome 21, have an increased risk of AD. Mothers who deliver such children prior to age 35 also have an increased risk because they may carry the marker gene. There may not be a gender difference in AD until the age of 90, after which the incidence of the disease is higher among women (Ruitenberg et al., 2001).

Psychological Risk Factors

There are no known psychological causes of Alzheimer's disease. When people begin to experience the symptoms, however, depression and anxiety are common. People may exhibit mood swings, become distrustful of others, and show increased stubbornness. Those emotional states and behaviors may be in response to frustration and changes in self-image, but biological reasons have also been offered to explain why depression is often present with AD (Bonavita, Iavarone, & Sorrentino, 2001). Higher rates of depression are found among first- and second-degree relatives of people with AD that includes depression in comparison with relatives of people who experience AD without additional cognitive or affective symptoms. This may be because the characteristic neurofibrillary tangles are higher in cerebral areas, where the pathogenesis of depression takes place, and thus the two disorders may share a biological association.

Social Risk Factors

Lifestyle factors may contribute to negative health conditions that put some people at greater risk for the disorder, although the role of these factors is somewhat speculative (Lyketsos et al., 2000). The prevalence of various possible contributing factors, including infections, nutritional deficiencies, brain injury, endocrine conditions, cerebrovascular diseases, seizure disorders, substance abuse, and brain tumors, varies across cultural groups. People with higher risks of these types may have relatively modest educational backgrounds and occupational status. They may consume high-fat foods, have low blood levels of folic acid and vitamin B_{12}, and have elevated levels of homocysteine, an amino acid that has been linked to circulatory problems. Their lifestyles may include poor exercise habits, a greater likelihood of smoking cigarettes, and the ingestion of environmental toxins such as water pollutants and aluminum.

Vascular Dementia

Vascular dementia (VaD) is a progressive, irreversible cognitive disorder caused by blocked blood vessels to the brain due to cerebral infarction or hemorrhage. (The word *vascular* refers to blood vessels.) It accounts for 10 to 15% of all types of dementia (Morrison, 1995). VaD was once known as *multi-infarct* dementia because it typically results from a person's experiencing several strokes (episodes of sudden paralysis due to breaking blood vessels in the brain). The physiological disturbances affect small and medium-size cerebral brain vessels, which undergo disruption and produce permanent areas of injury. The onset of VaD is usually abrupt and features a fluctuating course that includes periods of stability followed by periods of rapid decline in functioning (in contrast to the slower progression of Alzheimer's disease). The diagnostic criteria for VaD include:

- Memory impairment
- One or more of the cognitive disturbances (aphasia, apraxia, and agnosia)
- Disturbances in executive functioning
- The presence of specific neurological signs and symptoms or evidence of cerebrovascular disease that is judged to be etiologically related to the disturbance

The *DSM-IV* diagnosis may include the specifiers with *delirium, delusions, depressed mood,* or *uncomplicated*. The specifier *with behavioral disturbance* may also be used. Prior to diagnosis, several medical conditions must first be ruled out, including delirium from underlying physical illness, adverse drug reactions, infections, and reactions to sensory disturbances and environmental stresses. Unlike Alzheimer's disease, the central nervous system damage can be assessed with computerized tomography and magnetic resonance imaging.

The pattern of deficits in VaD is variable, depending on which regions of the brain are damaged. Severity of the disorder can range from minor to excessive symptom presentations (Raicu & Workman, 2000). VaD is more common in men, who are likelier to develop hypertension and other cardiovascular diseases (Ruitenberg et al., 2001).

The symptomatic heterogeneity of VaD often hinders accurate diagnosis (Dib, 2001). In fact, the symptoms often overlap with those of AD (10–15% of patients have both types of dementia). Researchers disagree about the appropriate means of diagnosing vascular dementia. The *DSM* criteria are questioned because they allow a high degree of subjective judgment and require evidence of multiple cognitive deficits. These are serious concerns because dementia is most treatable in its early stages; thus, clients can benefit greatly from early diagnosis.

Researchers debate the level of cerebral vascular pathology that must be present to permit a valid diagnosis (Stewart, 2002). The initial stages of dementia are characterized by fatigue, difficulty in sustaining mental performance, and the tendency to fail in novel or complex tasks. Early diagnosis in high-risk people is difficult, and its accuracy will require the development of advanced imaging markers and global diagnostic tools. Some researchers have proposed subtypes of VaD. One such classification might include Type 1, for major diseases such as strokes, Type 2 for smaller lesions, and Type 3 for damage to certain areas of white brain matter.

Comorbid Conditions

Depression is a relatively frequent complication of VaD, more so than with Alzheimer's disease (Bonavita et al., 2001). Approximately 27% of people with VaD experience major depression. Psychological factors play an important role, but there may be organic reasons for the association because the severity of VaD is correlated with the proximity of lesions to the left frontal pole in the brain. People with the dementia also tend to have other health problems, which can be expected because the disorder is an outcome of cardiovascular conditions.

Risk and Protective Factors

Biological Risk Factors
As already described, biological processes are responsible for damage to the nervous system that results in the onset of vascular dementia. Although the precise health factors that put a person at risk for VaD are unknown, the health history often includes long-standing hypertension and vascular disease processes (Stewart, 2002). Other risk factors for vascular dementia include hypertension, smoking, diabetes, cardiac rhythm disorders, excess body fat, high cholesterol, and an imbalance in antioxidant activity (Table 16.2). Particularly high rates of dementia are observed following clinical

Table 16.2

Risk and Protective Factors for the Onset of Vascular Dementia

Risk Factors	Protective Factors
Biological	
Genetic vulnerability (APOE)	No genetic loading for APOE
High blood pressure	Normal blood pressure
High fat levelsDiabetes	Normal fat levels
Glucose intolerance	Normal insulin processing, glucose tolerance
Lifestyle factors (no smoking, exercise)	Lifestyle factors (smoking, lack of exercise)
CNS inflammation	Absence of CNS disease activity
Cerebral perfusion	
Neuroendocrine dysfunction	
Oxidative stress	
Excitotoxicity	
Vascular (blood vessel) disease	
Stroke	
Ischemia	
Amyloid deposits	
Psychological	
Stress experiences that affect blood pressure and and general health	Stress management skills
Depression	Stable mood
Social	
Lower educational level	Higher educational level
Inadequate social support	Functional social support
Poor access to health care	Access to health care
Lower socioeconomic status	Higher socioeconomic status

stroke, with a ninefold increase in risk over the first year, followed by a twofold annual risk each year afterward (Wells & Whitehouse, 2000). In a study of 438 subjects in a semirural area of the United Kingdom, people with vascular dementia were distinguished by a history of stroke and diabetes, compared with those who had AD or no cognitive impairment (Boston, Dennis, & Jagger, 1999). There were no differences between members of the comparison groups for falls, heart attack, hypertension, head injury, lipid levels, or substance abuse. This supports what are generally hypothesized as the primary biological risk factors for the disorder and the relative heterogeneity of other contributing risk factors.

Psychological and Social Risk Factors

No psychological factors are associated with the onset of VaD or a worsening of symptoms. As with Alzheimer's disease, however, it is highly likely that lifestyle factors influence a person's physical health in ways that may be protective of, or put the person at risk for, the dementia. Regarding psychological factors, stress has been shown to have a negative influence on cardiovascular functioning and could be a factor in sustaining a person's high blood pressure (Boston, Dennis, & Jagger, 1999). Regarding social factors, low educational and socioeconomic status is associated with exercise, smoking, and diet practices that may be significant factors (Atchley, 2000).

Comparing Alzheimer's Disease and Vascular Dementia

Alzheimer's disease and vascular dementia have different causes (with some overlap) and courses. These differences are manifested in clients' behaviors and overall physical health. One major research study compared the mental and behavioral disturbances of people with the two disorders (Lyketsos et al., 2000). A study of 5100 residents of a Utah county, which were 90% of the older adult residents of that county, found that most people with dementia had either AD or VaD, and only modest differences were observed in the prevalence of their mental or behavioral disturbances. People with AD were more likely to have delusions and less likely to experience depression. Agitation, aggression, and aberrant motor behavior disturbances were more common in people with advanced dementia of both types.

Ironically, there is an inverse relationship between the presence of other health, emotional, and behavioral conditions and the degree of cognitive impairment with the dementias. In a study of 161,106 patients over the age of 65 with cognitive impairment, those with AD were likelier to be younger, female, and Caucasian than VaD patients. AD patients also had fewer additional health problems and lower mortality rates relative to patients with VaD (Landi et al., 1999). Thus, people with Alzheimer's disease are otherwise healthier than people with vascular dementia. The latter disease is more clearly the result of preexisting cardiovascular health problems. Depression is also more common (up to eight times more so) in vascular dementia than in Alzheimer's disease (Newman, 1998).

There are conflicting reports about the status of diabetes as a risk factor for dementia. A 5-year study of 5574 subjects, initially without cognitive impairment, in the Canadian Study on Health and Aging revealed no association between diabetes and the incidence of AD, although such an association was found with vascular impairment (MacKnight, Rockwood, Await, & McDowell, 2002). Evidence of the role of vascular factors in the onset of AD was also found, supporting the idea that vascular health factors may play a role in the onset of both disorders.

Other Cognitive Disorders

The *DSM-IV-TR* includes two types of cognitive disorders in addition to the dementias. *Delirium* is the most common cognitive disorder and also the least debilitating. It is defined as any disturbance in a person's consciousness and cognitive ability that develops and persists during a short time period (just hours or days) (APA, 2000). A person with delirium experiences impairment in his or her awareness of the environment and a reduced ability to focus, sustain, or shift attention. The disorder may be characterized by impairments in orientation, the capacity to discriminate sensory input, and the ability to integrate present with past experiences, as well as rambling or incoherent speech and unwarranted expressions of fear. Delirium has a brief, fluctuating course and resolves rapidly when its cause is identified and treated. The symptoms generally recede in 3 to 7 days, although sometimes the process can take up to 2 weeks.

Unlike dementia, delirium originates outside the central nervous system. Its possible causes include metabolic and cardiovascular illnesses, electrolyte imbalances, the physical stress of surgery and postoperative pain, fever (children with high fevers commonly develop short-term delusions), infection, blood loss, insomnia, side effects or toxicity from some medications, intoxication, and alcohol withdrawal. Risk factors for the disorder include older age, preexisting brain damage or sensory impairment, alcohol dependence, diabetes, malnutrition, and a history of delirium (Lipowski, 1990).

The *amnestic disorders* feature impairments of memory that do not include any other type of cognitive difficulty (Simon, Aminoff, & Greenberg, 1998). They are relatively uncommon and are associated with the effects of substance abuse and various medical conditions. Unlike delirium, the amnestic disorders may result in temporary or permanent memory impairment, depending on the cause. Some people with the disorder develop a tendency to confabulate; that is, they attempt to fill in their memory gaps by making up information that they hope is true.

Transient forms of the amnestic disorders, with full recovery, can develop from epilepsy, the side effects of electroconvulsive therapy and some medications, thiamine deficiency, and hypoxia (temporary oxygen loss) (Sadock & Sadock, 2005). Permanent amnesia may result from head trauma, carbon monoxide poisoning, cerebral infarction (cell death in certain areas of the brain due to an obstruction of blood flow), hemorrhage (internal bleeding), and brain swelling related to herpes simplex.

Differential Diagnosis

Some symptoms of dementia and delirium are similar, but the two types of disorders can be differentiated by their course (Wells & Whitehouse, 2000). The symptoms of delirium fluctuate and are short term, whereas the symptoms of dementia are relatively stable or deteriorating. Amnestic disorder is characterized by memory impairment only, without any other significant cognitive difficulty.

Intervention

Medications for Alzheimer's Disease

No known medical treatment exists at the present time to cure AD or stop the progression of the disease. The FDA has approved four drugs since 1994 that are intended to have a mild to moderate effect on its presentation: tacrine (Cognex), donepezil, rivastigmine (Exelon), and galantamine (Reminyl) (Kalb & Rosenberg, 2004). The medications may at best slow the process and temporarily stabilize some of the symptoms. Several other drugs are in the testing process. Most of them are classified as *cholinesterase inhibitors*, which work by inhibiting the breakdown of a key brain chemical, acetylcholine.

Tacrine, the first drug approved by the FDA in 1993, has been the most extensively studied thus far, with only modest success. Many people cannot tolerate the drug because of side effects, and only 30% of consumers experience its intended benefits. A meta-analysis of the tacrine trials produced summary information about its effectiveness (Qizilbash et al., 1998). In their report, the researchers included 12 trials, all of which were randomized, double blind, and placebo controlled. A variety of measures indicated that tacrine's cholinesterase inhibition was most effective in reducing deterioration in cognitive performance and increasing global clinical improvement during the first 3 months of use. Effects observed on measures of behavioral disturbance were of questionable clinical significance, however, and the drug did not appear to affect functional autonomy. The clinical relevance of the benefits of cholinesterase remains controversial.

The ideal remedy for Alzheimer's disease would slow the production of amyloid by disabling the enzymes that fabricate it (Altman, 2001; Atchley, 2000). Current drug research is focused on the development of *beta secretase*, since the earlier *gamma blockers* seemed to interfere with normal brain function. Other drugs being targeted prevent the binding of amyloid fragments to form fibrils. Still other drugs may bolster the immune system to ward off development of amyloid or control the distribution of glutamate in the brain, which occurs when a person's amyloid burden rises and, when chronically elevated, destroys neurons. New drugs under investigation may mimic the protective actions of APOE-2 or 3, or block the effects of APP-4. Drug therapy (and perhaps diet) may be able to decrease blood levels of APOE-4, remove excess amyloid, and support growth factors that keep brains healthy. Although the role of APOE in the production of Alzheimer's disease is questionable, several insurance companies have investigated the possibility of requiring APOE blood tests for subscribers, a highly controversial move.

Alzheimer's Disease and Vascular Dementia: Drugs for Related Symptoms

Other types of medications may be effective for treating the symptoms of psychosis, agitation, and depression in persons with AD and VaD (Raicu & Workman, 2000). These are only briefly mentioned here because they are described more fully in other chapters of this book. In general, all psychotropic medications are prescribed in lower doses for elderly clients than for other age groups because of their slower metabolism and rates of clearance through the kidneys (Bentley & Walsh, 2006). The effectiveness of these medications may also be compromised by interactions with other medications the person might be taking. Older adults tend to be more sensitive than younger age groups to the adverse physical effects of all medications. Although it is the physician's responsibility to titrate medications appropriately, the social worker should participate in the process by monitoring their positive and negative effects through observation and discussion with the client and family.

The only effective medications for reducing or eliminating symptoms of psychosis and agitation are the antipsychotic drugs (Schatzberg & Nemeroff, 2001). No differences in effectiveness have been found between the older ("conventional") and newer ("atypical") medications. The choice of a drug often depends on the side effect profile. Some antipsychotic drugs tend to be sedating, and others are more likely to induce muscle stiffness, among other possible adverse effects. Formal evaluations of the efficacy of antidepressant drugs with dementia clients are also lacking, but clinical evidence tends to support their use (Bonavita et al., 2001). The newer selective serotonin reuptake inhibitors are generally the first choice of physicians because of their relatively mild side effect profiles. The antianxiety benzodiazepine drugs and the anticonvulsant drugs may also be helpful in reducing agitation among people with dementia (Stahl, 2000).

Psychosocial Interventions

Vascular Dementia: Prevention

Because vascular dementia results from some long-standing disease processes, the early control of its risk factors may help prevent or delay its onset or progression. A number of medical strategies being considered are intended to protect neurons, increase the quality of neurotransmission, and improve cerebral blood flow. The validity of all these medical strategies needs to be demonstrated with large clinical trials.

The modification of risk status in midlife is likely to be an important means of preventing the onset of vascular dementia, although it will not affect the course of the disorder. The potential for preventive interventions was supported by one study of 296 Australian volunteers that investigated older people's knowledge and practice of lifestyle behaviors that may prevent vascular dementia (Coulson, Marino, & Minichiello, 2001). Relevant knowledge variables included the effects on health of interpersonal relationships, physical activity, medical knowledge, medical history, self-assessment of general health, and use of alcohol. Results indicated that knowledge by itself does not necessarily ensure that people will engage in healthy lifestyle behaviors. The authors concluded that professionals and family members should be trained to help older adults reinforce and apply their existing knowledge of healthy lifestyle factors. Such interventions should include the importance of ongoing relationships, how to approach health professionals, professionals' awareness of the difficulty of older adults in reaching out to and communicating with them, and how to create environments supportive of healthy lifestyle behaviors.

Alzheimer's Disease and Vascular Dementia

Because of the inevitable progression of both of these dementias, nonmedical interventions are focused on promoting the client's safety, comfort, and productivity for as long as possible and helping the family or other caregivers be more competent and capable of managing the stress that often accompanies their role. Unfortunately, it was not until the 1980s that health care professionals demonstrated a commitment to working with clients who have dementia, as evidenced by staffing and resources, and began developing formal intervention protocols (Cohen, 2001). Many psychosocial interventions are widely accepted by professional caregivers as effective, but there is not yet extensive research supporting these assumptions. Practice guidelines regarding the range of interventions that social workers and other professionals might apply with clients follow (Rabins et al., 2002).

Establish and maintain an alliance with the client and family. Unterback (1994), a social worker, has developed some useful principles for developing a positive worker–client relationship with people who have dementia: maintaining a calm, reassuring demeanor with the client, using simple language, asking one question at a time, speaking slowly, always referring to the client by name, being alert to certain words to which the client consistently responds, trying to interact with the client when he or she is calm, being alert to nonverbal communications, and moving slowly in the client's presence.

Arrange and participate in a diagnostic evaluation, and link the client with resources for any needed medical care. Although the social worker cannot directly engage in medical testing, he or she can provide appropriate case management activities (referral, linkage, follow-up, and advocacy) to make sure that a thorough evaluation is conducted.

Assess and monitor the client's noncognitive (emotional and behavioral) mental status. This includes being alert to the possibility of the client's developing problems with depression and anxiety.

Monitor provisions for the client's safety and intervene when appropriate. Some standard guidelines for family members who have a client living at home are providing the client with a safe, structured, predictable routine; minimizing the intrusion of environmental stimuli that may be overwhelming; minimizing the demands to which the client must respond; and distracting the client from confusing or agitating situations (Epple, 2002; Finkel, 2001).

Intervene to decrease the hazards of the client's wandering behavior (if applicable). Families may be helped to minimize the potential dangers of this behavior by locking doors, putting small "gates" at the top of staircases, or simply becoming alert to signs of the client's tendency to wander.

Advise the client and family concerning driving and other client activities that put people at risk. Family members often feel guilty or cannot agree on when to set limits on some of these activities, and the practitioner's "objective" point of view may be useful in resolving dilemmas.

Educate the client and family about the illness and available interventions. Families may have no knowledge of the process of cognitive decline or the many services available in (some) communities to manage it.

Advise the family regarding sources of care and support. Psychoeducational interventions with family members and caregivers are essential, and their positive outcomes are supported by the literature (Gallagher-Thompson, 1994; Mace & Rabins, 1999). Families need to be educated about how to interact with the client, modify the client's environment, provide appropriate types of support, and manage their own sense of burden. Respite care should ideally begin during the early phase of the disorder so that the client comes to accept it as a standard part of the routine. As dementia progresses, the client may resist any such changes.

Assess and refer the family for assistance with any related financial and legal issues. The stresses related to long-range money management and decisions about conservatorship require professional consultation if available.

Empirically Validated Interventions

A meta-analysis of interventions for older adults with cognitive (and other) disorders provides empirical support for several of the strategies described later in this section (Gatz et al., 1998). Specifically, behavioral and environmental interventions for behavioral problems in persons with dementia are "well established," meaning that they have been subjected to at least two group experimental studies conducted by independent investigators or at least nine single-case design experiments. Further, memory and cognitive retraining interventions and support groups for caregivers are classified as "probably efficacious." That is, they have been validated by at least two experiments with wait-list control groups, one or more group experiments by a single investigator, or less than three single-case experiments that used comparison groups. We now consider some details of psychosocial interventions for older adults with dementia.

There is wide agreement among practitioners that *behavioral* interventions can be effective in reducing or abolishing certain problem behaviors characteristic of clients with dementia, including aggression, screaming, poor hygiene, and incontinence (Cohen-Mansfield, 2001; Grassel, Wiltfang, & Kornhuber, 2003). Even so, empirical evidence of effectiveness is modest. For the behavioral interventions to be effective, the social worker needs to first clarify the target behavior, breaking it down into steps if necessary (for example, the act of bathing involves a variety of steps). The social worker then identifies the relevant antecedent and consequent reinforcers of the target behavior (by steps, if appropriate) as clearly as possible, including the roles of significant others. The social worker then enlists the assistance of caregivers in developing new environmental conditions (antecedents) that will increase the likelihood of the client's exhibiting the desired behavior. Again using the example of bathing, the social worker may suggest reducing its frequency or moving the activity to a different (more agreeable) time of day. Additionally, the social worker should teach caregivers how to reinforce the client's performance of desired behaviors (with praise, hugs, or a special "reward" activity, for example). When devising behavioral interventions, the social worker must be careful not to exceed the client's cognitive capacities to manage certain adjustments.

The *reminiscence* and *validation* therapies, which stimulate the client's memory and mood in the context of systematically discussing events in his or her life history, have been shown to improve short-term mood, behavior, and cognition in several studies (Burnside & Haight, 1994; Nomura, 2002). *Reality orientation* and *skills training*, which are both used to increase the client's awareness of the present and ability to focus on self-care, also seem to have modest benefits, although these tend not to persist beyond the situation in which they are applied (Metiteri et al., 2001; Williams, 1994). These two interventions include some possible adverse effects, however, including increased agitation and frustration in clients *and* stress in caregivers who apply them.

The *recreational* and *art* therapies provide stimulation and enrichment for people with dementia, mobilizing their cognitive processes. These interventions also seem to produce short-term improvements in mood and decreases in behavioral problems (Fitzsimmons & Buettner, 2003; Rovner, Steel, Shmuely, & Folstein, 1996). Data on their effectiveness are limited, but they are widely accepted as appropriate commonsense interventions. One group of researchers has developed a behavioral protocol for managing Alzheimer's disease that offers clients a variety of pleasant activities, a process that improves the overall moods of both clients and caregivers (Teri, 1994; Teri & Logsdon, 1991).

One issue that often arises in working with impaired older adults is that professionals, like family members and other caregivers, are inclined to become controlling of the behavior and choices of clients. A study of 80 social workers in three northeastern states indicated that less support is held for the autonomy of people with Alzheimer's disease than for people with vascular dementia (Healy, 1999). That is, the practitioners tended to become authoritarian and highly directive in working with these clients. Social workers were most controlling if they had concerns about client safety and caregiver burden. These professional behaviors may be appropriate, but when working with these clients, social workers should be careful to uphold the value of self-determination to the extent possible.

The fact that many psychosocial interventions with clients who have dementia have only short-term benefits should not deter the social worker from using them. The client's quality of life is usually enriched by the opportunity to participate in these programs and activities.

Critique of the Diagnosis of Dementia

Research on Alzheimer's disease and vascular dementia overwhelmingly concludes that both disorders result from degenerative biological processes in the brain. There appear to be no significant psychological or social factors that directly affect their onset, although their ultimate course (particularly with vascular dementia) may be either exacerbated or slowed in response to some emotional and social factors. For these reasons, the dementias are universally accepted as medical disorders. Disorders that have strong biological components such as these do not generate much debate within the social work profession about negative labeling, stigma, subjectivity, and the effects of values on diagnosis. Alzheimer's disease and VaD are among the more easily accepted *DSM* disorders by social workers.

Case Illustration

Mary Louise Hollman was an 80-year-old married mother of three grown children, two of whom lived nearby. She and her retired husband, John, also had nine grandchildren. Since her husband retired 15 years ago, they had led moderately active lives, including daily walks and frequent visits with their children and friends. Having emigrated from Germany in early childhood, the couple had never been sociable with their more "Americanized" neighbors. Mary Louise was in generally good physical condition, but John had a history of heart problems and was now using a pacemaker. His activities were restricted because he needed to be careful about his level of exertion. They had limited financial resources and were living in a trailer park.

Mary Louise had been complaining of forgetfulness for the past 5 years. She had trouble remembering where she put such items as her keys, money, books, grocery store items, and other small personal items. Occasionally her memory slips were dangerous, such as when she forgot to turn off the stove after cooking. Mary Louise usually laughed about these oversights, making jokes about the trials of the aging process. Her children were only mildly concerned about her cognitive functioning. They assumed that forgetfulness was typical of most people in their mid-70s and beyond. Indeed, they were all over 40 years old and had begun to notice that their own memory skills were not as sharp as they once were. Mary Louise's own mother, however, had experienced Alzheimer's disease for the last 7 years of her life, so Mary Louise and her family members carried a quiet concern about her welfare. One afternoon when her daughter Kathleen was visiting, Mary Louise asked where the bathroom was. This startled Kathleen and convinced her that Mary Louise's memory problem had become serious.

Assessment and Diagnosis

Kathleen persuaded her reluctant father to schedule an appointment for Mary Louise with the family physician. After John described the presenting problems, Dr. Hinson suspected dementia, considering Mary Louise's age and reported course of memory decline. The doctor first conducted a mental status examination of Mary Louise's sense of time and place and her ability to remember, understand, communicate, and compute simple math problems. In assessing the family history, Dr. Hinson learned that Mary Louise's mother had experienced similar signs of memory loss at about the same age. The patient's mother had in fact lived with the Hollman family during the last 5 years of her life. This established a genetic link to AD.

Dr. Hinson completed a comprehensive physical exam to more systematically investigate the possibility of dementia. He wanted to rule out any physical conditions that might be causing Mary Louise's worsening memory, such as hypothyroidism, vitamin B_{12} or folic acid deficiency, niacin deficiency, neurosyphilis, and infections. Blood and urine tests yielded no support for these factors. Mary Louise had suffered no head trauma, so it was unlikely she had suffered a subdural hematoma (brain swelling). John confirmed that Mary Louise had never been much of a drinker and had never used nonprescription drugs.

Following his tests, Dr. Hinson concluded that no physical or medication-related conditions were contributing to Mary Louise's memory loss and confusion. Prior to diagnosis, however, he referred Mary Louise for a neurological exam, cognitive screening exam, and brain scan (MRI) to further assess possible medical causes of her condition. He also recommended a full psychiatric examination to rule out mood factors (especially major depression) that might be contributing to the symptoms. These tests confirmed significant deficits in Mary Louise's memory, vision-motor coordination, and language skills but yielded no signs of strokes, tumors, or other medical problems. The psychological testing revealed that Mary Louise was experiencing moderate anxiety and depression, but these symptoms appeared to center around an awareness of her memory loss.

With all of this information, the following diagnosis was made for Mary Louise:

Axis I: Dementia of the Alzheimer's Type, With Late Onset, Uncomplicated (Mary Louise displayed no significant symptoms of delusions or delirium, and her depression appeared to be only moderate. It is possible that over time her condition might change, and one of these specifiers would be added.)

Axis II: No diagnosis

Axis III: Alzheimer's disease (Because it is a medical condition, AD is recorded on this axis even though it may seem redundant with the axis I diagnosis.)

Axis IV: None. Although the Hollman family had limited material resources, they were accustomed to living within their means and had experienced no stress related to this issue.

Axis V: Current GAF = 40 (serious impairment in reality testing),
Highest in Past Year = 55 (moderate symptoms)

Goal Formulation and Treatment Planning

After reviewing the full medical report, Dr. Hinson prescribed donepezil
(Aricept) for Mary Louise, one of the four FDA-approved drugs for the
treatment of AD. The medications do not stop the onset or progression of
the disorder, but it was hoped that the drug would slow the process and
temporarily stabilize some of the symptoms. He also referred Mary Louise
and her husband to a comprehensive senior citizens service center in her
community. A social worker there helped the couple develop an intervention plan. The goals included:

- To maintain Mary Louise's current levels of cognitive and physical
  functioning as long as possible
- For Mary Louise to function as a contributing member of her family
  and community
- To reduce Mary Louise's feelings of sadness and anxiety
- For Mary Louise's family members to become more knowledgeable
  about dementia, including an awareness of all community support
  services

The first two goals would be addressed by Mary Louise's participation in
three formal group activities provided at the community center. *Reminiscence* group therapy, a process of sharing memories of major events and
transitions in one's life, was appropriate because older memories are more
durable than newer ones in persons with AD (Altman, 2001). The purposes
of the group are to reduce apathy, alleviate depression, and increase social
interaction, life satisfaction, morale, self-esteem, and the client's sense of
control (Burnside, 1994). The *remotivation* group is a structured discussion
program that includes the goals of stimulating and revitalizing individuals
who have lost interest in the present or the future (Dennis, 1994). It serves
to resocialize members to events in their social worlds and encourage their
pursuit of interests to the extent possible. Each session revolves around a
common topic like pets, gardening, art, hobbies, holidays, and vacations.
The *reality orientation* group provides repetitive orienting activities and continual stimulation to help alleviate and in some cases stop memory deterioration (Williams, 1994). It focuses on concrete activities and events of the
day to enhance members' awareness of the world around them. All of the
group sessions were 30 minutes in duration, which is considered appropriate for older adults with mental and physical limitations. For people

with AD, however, reality orientation efforts should be constant and involve every staff member at the center throughout the day.

Mary Louise's third goal would be addressed through her participation in exercise groups and other activities with her family and friends, such as walking, housekeeping, gardening, and maintaining contact with her friends in the neighborhood. Mary Louise was in good physical condition, but to sustain her activity routine she would need to be regularly encouraged and directed or she may begin to forget about these activities. Mary Louise's final goal would be addressed through the family's modulating her environment and reducing stimuli when she becomes anxious. Soothing music and designated quiet areas often help with this. Surrounding her with mementos from her children and friends might promote a positive attitude, by keeping alive memories of her loved ones. Helping her family members learn to offer reassurance when she is anxious or sad would also be important. Mary Louise can be helped to learn and practice relaxation exercises to manage her anxiety.

The final goal would be addressed by the social worker meeting with Mary Louise's husband, John, and their two children who lived in town on a weekly basis for 4 weeks to provide them with a structured family education series about Alzheimer's disease and the typical challenges experienced by caregivers. The family would be encouraged to share responsibility for Mary Louise's supervision and monitoring and to take advantage of respite opportunities, particularly as the disease progresses. They would also be encouraged to participate in the senior center's monthly support group for the relatives of dementia patients.

None of the health care professionals who worked with Mary Louise could predict the course of deterioration of her cognitive functioning. All of them agreed, however, that while the medication might provide some benefit, the group and family interventions were most critical for maximizing her potential for ongoing quality of life. They were advised by the social worker to frequently encourage the client and family's participation because, as noted earlier, they did not have a history of extensive social integration.

Summary

All of the cognitive disorders have primarily biological origins. Not all of them are degenerative, although this chapter has focused on two types of dementia that are. It is fortunate that delirium, the most common cognitive disorder, is always temporary (it can also be a symptom of many other *DSM* disorders) and that the amnestic disorders are reversible in many cases. Further, the mental status of clients with several of the dementias related to specific health problems may also be stabilized and improved. Social workers who intervene with any of these clients are likely to do so as members of interdisciplinary health care teams. They can provide a variety of psychosocial therapies that may be beneficial to clients' functioning levels and quality of life, and they may be particularly helpful in providing supportive services to family members and other caregivers. Despite the biological causes of the dementias, attention to all aspects of the client's functioning is significant to their course.

Appendix. Instruments Used to Assess Dementia

The Mini-Mental Status Examination

Folstein, Folstein, & McHugh (1975)

Description

- Assesses a client's orientation, recall, attention, ability to perform basic calculations, and language comprehension.
- Tracks changes in a client's cognitive state over time.
- A client responds to questions, makes calculations, is asked to complete several tasks, and copies a design.
- A person can score between 0 and 30 points; a score below 23 suggests significant impairment, and a score below 20 indicates definite impairment.

Reliability

- Tested with 206 respondents diagnosed with dementia, psychotic disorders, and personality disorders, and 63 controls.
- 24-hour test-retest reliability was .89 with the same examiner, .83 with multiple examiners.
- Clinically stable respondents had a .98 score correlation over 28 days.

Validity

- Test scores accurately separated the clinical sample into those with dementia, depression, and depression with cognitive impairment.
- Concurrent validity was demonstrated by correlating MMSE scores with WAIS scores; resulting Pearson's Rs were .78 for verbal IQ and .66 for performance IQ.

The Pocket Smell Test

Duff, McCaffrey, & Solomon (2002)

Description

- Olfactory dysfunction has been noted in Alzheimer's disease and other neuropsychiatric conditions. This test is a three-item "scratch and sniff" measure used to discriminate elderly people with AD from those with VaD or major depression.
- On each item, the examiner releases an odor by scratching the odor patch with a pencil. The client smells the odor and chooses one of four response alternatives. These may be read to clients, and they are encouraged to guess if they are not sure of a response. Correct responses are lemon, lilac, and smoke.
- Two or more errors are highly suggestive of Alzheimer's disease.

Reliability

Not reported

Validity

Among clients previously diagnosed with AD, VaD, and major depression ($N = 60$), classification accuracy was 95%, sensitivity was 100%, and specificity was 92.5%.

The Ten-Point Clock Test

Moretti, Torre, Antonello, Cassato, & Bava (2002)

Description

- Assesses cognitive impairment and is helpful in distinguishing disease processes from normal aging. Also helps to distinguish AD from VaD.
- An 11.4-cm diameter circle is traced with a template. The client is asked to put the numbers on the face of the clock and then make the clock read 10 minutes after 11. A 10-point scoring system is used to quantify the accuracy of the spatial arrangement of the numbers and setting of the hands.

Reliability

Not reported

Validity

Significant correlations were reported with client scores on a variety of other measures (Mini-Mental Status Examination, a proverb test, tests of language fluency and visual-spatial skills). Scores of clients with AD and VaD also correlated significantly with different measures.

References

Altman, L. J. (2001). *Alzheimer's disease*. San Diego, CA: Lucent.

American Psychiatric Association. (2000). *Diagnostic and statistical manual of mental disorders* (4th ed., text rev.). Washington, DC: Author.

Atchley, R. (2000). *Social forces and aging: An introduction to social gerontology.* Belmont, CA: Wadsworth.

Beck, A. T., & Weishaar, M. (1995). Cognitive therapy. In R. J. Corsini & D. Wedding (Eds.), *Current psychotherapies* (5th ed., pp. 229–261). Itasca, IL: F. E. Peacock.

Bentley, K. J., & Walsh, J. (2006). *The social worker and psychotropic medication (3rd ed.).* Pacific Grove, CA: Brooks/Cole.

Bonavita, V., Iavarone, A., & Sorrentino, G. (2001). Depression in neurological diseases: A review. *Archives of General Psychiatry, 58*(Suppl. 7), 49–66.

Boston, P. F., Dennis, M. S., & Jagger, C. (1999). Factors associated with vascular dementia in an elderly community population. *International Journal of Geriatric Psychiatry, 14,* 761–766.

Burnside, I. (1994). Reminiscence group therapy. In I. Burnside & M. G. Schmidt (Eds.), *Working with older adults: Group process and techniques* (pp. 163–178). Boston: Jones and Bartlett.

Burnside, I., & Haight, B. (1994). Reminiscence and life review: Therapeutic interventions for older people. *Nursing Practitioner, 19*(4), 55–61.

Cohen, G. D. (2001). Criteria for success in interventions for Alzheimer's disease. *American Journal of Geriatric Psychiatry, 9*(2), 95–98.

Cohen-Mansfield, J. (2001). Nonpharmacologic interventions for inappropriate behaviors in dementia: A review, summary, and critique. *American Journal of Geriatric Psychiatry, 9*(4), 361–381.

Coulson, I., Marino, R., & Minichiello, V. (2001). Older people's knowledge and practice about lifestyle behaviors that may prevent vascular dementia. *Archives of Gerontology and Geriatrics, 33,* 273–285.

Cowley, G. (2002, June 24). The disappearing mind. *Newsweek, 139*(25), 42–48.

Cummings, L. J., & Cole, G. (2002). Alzheimer's disease. *Journal of the American Medical Association, 287,* 2335–2339.

Dennis, H. (1994). Remotivation groups. In I. Burnside & M. G. Schmidt (Eds.), *Working with older adults: Group process and techniques* (pp. 153–162). Boston: Jones and Bartlett.

Epple, D. M. (2002). Senile dementia of the Alzheimer's type. *Clinical Social Work Journal, 30,* 95–110.

Farrer, L. A., Cupples, L. A., & Haines, J. L. (1997). Effects of age, sex, and ethnicity on the association between apolipoprotein E genotype and Alzheimer disease: A meta-analysis. *JAMA: Journal of the American Medical Association,* *278*(16), 1349–1356.

Finkel, S. I. (2001). Behavioral and psychological symptoms of dementia: A current focus for clinicians, researchers, and caregivers. *Journal of Clinical Psychiatry,* *62*(Suppl. 21), 3–6.

Fitzsimmons, S., & Buettner, L. L. (2003). Therapeutic recreation intervention for need-driven dementia-compromised behaviors in community dwellers. *American Journal of Alzheimer's Disease & Other Dementias, 17*(6), 367–381.

Gallagher-Thompson, D. (1994). Direct services and interventions for caregivers: A review and critique of extant programs and a look ahead to the future. In M. M. Canter (Ed.), *Family caregiving: Agenda for the future* (pp. 102–122). San Francisco: American Society on Aging.

Gatz, M., Fiske, A., Fox, L. S., Kaskie, B., Kasl-Godley, J. E., McCallum, T. J., et al. (1998). Empirically validated psychological treatments for older adults. *Journal of Mental Health and Aging, 4*(1), 9–46.

Grassel, E., Wiltfang, J., & Kornhuber, J. (2003). Non-drug therapies for dementia: An overview of the current situation with regard to proof of effectiveness. *Dementia & Geriatric Cognitive Disorders, 15*(3), 115–125.

Healy, T. C. (1999). Community-dwelling cognitively impaired frail elders: An analysis of social workers' decisions concerning support for autonomy. *Social Work in Health Care, 30*, 27–47.

Kalb, C., & Rosenberg, D. (2004). Nancy's next campaign. *Newsweek, 143*(25), 39–44.

Landi, F., Gambassi, G., Lapane, K. L., Sgadari, A., Mor, V., & Bernabei, R. (1999). Impact of the type and severity of dementia on hospitalization and survival of the elderly. *Dementia and Geriatric Cognitive Disorders, 10*, 121–129.

Lipowski, Z. J. (1990). *Delirium: Acute confusional states.* New York: Oxford University Press.

Lopera, F., Ardilla, A., Martinez, A., Madrigal, L., Arango-Viana, J. C., Lemere, C. A., et al. (1997). Clinical features of early-onset Alzheimer's disease in a large kindred with an E20A presenilin-1 mutation. *Journal of the American Medical Association, 277*, 793–807.

Lyketsos, C. G., Steinberg, M., Tschanz, J. T., Norton, M. C., Steffens, D. C., & Breitner, J. C. S. (2000). Mental and behavioral disturbances in dementia: Findings from the Cache County study on memory in aging. *American Journal of Psychiatry, 157*, 708–714.

Mace, N. L., & Rabins, P. V. (1999). *The 36-hour day: A family guide to caring for persons with Alzheimer's disease, related dementing illnesses, and memory loss in later life.* Baltimore: Johns Hopkins University Press.

MacKnight, C., Rockwood, K., Await, E., & McDowell, I. (2002). Diabetes mellitus and the risk of dementia, Alzheimer's disease and vascular cognitive impairment in the Canadian study of health and aging. *Dementia and Geriatric Cognitive Disorders 14*, 77–83.

Metiteri, T., Zanetti, O., Geroldi, C., Frisoni, G. B., DeLeo, D., Dello Buono, M., et al. (2001). Reality orientation therapy to delay outcomes of progression in patients with dementia: A retrospective study. *Clinical Rehabilitation, 15*(5), 471–478.

Morrison, J. (1995). *DSM-IV made easy: The clinician's guide to diagnosis.* New York: Guilford.

Newman, S. C. (1998). The prevalence of depression in Alzheimer's disease and vascular dementia in a population sample. *Journal of Affective Disorders, 52*(169–176).

Nomura, T. (2002). Evaluative research on reminiscence groups for people with dementia. In J. D. Webster & B. K. Haight (Eds.), *Critical advances in reminiscence work: From theory to application* (pp. 289–299). New York: Springer.

Qizilbash, N., Whitehead, A., Higgins, J., Wilcock, G., Schneider, L., & Farlow, M. (1998). Cholinesterase inhibition for Alzheimer's disease: A meta-analysis of the tactrine trials. *Journal of the American Medical Association, 280,* 1777–1791.

Rabins, P., Bland, W., Bright-Long, L., Cohen, E., Katz, I., Rovner, B., et al. (2002). Practice guidelines for the treatment of patients with Alzheimer's disease and other dementias of late life. In American Psychiatric Association (Ed.), *Practice guidelines for the treatment of psychiatric disorders* (pp. 67–135). Washington, DC: Author.

Raicu, R. G., & Workman, R. H. (2000). Management of psychotic and depressive features in patients with vascular dementia. *Topics in Stroke Rehabilitation, 7*(3), 11–19.

Rovner, B. W., Steel, C. D., Shmuely, Y., & Folstein, M. F. (1996). A randomized trial of dementia care in nursing homes. *Journal of the American Gerontological Society, 44,* 7–13.

Ruitenberg, A., Ott, A., van Swieten, J. C., Hofman, A., & Breteler, M. M. B. (2001). Incidence of dementia: Does gender make a difference? *Neurobiology of Aging, 22,* 575–580.

Sadock, B. J., & Sadock, V. A. (2005). *Kaplan & Sadock's Comprehensive Textbook of Psychiatry.* Philadelphia: Lippincott Williams & Wilkins.

Schatzberg, A. F., & Nemeroff, C. B. (Eds.). (2001). *Essentials of clinical psychopharmacology.* Washington, DC: American Psychiatric Press.

Simon, R. P., Aminoff, M. J., & Greenberg, D. A. (1998). *Clinical neurology.* Stamford, CT: Appleton & Lange.

Stahl, S. M. (2000). *Essential psychopharmacology: Neuroscientific basis and practical applications* (2nd ed.). New York: Cambridge University Press.

Stevenson, J. (1994). A mixed blessing. *Harvard Health Letter, 20,* 1–15.

Stewart, R. (2002). Vascular dementia: A diagnosis running out of time? *British Journal of Psychiatry, 180,* 152–156.

Suh, G. H., & Shah, A. (2001). A review of the epidemiological transition in dementia: Cross-national comparisons of the indices related to Alzheimer's disease and vascular dementia. *Acta Psychiatrica Scandinavia, 104,* 4–11.

Teri, L. (1994). Behavioral treatment of depression in patients with dementia. *Alzheimer's Disease and Associated Disorders, 8*(3), 66–74.

Teri, L., & Logsdon, R. G. (1991). Identifying pleasant activities for Alzheimer's disease patients: The Pleasant Events Schedule–AD. *The Gerontologist, 31,* 124–127.

Unterback, D. (1994). An ego function analysis for working with dementia clients. *Journal of Gerontological Social Work, 22,* 83–94.

Wells, C. E., & Whitehouse, P. J. (2000). Dementia. In B. S. Fogel, R. B. Schiffer, &

S. M. Rao (Eds.), *Synopsis of neuropsychiatry* (pp. 425–435). Philadelphia: Lippincott Williams & Wilkins.

Williams, E. M. (1994). Reality orientation groups. In I. Burnside & M. G. Schmidt (Eds.), *Working with older adults: Group process and techniques* (pp. 139–152). Boston: Jones and Bartlett.

References for Assessment Instruments for Dementia

Duff, K., McCaffrey, R. J., & Solomon, G. S. (2002). The pocket smell test: Successfully discriminating probable Alzheimer's dementia from vascular dementia and major depression. *Journal of Clinical Neuropsychiatry, 14*(2), 197–201.

Folstein, M. F., Folstein, S., & McHugh, P. R. (1975). Mini-mental state: A practical method for grading the cognitive state of patients for the clinician. *Journal of Psychiatric Residency, 12,* 189–198.

Moretti, R., Torre, P., Antonello, R. M., Cassato, G., & Bava, A. (2002). Ten-point clock test: A correlation analysis with other neuropsychological test in dementia. *International Journal of Geriatric Psychiatry, 17,* 347–353.

AA. *See* Alcoholics Anonymous
AAMR. *See* American Association of Mental Retardation
ABC. *See* Aberrant Behavior Checklist
Aberrant Behavior Checklist (ABC), 56–57
abnormality, 11, 12, 13
acetylcholine, 274, 491
ACT. *See* assertive community treatment
ACTeRS-Second Edition, 154–55
active symptoms. *See* positive symptoms
acute stress disorder, 164, 167t
ADA. *See* Americans with Disabilities Act
Adaptive Behavior Scale-Residential and Community (ABS-RC:2), 54–55
adaptive inflexibility, 449
addiction. *See* substance use disorders
ADHD. *See* attention-deficit/ hyperactivity disorder
ADHD Rating Scale-IV, 151–52
ADHD Symptoms Rating Scale, 153

Adolescent Alcohol Involvement Scale, 334–35
adolescent disorders, 229–378
  of anxiety, 197
  bipolar, 390, 392
  depressive, 261–72, 267t, 275–80, 289–92
  of eating, 231–56
  sexual, 349–69
  substance use, 304–28, 309t, 333–35
Adolescent Drug Involvement Scale, 335
adolescents
  cognitive-behavioral therapy for, 109
  lithium ingestion, 392
  multisystemic therapy for, 105, 322
  sexually victimized, 359
  smoking among, 197
  stimulants for, 146
adult disorders, 379–475
  bipolar, 381–406
  cognitive, 479–503
  of personality, 448–72
  schizophrenic, 412–41
advocate, 424

African Americans, 192, 239, 270, 415–16
agoraphobia, 192, 197, 217–19
akathisia, 422
Al-Anon, 327
alcohol abuse. *See* substance use disorders
Alcoholics Anonymous (AA), 322–24, 327
aldehyde dehydrogenase, 327
Altman Self-Rating Mania Scale, 403
Alzheimer's disease, 479, 481–83
  biology of, 482–83
  case illustration, 497–500
  and dementia, 480
  diagnosis of, 496–99
  effects on family, 482
  goal formulation and treatment planning, 499–500
  interventions for, 491–96
  medications for, 491–92, 499
  risk and protective factors, 483–86, 484t
  and vascular dementia, 489–90
amenorrhea, 231, 233
American Association of Mental Retardation (AAMR), 35, 49, 50
American Psychiatric Association (APA)
  categorization of personality patterns, 467
  definition of mental disorder, 12
  and *DSM*, 14, 16–18, 23, 27
  mental disorders recognized by, 4
  and mental retardation, 49, 50
Americans with Disabilities Act (ADA), 140
amnestic disorders, 479, 490–91
amphetamines, 142, 143, 144
AMR Adaptive Behavior Scale-School (ABS-S:2), 54–55
amyloid beta, 483, 491–92
amyloid-precursor protein (APP), 483
androgens, 362
anger control, 109
anorexia nervosa, 231–56
  comorbidity, 232–33
  diagnosis of, 246
  interventions for, 240–46
  prevalence of, 232
  risk and protective factors, 234–40
  treatment settings, 241–43

Antabuse. *See* disulfiram
antiandrogen agents, 362–63
anticholinergic medication, 423
anticonvulsant medication, 392–94
antidepressants, 145, 146, 206–7, 245, 274, 278, 284, 394
antidipsotropics, 327
antihistamines, 207
antipsychotic medication, 110, 394–95, 422–23, 492
antisocial personality disorder, 450, 451
anxiety, 191
anxiety disorders, 191–212
  assessment of, 195–96
  case study, 208–12
  comorbidity, 194–95
  diagnosis of, 209–11
  family factors, 198–99
  interventions for, 200–208, 201t, 202t
  measures of, 212, 215–28
  medications for, 201, 202t, 205–8
  risk and protective factors, 196–200, 197t, 198t, 211
  types of, 192–94
anxiety hierarchy, 174
anxiety sensitivity, 196–97
APA. *See* American Psychiatric Association
APOE. *See* apolipoprotein (APOE) genes
apolipoprotein (APOE) genes, 483–85, 492
APP. *See* amyloid-precursor protein
applied behavior analysis, 47
approach-automatic pattern, 366
approach-explicit pattern, 366
art therapy, 496
Asperger's disorder, 69, 81
ASQ. *See* Autism Screening Questionnaire
assertive community treatment (ACT), 429–30
Association of University Centers on Disabilities, 40
atomoxetine, 143, 145, 147
attachment, 101, 136, 198–99, 365
Attention Deficit Disorder Evaluation Scale-Second Edition, 153–54
attention-deficit/hyperactivity disorder (ADHD), 129–57
  adjustment and recovery, 136–37

in adulthood, 131–32
and bipolar disorder, 384
case example, 147–48, 150t, 151t
comorbidity, 132
course of, 131–32
diagnosis of, 132–34
guidelines for treatment, 138t
interventions for, 137–47
measures for, 149–57
medications for, 142–44, 143–45t, 146–47
and posttraumatic stress disorder, 167–68
prevalence of, 130–31
risk and protective factors, 134–37, 134–35t, 150t, 151t
auditory changes, 412
auditory hallucinations, 413, 432
autism, 64–69, 73–86
assessment of, 66–69
case illustration, 82–84
diagnosis of, 81–83
differential diagnosis and comorbidity, 71–73, 72t, 73t
interventions for, 79–81, 84
prevalence of, 65–66
recovery and adjustment, 77–78
risk and protective factors, 73–78, 74t, 78t, 83
scales, 84–86
Autism Behavior Checklist (ABC), 85–86
Autism Screening Questionnaire (ASQ), 85
autonomic nervous system hyperactivity, 191
autonomic nervous system reactivity, 100
avoidance, 164, 202
avoidance-active pattern, 366
avoidance-passive pattern, 366
avoidant personality disorder, 450, 451

BADDS. *See* Brown Attention-Deficit Disorder Scales for Children and Adolescents
Beck Anxiety Inventory, 225
Beck Depression Inventory II, 292, 293
Behavioral and Emotional Rating Scale (BERS), 57–58
behavioral inhibition, 196, 197

behavioral intervention, 495
behavioral marital therapy, 281
behavioral models, 275
Behavior Problems Inventory, 58
benzodiazepines, 205–6
bereavement, 167t
BERS. *See* Behavioral and Emotional Rating Scale
beta-blockers, 207
beta secretase, 492
binge-eating, 231
biopsychosocial framework. *See* risk and resilience biopsychosocial framework
bipolar disorder, 381–406
case illustration, 398–402
diagnosis of, 384–85, 400–401, 402
evidence-based intervention, 390–95
frequency of manic and depressive episodes, 383–84
instruments used to assess, 403–6
medications for, 390–95
nature of, 381–84
psychosocial interventions, 395–98
risk and protective factors, 385–86, 387t, 388–90
subtypes of, 382–83
in youth, 384
bipolar I disorder, 382, 383
bipolar II disorder, 382, 383
borderline personality disorder, 450, 451, 452–53
biological factors, 455
case illustration, 464–68
comorbid disorders, 457–58
course of, 457
diagnosis of, 466–67
dialectical behavior therapy, 462–63
interpersonal group therapy, 463–64
interventions for, 458–64
medications for, 461–62
psychological factors, 455–56
risk and protective factors, 453, 454t, 455–56
social factors, 456
BPRS. *See* Brief Psychiatric Rating Scale
brain, 75, 482
breathing retraining, 202
Brief Psychiatric Rating Scale (BPRS), 436–37
Brief Strategic Family Therapy, 322

Brown Attention-Deficit Disorder Scales
for Children and Adolescents
(BADDS), 155–56
bulimia nervosa, 231–56
comorbidity, 232–33
diagnosis of, 246
interventions for, 240–46
prevalence of, 232
risk and protective factors, 234–40
bupropion, 145, 147, 394
buspirone, 206

carbamazepine, 392–95
case management, 429–30
catatonic schizophrenia, 413
CD. *See* conduct disorder
CDD. *See* childhood disintegration
disorder
Center for Epidemiologic Studies-
Depression for Children and
Adolescents, 291
Center for Epidemiologic Studies
Depression Scale, 293–94
Center for Sexual Assault and
Traumatic Stress, 367
chemical addiction. *See* substance use
disorders
child abuse, 101
Child Behavior Checklist, 121–22
childhood disintegration disorder
(CDD), 70–71
childhood disorders, 33–228
of anxiety, 191–212
attention-deficit/hyperactivity
disorder, 129–57
autism, 64–69, 73–86
mental retardation, 36–61
oppositional defiant and conduct
disorders, 90–122
posttraumatic stress disorder in
children, 164–87
child molestation. *See* pedophilia
Child PTSD Symptom Scale, 183
Children's Depression Inventory, 290
Children's Impact of Traumatic Events
Scale, 183–84
Children's PTSD-Reaction Index, 181
Children's Social Behavior
Questionnaire (CSBQ), 84–85
cholinesterase inhibitors, 491
circular causality, 321

clinical social work practice, definition
of, 14
Clinician-Administered Rating Scale:
Mania, 403–4
clomipramine, 207
clonidine, 143, 145
clozapine, 394, 395, 423
cocaine, 307
cognition, definition of, 479
cognitive adaptation training, 426
cognitive-behavioral treatment
for anxiety disorders, 201–5
for bipolar disorder, 398
for child molestation, 368
for depression, 275–77, 281
for eating disorders, 243–44
for mental retardation, 47
for oppositional defiant and conduct
disorders, 108–10
for schizophrenia, 425–27
for substance use disorders, 319–20
cognitive changes, 412
cognitive disorders, 479–503
definition of, 479
instruments to assess, 501–3
See also Alzheimer's disease;
dementia
cognitive models, 275
cognitive restructuring, 174, 202
community intervention, 429–30
community reinforcement, 320
conditioned reactions, 201
conduct disorder (CD), 90–122
assessment of, 92–93
case illustration, 111–17
comorbidity, 95
course of, 94–95
diagnosis of, 112–14, 117–18
interventions for, 103–10
measures for, 118–22
prevalence of, 92
risk and protective factors, 95, 96–
97t, 98–102, 106t, 115–17t
confrontation, 326
Connors Ratings Scales-Revised, 149–
50
consultant/collaborator, 424
Coping Cat program, 204
"Coping with Depression" course, 279–
80
covert sensitization, 363–64

CSBQ. *See* Children's Social Behavior
    Questionnaire
cyclothymic disorder, 385

Davidson Trauma Scale, 186
degenerative disorders, 479
delirium, 479, 480, 486, 490
delusion, 413, 432, 480, 486
dementia, 479
    case illustration, 497–500
    diagnosis of, 480, 496–99
    instruments to assess, 501–3
    multi-infarct, 486
    symptoms of, 480–81
    See also vascular dementia
denial, 363
dependent personality disorder, 450,
    451
depot leuprolide acetate, 363
depression
    in adolescents, 261–72, 275–80, 289–
        92
    in adults, 264, 265, 266, 272–75, 280–
        85, 292–94
    and anxiety disorders, 194–95
    and autism, 76
    biological factors, 272–74
    case study, 286–89, 289t, 330–31
    cognitive triad of, 267–68
    comorbidity, 265–66
    course of, 264–65
    and dementia, 480, 487
    diagnosis of, 262–63, 288
    and eating disorders, 232, 249
    experiences of maltreatment, 269–70
    family factors, 268–69
    interventions for, 275–79
    measures, 289–94
    medication for, 278–79, 282–83t, 284–
        85
    prevalence of, 263–64
    prevention of, 279–80
    psychotherapy for, 275–79, 281–84
    risk and protective factors, 266–75,
        267t, 273t, 288–89
    See also bipolar disorder
developmental disability, 36
deviance, 13
deviant fantasies, 365
dextroamphetamine, 142, 143, 144
diabetes, 489–90

*Diagnostic and Statistical Manual of
    Mental Disorders (DSM)*, 3–4
    classification system, 11, 18–20, 27
    and comorbidity, 27
    criticisms of, 4, 23, 25–28
    DSM-III, 18–20
    DSM-III-R, 21–22
    DSM-IV, 22, 468–72
    DSM-IV-TR, 4, 22–23
    evolution of, 16–23
    first edition (*DSM-I*), 16–17
    first revision (*DSM-II*), 17–18
    hierarchical exclusionary rules, 21
    influences on, 14
        multiaxial system of diagnoses, 19,
            23
    procedure for completing diagnoses,
        24–25t
    purpose of, 11
    and social work, 15–16
    symptom clusters as basis for
        diagnoses, 15
    V-codes, 20
    See also specific disorders
dialectical behavior therapy, 462–63
dieting, 236–37, 245
Dimensional Assessment of Personality
    Pathology Basic Questionnaire,
    468
disease model, 12
disorder(s)
    cognitive, 479–503
    concept of, 11–14
    with onset in adolescence, 229–378
    with onset in adulthood, 379–475
    with onset in childhood, 33–228
    with onset in the elderly, 477–506
    personality, 448–72
    See also mental disorder(s); *specific
        disorders*
disorganized schizophrenia, 413
disulfiram, 326–27
donepezil, 499
dopamine, 274, 422
Down syndrome, 41
DPI. *See* Drinking Problems Index
Drinking Problems Index (DPI), 337
drug abuse. *See* substance use disorders
Drug Abuse Screening Test, 336–37
drugs (pharmaceuticals). *See*
    medication; *specific drugs*

DSM. *See Diagnostic and Statistical Manual of Mental Disorders*
dysthymia, 232, 261, 330
dystonia, 422

early intervention programs (EIPs), 45
Eating Attitudes Test, 251
Eating Disorder Inventory–2, 255–56
eating disorders, 231–56
  assessment of, 233–34
  biological factors, 236–37
  case study, 247–51
  comorbidity, 232–33
  diagnosis of, 246–47, 249–51
  family factors, 237–38
  interventions for, 240–46
  measures, 251, 254–56
  medications for, 244–45
  prevalence of, 231
  prevention of, 245–46
  psychological factors, 237
  risk and protective factors, 234–240, 234–35t, 251, 252–53t
  societal influences, 238–39
  treatment settings, 241–43
Eating Disorders Examination-Questionnaire Version, 254–55
educator, 424
EE. *See* expressed emotion
EIPs. *See* early intervention programs
elderly
  depression, 263, 294
  disorders of, 477–506
  See also Alzheimer's disease; dementia
electrolyte imbalances, 233
EMDR. *See* eye movement desensitization and reprocessing
erotomanic delusions, 413
ethnic minorities, 270, 305, 324–25
evidence-based practice, definition of, 6–7
exercise, 285
exposure treatment, 174–75, 201, 203–4
expressed emotion (EE), 421, 428
Eyberg Child Behavior Inventory, 120–21
eye movement desensitization and reprocessing (EMDR), 175

family-focused treatment, 396–97
family intervention
  for attention-deficit/hyperactivity disorder, 138–39
  for bipolar disorder, 395–97
  with conduct problems, 103–8
  for depression, 277–78
  for eating disorders, 244
  with mental retardation, 48
  for schizophrenia, 428–29
  for substance use disorders, 320–22
family structure, 321
fantasies, 349, 351, 365
fear/avoidance behaviors, 201–2
Fear Questionnaire, 226–27
female identity, 238
FFT. *See* functional family therapy
firearms, 272
fluoxetine, 245, 284
fragile X syndrome, 41, 67
Frost Multidimensional Perfectionism Scale, 227
Functional Family Therapy (FFT), 107, 322

GABA neurotransmitter, 205, 274, 392
GAD. *See* generalized anxiety disorder
gamma blockers, 492
gender, 193, 270–71, 307, 325
gender identity disorders, 349
General Behavior Inventory (Adapted), 404
generalized anxiety disorder (GAD), 193–94, 197, 199, 222
genetics. *See* heredity
Geriatric Depression Scale, 294
gonadotropin-releasing hormone agonists, 363
grandiose delusions, 413, 432
gustatory hallucinations, 413

hallucinations, 413, 416
haloperidol, 423
heredity
  and anxiety disorders, 196–97
  and attention-deficit/hyperactivity disorder, 134–35
  and autism, 76
  and bipolar disorder, 385–86
  and conduct disorder, 98–99
  and depression, 272–73
  and eating disorders, 236

and mental retardation, 41
and schizophrenia, 417–19
heroin, 307
histrionic personality disorder, 450, 451
HIV infection, 307, 328–29
homeostasis, 321
Home Situations Questionnaire, 156–57
homosexuality, 18, 324
hyperactivity, 129
hyperventilation response, 201
hypervigilance, 168, 191
hypomanic episode, 382

ICAP. *See* Inventory for Client and
Agency Planning
*ICD. See International Classification of
Diseases*
IDEA. *See* Individuals with Disabilities
Education Act
impulsive behavior, 129, 452
inattention, 129
Incredible Years program, 104
Individuals with Disabilities Education
Act (IDEA), 45, 140
integrated psychological therapy
program, 427
intelligence. *See* IQ (intelligence
quotient)
Internal State Scale, 404–5
*International Classification of Diseases
(ICD)*, 17
interoceptive cues, 202
interpersonal sensitivity, 456
Interpersonal Therapy, 244, 277, 281,
463–64
Inventory for Client and Agency
Planning (ICAP), 55–56
Inventory of Drug Use Consequences,
337–38
IQ (intelligence quotient), 35, 36, 49, 99–
100
irritable mood, 262

lamotrigine, 392
language-based verbal skills, 100
learning disorders, 36
life-span approach, 7–8
limbic system, 386
lithium carbonate, 390–95

major depressive disorder, 385
major depressive episode, 261, 381, 382

manic episode, 381–82, 383–84
marital therapy, 281
masochistic personality disorder, 21
maternal depression, 262, 268
maternal smoking, 99, 135
measurement, 6–7
medication
for Alzheimer's disease, 491–92, 499
for anxiety disorders, 201, 202t, 205–8
for attention-deficit/hyperactivity
disorder, 142–43, 143–45t, 146–47
for autism, 80–81
for bipolar disorder, 390–95
for borderline personality disorder,
461–62
for depression, 278–79, 282–83t, 284–
85
for eating disorders, 244–45
for pedophilia, 362–63
pharmaceutical companies, 27, 147
for posttraumatic stress disorder, 173,
176
for schizophrenia, 422–24
for substance use disorders, 326–27
for symptoms of mental retardation,
46–47
See also specific medications
memory, 412, 479–81, 490, 498
mental disorder(s)
definition of, 12, 18
in *DSM*, 4, 18–20
medical (psychiatric) perspective, 12
psychological perspective, 12–13
social work perspective, 13–14
sociological approach, 13
See also specific disorders
mental retardation, 35–61
assessment of, 38–40
case illustration, 50–54
cognitive functioning, 38–39
comorbid disorders, 37, 40
diagnosis of, 35–37, 48–49
individualized plans, 40–41
interventions for, 45–48
interview session, 39
levels of severity, 36, 49–50
measures of adaptive behavior, 54–56
measures for emotional, behavioral,
and mental problems, 56–61
medications for symptoms, 46–47
multidisciplinary teams, 40
normalization, 45–46

mental retardation (*continued*)
   physical exam findings, 38
   prevalence of, 37
   risk and protective factors for course,
       43–45, 44t
   risk and protective factors for onset,
       41–43, 42t
meta-analysis, 6–7, 280, 281, 427, 428
methylphenidate, 142, 143, 144
Michigan Alcoholism Screening Test,
       335–36
Millon Clinical Multiaxial Inventory,
       468–69
Mini-Mental Status Examination, 501
minimization, 364
Mississippi Scale for Combat-Related
       PTSD, 186–87
modeling, 204
mood disorders. *See* depression; bipolar
       disorder
motivational interviewing, 243–44, 318–
       19, 327, 331
Multidimensional Family Therapy,
       322
multi-infarct dementia, 486
Multiphasic Sex Inventory, 373–74
multisystemic therapy, 105–7, 322

naltrexone, 327
narcissistic personality disorder, 450,
       451
National Crime Victims Research and
       Treatment Center, 367
negative cognitive style, 267–68
negative symptoms, 412
neighborhood factors, 102
NEO Personality Inventory-Revised,
       469
neurofibrillary tangles, 482
neurotransmitters, 75–76, 274, 482–83
non-right-handedness, 358
norepinephrine, 206, 207, 274
normalcy, 11, 12, 13
numbing, 164

obesity, 236
obsessive-compulsive disorder (OCD),
       167t, 194, 195, 197, 203t, 204, 207,
       223–24, 450, 451
OCD. *See* obsessive-compulsive
       disorder

ODD. *See* oppositional defiant disorder
olanzapine, 394, 423
olfactory hallucinations, 413
oppositional defiant disorder (ODD), 90–
       122
   assessment of, 92–93
   comorbidity, 95
   course of, 94–95
   interventions for, 103–10
   measures for, 118–22
   prevalence of, 92
   risk and protective factors, 95, 96–
       97t, 98–102, 106t
overanxious disorder, 193

Padua Inventory, 224
panic disorders, 192, 197, 199, 200, 202,
       217, 219
paranoid personality disorder, 450
paranoid schizophrenia, 413
paraphilias, 349–51
parent training, 104–5, 106t
parkinsonism, 423
PDD. *See* pervasive developmental
       disorder
PDD-NOS. *See* pervasive
       developmental disorder not
       otherwise specified
pedophilia, 351–75
   assessing, 354–55
   case illustration, 369–73
   diagnosis of, 352–54, 371–72, 373
   disorders comorbid with, 355
   instruments used to assess, 373–75
   interventions for, 361–69
   Justice Department intervention
       guidelines, 367–69
   medication for, 362–63
   recidivism, 365–67
   risk and protective factors, 355–61,
       356–57t, 372
   varieties of, 352–54
pemoline, 143, 144
penile plethysmograph, 355
Penn Inventory for Posttraumatic Stress
       Disorder, 187
persecutory delusions, 413, 432
Personal Experience Inventory, 334
Personal Experience Screening
       Questionnaire, 333–34
personality, definition of, 448–49
Personality Assessment Inventory, 470

Personality Diagnostic Questionnaire
for *DSM-IV*, 470–71
Personality Disorder Interview-IV
Schedule for Nonadaptive and
Adaptive Personality, 471
personality disorders, 233, 448–72
assessment instruments, 468–72
characteristics of, 449–50
diagnosis of, 451–52
three clusters of, 450–51
See also borderline personality
disorder
person-in-environment (PIE), 13–14, 28,
29t, 448
pervasive developmental disorder
(PDD), 36–37, 69–71, 81
pervasive developmental disorder not
otherwise specified (PDD-NOS),
71, 81
phallometric assessment, 354
pharmaceutical companies, 27, 147
phobias, 192, 193
physician's assistant, 424
PIE. *See* person-in-environment
PIMRA. *See* Psychopathology Inventory
for Mentally Retarded Adults
plaques, 482
Pocket Smell Test, 501–2
Positive and Negative Syndrome Scale
for Schizophrenia, 438
positive symptoms, 412, 413
Posttraumatic Stress Diagnostic Scale,
185–86
posttraumatic stress disorder (PTSD),
164–87
behavioral factors, 170, 172
biological processes, 170, 171
case study, 176–80
cognitive factors, 172
comorbidity, 168–69
course of, 169
diagnosis of, 165–68, 167t
interventions for, 172–76
measures for, 181–87
medications for, 173, 176
prevalence of, 165
risk and protective factors, 169–70,
171t, 172, 178–79
pregnancy
and attention-deficit/hyperactivity
disorder, 135
and autism, 76

and conduct problems, 99
and lithium ingestion, 392
and mental retardation, 41
and schizophrenia, 419–20
premenstrual dysphoric disorder, 21
Present State Examination, 438–39
Pressures to Change Model, 320
problem solving, 100–101, 203, 450
progressive muscle relaxation, 202–3
Project MATCH Research Group study,
319
protective factors
for Alzheimer's disease, 483–86, 484t
for anxiety disorders, 196–200, 197t,
198t, 211
for attention-deficit/hyperactivity
disorder, 134–37, 134–35t, 150t,
151t
for autism, 73–78, 83
in biopsychosocial framework, 5, 6
for bipolar disorder, 385–86, 387t, 388–
90
for borderline personality disorder,
453, 454t, 455–56
for conduct and oppositional defiant
disorder, 95, 96–97t, 98–102, 106t,
115–17t
for depression, 271–75, 288–89
for eating disorders, 234–39, 252–53t
for mental retardation, 41–45
for pedophilia, 355–57, 356–57t, 361,
372
for posttraumatic stress disorder
(PTSD), 169–70, 171t, 172, 179
for schizophrenia, 417, 418t, 419–22
for substance use disorders, 308, 309–
10t, 310, 311t, 332t
Prozac. *See* fluoxetine
Psychiatric Symptoms Assessment
Scale, 437
psychodynamic therapies, 200, 425, 460–
61
psychoeducation, 202
Psychopathology Inventory for
Mentally Retarded Adults
(PIMRA), 60–61
psychosocial intervention
for anxiety disorders, 201
for attention-deficit/hyperactivity
disorder, 138–42
for bipolar disorder, 395–98
for cognitive disorders, 493–95

psychosocial intervention (*continued*)
   for eating disorders, 243–44
   for mental retardation, 47
   for pedophilia, 363–65
   for substance use disorders, 316, 317–18t
psychostimulants, 142–44, 146
psychotic disorders, 167t
   See also schizophrenia
psychotropic medication, 244, 362, 424, 492
PTSD. *See* posttraumatic stress disorder
PTSD Symptom Scale-Self Report, 184
puberty, 236
Purdue PTSD Scale-Revised, 184–85
purging, 231

Quality of Life Interview, 441
quetiapine, 394

RADS. *See* Reynolds Adolescent
   Depression Scale
reality orientation, 496, 499
recreational therapy, 496
reexperiencing, 164
reference delusions, 413
reinforcement training, 320
Reiss Scales for Children's Dual
   Diagnosis, 58–59
Reiss Screen for Maladaptive Behavior,
   59–60
relapse prevention, 364, 365
reminiscence therapy, 495, 499
residual schizophrenia, 414
resilience, 4–5
response prevention, 204
restricting anorexics, 231
Rett's disorder, 70
Reynolds Adolescent Depression Scale
   (RADS), 290–91
risk and resilience biopsychosocial
   framework, 4–6, 239–40, 251
risk factors
   for Alzheimer's disease, 483–86, 484t
   for anxiety disorders, 196–200, 197t,
      198t, 211
   for attention-deficit/hyperactivity
      disorder, 134–37, 134–35t, 150t,
      151t
   for autism, 73–78, 74t, 78t, 83
   in biopsychosocial framework, 5–6

for bipolar disorder, 385–86, 387t, 388–90
for borderline personality disorder,
   453, 454t, 455–56
for conduct and oppositional defiant
   disorder, 95, 96–97t, 98–102, 106t,
   115–17t
for depression, 266–75, 267t, 273t, 288–89
for eating disorders, 234–40, 234–35t,
   252–53t
for mental retardation, 41–45, 42t, 44t
for pedophilia, 355–61, 356–57t, 372
for posttraumatic stress disorder
   (PTSD), 169–70, 171t, 172, 178–79
for schizophrenia, 417, 418t, 419–22
for substance use disorders, 308, 309–10t, 310, 311t, 332t
for vascular dementia, 487–89, 488t
risperidone, 80, 81, 394, 423
Ritalin, 142
role playing, 365

St. John's wort, 285
SANS. *See* Scale for the Assessment of
   Negative Symptoms
SAPS. *See* Scale for the Assessment of
   Positive Symptoms
satiation techniques, 364
Scale for the Assessment of Negative
   Symptoms (SANS), 439–40
Scale for the Assessment of Positive
   Symptoms (SAPS), 439–40
schizoaffective disorder, 385, 414
schizoid personality disorder, 450
schizophrenia, 412–41
   assessment instruments, 436–41
   biological factors, 417–20
   case illustration, 432–36
   course of, 416–17
   diagnosis of, 413–15, 433–34, 436
   interventions for, 422–32, 434–36
   medications for, 422–24
   neurodevelopment hypothesis of, 419
   prevalence of, 415–16
   primary prevention, 431–32
   psychological factors, 420–22
   risk and protective factors, 417, 418t,
      419–22
   vocational rehabilitation, 430–31
schizophrenia spectrum disorders, 415
schizophreniform disorder, 414

schizotaxia, 415
schizotypal personality disorder, 450
school intervention, 140–42
school performance, 98, 146
school refusal, 192
selective serotonin reuptake inhibitors
    (SSRIs), 206–7, 278, 284, 362, 461,
    492
self-mutilation, 453
Self-Report Delinquency Scale, 118–19
separation anxiety disorder, 192
serotonin, 206, 207, 274, 358, 423
sertindole, 423
sexual abuse, 101, 238, 359–60, 466
sexual arousal reconditioning, 364
sexual disorders, 349–75
    See also pedophilia
sexual function disorders, 349
skills training, 496
smoking, 99, 135, 197–98
SNAP-IV. See Swanson, Nolan, and
    Pelham-IV Questionnaire
social functioning, 13–14
social phobia, 193, 197, 202, 220–21
Social Rhythm Metric (SRM), 405–6
social skills training, 426–27
socioeconomic factors, 102, 193, 270
somatic hallucinations, 413
splitting, 452, 460
SRM. See Social Rhythm Metric
SSRIs. See selective serotonin reuptake
    inhibitors
State-Trait Anxiety Inventory: Form Y,
    228
Static–99 Sex Offender Risk
    Assessment, 374–75
stimulants, 142–44, 146
stress, 388, 449
stress/diathesis theory, 417
Structure Interview for *DSM-IV*
    Personality, 471–72
substance abuse, 304, 305
substance dependence, 304, 305
substance-induced disorders, 304
substance use disorders, 304–39
    Alcoholics Anonymous, 322–24, 327
    and anxiety, 195
    assessment of, 308, 310
    and borderline personality disorder,
        458
    case study, 328–33
    course of, 305

intervention goals, 312–13
intervention strategies, 313–27
measures of, 333–39
medical comorbid disorders, 307
medications for, 326–27
and posttraumatic stress disorder,
    169
prevalence of, 304–39
psychiatric comorbid disorders, 306,
    326
psychosocial treatments, 316–18
relapse prevention, 313
risk and protective factors, 308, 309–
    10t, 310, 311t, 332t
treatment settings, 315–16t
suicide, 272, 276t, 286, 389–90, 453
Swanson, Nolan, and Pelham-IV
    Questionnaire (SNAP-IV),
    150–51
symbolic interactionism, 13
systems, 5, 13

tacrine, 491
tactile hallucinations, 413
tardive dyskinesia, 423
teenagers. See adolescent disorders;
    adolescents
temperament, 99, 196
temperamental sensitivity, 196, 197
Ten-Point Clock Test, 502
TFC. See treatment foster care
thought broadcasting, 413
thought disorders, 412
thought insertion/withdrawal, 413
tic disorders, 195
Tourette's disorder, 195
Transtheoretical Stages of Change
    Model, 316, 317–18t
trauma
    childhood, 456
    See also posttraumatic stress disorder
Trauma Symptom Checklist for
    Children, 182–83
treatment foster care (TFC), 107–8
tricyclic antidepressants, 145, 146, 206–
    7, 245, 274, 278, 284

UCSD Performance-Based Skills
    Assessment, 440
undifferentiated schizophrenia, 413
unilateral therapy, 320, 327

University of Rhode Island Change
    Assessment Scale (URICA), 338–
    39
URICA. *See* University of Rhode Island
    Change Assessment Scale

VADPRS. *See* Vanderbilt ADHD Parent
    Rating Scale
validation therapy, 495
valproate, 392–95
Vanderbilt ADHD Parent Rating Scale
    (VADPRS), 152–53
vascular dementia, 479, 486–90
  and Alzheimer's disease, 489–90
  drugs for related symptoms, 492–93
  psychosocial interventions, 493–95
  risk and protective factors, 487–89,
    488t
venlafaxine, 394

verbal skills, 100
vicious cycles, 450
victim empathy, 365
visual changes, 412
visual hallucinations, 413
vocational rehabilitation, 430–31

weight, 238–42, 245, 262
Wellbutrin. *See* bupropion
Wender Utah Rating Scale (WURS), 157
Wisconsin Personality Inventory, 472
women, 238, 307, 325–26
WURS. *See* Wender Utah Rating Scale

Young Mania Rating Scale, 406
Youth Self-Report, 119

Zung Self-Rating Depression Scale, 292–
    93